THE
BROEDERBOND

Ivor Wilkins
Hans Strydom

PADDINGTON
PRESS LTD
NEW YORK & LONDON

Library of Congress Cataloging in Publication Data

Wilkins, Ivor, 1951–
The Broederbond.

Includes bibliographical references and index.
1. Afrikaners—Politics and government. 2. Broederbond. 3. South Africa—Politics and government—20th century. 4. South Africa—Race relations.
I. Strydom, Hans, 1936– joint author. II. Title.
DT888.W54 1979 320.9'68'05 79-12029

ISBN 0 448 22981 1 (U.S. and Canada only)
ISBN 0 7092 0734 4

First published in 1978 by Jonathan Ball Publishers, South Africa.
Printed and bound in the United States.

In the United States
PADDINGTON PRESS
Distributed by
GROSSET & DUNLAP

In the United Kingdom
PADDINGTON PRESS

In Canada
Distributed by
RANDOM HOUSE OF CANADA LTD.

In Australia and New Zealand
Distributed by
A.H. & A.W. REED

To my wife, Gertie, for the endless hours spent on deciphering codes and preparing the most extensive membership list of the Broederbond ever published ...
To my children, for understanding a disrupted household at a difficult time in their careers ...
To all my friends for their assistance and moral support.

Hans Strydom

To my family and friends.

Ivor Wilkins

Contents

"Do you realise what a powerful force is gathered here tonight between these four walls? Show me a greater power on the whole continent of Africa! Show me a greater power anywhere . . ."

H J Klopper

First chairman of the Afrikaner Broederbond in a celebratory speech on the occasion of the organisation's 50th anniversary in 1968.

Acknowledgements

Many people have assisted in the publication of this book. In the nature of the subject, some of them have to remain anonymous. We extend our sincere appreciation to our main informant, who took a lonely decision to break ranks; also to other members and former members of the organisation who were prepared to co-operate, as well as to non-members who shared their knowledge. For technical assistance and encouragement we would like to record our thanks to Avril Hickman, Alison Lowry, Tessa Paul, Toni Tickton and Melanie Yap.

I Wilkins
H Strydom

Preface

In January 1977 a letter arrived at the offices of the *Sunday Times* in Johannesburg offering information about the Broederbond, the exclusively Afrikaans, awesomely influential South African secret society. No telephone number or street address was given with the letter, only a Johannesburg post office box number. It aroused immediate scepticism.

"Probably a crank. Breaks into the Broederbond just don't come this way," was the general response. But the letter was investigated as a matter of routine.

Ivor Wilkins wrote to the box number asking the informer to telephone and several days later he rang the *Sunday Times* and arranged a meeting at the offices. At that stage security precautions did not figure in the calculations. Nobody really believed a break into the organisation was in fact beginning to materialise.

The appointed time came and went and the informer did not turn up. There was no way to contact him as he had refused to leave a telephone number, so all that remained was to wait, and hope he would call in again. But there was a nagging feeling that it was all a hoax.

He did call again, about a week later, and another meeting was arranged in the *Sunday Times* office. He seemed completely happy with this arrangement, declining an offer to choose a different rendezvous. Again he refused to leave a telephone number.

And again he failed to keep the appointment.

This happened a third time as well. And then there was silence. No word was heard from him and gradually he was forgotten, just another of the thousands of false leads that find their way into newspaper offices the world over. A year passed. Early in January 1978, Wilkins was phoned by a security guard at the *Sunday Times* reception desk. A man wanted to see him, could he come up to the newsroom?

"The name given didn't mean a thing," recalls Wilkins. "But obviously he knew me, as he had asked for me by name. I told the reception desk to send him up." Minutes later, a small insignificant-looking man sat down at the desk and said: "I'm sorry, I know I'm a year late for our appointment, but I've come at last." His handshake was soft, and damp; his quietly-spoken English was competent, although laced with a heavy Afrikaans accent. He was agitated and glanced around the busy newsroom constantly, continuously wringing his hands.

Wilkins said he could recall no appointment with the man facing him.

"I've come to talk about the Broederbond," came the soft reply. There was a pause as the message sank in. "I've got documents. It's genuine. I want to talk. I'm sorry I didn't come before, but I've been so nervous and confused.

"I just didn't know whether I was doing the right thing. I knew I wanted to talk, but I didn't know whether I could trust you, or quite how to start.

"I've been reading my Bible constantly, and thinking. Now I feel certain I want to expose the Broederbond."

The man was clearly in an agonising state of nervousness and, despite his protestations that he had come to a firm decision about what he wanted to do, still torn by a terrible doubt.

Wilkins recalls: "I had my doubts, but his nervousness could not have been contrived." He hustled his mysterious visitor out of the building and arranged a meeting at his home later that afternoon. Then he went to tell news editor, Hans Strydom, that a break into the Broederbond was under way.

Instead of the enthusiasm he expected, his announcement met with a heavy, doubtful silence. Strydom clearly disbelieved the man's story. Worse, he feared a trap.

Newspapers in South Africa were under the very real threat of Government clampdowns at the time. The Prime Minister, Mr John Vorster, had given the Press a year to put its house in order. Powerful legislation, carrying heavy penalties, had been prepared to deal with newspapers failing to heed the warnings.

The Broederbond was an extremely sensitive subject in this unpredictable situation. Little was known about the organisation, apart from its reputation for influence in high places. It was suspected that it was a secret arm of the Government; that the highest figures in Afrikanerdom – including Vorster – were numbered among its ranks. Make a mistake on the Broederbond, and a newspaper would be wide open to trouble. One of the problems with a story of this sort was the necessity to trust the source implicitly: there would be nobody with whom to check.

After discussing the matter at some length, it was agreed that Strydom would accompany Wilkins to the informer's house to judge for himself whether the information was genuine or not. The two men drove up to the modest home (for obvious reasons its location cannot be disclosed) and were greeted by their nervous host. Seated in his lounge, they were at last shown a small pile of documents, duplicated on foolscap. Strydom, who had seen Broederbond documents before, quickly confirmed that they were genuine. What was more, they were the latest documents in circulation. The three men sat and talked. Eventually, the informer agreed to let them take the documents away to be photocopied, with a strict admonition to return them straight away.

He had taken his first step in defiance of the organisation to which he had belonged for nearly twenty years. He was committing its most serious offence: betraying its secrets. Sixty years of tradition glared down on traitors.

That weekend the *Sunday Times* ran the first of a six-part series on the organisation. It started with a report on a secret masterplan to ensure white survival in South Africa. In effect it was an accelerated version of Verwoerd's Bantustan plan, with all the details and ramifications painstakingly worked out.

It had been decided that from the first week of publication that strict security should be maintained on the story. Particularly stringent precautions must be taken when meeting the informer. There had been warnings from well-disposed people who knew enough about the organisation to predict that once it felt endangered, all possible steps would be taken to repair its breached defences. The two newspapermen were warned that they might be followed, their telephones tapped. The warnings were not fantasy. After a previous exposé of the Broederbond by the *Sunday Times,* the newspaper's offices had been raided by members of South Africa's security police. Broederbond documents in the newspaper's possession were taken away.

The following week a rendezvous was set up outside a post office in a suburban shopping centre. The informer was there and the three men went to a seedy local hotel and sat talking. Bare floorboards, bare formica-topped tables and chairs. This cheerless setting became a regular meeting place.

Strydom was concerned that the organisation might quickly

find out who was responsible for the leak, and confiscate all the documents. Tentatively, he suggested that all of them be handed over for photocopying. That way, there would at least be a second set available. It was agreed and, to the almost incredulous delight of the two journalists, the informer revealed that he had documents going back 15 years locked away at home. He had violated another of the organisations's strict security measures, which insists that documents are not to be kept for longer than two years before being destroyed.

Boxes of papers were passed over to the two reporters. Teams of volunteers from the newspaper's reporting and administrative staff manned a battery of photocopying machines to duplicate the invaluable collection. The newspaper office buzzed with excitement. On Saturday, their busiest production day, the editor, Mr Tertius Myburgh, could scarcely contain himself, rushing in and out of the rooms where the collection was being compiled, picking up documents at random and reading them with fascination.

That night the mammoth copying job was completed. Wilkins piled the originals into a car and drove out to return them. He found the informer in a renewed state of agitation.

A circular had arrived that morning from the Broederbond's headquarters in Auckland Park, Johanesburg, concerning the previous week's reports in the *Sunday Times*. All document-holders in the organisation were told to call a meeting of their branch executives, and account immediately for the papers quoted in the reports. The witch-hunt had begun. The following morning the *Sunday Times* was able to show how deeply it had penetrated, by quoting from the day-old circular itself.

According to later disclosures, this caused deep anxiety in the organisation's hierarchy. The rest of the reports in that Sunday's edition of the paper must also have hurt badly the custodians of the organisation's security. They learned that this was no isolated leak of a few documents; the newspaper possessed a comprehensive set of Broederbond secrets.

That weekend, armed guards patrolled the homes of the editor and the two reporters. There were no incidents. The following week, Strydom and Wilkins moved out of town and sifted through more of the documents. The result was a two-page spread, taking *Sunday Times* readers into the very heart of the organisation. The swearing-in ceremony, which had never before been described, was detailed along with the induction mechanisms and evidence of the close links between the organisation and Prime Minister Hendrik Verwoerd and the former premier, John Vorster.

During that week the informer had been telephoning the *Sunday Times* offices virtually every day: a breach of the agreed arrangements. Wilkins made an arrangement to meet him. The meeting again took place in the sordid hotel lounge. He was waiting when Wilkins arrived, and apologised profusely for having telephoned the office. Clearly very shaken, he complained that he had not been sleeping well. It turned out that all he wanted was reassurance.

He again went tortuously through his reasons for exposing the organisation. He said he was disillusioned with the way South Africa was developing. He had been deeply shocked by the Soweto riots and subsequent widespread black unrest in the country in mid-1976. This was the first time the depth of black dissatisfaction with the status quo had been brought home to him. He had considered breaking silence on the Broederbond at that stage, but had decided against it.

Then came the death in Security Police detention during September 1977 of Mr Steve Biko, the black consciousness leader. The outcry that followed had disturbed him deeply. The callous reaction of the Minister of Justice, Mr Kruger, who told the Transvaal congress of the ruling National Party that Biko's death "leaves me cold", had particularly upset him. He felt the National Party Government was on the wrong road.

The informer is a profoundly God-fearing man in the strict Calvinist mould of the Afrikaans churches. He said his conscience was bothering him about the path South Africa had chosen and was following. But he was in a turmoil because he had sworn a solemn oath before God never to reveal to any outsider anything about the Broederbond.

Meanwhile, the Broederbond continued to try to find the crack in its jealously guarded defences. A special meeting of the supreme body, the Executive Council, was called to discuss the matter and plan counter-action. According to authoritative sources, secret service agents were again called in.

During this period a sobering thing happened. A new system of computer-controlled electronic editing was introduced to prepare the book. Close security was emphasised in the new system. Each operator was given a confidential code enabling him to store exclusive information in the system. Access to that information was confined to the operator alone and, in exceptional cases, to four highly senior management members.

While the data was being compiled on the Broederbond, lists of names (which appear at the end of this book) were painstakingly put together from the documents in the journalists' possession. As these lists grew, they were fed into the computer store under Strydom's code. For security reasons, the lists were split into four groupings under different code-names. Eventually the list of names was virtually complete. The reporters had by then managed to identify about 3 000 of the 12 000 members of the organisation. In the system, the names were safe. Its designers had given an assurance that the security was to all intents foolproof.

First thing one Tuesday morning, Strydom coded himself onto one of the computer terminals and stared in horror. All the Broederbond names had been wiped out. The four Broederbond groupings were selectively removed, leaving behind innocuous items such as telephone numbers and contact information.

The system engineers were summoned to investigate, but had to confess they were baffled.

Then, after the series had been running in the *Sunday Times* for about a month, an extraordinary message reached the two writers. It was given to one of their colleagues by a Government source who said he was merely acting as a go-between for another party whom he refused to identify. This party was willing to pay R50 000 for the series to stop, and for the name of the source. The series continued until the newspaper felt it had run its course.

It is in the nature of newspaper reporting that much of the detail in the documents handed over remained undisclosed. It is in an effort to complete the picture that this book has been written.

Profile of Power

World attention is focused on South Africa: a vast, rich country of extremes and diversity, the country of gold and diamonds, apartheid and Soweto, Biko and Botha. Hardly a week goes by without South Africa making international headlines.

Yet despite the probing spotlight of critical world attention, a crucial element of South African political reality has largely escaped detection. This strange, unique society is not ruled, as is generally believed, by "whites" or "Afrikaners". It is not as simple as that. A dominant force is an ultra-secret organisation, the most exclusive and influential underground movement in the Western world.

It is called the *Afrikaner Broederbond* (Brotherhood).

Although it has only 12 000 scrupulously selected members, it plots and influences the destiny of all 25-million South Africans, black and white. By stealth and sophisticated political intrigue, this 60-year-old organisation has waged a remarkable campaign to harness political, social and economic forces in South Africa to its cause of ultimate Afrikaner domination. And, to an extent beyond the most optimistic dreams of its founders, it has succeeded.

The South African Government today is the Broederbond and the Broederbond is the Government. No Afrikaner government can rule South Africa without the support of the Broederbond. No Nationalist Afrikaner can become Prime Minister unless he comes from the organisation's select ranks.

Mr P W Botha, the current Prime Minister, is a member – as were his four predecessors, Dr D F Malan, Advocate J G Strijdom, Dr H F Verwoerd and Mr John Vorster. Every member, except two, of the Botha Cabinet is a Broederbonder.

From this pinnacle of executive control over South Africa's affairs, the organisation's 12 000 members permeate every aspect of the Republic's life. Through its network of more than 800 cells in the villages and cities of South Africa, the organisation has infiltrated members into town and city councils, school boards, agricultural unions, the State-controlled radio and television networks, industry and commerce, banks and building societies.

Its membership spirals insidiously upwards through the strata of South African society, into the provincial administrations, the departments of education, planning, roads and works, the hospital services, universities, the quasi-state corporations, the civil service, the National Party caucuses, working through the administrators of the provinces, through Parliament and the seat of government, until it finally reaches its apex in the offices of the Prime Minister.

Its all-pervading influence has made its indelible mark on South Africa. The Bantustan policies, the Christian national education policy, the sport policy, the coloured and Indian policy – all the major political peculiarities which have shaped South Africa into a constitutional oddity bear the stamp of the Broederbond on their formulation and execution. Beneath the trappings of Parliamentary "democracy", and behind the remarkable success of South Africa's ruling National Party, lies the extraordinary power of the Broederbond.

In 1934 when the organisation was 16 years old, the then chairman, Professor J C van Rooy, set an ambitious goal for the Broederbond. Probably more than any other single statement in its history, this sums up the organisation's fervent purpose. Van Rooy wrote, in a secret circular to its members:

"The primary consideration is whether Afrikanerdom will reach its ultimate destiny of domination in South Africa. Brothers, the key to South Africa's problems is not whether one party or another shall obtain the whiphand, but whether the Afrikaner Broederbond shall govern South Africa."

Since then, the organisation has been an abiding force in the shaping of modern South Africa's destiny. From the time the Broederbond scored its first major political triumph in the 1948 general election victory of the National Party, it has gone from strength to strength. Through periods of changing fortunes the organisation has weathered crises and setbacks, but has tenaciously sought its "holy grail" of ultimate control.

Whether Van Rooy's dream of the Broederbond *governing* South Africa has been achieved or not may be open to debate. But that it is *Broederbonders* who govern South Africa is beyond all doubt.

The first chairman of the organisation, H J Klopper, summed it up in a celebratory speech at the 50th anniversary of the Broederbond in 1968, when he said: "From the time the Afrikaner Broederbond picked up momentum, it has given the country its governments. It has given the country every Nationalist Prime Minister since 1948. However indirectly, its efforts gave the Republic to our nation. It has given the country two State Presidents.[1]

"Do you realise what a powerful force is gathered here tonight between these four walls? Show me a greater power on the whole continent of Africa! Show me a greater power anywhere, even in your so-called civilised countries!

"We are part of the State, we are part of the Church, we are part of every big movement that has been born of the nation. And we make our contributions unseen; we carried them through to the point that our nation has reached today."

An extraordinary achievement. From humble but determined beginnings in the hills around Johannesburg in 1918 when the Afrikaners were confused, dispirited, spent, the organisation has

Dr Verwoerd. Leading Broeder and South Africa's third Nationalist Prime Minister.

built a government that today holds a world record of unbroken rule, and a party that, following the 1977 general election, holds the biggest-ever majority in the South African Parliament (135 seats in the 165-seat Assembly).

South Africa's present power structure is a tribute to the Broederbond's tireless efforts on behalf of Afrikanerdom. The present Prime Minister is Broeder number 4487. His predecessor, Mr Vorster, was member number 3737 and Dr Hendrik Fransch Verwoerd was member number 1596. Dr Verwoerd, whose term of office saw two of the Broederbond's most cherished achievements – the advent of Republic in 1961 and the acceptance of the Bantustan policy – maintained a very close relationship with the organisation. He became a member on February 17 1937 and was elected to the Executive Council, the organisation's supreme body, in October 1940. He remained on the Executive Council for 10 years until 1950 when, as he said, he exchanged "the Cabinet of the Afrikaner Broederbond for the Cabinet of the nation." During his term as an Executive member he attended 51 meetings and was absent,with apologies, on only two occasions.

Shortly after his election as Prime Minister in 1958 he attended a national meeting of the Broederbond where he told his fellow members: "Friends, there is nothing that gives me greater pleasure than to be with you. When the invitation arrived I knew there would be people who would have doubts about my coming, doubts reflecting caution. But I never had one moment of doubt and the reason is simple.

"I do not see that the opponents of our national organisation, the opponents of our Afrikaner ideal, may dictate the movements of the Prime Minister of the country.

"I saw it not only as my privilege, but also as my duty to draw closer by my presence the ties that always existed unobtrusively between our Afrikaner organisation and our Afrikaner Government. And that is why I am here: to draw the Broeder bonds tighter."

A former chairman of the Broederbond, Dr P J (Piet) Meyer, referred to this close relationship in his address at the 50th anniversary meeting of the organisation in 1968. He told the meeting that Dr Verwoerd had consulted the Broederbond in July 1959 about the Republic referendum – six months before he told Parliament he was going to the country to test national support for the Afrikaners' republican dream."He asked the Afrikaner Broederbond to accept co-responsibility for the new Republic, a task that the AB accepted with great eagerness and the provision of large amounts of money."

Dr Meyer added that he had seen Dr Verwoerd a week before he was stabbed to death in Parliament by an insane messenger, Dimitri Tsafendas in September 1966. According to Dr Meyer: "He gave me, as chairman of the Executive Council, permission to start planning for a new Republican flag and a change in the State President system to bring it more in line with the old Transvaal and Free State presidencies – obviously with the necessary adaptation to comply with the present circumstances...We will give attention to the State Presidency when the time is right." Significantly, the new constitutional proposals for South Africa announced in 1976 include a strengthened State Presidency with executive powers.

After Dr Verwoerd's assassination, and after the flurry of activity over his succession by Mr Vorster, the ties between the Broederbond and the Prime Minister's office were quickly renewed. On August 2 1967 the Broederbond chairman, Dr Meyer, reported that "during the recent Parliamentary sitting, the chairman of the Executive Council personally conveyed our organisation's heartfelt thanks and appreciation to our friend (the organisation's term for member), the Prime Minister, for everything that the Government has done to the advantage and in the interests of our country and all its peoples" (Broederbond circular entitled *Us and Our Political Leaders)*.

He noted that the "doors of the Prime Minister and of our other political leaders" were always open to the Executive Council.

The relationship was rocked soon after, however, by the bitter struggle in the National Party between pro-Vorster faction and the extreme right-wing group under the Minister of Posts and Telegraphs, Dr Albert Hertzog. The debilitating struggle, which ended in a split in the party, seriously dented the new Prime Minister's position and also caused a major crisis in the Broederbond where the divisions sapping the party were mirrored.

In the early stages of the revolt, the Broederbond chiefs called on Vorster to discuss the problem. The meeting is reported in a Broederbond document, number 8/67/68 of November 2 1967. Dr Meyer reports:

"The Executive Council delegation held an open-hearted discussion with our friend (Mr Vorster) about:

(a) The contribution of our organisation to the desired and essential unity of our nation, among our own members and in all spheres;
(b) The role in this connection of all communications media, particularly the Press – including our own;
(c) The areas of activity, tasks and problems of our Afrikaans cultural organisations;
(d) The undermining philosophies that are threatening the spirit and soul of our nation – namely humanism, communism and liberalism – and measures to combat them;
(e) The dangers of increasing economic integration under the leadership of businessmen who do not subscribe to the policy of separate development, and the complementary problem of the Afrikaner continuing in the subordinate economic role;
(f) The application of our national education policy which has now been ratified by legislation.

"Our honourable Prime Minister thoroughly informed the delegation about his and his Government's standpoints in connection with all these matters, and informed us confidentially on the immediate and urgent problems to be tackled by the Government."

Despite the encouraging and placatory tone of this report, all was not well for a long time and the lingering divisions in Afrikanerdom continued to strain the Broederbond-Cabinet relationship considerably. It was clear that Dr Meyer himself was in two minds about which side to back, and it was only Vorster's bulldozing personality and his highly efficient information network that enabled him to scrape through.

The 1968 Broederbond annual report mentions the divisions among Afrikaners, Vorster's controversial sports policy, unity between Afrikaans and English-speaking South Africans, and the contentious issue of black diplomats in the Republic – all issues causing bitter dissent in the National Party at the time. The vital importance to the Premiership of the Broederbond's support is illustrated by a remarkable speech Vorster made to the organisation that year in which he explained each point at issue. Clearly he felt compelled to account for the more flexible line he was adopting in contrast with the rigid, preordained style of his predecessor. He was fighting desperately to keep the Broederbond on his side, for he was well aware that failure to do so would seriously jeopardise his position.

During the speech he made a major concession to the organisation, strengthening its position even further, when he gave permission for Cabinet Ministers to serve on the Broederbond's Executive Council.

In 1969, the year Dr Hertzog and his dissidents broke from the National Party to form the Herstigte Nasionale Party (HNP), an Executive Council delegation again went to see Vorster – this time at the Prime Minister's official residence, Libertas, in Pretoria.

"Broeder Vorster said he appreciated and welcomed the Executive's co-operation," after receiving the seldom-awarded Broederbond badge "as a token of our unifying brotherhood," reported Dr Meyer in the secret circular to members of October 7 1969. Obviously relieved by this sign that the Broederbond would back him, Vorster described the meeting as a "lovely day", Meyer reports.

By 1972, after about 200 extreme rightwingers had been expelled from the Broederbond's ranks for refusing to dissociate themselves from the HNP, Vorster could breathe easily again. He had carried the day and the Broederbond-Cabinet relationship was well and truly healed. The organisation's annual report of the year notes: "The relationship between the Executive Council and our Broeders in responsible circles (the organisation's term for the Government) has never been better."

From the Prime Minister's office the Broederbond's representation can be traced down the line of executive control, threading its way through every Cabinet Minister's office with only two exceptions. These exceptions are the Minister of Finance, Senator Owen Horwood, and the Minister of Indian Affairs and of Tourism, Mr Marais Steyn. Their respective disqualifications are that Senator Horwood's English-speaking background precludes him from membership of the rigorously Afrikaner organisation, while Mr Steyn is a second-choice Nationalist. He crossed the floor from the opposition benches where, for years, he had the reputation of being the only opposition member who could harass the formidable Vorster in debate.

When Vorster reshuffled his Cabinet early in 1978 the brotherly tradition of power was maintained. The only newcomer to the Cabinet itself was Mr F W de Klerk who became Minister of Posts and Telegraphs and of Social Welfare and Pensions. He too is a member of the Broederbond, having been invited to join in 1964 at the unusually young age of 27 (*Sunday Times,* January 29 1978).

Present chairman of the Afrikaner Broederbond, Prof Gerrit Viljoen.

Thus whenever the South African Cabinet meets, it is a tribute to Van Rooy's ideal expressed more than 40 years ago – that the Broederbond should govern South Africa.

The Executive Council of the Broederbond are all leading Afrikaners in their own right. The chairman is Professor Gerrit Viljoen, Rector of Rand Afrikaans University in Johannesburg. A highly talented and articulate man, he was described as "brilliant" by the former American Secretary of State, Henry Kissinger, during a visit to South Africa in 1976.

The vice-chairman is a highly significant and powerful figurehead in Afrikanerdom, their spiritual leader, the Reverend D P M Beukes, moderator of the Nederduitse Gereformeerde Kerk, the largest of the three main Afrikaans churches.

The other Executive members are Dr F C Fensham, Professor of Semitic Languages at the University of Stellenbosch; Mr J M de Wet, former Commissioner General of South West Africa; Dr W J (Wimpie) de Klerk, managing editor of the National Party's Transvaal mouthpiece, *Die Transvaler*, a 60 000-circulation daily morning newspaper; Mr Gabriel Krog, director of Indian Education; Professor E J Marais, Rector of the University of Port Elizabeth; Mr S A S Hayward, Nationalist MP for Graaff-Reinet; Professor H J Samuels, retired chairman of the South African Armaments Board; Dr C W H Boshoff, head of the South African Bureau of Racial Affairs (a Broederbond front organisation); Mr Eben Cuyler, a former Nationalist senator; Mr D P de Villiers, head of the giant oil-from-coal corporation, Sasol; Professor B Kok, chancellor of the University of the Orange Free State; Professor W A van Niekerk of the Department of Obstetrics and Gynaecology at the University of Stellenbosch; and Mr S W van der Merwe.

It is the fusion of these two bodies, the Cabinet and the Broederbond Executive Council, and the forces they individually and collectively represent, that gives the National Party its present position of extraordinary power in South Africa.

From this rarified summit of political influence the Broederbond's authority is disseminated through the other ranks of society. The President of the Senate, the upper house in South Africa's present Westminster-type constitutional arrangement (under the new constitutional proposals the Senate will disappear) is a Broederbonder, Mr Marais Viljoen. The National Party's Parliamentary caucus of 135 is dominated by Broederbond members, among them, of course, Mr Hayward of the organisation's Executive Council. There are 186 full-time politicians on the Broederbond's membership lists, according to one of their secret documents, *Professions and Ages Breakdown*, compiled in 1977. These include Administrators of South Africa's provinces: Mr Sybrand van Niekerk, the controversial rightwing Administrator of the Transvaal (member number 2296), the Administrator of Natal, the amiable Mr Ben Havemann (Broeder number 4405); Mr A C van Wyk, the Orange Free State's Administrator (member number 3108). There is every likelihood that Dr L A P A Munnik, the Cape Administrator, is a member, although this has not been established beyond all doubt.

Most of the members of the Provincial Executive Committees in the Transvaal, Cape and Free State are Broeders. In Natal the ruling political party in the Provincial Council is the New Republic Party, an opposition party, so there is no Broederbond representation in that Executive Committee.

It is not only the policy-makers, but also the policy-executors that are to be found in the Broederbond's ranks. Examples from the former Prime Minister's Department were his private secretary, Mr Johan Weilbach, the liaison man, Mr Neville Krige, and the secretary to the department, Mr Wessel Meyer. It is significant that Mr Krige, who was recruited to the Prime Minister's Department from the South African Broadcasting Corporation, was brought into the Broederbond at the recommendation of the Executive Council itself soon after his appointment had been announced. The clear implication is that one of the qualifications for the job was membership of the organisation.

Many of Vorster's top advisers were also members of the Broederbond. His economic adviser, Dr P J Rieckert, is a member. His Security Council was made up almost entirely of Broederbonders. It included the Minister of Defence, Mr P W Botha, the Minister of Justice and Police, Mr J T Kruger, the Minister of Foreign Affairs, Mr R F (Pik) Botha, and the former head of the secret service, General Hendrik van den Bergh.

Other notable members include the Secretary for Coloured, Rehoboth and Nama Relations, Mr J H T Mills; the Secretary for Sport and Recreation, Mr B K de W Hoek; and the Secretary for Plural Relations, the department which controls every facet of life for South Africa's 18-million blacks, is also a Broeder. So is Mr P T C du Plessis, Nationalist MP for Lydenburg and Chairman of the Plural (formerly Bantu) Affairs Commission, an important post in terms of South Africa's Bantustan policy.

Among the Bantu Administration Boards under Broederbond control the most important are: the West Rand Administration Board which controls the brooding giant black city of Soweto just outside Johannesburg, the East Rand Administration Board under Mr S van der Merwe, the Vaal Triangle Board under Mr C H Knoetze and the Cape Peninsula Board under Brigadier J H van der Westhuizen. The chairman of WRAB, Mr Manie Mulder (brother of the Minister of Plural Relations, Dr Connie Mulder) is a prominent Broeder. These administration boards play a vital role in the execution of South Africa's apartheid policy. Through a baffling system of permits they control every aspect of black urban dwellers' lives.

There are 518 civil servants in the Broederbond, the most notable being the chairman of the enormous service, Dr P S Rautenback (number 6142), the Secretary, Dr W I Steyn and one of the commissioners, Mr W G Schickerling, who has since been appointed Auditor-General. There are 61 Broeders in the provincial administrations. A significant proportion of these are in the education departments of the four provinces where they exert particular influence on the 2424 Broeder teachers who in turn "spread the gospel" in the classrooms. The teacher corps of the Broederbond is held in high esteem because of its unique potential for moulding the minds and attitudes of future white generations.

In modern South Africa, fast becoming one of the world's most isolated pariah states, the military plays an increasingly important role. Its sphere of activity and influence has spread in recent years to include a regular place in the inner sanctums of power, where major political decisions are taken. The Minister of Defence, Mr P W Botha, is a Broeder. The Head of the Defence Force, General Magnus Malan, is also in the organisation's ranks along with 143 Defence Force personnel, most of them senior officers.

General Hendrik van den Bergh, whose membership number is 6745, is an important member of the secret organisation. He shared internment during World War Two with Vorster, forming a lifelong friendship. In his position at the head of Security Services, from which he has recently retired, he played a vital role in South African politics. Throughout his career he had been a close lieutenant and confidant of Vorster, particularly during the detente years in the early and middle 1970s when he made numerous secret diplomatic sorties into Africa. Information about the other links between BOSS (DONS) and the Broederbond may not be disclosed here because of new legislation in South Africa preventing the publication of any details about personalities and activities of the secret service. In South Africa, where the economy increasingly takes on the look of a socialist state, there are a large number of semi-State corporations, all of which have powerful Broederbond representation in their top echelons. In terms of political influence the most important of these is the State-controlled South African Broadcasting Corporation (SABC) which holds a jealously-guarded monopoly of radio and television.

Its chief executive, Dr Piet Meyer, was chairman of the Broederbond from1960 to 1972. For the major part of this period he was simultaneously chairman of the SABC. He is no longer on the Broederbond Executive but remains an important and highly influential member of the organisation. His membership number is 787. At least three members of his SABC board, Mr W A Maree, Professor S J Terreblanche and Professor H O Mönnig are Broederbonders. Dr Meyer also serves as chairman of the SABC's Bantu Programme Control Board (the SABC, like South Africa, is divided on ethnic lines with different services for the various language and colour groups). This control board includes at least one other Broeder, Professor E F Potgieter. Television and radio programmes are the responsibility of Dr J H T Schutte, recently promoted to Director General (Programmes) of the corporation. He belongs to the Broederbond's Oom Paul branch in Johannesburg.

Other top executives of the corporation, who influence the viewing and listening of all racial groups, include the following Broeders:

- Mr Jan Swanepoel, director-general of the corporation;
- Mr Steve de Villiers, director of English and Afrikaans radio;
- Mr T van Heerden, who was recently appointed director of Bantu and External Services. Mr van Heerden's new position indicates that listeners to the SABC's African language services, future black TV viewers, and people who tune in to the worldwide Radio RSA service, are likely to have only what the Broederbond wants them to see and hear;
- Mr B J Steyn, recently appointed head of the SABC in the Orange Free State. Before that, he was head of Radio Bantu's Nguni language service;
- Mr L S Seegars, now director of Schools Radio Service. He was formerly head of SABC's South Sotho service.

Other areas of the SABC's administration also have their share of Broederbond representation. Deputy Director General (Administration) Mr Gert Yssel is a member, as is the head of Stores and Supplies, Mr E van H E Mischke. The viewers' watchdog, the Television Programme Advisory Board, includes at least one Broeder, Mr P R T Nel. Mr Nel, a former Director of Education in Natal, is also a former member of the Broederbond's Executive Council.

The importance of the SABC to the Broederbond-National Party alliance and the extent to which it is manipulated for party political ends is indicated in two secret Broederbond documents.

The first, *Masterplan for a White Country: the Strategy*, explains the importance of having Broeders in control of the so-called Bantu Services. The masterplan calls for the use of organisations, including the SABC and its Bantu Services and the planned black TV service, to "compel" compliance with the plan whose main purpose is to see that overwhelming numbers of the black population live and work in their own homelands, or Bantustans, as soon as possible. The second is a secret circular to members, number 5/70/71 dated August 3 1970, which deals with the introduction of television in South Africa, a hot political issue for many years. The document shows that while Dr Meyer was simultaneously head of the SABC and of the Broederbond, he headed the Commission of Inquiry into television in South Africa. More important, he informed the Broederbond on his findings *before* passing them on to the Government and Parliament.

After the *Sunday Times* published information about the SABC's Broederbond connection there were two fascinating reactions. The first was official, in the form of a letter of complaint to the newspaper from the SABC public relations department's Mr Andre Walters. Among other things he wrote: "The SABC, in the selection of the nature and contents of its programmes, is under the control of its board as determined by the Broadcasting Act and we challenge you to prove that its programmes are subject to consistent influence by ominous, menacing, subversive or collusive outside persons, organisations or pressures."

The first point to make is that the Broadcasting Act, by the nature of the Broederbond's position of power in the South African Cabinet, is a Broederbond-sanctioned piece of legislation. Whether the Broederbond's undeniable influence in the SABC's affairs is ominous, menacing, subversive or collusive can only be a matter of subjective judgement.

The second reaction came in the form of telephone calls and conversations with other SABC employees who were disappointed that more names of members in the corporation were not exposed. The authors were told that many more people, particularly in top positions in the radio and television news services of the corporation, were Broederbonders. Altogether there are, at latest count, 49 Broederbonders involved in broadcasting in South Africa.

The South African Railways, the largest single employer in South Africa, is also under the control of a Broederbonder general manager, J G H Loubser. The SAR's Financial Manager, Dr E L Grove, is also a member. There are 221 railways and airways Broeders.

Dr Ampie Roux, chairman of South Africa's Atomic Energy Board, is an important Broeder. With constant speculation that

South Africa is technically capable of developing nuclear capability, Dr Roux's position takes on added significance. In any event, his position is a major one in South African affairs. Iscor, the semi-State Iron and Steel Corporation, also has tremendous strategic importance for South Africa. Six of its board members are Broeders. They are the chairman, Mr Tommy Muller, Mr J P Coetzee, Mr P K Hoogendyk, Dr M D Marais, Professor H J Samuels and Mr J J Vermooten. The top position in the Electricity Supply Commission (Escom) is also held by a Broeder, Dr R L Straszacker. Mr T W de Jongh, Governor of the South African Reserve Bank, is also a member.

As we have mentioned, another leading member of the Broederbond is Mr D P de Villiers, managing director of Sasol, the corporation that produces oil from coal – an organisation of enormous importance to South Africa facing constant threats of oil boycotts.

Afrikanerdom's large business undertakings are also generally under Broederbond patronage. The big Afrikaner financial combine of Sanlam is headed by Broeder Dr A D Wassenaar. The former managing director, Mr Pepler Scholz who retired recently, is a Broeder and so is his successor, Dr Fred du Plessis. Dr P E Rousseau, chairman of another Afrikaans finance house, Federale Volksbeleggings, is also a Broeder.

Afrikanerdom's Press barons are also members of the organisation. They are Mr Marius Jooste, the head of the huge Perskor group which, apart from its newspapers, handles a large slice of the South African Government's printing contracts and Mr D P de Villiers, the head of the Nasionale Pers group.

The Broederbond has an abiding passion for control of education because of the obvious advantages this holds for any organisation wishing to influence the lives and minds of young people. Consequently its representation in the top echelons of all the Afrikaans universities in South Africa is extremely strong. The list includes the following:

- Rand Afrikaans University – former chancellor, the late Dr Nico Diederichs (former State President of South Africa); rector and vice-chancellor, Professor Gerrit Viljoen (number 6197 and present chairman of the Broederbond); chairman of the council, Dr Piet Meyer (a former Broederbond chairman); vice-chairman of council, Dr R L Straszacker; former vice-principal for business administration, Mr R S de la Bat.

Broeders B J Vorster and Prof H B Thom at Mr Vorster's installation as Chancellor of the University of Stellenbosch.

- University of Stellenbosch – chancellor, Mr John Vorster (the former Prime Minister); vice-chancellor and chairman of council, the Reverend J S Gericke (number 1999 and a top executive in the Nederduitse Gereformeerde Kerk); rector, Professor J N de Villiers.
- University of Pretoria – chancellor, Dr Hilgaard Muller (former Minister of Foreign Affairs); principal, Professor E M Hamman; vice-principal, Professor A N Pelzer (number 3381); chairman of council, Dr S M Naude (number 233).
- University of Potchefstroom – chancellor, Mr Jan de Klerk (number 2490 and former president of the Senate); principal, Professor Tjaart van der Walt.
- University of Port Elizabeth – chancellor, Dr Anton Rupert; chairman of council, Dr A D Wassenaar; principal, Professor E J Marais (number 4955 and a member of the Broederbond Executive Council).
- University of the Orange Free State – chancellor, Professor B Kok (a Broederbond Executive Councillor); principal, Professor W L Mouton; chairman of council, Dr S J Naude.

The surviving white rectors of "non-white" universities are members, as were those who have been replaced by blacks. They include:

- The rector of the University of Durban-Westville (for Indians), Professor S P Olivier (number 6991).
- The rector of the University of Fort Hare (for blacks), Professor J M de Wet.
- Professor J A Mare (number 5340), the former rector of the University of Zululand.
- Professor J L Boshoff, former rector of the University of the North.
- The former rector of the University of the Western Cape, Professor C J Kriel.

These are some of the elite, the enormously influential brokers of power in South Africa. It is through the patronage of men like these that, after 1963 and 1964, the two most traumatic years of the organisation's existence, the chairman, Dr Piet Meyer, was able to report: "The Afrikaner Broederbond continues to show it is still the organisation that exercises the greatest influence among Afrikaners." He went on to spur the organisation to greater efforts to make a positive contribution to the "security of the Republic of South Africa as a white man's country."[2]

Dr Meyer's proud assertion of the organisation's influence is revealing. In the secrecy of internal communication with fellow members he placed a value on the organisation's importance which is invariably denied in public. Its response to accusations that it exerts influence at all is invariably one of injured innocence. When the allegation is made that it exerts political influence, its rebuttals become even more shrill. But a detailed examination of the organisation's history and record in the public affairs of South Africa will soon reveal that this is very much a matter of "methinks she doth protest too much".

The organisation itself provides ample evidence within its secret documents that it has been closely involved in every major political development in South Africa. These secret documents also clearly show that its links with the National Party are intimate and inseparable. At the *Bondsraad* meeting held on April 6 1972 the members heard a paper on *Ons Taak op Staatkundige Terrein* (Our Task in the Constitutional Field). The document begins with the peculiar form of "double-speak" the organisation has evolved. This is a cynical ploy whereby the organisation, with pious innocence, always declares that it is above party politics and may not involve itself in political or clerical matters.

It is, however, nothing more than a safety valve to be used in emergency. If the organisation comes under suspicion, and is under such pressure that it must submit to investigation, it can hastily produce documentary evidence that it has declared politics, among other things, "out of bounds". But its own documentation exposes the transparency of its claims. "That our organisation stands outside party politics does not, however, mean that our organisation ... has no task and duty in connection with organised endeavour on the other areas of life. Our members are, and indeed should be, simultaneously active members of their own Afrikaans churches and of their own national-political party and must continue to receive leadership from our organisation – that also goes for our church and party in regard to our cultural field. It is so, and should always remain so, that cultural leaders are at the same time church and political leaders; that political leaders are simultaneously cultural and church leaders; and that church leaders are likewise cultural and political leaders. Although our organisation stands outside organised party politics, there is nothing to prevent it from co-operating with any political party, even a ruling non-national political party, for the promotion of our Afrikaans-cultural ideals. That especially implies that our organisation will continue to remain in the closest contact with the leaders of our own national-political organisation and will co-operate intimately with them ... thereby ensuring that the Afrikaner's cultural struggle is also politically assured. While a nation's form of government is also an inherent part of its culture, it is obvious that a cultural organisation will directly involve itself therewith.

"Therefore, it was from the beginning an important objective of our organisation to strive for a peculiar Republican form of government in our country. We are giving constant attention to a greater historical-Afrikaans content to our form of government.[3] Our organisation has, from its formation onwards, had to do with the constitutional-political terrain. It was set as the general duty of our organisation on the political front that our members should continue to strive to combat Afrikaner division in this area, and to achieve and promote the greatest possible national-political unity.

"In the years of fusion, when there was serious political division among Afrikaner nationalists, we began to recruit leading national politicians as members of our organisation, namely Dr D F Malan,

J G Strijdom, Dr N J van der Merwe, C R Swart, H F Verwoerd and others. In these years our organisation propagated clearly and powerfully the Republican ideal as the most important medium for Afrikaner unity on the constitutional domain."

The document then deals with attacks on it by Generals Hertzog and Smuts until "in 1948, with the change of government by the National Party, under the leadership of Dr D F Malan, a staunch co-operation came into being between the Afrikaner Broederbond and the Broeder-leaders of the party. This co-operation already existed during the war years (1939–1945) with the support that our organisation gave to the attempts to overcome the serious divisions of nationalist Afrikaners.

"The big reunifying gathering at Monument Koppie (at the climax of the 1938 Oxwagon Trek) was organised by our organisation. Our organisation also initiated the Unity Committee *(Eenheidskomitee)*. In addition the Executive Council formed a Policy Committee, which drew up a Republican constitution for our country. Our political leaders were also represented in this.

"During the Prime Ministership of Advocate J G Strijdom, we co-operated with the National Party to develop South Africa as quickly as possible towards a Republic. At a special annual meeting, where Advocate Strijdom took part, the basis and form of the coming Republic was thoroughly thrashed out. It was, however, Dr H F Verwoerd, who was for a long time a member of our Executive Council, who called in the active co-operation of our organisation when he, as Prime Minister, decided to call a referendum for or against our becoming a Republic. We not only used our funds to elicit public support for the Republic, but also used the powers of our own members, and of outside supporters, to this end.

"As a result of hostile reaction engendered against our organisation, particularly by Freemasons within the ranks of the National Party, we co-operated with Dr Verwoerd in allowing the establishment of a judicial investigation into the activities of secret organisations. In the report of the judge concerned, our organisation was acquitted of any form of illegitimate behaviour and activity, particularly in connection with interference in party political matters (not strictly true: the commission did not investigate this aspect, see Chapter 17).

"Our staunch and intimate co-operation with our national political leaders was continued when Advocate John Vorster became our new Premier. We did everything in our power to prevent a small group of nationalists from forming their own party in opposition to the National Party, which is under the leadership of members of our organisation. And where some of our own newspapers tried to wage their own campaign in this matter, we tried to keep the split as confined as possible.

"Our organisation has, as in the case of our former national premiers, closely liaised with Advocate Vorster on all matters of great significance for the Afrikaner and which directly touch our nation as a language and cultural community. Not only his door, but those of all the members of his Cabinet, continuously stood wide open to use in this regard. Requests for support for specific matters have never fallen on deaf ears.

"In all the mentioned Nationalist Prime Ministerships, our organisation experienced the closest co-operation and sympathetic support for matters affecting the future of our nation. We name only the important ones: The Afrikaner's responsibility, role and place in the civil service, or semi-civil service: with the help of our own political leaders, success was achieved in opening the way to the top of these services ... for culture-conscious Afrikaners. There were no longer any obstacles for qualified and hard-working Afrikaners to reach the highest posts in all the State and quasi-State services. With the sympathetic understanding of our political leaders, the good Afrikaans businessman could tackle the road ahead with greater confidence as a result of our organisation's struggle for complete equal rights. The result of this was greater participation by the Afrikaner in the private business life of our country, although his disadvantage continues to give concern today.

"Perhaps the most important fruit of mutual consultation and co-operation is our progress in the educational field in the interest of the children of our nation. Afrikaans mother-language schools, which, under our Nationalist government, came into their own, indeed form the basis ... of our survival as a separate language-cultural national community. In addition, mutual co-operation also led to the development of a complete national education system for our country – surely one of the greatest national-political achievements of our time.

"Our organisation also placed its resources fully at the disposal of our political leaders for the consistent execution of our policy of separate development. It is not possible, within the framework of this short exposition, to fully reflect our contribution in this connection. This concerns not only theoretical contributions, but practical actions which are not even yet fully calculable. I mention only two in this connection, namely the contributions of SABRA and of Radio Bantu, in which our members play a large role.

"In the most recent period, concerning our multi-national sports policy, we have made a special contribution in organising this important matter in the interests of our country and all its national groups, and that on the basis of our policy of separate development.

"A matter which also continues to demand the closest co-operation of our organisation and our national-political action, is the need for continued immigrant contributions to the full development of our national economy. Without a powerful expansion of our national economy, our independent survival, as well as the execution of our policy of separate development, will come into serious jeopardy.

"On the other hand, we must be extremely careful that our own national composition, nature and character, as well as our own religious attitude, are not permanently damaged by immigration. Our organisation acts strongly and purposefully in this regard. We also continue to enjoy the support of our political friends in this connection. The naturalisation of immigrants into our own community is, for our organisation, of the highest priority.

"Dozens of other national-political matters in which we keep ourselves busy, are invariably summed up in our annual reports.

"Our current task in the constitutional field flows particularly from the fact that many Afrikaner nationalists recently have begun either to lose their enthusiasm for our language-cultural and national-political action, or are becoming so ensnared in petty personal grudges, that they are losing sight of the greater Afrikaner cause. According to a very reliable calculation, 70 000 Afrikaner nationalists in the Transvaal did not vote for Nationalist candidates in 1970. Of them, 33 000 voted for the Herstigte Nasionale Party, 15 000 for the United Party, while 22 000 abstained. That apart, about 7 to 10 per cent of urban Afrikaners and between 15 and 20 per cent of rural Afrikaners in the Transvaal continue to vote for the United Party.

"It is not the task of our organisation and besides we are not in a position, to analyse this situation correctly and thoroughly – what is our task is to stimulate the enthusiasm of culture-conscious

Afrikaners for our national-political action in the interest of our nation's own and separate survival, and to help overcome political division in our own ranks. It is self evident that any effective co-operation we can give in this regard, can and must be with the leaders of the ruling National Party. Not only are the members of the current Cabinet, with one or two exceptions, members of our organisation, but they are also the purveyors of our close mutual co-operation on the national-political front since 1948.

"As far as the Herstigte Nasionale Party is concerned, the Executive Council made it clear from the foundation of this party, which took place under leadership of certain of our members, that our organisation denies no member the right to have his own opinion on party political matters, or to join a political party of his own choice, as long as he does not, as a result, come into conflict with our Bond's basis, spirit, policy and objectives. And, where the Executive Council took disciplinary action against a member, it did so not on the grounds of his membership of a particular party or group, but because of his own individual actions, if they were in conflict with his personal undertakings of our organisation.

"Our most recent task in the constitutional field was, therefore, also to try to prevent the establishment of a second national-political party. We did not succeed. Thereafter, we did everything in our power to contain this division as much as possible. It was particularly our job to prevent this division from being brought into our own organisation. Here we succeeded to a great extent.

"Against the background of the outlined current situation, it is clear that we as Afrikaners, especially as members of our organisation, must fill our own people again with enthusiasm for our exceptionally important national-political action, and ... in this way demonstrate our own maximum political unity to the internal and external underminers and enemies of our country. We must not only now tackle the next election in a positive manner, but must carry it through under the banner of our unified Afrikanership, to the biggest-ever Nationalist victory.

"To do this in the closest co-operation with our political leaders, our organisation's specific task must include the following:

(a) We must systematically inculcate into every member, every Afrikaner and especially our young Afrikaners, the national-political responsibility and duty to achieve a massive victory in the next election on the basis of united Afrikaner resources.

(b) We must now inspire the national Afrikaner to give himself a positive national role, and to desist from the hairsplitting search for reasons for the birth of the present situation. Our political leaders know better than us what possible shortcomings on an organised national-political level must be rectified.

(c) As a cultural organisation, it is our particular task to start now to plan and organise unifying and inspiring cultural functions on a large scale throughout the country, functions like the Ox-wagon Trek, the Monument meetings, the language festivals and others from the past. In 1974, it will be 50 years since our first National government, with its policy of South Africa First, came to power – a rule which has been of the greatest significance to Afrikanerdom, not only politically and economically, but also culturally. This could, for example, provide good reason for large folk *(volk)* festivals before the next election.

(d) We must fight with all our might and completely eradicate all old-womanish slander about each other and underhand criticism of our leaders. To speak frankly to each other means to understand each other and to pool our strengths.

(e) We must marshall positively all our communication media to unite and not divide the Afrikaner's national-political power for the struggle for survival. In this our leaders must take the initiative ..."

The most vehement opponent of the Broederbond, seeking to prove its interference in, and influence on, political affairs in South Africa, including party political matters, could hardly have drawn up a more comprehensive indictment than the one which the organisation itself provides in this document. Another such indictment is contained in the Broederbond document *Ons Taak Vorentoe* (Our Task Ahead) which contains the following passage:[4]
"The most important and effective manner of ensuring our white future is to support with all our resources the current government, under the leadership of Dr H F Verwoerd, and to help keep it in power for as long as possible, in so doing not only to repel the leftist onslaught on our future, but also to successfully carry our the Transkei undertaking, with which our future is narrowly bound."
The organisation, continues the document, should help establish the public climate for effective government action in the so-called "Cold War", particularly where this involved unorthodox

methods. It should also support the government in its attempts to strengthen the police and defence forces. There are countless other documented examples of this kind of political involvement by the Broederbond. Many of them will be fully exposed in this book as it related the organisation's inexorable advance on behalf of Afrikanerdom and all its interests.

This ardent purpose presents the organisation with an enormous task, affecting virtually every aspect of South Africa's national life. It is a function the organisation undertakes with grave determination and collective dedication on an impressive scale. No project is too big or too small.

The organisation will apply itself to the problems of why Afrikaans schoolchildren sing English rugby songs (Circular 7/75/76 of August 27 1975) with the same diligence and fervour as it brings to matters of national and international significance. The Broederbond has achieved its position of extraordinary influence over South Africa's affairs by skilful manoeuvering, persistent application to its task, and sheer dogged hard work. Whether or not one agrees in principle that such an organisation ought to wield, from the shelter of absolute secrecy, such tremendous influence on public affairs; whether or not one agrees with the formulae it propounds as solutions to the problems of South Africa, one cannot but feel awed by the scope of its work, the success it has achieved, and the efficiency of its operations.

How does it operate and how has it been able to achieve so much? The current chairman, Professor Gerrit Viljoen, described the methods in his 1976 chairman's address to the national congress. "We are not an executive or governing organisation; we do not have the financial means or the manpower for that. In general, we comprise part-time amateurs and not full-time experts working only for the AB.

"Our task, therefore, is primarily to negotiate and to work through the activation, motivation and preparation of our own members, scores of whom carry high level management and policy responsibilities in their daily lives, and in this way 'do the AB's work' every day.

"The AB achieves most of its successes, and the greatest of them, not so much by working organisationally as the AB but far more through the daily work activities of its network of responsible, informed and motivated members.

"When expert committees are formed from AB members in

connection with national matters, we usually find that the majority of key figures in the relevant field are already our people, have already taken a lead, and are carrying responsibilities."

The organisation *has* succeeded in capturing major areas of influence in virtually every sphere of South African life, both in public affairs and in the private sector. These are goals for which it has worked with implacable resolve. It is insatiable in its hunger for influential positions throughout all strata of society, and is a hard taskmaster continually pushing and urging its members to extend that influence. The monthly circular letters are replete with instructions like the following:

1. "A by-election to fill an Orange Free State vacancy in the (South African) Medical (and Dental) Council will be held soon. All doctors can participate. Dr Izak J Venter, a Bloemfontein dermatologist, has been mentioned to us by friends as somebody who ought to be supported. Secretaries must convey this announcement to doctor friends who are absent when this circular letter is read (Circular 77/77/78 of September 1 1977).
2. "The attention of friends involved in education in the Transvaal is drawn to the fact that in the new education structure provision is made for the appointment of a head of department for vocational guidance at each school.
   It is of the utmost importance that these posts which were advertised in August are manned by teachers with the right attitudes, capabilities and motivation, as is the case with all heads of departments.
   In view of the responsibilities of this post, further explanation is hardly necessary: they encompass religious education, youth preparedness, the education programme in the hostels, cadets, and visits to the veld schools. Friends are asked to apply for these key positions (Circular 6/77/78 of August 1 1977).
3. "It is important that Afrikaners working in the newspaper industry are considered for membership. These people, because of their working conditions, cannot always take part in public affairs or serve on public bodies. Their work gives them exceptional opportunities to exercise leadership and influence so they merit consideration, especially as they perform, or can perform, a service to the Afrikaner cause (Circular 5/77/78).
4. "Branches and friends are asked to consider how to attract young people to Afrikaans organisations like Rapportryers.

Various branches have pointed out that promising young Afrikaners are being recruited by alien organisations like the Rotarians, Round Table and the Freemasons when they should have been won over to the Afrikaner cause. Young officers in the Defence Force and the police are often lost to our cause through recruitment by these organisations.
Branches with military bases in their areas, or where there are significant number of police or prisons officers, must give attention to this (Circular 9/76/77 of October 29 1977).

5. "Following requests from branches, we wish to emphasise the importance of the right influence in public organisations like municipal associations and agricultural associations. Friends must strive to ensure that people with the right attitudes are elected as executives of these bodies (Circular 5/75/76 of July 1 1975).
6. "It is important that senior officials of Afrikaner business undertakings and financial institutions render public service in fields where they can help develop and strengthen Afrikaner interests. Here we think particularly of local government, where people with a different outlook from ours often play a major role because Afrikaner businessmen are not available.
The Executive Council therefore calls on the appropriate friends to influence the directorates of large undertakings in this direction (Circular letter 4/75/76 of June 2 1975)."

Not only is the Bond's quest for influence insatiable, so is its hunger for information. It is never content merely to postulate theories or solutions. Intense investigation is its hallmark. "Our task is not only the formulation of policy but, even more so, the discovery of the best methods of carrying through proven policy at all levels and in all fields. This demands intensive and co-ordinated scientific research, sophisticated testing of methods, and their expert application" (Extraordinary circular of May 4 1961).

The Executive Council always comprises top people in a diversity of fields, and can draw upon a vast reservoir of highly trained experts on any aspect of the nation's life. They constantly form think-tanks and hold brainstorming sessions on virtually every subject imaginable: "Recently 14 work groups were constituted from 156 members representing the best brainpower, not only in South Africa but in the whole world, on virtually every aspect of life" (Extraordinary circular of June 12 1963).

So, in his last year as chairman, Dr Piet Meyer, head of the

South African Broadcasting Corporation, was able to report to the 1972 Broederbond National Congress: "To a greater or lesser extent the following matters were also given attention: the Association of Rhodesian Afrikaners, our relations with the Chinese and Japanese, liaison with Broeders abroad, South Africa's position abroad, methods whereby Afrikaner unity can be promoted and strengthened, the role of the State President and his public activities, constitutional relationships, the closing of the Heidelberg Training College, the American Field Service, the United States-South Africa Leadership Exchange Programme, the introduction of off-course totalisator boards in the Transvaal, the marked increase in snobbishness among Afrikaners, the Afrikaner worker, road safety, the Southern Cross Fund, the Springbok Legion, the so-called necessary lie.

"Brochures were compiled on our Christian national viewpoint and the basis and objectives of our struggle, the executive arts, coloured voting rights in municipal elections, the University of South Africa, municipal affairs, us and our church, etc.

"Study papers and documents on the following subjects, among others, were circulated from time to time: the Publications Control Board and its work, South Africa's capital requirements in the coming years, labour integration in South Africa, the administration of the AB, the attacks on the AB, the influence of foreign investment in South Africa, Indian education, Bantu education, Bantu population in white areas, the greetings and handshakes of the non-whites, the sports policy, sport and the current campaign against South Africa, parallel development as a guarantee of the future of the coloured people, who are the coloured people, our relationship with the coloured people, self-protection in a hostile world, pop music and the South African Broadcasting Corporation, the National Union of South African Students, the stranger in our midst, the agricultural industry in perspective, the importance of local authorities." This list reveals a remarkable degree of foresight anticipating the problem areas looming on the South African horizon.

The year 1972 was a watershed for South Africa. After a boom-decade, the Republic was about to go into a dramatic slide, economically, politically and internationally. Yet even in the days of heady prosperity and plenty, the organisation was paying attention to the vulnerable areas; preparing by study and investigation for the stormy passage ahead.

By 1972 sport was feeling the pinch of international isolation: the Broederbond was studying South Africa's sports policy and the campaign against it. Sport was to become a major preoccupation for the organisation, which has been closely involved in the policy modifications that have been effected over the years (see Chapter 14).

The following year, 1973, saw the oil crisis spread economic gloom over the Western world, and South Africa felt the early intimations of lean years ahead: the Broederbond had already examined the country's capital requirements for the future.

Three years later, in 1976, Bantu education and the problems of urban blacks exploded onto the national and international scene in a horrifying outbreak of protracted violence in the black townships, particularly Soweto. The Broederbond had looked at the education policy (stated by the leaders of the riots to have been the cause of the rising), and the question of blacks in "white" areas.

In the wake of the riots, international attention was focused even more closely on South Africa. By 1977 President Carter was in the White House and human rights was the issue of the day. The South African Government's harsh security clampdown in October that year, the widespread detention and banning of people and organisations, and the death in detention of black consciousness leader Steve Biko, followed in rapid succession, evoking bitter condemnation from the West and a determination to do something positive.

Sanctions and further isolation from the international community faced South Africa and the Broederbond had already investigated the influence of foreign investment in South Africa and the question of self-defence in a hostile world. In his 1972 report Dr Meyer had sounded an early warning, saying: "It appears that South Africa's position in international politics is not generally appreciated."

The question of the coloured people's place in South African society could be deferred no longer. South Africa needed to show the world at least some measure of progress towards solving its race problems. Late in 1977 the ruling National Party announced a major departure from the Westminster system of Government to a de Gaulle-style presidency in which coloured and Asian people would have a direct role; the Broederbond had been particularly active in connection with the coloured issue in 1972.

This, like sport, was a major matter that was to involve the

Broederbond intimately. The Government response to the Erika Theron Commission of Inquiry into the Coloured People and the proposals to change South Africa's constitution were issues to which the Broederbond applied particular study and energy, and over which it wielded tremendous influence (see Chapter 10).

All this investigation does not go to serve some esoteric, introspective Broederbond purpose. It is used for the South African Government. The Executive Council is in close and regular contact with the Cabinet and through its research, provides early warnings in important areas of national and international policy.

In his 1972 report, Dr Meyer told the Broederbond national congress: "We have worked in the period just past to maintain the closest liaison with Broeders in responsible circles. To this end we have held discussions from time to time with such Broeders at full meetings of the Executive Council.

"Apart from that, delegations have been formed to put specific problems to leading Broeders ... It is obvious that the Executive Council cannot expect its requests to be implemented in every instance. The Executive responsibility remains with our Broeders charged with specific tasks and answerable to the highest authority.

"The Executive Council would like to express sincere gratitude to the Prime Minister and the Broeders in his Cabinet for their readiness to receive delegations from our organisation.

"The relationship between the Executive Council and our Broeders in responsible circles was never better than it is now."

There can be little doubt that it is due at least in part to this relationship, and to the Broederbond's function as an early warning system, that Government spokesmen were able to say "We were prepared" when issues such as international pressure began to impact on South Africa. The chairman's summary of the events of 1975 (Circular 11/75/76 of February 4 1976) shows that the organisation remained involved in vital issues of the day.

Professor Viljoen again mentions "regular discussions at high level" and lists some of the subjects to which the organisation attended: the detente policy, relations with Rhodesia, the removal of unnecessary discrimination, shifts in the sports policy on the international front, the Turnhalle Conference in South West Africa/Namibia,[5] security matters, the education crisis, progress with separate development (particularly development of the homelands), the coloured question.

The detente policy provides another example of the Broederbond using its expert members to provide information to the Government on matters of crucial importance, and again highlights the very close working relationship between the organisation and the Government.

The previous monthly circular letter (10/75/76 of February 3 1976) contains the chairman's report on discussions with "friends in responsible circles" about the detente policy. He describes the pressure under which the South African team had to operate. "Often decisions with far-reaching implications have to be taken amid great uncertainty and risks. There can be no waiting or postponement to reach absolute certainty or greater clarity. There simply has to be progress; decisions and choices have to be made.

"In order to provide our members with the necessary expert information, the Executive Council has decided to establish a special committee on foreign relations, particularly on relations with Africa." This committee would collate information, analyse it, formulate strategy suggestions, and pass on valuable tactical information to the Prime Minister and his detente team.

A picture emerges of an organisation whose activities extend far beyond the realms of purely cultural endeavour to which it claims to confine itself. Broederbond documents show clearly that the organisation also involves itself and its members in party political matters. If it is axiomatic that the objectives of a political party are to assume power, and once in power to retain it, then the National Party in South Africa has a very valuable asset in the Broederbond. Although the organisation's constitution excludes party politics, the general aims of the organisation – furthering the interests of Afrikanerdom – provide a convenient rationale for supporting the National Party on the ground that, politically, it is the best agent for the purpose.

"It is obvious that we also guard the interests of the Afrikaner on the political front. We must be actively involved in the routine organisation and activities of the political party and so enable the standpoints and ideals of the Afrikaner to work their way through . . .

"But we want to add this: we call ourselves Afrikaners aware of our calling. If our members exclude themselves from politics on the pretext of being concerned with cultural matters they will in practice be neglecting their cultural concerns to an extent, because a nation's politics is a part of its culture"(Circular 2/74/75 of March 22 1974).

This provides part of the explanation for the Broederbond's continued existence as a secret organisation of fundamental importance to South African politics. It has been contended – both within the organisation and outside – that with the National Party's accession to power in 1948, and the advent of republic in 1961, the Broederbond has completed its programme. Whether or not the National Party per se played any role in convincing the organisation otherwise, its decision to remain cloaked in secrecy must have caused heartfelt relief in party circles.

The Broederbond in fact performs a significant role in keeping the National Party in power. There is documentary evidence that the local branches of the Broederbond take it upon themselves, as an official part of their work programme, to help the National Party during elections.[6]

There is also evidence of the Executive Council urging Broeders to work for the party. "Friends are again requested to involve themselves actively in the National Party organisation. That is the most effective and, in fact, the only way in which influence can be exercised in the nomination of candidates. Members of our organisation should play an active role, *as members of the party,* for the duration of the election" (Circular 6/69/70 of September 2 1969).

But, important as this is, it is not the organisation's most useful feature where the National Party is concerned: the organisation also provides the Government with its own private and, more important, secret opinion poll. Just as Western politicians regularly use opinion polls to check the grassroots feelings of the electorate, so does the National Party use the Broederbond. The unique advantage in this case is that the Government has at its disposal as a sounding board for any proposed policy innovations a streamlined, highly disciplined organisation of nearly 12 000 members representing the main body of its support, and covering the broadest possible spectrum of interest groups.

It works quickly and efficiently, costs the Government nothing, and is secret. This works in several ways: some of the study documents sent out by the Executive Council to the general Broederbond membership are drawn up specifically to guage the reaction of the members.[7]

On important policy matters this system provides "friends in responsible circles" with quick access to 12 000 confidential opinions. Another way it performs this function is through questionnaires on specific subjects. This was explained in a detailed

Broederbond document *Our Organisation,* circulated in June 1974. Under a sub-heading "Activities and Work Methods of the Executive Council" it says: "As far as is practical, opinion polls on specific subjects will be provided more often by the distribution of short questionnaires to branches and even individual members. The results of such studies will be made known to the branches by the Executive Council and will be used in representations to friends in responsible circles."

Both these methods were used to supply the Government with detailed information on the sports policy and the coloured issue. It is, of course, doubly valuable. While it is of enormous value to the Government to have this secret facility available, it also provides the organisation with a formidable weapon. If it wants to initiate changes or innovations, or prevent them, it can bring this considerable bargaining counter to the conference table, further strengthening its already well-stocked arsenal as a pressure-group extraordinary in South Africa.

Similar benefits accrue from the organisation's national congresses, held every two years. These take a form similar to political party congresses in the sense that they pass resolutions on major aspects of public policy such as education, foreign affairs, finance, agriculture, defence and internal security. They also, of course, handle internal matters, such as organisational affairs, cultural and work programmes, finances and the election of the Executive Council.

Cabinet Ministers attend these congresses and take careful note of the attitudes, criticisms and trends. This has the double effect of providing the Government with secret access to candid and often outspoken opinions and at the same time adding one more link to the organisation's chain of influence.

1. The third, the late Dr Nico Diederichs, was also a member and one-time chairman of the Broederbond. T E Dönges, who was State President-elect before his death, was also a member.
2. Sekretariele Verslag van die Uitvoerende Raad oor die tydperk 1 Maart 1963 tot 28 Februarie 1965, p 27.
3. This envisaged giving executive power to the State President, as was the case of the presidents of the former Boer Republics. It is a tribute to the organisation's influence that this is part of the new constitutional proposals to be introduced in South Africa at the turn of the decade.
4. *Ons Taak Vorentoe,* p 13.

5. Later in the same report he says the constitution's conference was taking place "under our direction."
6. The nature of the evidence in this case cannot be revealed as it would lead straight back to one of our confidential sources.
7. For example, the paper *The Coloureds – an Approach to their Future* which, according to Circular 6/76/77 of August 3 1976 was "sent out in August 1975 *for comment*."

Part one
Ascent to power

1 *History of the Afrikaner Broederbond*

Vereeniging, May 1902 and the bedraggled, tattered leaders of the Boer forces gathered to talk about peace after three years of exhausting, bitter war. Slowly they dribbled into the camp which had been set up on the Transvaal side of the Vaal River. Indomitable, proud men, whose small bands of farmer soldiers had seriously embarrassed the British forces, the mightiest fighting machine in the world at the time. Under a lull in the war, negotiated with the British commander, Kitchener, the Boer warlords, many of whom had not seen each other for months, years of fighting, greeted each other tiredly and sat down to talk. Travelling under guaranteed safe conduct through the British lines, Botha, De Wet, De la Rey, Kemp, Beyers, names which had become legends throughout South Africa and across the Atlantic in the rich, leathery clubs and stately homes of Britain, rode dustily into the camp. Smuts, interrupting his siege of O'Okiep in the north-west Cape, arrived by train, having been uneasily entertained by the British themselves, including Lord Kitchener, who rode up on a magnificent black charger to greet him at Kroonstad. Accompanying him was the young Deneys Reitz, who described the Transvaal commandos as "starving, ragged men, clad in skins or sacking, their bodies covered with sores, from lack of salt and food ... their appearance was a great shock to us, who came from the better-conditioned forces in the Cape."[1]

In due course, on May 15, all sixty delegates from the Transvaal and Orange Free State converged on Vereeniging and, with their governments, commenced their discussions. The arguments ranged endlessly back and forth, moving from extremes of optimism, through a spectrum of harsh experience, to extremes of pessimism. But, reports Kruger,[2] "Submission was inevitable: it was palpable in the tattered clothes of many delegates, in the absence of Steyn who was too sick to appear publicly, in the vivid recollection of ruin from end to end of the country."

But still the talking and arguing dragged on. While some urged peace, others supported the fiery Kemp, who declared: "As far as I am concerned, I will fight on till I die."[3] From Vereeniging, a small delegation moved to Pretoria to try to negotiate terms with the British, but the hated Milner was obdurate, and they returned empty-handed. Slowly the deadline for a decision drew near, until on the last day, May 31, the young Transvaal State Attorney, Jan Christian Smuts, stood up to speak. "We are here not as an army, but as a people," he said. "We have not only a military question, but also a national matter to deal with. No one here represents his own commando. Everyone here represents the Afrikaner people, and not only that portion which is still in the field, but also those who are already under the sod and those who will live after we have gone. We represent not only ourselves, but also the thousands who are dead and have made the last sacrifice for their people, the prisoners of war scattered all over the world, and the women and children who are dying out by thousands in the concentration camps of the enemy; we represent the blood and the tears of an entire nation. They call upon us, from the prison-of-war camps, from the concentration camps, from the grave, from the field, and from the womb of the future, to decide wisely and to avoid all measures which may lead to the decline and the extermination of the Afrikaner people, and thus frustrate the objects for which they made all their sacrifices. Hitherto we have not continued the struggle aimlessly. We did not fight merely to be shot. We commenced the struggle and continued it to this moment because we wished to maintain our independence, and were prepared to sacrifice everything for it. But we may not sacrifice the Afrikaner people for that independence. As soon as we are convinced that, humanly speaking, there is no reasonable chance to retain our independence as republics, it clearly becomes our duty to stop the struggle in order that we may not perhaps sacrifice our people and our future for a mere idea which cannot be realised." Continuing his eloquent plea for peace, he said the result of the struggle should be left in God's hands. "Perhaps it is His will to lead the people of South Africa through defeat and humiliation, yea, even through the valley of the shadow of death, to a better future and brighter day."[4]

About an hour before the midnight deadline, the talking was exhausted and after the hawklike De Wet suddenly switched and gave the nod for peace, a statement drawn up by Smuts and his legal colleague Barry Hertzog was signed that "We, the national representatives of both the South African Republic and the Orange Free State ... have with grief considered the proposal made by His Majesty's Government in connection with the conclusion of the existing hostilities, and their communication that this proposal had to be accepted, or rejected, unaltered. We are sorry that His Majesty's Government has absolutely declined to negotiate with the Government of the Republics on the basis of their independence ... Our people ... have always been under the impression that not only on the grounds of justice, but also taking into consideration the great material and personal sacrifices made for their independence, that they had a well-founded claim for that independence."[5]

After setting out the reasons for laying down their arms, the statement ended: "We are therefore of the opinion that there is no justifiable ground for expecting that by continuing the war the nation will retain its independence, and that, under these circumstances, the nation is not justified in continuing the war, because this can only lead to social and material ruin, not for us alone, but also for our posterity ..."

England rejoiced. In Holland, one of the protagonists who started the war, Paul Kruger, placed his hand on the open Bible and murmured, "God will not forsake His people."[6] In South Africa some of the Boers smashed their rifles rather than hand them over, some refused to swear allegiance to the Crown and were deported, but most conceded defeat and trudged off to a forbidding future.

As the silent groups of guerilla fighters returned to their desolate farms, their bitterness fanned the flames of a new nationalism. Materially the war had taken a heavy toll. Towards the end, the British had adopted a scorched earth policy and had laid waste the Boer farms. They had also established concentration camps for the "protection" of Boer women and children. Although many gave themselves up voluntarily to these camps, they led to one of the most bitter aspects of the war – 26 000 Afrikaner women and children died in conditions of terrible disease and hardship. The fact that scores of British died of the same diseases did little to expatiate the bitter grief of the Boer veterans. Hardly an Afrikaans family did not lose a mother, young son or daughter in the camps, and even today accounts of the deprivation and hardship they caused are passed on from one generation to the next. Spiritually, the Boers emerged in better shape. They could hold their heads high in any company as fighters. Britain had put 448 000 men in the field, while the Boers could at no time call upon more than 70 000, and probably never had more than 40 000 in active service. The British were trained soldiers, while the sharpshooting Boers were almost exclusively civilians under arms. In round figures, 7 000 British soldiers were killed and 20 000 wounded. The Boers lost 4 000 men. They were justifiably proud of their war record. With this pride was a burning nationalism and a determination to become the rulers of their land – one day.

And, of course, they had their bitterness and hate to sustain them. Lord Salisbury was prophetically accurate when he said that if the Boers submitted without fighting, they would hate the British for a generation; if they fought and were beaten they would hate much longer.[7] The imprint has not faded and there is an unhappy measure of truth in the persistent South African cliché that the Boer War is still being fought today.

A fundamental and powerful factor in that abiding hate was Lord Milner, the tyrannical High Commissioner whose rigorous imperialism so antagonised the Boers. As Kruger[8] points out, the great achievements of British colonial administrators all over the world have usually stemmed from their love of the country and people they administered. When Milner wrote from South Africa, "I have always been unfortunate in disliking my life and surroundings here," he laid bare a fundamental disqualification for his job. If Milner disliked South Africa, the Boers detested him and all he stood for. They particularly detested his policy of anglicising the Afrikaner. Under the British regime, Afrikaans became a despised language. Children were allowed to speak it only three hours a week at school, otherwise they had to carry a placard proclaiming, "I am a donkey, I spoke Dutch." O'Meara[9] observes: "Within the imperialist colonial states, a clear cultural oppression operated against Afrikaans speakers. Long before the war ended the independence of the Republics, so generating a fierce cultural response, the language of the Cape had inspired a strong cultural nationalism. More importantly, in an essential peripheral economy dominated by the ideology of imperialist interest, for those Afrikaners unprepared to accept cultural assimilation, and who possessed a modicum of training, rendering them unsuitable for manual labour, employment opportunities were limited. English was the language of the economy."

Herein lay the seeds of more Afrikaner resentment. The devastation of their lands by the British during the war, crop failures, drought and depression forced many of them off the land and into the cities, particularly the goldfields of the Witwatersrand. Here, proud landowners became labourers – a pathetic, dejected group, whose bitterness and family responsibilities were all that kept them going. From the bitterness of military defeat, they were forced to the greater bitterness of economic subjection by the same foe, British imperialism.

But in this ravaged emotional and spiritual wasteland, little breezes were kicking up dusty hopes. Poets like Eugene Marais, Totius, C Louis Leipoldt and others were giving dignity, depth and cultural validity to the Afrikaans language. Politically, there were stirrings as well. General Louis Botha in the Transvaal organised his people in a new political union called Het Volk, with an underlying philosophy of "forgive and forget". Four years after defeat, Botha became the first premier of the Transvaal. In the Orange Free State, Abraham Fischer, with Hertzog and De Wet, organised the Orangia Unie and in 1907, he became its Prime Minister. In the Cape the following year, John X Merriman rejuvenated the Afrikaner Bond and came to power under the banner of the new South African Party. The elements of Afrikaner reconstruction were beginning to grow.

On May 31 1910, the Act of Union was passed, moulding South Africa into a constitutional unit. The parochial, provincial elements of Afrikaner political expression combined under Botha, the first Union Prime Minister, in the form of the National South African Party. The party was only formally founded in November 1911, after it had won the election and had ruled for some time. At the formation, speeches were given by most of the Boer heroes, including General Botha, President M T Steyn, Generals J H de la Rey, J B M Hertzog and J C Smuts. But it was an uneasy and artificial alliance, the first signs of which came when "National" was dropped from its title. General Hertzog, particularly, was an uncomfortable presence. He was unpopular with the English section of the population and with the Press, largely because of his record in education matters. While he was Minister of Education in the Free State in 1908, he passed a law which put Dutch and English on a par in the schools and also made mother-tongue instruction compulsory until Standard Six. General Botha tried to keep Hertzog out of the Cabinet by offering him a post as an appeal judge, but he refused.[10] Constitutionally, South Africa was indeed unified, but emotionally and politically deep divisions remained. Afrikanerdom split into two distinct camps inside the same party. On the one hand, there were those who subscribed to Botha's dictum of forgive and forget, which led to the accusation that he began to ignore the interests of his own people, giving preference to the British. On the other hand, there was the Afrikaans language champion, Hertzog, pursuing a policy of South Africa First, which sought to unite South Africans into one Afrikaner nation, free from any form of imperialism.

Eventually, Botha felt compelled to drop Hertzog from his Cabinet, but, as if nothing had happened, Hertzog stayed on in the party. Then, on December 28 1912, he made a ringing speech in Pretoria and outraged British sensibilities when he said he would rather live with his own people on a dunghill than stay in the palaces of the British Empire. Botha was appalled, but was unable to subdue his outspoken compatriot.

The inevitable split came the following year at the united congress of the SAP in the Cape in November, where voting was 131 to 90 in favour of Botha continuing without Hertzog. The latter walked out of the congress, followed by the revered Boer commander, General de Wet, who, with a flourish, waved his hat at the congress and called out "adieu". And it really was goodbye; the split was irrevocable.

In January 1914, Hertzog called a special congress of his supporters where the National Party was formed.

The first acid test for the separating streams of Afrikanerdom came the same year when World War 1 was declared. Botha felt that South Africa, as part of the Empire, was compelled to enter the war. Constitutionally, he was left little alternative. But it was too soon to put the Union of South Africa to such a test. Afrikanerdom was seriously divided within itself, and the Boer War, concluded only 12 years previously, loomed large in the memories of the Afrikaner people. Botha's quandary became agonising when Britain accepted his offer of assistance and, moving outside the limits of its intentions, immediately requested him to seize the German territory of South West Africa. Hertzog won enormous Afrikaner support by strenuously opposing this proposition, saying it was contrary to "South Africa First" and was really only in the interests of the British Empire. Only 12 years after the Boer War, with heartbreak and grief still deep in Afrikaner hearts, the stage was being set for an even more traumatic experience – *Broedertwis,* brother taking up arms against brother.

A remarkable set of coincidences lit the fuse of the Afrikaner fratricide. Botha was quietly, behind the scenes, setting in motion the training of a force of men to march on South West Africa. General de la Rey, a Senator in Botha's party, had other ideas and saw in the war an opportunity to win the final victory of the Boer War and gain republican independence for South Africa. General Beyers, Botha's Commander-in-Chief was also against active participation in the war, but remained irresolute. De la Rey brooded in restive agitation at home in Lichtenburg. Nearby lived a man, Niklaas van Rensburg, who was reputed to be a seer and prophet, gifted with second sight.

It was said that during the Boer War, while serving with De la Rey, he had used this gift to save many military situations in the nick of time. As a consequence many people, including his former general, believed in him implicitly. During this period of torment over whether to fight Britain's war or not, Van Rensburg claimed to have had a vision in which a red bull and a grey bull had a fight to the death. The red bull was trampled in the dust. This was taken to be a sign that Germany, associated with grey, would defeat Britain, unmistakeably represented by red. Van Rensburg, in his vision, also saw the number 15 against a dark cloud from which blood poured. He saw De la Rey, with his head bare, coming home and he saw a carriage filled with flowers. These visions were interpreted as the scenes of the restoration of the republican flag and as the triumphant return of De la Rey on the 15th of the month. The story of Van Rensburg's vision spread like wildfire across the western Transvaal and gave rise to the belief that the Great War in Europe was the opportunity for the realisation of the Afrikaners' republican dream.

De la Rey began seriously to think in terms of a revolt against Botha. He prevailed upon the less convinced Beyers and a conspiracy of officers was hatched. It included Major J C G Kemp, commanding the 1 400 men in training for the South West expedition at Potchefstroom, and Lt. Col. S G Maritz, in command of the training camps in the north western Cape. On 15 September Beyers resigned his commission as Commander-in-Chief of the armed forces. On the same day, he and De la Rey left Pretoria for Potchefstroom, where Kemp was waiting to start the revolt. Also on that day, on the instructions of the Botha government, armed patrols were out, manning roadblocks and searching for the notorious Foster gang, a band of robbers and murderers who had escaped the law for months. On the way to Potchefstroom, De la Rey and Beyers came upon one of these roadblocks and, thinking their plot had been revealed, crashed through it. Further on, they attempted the same at a second roadblock. A policeman, aiming at the wheels of the speeding car, opened fire and a bullet, ricochetting off the road, found De la Rey's heart. He died in the arms of his stunned friend and co-conspirator. His death was also the death of the planned revolt. Beyers, never absolutely convinced about the course he was on, quickly pulled out and Kemp, when he heard the news, hastily countermanded all the steps he had taken. Five days later, thousands gathered at De la Rey's home town of Lichtenburg for the funeral of one of the most respected and well-loved of the Boer leaders. Botha and Smuts attended as well as De Wet and Beyers, not yet openly rebels. The prophet Van Rensburg had not been entirely wrong. There was De la Rey, bare-headed on his bier; there was a carriage festooned with flowers and wreaths; and there was the bloodstained car. An ugly mood prevailed at the graveside, where grief-stricken Afrikaners believed that the famous old fighter had been killed, not by accident, but on instruction from the Government. In vain, Botha and Smuts tried to explain what had happened and eventually the crowd dispersed, muttering threats against the Prime Minister.

This sullen mood spread throughout the western Transvaal and northern Free State, stoking up emotions to exploding point.

H S Webb in his *Oorzaken van de Rebellie* described some of the scenes which led up to the rebellion.

"At a National Party meeting at Potchefstroom on October 2, a wild mob interrupted the meeting and threw rotten eggs and dead cats at the General (de Wet) – the hero of heroes of the Afrikaners" (p 48). And at a concert in Pretoria to celebrate Kruger's birthday on October 10, at which General Beyers was to speak, "eggs, tomatoes and sinister objects were thrown at him, while the British National Anthem was sung" (p 50).

The fuse was lit when Maritz, far away in the Cape, raised the standard of revolt and, after some hesitation, declared the independence of the Union. In itself, Maritz's action was doomed, but it provided the charge to galvanise the rest of the country into armed rebellion. Botha, faced with a massive crisis, took to the field himself. It was Boer commander against Boer commander as De Wet called his Free Staters to arms and Kemp did the same in the Transvaal. Beyers, who ostensibly should have led the Transvaal rebels, did not have his heart in the fight against fellow Afrikaners and took to the bush, eventually to be forced into the fray. Botha, able to mobilise huge resources, soon scattered the rebels. Kemp and Beyers, nearly out of ammunition, began to pin their hopes on Maritz soldiering on near the German South West border. Eventually Kemp, with 600 mounted men, struck out across the Kalahari to join forces with Maritz. Beyers, hounded by Government forces tried to recross the Vaal River, from the Free State back to the Transvaal. He met his death from heart failure in the swollen waters of the river. When his body was recovered, it was found that he had not fired a single shot from his Mauser pistol. He had been a rebel by circumstance, never by conviction.

Meanwhile, in the Free State, De Wet continued the rebel struggle, but Botha's superiority soon began to tell and, like Kemp, De Wet decided to strike out to join forces with Maritz. He never made it; with dwindling support and with his resources rapidly exhausting themselves, he was harried across the veld until he was cornered on a farm near Kuruman. The legendary warrior, who had fought so successfully against the British, finally gave himself up to a fellow Afrikaner, Colonel J F Jordaan, and was locked up in the Johannesburg Fort to await trial.

With the capture of De Wet and the death of Beyers, the fire of resistance in the rebel forces was extinguished, except for Kemp and Maritz and a small band of die-hards in the Pretoria district under the leadership of Captain Joseph Fourie. "Jopie" Fourie joined the rebellion, but made the cardinal error of not first resigning his commission from the Government forces. After a sharp skirmish, in which the Government troops lost heavily, Fourie was captured, arraigned at a field court marshall and condemned to death for treason. Leading Afrikaners, like Dr D F Malan, the Cape Dutch Reformed Church minister, pleaded with the Government for leniency, but with no success. On December 20 1914, Jopie Fourie, bravely singing a hymn, faced a firing squad. The shot that killed him became a symbol to Afrikaner nationalism, that imperialism, and Afrikaners who co-operated with it, could be trusted never again.

Kemp, after an epic trek across the desert, managed to join up with Maritz and for a while they together scored a number of victories over the Government soldiers. But it could not last.

Eventually, Maritz fled to Angola and then to Portugal and Spain. Kemp surrendered and, with his officers, was taken to Johannesburg to stand trial.[11] In the first half of 1915, the rebel leaders were tried and convicted to varying terms of imprisonment and fines. De Wet was sentenced to six years' jail and a £2 000 fine, Kemp to seven years' imprisonment and a £1 000 fine. None served the full prison terms, however, and by the end of 1916 all had been released after their fines were paid by public subscription. Krüger[12] sums up: "The rebellion was over, but it had been no slight affair. Thousands had taken part, hundreds of lives had been lost and the cost in money was high. The rebellion had important political consequences. All ex-rebels, who had not been political supporters of Hertzog before now became such, and their relatives and friends speedily joined their ranks. They bitterly hated Botha and Smuts and their policy which they blamed for the whole affair. Memories of the South African war with its destruction of property and its concentration camps revived and Botha and Smuts were henceforth classed as renegade Afrikaners. Botha's opponents did not realise that for him also it had been a terrible experience, that in his heart poignant memories had been revived and that the rebellion was to hasten him to his end."

Botha paid the political price of the rebellion in the general election later that year. During his campaign, he suffered the terrible humiliation of having insults like "bloodhound", "murderer", "traitor", "Judas" thrown in his face.[13] Hertzog scored huge dividends and in the end Botha's South African Party and its Independent supporters received 95 000 votes as against Hertzog's 77 000, forcing Botha into coalition with the ardently pro-war Unionists, who were hated by many Afrikaners as "British Jingoes".[14]

Deep Afrikaner divisions persisted throughout World War 1. Politically in turmoil, economically oppressed, culturally confused, the Afrikaner by the end of the war was a dispirited, demoralised, broken soul. It was into this grim scenario that the Afrikaner Broederbond was born. It was a birth marked by fire and violence. On the night of April 17 1918 a Nationalist meeting, addressed by the party's Cape leader, Dr D F Malan, who had left the church for politics, was broken up by a mob. The National Club building in Johannesburg was vandalised, fittings and furniture were smashed up and set alight in the street. In the mayhem, members of the audience were beaten up. It had a marked effect on three young Afrikaners, H J Klopper, H W van der Merwe,. and

D H C du Plessis. Still in their late teens, the three met on a koppie in Kensington, Johannesburg the following day and pledged themselves to form an organisation to defend the Afrikaner and return him to his rightful place in South Africa. They were helped in their task with advice from the Reverend J F Naude, a Dutch Reformed Church minister. On the evening of June 5 1918, they held a meeting with a few others at the home of Danie (D H C) du Plessis in Malvern. This meeting can really be taken as the formation of the Afrikaner Broederbond, at that stage called Jong Suid-Afrika.

In his review, O'Meara ascribes the birth of the organisation firmly to imperialism which "was seen as having operated since 1806 to divide Afrikaans-speakers with conflicting classes, and, since the Slagtersnek rebellion, the (Great) Trek, and 1877 annexation of the Transvaal, and finally the conquest of the Republics, subjected them with increasing oppression, impoverishment and division. The Afrikaner Broederbond was born into, and self-consciously as a result of, these divisions."[15]

Professor A N Pelzer, a leading Broeder, explained the organisation's initial problems in his historical review given at the Broederbond's 50th Anniversary in 1968. "For understandable reasons," he said, "it was difficult to explain the aims of the Bond clearly in words, with the result that, in the beginning, people were allowed in to the movement who thought it was just another cultural society. In this way, many disappointments were suffered and it took more than two years before the Bond took on its final shape. On September 21 1920, the rules of the Bond were accepted, which made an end to the initial uncertainty."

At that stage, the Broederbond consisted of 37 members, who declared themselves the founders of the Bond.

One of the earliest members was Mr L L du Plessis, (not to be confused with Professor L J du Plessis), who said the Broederbond was originally an Afrikaans organisation to propagate the Afrikaans language and bring together serious-minded young Afrikaners in Johannesburg and on the Reef.

"It was nothing more than a semi-religious organisation," Mr du Plessis added. "Meetings were held in the parsonages of the Jeppe and Irene congregations, as well as in the Irene church hall, where the late Reverend W Nicol (later moderator of the Nederduitse Gereformeerde Kerk and Administrator of the Transvaal), was Minister."

It was an open organisation then and the members were expected to wear Broederbond buttons on their coats. Of the founder, Henning Klopper, Mr du Plessis said, "We were at school together and we worked together for years in the railway service. He is an idealist of the first magnitude and a man who never touches alcohol and tobacco."

One of the first 18 young Broeders, Lourens Erasmus Botha van Niekerk, pondered in a newspaper interview in 1964: "I wonder why the Broederbond has become the way they say it has?"

He found it puzzling that the organisation had become such a potent underground force, that it had seized sufficient power to take upon itself the guidance and administration of an entire nation. "It was never intended to be like that, I can assure you," Mr van Niekerk said. "I can remember the first days of the Bond. It was in the year of the great 'flu when 18 of us got together one night in the old Irene church hall in Plein Street, and decided to form an Afrikaner society. There were 11 railwaymen, six policemen and one outsider. The driving force behind the establishment of the society was Henning Klopper.

"We formed the Broederbond as a kind of counterpart to societies and clubs which, in those days, were exclusively English-speaking. Those were hard days for the Afrikaner. Everything was English and Afrikaans-speaking people found it hard to make out. We decided the Broederbond would be for Afrikaners only – any Afrikaner – and that it would be a sort of cultural society. We started raising funds to build up a library and we invited prominent Afrikaners to give lectures. There was nothing sinister about the Bond in those days. We had our own colours – green, gold and grey – and we had some good times. In 1922, I was transferred by police headquarters to Port Elizabeth and later to Bloemfontein, where I lost touch with the Bond. They never communicated with me after that."

On August 26 1921, at a meeting in the old Carlton Hotel, the members decided to transform the Bond into a secret society (Oelofse report, p 8).

At the 50th anniversary of the Broederbond in 1968, only nine founder members were still alive and Henning Klopper made a rousing speech about the organisation he formed and which had taken over effective control of almost every public position.

According to another founder member, Mr L J Erasmus, who later left the organisation, the Bond's decision to go "underground" was justified. "The confidential nature of its activities and membership was only decided upon under pressure of the cruel realities of those post 1918 days as a matter of tactics, and self-preservation strategy." Members, particularly civil servants and teachers, claimed they were persecuted because of their open association with the Bond. If the Bond went underground, they could carry on the furtherance of its aims unharmed.

The tide had turned. From an idealistic, open society for the Afrikaner, the Bond was on its way to becoming a secret Afrikaner elite organisation, determined to rule South Africa.

After the decision in favour of secrecy the members spent their time planning the expansion of the organisation and implementing a masterplan for ruling South Africa. A rigorous set of rules guarding its secrecy was laid down, so that no outsider knew who its members were, its plans, or even its successes and failures. The first branch of the Broederbond existed for three years before a second was formed – on the West Rand on August 26 1921. The next year, on March 3 1922, an East Rand branch was formed.

From the time that Mr Iwan Lombard became the Broederbond's first full-time secretary on January 1 1931, the organisation really expanded, as shown below:

	Number of Cells	*Members*
1920	1	37
1925	8	162
1930	23	512
1935	80	1 395
1940	135	1 980
1945	183	2 811
1950	260	3 662
1955	332	4 749
1960	409	5 760
1965	484	6 966
1968	560	8 154
1977	810	12 000

By 1968 – 50 years after formation – the three Transvaal branches had increased to 237, Cape to 191, Orange Free State 97, Natal 19, South West Africa 11, and Rhodesia 5. The one branch in Lusaka, Zambia, was disbanded in 1965/66.

In its 60 years of existence, the Broederbond had only 12 chairmen:

H J Klopper – June 5 1918 to June 26 1924 – later Speaker of the House of Assembly.
W. Nicol – June 26 1924 to March 13 1925 – later Administrator of the Transvaal.
J H Greybe – March 13 1925 to May 26 1928.
J W Potgieter – May 26 1928 to September 6 1930.
L J du Plessis – September 6 1930 to August 13 1932 – later Professor at Potchefstroom University.
J C van Rooy – August 13 1932 to October 6 1938 – Professor at Potchefstroom University.
N Diederichs – October 6 1938 to October 3 1942 – later Minister of Finance and State President.
J C van Rooy – October 3 1942 to February 23 1952.
H B Thom – October 1 1952 to November 24 1960 – later Rector of Stellenbosch University.
P J Meyer – November 24 1960 to 1972 – Chairman Board of Directors, SABC.
A P Treurnicht – 1972 to 1974 – Deputy Minister.
G Viljoen – 1974 – Rector of Rand Afrikaans University.

All the Broederbond chairmen – with one notable exception – remained faithful to the secret society until the end. The exception was Lodewicus Johannes du Plessis. One of Afrikanerdom's most talented sons, he became one of the leaders of the Super-Afrikaners, later tried to break its ranks, became a rebel, and died a lonely man. The Du Plessis story illustrates the strong hold the Broederbond can take on individuals, no matter how brilliant they are. For even when he was at his bitterest and in an open feud with the Prime Minister, Dr H F Verwoerd, he never dared attack the Broederbond openly.

Wikus du Plessis, son of a professor at a theological school, was born on February 10 1897, at Burgersdorp. He was a brilliant scholar in four disciplines: economics and political science, in which he got an M. Econ; classics, in which he obtained an M.A.; and law, in which he obtained an L.L.B.

He was elected chairman of the Broederbond on September 6 1930, and served until August 13 1932. On April 1 1933, he became professor in political science and law at the Potchefstroom University College for Christian Higher Education. Also in 1933, he became chairman of the National Party in the Transvaal. He was professor until the end of December 1946 when he moved to

Johannesburg, to immerse himself in the economic struggle of the Afrikaner.

"Undoubtedly, it was worry over the economic position of the Afrikaner and his own calling to make a contribution to the improvement thereof which made him take that step."[16] Du Plessis was one of the founders of *Volkskas* and for eleven years he was chairman of the board of directors. He also played a key role in forming *Asokor, Kopersbond* and *Dagbreekpers,* one of the pillars on which the mighty Afrikaans Press group, Perskor, was based. The present chairman of Perskor, Mr Marius Jooste, said of him: "Up to that time (the beginning of the fifties), I do not know of a single foundation in the north, as well as many in the southern part of South Africa, in which Wikus du Plessis did not have a share – I go so far as to say that no other Afrikaner of which I know, can be compared to this, when it comes to the forming of Afrikaner businesses."[17] Du Plessis was an outstanding political theorist, rather than a leader. After fusion, he became the first chairman of the Transvaal National Party. "He played a leading role in it (the NP), especially in policy formulations. The constitution (draft republican constitution) was almost exclusively his creation. It is no longer any secret that Dr Malan at one stage considered Professor du Plessis as his successor."[18]

Du Plessis served on the Supreme Council of the militant Ossewabrandwag, and was its policy chief until 1946. He became chairman of the unity committee which had to try and establish reconciliation between the Ossewabrandwag and the National Party. He was never a conformist, except, perhaps, for the period he was in the Broederbond leadership. But even of that time he said: "I was not a founder, but a reformer of the Broederbond."[19] He did not explain what he meant by it, probably because he still felt bound by the oath of secrecy.

The rift between Du Plessis and the party and Broederbond leaders became deeper and deeper. He challenged concepts such as White *baasskap,* and said colour discrimination should go. He pleaded for proper consolidation of the homelands and diplomatic ties with Africa – views with which any *verligte* Nationalist would today agree, but in the late fifties, were regarded as heresy. Du Plessis was so far ahead of his time that the strain between him and Verwoerd reached breaking point. In 1959, he was expelled from the National Party by the Transvaal Head Committee, and also replaced as chairman of the *Dagbreek* board of directors. On his expulsion from the party, he said: "Dr Verwoerd has not silenced me; only God Almighty can do that. I am only to be in abeyance for a while, like Nehru."

The final humiliation was his expulsion from the Broederbond, the organisation he joined and steered in its formative years. In 1960, he wrote to Mr J P van der Spuy, the Secretary of the Broederbond:

"I do not write to justify myself or to persuade anybody, but only as witness to my own conscience. And I hope I write with no self-glorification or personal grief, but straightforward, and to the point . . . in deep sorrow over the wonderful opportunities missed by Afrikanerdom, because of the narrow-mindedness and imperiousness of the leaders – who dare not accept heroic vision because the nation *(volk)* is supposedly not ready for it, but at the same time try to destroy everyone who undertakes to prepare the nation (for change). However, I hope, through the grace of God, that they will not be able to destroy me – because I fear nobody and I believe only and exclusively in God Almighty, through Jesus Christ our Lord."[20]

Soon after the break between Du Plessis and the Super-Afrikaners, the rumours started – that he was an alcoholic, that he was "off his head", and did not know what he was doing.

In 1963, he underwent a brain operation.

According to Potgieter: "After that, his life became still. His voice no longer heard in clear and persuasive tones. His crafty pen no longer writing. His energetic life came to such a sudden end . . ."[21] It was a chilling epitaph. Wikus du Plessis died in 1968, a lonely man, rejected by the men he helped to unite Afrikanerdom, and through their propaganda, by Afrikanerdom at large.

1968 was the year of Du Plessis' death, but it was also a year of triumph for the Afrikaner Broederbond. It marked fifty years of its existence, fifty vigorous years during which it left its insidious imprint on every major political event in South Africa's development. It had grown from small, desperate beginnings to become a giant shadow, a spectre of enormous power working behind the scenes, manipulating, squeezing, forming South Africa's policies and strategies for the sake of Afrikanerdom. But mingled with the triumphs, those 50 years also saw their setbacks and crises.

Ironically, the Broederbond came into being on a wave of emotion and fervour largely symbolised by Hertzog in the World War

1 years: ironically, because Hertzog was destined to be the first person publicly to deal the organisation a punishing body blow, the first to present it with a real crisis.

1. Kruger, R, *Goodbye Dolly Gray,* p 496.
2. Ibid. p 497.
3. Ibid.
4. Kestell, D E, and van Velden, J D, *The Peace Negotiations between Boer and Briton in South Africa,* pp 188-191.
5. Kruger, R, Goodbye Dolly Gray, p 503.
6. Krüger, D W, *The Making of a Nation,* p 19.
7. Troup, F, South Africa: An Historial Introduction, p 190.
8. *Goodbye Dolly Gray,* p 509.
9. O'Meara, Dan, *The Afrikaner-Broederbond 1927–1948: Class Vanguard of Afrikaner Nationalism,* Journal of Southern African Studies, Vol 3, April 1977, p 161.
10. Van Rooyen, Jan J, *Die Nasionale Party – Sy Opkoms en Oorwinning – Kaapland se Aandeel,* p 2.
11. Under a general amnesty non-commissioned rebels were released. It was a heavy factor against the rebel leaders, because with the lure of a pardon, much of the fight went out of their men, who quit and went home.
12. *The Making of a Nation,* p 95 (from which the bulk of the account of the rebellion was taken).
13. Ibid. p 102.
14. Ibid. p 103.
15. O'Meara, Dan, *The Afrikaner-Broederbond 1927–1948: Class Vanguard of Afrikaner Nationalism,* Journal of Southern African Studies, Vol 3.
16. Potgieter, P J J S, *L J du Plessis as Denker oor Staat en Politiek,* p 9.
17. Die P U Kaner, November 19 1968, p 5.
18. Potgieter, P J J S, *L J du Plessis as Denker oor Staat en Politiek,* p 13.
19. Letter to the *Sunday Express,* June 22 1958.
20. Potgieter, P J J S, *L J du Plessis as Denker oor Staat en Politiek,* p 17.
21. Ibid. p. 18.

Prime Minister Barry Hertzog. The first outspoken opponent of the Broederbond.

2 *Hertzog*

The morning of November 6 1935 dawned fresh and clear in the Orange Free State. In the dusty rural constituency of Smithfield, there was much activity because that afternoon the member of Parliament was to make a speech. At any time this would have been a highlight of the local farming community's year. On this occasion interest was heightened because the MP had been ill and the meeting put off several times.

The MP was the Prime Minister, General Barry Hertzog, the veteran Boer campaigner and an architect of the guerilla tactics the ragged farmer army had used with devastating effect against the British some 30 years previously.

Now in coalition with General Smuts, he was ardently pursuing the goal of national unity in South Africa, trying to weld English-speakers and Afrikaans-speakers into one Afrikanerdom, pledged to put "South Africa First." The Fusion policy of the two Boer generals was proving a viable and vibrant force in South African politics.

But there were new forces growing among Afrikaners; restless, rebellious mutterings against the reconciliation politics of Hertzog and Smuts; forces of exclusive nationalism that wanted nothing to do with outside, foreign influences; forces that in their time would destroy both Hertzog and Smuts. It was a new nationalism on the march under the banners of D F Malan and similar intellectuals including N J van der Merwe, T E Dönges, Eric Louw, C R Swart, J G Strijdom, H F Verwoerd.[1]

This new breed of nationalists had little in common with the two generals governing South Africa at the time. They lacked war experience, they had been born in the platteland, and had studied at South African and European universities. They had become members of a new political intelligentsia emanating from the *burgerstand*. The remodelled National Party held them together, but so did an older and in a sense more inclusive organisation, the Afrikaner Broederbond.[2]

By 1935 the Broederbond was a flourishing concern. Its membership had grown from small beginnings in the Transvaal 17 years previously, to include members from all the provinces apart from Natal – disparagingly known as the last bastion of the British Empire. By 1935 it had harnessed to its exclusive nationalist, republican cause significant numbers of farmers, civil servants, railway workers, budding businessmen and politicians. It also enjoyed the support of a large number of Afrikaner *dominees* and schoolteachers. With the spiritual and educational leaders well and truly in the fold, it was beginning to shape up as a durable power in South African affairs. At that stage, South Africa as a whole was unaware of this growing force in its midst. The secrecy on which the organisation's founding fathers had so strictly insisted ensured that.

However, when the sun set over Smithfield that clear November day the carefully nurtured, closely guarded secrecy lay shattered. The venerable old Boer general, Hertzog, had launched a blistering attack on the Broederbond and poured scorn and contempt on its creators' claims to be better Afrikaners than anybody else.

The echoes of that speech, delivered in a strained and croaking voice by Hertzog, who was suffering from a throat infection, were to reverberate around South Africa for years to come. Even today, the organisation must look back at what became known as the Smithfield address with a shuddering distaste for the unwelcome memories it recalls. Smithfield was a watershed for the Broederbond, from which it has never fully recovered. It launched a wave of suspicion and mistrust which has worried the organisation ever since.

It also marked the beginning of the end for Hertzog, who had given his all for his people and country. At Smithfield he joined battle with a force that was to prove more than a match for him and drive him into lonely defeat. Author W A de Klerk[3] sets the scene. "For more than 30 years, Hertzog had accepted the growing burden of serving his people and country ... In the Anglo-Boer War he had been among the successful commando leaders who had invaded the (Cape) Colony, and had ultimately managed to establish Boer control over a large part of the north-western territory ... He had led a ragged band of burghers over the endless Karroo, often being forced to proceed on foot, because of horsesickness. In many encounters with the British, his commando had miraculously survived. His most notable victory had been the capture of Calvinia on January 10 1901. This town was later to be represented in Parliament by D F Malan. Meanwhile, his wife had suffered deeply in a British concentration camp.

"After the war, in the days of the Orange River Colony, he had fought and won the battle for equality of the languages in the schools. At De Wildt, in 1912, he had stood under a korri tree and had announced his championship of the *eie* (literally, own). All who gave their unconditional loyalty to South Africa, he said, were Afrikaners. In 1924, he had formed a most successful coalition with the English-speaking Labourites. He had fought for and established iron and steel and other industries. He had expanded the railways. He had cared for the dispossessed of his people. He had fought, against the most impassioned opposition, for a national flag. He had been the decisive factor behind dominion sovereign independence and diminishing colonialism. South Africa had been hit by drought and depression and his people had suffered. He himself had gone through difficult times, but he had always survived. He was still deeply, reverently attached to the *eie* and to the ideal of national unity. He visualised both great cultural traditions flowing in two parallel streams. With Smuts, he had found a *modus vivendi.* They were fully agreed on the deep necessity of encouraging a true South African spirit, a feeling of national self-respect. After the many years of unrelenting political conflict, the country overwhelmingly supported Fusion.

"The only serious opposition came from the Cape Nationalists, under the leadership of Malan. In a speech at Stellenbosch on June 29 1934, Malan had openly accused Hertzog of dealing on his own initiative with Smuts, who had been rejected by the volk, at the cost of principle. 'Principles?' Hertzog angrily expostulated. What did these political *parvenus* know about principles when they libelled a man of the stature of Smuts in the way they did? They, the Malanites, were, according to themselves, the only true believers. Hertzog himself had become 'the poor old general ...'

"Hertzog himself gave no quarter. His intolerance and angry invective towards his former political comrades remained unsurpassed. His abhorrence was unmitigated and complete. What, Hertzog was to inquire with mounting bitterness, had these 'super-nationalists' ever done for their country to warrant their fantastic claims? All they ever seemed to do, he might have thought, was to gather in the Koffiehuis in Cape Town. There they sat, morning after morning, listening to the pronouncements of a man who had watched the Anglo-Boer war from the comfort of the Netherlands (Verwoerd) ...

"Hertzog was right in judging the behaviour of the new political intellectuals as being – to use a modern term – one-dimensional. They were concerned only with Afrikaner ascendancy in an Afrikaner nation. But he was wrong in trying to explain everything in terms of an unadorned power struggle. What he failed to recognise was the intimation of revolutionary thought among the political intellectuals of the expanding *burgerstand.* Increasingly it became for him a personal struggle. In the Koffiehuis, discussions tended to be directed to the idea of a completely new South African order. It would not only be a republic, it would be an Afrikaner republic of a particular kind. Its shape could not yet clearly be seen, but it would be fundamentally different from what had always been obtained. What was being discussed in the Koffiehuis was only a reflection of ideas being deeply considered in the Broederbond ..."

On November 7 1935 at Smithfield, then, Hertzog went to the heart of the new force spreading unease in the South African political scene – the Broederbond itself. Said *The Star's* headlines that afternoon: "Aims of the Afrikaner Broederbond – Secret Society Backed by Nationalists – Dangerous Policies – Folly of Domination By One Race in Union." The following morning, the *Rand Daily Mail* followed up in the peculiar, multi-tiered headlines fashionable at the time: "Premier Denounces Underground Racialism – Secret Anti-British Broederbond Attacked – Misuse of Voortrekker Movement Alleged."

The Star, from which the bulk of this account is drawn, began its report: "In his speech at Smithfield this afternoon, the Prime Minister, General J B M Hertzog, referred at length to a secret society, known as Die Afrikaner Broederbond, and pledged to secure dominance of South Africa by the Afrikaans-speaking section, or, as it had appeared recently, by the 'purified Nationalist Party.'

"In this organisation, which had originally been cultural, but was now frankly political, Dr Malan and his lieutenants were prominent members. The Broederbond, stated the Prime Minister, sought to advance its members in the civil service and in political life and to induce Afrikaners to buy only from shops owned by Afrikaners.

"General Hertzog described this movement as a dangerous attempt to spread disunion in the country and said it was a further reason why the people should back the United Party solidly."

General Hertzog went on to apologise for appearing before his constituents somewhat later in the year than usual. The "vicissitudes" of his advancing years were making an increasing impact on his life, he said. Then he dealt at length with farming matters, how to combat weeds and erosion, rural housing schemes, provisions for labourers, the availability of food, clothing and the "usual necessities of life," wages, and labour conditions generally, the state of the gold mining industry, prosperity in the Union – all matters of vital importance to a South Africa emerging from the debilitating years of Depression.

Winding up the "state of the nation" part of the speech, General Hertzog said no unprejudiced person could doubt that the success which had crowned the efforts of the Government and the circumstances which had made these efforts possible were due above all to the fact that the grave problems which had been solved so successfully were made the responsibility, not of a party political group, but of the whole nation joined together in one united national party, and operating through a Government which could act, and did act, as an authoritative body on behalf of, and in the interests of, the whole South African nation, the Afrikaans-speaking as well as the English-speaking sections.

Emphasising the vital importance of harmony and cordial relations between these two sections of the population, General Hertzog continued: "Unfortunately storm clouds are already beginning to gather and, unless we are on our guard, the foundations of our whole state structure – freedom, language equality and the rest – will soon be wrenched asunder and our state structure will crash to pieces in its fall.

"What do we see about us today? Restless and feverish attempts in all directions to create dissension among the people; to incite one race against the other in irreconcilable aversion and hate towards each other; to exploit our cultural possessions, our language and our religion, our history and our derivation as inimical means of attack and for the purpose of fighting, libelling and abusing one another. The political platform is no longer looked upon as a place or opportunity for imparting information or guidance to the people, for reasoning and convincing, but rather for malicious demonstrations, for incitement and fisticuffs.

"Why all this nervous excitement, these ill-mannered cad displays? Does not every one of us feel that this is an unusual phenomenon, something foreign to the nature and character of the Afrikaans-speaking South African? Why then this passionate political disorderliness, in which even fist assaults on men and defenceless women are no rare occurrences? What lies behind all these outbursts, accompanied by excessive political activities?

"That the division among the Afrikaans-speaking section of our nation is the contributing cause towards all this misconduct and nation-violation is responsible for this division among our people is therefore of the greatest importance.

"We shall thereby not only discover with whom the fault lies, but also what the aim and motives are of those to whom the guilt attaches, while we shall further be placed in a position to exercise the necessary restraint on the mischief that is at present threatening our entire national existence."

At this point Hertzog quoted at length from previous speeches by Malan showing that the latter had declared himself on numerous occasions to be in full support of attempts to unify English and Afrikaans-speaking sections of the South African population. Then, said Hertzog bitterly, within four months of pleading for national unity, Malan had spoken at the Federal Council of the National Party in Pretoria, where, in collaboration with Dr N J van der Merwe, he did all in his power to wreck national unification. When he found he could not do this, he had isolated himself in a separate party of purified nationalists. Instead of proceeding with his plea for a united Afrikanerdom, Malan had suddenly swung round and become the champion of division and controversy among Afrikaners. He accused Malan of being motivated by racial animosity in deciding not to take part in unification.

He went on: "Before I proceed to deliver proof of what I have just said, however, permit me to inform you of a disclosure made to me recently. It affects a secret society called Die Afrikaner Broederbond and the relation in which Dr Malan and other prominent leaders of the Purified National Party stand to the society. Die Afrikaner Broederbond is a society established in 1918. At inception it was entrusted with the task of guarding the cultural interests of Afrikaans-speaking Afrikanerdom, with the definite provision in its constitution: 'Party politics are excluded from the Bond.'

"No objection could, therefore, be raised against the Broederbond restricting its membership to Afrikaans-speaking persons, and I want to accept that, as a purely cultural body, the Bond did good work.

"So long as the Bond remained a purely cultural body, with purely cultural objects, no particular objection could be taken against its establishment as a secret society, except that it might be misused – as so often happens with secret organisations, owing to their nature – for purposes other than its defined objects and thus become a danger. Unfortunately, this was precisely what was soon to happen with the Bond. In the long run party politics could not be kept out of it and as the influence and political views of a certain section in our public life gained ascendancy in the Bond, it was converted from a cultural to a party political organisation.

"In August 1932, the Broederbond had proceeded so far along the road of party politics that the chairman of the Executive Council, which is the highest authority of the Bond, could, as chairman of the Bond's congress, make the following statement with the general approval of the congress. 'Our Afrikaner Broederbond must not withdraw its hand from the cultural work, merely because sufficient vigilant defenders have now come to the fore. But for a start, provision has been made for that primary national need.

"'In conformity with this new situation we find that the Broederbond is gradually making over its cultural work to its considerably bigger son, the FAK[4] and I think that we should be acting wisely if we pursue this course also at this Bond council. I consider that national culture and national welfare cannot unfold fully if the people of South Africa do not also constitutionally sever all foreign ties.

"'After the cultural and economic needs, the Afrikaner Broederbond will have to devote its attention to the constitutional need of our people. Added to that, the objective must be an entirely independent, genuine Afrikaans form of government for South Africa ... a form of government which ... through its embodiment in an own personal head of State, bone of our bone and flesh of our flesh ... will inspire and cement us to irresistible unity and strength.'

"But the Bond was soon to proceed much further along the political course. On January 16 1934 a circular letter was issued by the highest executive authority of the Bond, namely, the Executive Council, signed by the chairman, Professor J C van Rooy, and the general secretary, Mr I M Lombard. This letter, which was directed to all members of the Bond, reads as follows, 'Our test for brotherhood and Afrikanership does not lie in a political direction, but ... in aspiring after the ideal of a never-ending existence of a separate Afrikaans nation with its own culture.

"'It has been made sufficiently clear at the previous meeting of the Bond council that what we expect of members is that they should have as their object the Afrikanerising *(verafrikaansing)* of South Africa in all aspects of its life. Brothers, your Executive Council cannot tell you to promote party political fusion or union, or to fight it ... but we can appeal to every brother to choose in the party political sphere that which, according to conviction, is most helpful for the Bond's object and the Bond's ideals as outlined above and as is known to you all.

"'Let us focus our attention on the fact that the primary consideration is whether Afrikanerdom will reach its ultimate destiny of domination *(baasskap)* in South Africa. Brothers, our solution for South Africa's ailments is not that one party or another shall obtain the whip hand, but that the Afrikaner Broederbond shall govern South Africa.' (The organisation began recruiting Afrikaner Nationalist political figures about 1934. Among the first nationalist MPs to join the Broederbond were D F Malan, C R Swart, J G Strijdom, N J van der Merwe, and H F Verwoerd. Later, through the organisation's active participation in the Republican struggle, "the Afrikaner Broederbond bound itself more closely to the national organising of the political struggle for State power ..." The document also boasts that after the clash with Hertzog, "with the leadership of the National Party ... in the hands of Broeders, the Afrikaner Broederbond was in the fortunate position of being able to discuss any differences of a serious nature with our Broeder leaders in the political field ..." Still later in the document, in a remarkable example of "double-talk", the statement is made: "The Afrikaner Broederbond as a non-party political cultural organisation devotes its support more and more to the National Party's political struggle ...")

"In order to realise the precise tendency and meaning of the words I have just quoted from the address of the chairman and from the circular of the Executive Council of the Bond, it must be explained here that a person, in order to be admitted to membership of the Bond, must conform, *inter alia,* to the following demands: (1) He must be Afrikaans-speaking; (2) His home language must be Afrikaans; (3) He must subscribe to the ideal of a never ending existence of a separate Afrikaans nation with its own culture.

"As stated by Professor van Rooy, Mr du Plessis and others on various occasions, the word 'Afrikaner' in Broederbond circles conveys the exclusive idea of a Dutch Afrikanerdom. This is also made abundantly clear in the constitution and other articles of the Bond.

"Now, when we consider that wherever these two Potchefstroom ministers of religion use the words 'Afrikaner' and 'Afrikanerdom', they mean Afrikaans-speaking Afrikaner and Afrikaans-speaking Afrikanerdom, and when we consider, moreover, that the membership of the Broederbond is strictly confined to Afrikaans-speaking persons, then the words of Professor van Rooy as well as those of Mr du Plessis, allow of no doubt as to what is intended by it all.

"The Broederbond's high ideal and aspiration, according to what they themselves inform us, is to let Afrikaans-speaking Afrikanerdom attain domination in South Africa, and to get the Afrikaans-speaking Broederbond to govern South Africa. Very pretty, surely! Flattering to the soul of Afrikaans-speaking Afrikaners such as you and I! But it suffers from one great deficiency – a deficiency that must of necessity lead to the downfall of the Afrikaans-speaking Afrikanerdom itself, if this form of Afrikaner jingo self-glorification is persisted in. It is forgotten that there are also English-speaking Afrikaners in South Africa, who are also entitled to a place in the South African sun.

"When will that foolish, fatal idea cease with some people that they are the chosen of the gods to govern over all others? The English-speaking section has tried this with the Afrikaans-speaking section, but they did not succeed. The Afrikaans-speaking section has also tried it with the English-speaking section, but they also have failed. Neither the one nor the other will ever succeed in a policy of domination, and where the Potchefstroom fanaticism is out once again to incite Afrikaans-speaking Afrikanerdom to a repetition of the past, I want to ask Afrikaans-speaking Afrikanerdom – my own people – whether South Africa has not suffered sufficiently in the past from Afrikaner strife and dissension? I want to ask you whether our language and our freedom are of so little value and significance to us that we should once again stake it in a gamble from pure racial animosity and fanaticism?

"When I exclaimed, 'Very pretty, surely flattering to the soul of the Afrikaans-speaking Afrikaner such as you and I,' I had unfortunately forgotten one thing – that it is clear from the provisions of prescriptions of the Broederbond as well as from the circular letter of the Executive Council, and of Professor van Rooy, that where they speak of the Afrikaner, or of Afrikanerdom, which must dominate in South Africa, you and I, who are not brothers, are not included. You and I will have to be satisfied that we shall never have the privilege to share in the Broederbond domination in South Africa. We are not Afrikaners.

"But, what is more, not even all the brothers count as Afrikaners or are considered worthy of sharing in that superlative privilege of domination. According to the test laid down by the Executive Council and Professor van Rooy, for true Afrikanership nobody can have a claim to Afrikanership other than persons who have set themselves the ideal of the Afrikanerising which excludes the English language and the English-speaking Afrikaner. The Fusion brother, such as you and I, and any other protagonists of national unity are isolated from the privileged circle of true Afrikaners predestined by Professor van Rooy and his Executive Council for domination in South Africa.

"By this opening address of Mr du Plessis and the circular letter of the Executive Council signed by Professor van Rooy, the cultural mask of the Afrikaner Broederbond has been removed, and it has entered the political arena with no ambiguous battlecry. As will be clear to you in a moment, the Broederbond has been converted into a secret purified National Party that is occupying itself with that secret propaganda work for the promotion of the interests of the purified brothers and of the purified National Party. As could be expected, the Bond has been put at the disposal of the Purified National Party in ever increasing measure since 1932[5] and its doors have been thrown wide to all who can pass as leading or prominent purified nationalists. But the wider the doors of the Bond are opened for the purified party, the tighter they are closed on the United Party, so that since 1932 not a single leading political person taking an active part in politics and belonging to the United Party, has been taken up by the Bond.

"The membership list of the Broederbond has been swelled almost exclusively by prominent musket-bearers and propagandists of the Purified National Party. The Broederbond has, since that time, fallen almost exclusively into the hands of the purified Nationalists, while all brothers not belonging to the purified party have been pushed aside as far as possible. It is the purified nationalist brothers to whom must be ascribed the fact that the Bond, since that date, has been misused in various ways for purposes and objects for which it was never intended and which have shocked the feelings of right and justice of those among the brothers who do not belong to the Purified National Party to such an extent that some were obliged to take part in active protest.

"I have just said that since 1932 the Bond has been placed more and more at the disposal of the Purified National Party and its objects. How, it is asked, was this possible without the joint knowledge of the Fusion brothers in the Bond?

"The answer is simple. The non-purified section who were known not to sympathise with purified politics or known to be active Fusionists were simply ignored and shunned as apostate brothers and kept in the dark as much as possible as to what was transpiring. Where, thus, it concerned matters in the interests of the purified National Party, they were not consulted, and were left in ignorance of what was being done.

"How easy it is for a section or branch to intrigue to its heart's content is evident when I tell you that it is an instruction to every member of the Bond that each member must be well known to every other member in his section. Everyone knows, therefore, who is a Fusionist or not, and who must be shunned as apostate. No matter what the cultural object and striving of the Afrikaner Broederbond may have been in the past, in the light of what I have submitted to you here today, there can be no doubt that in the Broederbond we now have to do with a secret political society accessible only to, and consisting only of Afrikaans-speaking Afrikanerdom to domination in South Africa, ignoring the rights and claims of the English-speaking section of our population ...

"Of this secret Broederbond, which has as its ideal dissension among the Afrikaner nation, through the exclusion of the English section from the government of the land, Dr Malan has been a member and brother since coalition. It must be clear to everyone why Dr Malan was suddenly converted from a protagonist to an antagonist of Afrikaner national unity. His membership of this anti-English movement of necessity compelled him to depart from the policy of national unity, which included the English-speaking Afrikaner; he was further compelled by his connection with the Broederbond to pursue the course of national division and strife.

"Three things emerge crystal clear from what I have just divulged: (1) that membership of this secret society is entirely in conflict with co-operation for the establishment of a united Afrikanerdom of English-speaking and Afrikaans-speaking sections; (2) that Dr Malan, by becoming a member of this secret society, had of necessity to become disloyal to his earlier doctrine of a united nation and had of necessity to refuse co-operation with the United Party; (3) that when Dr Malan denies that he was influenced, and is still influenced, in his refusal to co-operate with the United Party and national unity, by racial animosity and the desire to dominate over the English section of our population, he makes an inaccurate statement.

"The question with which I commenced my address on this subject has now been answered. We know now decidedly who and what is responsible for the national division and strife among us. What a pathetic figure Dr Malan strikes in this sorry episode of our national history!

"But what I have said here about Dr Malan applies no less to his first lieutenants, Dr van der Merwe, Advocate Swart, the Reverend C W M du Toit, Advocate Strydom and Messrs Werth, Haywood, Martins and others, all members of the Broederbond and thus all obliged, with Dr Malan, not to support any national unity in co-operation with the English section of our fellow citizens ...

"We see now in what close relationship the Afrikaner Broederbond stands to the Purified National Party. The leaders and moving spirits of the one are the leaders and the moving spirits of the other. There can be no doubt, therefore, that the secret Broederbond is nothing less than the Purified National Party busy working secretly underground, and that the Purified National Party is nothing but the secret Afrikaner Broederbond which conducts its activities on the surface. Between the two, the unification of Afrikanerdom is being bartered for a republican-cum-Calvinistic Bond.

"By departing from the sphere of national culture and mixing in politics, the Afrikaner Broederbond has shed its youthful innocence and has suddenly become a grave menace to the rest and peace of our social community as well as to the irreproachable purity of our public life and of our civil administration, even where it operates in the economic-cultural sphere.

"To realise the nature and extent of the danger with which we are now being threatened by the secret machinations and activities of the Broederbond, it is necessary for me to impart to you certain information from secret documents of the Bond regarding its organisation, members and several other particulars. The strictness with which the Bond's activities are kept a secret appears from the fact that only very few persons outside its organisation know of its existence, although it has existed for 17 years and although there are few towns or villages in the Free State where it is not in operation, or where it has no organisation.

"The members of the Bond are not many – at the outside 2000. But the power of the Bond does not lie in its membership, but in its secret organisation, which, for instance, is spread over the whole Free State like a network for the purpose of active propaganda. In this network, every vestige of information of any sort that may be useful to the National Party, true or untrue, is caught up and disseminated. The sort of propaganda that emanates from this network is of a nature similar to that employed by *Die Volksblad* and *Die Burger*.[6]

"In this network of secret propaganda lies the main power and influence of the Broederbond. Not solely in this. It is closely connected secretly with a number of institutions deliberately exploited by interested politicians and semi-politicians to be used secretly as instruments for the furtherance of secret motives. The Federasie van Afrikaanse Kultuurverenigings, the Handhawers-Bond, the Helpmekaar, the Voortrekkers, the Republican Bond, the Calvinistic Bond – all these, no matter how useful and necessary some of them may be to the Afrikaner nation and its interests, are systematically used and misused, through the medium of the Broederbond for those ends.

"Each member, under solemn promise, is obliged to maintain the strictest secrecy. Nothing affecting the Bond, its existence, its members, its activities, or its organisation dare be divulged. The Bond is organised into local divisions or branches of at least five members each, each branch having its own executive and its own domestic rules. For the rest, each branch stands by itself and acts as its executive thinks fit as a separate, independent entity, if necessary without the knowledge of the rest.

"At the head of the Bond is an Executive Council of nine members elected annually by the Bond council or congress and vested with illimitable power of control over the affairs of the Bond. To become a member, each person concerned must undergo a very strict and secret test on the lines of the Freemasons ...

"In the secret manual of instructions, printed for the use of members of the Bond, it is laid down that brothers must endeavour to support the interests of brothers, and that brothers should support one another's undertakings as far as possible. The spirit of preference between brothers and their interests is obvious throughout the rules of the Bond and controls the relationship between brother and brother everywhere. So much so that in the domestic rules of certain branches of the Bond, which have received the approval of the Executive Council of the Bond, the following, *inter alia,* is definitely laid down: 'The promotion of each other's interests in the community ... shall be the duty of Bond members ... brothers shall, wherever possible, support one another's business by word and deed, and be one another's intercessionary wherever the opportunity offers.'

"Even if the Broederbond had never become a political society and had contined to exist as a purely cultural body, gross injustice would have been done whenever a brother furthered the interests of a fellow brother along secret channels to the detriment of a non-brother who might have equal or greater claims to support. Hence the Bond is a secret body with the strictest injunction against each member to maintain the utmost secrecy of what happens, and it is therefore impossible to discover what is transpiring behind the scenes; there is no protection for the non-brother against the secret supporters of the brother.

"Generally, there is nothing to prevent the Bond from being misused as an instrument of organised injustice towards non-brothers – or even as an instrument of organised action in conflict with the best interests of the State and the public service.

"As an instance of how the Broederbond abuses its powers as a secret political society, I must remind you of what happened recently when the so-called Le Roux motion[7] was before Parliament. While the motion was being discussed, the Broederbond set to work secretly and a secret organisation was set afoot by brothers on the platteland for the purpose of making propaganda in support of the motion. The brothers, encouraged by the Purified Nationalists in Parliament, succeeded in manoeuvring matters in such a way that numbers of telegrams were sent to practically every platteland member of Parliament for the purpose of bringing pressure to bear on him to support the motion.

"Through this secret activity, the Bond endeavoured to create the impression that the members of Parliament had to do with a spontaneous expression of feeling on the part of the people of the respective constituencies. The Bond in this instance, therefore, deliberately assumed a role in a play of deceit, by which it endeavoured to influence the free vote of members of Parliament in favour of the purified Nationalists in Parliament. The Broederbond, a secret society, deliberately availed itself of its secret nature to mislead representatives of the people of the Union in the execution of their national duties.

"Another instance of the secret interference and the secret misuse of the Broederbond is provided by the following. The purified brothers in Parliament were apparently embarrassed in Cape Town recently by a lack of co-operation among themselves on a matter in which it was desired that they should all vote against the Government. To obviate a similar occurrence in the future, some of the purified brothers, without the knowledge of other brothers, agreed to avail themselves of the secret existence of the Bond with its secret authority and influence.

"Suddenly one day the brothers in Parliament received notice that a certain gentleman from Potchefstroom had been appointed, or would be appointed, as political commissioner for the Bond in Parliament, and that he had been entrusted with the task of attending the sittings of Parliament from a vantage point somewhere in the gallery, with power to issue instructions from time to time to Parliamentary brothers, telling them how to vote etc. This was a bit too much for the brothers in Parliament who were not prepared to submit themselves as puppets to a Bond dictator. Mutiny and revolt on the part of Fusion brothers was the result, and the Broederbond had to pocket its commissioner and depart.

"The Fusion brothers in Parliament deserve our compliments. But I cannot help warning them that those who wish to dine with the devil must provide themselves with long spoons. From this again it transpires how much the Bond and the purified National Party is one and the same body, functioning in two separate compartments – the one underground and the other above ground.

"What is there to prevent brothers seeking to promote one another's interests in respect of appointments and promotions in the public service to the detriment of more deserving non-brothers? Has this not already happened without its being discovered? I put it to you, what protection have you and I and our children, who are not members of the Broederbond, against the misuse of secret influence by brothers whereby we are prevented from attaining what is legitimately and rightfully our due?

"This I do know, that brothers have urged their prior claims over non-brothers before responsible officials of the State, who are also members of the Broederbond. If I understood the matter aright, these claims of brothers went so far as to demand that the prescriptions of the Broederbond should weigh more with brothers occupying responsible positions than the legitimate rules of the public service. Fortunately, these attempts failed, by reason of the courageous opposition which these presumptuous demands met at the hands of the officials concerned.

"If the prescriptions of the secret manual of instructions to which I have referred, or of the domestic rules of the branch quoted by me, are strictly carried out, then a brother who has a shop can lay claim to the support of his fellow-brothers. This would be a Bond obligation as expressed in the rules quoted by me. Wherever an opening in the (public) service occurred, either for an appointment or for promotion, one brother would have to exert himself to get a fellow-brother competitor appointed or promoted.

"This would be a Bond obligation in terms of the rules. To the Broederbond and the brother it would matter little what your or my claims may be for support for our shop, or what claims you or I may have to an appointment or for promotion. We are not brothers and we therefore do not count at all. In the meantime, we are deprived of the opportunity of acting honestly and openly in the protection of our threatened interests. All measures adopted against us are conducted in secret, underground, where you and I cannot possibly discover what is being done to deprive us of what is due to us.

"With reference to the Broederbond, I have to address a very serious word to our teachers. Recently, I addressed a circle conference of the United Party at Oudtshoorn, and when the conference had gone into committee, a number of persons unexpectedly complained of the participation of teachers in politics. At the end of the discussion an earnest appeal was made to me by a prominent delegate in the following terms. 'In the name of God, General, we mothers appeal to you to do all in your power to prevent that our children should be incited on the school benches against their parents. You have no idea how bad it has become.'

"These complaints of improper influence imparted by teachers to children on the school benches have reached me before here in the Free State. What are the facts of the case? If these allegations are true, then all I can say is that a grosser and more serious abuse of position and profession is hardly conceivable. Whether it is true or not, I cannot tell, but what I do know is that the number of teachers in the Broederbond comprises more than one-third of the Bond's membership.

"I know also that there are very few towns or villages in the Free State where the Bond has not created for itself a little nest of five or more brothers, who must serve as the focal point for Bond propaganda. I know furthermore, that there is hardly one of these nests on which one or more teachers are not brooding. Assuming that there is an average of only two teachers to each of these little nests in the Free State, we can form a fair idea of the subterranean activities and machinations that are being conducted by teachers in respect of the children. When to the number of these subterranean purified teacher Nationalists is added the number of surface purified teacher Nationalists, then I can imagine that the parents of children from non-purified homes will have a lot to complain of.

"Is this a condition of affairs that can be tolerated by the State? We have seen that the Broederbond is a secret political society which has as its object the domination of the Afrikaans-speaking section over the English-speaking section, and whereby the nation has been torn apart into dissension and bitter strife.

"Should one allow the teachers, who are paid by the State to educate the children of the nation, to abuse the opportunity thus provided them of coming into contact with the children, for the purposes of commotional political propaganda? But, what is more, is it right that a teacher should be allowed, by membership of the Broederbond to reveal his inimical attitude towards the English-speaking section of parents whose children have been entrusted to his care, bearing in mind also that the English-speaking parents pay the salaries of the teachers as well as the Afrikaans-speaking parents?

"The vulgar public participation of some teachers in ordinary party politics has already been so objectionable to the parents and to the educated public in general that protests – which have led to a measure of restraint – have had to be lodged against this state of affairs. Now, however, that the impression has been created in the mind of the parents of a secret devotion on the part of the teacher to the ignoble task of bringing the youthful mind secretly into revolt against their parents, the whole matter may easily lead to a most deplorable loss of that respect and goodwill, which the public has entertained towards the teachers as a class.

"Membership of a secret society must of necessity immediately place the person concerned in a position of suspicion, as against his fellow beings, and cause him to be lowered in proportional measure in that trust, if not the respect of his environment. Where suspicions of that nature are evinced in the direction of parental fear for corruption of the youthful minds of their children, they will unfailingly give rise, in whatever measure, to a feeling of hate and disdain.

"The deeply unfortunate aspect of disdain or hate of this nature is that it does not confine itself to the guilty individual, but spreads and rapidly embraces the whole class to which that individual belongs. It is to be expected that this will be the outcome to teachers as a class arising out of the relationship some of them bear to the Broederbond.

"Where the teacher is today acting in secret, he must come out into the open. There is nothing which requires the clear daylight so much to stay sound as our education. The teaching class has never yet received anything but the biggest and most upright friendliness and respect from me, and as long as they remain the trusted keepers of the happiness and education of the youth of South Africa, they will continue to receive that friendship and respect from me. But, as has again appeared here this evening by what I have just said, it cannot be expected from me that I shall keep silent in regard to individual pedagogic abuses and misdeeds on the ground of my goodwill towards the teachers as a class.

"That an outcry occurs every time I draw attention to abuses and misdeeds perpetuated by individual teachers, as was the case at the recent Free State Teachers' Congress, cannot deter me from doing my duty towards my nation. I am prepared to leave it to the judgement of men and women who still harbour sentiments of honesty and decency as to whether I was justified in speaking as I did at the congress in Bloemfontein two months ago and as I have spoken here again today.

"Suffice it further for me here to impart a little communication to the head committee of the Orange Free State Teachers' Association that will interest them. In August of last year they were so kind as to give me the unsolicited assurance, through their secretary, that they as a teachers' association have never taken part in party politics and they did not approve the active participation of teachers in politics; further, that they were not aware of teachers in the Free State having actively participated in party politics.

"I accepted this assurance. Now, however, that better information has come into my possession, I wish to inform them that they would not have given me this assurance had they not been deceived and kept in the dark by their fellow-teachers who are members of the Broederbond. The head committee will forgive me if I inform them of the fact that just recently I had in my hands the minutes of a Broederbond congress together with an agenda, no less inclusive of all manner of political and party political motions than one associated with any party political congress; and that congress was attended by no fewer than 21 teachers, among the hunderd or so delegates including six teachers from the Free State.

"The facts I have submitted to you today reveal a state of affairs that will wring from everyone who loves South Africa and who possesses a sense of responsibility the question: Has the Afrikaner nation sunk to so hopeless a level that it must seek its salvation in secret conclave for the furtherance of race hatred, or national dissension and of strife among brothers? Is there no higher aspiration for the sons and daughters of South Africa, no nobler task, than that of racial strife and dissension? Is there no higher ideal for our children to attain than that of racial domination . . .?

"We are confronted here by a question that affects not only the Afrikaans-speaking Afrikaner. The same racial feelings of ill-will and aversion which are actuating Dr Malan, Dr van der Merwe and their followers, the same passion for racial domination, are also prompting Colonel Stallard, Messrs Coulter and Marwick and their followers.

"The one, as much as the other, finds inspiration in blind race animosity, which secretly seeks racial domination and bossism *(baasskap)*; and while the better self of each is ashamed of the motives by which he is actuated and guided, they must all eventually resort to inevitable secret associations and subterranean activities that cannot stand the test of honest and open criticism."

Hitting out at both the Purified Nationalists and Colonel Stallard's Dominion Party followers, he warned that their extreme courses could lead to violence and eventually, national ruin and self-destruction. He thanked God that the majority of South Africans had demonstrated clearly that their sentiments were fully behind the United South African National Party, a state of affairs that he confidently predicted would continue. History shows, however, that he was wrong. In four years the Fusion was split by the war, Hertzog himself was in the wilderness and nine years after that Dr Malan was Prime Minister of South Africa.

General Hertzog wound up his Smithfield address with the words: "The Purified National Party, with its purified leaders, now stand revealed in all their racial nakedness, covered only by one single fig leaf: secrecy!"

It was out at last. The Broederbond lay exposed and vulnerable. It reacted in two ways: it burrowed deeper underground to repair the broken defences of its secrecy; and it swore vengeance on General Hertzog.

As large numbers of Hertzog supporters quit the organisation, a special meeting of the Broederbond Executive was called and undying vengeance sworn against the Prime Minister. He had committed the unforgiveable sin and a dire nemesis was planned for him.[8]

One of the first gratifying fruits of this vengeance campaign came soon, when the Broederbond managed to force General Hertzog to withdraw from the centenary Oxwagon Trek in 1938,[9] a terrible humiliation for the venerable Afrikaner and erstwhile hero of the Free State.[10] Later that year, the electorate gave overwhelming support to the Hertzog-Smuts coalition. But the divisions among Afrikaners grew deeper.

General Hertzog, says his biographer C M van den Heever[11] was deeply sorry that he could not bridge the gap. He was, however, equally adamant that he would not sacrifice his firm belief in unity and co-operation between English and Afrikaner sections of the population – that unity he so ardently sought to achieve through his rallying cry of South Africa First.

About this time, General Hertzog's son, Albert, was a hot-blooded Purified Nationalist – and a member of the Broederbond. On behalf of a group of young Afrikaner intellectuals, all of them almost certainly members of the secret organisation, he wrote to his father demanding action to restore Afrikaner unity. In reply, Hertzog wrote a remarkable letter, which was released to the Press at the time, reaffirming his firm commitment to foster good English-Afrikaans relations.

"I want to assure you," he wrote to his son and the young intellectuals, "that under no circumstances will I ever in politics give my co-operation to people who are not prepared to recognise and accept the principle of complete equality and equal rights between our Afrikaans- and English-speaking national components on the basis laid down in the programme of principles of the United Party."

He too longed for the unity of the Afrikaans-speakers, but was not prepared to buy that unity at a price which would inevitably doom the whole of Afrikanerdom to an endless condition of divison and dissent with eventual self-destruction as its result. Although he did not go so far as to name the Broederbond in his letter, it was a clear repudiation of the sectional interests the organisation was energetically pursuing and must have strengthened the organisation's deep antagonism and, correspondingly, its resolve to exact revenge.

World War Two intervened, however, and for a short while the Broederbond suppressed its drive to repay its debt to Hertzog. For a time they were in accord: both Hertzog and the Broederbond were implacably opposed to South Africa's entry into the war, while Hertzog's Fusion partner, Smuts, argued strongly for involvement. The matter was put to Parliament and Hertzog's neutrality motion was defeated by 80 votes to 67. Hertzog resigned as Premier; Smuts took over the reins of government and immediately began to prepare for war. Hertzog and Malan came together in a brief but uncomfortable union in the form of the Herenigde Nasionale Party. But the Broederbond had not forgotten Smithfield and the campaign to destroy Hertzog proceeded.

A whispering campaign was started to the effect that Hertzog was a member of the Freemasons, an ironical charge in the light of his Smithfield attack on the Broederbond. According to C M van den Heever, Hertzog's biographer, the so-called Freemason Letters used against Hertzog were supposedly found in a box in Bloemfontein. According to the charge against Hertzog they revealed a plan by him and Smuts to establish an English republic. The malicious smear story was skilfully spread by a "confidential" whisper campaign (*Generaal J B M Hertzog,* pp 722–3).

It was an effective tactic and the final act of vengeance by the Broederbond. In 1940, following this consummate plotting and manoeuvring, Hertzog failed to secure election as chairman of the HNP congress in Bloemfontein, a degrading snub right on his home gound. When English-Afrikaans relations – the ideal to which he had devoted so much of his political career – was made an issue, he walked out of the congress in disgust. On December 11 1940, General Hertzog and his trusted friend, confidante and lieutenant, Klasie Havenga, resigned as members of Parliament.

He was approaching a devastatingly lonely road. Hertzog was thereafter spurned and rejected by the Afrikaners whom he had loved and served through war, famine and hardship, and whose cause he had sought to further in the way he considered best: union with the English-speaking section of the population.

Hertzog withdrew to his farm Waterval, where he lived in solitary seclusion. C M van den Heever[12] described his new lifestyle poignantly.[13]

"On the farm General Hertzog was now alone, and the rare visitor that in a time of petrol shortage arrived there must have been deeply struck by the loneliness in which the former Prime Minister now lived as the simple farmer of Waterval. In his woodcutter's jacket he was sometimes to be seen on his horse as he rode through the warm fields of his huge farm; then again, he gave work to a native close to the house and there he stood by, a thin and made-lonely figure amongst the thorn trees."

One night, alone, he arrived at a Pretoria hospital and asked to be admitted. The nurse, taking down personal details, did not recognise the frail, bespectacled man with a bushy moustache standing before her. He gave his name as J B M Hertzog, farmer. Shortly afterwards, on 21 November 1942, back on his farm Waterval, he died.

After Hertzog's death the Broederbond tried to claim that he had come to accept the organisation. They obviously realised that they could not break his image and that history would judge him as one of the greatest Afrikaners ever. It was asserted[14] that after the Smithfield address two executive members of the organisation had had a meeting with him where they had enlightened him about the "real" facts of the Broederbond and had convinced him of its innocence.

That he found some *modus vivendi* with the Broederbond is, however, unlikely. Its ideals and his were too far apart. As far as can be ascertained, he never retracted anything he said at Smithfield and it seems highly improbable that his forbearing to follow up his Smithfield attack can be ascribed to tacit approval of the organisation whose objectives he so staunchly scorned.

1. De Klerk, W A, *The Puritans in Africa,* p 114.
2. ibid, p 114.
3. *The Puritans in Africa,* pp 115–117.

4. Federasie van Afrikaanse Kultuurvereenigings.
5. When Hertzog went into coalition with Smuts.
6. Newspapers sympathetic to the Nationalists' cause.
7. Part of the no-confidence debate in 1935, it was vehemently anti-Fusion.
8. Malherbe, E G, *Education in South Africa,* Vol 2 p 24.
9. See chapter 4.
10. Malherbe, E G, *Education in South Africa,* Vol 2 p 29.
11. *Generaal J B M Hertzog,* p 887.
12. A fascinating aspect of van den Heever's biography is that it nowhere mentions the Broederbond. Even in the account of the Smithfield address there are no references to the organisation, raising the possibility that van den Heever was a member.
13. *Generaal J B M Hertzog,* pp 758–759.
14. *Hansard,* March 21 1945, Col 3919.

3 *Smuts*

No sooner had the Broederbond disposed of Hertzog than a new and even more dangerous enemy appeared. He was General Jan Smuts. If Hertzog's years as Fusion Prime Minister had been marked by Afrikaner division, Smuts's rise to power heralded prolonged and bitter hostility. World War Two, the issue on which he came to power, split the country's white factions far apart.

A great many Afrikaners vigorously condemned Smuts's determination that South Africa should participate in "England's war". For some this feeling went even further, to an open sympathy with the Nazi cause. Hitler's quick climb to ascendancy greatly attracted a number of Afrikaner Nationalists, as did developments in Nazi Germany. So much so, in a number of cases, that a feeling of general sympathy was translated into active support for Germany's struggle. The Broederbond numbered among its ranks many such supporters. The organisation which had striven in cultural matters to keep English- and Afrikaans-speaking elements apart, and thus reinforce Afrikaners of an exclusive Afrikanerdom, arranged for a few selected Afrikaans students to go to Germany and study methods employed there in the education of the nation's youth.[1]

Dr Nico Diederichs[2] was one who went across to study and report, and qualified as a quisling in the Nazi's Anti-Komitern training school.[3] According to Malherbe[4] who was Smuts's Director of Military Intelligence, as early as 1934 Hitler had sent a spy to South Africa, a German professor, Graf von Duerckheim Montmartin, to ascertain what elements in South Africa could be relied upon to collaborate with Nazi Germany in the event of a war with Great Britain.

His findings were said to have been sent to Hitler in a secret report. A copy of this report was found by South Africa's military intelligence among the papers seized at the headquarters of the German diplomatic representative in South West Africa in 1940 when the South African forces moved in. The report stressed, *inter alia,* the furtherance of German *Kultur* by means of subtle propaganda and by encouraging South African students to go to German universities, and the exploitation of anti-English sentiments among Afrikaners. Von Duerckheim held a prominent position in von Ribbentrop's organisation during the 1939–45 World War. He was, however, liquidated towards the end of the war when it was found that he had a Jewish grandmother. Dr Malherbe goes on: "With South Africa's participation in the war, anti-British feelings flared up with renewed fervour. A number of prominent Afrikaner leaders became openly pro-Nazi and found expression of their ambitions in flamboyant organisations such as the Grey Shirts and the Ossewabrandwag. The latter organisation, under the leadership of Dr Hans van Rensburg, was openly militant and opposed to General Smuts's war effort. He soon counted more members than there were in Smuts's army. Among these were a large number of teachers and even Dutch Reformed ministers. South Africa's former Premier, Mr Vorster, occupied a high position as Assistant-hoof Kommandant. Dr Verwoerd had strong Nazi sympathies, and his paper, the *Transvaler,* was jubilant over the initial reverses of the Allied forces on land and sea. Likewise it was filled with gloom when the Nazis started losing.

"It was hoped that with a German victory South Africa would become 'freed from the British yoke' and at last achieve the Broederbond ideal of an independent Afrikaner republic, excluding the British and the Jews. In the anti-war propaganda Smuts was made out to be a traitor to the Afrikaner cause in fighting *for* the British – not (as was the case) *with* the British ... Meanwhile, through a powerful broadcasting station at Zeesen (Germany) pro-German propaganda in Afrikaans was pouring into South Africa over the radio. Its programmes were avidly listened to because of the excellent music and good reception, far better than that of the British Broadcasting Corporation or the local South African Broadcasting Corporation.

"Immediately following on the music programme came the most venomous anti-British and anti-Jewish talks in Afrikaans by Dr Erik Holm, a young South African teacher who was studying in Germany at the time.[5] He was employed by the Nazis and paid by Goebbels himself ... There can be no doubt that this slimy, hate-generating stuff which was poured nightly in Afrikaans into South African homes must have left its mark on the receptive minds of the Afrikaner youth at the time. Many of these today are teachers and political leaders ...

"Racial separation, which had been part of South Africa's way of life for generations, received a new impetus from Nazism and German-orientated Afrikaners. This attitude spilled over on to English-Afrikaner relationships as well as between white and non-white. As indicated before, a number of leading Afrikaners had become impressed by Hitler's success in propagating the doctrines of national socialism in Germany. The Nationalists, particularly, found themselves in sympathy with his ideas of building up a pure Nordic race which would rule Europe after getting rid of Jews and capitalists. Hitler's regimentation of the German youth and particularly his use of symbol slogans and national rallies to create a feeling of national consciousness were soon copied in building up an exclusive Afrikaner nationalism. Behind it all was the thoughtful planning and pervasive organisation of the Broederbond ..."

The Government,[6] through its intelligence service, was kept informed of all the Broederbond's activities and those of its associated organisations working against the war policy. General Smuts could have banned the Broederbond and acted against its outspoken members with the extensive powers granted him by Parliament under the special war measures (Number 4 of 1941). This, however, he did not do, although he did restrict some of the leading activitists in the Ossewabrandwag. Vorster, for example, spent the war interned in Koffiefontein, along with a number of other leading Afrikaners, many of whom rose to great prominence in public life after the war.

"His reluctance to prosecute the Broederbond, was," says Malherbe, "partly due to the fact that he was quite too much preoccupied with the conduct of the war on an international front, but mainly because he did not want to involve the Dutch Reformed Church and the teaching profession, for the traditions of both of which he had a great regard."

Smuts knew that a large number of Dutch Reformed ministers as well as teachers were active in the Broederbond. Through his intelligence service, which monitored the organisation closely, he knew many of their names. He particularly avoided acting against university students and staff, only doing so when they were convicted of criminal deeds, in spite of wild pro-Nazi and revolutionary comments in student organisations during the war.

But when it came to the civil service, it was even more worrying to the government, although Smuts steadfastly refused to act against the Broederbond. One detects a sense of deep frustration at this caution in this passage by the former Intelligence Director.[7] "By that time the Broederbond had infiltrated every Government department ... Many of these Broederbonders were Nazi sympathisers. A secret organisation of this nature therefore proved to be a security risk at a time when South Africa was involved in a bitter war aginst the Nazis, who had their spies and informers all over the country. They had secret radio transmitters with which they were in constant communication with Germany ...

"Just as in recent times, certain religious and educational organisations were stigmatised (for example by men like Dr J D Vorster, former Moderator of the Dutch Reformed Church) as nothing but a front for the communists, so during the Second World War the Broederbond, the Ossewabrandwag, the Grey Shirts, etc, came to be regarded as Nazi fellow-travellers. This was not without justification. Despite the great security risks involved during the war, General Smuts refused to authorise a raid being made by the Security Police on the headquarters of the Broederbond – a precedent not followed in later years under the National Party rule, when South Africa was not at war, when raids were made on the offices of religious and student organisations as well as on the homes of private persons."

One of the methods suggested to Smuts by his military advisers for dealing with the Broederbond was to publish the whole picture of the organisation, with all its affiliated organisations. This, with a list of the names of known members, would sufficiently emasculate the organisation, he was urged. It was felt that the public, thus alerted, would treat the organisation and its individual members with due suspicion, which would rob the Broederbond of much of its power. Otherwise inexplicable appointments would become clear cases of Broeder nepotism and there would be no doubt in the public mind as to why nominations in church, educational and Government bodies were made and why prominent Afrikaners, who were ardent nationalists, were passed over.

In fact, the Broederbond had a "black list" of such prominent Afrikaners who were not members. Exposure would have revealed to the public the extent to which the organisation breached its own constitution which pledged it would remain clean of party politics, argued Smuts's advisers. But he would not bend, even though the Press was ready and willing to lend its co-operation.

He refused to take any action against the Broederbond, other than to instruct his security men to keep a close watch on its activities and its links with avowedly subversive organisations like the Ossewabrandwag.

At last the war came to an end in 1945. It had done much to enhance Smuts's status as a statesman of international stature. It had done little to settle the burning divisions inside South Africa. Afrikaner sentiment smouldered in angry hostility against Smuts, who had plunged South Africa into an unpopular war. Worse, he had thrown leading Nationalists into incarceration, a drastic step that recalled all the hated indignity of the Boer War concentration camps. The Broederbond's own history refers to entry into the war as "the political degradation of 5 September 1938."[8] In the postwar period, Smuts's detractors charged that he spent more time being an international figure than worrying about the major problems looming in his own country. His administration laboured under all the tribulations of a country readjusting from the ravages of war to the more insidious ravages of peace.

Over all this ferment loomed the inevitable conflict with the Broederbond. Smuts, like his predecessor Hertzog, could not escape it, even though he was reluctant to enter the struggle. Perhaps he had seen the results of such rashness in Hertzog's lonely death. Perhaps it was just that his overseas preoccupations took up too much of his time.

W A de Klerk[9] describes it thus: "The impotence, confusion and disarray of his opponents had also lulled Smuts into a sense of false security. What he saw was only what was taking place on the surface. In a sense, it was the price he was paying for having lived and moved for so long on a world platform. As a national leader and as a field-marshal in perhaps the greatest struggle of the age, there was even less possibility of his understanding the dangerous earnestness of the new elite the *burgerstand* had produced; or of the way in which their nationalism differed profoundly from anything which hitherto had been a part of the South African political landscape. Smuts had long since lost all real contact with the thinking of a large and important part of his own people . . .

"Whether it was a complacency induced by supreme confidence, the shrewdness of the wily politician or a lack of sufficient contemporary sense, is debatable. It was, probably, a combination of all these things. Smuts had his gaze fixed on the fine new world which would arise from the ruin of the war and in which the

British Commonwealth of Nations would play such a tremendous role. He could hardly take parochial politics too seriously. The more adventurous of his opponents had had to be curbed by internments and imprisonments. For the rest, as he was fond of saying, 'the dogs may bark, but the caravan moves on.'

"But the barking of the dogs was mostly so much misleading fury. There was a quieter, more effective and earnest core of people meeting within the innermost *binnekring* of the Broederbond, thinking, talking, into the small hours of the morning."

Smuts's advisers at home urged him to take action against this underground organisation. It was politically dangerous and would have to be confronted, they stressed. Apart from more sober counsel, a great deal of the heat generated against the Broederbond came from the fiery Senator Andrew Conroy, Smuts's Minister of Lands. He rarely allowed an opportunity to go by without launching vitriolic tirades against the organisation. An indication of some of the pressure on Smuts to take action is found in a brief newspaper report dated February 21 1944.[10]

It reads: "United Party's Senator ... Conroy ... was another who went political game-hunting. He sought Broederbond buck.

"In an 'insdious and underground way,' he declared at Dundee, the Broederbond had decided to get hold of school boards, municipalities and other local bodies. The Broederbond had control of the Nationalist Party. For years it had infiltrated into the public service. They could sabotage the Government.

"'If we want to save South Africa, something will have to be done soon.'

"Whereupon Maritzburg's *Witness* declared: 'Beating his wings helplessly in a vacuum, like Mathew Arnold's angel, won't get Senator Conroy or the Government anywhere ...

"'Unless all this brave talk about stamping out the Broederbond is followed by determined action, it will be worse than useless. Inaction will virtually be a confession that the Broederbond is stronger than the Government. Then one day the Broederbond will be the Government.'

"On the other hand, J W Higgerty, the United Party's Chief Whip, said very few of the charges that disloyal civil servants sometimes sabotaged Government policy could be substantiated.

"Meanwhile, General Kemp issued an appeal to Nats to take immediate action to see that Nats were elected to all possible administrative bodies and committees.

"In the course of an attack on Senator Conroy, Kemp warned that, 'When the Nationalist Party comes into power, care will be taken to see that only Nationalists stand at the head of affairs.'

"Echoed Strijdom: 'Nationalists must be elected to every possible local board ... whether it be a school board, a hospital board, or any other kind of board.'

"This warning, said Strijdom's paper, *Die Transvaler,* was retaliation for recent United Party demands that all Nats should be removed from local boards. 'Fight with gloves off,' was the paper's advice."[11]

Smuts's military intelligence advisers added to the pressure with a report on the Broederbond influence in South Africa, concluding: "In 1935, in full peacetime ... General Hertzog judged it necessary to try to destroy the Afrikaner Broederbond by dragging all their unsavoury doings into the open. No action was taken, however ... Today, with the bitter experience of the Broederbond's influence on the war effort, and its strong hold on South African public life, the need for action is much more urgent. If we are to dwell together in peace and amity in South Africa, the Broederbond must be destroyed."[12]

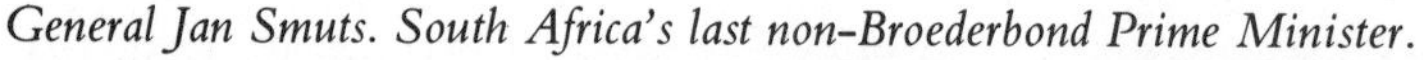

General Jan Smuts. South Africa's last non-Broederbond Prime Minister.

Eventually the advocates of action prevailed. Smuts joined battle with the Broederbond. The practical handling of the affair was, however, politically disastrous. He launched a campaign to root out all the Broederbond members from the civil service. On December 15 1944, using emergency powers granted to him by Parliament during the war[13] he gave Broederbond members of the public service, including teachers, the alternative of resigning from one or the other.

The same month, at the United Party congress in Bloemfontein, he attacked the Broederbond, describing it as a "dangerous, cunning, political, Fascist organisation of which no civil servant, if he was to retain his loyalty to the State and the administration, could be allowed to be a member."[14]

As a result, 1 094 civil servants quit the Broederbond. The others ducked the issue and lay low. Four years later, when the National Party had come into power, 807 resumed membership.[15] The tactic failed miserably, as even Smuts later admitted. It did nothing significant to damage the Broederbond. In fact, if anything, public sympathy to a large extent went to the organisation, particularly when a group of prominent civil servants resigned from the administration rather than quit the Broederbond. This report appeared in the *Sunday Times,* February 25 1945, under the headline *Broederbond Members Fired.* "Two senior public servants have been dismissed by the Government for refusing to resign from the Broederbond. They are Mr Wentzel du Plessis, head of the Division of Diplomatic and Consular Affairs, and Mr Jan Cloete, chief clerk in the treasury.

"Mr du Plessis has been in the Government service since 1924 and in the Department of External Affairs since its inception in 1927. He was at one time private secretary to General Hertzog, then Prime Minister, and was secretary of the Union legation in Holland from 1933 to 1938. Mr Cloete had had 20 years' service.

"Professor H O Mönnig, a well-known parasitologist of Onderstepoort, and Mr A J Bosman, under-secretary for Commerce, have resigned rather than end their membership of the Broederbond. Others who have been found guilty of contravening the emergency regulations by declining to resign from the Broederbond are Mr J Combrink, secretary of the National Housing and Planning Commission, and Professor A I Malan, a biochemist of Onderstepoort."Mr du Plessis, who was three years later to enjoy the satisfaction of defeating Smuts in his own constituency of

Standerton, has given a detailed account of this period in his book *Die Goue Draad – Op die Trekpad van 'n Nasie.*[16] In it he discloses that the Broederbond, as early as 1943, was aware that it was under Smuts's scrutiny and had foreknowledge that pressure was mounting on him to clamp down on members of the organisation. The matter was discussed "calmly – the pros and cons" within the organisation. The following morning, an informer went to Smuts chief lieutenant Jan Hendrik Hofmeyr and told him what had transpired.

The question was again discussed inside the organisation and it was decided that the Broederbond could not dictate to its members how they should respond to the expected action against civil servants. They would have to decide for themselves. Apart from those mentioned in the *Sunday Times* report above, those that decided to quit the civil service rather than the Broederbond, were Barend de Klerk, an expert in agricultural education, and Piet Basson, who worked for the most notable thorn in the organisation's flesh, Senator Conroy.

The day Smuts's proclamation was issued, du Plessis was on leave. He hurried back to his office where he wrote a memorandum to the Secretary for Foreign Affairs: "I must hereby inform you that I am a member of the Broederbond and that, after careful consideration, I do not see my way open to giving up my membership." He rejected allegations that the organisation was born in darkness *(duister),* that it carried on its work in darkness, or that it was Fascist and busily undermining the Government. He denied that party politics had ever played any part in his association with the organisation, or that he had been guilty of any dereliction of duty.

"No information about the official matters of this, or any other Government, has ever been given by me to the Broederbond. It was never asked or suggested by the Broederbond, nor was it offered ... The right to associate with my compatriots for the purpose of doing good to my fellow beings, without thereby interfering in party political affairs, is for me an elementary right which is unassailable by any government. I trust that you will accept this letter in that spirit," he wrote.

He was immediately suspended from his duties. Later, asked by the Secretary for Foreign Affairs, D D Forsyth, whether he would reconsider, he replied that he would gladly do so if General Smuts would make it possible for him. This would involve forbidding civil servants to be members of any secret organisation, including the Sons of England, the Freemasons and the Truth Legion. Several days later, a message was conveyed from Smuts to du Plessis that such a ban was considered "unnecessary". In his subsequent "admission of guilt" letter to Forsyth, du Plessis wrote: "That one group is being denied what is allowed for another group, I regard as discrimination that borders on racial persecution."

He was informed that his hearing would be held on February 7 1945 in Room 88, Union Buildings, Pretoria. Ironically his "courtroom" was the office he had previously occupied for many years as private secretary to General Hertzog. He recalls the hearing, which took place before a Johannesburg magistrate, Mr R F Plewman. "Nobody was allowed into the courtroom, just us two, apart from the former private secretary of the Prime Minister, then under-secretary of the department, who explained he was busy looking for a file.

"*Question:* Is your name Wentzel Christoffel du Plessis?

Answer: Yes.

Question: Are you a member of the Civil Service?

Answer: Yes. (The head of personnel was called in to confirm- this under oath.)

Question: Are you a member of the Broederbond?

Answer: Yes.

Question: Do you refuse to resign from the Broederbond?

Answer: Yes.

Question: Do you hold any executive position in the Broederbond?

Answer: No (what a remarkable question, I thought)

Sentence: Then I must find you guilty of the offence as specified."

The issue caused indignant and prolonged outcry from the Nationalist Press. The public in general, unconvinced of the subversive influence of the Broederbond, thought Smuts foolish to get rid of such able and prominent public administrators.[17]

In reply to Smuts's attack on the Broederbond, the organisation's chairman, Professor J C van Rooy of Potchefstroom, and its secretary, Mr I M Lombard, issued a series of five articles explaining the aims and objects of their organisation. The series was run in *Die Transvaler* on December 14, 21, 28 1944 and January 4 1945. They were summarised in *The Friend* published in Bloemfontein. The articles rejected allegations that the Broederbond was a subversive organisation "which incites sabotage or will tolerate it from members in any form"; that members consisted mostly of teachers and civil servants as General Smuts had claimed – of a total membership of 2 672, at the most 8,4 per cent were civil servants and 33,3 per cent teachers; that the organisation was fascist or undemocratic; that the "Bond at any time declared itself in favour of a national-socialist system for South Africa, or that it has ever had, or sought, any connection with the Nazi rulers of Germany."

Dealing with its secret nature, the articles said "the confidential character of the Broederbond is comparable with what one finds at a Cabinet meeting, at a meeting of directors or a decent business undertaking, or at an executive meeting of a church or cultural organisation before it comes to a decision which can be conveyed to its members." Quoting from the constitution, Lombard wrote, "In connection with the activities of general district meetings, the meetings may discuss any national problem or historical point with a vew to ascertaining, in an impartial manner, what is the best for the moral, intellectual, social and political progress of our nation. No speaker may, however, act as a propagandist for any existing political party or for party politics as such."

To a general public already dubious about the wisdom of Smuts's action, the ardent denials from the Broederbond leaders must have presented fresh doubts. The debate on the issue that followed in Parliament on March 21 1945 could have done little to change this. The Government speakers, including Smuts, under sustained and bitter attack from the Nationalists, generally put their case weakly. General statements were made about the organisation's secret involvement in politics without furnishing concrete evidence, which surely must have been available by them from all the surveillance to which the organisation had been subjected. Malherbe had supplied Smuts with detailed name lists of Broederbonders and a comprehensive report of its activities.[18] But the main thrust of their argument was left to Hertzog's Smithfield address 10 years previously.

In the arguments presented by the Nationalists, there was a paradoxical shrill insistence that action should not be taken against an organisation without firm evidence of misdemeanours. Why was there no trial; where was the proof? they demanded. How this elevated concern for the requirements of justice has changed over the years. Since coming into power, the Nationalist Government has placed on the statute book a battery of legislation which enables it to take unlimited arbitrary action against organisations and individuals. Bannings and detentions without recourse to the courts, and without the persons or organisations concerned ever knowing the nature of the charges, has become a common feature of Nationalist rule in South Africa. It is a feature that invites the accusation both at home and abroad that it is a "police state".

The debate opened with a two-pronged attack. Smuts was discriminating against Afrikaners. "I just want to ask the Prime Minister whether this attack on the Afrikaner Broederbond is just the beginning of the death of every Afrikaans organisation in the country. There are the Sons of England. We know that that organisation has a strong political colour ... there are the Sons of Scotland; and also the Sons of Palestine have their organisation. There is an Empire League, the Truth Legion and all sorts of organisations, and we now want to know from the Prime Minister why he selected an Afrikaner organisation."[19]

"He passed over the Civil Service Act and sheltered behind emergency regulations... Prominent officials in the service were put out of the service one after the other, not because they were convicted under the Civil Service Act, but simply because an emergency regulation was issued which they had contravened by belonging to the Broederbond ..."[20]

The Nationalists were also aggrieved that his action had been taken without proof being delivered of any subversive activities by the civil servants concerned. Mr C R Swart:[21] "I would like to know from the Prime Minister whether there has ever been any member of the Afrikaner Broederbond in the department controlled by him who committed subversive acts, who committed sabotage, who was unfaithful in his work. I consider that we have the right to know it. Was one of them ever tried? Can he deliver the proof ...? Will he tell us whether Mr Wentzel du Plessis ever committed any subversive act or was unfaithful in his work?"

The debate raged on through the morning. At the start of the afternoon session, Smuts was urged to reply because time was being wasted. There was a hush in the packed house as he rose to speak. He began by saying that only one aspect of the Broederbond's activities had been touched on; there were much wider activities in which it was involved. "The Government has acted on a firm principle," he said. "We proceed from the standpoint of the law. We have based our action on the law of the land, and that law is that our State officials should not take an active part in the politics of the country. That is the law; it is prohibited. Officials must not take part in the politics of the country, and in respect of the action that has been taken in reference to the Broederbond in this case, we have only acted in connection with that aspect of the matter ...

"My charge is in the first place against those officials who have not complied with the law of the land. Now I go further and I say that the Broederbond, the secret Broederbond, is a political organisation which is more dangerous from the point of view of the official and the Government service than any other political organisation in the country. The whole standpoint of the Broederbond is a political one. That is admitted.

An Hon. Member: Who admitted it?

The Prime Minister: We know it.

Mr Swart: What proof have you?

The Prime Minister: Now we come to one of the difficulties in which the Broederbond has landed us. It is a secret organisation, as secret as the grave.

Mr Swart: Is that the first objection?

The Prime Minister: Yes, that is an objection. It is a secret organisation, but it is also the calculated object of the organisation to foster the interests of one section of the population as against the other section ...

"In all respects where we thrashed out matters, it became clear that it was a political organisation working in secret, that it adopted a stealthy attitude, that did not disclose who its members were, and that kept everything secret. In my opinion there is nothing more un-Afrikaans than that sort of action. It was the combination of a number of people to get the key positions of the country into their hands, and to get all the key positions in the administration of the country, and in that manner to try to control the policy in the country. That was the object of the Broederbond and it was all done in secret. Everything was *sub rosa*. I think that anything like that is worse than any political organisation.

Mr Klopper (one of the Broederbond founders): Have you any proof of that?

The Prime Minister: I well know what I am talking about. The Government is convinced in regard to everything that has come before it. It has been convinced from the evidence that it has had before it and much of that has been derived from members of the Broederbond itself.

Mr Swart: You flourish on traitors in the British Empire.

The Prime Minister: When we have an organisation that wants to promote the interests of one section or of one race by an attitude of secrecy and keeping everything shrouded in darkness, you have to be careful. The Government is convinced that this is the case with this organisation.

"There was a series of articles in the Press from the secretary of the organisation[22] who wished to defend the organisation and one line of the defence was this, 'Why do you complain that this as a secret organisation? Is the Government not a secret organisation; is the Cabinet not secret; is the caucus not secret?' This is the official explanation of the attitude of secrecy that was given by the secretary, that all the resolutions remained secret, and that everything is kept as silent as the grave. No, this is a position that cannot be tolerated, at least not where officials are concerned. Whether it can be allowed in the country itself is another question to which I shall return; but as far as regards the public service, it is my opinion that they cannot serve two masters. They cannot take an oath and submit themselves to the discipline of a secret oganisation to carry out the orders of that organisation, and continue to do their duty towards the State. They cannot serve two masters. Accordingly, I say that the officials who are Brothers should resign from the organisation."

Mr Klopper: And the Sons of England and the Jewish organisations are all secret.

The Prime Minister: The Hon member may believe in that argument, but no one else will accept it.

Mr Serfontein: There is a Freemason sitting beside you.

The Prime Minister: To say that the Freemasons are a political organisation and that they pursue politics in secret is the greatest rubbish in the world. I say today to this House and to the country, that in my opinion the Broederbond is a dangerous organisation resting on a foundation that is in conflict with the interests of the country and that is un-Afrikaans.

Mr Serfontein: Mention the foundation.

The Prime Minister: It is purely exclusive race politics, the promotion of race interests.

Mr Klopper: Mention one proof.

The Prime Minister: This is the position. We have dealt to this extent with the officials; whether we may have to go further later on and place a ban on the organisation itself is another matter."

"Those whom the gods wish to destroy, they first make mad,"

retorted Dr Eben Dönges. At the time vice-chairman of the organisation, he stood up to reply to Smuts's attack. His first point of attack was that Smuts, with his legal training, should have known a person could not be condemned on secret evidence. If anything remained of his legal training and his legal instincts then he would not in this manner come and say he was going to judge a body like the Broederbond on secret evidence.

Continuing, he said: "Time and again we have heard outside about sabotage, of the fascistic nature of the movement, we have heard that it is national socialist, that they stand for a national socialist state. Now the Prime Minister says, 'No, politics, that is their only sin.'

"Let me say in the first place that no party politics are permitted in the organisation. That is one of the points of the constitution ... Let the Prime Minister say what politics there are in it. Is it party politics, is it a political organisation, because it is only open to Afrikaans-speaking people? What about the Dutch Reformed Church? It is for Afrikaans-speaking people, it is for the Afrikaner, but not in the narrow sense. Is it now being called a racial association?

"Now I want to say something on the subject of secrecy. The Prime Minister knows it is not secret. He knows this. Where does he get the other information he has? It is true that the organisation does not work in public and the reasons will be readily understandable by the Prime Minister. The reason is that it is an organisation of service, and our view is that the highest service that is not brought to light, that does not catch the public eye ...

"There are many things on which you make resolutions which for many reasons are not displayed in public or hung on the big clock ... One of the reasons why membership is not made public and why activities are not made public, is the same reason that Plato gave the Guardians of the State should not possess any property, namely that they should not be exposed to the temptation to seek their own glory and their own profit. It is for this reason that in a service organisation such as this that is only there for service does not advertise itself, and does not wish to place itself or its members in temptation to gain advertisement for themselves."

Denying the charges against the organisation, he said Smuts knew that detectives had visited the offices of the Broederbond, had been given access to its documents and had gone away satisfied. Why then did he allow his colleagues to go around the country spreading gossip about the organisation that he knew to be unfounded?

He accused Smuts of being in conflict with the fundamental principles of justice, the first of which was that the accused was entitled to a hearing. "Here we have a condemnation without a hearing, without the opportunity being afforded to refute it and without a proper examination of the evidence which has come into the possession of the Prime Minister behind the scenes from people, as he admits himself, who are apparently traitors; and that on that evidence of these traitors, which has not been examined, condemnation has been expressed. We say that is not right ..."

The third "and most serious complaint" Dr Dönges levelled at Smuts was that his action had been "nothing less than an offence against racial peace." The most important of all the post-war problems of reconstruction facing South Africa was the healing of the disturbed relationships between the English- and Afrikaans-speaking people in the country. That attitude had been hopelessly aggravated and inflamed by the action of the Government in recent times.

"In the course of the last five years we have had it in every respect that when the Prime Minister has acted, he has acted against the one race and not against the other race, and thereby he has disturbed and aggravated that attitude ... I do not want to make this accusation, but there is another conclusion which is arrived at by many – and which is almost unavoidable when one reviews the Prime Minister's deeds since 1939 – namely that he has been driven by that small-minded section in his party to attempt the destruction of everything that is Afrikaans...

"Like his spiritual predecessor, Milner, it is apparently his object today 'to break the back of Afrikanerdom'. I am a young man and I say this with the respect that is due to the Prime Minister's age and experience, that if he wishes to follow Milner's road ... he is on the road that leads to a dishonourable grave to which he will descend unhonoured and unwept by all Afrikaans-speaking and English-speaking people who perceive in racial peace the only future for South Africa. This injustice to the Afrikaans-speaking people can only make them stronger, the immoral exercise of the authority of the State towards its officials will only be temporary; the crime of the Prime Minister is that he has dealt a blow at the future of South Africa."

The implication that the Broederbond was pursuing racial peace in South Africa, was, of course, pious nonsense. Its fundamental raison d'être was and remains the exclusive promotion of a strictly sectional, Afrikaans cause. The warning that action against the Broederbond would strengthen Afrikaans-speaking people, had a firmer basis. It was one of several warnings issued by the Broederbond during that debate that Smuts ought to have noted. As Mr Nel exclaimed: "I must . . . openly say that by its action in this case, a real feeling of bitterness and hatred has arisen in my heart." And Dr Bremer predicted, with impressive accuracy: "In passing I might say that I believe that this is one of the steps which will lead to the speedy fall of the Government." In three years he was proved right.

But there were three years of glory for Smuts, until that dramatic and unexpected crash. Bearing the rank of Field Marshal, an honour conferred on him by King George VI for his valuable services to the war effort, he enjoyed immense prestige overseas. The collapse of Germany's armed resistance in 1945 and the end of hostilities in Europe created the opportunity for building the new world order of which he spoke with such enthusiasm. He was ready to play his part.[23]

Accordingly, he headed the South Africa delegation at the inauguration of the United Nations Organisation at San Francisco. He was there given the singular honour of drafting the Preamble to the UN Charter, an historic task he accomplished with skill and erudition. When he returned to South Africa, he was greeted with acclaim. Only the Nationalists stayed unmoved, pouring derision over the UN, which they said would end in the same disarray as the League of Nations.

"Smuts," says Friedman[24] "could afford to ignore his opponents. His star was definitely in the ascendant. After the general election of 1943 he was at the height of his power. After V E Day – victory in Europe – he was at the height of his prestige. He had brought his country through years of bitter adversity to ultimate triumph. At home, his authority as Prime Minister was complete and unchallengeable; he was in full control of the destiny of his country. Abroad his prestige was immense – no other Commonwealth statesman outside of Britain had ever attained such heights.

Alas! from those heights there was a sharp decline. Three short years later he fell from power. He was rejected by the electorate and had to yield office to his political opponents who had opposed his participation in the war, derided the men in the armed forces, rejoiced in the Allies' reverses, had demanded a separate peace with Hitler and declared openly that the future of South Africa depended on a Nazi victory.

For Smuts it was a personal defeat of staggering magnitude. For the Broederbond, it was sweet triumph. In Smuts's constituency of Standerton he had been defeated by one of the civil servants who had been hounded out of office, rather than quit the Broederbond: Wentzel du Plessis.

Strangely, the question of the Broederbond was never mentioned during that campaign in Standerton. "Some of my people insisted that we should do it, but I refused. Not even a question on it, I said, unless the United Party does it. They also didn't, although Senator Conroy's mouth was still full of it. But in Standerton he didn't count," writes Du Plessis.[25]

This is not the place to speculate on the causes of Smuts's ignoble defeat, or that of his party in 1948, although it should perhaps be pointed out that the Broederbond's role, active or passive, in that downfall is not given high priority by most historians. But Smuts's own words in the first anguish of that defeat are revealing. "To think," he exclaimed, "that I have been beaten by the Broederbond."[26]

After the election, he was offered a straw with which to pull himself back into power. Malan's Nationalists had risen to power on a minority vote and by dint of an uneasy coalition with Havenga, Hertzog's lieutenant, and his Afrikaner Party, which had won nine seats in the election. Bearing in mind the Nationalists' rejection of Hertzog in 1940, it was a fragile pact and within a short time Havenga let it be known he would like to break with Malan. He conveyed this information to Dr Malherbe, Smuts's erstwhile military intelligence director, then principal of the University of Natal.

Malherbe immediately wrote a long letter to Smuts urging him to join forces with Havenga. "The United Party as such is finished," he said. Lacking a positive, aggressive policy, it took too much for granted its moderate elements without protecting and fostering them. This was demonstrated in the way the bilingual school policy had been torpedoed by the English jingoes on the one hand and the Broederbond on the other. Pressing his argument, Malherbe emphasised that all was not well with the Nationalists either. There were deep divisions in the party and an atmosphere of suspicion prevailed; Broeders and non-Broeder nationalists and the Ossewabrandwag stalwarts distrusted each other. What was needed was for Smuts and Havenga to abandon party identities and draw up a programme of principles to present to the country.

Among these principles should be: co-operation between the English- and Afrikaans-speaking sections and the maintenance of "our democratic way of life and the combating of fascism, whether in the form of a Broederbond-Gestapo government or in the form of totalitarian communism."[27]

Smuts reported that he was not prepared to work with "a lot of fascists."[28] Malherbe bluntly replied that this evaluation of the situation was "superficial", which he ascribed to the weakness of Smuts's information service. "The facts," he said, "are as follows: (1) Havenga uses the Ossewabrandwag[29] chiefly to intimidate the Nats and to strengthen his bargaining power, and not because he has liking for the OBs or their ideology. Besides, with the exception of a small group of ideological leaders, fascism does not penetrate very deeply into the rank and file of the OBs. It is not in the nature of our people and does not fit in with our indigenous institutions . . . I would, therefore, not attach too much weight to Havenga's opportunistic affiliation with the 'Fascists'; and (2) Havenga hates the Broederbond. It was they who stabbed his old friend, General Hertzog, in the back. That he will never forgive them."[30]

There were two catches in Malherbe's scenario for a pact with Havenga. Jan Hofmeyr, the leader of the liberal faction in Smuts's party would be an "indigestible lump"[31] in the scheme of things; and Smuts himself might have to sacrifice his position as leader, stepping down for Havenga as he had done for Hertzog in 1933.

After weighing the options, Smuts, who remained unsure of what Havenga stood for, decided to "hold fast to what we have." By 1949 Smuts's opportunity had gone. Havenga was still with Malan, and his key role in the maintenance of Nationalist power, in any case, was no more. Malan introduced an Act[32] which brought six white representatives of South West Africa into the Union's House of Assembly. Predictably Nationalists, their arrival freed Malan once and for all of his dependence on Havenga.[33]

Smuts, appalled by his enforced removal from the stage centre, died at his home Doornkloof the following year. "Never did he speak any words of criticism or bitterness of his political foes," his physician recounted. "The only slight tone of disappointment I ever noted during my conversations was against those of his fellow-Afrikaners who, he thought, did not regard him as one of them, because he thought wider than the South African scene."[34]

In one striking aspect, there is a close parallel between Smuts's death and Hertzog's. Both died in isolation from their own people. Smuts, suggests de Klerk[35] "did not understand these new Afrikaners with their involved and sweeping oratory." Afrikaner nationalism was gathering momentum in its inexorable march across South Africa's history. Behind the new "involved and sweeping oratory" lay the eternal industry of the Broederbond, drafting a new, radical course for South Africa.

1. Malherbe, E G, *Education in South Africa,* Vol 2, pp 24–25.
2. Later to become State President of South Africa.
3. Military Intelligence report on the Afrikaner Broederbond, March 29 1944.
4. *Education in South Africa,* Vol 2, p 25.
5. In 1947 Holm was tried in South Africa and found guilty of high treason. He was given a prison sentence of 10 years. When, however, the Nationalist Party came into power in the next year, he was liberated and received an appointment in the Union Department of Education. The British 'Lord Haw Haw', who played a similar role in Germany over the radio against Great Britain, was tried in the British courts after the war, and executed for high treason.
6. *Education in South Africa,* Vol 2 pp 676–679.
7. Ibid p 677.
8. Secret Broederbond document, *Fifty Years of Brotherhood,* chairman's address, 1968, p 5.
9. *The Puritans in Africa,* pp 197 – 199.
10. The name of the newspaper is not indicated on the cutting, but it appears to be either *The Star* or the *Rand Daily Mail.*
11. Both Strydom and Kemp were Broeders. Strydom was later to become Malan's successor as Prime Minister, when he insisted on the Dutch spelling of his name: Strijdom.
12. Military Intelligence report on the Afrikaner Broederbond, March 29 1944.
13. Proclamation No. 255 in terms of Article Six of the National Security Regulations.
14. Vatcher, H W, *White Laager.*
15. Malherbe, E G, *Education in South Africa,* Vol 2, p 678.
16. From p 101.
17. Malherbe, E G, *Education in South Africa.* Vol 2, p 678.
18. A copy of the Malherbe report is contained as an appendix in *White Laager: the Rise of Afrikaner Nationalism,* by W H Vatcher Jr, Pall Mall, London, 1965.
19. Mr Werth, *Hansard* March 21 1945, Cols 3854, 3855.
20. Dr D F Malan, ibid, Cols 3862, 3863.

21. Later to become South Africa's first State President.
22. Referred to earlier in this chapter.
23. Friedman, Bernard, *Smuts: a Reappraisal,* p 156.
24. Ibid
25. *Die Goue Draad – Op die Trekpad van 'n Nasie,* p 148.
26. Hancock, W K, *Smuts, the Fields of Force,* p 506.
27. Van der Poel, Jean, *Selections from the Smuts Papers,* Vol VII, p 242.
28. Hancock, W K, *Smuts, the Fields of Force,* p 513.
29. Smuts's main objection was a form of alliance between Havenga and the OB.
30. Brotz, H. *The Politics of South Africa: Democracy and Racial Diversity,* p 18.
31. Van der Poel, Jean, *Selections from the Smuts Papers,* Vol VII, p 241 f.
32. No 23 of 1949.
33. Hancock, W K, *Smuts, the Fields of Force,* p 516.
34. de Klerk, W A, *The Puritans in Africa,* p 227.
35. ibid. p 226.

4 *The Symbolic Oxwagon Trek of 1938*

It is difficult to find another single event which stirred Afrikaner emotions more between the Anglo-Boer War and the Second World War than the symbolic oxwagon trek of 1938. Not even the people who planned and organised it, the Afrikaner Broederbond, had the faintest idea it would be such an overwhelming success. It served to reunite Afrikaners in one nationalism and played a most significant role in the 1948 election victory.

A year after the Trek, the war divided the Afrikaners and the Ossewabrandwag created a split in the National Party; but it was all temporary. Deep down the Afrikaners wanted unity, and the symbolic trek emphasised this. As soon as the war was over the deep divisions healed and a political unity was found which led to a victory through the ballot box. Looking back today, it is impossible to see how this could have been achieved without the emotional binding force of the symbolic trek. It created the opportunity for Afrikaners to be together, to experience the satisfying feeling of a nation on the march, of agreement rather than divisions.

What started as a fairly inconspicuous attempt to celebrate the centenary of the Great Trek by sending a team of oxwagons from Cape Town to Pretoria became a rousing national movement. At the final celebrations 200 000 Afrikaners camped for days at Monument Koppie, the site chosen for the Voortrekker Monument to be completed about 10 years later. Along the route to Pretoria thousands of Afrikaners – some travelling hundreds of miles – came to see the oxwagons, to touch them, to pray by them.

The oxwagon trek was one of the Broederbond's greatest master-strokes. Realising the division in Afrikaner ranks and the absolute necessity for unity to prepare for political victory, they staged it as an emotional rally. The opportunity was ideal. It was 100 years since the Great Trek when the Voortrekkers went north, one of the most important reasons being the desire to escape British rule. The celebrations planned by a central committee headed by

Dr E J Jansen, a prominent Broeder and then Speaker of the House of Assembly, were to peak on December 16, Dingaan's Day, at Monument Koppie where the foundation stone for the Voortrekker Monument was to be laid.

No doubt this would have been an impressive ceremony on its own, but it was the oxwagon trek which turned it into a national crusade. The idea came from the *Afrikaanse Taal en Kultuurvereniging* of the Railways (Afrikaans Language and Cultural Society of the Railways), a cultural front organisation of the Broederbond. The ATKV was formed by Henning Klopper, one of the three young men who founded the Broederbond on the koppie in Johannesburg in 1918. When he formed the ATKV on the Railways it had only 200 members; five years later it had 50 000 and today it is probably the largest formally organised Afrikaans cultural association.

Who was Henning Klopper who had played such an important part in forming the Broederbond and the ATKV? Like other prominent Broeders, Danie du Plessis and Willie Heckroodt, he worked on the Railways. He joined when he was 15 at a salary of £4 a month, and worked hard to spread his belief in Afrikanerdom. His role in the oxwagon trek made him a national hero among Afrikaners. Not only was he the founder of the ATKV who had organised the trek, but they had nominated him as trek leader. At all the main celebrations along the route he was the central figure, making speeches and passing on the message of Afrikaner unity.

Henning Klopper is convinced that it was the symbolic oxwagon trek that paved the way for the 1948 election victory for the National Party and the subsequent referendum majority which led to the Republic. "It was this dynamic movement which gave expression to the aspirations of the Afrikaners, and united them at the time when division among Afrikaners was at its greatest, and their feelings were bitterest," he says. When Klopper left home to join the Railways, his mother gave him a Bible and said: "Read it every morning and evening." Fifty years later he said: "I never let her down." At that stage he had read the Bible from cover to cover 22 times. It takes him 10 to 18 months to read it though once.

He does not smoke or drink and in the true spirit of the Broederbond, abhors "loose morals". Like the Broederbond, which expels members involved in a divorce, he sees divorce as an evil practice "undermining the morals of the people." He feels clergymen should "put their foot down and take the lead in stamping out this evil."

In all his readings of the Bible, he says he has found nothing to shake his belief in apartheid. "We are not all created the same. We are created to be what we are – not something different from what the Creator wants us to be. But there is room for everyone."

As international pressure intensifies around South Africa, Klopper remains unshakeable in his faith in the future of the Republic his Broederbond created. "We are in South Africa to stay, no matter what the United Nations or any other body decrees. We are here in accordance with the will and by the grace of God. Our road is forward – only forward and always forward."

After the oxwagon trek Klopper became active in politics and in 1943 he was elected MP for Vredefort. He became Speaker of the House of Assembly in 1961, a post he held until 1974 when he retired to his farm near Parys in the Free State.

Initially the trek featured two wagons sponsored by the ATKV, but the idea captured the imagination of the people to such an extent that further wagons were added on routes far away from the original ones. Some of the wagons were more than 100 years old. Eventually the routes covered almost the whole of South Africa, the wagons visiting an amazing number of places before they congregated at Monument Koppie.

The wagons were named after national heroes. The *Johanna van der Merwe* trekked through Namaqualand, the *Magrieta Prinsloo* through the western and northern Cape, the *Hendrik Potgieter* and *Andries Pretorius* through the southern and eastern Cape and Orange Free State. This last route was also followed by the *Piet Retief* and *Vrou en Moeder* while the *Hendrik Potgieter* and *Andries Pretorius* also visited the eastern Transvaal.

All over the country men started growing beards and women fashioned Voortrekker dress for the day the wagons would reach their district. Town and city councils renamed streets, squares and buildings in honour of the Voortrekkers, sometimes creating disputes between Afrikaans- and English-speaking members of the communities.

The Government of the day was a coalition between General Hertzog, the Prime Minister, and General Smuts, his deputy. On their right were Dr Malan and his purified Nationalists. The brimming Afrikaner emotionalism of the symbolic trek presented a

The Bond-organized oxwagon trek gave fresh impetus to Afrikaner nationalism.

problem to General Hertzog who was trying to keep Afrikaner and English together. It delighted the Malanites, however. It was a rallying cry for Afrikaner nationalism, bringing the *volk* together, at least in spirit. The strains it created in the Government party could only benefit the Nationalists.

All along the route Broeders served on the welcoming committees arranging local celebrations for the oxwagons. They made the most of their opportunity to stress Afrikaner unity, the need for a republic and the dominant role to be played by Afrikaners in South Africa. In Pietersburg they tabled a motion of no confidence in the mayor because he did not attend the arrival of the oxwagons. His claim that it was all a misunderstanding was rejected. The Benoni Town Council was not invited to the celebrations after a bitter row between the mayor and festival committee. The "Christian spirit" of the festival was given as one of the reasons, the mayor's followers claiming that it was because he was Jewish that he was not invited.

While the mayor of Bloemfontein, Mr W F Prophet, stood watching the arrival of the wagons, the chairman of the local branch of the ATKV, Mr P J Goosen, said he should be requested not to take part in the proceedings. The announcement was loudly cheered by the crowd. The protests were made as a result of a controversy over the renaming of certain streets which arose between the committee and the Bloemfontein Town Council. Young men drew the wagons through the streets in place of the oxen provided by the Bloemfontein municipality. The Voortrekker choir and guard of honour refused to use municipal transport, and were driven in private cars.

The atmosphere of the time, and the message from the Broederbond during the trek, could be perceived in a speech that day by one of the trek leaders and a prominent Broeder, Mr M C (Oom Tinie) van Schoor. He deplored the cold reception of the wagons in the Orange Free State – the model State of South Africa. Why should the Afrikaner feel himself a stranger in his own city?[1] "In the slums we are permitted," Mr van Schoor said, "but in those parts which rightly belong to us admission is refused." The time had come, he declared, when the Afrikaners would no longer be strangers in the land which had been dearly bought by the blood of their ancestors.

"While the Afrikaner is working with the pick and shovel, the stranger is occupying the offices. The time has come when we should erect monuments to our heroes who gave their lives for us, and those monuments should be erected in the cities where they belong. There are sufficient monuments to the men who offered their lives to foreign countries, but where are the graves of our own heroes of the past century?"

Realising the danger of even deeper divisions between the Afrikaans- and English-speaking sections over the trek, the Government and English-speaking leaders encouraged their people to support local celebrations, to avoid conflict and turn the occasion into an event for all sections.

This was successful to a large extent, and apart from minor incidents the two sections co-operated well. In Durban, heart of English-speaking Natal, thousands of people formed a mile-long crowd to welcome the wagon. Scenes of wild enthusiasm greeted it as it made its way slowly down West Street which was packed with thousands of people, 40 deep in places. The crowd rushed up to the wagon singing *Sarie Marais*. At the city hall 15 000 people waited for the wagon.

Clearly, many thousands of those people must have been English-speaking. The spirit was the same throughout the country. But deep down there was always the feeling that it was really an Afrikaner celebration. The Broeders who took an active part in the trek knew exactly how far to go in whipping up Afrikaner emotions without antagonising the English section. The delicacy of the situation was clearly illustrated by General Hertzog's dilemma over the foundation stone ceremony at Monument Koppie. The controversy centred around the playing of the then national anthem, *God Save the King,* at the ceremony. If the foundation stone laying was a State occasion attended by the Governor General and General Hertzog, *God Save the King* would have had to be played. This was too much for the Broeders and Dr Malan's National Party, and even some Afrikaners in General Hertzog's Government, like Dr E G Jansen, Speaker and chairman of the central committee. The Broeders took over the occasion and turned it to their advantage, pressing for Afrikaner unity, a stronger National Party, *Die Stem* as the national anthem, and ultimately a republic. In all these respects they totally outmanoeuvered the coalition Government of Hertzog and Smuts.

The Government had decided in 1935 to assume responsibility for the celebration of the Voortrekker centenary and issued the following statement.[2] "The decision to which the Government has come contemplates the celebration of the centenary on a broadly national basis worthy of the occasion and in such a manner that all sections of the people of South Africa can take part... For these reasons the Government felt that it should in the name of the State and the people as a whole, assume responsibility for the erection of a worthy monument and take steps to ensure that all arrangements in connection therewith should be made on a broadly national basis. It was the opinion that in order to attain this end, the laying of the foundation stone of the monument should be a State ceremony..."

There would probably not have been a dispute had the celebrations featured only the foundation stone laying at Monument Koppie. It would have been a much tamer event, with much smaller attendance, than eventuated. The Broederbond saw its chance to control the event by arranging the symbolic oxwagon trek, carrying the emotion and the crowds with it on the way to Pretoria. The number of wagons had to be increased in response to popular demand, and the Voortrekkers, the youth organisation formed by the Broederbond, organised a torchlight procession to Pretoria. As the emotion increased, the prospect of hearing *God Save the King* at the climax of the celebrations became a thought too horrible for Afrikaner minds to contemplate – a development the Broeders were quick to exploit. This finally forced Generals

Hertzog and Smuts out of the celebrations. Although a compromise was reached which also excluded Dr Malan and all active politicians, the Broeders took over the leading role and worked on the same lines as Dr Malan.

On July 26 1938 General Hertzog issued a statement that "in present circumstances it appeared such a course (playing *God Save the King* at the koppie) would lead to much unpleasantness and bitterness and the fear had been aroused that in consequence the peaceful development of our national unity would be impeded." General Hertzog said that accordingly English-speaking members of the United Party had said they would welcome a decision to depart from the intention of making the foundation stone laying a State ceremony. The event would therefore be non-political and descendants of the Voortrekkers would lay the foundation stone.

In October, another attempt was made by the Centenary Committee to persuade General Hertzog to lay the foundation stone. He agreed – provided the English-speakers in the United Party caucus and Dr Malan's Nationalists supported the move. General Hertzog already had the support of his caucus, but Dr Malan refused point-blank to give his support. He agreed with the Government's July statement that no politicians should take part in the ceremony. Once again it was seen how cleverly the Broeders squeezed General Hertzog into a corner, and out of the limelight. Dr Malan could accept exclusion because others were doing his work for him.

The strange role played by Dr Jansen was never fully explained. As Speaker he was regarded as above party politics. He was a top Broeder, and as chairman of the Centenary Committee he supported the move to ban *God Save the King* from the proceedings. However, it was clearly accepted that if the ceremony was no longer a State occasion, in the interest of national unity *Die Stem* would not have been played either, yet it was Dr Jansen who appealed in his speech at Monument Koppie for all sections to help make *Die Stem* the national anthem. According to the *Rand Daily Mail*[3] "this was greeted with thunderous applause from the crowd of ten thousand and they rose to their feet to sing the anthem once more."

Dr Malan and General Hertzog agreed on one thing – a political truce until after December 16. But there was an unease in Government ranks as the wagon wheels started rolling in Cape Town's Adderley Street on August 8 1938. A Government Minister, Mr

Oswald Pirow, made a speech and that was the last time the Government of Hertzog and Smuts had any significant part: from then on the Broeders took over. As Henning Klopper said, before the whip cracked in Adderley Street: "Let us build a monument of united Afrikaner hearts stretching from the Cape to Pretoria. We trust that the wagons will be the means of letting Afrikaner hearts, which today may not beat in unison, beat as one again."[4] By the time the wagons reached the Reef on December 2, it was clear that his wish had come true – Afrikaner hearts were indeed beating in unison and the fever of nationalism was building.

Some of the most vivid descriptions of the scene, the atmosphere and emotions appeared in the *Rand Daily Mail* and *Sunday Times* under the by-line of that remarkable journalist, T C Robertson. He captured the spirit of the trek as no other reporter of his time did. This is how he described the entry of the wagons into Johannesburg.[5] "Modern Voortrekkers – Afrikaners whose pulses beat to the rhythm of the wheels of industry – heard the rumble of wagon wheels among the skyscrapers in Johannesburg yesterday. Grandchildren of the men whose flocks once grazed on the hills of the Witwatersrand stood among the cheering thousands in the city of gold, the gold the old Voortrekkers feared.

"Girls in Voortrekker *kappies* leaned out of the windows of factories in Fordsburg, where the relentless assembly belts stopped moving as the wagons passed ... miners came up from underground and raced off to watch the procession ... Voortrekker costumes made vivid splashes of colour on the balconies of skyscrapers... As the wagons passed through the far-flung suburbs, where Afrikaner workers live, thousand of people lined the route, their enthusiasm not damped by the steady rain."

And on the evening's events: "Fifteen thousand Afrikaners, stirred by deep emotions of patriotism, last night sang the old Dutch psalms and anthems that had once echoed through the laagers of the Voortrekkers. Above the head of the vast crowd gathered on the Brixton Ridge the two Centenary Trek wagons stood on high platforms like images on a shrine. Floodlights illuminated the white tents and brown stinkwood of the wagons... Men and women gazed at the cumbersome vehicles that had cradled a nation, and were silent with adoration... Fathers lifted their children on to their shoulders to show them the wagons... The Afrikaners on the Rand had made a pilgrimage to a new symbol of nationhood."

On December 13 Robertson reported: "The great Voortrekker camp on Monument Koppie stirred with life tonight. Ten thousand visitors from all over South Africa had trekked in, and the smoke from their campfires drifted low over the long rows of white tents. It was a scene with those hard contrasts of light and shade, of silence and noise, which provided the stark qualities of a film set.

"Powerful floodlights played on the tents and accentuated the red glare of the campfires against the white canvas. In the valley, a mile below the hill where the foundations of the Voortrekker Monument were silhouetted against the evening sky, a choir of 1 000 children were singing Afrikaans songs. The echo of the melodies vibrated among the tents, and men and women round the campfires stopped to listen.

"But the heroes of the camp are the burghers of the commando. They sit loosely in their saddles and yet manage to ride with the swagger and bravado of Roman cavalry in a triumphal procession. Looking at these commandos one can understand why they have been described as the greatest and most mobile fighting unit in the world."

The eight wagons reached Pretoria on December 13 after four months of trekking across the country. "Scenes of enthusiasm and crowds of a size never before seen in Pretoria marked the arrival of the wagons, and their progress through the flag-bedecked streets was the signal for the pealing of church bells, the firing of guns and the ceaseless cheering of thousands of people".[6] On December 15 Robertson told of the "river of flame." "The two torches brought by relays of Voortrekkers from Cape Town and Dingaan's Kraal, arrived in the valley below the Monument tonight. Three thousand boys and girls, carrying torches, met them on the hill above the aerodrome. They marched down towards the camp like a winding river of fire more than a mile long. There a crowd of 60 000 stood waiting in silent amazement.

"Then, as the chain of light wound past them, they started cheering – more lustily and enthusiastically than I have ever heard a South African crowd cheer. Women rushed forward and burned the corners of their handkerchiefs and *kappies* in the flame of the two torches, to keep as mementos of the great event." The next day he reported: "A score of women knelt in silent prayer in the darkness round the bare foundations of the Voortrekker Monument tonight. I saw the outlines of their *kappies* silhouetted against the brilliant lights of Pretoria – the Voortrekker city – in the valley below. The action of these 20 women was characteristic of the reverent spirit that is prevailing at the Monument. Although a soft rain was falling they climbed the steep slopes of Monument Koppie through the thick growth of protea bushes and long grass. From the camp the echo of the massed choirs singing hymns could be heard. In the south the lights of the city of gold, where the modern Voortrekkers are fighting their battle, could be seen twinkling over the hills."

And so the great day arrived. More than 200 000 Afrikaners attended the ceremony, the biggest and most enthusiastic gathering of Afrikaners ever. There was no revolution or attempted coup d'etat as some had feared. Rumours had been spread, fanned by the fervour of the trek and the mood of Afrikanerdom, that they would plan to take over the Government. But it was based only on an interview an Afrikaner *dominee* had with the famous Boer "prophet" Niklaas van Rensburg. Dr S H Rossouw, minister of the Dutch Reformed Church at Swellendam, told a Nationalist newspaper of van Rensburg's "flag of blood" prophecy which led to all kinds of rumours about a revolution.

Van Rensburg was the famous visionary who helped General Koos de la Rey in the Anglo-Boer War. According to Dr Roussouw, Van Rensburg had predicted the 1938 trek in 1920 when he said: "In our country I see in the turbulent times oxen and donkey wagons trekking from the south to the north. The donkey wagons, however, gradually lag behind, while the oxwagons gradually increase in numbers. They are escorted by equestrians. From all sides people will gather in tens of thousands at a spot somewhere north of Lichtenburg.

"It will be the greatest gathering of Afrikaners in our national history. All this will happen without any leader summoning the people together. The people will take things into their own hands and those who do not want to stand out of the way, they will trample to death. Then a great silence will ensue before the storm. That storm will be severe but of very brief duration. One pail of blood will tumble over in which our flag will be dipped and the flag of blood will then fly over a free people."

But although the feelings on Monument Koppie were intense, there was also a lot of goodwill; even the King's message (in Afrikaans) was cheered. Then, suddenly, it was all over and life could return to normal – but the Broederbond's intervention in the trek had ensured that Afrikanerdom would never be quite the same again.

As T C Robertson said in his final report from Monument Koppie:[7] "The Great Trek of 1938 is only a vivid memory. But the emotions that it stirred up are still alive. Those Afrikaners who came from their karakul farms in South West Africa, from their cattle ranches in the bushveld, from the vineyards and orchards of the Cape, are going back with an intenser feeling of patriotism.

"Eight thousand schoolchildren, in the uniforms of the Voortrekker movement, will remember the ceremony as the greatest experience of their lives. I listened to their shrill cheers on Saturday morning as they left their tents to march to Pretoria station ... heard them singing *Die Stem* as a final salute to the greatest monument that will be built on the koppie.

"Over the hill in the east, with the rising sun glinting on the barrels of their rifles, the commandos rode homewards ..."

1. *Sunday Times,* October 23 1938.
2. *Rand Daily Mail,* July 27 1938.
3. Ibid. December 17 1938.
4. Ibid. August 9 1938.
5. *Sunday Times,* December 1938.
6. *Rand Daily Mail,* December 14 1938.
7. Ibid. December 13 1938.

5 *Political Triumph – the 1948 Election Victory*

The Broederbond played a decisive role in the unexpected Nationalist victory of 1948, which placed South Africa on a totally new course. The Broederbond supplied the political leaders to make the victory possible. Virtually all the members of Dr D F Malan's Cabinet were also members of the Super-Afrikaner society. They were imbued with the same idealism and determination to ensure an Afrikaner victory at the polls.

They masterminded the symbolic oxwagon trek of 1938, which united Afrikaners emotionally and facilitated the later political unity (see Chapter 4).

They supplied the National Party with the policy of apartheid or separate development, which became a powerful political slogan in contrast to General Smuts's indecisive attitude to racial matters (see Chapter 3).

They united Afrikaners politically, in spite of sharp differences of opinion and approach between, for instance, the Ossewabrandwag and the National Party. They took over the Mineworkers' Union, which swung six vital seats on the Witwatersrand and enabled the National Party to win the election with a majority of six seats.

Soon after the emotion of the oxwagon trek had died down, the shadow of the Second World War also fell over South Africa – and Afrikanerdom. Even the emotional unity experienced at Monument Koppie was shattered, and division in Afrikaner ranks became deeper then ever. Smuts won the vote in Parliament supporting the war, and Hertzog had to resign as Prime Minister. For a short while he and Malan were reconciled but that, too, was to be shattered. Smuts called for volunteers to go and fight and, according to F A van Jaarsveld,[1] "a great percentage, if not the majority, of the white military forces consisted of Afrikaners."

In the anti-war emotion characterising a strong section of Afrikaners, a new militant organisation, the Ossewabrandwag, thrived. It soon had 300 000 members, held military parades and rallies, cheered British setbacks and Nazi triumphs. Sporadic sabotage occurred, and some members of the organisation were interned without trial by the Smuts Government. Among those jailed at Koffiefontein, but never proved guilty of anything, was young Advocate John Vorster, then an OB general, and later Prime Minister of South Africa, Hendrik van den Bergh, later to become his security adviser, and P J Riekert, his economic adviser.

The confusion, division and political impotency in Afrikaner ranks had hardly ever been greater, says van Jaarsveld. "It was a condition which reminded one of the period of civil war in the Transvaal from 1860–1864."

Apart from Malan's National Party and Hans van Rensburg's Ossewabrandwag, there was also the Afrikaner Party, made up mostly of Hertzog followers and led by Klasie Havenga.

The Broederbond's first attempt to heal the breach in Afrikanerdom came after the split between Hertzog and Malan in 1940. The reason for the split, a smear story in Nationalist ranks that Hertzog was collaborating with the Freemasons, was investigated by a committee of Nationalist Members of Parliament, headed by the chairman of the Broederbond, Professor J C van Rooy of Potchefstroom.

The commission found that the Freemason story could not be regarded as "the primary reason" for the break, but that it created confusion and mistrust and "indirectly affected detrimentally attempts at reunion."[2] It exonerated the Free State Nationalist leaders, Dr N J van der Merwe and Advocate C R Swart, from blame for the Freemason gossip story. As the reason for the break, it cited a misunderstanding on General Hertzog's part as to the form of the party he and Malan had tried to establish.

General Hertzog was obviously being written off as a force in the political war that was to come. In spite of his stature, he was regarded as too soft on Republicanism and too conciliatory on English-Afrikaans co-operation.

Because the Ossewabrandwag did not have a specified role in the Afrikaners' political and cultural life, negotiations between the militant organisation and the Herenigde Nasionale Party took place. At the Cape Congress of the party held at Cradock in 1940, Dr Malan announced that agreement had been reached: although the two organisations would co-operate, the party would be active politically and the Ossewabrandwag in non-political areas such as the economic, moral and religious advancement of the Afrikaner nation. The Ossewabrandwag would work for Afrikaner unity and refrain from underground revolutionary activity.[3]

The anticipated new unity was shattered in January 1941 when a group of Hertzog supporters split off and formed the Afrikaner Party under the leadership of Senator E A Conroy, (later replaced by Havenga) with 12 other members of Parliament supporting him. This would become the political home of many OB members.

The Broederbond entered the struggle again in June 1941, realising that only a combined Afrikaner vote had a chance of defeating Smuts.

Representatives of the Broederbond's cultural and economic front organisations, the FAK and *Reddingsdaadbond,* negotiated respectively with Dr Malan and the Ossewabrandwag. The organisations found common ground, and a unity committee, under the chairmanship of Professor L J du Plessis, former Broederbond chairman, was formed. The committee put the following motion to the Union Congress of the HNP in Bloemfontein:

"The Congress declares that the Herenigde Nasionale Party or *Volksparty,* is the only organisation representing nation-orientated Afrikanerdom in the field of political leadership... Congress, therefore, makes a serious appeal to all Afrikaners in this hour of South Africa's decision of destiny, to work enthusiastically and actively together, and to close our ranks..." This motion was carried unanimously and Professor du Plessis said: "When Dr Malan talks in future, it will not only be on behalf of the Party, but on behalf of Afrikanerdom."[4]

But only a month afterwards the Commandant-General of the OB, Dr Hans van Rensburg, made a veiled attack on the party at a speech at Elsburg. Professor du Plessis declared that Dr van Rensburg "undermined, rather than supports the party."[5] The OB also distributed 100 000 pamphlets, setting out the kind of republic it wanted, and Dr Malan demanded their immediate withdrawal, because this was interference in politics – the party's sphere. Once again the Broederbond-controlled unity committee intervened, and the pamphlet was withdrawn. The position between the two organisations kept on deteriorating, until Dr Malan said he could no longer ask members of his party to be members of the OB as well. Those who wanted to leave the OB were free to do so. An increasing number of HNP members followed his advice, but it did not bring unity.

The 1943 election was round the corner, and Dr Malan had 41 MPs. In spite of the divisions in Afrikaner ranks, the HNP improved its position slightly, to return 43 MPs against General Smuts's 89 who also had the support of two Independents, the Labour Party (9) and the Dominion Party (2).

In its annual report the Federal Council of the HNP said: "This victory is only as temporary as the war – if not shorter – and the task resting on the HNP, South Africa's only alternative Government, is bigger than ever."[6]

The sights were, therefore, firmly set on the 1948 election, although the HNP and Broederbond leaders realised a small miracle was needed to defeat Smuts's massive majority. The Broederbond was working hard on shaping the apartheid policy (see Chapter 12), which became an HNP trump-card in the election. It was also pressing the HNP to come out more firmly for a republican form of government – another policy which appealed strongly to Afrikaner voters. The Broederbond's policy of mother-tongue education became a national issue, once again receiving wide support from Afrikaners.

The OB was dying as the emotionalism of the war effort wilted, and in 1944 when Dr van Rensburg further undermined the HNP all the party's congresses decided that members must resign from the OB. The party emerged strengthened from the conflict because more and more Afrikaners realised that victory through the ballot box – something the OB sneered at – was the only way of getting power.

The last objective, unity between the HNP and Mr Havenga's Afrikaner Party, now had to be achieved. Before the 1948 election on March 22 1947, Malan and Havenga announced that an election pact had been made whereby the parties would not oppose each other but allocated a certain number of constituencies to each other to avoid splitting the Nationalist Afrikaner front.

On another front the Broederbond was feverishly working to swing the Afrikaner workers on the Witwatersrand in favour of the HNP before the election.

Dr Piet Meyer and Dr Albert Hertzog, the longest-serving member with 20 years on the Executive of the Broederbond, took the lead in this drive. Joining the battle on their side were two prominent Broeders, Frikkie de Wet, Faas de Wet, Paul Couzyn and, later, Daan Ellis. They concentrated on the Mineworkers' Union which had a membership of 22 000. With their families they held the balance of power in a number of vital Witwatersrand seats. The Broeders decided the leadership of the union must be taken from "foreign elements" and put in the hands of Afrikaners who could influence the members "positively" in the coming political battle. On October 4 1936 the Broederbond arranged a meeting at which Dr Hertzog, Dr Meyer, Frikkie de Wet and Professor Nico Diederichs formed the National Council of Trustees "to establish right-minded trade unions which must serve as links with the Afrikaner nation."[7]

The National Council was financed by the Broederbond. Several prominent Broeders including Professor Dr J D du Toit (Totius), Professor Joon van Rooy (Chairman of the Bond), I M Lombard (Secretary of the Bond) and Mr J J Bosman (founder of Volkskas and the Broederbond's Christiaan de Wet Fund) served on the committee.

Because the struggle ahead demanded substantial funds for organisational purposes, the Broederbond could contribute to only a limited extent at that stage – more sources had to be tapped. Mrs Jannie Marais, widow of an Afrikaner leader from Stellenbosch, was approached by Dr Hertzog and she contributed £2 000.

On November 24 1936 Dr Hertzog, Dr Meyer and Faas de Wet addressed a meeting of mineworkers in the Krugersdorp City Hall and formed the Afrikanerbond of Mineworkers. Faas de Wet became its first organiser. When a closed-shop agreemeent was granted to the Mineworkers' Union in April 1937, under which only their members could work in mines, the position of the Afrikanerbond became impossible. They had to change tactics – to take over the Mineworkers' Union from within. With that aim in mind the Afrikanerbond became the "Reform Organisation in the Mineworkers' Union" in February 1938.

At the same time, the Broederbond leaders also launched a drive to get the clothing workers' trade unions into Afrikaner hands. Dr Hertzog made repeated trips to the more affluent Cape farmers, collecting money for the struggle. He also formed *Koopkrag* through which people could get discounts on purchases, a commission being retained by the organisation. *Koopkrag* later became a huge success in Pretoria.[8] An Afrikaner philanthropist, Mr Frederik Ziervogel, donated a huge amount for the establishment of the Johanna Ziervogel Fund. The interest was to be used for the struggle of the Afrikaner worker, and especially the women in clothing factories. The fund is still under Dr Hertzog's control today. Hertzog also persuaded a rich Stellenbosch farmer, Mr Pieter Neethling, to donate his estate to a trust to be used in the interests of the Afrikaner. The Pieter Neethling Building in Pretoria today houses the Hertzog network, and he is in control of the trust. When the battle for power in the Mineworkers' Union was finally won by the Broeders, the Pieter Neethling Fund had contributed £23 519 to the victory.

It was a bitter struggle during which Mineworkers' Union leaders changed the constitution, delayed elections, and even used false-bottomed ballot boxes in order to keep the Reformers out. But the tide was turning against the United Party Government which appeared to be in collusion with the Mineworkers' Union leaders, desperately clinging to power, and the Chamber of Mines which also feared a takeover. The Reformers were making constant progress and forming the Afrikaner mineworkers into a political force which had major influence in the marginal Witwatersrand seats. Although the final takeover took place only in 1949, the swing towards the HNP was almost complete among mineworkers when the election took place on May 26 1948. "Where the Nationalists had only two Reef seats before the election, they now gained six. In all these constituencies the mineworkers' vote was decisive. Those six constituencies brought the Nationalists to power."[9]

De Klerk[10] observes: "With almost nothing to raise expectations that the Government was in danger, the country went to the polls in May 1948. The rhetorical confidence which had been a feature of the planning of intellectuals like Diederichs, Meyer, Cronje and others, suddenly, astoundingly, proved to be of substance. The Herenigde Party, under D F Malan with 70 seats, supported by the Afrikaner Party under N C Havenga with nine seats, had a majority of five over the United Party under Smuts with 65, the Labour Party, under Madeley with six, and the three Native Representatives."

It was, indeed, the Broederbond's hour of greatest triumph. A small band of brothers in 1918, they were now the group with political control of the whole country. Never would they let power slip from the hands of the Super-Afrikaners. They would reform the country politically and socially on racial lines, with a zeal never witnessed before in the world. The campaign they had planned so painstakingly over the years to build up their secret structure had finally given them the biggest prize of all – absolute control. Not a day, not an hour, could be lost in putting their stamp on everything.

The world would look in wonderment at a secret society that gained political control and transformed a sophisticated country almost beyond recognition. It must surely rank as one of the most fascinating political stories of our time.

1. Van Jaarsveld, F A, *Van Riebeeck tot Verwoerd,* p 247.
2. Malan, M P A, *Die Nasionale Party van Suid-Afrika,* p 202.
3. Brochure: *Ons Party en die OB,* p 3.
4. Ibid. p 4.
5. Malan, M P A, *Die Nasionale Party van Suid-Afrika,* p 206.
6. Ibid. p 214.
7. Naude, Louis, *Dr Albert Hertzog, die Nasionale Party en die Mynwerkers,* p 27.
8. Ibid. p 100.
9. Ibid. p 239.
10. De Klerk, W A, *The Puritans in Africa,* p 224.

Part two
Power

6 *After the Victory*

The Broederbond was elated by the election result. It had good reason to be: after all, it was Broederbond strategy and tactics that had put the Nationalists in power. Many leading Broeders doubted that victory at the polls could be achieved so soon after they had implemented their plan to restore Afrikaner unity, though they worked day and night for it. Dr Malan, the new Prime Minister, did not even have his shadow Cabinet ready when the result was announced.

His train trip from Cape Town to Pretoria became a triumphant victory tour. On every station platform crowds were waiting to cheer him on to the north where the Governor-General, Mr G Brand van Zyl, would ask him to form the Government.

Before the election, General Smuts's United Party had 89 seats in Parliament but could count on 107 votes, including Labour Party MPs and Native Representatives. After the election he was left with only 65 seats, plus six Labourites and three Native Representatives who normally supported him: a total of 74, five less than the National and Afrikaner Parties' 79. After appointing the Speaker, the Nationalists had a majority of only four.

But a majority it was. Its importance could be seen in subsequent elections when the Nationalists went from strength to strength. Today, after 30 years in power, they are stronger than ever. The Broederbond was right: achieving Afrikaner unity, maintaining it at all costs, would probably keep an Afrikaner Government in power for ever in *normal* circumstances in South Africa.

From the Broederbond point of view, the new Nationalist Government, their political arm taking control, represented a massive breakthrough. It would mean the end of official campaigns against them. Quite the opposite: the new regime consisting mainly of Broeders would give the Broederbond its blessing to expand its activities. For the Bond it was the day of the political pay-off. For years they had been struggling to get their people in key positions: they achieved a measure of success only because of their absolute secrecy and cunning. But this was a God-given opportunity to reward those who had been working so hard for the success of the Bond.

All of a sudden the whole civil service, government boards and corporations, had opened up and could be packed with Broeders. Not only would this expand the influence of the Bond, it would create new bonds of loyalty between the Bond and members who were rewarded with top positions.

The 1948 election produced a number of "firsts" for the Broederbond. Dr Malan was the first Broederbonder to become Prime Minister. The top position in the country had fallen to them. His cabinet was not only the first exclusively Afrikaner cabinet in South Africa's history, it was also the first Broederbond Cabinet. Minister Broeders were J G Strijdom, C R Swart, E G Jansen,

Dr D F Malan. The first of a continuing line of Broederbond Prime Ministers.

Eben Dönges, Ben Schoeman, F C Erasmus, A J Stals and Paul Sauer. Only Eric Louw and Klasie Havenga were not Broeders.

It was an unbelievable coup for an organisation which had such humble beginnings only 30 years before, and only three years previously was outlawed in the civil service. With Broeders ensconced right at the top of the administration, the process of "Broederising" went down to the lowest level. For the first time Broeders were in the position to push their members, the Super-Afrikaners, into key positions with the approval – and sometimes active support – of the Prime Minister and the Cabinet.

In most cases it happened as positions became routinely available through retirement or death, but in some celebrated instances the Broederbond could not wait – they provided vacancies for some of their top members simply by giving civil servants golden handshakes and retiring them prematurely. The three most famous cases were those of Major-General Evered Poole, CB, CBE, DSO, of the Defence Force, Mr W Marshall Clark of the Railways and Mr Gideon Roos of the SABC. The Broederbond's reasoning was obviously that these were key strategic, military and propaganda posts. It was enlightening though, because these cases were forced into the open and South Africa could get a glimpse of how serious the Broederbond was when it proclaimed that it wanted to "control every sphere of South African life" (Dr Verwoerd).

Only 43 days after the Nationalists' surprise victory the new Minister of Defence, Mr F C Erasmus, dropped a bombshell on the South African Defence Force. "The position of Deputy Chief of the General Staff now held by Major-General Poole was created during the war. The Government does not intend to fill the post of Deputy Chief of the General Staff now vacated by Major-General Poole."[1]

Just like that.

South African soldiers were shocked to the core because General Poole was a highly respected officer and the clear front-runner to take over as Chief of the Defence Force. And here a new Minister who had actually opposed South Africa's war effort bitterly, and who never wore a uniform himself, squashed Poole's chances in a two-line statement. The fact was, of course, that General Poole did not vacate his post as Erasmus put it: he was demoted and kicked out of the way to clear the way for Afrikaner Broederbonders.

In a debate in the Assembly on September 17 1948 the Minister of Defence said that although he had made it perfectly clear that he was not prepared to appoint General Poole to the position of Chief of the General Staff, he would make use of his services. That was why he had appointed him Head of the South African Military Mission in Berlin.[2] The Berlin post was almost a non-post. It was little more than a consulate under another name. Germany was a defeated country, not a sovereign or military power, and merely an occupied territory. On July 13 1948 the *Rand Daily Mail's* London correspondent reported that General Poole's appointment to Berlin "has been received with a great deal of surprise in London. As a soldier he ranks high in the estimation of the British military chiefs, and considerable surprise is being expressed at his appointment to what is for all practical purposes a non-military post."

According to all accounts, especially those of the soldiers who served under him, Poole was one of the greatest soldiers South Africa ever produced. General Smuts appointed this career soldier in 1943 to succeed the immensely popular General Dan Pienaar in command of the 1st South African Division. Most of Pienaar's loyal soldiers doubted whether Poole – or for that matter anybody else – could take Pienaar's place. Yet Poole succeeded through his example as an outstanding soldier, loyal at all times to his men. General Smuts's citation when he appointed Poole Major-General said: "During hard and intense fighting, Major-General Poole controlled the battle of his brigade in such a calm and determined manner that all enemy resistance was overcome." At only 40, Poole became the youngest general in the South African Army.

Major-General Poole led the famous attack which pierced the Gothic Line in Italy and the message to his men afterwards gives an insight into his relationship with them. "It is with unbounded pride that I look back on the great events of the last year. During these 12 months of bitter fighting in Italy, every man in this division has played a most worthy part, both in and out of battle. The fighting men have never flinched either in the heat of battle or during the grim static phases when we held our positions throughout the winter.

"We are proud and honoured to have represented our country in this momentous period in the history of the world. We are thankful for our speedy and decisive victory in the final phases of this campaign. Even the most optimistic appreciation did not foresee such a rapid and complete defeat of the German forces in Italy.

"In three short weeks a powerful enemy was destroyed and

nearly one-third of the country and a half of the Italian population was freed. I need hardly add how grateful we are to have been present at the coup de grace of Nazidom and to have made our contribution to its downfall."[3]

It was generally assumed that General Poole would succeed General Sir Pierre van Ryneveld as Chief of the General Staff. General van Ryneveld was due to retire about 10 months after the Nationalists took power, but within days it became clear that they had their own ideas for this important post. One of the reasons the Nationalists would not give the post to Poole was that he was relatively young, only 46, and would have been Chief of the General Staff for at least 10 years. He would have blocked the way for an Afrikaner Broederbonder for far too long. It must be remembered that there was no Broeder ready to take over immediately: they were bitterly opposed to the war effort. Yet they planned ahead, and opened the way at least by removing Poole.

Another reason, some ex-soldiers believe, was that Poole as head of the Army would have been totally incompatible with the new Nationalist administration. Here on the one hand was the English-speaking career soldier who threw himself with gusto into the war against the Nazis and made no secret of his delight, in statements and interviews, every time the "Huns" were beaten. On the other hand, Frans Erasmus and his Super-Afrikaner colleagues in the Cabinet, had opposed the war against the Nazis with equal gusto and whimpered every time the Nazis suffered a defeat.

It just could not work. The Broederbond had to show publicly what the new criteria would be. On August 8 1948 the tall, distinguished-looking General Poole arrived early in the morning at Zwartkop Air Station to leave for his new post in Berlin. A large party of Defence Force officers came to say goodbye. General Poole did not refer to his deep disappointment.

He did valuable work for his country in the diplomatic field, and was promoted on a few occasions. But his yearning was still for the military and his officers and men in the Defence Force always missed him. He died in March 1969, having declined a full military funeral offered by the State. The *Sunday Times* said: "It was his only gesture reflecting his deep disappointment and bitterness – which he kept hidden – at being cursorily debarred from becoming Chief of the Defence Force."[4]

The second case where the new Broederbond administration showed its hand was in the South African Railways, the largest single employer in South Africa and a breeding-ground for the Broederbond. From the time the Broederbond was started in 1918, Railway personnel played an important role in it. As a result the Broederbond also played an important role in the Railways after the Nationalists came to power in 1948. In fact, every single general manager of the Railways since 1948 was a Broederbonder – that is, after they had removed the stumbling-block called Clark. W Marshall Clark, OBE, at 45 was the youngest man ever to be appointed General Manager of the Railways (on July 27 1945).

Marshall Clark. (Reproduced by kind permission of *The Star*).

Therefore, when the Nationalists came to power he had a full 13 and perhaps 18 years to serve as general manager ... the prospect was unacceptable to the Super-Afrikaner Cabinet and to the leading Broeders, H W Heckroodt and D H C du Plessis, waiting in the wings. So Marshall Clark was forced out on early retirement and given a golden handshake of about £80 000 – a small fortune in those days. W H Heckroodt was installed as general manager, and when he retired not long after, Danie du Plessis took over.

Marshall Clark was a career railwayman, joining as a pupil engineer in 1921. He was a lieutenant-colonel in the war. He built the Allies' railway line through Syria, a strategic track through the mountains of Syria linking the Palestinian port of Haifa with the Syrian oil pipeline terminus of Beirut. War correspondents described this work as "an epic of railway construction."

In a farewell message to the railway staff he said on February 8 1950: "At the repeated and earnest request of the Prime Minister and the Minister of Transport (Paul Sauer) I have agreed to retire immediately from my position as General Manager of the Railways to undertake other work which they have asked me to do. As a lifelong railwayman, and the son of a railwayman, I have always thought of the South African Railways as my life's work. It is with a sad heart that I leave you."[5]

The "other work" that Marshall Clark referred to was a feeble pretext to get him out of the way. He was asked to become secretary general of an interim organisation for Central and Southern African Transport. The half-baked idea never really got off the ground and Marshall Clark pulled out of it soon after it had started. Fortunately for him, he had insisted on compensation from the Government. They were so keen that they agreed and paid him a pension as if he had completed his full term of service. They took into account that at the age of 50, Mr Clark had "a natural life expectancy of 20 years." Special legislation condoning the Government's financial arrangements for Mr Clark's retirement had to be approved. At that stage a figure of £40 000 was mentioned, but it turned out to be £80 000.

During the debate in the Senate, Senator D Jackson (United Party) on June 13 1950 quoted rumours that the Broederbond had said, "Either Mr Clark goes or the Minister goes."[6] Mr Clark had been sacrificed. The Railway Grievances Commission, giving railwaymen the opportunity to complain about treatment under the Smuts Government, had cost £23 000. Add to that Mr Clark's pension and it had cost the country £95 000 to put one Broederbonder (M Heckroodt) in power for two years until retirement, Senator Jackson said. He added that there should be a judicial inquiry to discover why Mr Heckroodt was enjoying such consideration. Senator A M Conroy (United Party) said the removal of Mr Clark resulted from the Broederbond constitution's demand for all key positions to be held by Broederbonders. When the case was discussed in Parliament on February 24 1950, Mr S F Waterson, former Minister of Economic Development, said: "The size of the compensation which the Minister of Transport has arranged for Mr Clark is a measure of the sense of his guilt."

Mr Clark did not remain idle for long. He was an extremely competent man and was snapped up to become a director and manager of Anglo American, a director of De Beers, General Mining and Finance Corporation, Rand Mines, and other companies.

Mr Heckroodt was one of the earliest members of the Broederbond. He was born in the Free State in December 1892 and joined the Railways at the age of 16. He advanced through the clerical and station-master grades to reach head office. On the same date in 1945 that Marshall Clark became General Manager of the Railways, Mr Heckroodt was appointed Deputy General Manager.

The new Broederbond Cabinet was faced by the problem here that Marshall Clark was blocking the way for two of their top members to become chief of the Railways. They could not wait that long. The Railways was a massive undertaking of the kind that the Broederbond had prepared for years to take over. Heckroodt had only three years to retirement in 1950, and du Plessis eight. Leaving Marshall Clark in the job would have stymied the Bond. It was a matter of principle for them that their long-serving Broeder be rewarded, that the Bond's policy of controlling all the top positions be fulfilled, and that other Broeders should become aware of what was waiting at the end of the line for them if they stayed loyal to the Bond and the party. Daniel Hendrik Cilliers du Plessis became Deputy Manager when Heckroodt became General Manager. When Heckroodt retired three years later, Du Plessis took over the top position.

Du Plessis was born in the Colesberg district in 1898. He joined the Railways as a messenger when he was 16. It was only a few years later in Johannesburg that he met Henning Klopper, about the same age and also on the Railways. They had the same political outlook, and felt strongly about the plight of the urbanised

D H C Du Plessis. Broederbond founder member and Railways Manager until 1961.

Afrikaner after the Boer War. So Du Plessis became one of the three young Afrikaners who met on a koppie near Johannesburg in 1918 to plan the Broederbond. Their ranks had been expanded by the time they met again for the official inauguration and Du Plessis's Broederbond number was 8. All the same, it indicated a powerful position in the organisation. According to the Bond, he was entitled to the reward of becoming General Manager before retirement. Du Plessis in his own right was an extremely capable man, but the fact of the matter is that if Clark had not been removed he would not have reached the top position.

Du Plessis served the Railways for 46 years, and in that time been absent from work only once when he had mumps. When he became General Manager in 1953 the Railways employed 220 000 people and the daily wage bill was R610 000. He was proud of the role that the Railways under his direction played in implementing the apartheid policy. In September 1956 he told a group of overseas business men that the Government's plan for the large-scale resettlement of blacks would have meant Railway expansion of £50-million. He said that between 1956 and 1963 about 932 000 blacks would be housed in their own townships near Johannesburg, Germiston, Benoni, Pretoria, Cape Town and Durban. Of this number, about 400 000 would travel to and from work in electric trains.

By the time Du Plessis retired in 1961 the Broederbond was firmly entrenched in top positions in the Railways. Since his time every general manager has been a Broederbonder, and the top echelons of the organisation have been packed with members. Obviously there has also been a ripple effect in other departments, and in industries interwoven with the operations of the transport giant.

The case of the South African Broadcasting Corporation was slightly different from the previous two cases. Taking control of such a powerful propaganda medium with monopolistic authority was, of course, one of the main aims of the new Broederbond Government. Strangely enough, although they thought they had it all sewn up it did not work out exactly as planned.

As chairman of the SABC Board of Governors they appointed a veteran Broederbonder, Dr S H Pellissier, father of *volkspele* in South Africa. But the chairmanship did not carry much weight. Dr Pellissier was getting old, and he did not have enough drive. Real power in the corporation was vested in the Director General. Here they took a calculated risk which did not pay off. As in the Defence Force, there was no Broeder in line who could possibly be appointed on merit. The man they appointed appeared to have credentials, although he was not a Broeder. He was Gideon Roos, son of a former Springbok rugby captain and MP for Stellenbosch, Mr Paul Roos. Gideon Roos was a qualified advocate who had devoted his life to broadcasting. One of the strong points in his favour, as far as the Broederbond was concerned, was that he "popularised" the symbolic trek in 1938 over the radio to such an extent that it became an emotional mass movement reuniting the Afrikaners, and contributed substantially to the election victory 10 years later.

Roos was only supposed to accompany the trek to its first stop outside Cape Town. The rest of the long journey to Pretoria would have gone almost unnoticed if his broadcasts had not been so outstanding. They gripped the imagination and emotions of the Afrikaner nation to such an extent that the demands for Roos to

SABC Director, Gideon Roos. His position was undermined by the Broederbond.

accompany the trek to Pretoria became irresistable. Unbeknown to him, Roos ensured with his broadcasts exactly what the Broederbond had hoped the trek would achieve.

When they had to appoint a new Director General in 1949, the Cabinet chose Roos – but they had misread him. He insisted on scrupulously fair reports and comment, not favouring one party over the other. He would not allow the SABC to be used as a progaganda machine for the National Party.

At first they thought the fault lay with the weak chairmanship of Dr Pellissier, so in 1959 they replaced him with a prominent Broederbonder, Dr Piet Meyer. But still the SABC did not turn into a propaganda machine overnight, because the chairman did not have the necessary power to enforce his will and, secondly, Gideon Roos resisted biased broadcasting. In order to get the SABC completely under Broederbond control the problem had to be aproached from two sides: the chairman had to be given more powers, and Roos had to be ousted.

In April 1961 Roos found his position untenable and resigned. Like Marshall Clark he received a golden handshake. *The Star* on April 12 1961 said his resignation had come as no surprise. "His executive tasks as Director General had been whittled away one by one until he was left with almost nothing to do." As in the case of General Poole in the Defence Force, the SABC Board now announced that Mr Roos's post had fallen away.

The Board of Governors, initially advisers to the Director General, took over the function of the Director General. The chairman of the board, Dr P J Meyer, became the effective head of broadcasting in South Africa. Commented *The Star:* "In his 24 years of broadcasting Mr Roos had persistently championed the cause of impartiality in the function of the SABC and the maintenance of democratic principles in broadcasting. He always fought vigorously any attempt to convert the SABC into a Government propaganda machine."

The *Sunday Times* of April 16 1961 said: "The Government and the Broederbond have won their four-year struggle to get rid of Mr Gideon Roos. With his departure, the last obstacle has been removed for the control of broadcasting in South Africa to fall completely into political hands."

The *Sunday Times* reported that Mr Roos had told them some time earlier: "The SABC provides a service to the public, and is therefore a servant of the public, not a servant of the Government."

When Dr Meyer was appointed chairman of the board in 1959, a new post of executive chairman was created. This gave Dr Meyer not only control of legislation in the Corporation, but overriding administrative and executive powers. He kept a tight rein, especially on matters of political importance.

Dr Meyer's and Mr Roos's views on broadcasting had clashed head-on. Somebody had to yield, and as usual it was not the Broederbond. A case in point was that of Mr Jannie Kruger, who resigned as editor of the *Transvaler* in 1961 to become "cultural adviser" to the SABC. This was a new post created by Dr Meyer, by the then Boss Broeder, for another leading Broeder. Mr Kruger's series of talks *The South African Scene* provoked a public and parliamentary outcry against political slanting in the SABC. Mr Roos said he had no authority to censor the talks. They were "sanctioned at a higher level." The next step Dr Meyer took to limit Mr Roos's power, was to appoint directors with specific tasks. Although Mr Roos was one of them, control was split among five men – three of them Broederbonders – given functions which were previously his. Administration was allocated to Mr J P A van der Walt, formerly secretary of the corporation, Finance to Mr J N Swanepoel, a surprise appointment of a man who was formerly a railway clerk – until one learns that he came from the breeding-ground of the Broederbond – and Mr C D Fuchs, another Broeder, took another giant step in his meteoric rise to power in the SABC by getting the post of Director of Programmes. (Incidentally, Dr Meyer was to revive the post of Director General which he abolished when he ousted Mr Roos. First, Mr Fuchs held it, and it is now Mr J N Swanepoel's.) Mr Norman Filmer was put in charge of planning and development. Mr Roos, stripped of all these tasks, was left with only Springbok Radio and the Africa service. These involved very little policy direction or administration.

Most of the staff were very upset. They felt that Mr Roos's influence had been undermined and that he was being humiliated. He had built up a reputation for being scrupulously fair and creating harmony between English and Afrikaans-speaking personnel. At a farewell party at Broadcast House on June 1 1961 he told his staff who had presented him with a stinkwood display cabinet: "I would like to have spent the rest of my life working for radio in South Africa, but a man can't always do what he wants to do."[7]

In an interview with *The Star* (May 30 1961) he said: "It is not easy to pull up roots and break away after a quarter of a century in a profession I love as much as broadcasting. I had hoped I would have the privilege of serving my country and my people in broadcasting until the day of my retirement." The Broederbond was now firmly in control of a mighty propaganda machine. Another key to control of all spheres of influence in South Africa had been seized.

By 1961 the undisputed boss of the SABC was Dr Meyer. He had become boss of the Broederbond in 1960. He now held two of the most powerful positions in South Africa.

Pieter Johannes Meyer was born in January 1909 in Ladybrand, Orange Free State. His educational qualifications are impressive: Bachelor of Arts, Higher Teachers' Diploma, Master of Education, Master of Arts (Psychology), Master of Arts (Philosophy), Doctorates in Literature and Philosophy (Amsterdam) and Philosophy (South Africa). He became a primary school teacher in 1931, moved to a high school the next year, and in 1933 became a lecturer at the Pretoria Teachers' College. Dr Meyer was the FAK's secretary from 1936 to 1943. According to HNP sources, he was axed as assistant secretary of the Broederbond in 1942. He then occupied two other important positions apart from that as secretary of the FAK: he was also assistant secretary of the Broederbond and secretary of the Reddingsdaadbondfonds.

Apparently the Executive Council discovered that Meyer was strongly under the influence of the Ossewabrandwag of which he was a staunch member. He used his Broederbond position to favour the OB at a time when it was the Executive Council's policy not to take sides between the Afrikaner organisations, but to work towards reconciliation. To keep him under control the Executive Council told him his responsibilities were too heavy and that he must resign the Broederbond post. Dr Meyer then resigned all his posts and from 1942 to 1951 he was with the newspaper *Dagbreek* and *Sondagnuus,* first as a journalist and then as a secretary. From 1951 to 1959 he worked for Dr Anton Rupert's Rembrandt Tobacco Corporation as Chief Public Relations Officer. On August 1 1959, he was plucked from this obscurity to become a national figure.

The man who put him in this powerful position was Dr Albert Hertzog, a lifelong friend who joined the Broederbond at about the same time as Meyer. In the 1930s they started their campaign to take over the Mine Workers' Union and turn it into a pro-Nationalist organisation. In the late 1940s Hertzog and Meyer succeeded in this, and the mineworkers on the Reef swung a number of vital seats to the Nationalists.

Hertzog was appointed Minister of Posts and Telegraphs in 1958 by Dr Verwoerd. This gave him the direct say in the affairs of the SABC and he started scheming immediately to get the key post of chairman of the board for his friend Meyer. In fact, he promised Meyer the post before he had even discussed the matter with Dr Verwoerd! Verwoerd was upset because he wanted to appoint somebody with more prestige.

Although Meyer was well-known and respected in Broeder circles, the general public only knew him, if at all, as PRO for Rembrandt. Verwoerd approached Mr M C Botha, later Minister of Bantu Affairs, but fortunately for Meyer – perhaps Hertzog and Meyer spoke to Broeder Botha – he turned it down. The way was then clear for Hertzog to give the plum job to Meyer, even though the majority of Cabinet Ministers opposed the choice.

Meyer now had one of the most powerful opinion-influencing positions in the country. As he told an Afrikaanse Handelsinstituut congress in Pretoria in September 1961, the spoken word was more powerful than the atomic or hydrogen bomb in today's uncertain world. He also held that radio listeners did not have the right to prescribe the policy of the SABC, any more than newspaper readers had the right to prescribe the policy of a newspaper.[8] What he failed to mention was that the SABC had a monopolistic position entrenched in the law, and people simply had to listen to it if they wanted to listen to the radio. Newspapers, on the other hand, were involved in serious circulation battles and people had a wide choice.

In spite of predictions to the contrary, Dr Meyer has been reappointed chairman of the SABC every time his term expired since 1959, the last time from January 1977 for a further three years. It is clear that through his position in the Broederbond he has established a powerful, almost unassailable position in Afrikanerdom. At the time when Mr Vorster faced a split in Afrikaner ranks, provoked by the Hertzog group, he had to consider the strong possibility that Dr Meyer would try to throw the powerful Broederbond behind his lifelong friend, Albert Hertzog. Mr Vorster and Dr Meyer were in constant contact and it is clear that deals were made between Vorster and the Broederbond, and between him and Meyer. That is the only explanation for Meyer's retention of power for so long and despite so many controversies.

It must also be borne in mind that Dr Meyer entrenched himself firmly in the SABC by surrounding himself with yes-men and Broeders. Almost the entire hierarchy of the SABC belongs to the secret society of Super-Afrikaners. Dr Douglas Fuchs, the former Director General, is a Broeder; the present Director General, Mr J N Swanepoel, is a Broeder; Dr Jan Schutte who was recently promoted to the post of Director General (Programmes), is a Broeder. Mr Steve de Villiers, Director of Afrikaans and English Programmes, is a Broeder. Mr T van Heerden, recently appointed

Director of Bantu and External Services, is a Broeder. The new head of the SABC in the Free State, Mr B J Steyn, is a Broeder, as is Mr L S Seegars, Director of Schools Radio Service. Deputy Director General (Administration) Mr Gert Yssel and Mr E van H E Mischke, head of Stores and Supplies, are Broeders. Dr Meyer has obviously left nothing undone to secure the Broederbond's position for ever and ever in the SABC. As the older ones retire, the younger Broeders will take over and even under another Government, the Broederbond will be firmly in control of the country's radio and television services.

Dr Meyer was also chairman of the commission which investigated the advisability of television. In fact the outcome was cut and dried before the investigation was started. The commission was appointed only after the Government had had discussions with the Executive Council of the Broederbond. The terms of reference were agreed between them. The Minister of Posts and Telegraphs, then Senator J P van der Spuy, who appointed the commission, was a leading Broeder – in fact the secretary at one stage. The commission's chairman, Dr Piet Meyer, was then Broederbond chairman. A member of the commission was the Reverend J S Gericke, a former deputy chairman of the Broederbond. The secretary was Dr Jan Schutte, also a leading Broeder. The TV era gave a new lease of life to Dr Meyer, who likes to do things on a grandiose scale. The new headquarters in Auckland Park would be the envy of many of the larger nations of the world and Dr Meyer's office is *out* of this world. No expense was spared; original paintings by South African artists are on the walls, and the furnishings are antiques. The restaurant and bar for SABC executives might be part of a five-star hotel. The Government hides behind the fact that the SABC is "autonomous" and refuses to give information on such matters, even in Parliament.

At the opening of the new TV complex, the SABC spent about R250 000. An instant lawn was laid for about R10 000, a planeload of overseas visitors was flown in, taken to the Kruger National Park, and then from Johanesburg to Cape Town in the Blue Train. The same extravagance is displayed every year at the SABC's Artes awards ceremony. It appears as if Dr Meyer, by throwing money around, is trying to tell the world that the Afrikaner has reached the top at last, that he no longer has to feel inferior, that anything a big English business house can do, he can do better.

In the first half of 1976 the SABC bought Dr Meyer's house in

Emmarentia at a price 52 percent above the municipal valuation of R52 400.[9] The SABC said it would be used by Dr Meyer until his retirement and then by his successors. But it did not explain why Dr Meyer got such a good price at a time when the property market was dead in South Africa. Of course the deal was tax-free, being a capital gain.

Dr Meyer's statements on various subjects can be found throughout this book, because a book on the Broederbond in which Piet Meyer was not prominent is unthinkable. He had publicly denounced Afrikaners who patronise non-Afrikaner businesses.[10] In 1961, speaking to the *Natalse Onderwysunie* he attacked the "superficial, sentimental attitude towards other peoples, the unscientific stories of equality of peoples and races, a spirit derived from a senseless, fatalistic outlook of doom."[11] This was not to educate but to undermine. Education's most important task today was to mould and equip children "in all their thoughts and feelings" against the threat of communist world domination. "Our children must learn to identify the fellow travellers and pathfinders of this anti-Christian, satanic warmongering, whose pretty phrases are slavishly being taken over by communism's opponents. It is the responsibility of all, especially of teachers, to complete this task," he said.

At a *Bondsraad* meeting in April 1972 he said the Broederbond had made practical contributions to the implementation of the Government's apartheid policy. Dr Meyer also made it quite clear that television would strengthen Afrikanerdom. "With the results of research, we shall be in the position timeously to detect and eliminate harmful and undesirable effects of television on the maintenance and strengthening of Afrikaner identity."[12]

But Dr Meyer's public statements and speeches are kindergarten stuff in comparison with what he had been telling the Broeders behind closed doors at secret meetings inaccessible to ordinary members of the public, let alone the Press. There Piet Meyer is seen in an entirely different light, because there he can speak as he really feels without fear of public criticism. There he can preach naked Afrikaner *baasskap* and Broederbond control.

Fortunately, documents containing some of his secret speeches will enable people to judge him more accurately than his public performance alone makes possible.

A few weeks after Dr Verwoerd's death in 1966, Dr Meyer addressed his Executive Council on the future of the Afrikaner nation. He said the Broederbond had a clear objective which it must disseminate. "This objective can be nothing less than the complete political nationalising and eventual cultural Afrikanerising of our English-speaking co-citizens – if it can still be done. We will not be able to stop the process of complete cultural integration of Afrikaans- and English-speaking if we have only limited control of this process. Therefore we can envisage only the deliberate Afrikanerising of the English-speakers, or tacit acceptance of the unintentional but certain anglicising of the Afrikaner. The objective of nationalising the English-speakers politically will be of permanent value, ensuring the continued existence of the Afrikaner, only if it is coupled with the Afrikanerising of the economy.

"The Afrikanerising of the English-speakers is an educational task – it must start in the schools. The Afrikanerising of the English-speaker entails the English-speaker accepting the Afrikaner outlook and philosophy as his own; integrating his ideals and lifestyle with that of the Afrikaner; recognising the Afrikaner's history as his history; and recognising Afrikaans as his national language next to English as the international language of the two white groups ... We will then talk of Afrikaans-speaking and English-speaking Afrikaners."

1. *Rand Daily Mail,* July 9 1948.
2. *Rand Daily Mail.*
3. *Sunday Times,* May 13 1945.
4. Ibid. March 16 1969.
5. *Rand Daily Mail.*
6. Ibid.
7. Ibid.
8. Ibid. November 23 1962.
9. *Sunday Times,* July 11 1976.
10. Ibid. December 23 1962.
11. Ibid. December 3 1961.
12. *Rand Daily Mail,* July 12 1974.

7 *Republic – A Dream Achieved*

Afrikaners never accepted that they had finally lost their republican form of government with the defeat of the two Boer republics in 1902. The republican dream remained with them and was carefully nurtured during the long years in which one constitutional concession after another – eventually leading to full independence – had to be won from Britain.

Ever since its inception in 1918, the Afrikaner Broederbond saw as one of its most important aims the cutting of all constitutional ties with Britain and the establishment of a free, independent republic ruled by Afrikaners. It played a tremendous part in achieving this aim by harnessing Afrikaner organisations such as the FAK, youth movements, churches, the National Party and its influential membership to strive towards the same objective.

Professor Pelzer referred to this in his historical review in 1968. "The way in which South Africa was drawn into the (Second World) War convinced Afrikaners that the establishment of a republic would be the only effective way to prevent a repetition. For the preparation of the republic, the Executive nominated a policy commission to draw up a Constitution Bill.

"With the National Party's victory in 1948, the Afrikaner Broederbond entered a new development phase. The most important aspects of this phase can be summarised as follows: a constant effort to overcome the ideological confusion created by the war; the formulation of the republican policy and the promotion of the practical steps for the establishment of the Republic of South Africa..."

The long-serving former chairman of the Broederbond, Dr Piet Meyer, referred in several speeches to the decisive role the organisation played in the attainment of the republican ideal. On May 21 1963 he told the annual meeting in his chairman's address: "In the second phase of our organisation's existence, from about 1934, it deliberately worked for the establishment of the Republic of South Africa, separate from the Commonwealth. It saw this as the most important condition and method through which English-speaking citizens could be persuaded to become loyal South Africans and, with the dedicated Afrikaner, safeguard the future of southern Africa as a permanent home for the separate white and non-white groups."

Dr Meyer here put into perspective the whole question of why South Africa did not remain in the Commonwealth. The fact is that the Broederbond never saw the new republic as part of the Commonwealth. Dr Verwoerd's statements that although he tried to keep it in the Commonwealth, this was made impossible for him by other States, must be seen in the light of the Broederbond commitment.

This commitment also came to light in a secret document of the Broederbond's policy committee circulated under the title *Study Document on the Republic: Policy and Task.* The document stated: "The decision as to whether the republic will immediately be established outside the Commonwealth will depend on practical considerations at the time. But departure from the Commonwealth as soon as possible remains a cardinal aspect of our republican aim."

In 1971 Dr Meyer again referred to the role played by the Broederbond and the National Party after 1948. "They placed South Africa clearly, firmly and inexorably on the road to an independent republic – they and Afrikanerdom had had enough of the road of "honour" which always ended in participation in British wars. The republican road was not a road of abstract constitutional freedom, but of embracing spiritual freedom in which the Afrikaner could always be himself..."

The ground had to be prepared slowly for the advent of the republic. There were many differences of opinion among Afrikaner leaders about the timing of the constitutional change. Victory was essential and so the referendum had to be held at a time when at least some English-speakers would vote for a republic. Dr Malan's majority was too small for such a risk; he was in his old age, and his new administration had many urgent tasks. Strijdom's reign was short and although he was the strongest republican of all his failing health prevented him from seeing his dream fulfilled. It was his successor, H F Verwoerd, who eventually took the calculated risk in calling the 1960 referendum. Verwoerd's stature had grown through the years among his Afrikaner supporters and also among many English-speakers who had come to regard him as a kind of father figure – a benign but strong ruler at a time when more and more whites had to flee for their lives from African states in the north. There was also an attempt on Dr Verwoerd's life on April 9 1960 which created more hero-worship for him.

None of the National Party's provincial secretaries could guarantee Verwoerd that he would win the referendum. He took the chance all the same but he could never have succeeded without the help of the Broederbond. In fact he told the Broederbond of his plan long before he even informed his own caucus or Parliament.

This was revealed by Dr Piet Meyer in his chairman's address in 1968. "It was the late Broeder Verwoerd, former Executive member and then Prime Minister, who invited the Broederbond in July 1959, six months before his Republican statement in Parliament, to accept co-responsibility for the establishment of the Republic. This task the Afrikaner Broederbond accepted with great enthusiasm and the expenditure of large amounts of money from our reserve and other funds."

The work Broederbonders did in the republican campaign can never be overestimated. Not only did they spend from their own funds, they also collected money for the campaign. Every one of the thousands of members became a dedicated organiser, knocking on doors, canvassing, persuading. Add to this their immense influence in radio and broadcasting, churches, universities, schools and scores of public bodies, and there can be no doubt that they swung the campaign in favour of the republicans. South Africa went to the polls on October 5 1960. The results were: republicans 850 458, anti-republicans 775 878, giving the republicans a majority of 74 580. One of the first things Dr Verwoed did was to write to the Broederbond to thank it for the part it had played in the referendum. His letter was read by the chairman of the Bond, Professor H B Thom, to the *Bondsraad* held in Bloemfontein on November 24 1960.

Dr Verwoerd wrote: "Inside the Cabinet and the party there has been unity, but it was also experienced outside the party as your organisation would know only too well. Apart from the blessing from Above we are thankful to everybody and I sincerely want to thank your council especially and everybody it represents for the support in many forms that was given to us. It is our common achievement and the achievement of the nation *(volk)* which will make the Republic a reality. I deeply appreciate the promise of co-operation in the days ahead."

The Broederbond's idea was always that the new Republic should be on the same lines as the old Boer republics with a new flag and an executive president elected by the nation. They accepted that it would have been unwise to insist on this in a referendum which could have gone either way. It would have been too alien to English-speakers whose support they needed. But this dream, too, never died. They had only to bide their time, advocate the idea in the background and wait for the climate to be right for changes in the presidency. This is exactly what has happened now, 18 years later: the Government's new constitutional plans include an executive presidency.

The Broederbond's role in getting this accepted is disclosed in the secret documents. Dr Meyer said in 1968 that one of the main tasks of the Broederbond was to give a greater Christian-Afrikaner content to the Republic. He added: "A week before Broeder H F Verwoerd was murdered in Parliament, he gave me, as chairman of the Executive, permission for the Afrikaner Broederbond to start campaigning for a new Republican flag and a change in the presidency to bring it more in line with the position in the Transvaal and Free State republics . . . We will give attention to this when the time is right for it."

The new chairman, Professor Viljoen, also referred to the Broederbond's role in this respect in his 1976 chairman's address. "There is already debate in government circles (Cabinet level) on political matters like the Westminster system, the role of a cabinet council to give brown people a say in political decision-making on a basis of consensus, a new role for the State President, especially in multinational consultations . . . We should make a contribution here."

Not satisfied to sit back after the attainment of the Republic, the Broederbond went into action immediately to make sure that its indelible stamp would remain on the country. As early as May 1961 it urged its members to increase their efforts to have their policies implemented. Under the heading *Our Task in the Republic* the chief secretary stated that the organisation's role would remain basically the same, but that its tasks would have to be defined more precisely and the organisation's effectiveness increased even further. "Our task is presently not only to formulate policy, but more so to find the best methods to implement our well-tried policies in every sphere of society. This demands intensive and co-ordinated scientific research, the prior testing of methods, and their expert application."

The most urgent inquiries to be conducted by the "expert brainpower" of the organisation was seen as how to maintain the white state in Africa and the world, and in the numerically superior black environment, how to get the English-speaker to co-operate more closely with the Afrikaner and to accept the Afrikaner dynamism as his own, and which existing and new public bodies and institutions could be used for the execution of these tasks.

"The Executive will see to it that experts over the whole country will start working on better methods for the successful implementation of our policy ... and will send the details, as recommended, to branches for implementation. Branches should not wait for this, however, but continue with the work as they have always done.

"Develop the existing public bodies through which you work to the outside as living, enthusiastic organisations, and see to it that the right people are represented in their managements."

The attainment of the Republic was, indeed, one of the Broederbond's greatest achievements. It showed, once again, how a relatively small group of highly organised and motivated people working in secret, could change a country's course and history. This amazing group of Super-Afrikaners could claim yet another monument for themselves.

8 *Afrikaans-English Relations*

"The Prime Minister (General Smuts) has unchained forces just as the first language struggle and the second language struggle did, and he ought to know what the result will be if he touches the sentiment of the people, if he touches the soul of the people and if he touches the life of the people. He must know what it means to run up against the Afrikaans-speaking section's church, its teachers, its cultural organisations . . . and the Prime Minister knows today that in the struggle he has now commenced these forces eventually will win. These forces stand foursquare against him."

The speaker was Dr D F Malan, leader of the National Party and only two years later South Africa's first Broederbond Prime Minister. The occasion was a debate in Parliament on the Smuts Government's "bilingualism" policy of bringing Afrikaans- and English-speaking children together in the same schools.

Dr Malan's statement[1] made quite clear the Broederbond's policy: to establish exclusive *Afrikanerskap,* a start must be made in the separated schools. That is still the organisation's stance today. It is unashamedly Afrikaans-oriented, for the promotion of everything identified with Afrikaans, indeed for Afrikaner domination of South Africa.

No matter what Nationalist leaders say about the need for unity between the Afrikaans- and English-speaking sections of the population, they know it is only half the story: the other half is to be found in the documents of the Broederbond. Instead of rejoicing at the success of the National Party in getting English-speakers' votes on a large scale in recent elections, some top Broeders found it disturbing. They see a danger in diluting the Afrikaner purity of the National Party, the Bond's political arm.

The Broederbond's policy on relations between the Afrikaans and English sections was spelt out clearly by the long-serving chairman, Dr Piet Meyer, a few weeks after Dr Verwoerd's assassination. Dr Meyer, addressing the Bond's Executive Council on the future of the Afrikaner, came out strongly in favour of

Afrikaans as the main language and the Afrikaner as the dominant partner in the relationship. He said the Broederbond had a clear aim which it should disseminate. "This aim can be nothing but the complete nationalising and eventual cultural Afrikanerising of our English-speaking co-citizens – if it can still be done. We will not be able to stop the process of complete cultural integration of Afrikaans- and English-speaking if we have only limited control of this process.

"Therefore we can only envisage either the deliberate Afrikanerising of the English-speakers, or the silent acceptance of the unintentional but certain anglicising of the Afrikaner. The drive to nationalise the English-speakers politically will not be of permanent value, ensuring the continued existence of the Afrikaner, unless it is coupled with the Afrikanerising of the economy.

"The Afrikanerising of the English-speakers is an educational task: it must start in the schools. It entails the English-speaker accepting the Afrikaner outlook and philosophy as his own, integrating his ideals and life-style with that of the Afrikaner, embracing the Afrikaner's history as his own, and regarding Afrikaans as his national language next to English as the international language of the two groups, while both remain official languages... We will then talk of Afrikaans-speaking and English-speaking Afrikaners."

The organisation's name reveals what it is all about: Afrikaner Broederbond. It was formed after the Anglo-Boer War to uplift Afrikaners living in poverty. It was a reaction against the English, whom they blamed for the war, their poverty and humiliation. It was a reaction against Lord Milner's policy of anglicising the Afrikaner. It was an attempt to organise the Afrikaners to overcome discrimination against them in commerce and industry.

The minutes of the formal inaugural meeting on June 5 1918 show the chairman, Mr H J Klopper, as saying: "Our aim is a Brotherhood of Afrikaners..." On July 2 1918 these aims were formulated: "A melting together of Afrikaners... To serve the interest of Afrikaners at all times... To bring Afrikaners to consciousness, to create self-respect and love for our own language, history, country and *volk.*"

The constitution of the Broederbond makes it quite clear that only Afrikaners – in fact only Super-Afrikaners – can belong to the organisation. Not even a top Nationalist is qualified for membership, unless he is also of the Afrikaner elite. A case in point is that of Senator Owen Horwood, Minister of Finance and Nationalist leader in Natal. His credentials as a Nationalist are impeccable, but because he is not an Afrikaner he is excluded from the inner circles.

Article 4 of the Broederbond constitution states these aims:
(a) The creation of a vigorous and increasing harmony among all Afrikaners striving for the welfare of the Afrikaner nation;
(b) The development of national consciousness within the Afrikaner and the inculcation of love for his language, religion, traditions, country and nation;
(c) The promotion of all the interests of the Afrikaner nation.

Article 5: The language of the Bond is Afrikaans

Article 8: Membership: The Bond consists of white males over 25 years of age who are:
(a) Afrikaans-speaking;
(b) Of the Protestant faith;
(c) Clean in character and holding strongly to their principles as well as to the maintenance of their *Afrikanerskap,* and who
(d) accept South Africa as their only fatherland.

Regulation 3 dealing with nomination says proposer and seconder must be fully convinced that they can reply affirmatively to these questions about the candidate: (i) Does he strive for the ideal of the continued existence of a separate Afrikaner nation with its own language and culture? (ii) Does he give preference to Afrikaners and other well-disposed persons and companies in his business, public and professional life? Other questions concern the institutions where he was educated, the origins of his wife or fiancee, and her home language.

Clearly then, no English-speaking person or Roman Catholic, for instance, could become a member of this Super-Afrikaner organisation. This exclusivity is reconciled with public appeals for national unity between the language groups in a striking way. The argument is that a strong South African white nation, united in its determination to survive, presupposes a strong, united Afrikanerdom; that in practice a divided Afrikanerdom would not only make unity between Afrikaans and English impossible – it would entail the downfall of the black groups as well.

When the Broeders call for national unity they envisage it on their own terms. They see themselves as involved in a continuous struggle against threats of domination by the English-speaking section, blacks, Roman Catholics and others. To frustrate this, they must be the dominating force themselves.

The Broederbond's attitude to Afrikaans-English co-operation is clearly demonstrated by its fanatical concern with separate "pure" Afrikaans organisations. Instead of modifying existing South African organisations to make them bilingual, they formed their own. The Broederbond counterparts of the Boy Scouts and Girl Guides are the *Voortrekkers;* the Chambers of Commerce are paralleled by the *Afrikaanse Sakekamers;* Rotary and Lions by the *Rapportryers;* the Red Cross by the *Noodhulplige;* the Teachers' Association by the *Onderwysverenigings;* the National Union of South African Students (NUSAS) by the *Afrikaanse Studentebond* (ASB); and there are many other examples of division along language lines which Professor E G Malherbe characterised as "the corrugated iron curtain."

Former chairman, Andries Treurnicht, now a Deputy Minister, put it like this at the 50th Bond meeting in 1968. "If there is one thing vital to keeping the Broederbond alive in the ranks of the Afrikaner nation, now and in the future, it is the conviction that fulfilment cannot be attained by the Afrikaner without maximum economic control. Especially now that we put so much emphasis on unavoidable co-operation between the Afrikaans- and English-speaking, we must ensure – even if it must be done discreetly – that the Afrikaner is the senior partner. Without that there will be something still missing from our status and independence. Therefore the Broederbond should give urgent attention to it now."

Then follows a clear indication that Dr Treurnicht even deplores marriage between Afrikaans-speakers and English-speakers. "I believe that the Broederbond and the Afrikaner nation must again be called to resist . . . the blurring of the Afrikaner consciousness into a kind of white unity that is neither Afrikaner nor English."

Mr Vorster obviously felt ill at ease listening to Dr Treurnicht's views, conscious of his own appeals for unity. The former Prime Minister emphasised in his speech that he was not prepared to trick the English, a statement he had made several times in public.

He warned: "One thing we must realise very clearly – the future of South Africa does not lie only with the Afrikaner. It is the future of the white man in South Africa and southern Africa that must be fought for." He then expressed the two-stream policy: the Afrikaner had a right to everything dear to him, and so had the

English-speaker. Common loyalty to the Republic would bind the two groups together. It sounds fine in theory but Mr Vorster's presence at a Broederbond meeting and his active support for the organisation must place a question mark over the Government's sincerity with regard to national unity. The Broederbond is not only pro-Afrikaner – it is so at the expense of other groups. There simply is not room for the Broederbond and another group to rule the same country. Behind the scenes the Broeders are constantly scheming to improve the Afrikaner's position economically, socially and politically. Every advance is made by displacing somebody else. It is an organised and deliberate process and Mr Vorster's association with it helped to explain why there was only one English-speaking Minister in his Cabinet during his term of office.

In a Broederbond secret document entitled *Unity* the question is asked: "Are the English-speakers really a nation in South Africa equal in nature and status to the Afrikaner nation? The answer cannot be 'Yes' so the question arises of whether we can speak of 'the two language groups' or 'the two national groups' as if an Afrikaner nation and an English-speaking nation were equal in status. With this usage we give a false status to the English-speaker and degrade the status of the Afrikaner nation. There are not two white nations in South Africa. There is only one. That nation is the Afrikaner nation...

"In view of this, it is time to invite the English-speakers to become absorbed into the (Afrikaner) nation. (Groups like Jews and Greeks are of course excluded here: 'English-speakers' means those of British descent)."

The document created a commotion and an instruction went out to have it destroyed on the ground that it did not represent policy. Its greatest fault was not so much what it said, but that it said it so bluntly and a publicised leak could damage the National Party considerably. Yet its essential message is not much different from that expounded by Dr Malan at the beginning of this chapter.

In an extraordinary circular (August 1 1962) Dr Meyer put it more moderately and diplomatically, but the meaning is unmistakeably the same. "Because many of our Afrikaners misinterpreted the appeal of the Prime Minister and his Government to the two white groups to combine their strengths, to solve the country's problems on the basis of the policy of the National

Party, the Executive Council wants to restate its viewpoint in this regard.

"English-speakers have co-operated so little with Afrikaners on the national policy level that their numbers in the National Party are very small... Co-operation between the white groups does not imply that we Afrikaners must suddenly, guiltily, submit ourselves to the English-speakers, asking for co-operation. We must do everything in our power to persuade them to co-operate with us on the basis of the principles of the National Party; there are no principles or institutions that we have to sacrifice to achieve this.

"English-Afrikaans integration has developed so far in such a way that the Afrikaner, in many important respects, is beginning to think and act like an English-speaker. This has been to the detriment of that which is truly Afrikaans... We must continually be on guard that the Afrikaner is not anglicised more than the English-speaker is Afrikanerised."

Dr Meyer reaffirmed these views in his chairman's address of 1971. "Self-protection is a moral right and a moral duty incumbent on us as a nation – the right and duty to promote and protect our separate existence as an Afrikaner nation, our own Afrikaner interests, our own identity and our own future. God did not call us ... to commit suicide, but to maintain ourselves and protect ourselves in order to fulfil the calling and discharge the tasks He has allotted to us."

The absolute dedication to the promotion of everything Afrikaans in every sphere of life runs like a thread through all the secret documents. Members are continually urged to see that "well-disposed" people are elected to influential positions and that Afrikaner business and professional people are supported. "Well-disposed" and "true Afrikaners" obviously refers to Broeders *first* and then other Afrikaners. The discipline is strict and the standing instructions on what every cell should do every year in this connection were set out in Circular 5/5/75:

3.1 "Observing first our general aim, namely the promotion of all the interests of the Afrikaner, every branch must take stock every year of the position of the Afrikaner cause in its local community, especially in organisations in which we should have influence. These are some of the matters that must be investigated:

3.1.1 "The extent to which our language received its due in public life; for instance in commerce, public bodies like city councils, public announcements etc;

3.1.2 "The status of Afrikaans culture in plays, concerts, music and recitals etc. by schools, cultural organisations etc;

3.1.3 "Vigorous leadership of opinion-forming and co-ordinating Afrikaans organisations such as cultural societies, liaison committees, cultural councils, Rapportryers, etc;

3.1.4 "The celebration of Afrikaner national festivals;

3.1.5 "The role of well-disposed Afrikaners in sports clubs and in school committees, agricultural unions, farmers' organisations, women's societies, etc;

3.1.6 "The role and vitality of youth organisations such as the Voortrekkers, church youth societies and *Landsdiens,* and their influence."

The circular summed up: "Branches should consider, in the light of this survey, how Afrikaans cultural life can be strengthened in their areas. We dare not neglect the promotion of our own interests. Local public bodies must be used in this process."

One of the main reasons South Africa was the last developed nation in the world to get television was the fear that it would undermine the Afrikaans culture and language. It was for this reason that the Broederbond resisted its introduction for many years, and it was only introduced after the Bond had given the green light. It was entirely up to the Broederbond to decide the issue. The Minister of Posts and Telegraphs at the time, Mr M C van Rensburg, appointed a commission of inquiry to consider television for South Africa. Mr van Rensburg appointed the then chairman of the Bond, Dr Piet Meyer, as chairman of the commission. The vice-chairman of the commission, Dr J S Gericke, was vice-chairman of the Bond and the commission's secretary, Dr Jan Schutte, was also a Broeder.

The secret documents disclose that the Broederbond recommended the appointment of the commission to the Cabinet on condition that Broeders ran the inquiry. Dr Meyer, as chairman of the commission, called on Broeders to give evidence and made it clear he would submit the commission's finding to the Executive Council of the Bond *before* he submitted them to the Cabinet. The decision was that South Africa should get one-channel television with equal time for Afrikaans and English.

One of the major considerations that overcame Broeder resistance was that programmes in Afrikaans would encourage bilingualism among English-speakers in cities where they got little opportunity of hearing and speaking it. This assumption appears to have been justified although no scientific study of it has as yet been made.

Broeders were assured that a group of Broeder experts would continuously scrutinise the service and the moment there was evidence that television was having a detrimental effect on Afrikaners, threatening neglect of their language and culture, steps would be taken to redress this. This finally convinced most of the doubting Broeders and the green light for the introduction of television was given.

Here are some examples of the instructions to Broeders on the promotion of the Afrikaner, his language and other interests.

3/63/64: "Afrikaner doctors must be encouraged to ask in a friendly and tactful way that reports from the Medical Research Institute be drawn up in Afrikaans. In this way the use of Afrikaans medical terms will be encouraged and people working on the reports will feel compelled to learn Afrikaans terms."

8/73/74: "During the summer holidays thousands of Afrikaners, including members, will scatter all over the country. Many opportunities will arise where our language can be promoted with courtesy and determination. An urgent appeal is made to our members to give an example in this way and influence others to do the same.

Afrikaans reading matter is often completely absent from waiting-rooms, hotels. Afrikaans newspapers are not made available in hotels. Menus are in English only, or in English and French. Service in Afrikaans is poor or just not available. These are only a few of the matters to which attention can be given."

6/75/76: "One of our branches draws attention to the fact that our members can do a lot to prevent genuine Afrikaans historical place-names being replaced by un-Afrikaans names. The branch mentions the example of *Vogelstuisbult* having become Copperton."

2/2/77: "After representations by the FAK to South African Airways it has been disclosed that airways tickets will be available in Afrikaans from January 2 1977 for internal flights. Members should please insist that their tickets are in Afrikaans."

10/70/71: "Medical members point out that Afrikaners in the profession can be more positive about giving Afrikaans its rightful place. This applies to laboratory reports, consultations and notices in nursing homes and hospitals, advertising material sent out by pharmaceutical firms etc. A friendly appeal is made to all our medical members to use their influence with their colleagues to promote Afrikaans in the medical profession."

4/70/71: "Members draw attention to the need to maintain our language through the singing of sporting and school songs. It is noticed that many Afrikaans schools sing English songs at sports meetings. Members in the educational field should use their influence to accord our language its rightful place."

6/70/71: "Hotels throughout the country tend to supply only English-language newspapers to guests. Our members who often stay in hotels should use their influence to promote Afrikaans newspapers. By refusing an English-language newspaper and insisting on the local Afrikaans newspaper or other Afrikaans newspaper of your choice, you can make a positive contribution."

6/63/64: "Broederbond members concerned with the arrangement of congresses, especially scientific congresses, are asked to see that Afrikaans is accorded its rightful place."

Circular 8/64/65 gave examples of laxity. Afrikaner attorneys were corresponding with each other in English and a DRC church official had made out a Volkskas cheque in English for a *dominee's* sermon! "Also see that our language gets its due in sports bodies. Here we think especially of golf, rugby, bowls and tennis clubs."

In Circular 2/4/75 members were asked to use the public arms of the Broederbond (FAK and others) to complain about literature and theatrical performances which upset them. It was also pointed out that every Afrikaner and his church had a duty to protect the dignity of the Sunday; legislation could not solve the problems on its own.

The secret Broederbond documents contain scores of warnings against Rotary, the Freemasons, Round Table, Lions International, Moral Rearmament and similar organisations. It is clear that the Broederbond regards these organisations as a threat to itself specifically and to the Afrikaner generally. For example: "In accordance with out organisation's traditional viewpoint the Executive Council feels it must warn once again against the denationalising influence of these organisations on the Afrikaner. Their activities in various spheres often have political implications. The fact is that these organisations are regarded in some semi-official circles as the innocent public arm of Freemasonry" (Circular 2/11/67). The same circular also warns: "It appears that Moral Rearmament encourages undesirable fraternisation and so undermines determination to remain true to the Afrikaner's own calling."

Even the American Field Service scheme in which South African and American children exchange homes for a period after their matric year is viewed with suspicion. "It is the Executive Council's view that children should be strongly advised against participating in the American Field Service programme. They are sent to America when youthful and vulnerable, and exposed there to all kinds of alienating influences. Parents should be persuaded of the undesirability and danger of this."

It is interesting that all the organisations the Broederbond warns against are English-orientated, and this may indeed be the main reason why they are not acceptable to the Super-Afrikaners. The Bond has copies of many of the organisational features of the Freemasons and this organisation has become its Number One Target. It is as if they realise the dangers inherent in an organisation operating on the same lines as their own. They are aware of their own power, and would not tolerate another organisation reaching the same level of effectiveness.

In Circular 5/67/68 another warning went out. "Various branches draw attention to the obvious increase in activity of the Freemasons and related organisations. More and more we find members of these organisations elected to public positions. Organisations like Rotary, Lions International, Round Table and Junior Chamber International are also more active than in the past." Then follows a definite instruction to all cells to spy in their neighbourhood and report to Broederbond head office. "The Executive Council asks therefore that branches try to establish what is happening in their areas and report by letter to the office. Register this mail to Mr J Naude, P O Box 9801, Johannesburg."

Circular 29/5/73 discusses the problem of Broeders offered honorary membership of an "alien" organisation. "The Executive Council requests friends (Broeders) not to accept such membership."

Freemasonry and its growing influence are again the topic of Circular 6/70/71. "Various branches draw attention to the increasing drive of the Freemasons to draw young Afrikaners into their organisation. It is also obvious that they are striving in certain areas to get into leading positions in co-operatives, agricultural unions, businesses, cultural organisations, sports clubs, political organisations etc. This development, and the influence of members of the alien organisations on young Afrikaners and youth organisations, must certainly be watched and counteracted. The best way to do this is to ensure that well-disposed Afrikaners take on the leading positions."

Circular 5/71/72 warns similarly that Freemasons "are pouncing on school committees and city councils and are not slow to seek control of cultural organisations. These fronts must be watched carefully therefore against Freemasons! Freemasonry, however innocent it might appear, is fundamentally anti-Christian and action must be taken with that in mind. It is the Executive's view that action against Freemasonry must start at church level, consistently with the synodal decisions of the various Afrikaans churches against Freemasonry. Once the minister and his church council have confirmed that Freemasonry is unacceptable to Christians, local action can be taken in the prescribed way. Furthermore, there should be positive attempts to elect to public office well-disposed and able Afrikaners, people who are prepared and able to live out consistently our Christian National philosophy."

In Circular 6/63/64 Broederbond doctors are urged to use their influence to ensure that Protestant patients are not sent to Roman Catholic hospitals and nursing homes. This is also the subject of Circular 1/64/65 which calls on Broeders to help establish a "Protestant maternity home" in Pretoria. "Branches and friends (members) are asked to promote this by using their influence in public bodies. To create such an institution an amount of R125 000 must be found. This has become a matter of urgency, because the Roman Catholic Church is busy concentrating on the provision of luxury maternity services to the young residents of Pretoria." The circular said the total cost of the Protestant maternity home would be R650 000 of which the State would give half and the *Suid-Afrikaanse Vrouefederasie* R200 000. The balance of R125 000 had to be found within 12 months.

The Broederbond's concern over the influence of "alien" organisations specifically relates to the youth – for example, Afrikaans youth leaders like head boys and girls of schools who were invited to Rotary lunches. No Broederbond member can join any of these "alien" organisations without applying for the Executive Council's permission, which is seldom given. Members already belonging to such organisations, if there are any, are usually directed to resign immediately.

The Broederbond was also instrumental in breaking the power of the National Union of South African Students (NUSAS) on the campuses of English-language universities. Not only did it create the *Afrikaanse Studentebond* which took all the Afrikaans students out of NUSAS, but it also kept a careful watch on NUSAS and the English campuses.

Various student movements on these campuses were financed by the Broederbond to counter the influence of NUSAS. It was a Broederbond think-tank which pinpointed the two main weaknesses of NUSAS: the fact that it was financed heavily from overseas, and the "automatic" membership of all English-speaking students whose SRCs were affiliated to NUSAS. When the Schlebusch Commission decided that certain South African organisations should no longer be financed from overseas contributions, it was a punishing blow to NUSAS. It withered without financial support, and lost a great deal of its influence. The system of "automatic" membership was also challenged at a number of universities, and the organisation was committed to an internal struggle which substantially damaged it.

The Broederbond's difficulties in formulating a clear-cut immigration policy have also become the Broederbond Government's problem. The concepts of white survival and Afrikaner domination were in conflict here. A more favourable balance in white and black population figures demanded large-scale immigration, yet if South Africa accepted English-speaking immigrants indiscriminately this could lead to the Afrikaner losing his dominant position in the white group. There was the added fear of too many Roman Catholics entering the country and "jeopardising" the position of the Protestants. Basically, the Broeders were frightened that they and the Afrikaner would lose the numbers game. After some years' residence, immigrants "not incompatible with the South Africa way of life" would be entitled to citizenship – and the vote. This could break the stranglehold that the Afrikaans-speaking group, 60 per cent of the white voting group, has on the central Parliament.

These considerations led to the formulation of a very strict "selective immigration" policy. Immigration boards are packed with Broeders who are there to see that the ratio of Afrikaans-speaking to English groups is maintained, as well as the ratio of Roman Catholics to Protestants. They also restrict entry to people they regard as future "good" South Africans – people who at least sympathise with Government policy and do not openly disapprove of "the South African way of life."

Immigration policy has caused deep rifts in the Broederbond and the National Party. Extreme right-wingers see it as a sure way of undermining Afrikaner domination, while others defend the policy by showing that a balance has been maintained in spite of large numbers of immigrants having entered the country in some years.

A Broederbond watchdog committee keeps a careful eye on the situation and reports back regularly to the Executive. Government immigration figures reach the committee almost as soon as they are compiled, because the Minister is a Broeder. At the first signs of a significant shift in the Afrikaner-English ratio, action will be taken. The Executive can discuss ways and means with the Minister, such as putting a brake on the admission of English-speakers as against Dutch and German immigrants. But such a shift is unlikely because the people deciding who will be allowed into the country – the immigration officials board – are predominantly Broeders. They are there to protect the Afrikaners' dominant position in the white group.

Many studies have been made over the years into the effect of immigration on the all-important ratio. The secret Broederbond documents make it clear that immigration is one of the most serious matters they have ever faced, and no effort is spared in seeking a solution. For example, studies of the birthrates of the two groups went right back to the turn of the century.

In a bid to Afrikanerise as many immigrants as possible, the Broederbond formed the *Maatskappy vir Europese Immigrasie* which is headed by Mr J H Hattingh, a prominent Broeder. The Broederbond financed this organisation, which also gets a Government subsidy like that of the 1820 Settlers Association looking after the interest of the English-speaking immigrants.

At a meeting of the immigration watchdog committee in 1969 Dr Piet Koornhof reported that a decision had been taken in principle that the provincial authorities (largely Broeder-dominated) would take over nursery schools, new nursery schools would be established, and Afrikaans would be used in them increasingly. Immigrant children enrolling at nursery schools would thus be forced to learn Afrikaans at a pre-school age. Dr Koornhof also reassured the meeting that figures of the previous two years indicated no change in the ratio between the two language groups.

The Broederbond encourages its members to use their positions in public bodies to facilitate the "incorporation" of immigrant families into the Afrikaner's cultural life. Members of women's organisations are invited to visit immigrant wives, arrange church services in the immigrants' languages, organise youth evenings and ask immigrant families into their homes.

But the Broederbond's continuing dilemma was set out in the September 1964 circular: "We are not prepared to sacrifice our traditional way of life, language and culture but are obliged today to accept large-scale immigration as one of the most important aids in our struggle. Yet recruitment overseas has raised doubts in the minds of the *volk* because the majority of immigrants are English-speaking ... and many belong to the Roman Catholic Church. Just as in the past, the Afrikaner feels threatened by foreign elements ...

"It should not be regarded as a threat to the Afrikaner's language and culture. The Afrikaner nation achieved predominance in language and politics over the last 300 years even though only a small number of immigrants joined it.

"The Afrikaner nation's growth was largely due to the birth-rate. This strong position developed in spite of the fact that the population at the time of the British take-over of the Cape in 1795 was only about 15 000. From that time onwards the British element has always been the major component in emigration to South Africa. It is not necessary to recall the deliberate attempts to destroy the Afrikaner's culture and language, (in another document reference is made to the 26 000 Afrikaner women and children who died in the concentration camps during the Anglo-Boer War) but they did not succeed and the Afrikaner nation went from strength to strength – to such an extent that in 1960 there were 1 790 998 Afrikaners against the 1 150 738 English-speakers. The annual increase between 1951 and 1960 was no fewer than 33 000 Afrikaners as against only 11 500 English-speakers of whom an average of 3 000 were English-speaking immigrants.

"As has already been pointed out, we should strive for a minimum of 30 000 immigrants a year. Suppose we succeed in getting that for the next ten years and that 26 000 would be English-speaking. Added to the natural growth of 8 500 we would get an annual increase in the number of English-speakers of 34 500 as against the natural growth of 33 000 Afrikaners.

"The composition of the population would then change as follows:

	English	*Afrikaners*
1960	1 150 738	1 790 988
1963	1 212 000	1 890 000
1973	1 557 000	2 220 000

"The Afrikaner attained political and numerical supremacy in the country under unfavourable conditions, and he should be able to hold his position, taking into account the natural increase. Of course we should maintain our vigilance, but this must be based on positive thinking."

According to the circular the position *vis á vis* Catholic immigrants is "under control" because Protestants increase by 67% annually and Catholics by only 24%.

In spite of all the assurances, crisis point was reached again by October 1967 when the Executive had to respond to concern expressed by some branches. It reported that it had given "more and longer" attention to immigration matters in the pevious year. It had been told of failure to honour assurances regarding the ratio of Protestants to Catholics and certain "unassimilable persons." The Bond had asked the Cabinet to formulate a policy that would maintain the respective positions of Afrikaners and English-speakers in matters of religion, language and culture.

As usual, the Cabinet had agreed to the Broederbond "request". Instructions had been given that led to a considerable decline in the number of immigrants from Portuguese territories, Greece, Italy and Mediterranean area as a whole. These immigration figures were quoted in the circular to indicate the decrease.

	1966 January to June	*1967 January to June*	*Difference*
Portuguese	5 179	2 410	2 769
Greeks	894	409	485
Italians	1 105	729	376

"The decrease from these areas will continue and will probably get steeper. The reduction especially affects people of the Roman Catholic conviction ... *Highly Confidential:* from January 1 to June 30 1967, 9 600 Protestant immigrants were selected as against 5 600 Roman Catholic immigrants, an entirely new pattern. *(This information would draw a sharp reaction from the Press if it became known.)*

"An assurance can therefore be given in all honesty. (1) The religious ratio between Protestants and Catholics will not be disturbed by immigration. (2) 'Unassimilable elements' will be kept out of South Africa, and everything will be done to remove those who enter illegally. (3) Care will be taken to ensure that immigration does not become a threat to the Afrikaner's future. (4) Immigrants will not deprive our people of jobs."

The circular then laid any doubts about the Immigration Selection panel whose members were appointed by the State President for periods of one or two years. "It consists of the following persons who are all members of one of the three Afrikaans churches, and are all Afrikaners. G Booysen, formerly deputy secretary, Department of Immigration; T H V Honck, formerly secretary, Department of Interior; S J P Eloff, representative, Department of Labour; P L J Wessels, formerly Chief of Security Police. Alternates: C H S van der Merwe, deputy secretary, Department of Immigration; H R W de Wet, deputy secretary Department of Immigration.

"Immigration is a serious matter which can decide a nation's future. Therefore our members must always remain vigilant, and use the right channels to make themselves heard in a responsible way when it becomes necessary in our *volk's* interests. The application of the immigration policy during the past 12 months provides the best example of this. It also demonstrates the close interaction between our organisation and the Government (friends in responsible circles.)" The Executive then repeated its call to "win immigrants, and especially their children, for the Afrikaner's language and his culture."

The Broederbond gave these details of its study of the fertility rate of Afrikaans- and English-speaking women to determine its influence on the population ratio.

In a comprehensive immigration report, circulated in March 1974, it said that Afrikaner women who completed their families between 1910 and 1945 produced about 70 per cent more children than English-speaking women. Afrikaner families completed between 1945 and 1960 were only about 50 to 60 per cent bigger than corresponding English-speaking families. The difference was even smaller, between 45 and 50 per cent, for women aged 35 to 44 whose families were probably close to completion. For women between 20 and 24 years of age the difference was only 25 per cent. The higher fertility rate of the Afrikaner women was therefore a temporary phenomenon and the advantage the Afrikaner has enjoyed has probably passed."

Throughout the secret documents' discussions of immigration, the central question is always: how will it affect the position of the Afrikaner? This demonstrates forcibly the Broederbond's belief that Afrikaans-English co-operation is possible only as long as the Afrikaner is in the dominant political and cultural position, and as long as the English-speaker is prepared to accept the Afrikaner's policies.

1. *Hansard,* January 25 1946.

9 *A View on the Indian Future*

When the National Party first came to power and for several years after that, its official policy was still that those Indians who so desired would get financial assistance for repatriation to India.

Over the years it became clear, however, that the Indians were not interested in the scheme. They had been in South Africa since the turn of the century and had accepted it as their fatherland.

As in all other matters of policy, the Broederbond started at an early stage to take an active interest in Indian affairs. Its permanent watchdog committee on this subject reports regularly to the Executive and over the years several study documents have been drawn up. In one of them entitled *The Future of the Indian Population* the idea of a separate homeland for the Indians is propounded. It concedes at the end, "the full implications of this idea have not been worked out fully . . . and a more detailed study is required before it can be considered seriously."

The detailed study on population increase stated that 83 per cent of all "Asiatics" in South Africa live in Natal, 75 per cent of them concentrated within a 90-mile radius of Durban. About 60 per cent of Natal's Indians live within the Durban metropolitan complex. If this ratio remains constant, at the end of the century there will be 1 million in Natal out of a total Indian population of 1 215 000. In 1960 there were 116 Indians to every 100 whites in Natal.

When the removal of Indians to their separate group areas has been completed, 50 per cent of Natal's Indian population will live north of Durban and on the north coast; 30 per cent immediately south of Durban; 6 per cent on the south coast; and 14 per cent scattered over the inland with the biggest concentration (7 per cent) in Pietermaritzburg.

"The Indians are presently accepted as an indigenous national group, as citizens of South Africa who must make a living in the white area. At the same time, the policy is clear that this must happen in a separate area. In the period exceeding the 100 years they have been in the country, the Indians have become less acceptable, rather than more, to other national groups in respect of possible assimilation. For everybody except the Indians, repatriation or resettlement in another country remains the most acceptable solution. If that is not possible, then an alternative plan is for a separate geographic home where the present process of physical and political separation can be completed."

One of the arguments favouring this separate "homeland" is that government policy already aims at strengthening the identity of the Indians as a separate national group – "nation-building is in progress. It is clear that there is no room for them in the white nation structure, socially, politically, or otherwise, as in the case of English speakers, Portuguese, Jews and other immigrant groups."

It is necessary that a bigger concentration of Indians and a city structure be established on which effective separate and independent management for Indians can be built.

"Homeland orientation is also urgently necessary, because of the increasingly uncomfortable position in which whites in Natal find themselves. The whole province is either Bantu or border area. A small corridor from Durban to the Transvaal and Free State border is all that remains for the whites, and if there is no separation between whites and Indians, the Indians would be numerically superior to whites in the corridor before the year 2000, so that the province will become increasingly unattractive to whites.

"From a policy point of view, it is urgently necessary that Indian capital be drawn to places where it will not be a danger to national policy. A homeland will encourage Indian entrepreneurs to use capital productively and create work opportunities for their own people."

The document stated that a "national home" should be established for Indians north of Durban. Its creation did not mean that all Indians in the Republic would have to move there. It would enable them to fulfil themselves politically and prevent them from threatening the white man's identity. It would, however, be important to prohibit emigration from Natal to other areas, and to strengthen the ties between the 'national home' and Indians in other areas. "To give support to the idea of an 'own home', investments in education, recreation, health etc, and the encouragement of industrial settlement, can already be directed to the area north of Durban.

"The new university for Indians is, for example, already situated in the right place and must be supplemented with a training hospital and the removal of the medical faculty from the University of Natal to the university for Indians. The development of independent self-management at Verulam, and the use of expensive sugar plantations for towns, is also right and must continue. It is important that the seat of the proposed Representative Indian Council be in the same area. Border areas, advantages for industries which employ Indians are already given at Verulam, Tongaat and Stanger, and considerable development has already taken place at Tongaat. There is thus encouragement for the creation of work opportunities in the area which will encourage the voluntary influx of Indians.

"Such an area does not have to be big, because the population is already relatively concentrated. The population can be envisaged as becoming increasingly involved in specialised manufacturing, wholesale trade and especially international trade. The community could function in South Africa as a kind of Singapore or Hong Kong... It should be possible to earmark an area of 610 square miles between the Umgeni and Tugela rivers for homeland development. This area has the advantage of already containing 20 to 30 per cent of Natal's Indians and, after resettlement, 50 to 60 percent; it is a rich agricultural area in which there are some wealthy and independent Indian farmers; and such an area is an obvious choice for resettlement in intensive urban development.

"Two stumbling blocks must be considered: the position of white farmers in the area, and the fact that such an area will eventually be the smallest and most densely populated territory in Africa."

One of the most revealing secret circulars is entitled *Indian Education in South Africa* (March 1971). It shows that Afrikaans is promoted vigorously in Indian schools, that the Broederbond is adamant that control must be kept in their hands, or in the hands of Indians supporting Government policy, and the Christianisation of the largely Hindu or Muslim population of Indians is a top priority.

The document sketches the progress made since the Government took over control of all Indian education in terms of the Indian Education Act of 1965.

It says the progress made since then has silenced most of the critics of the takeover. "Indian leaders are not blind to the progress made in education. The assertion that the Afrikaner (meaning the

Afrikaner Government) keeps his promises in education is often heard. Only now and then is an objection raised to the present control of education, notably by the venomous leftwing Indian newspapers, *The Leader* and *The Graphic,* published in Durban."

The circular adds that before the takeover, only two schools in Pietermaritzburg and one in Durban offered Afrikaans as a subject. "The teaching of Afrikaans was, therefore, shockingly neglected in Natal schools. With the takeover of education in 1966, a huge leeway had to be made up hastily, especially since Afrikaans was, from 1974 a requirement for Senior Certificate examinations. The problem was to find teachers to teach Afrikaans. Fortunately, a nucleus could be drawn from the small group of students who took Afrikaans in the three schools mentioned, but the problem of finding an adequate number of teachers of Afrikaans will persist for at least three years after 1974 when all new teachers will have met the bilingualism requirements.

"The drive to bring Afrikaans into Natal schools is facilitated by pupils' particular keenness to learn the language. In order to meet the 1974 matriculation requirement, Afrikaans has gradually been introduced as a compulsory subject. In 1970 it was made compulsory in Standard Six, in 1971 in Standard Seven, etc. But in fact some of the pupils were ahead of this arrangement; 3 848 wrote Afrikaans examinations in 1970 in Standard 8, 539 for matric. This represented increases of 1 078 and 196 respectively over the previous year. Indian languages are not taught in State and State-subsidised schools, and there is no demand for them."

The circular also dealt with *Further Aims in Education,* and stressed that facilities and the standard of education for whites and Indians must be the same. "Of much greater importance is the implementation of State policy through the medium of education. For this it is indispensable that the top structure of Indian education remains for considerable time in the hands of right-minded whites. Although it is Government policy that every racial group must be served more and more by its own group, and that eventually an Indian will fill the post of Director of Indian Education, this must not happen prematurely. The highest posts presently filled by Indians in education are those of inspectors of education, and the policy is that all new vacancies must be filled by Indians. It is, however, important that Indians who are sympathetic towards Government policy are appointed in these posts, because from their ranks the higher posts will have to be filled later.

"These people will have to be carefully selected, and prepared to identify and combat wrong influences in education. There must, for instance, always be a guard against integration in sport at schools and infiltration of leftwing influences on the campuses of teachers' colleges. It is known that Nusas aims to inflitrate these campuses and problems have already emerged there. Persons in these posts must be strong enough to withstand the pressure of certain groups such as the South African Indian Teachers' Association. It is known that the chairman of this association is collaborating with liberals and integrationists. It is thus essential that control of appointments to senior posts in education must remain for a considerable time in the hands of right-minded whites."

The deviousness with which the Broederbond achieves some of its aims is apparent from a section showing how the Indians are Christianised without being aware of it.

"It is furthermore our duty as Christians to help promote the Christianisation *(kerstening)* of Indians through the medium of education. This must be carefully handled. For this reason religious teaching as such is not provided in Indian schools, but what is called "Right Living". The intention is to bring home to the child basic attitudes such as honesty, obedience, gratefulness, neighbourly love etc. A considerable part of the syllabus consists of Bible stories or refers to Bible figures and texts. Every year a large sum is voted to provide Bibles to Indian schools. If religious teaching was allowed, every religious group would have the right to teach its faith in the schools. Because at least 95 per cent of the teachers are non-Christian, they would then have control."

By 1981 241 000 Indian pupils would attend school, 110 000 concentrated in the lower Umgeni-Tugela river areas: 45,6 per cent of the total school population. "In other words, this area will change in the next 10 years to comprise by far the biggest complex of Indians in South Africa, and geographically it is suited to further expansion. Indian education is planned to meet the demand as it develops from year to year."

In order to ensure Broederbond authority and overall control as envisaged, the key posts in Indian Education are manned by Broeders. The Director of Indian Education is Mr Gabriel (Gawie) Krog who serves on the Broederbond Executive. The Rector of the University of Durban-Westville (for Indians) is Professor S P Olivier, formerly on the Broederbond Executive, and the Registrar of the university, Mr Gawie Heystek, is also a Broeder.

10 *The Broederbond and the Coloured Policy*

When the former Prime Minister, Mr Vorster, finally withdrew the last vestiges of coloured representation from the South African Parliament in 1968, the Broederbond was ecstatic. At last the dream embodied in the organisation's earliest constitutions had been realised, "The segregation of all coloured races domiciled in South Africa with provision for their independent development under the trusteeship of whites."[1]

The Executive Council wrote joyful congratulations in their monthly circular letter 2/68/69 of April 8 1968, praising Mr Vorster for his courage. "The Executive Council is especially deeply grateful that our honoured Prime Minister, John Vorster, is currently taking one of the most important steps in our age-old anti-liberal struggle against political integration for non-whites – which would bring the downfall of whites in all spheres of life – namely the termination of coloured representation in Parliament. This courageous step will undoubtedly be recognised as one of the most important milestones in our struggle for white survival, and as being in line with General Hertzog's Native Legislation of 1936, Dr Malan's prevention of Indian representation in Parliament, and Dr Verwoerd's Transkei Act."

But it was in the very nature of things that the Broederbond should be well aware of its responsibilities in the new dispensation for coloured people. Not content merely to sit back, now that whites at last had exclusive sovereignty in South Africa's Parliament, the organisation set to with a will to ensure that the new coloured policy would work – or at least be seen to work

For a start this required that the first national elections to the Coloured Persons' Representative Council (CRC) should run smoothly with enough support from the coloured electorate; and secondly it required that the right man and the right party should command a majority in the CRC.

The Broederbond approached this task with its customary zeal and determination. Throwing its weight into the election, it flagrantly ignored the Prohibition of Political Interference Act (No 51 of 1968) which was specifically designed to prevent the involvement of whites in "non-white" political affairs. The Broederbond chose to back the conservative Federal Coloured Peoples' Party under the leadership of the pro-apartheid Tom Swartz.

Writing in the *Sunday Times,*[2] Mr Hennie Serfontein clearly exposed the extent of the Broederbond's role in the 1969 coloured elections: "It gave secret support on a large scale to the Federal Party of Mr Tom Swartz before and after Parliament had passed the Act in 1968 to prevent white political parties from interfering in non-white politics...

"In the light of information gained from the latest documents, the following points have emerged. In September 1966 the No Interference Bill was unexpectedly dropped two weeks after the death of Dr Verwoerd as a direct result of pressure by the Broederbond UR (Executive Council) on the Cabinet. The UR feared that if the Bill was passed at that time, it would wreck their secret operations to back the Federal Party of Mr Swartz.

"A special Broederbond committee was appointed in 1966 with the task of helping the Federal Party in its election campaign in a manner which would not directly involve the Government.

"In October 1968 the Broederbond sent out a special circular urging Broeders and divisions to assist with the registration of coloured voters and expressing the backing of the Broederbond for Mr Swartz. The Christiaan de Wet Fund – the secret R1-million fund of the Broederbond – contributed more than R50 000 to finance the election campaign of the Federal Party. Mr Louis van der Walt, a *verkrampte* (rightwing) full-time employee of the Broederbond, who was also employed by the Republiekeinse Intelligensie Diens (RID) – the ghost section of the Special Branch at that time – was a kingpin of this operation and controlled the Broederbond coloured campaign...

"In the middle 1960s, Dr Verwoerd, as Prime Minister, and Dr Piet Meyer, as chairman of the Broederbond, agreed that the Broederbond should actively involve itself in coloured politics by backing the Federal Party... The UR discussed the coloured political campaign of Mr van der Walt. There was apparently great consternation when they came to the conclusion that should the No Interference Bill be passed at that stage, it could seriously jeopardise the Broederbond involvement in the coloured elections.

"Dr Piet Koornhof, the former Broederbond secretary and then a member of the UR, was asked to convey an urgent message to Mr Vorster and the Cabinet. They requested the Government to postpone the passing of the Bill.

"In October 1968 the Broederbond Executive issued a special circular letter dealing with the CRC elections. Dealing with the political parties, it said, 'During the last few years a political consciousness has started to grow amongst the coloureds. In terms of our principle of guardianship, it is necessary that there should be guidance from the white man to ensure development in the right channels. The law on improper interference restricts active influencing.' The last sentence was obviously intended as a smokescreen to hide even from its own members the active involvement of the Broederbond," Mr Serfontein commented.

That the Broederbond was indeed not averse to flouting this law becomes clear in a subsequent special circular letter to members sent out on August 14 1969. "Whites, in terms of the Improper Interference Act, may not give help to coloured people in connection with the election. Yet we cannot just remain aloof in the face of indications that influence is being exerted by leftist institutions in specific support of the Labour Party. The successful execution of the policy of separate development is, after all, at stake here.

"There are, in fact, a number of matters to which whites can give attention, especially in areas with large concentrations of coloured voters. Firstly arrangements can be made to get them to the polling stations on September 24, and secondly the support of the Federal Coloured Peoples' Party led by Tom Swartz can be encouraged. It is the largest and best organised conservative coloured party in the country and will apparently put up candidates in 40 seats. Support for the other, smaller conservative parties can only benefit the Labour Party in three-cornered contests.

"Legal opinion on the transport of coloured voters indicates that a white can make his vehicle available to a coloured person to go and vote himself and/or transport other voters. The white must not drive and may not receive recompense. The coloured voter must provide the fuel himself. (In other words, a white can lend his vehicle but not hire it out.) Friends can make a contribution to a successful outcome in the following ways.

"(a) Explain to coloured people in your employ the importance of the democratic vote, and the necessity for every voter to cast his ballot. (b) Encourage them to go and vote on election day, and give them the opportunity to do so. (c) Talk with other well-disposed Afrikaners and get them to do the same. (d) Entrust vehicles to reliable drivers so that they can help transport other voters, if you can see your way clear to do this. (e) Influence coloured people in your employ to vote for the Federal Coloured Peoples' Party of Tom Swartz, otherwise the left-wing Labour Party (under M A Arendse) will gain by a split vote."

As it turned out the Broederbond's support for the Federal Party was a massive flop. Tom Swartz's party was severely trounced by the anti-apartheid Labour Party. There were 573 985 registered voters and the election result was as follows.[3]

Party	*Votes*	*Seats*
Labour Party of South Africa	140 631	26
Federal Coloured Peoples' Party	87 781	11
Republican Coloured Peoples' Party of South Africa and South West Africa	21 693	1
National Coloured Peoples' Party	17 759	1
Conservative Party	3 865	–
Independent candidates	13 351	1

However, because the composition of the CRC laid down by Parliament provided for 40 elected members and 20 members nominated by the South African Government, enough nominated seats were swung to the Federal Party to give it a working majority.

Tom Swartz, who had lost his deposit when beaten by the Labour Party candidate in the Kasselsvlei constituency, rationalised this by saying: "Although the Federal Party got only 12 seats in the election,[4] and the Republican and National Parties one each, these three, which underwrite Government policy, polled altogether 158 179 votes against the Labour Party's 136 845, a majority of 21 334 votes."[5] Swartz became chairman of the CRC and endured a five-year term of office in which he was repeatedly humiliated by the overwhelming popular support for the Labour Party. He became increasingly disillusioned with the Government, which granted him nothing to justify his loyal stand.

By the time the second coloured election came round on March 19 1975, the Broederbond had become slightly more circumspect in its advice, but nevertheless made it quite clear to members in a special circular of March 3 whom they should persuade their coloured employees and acquaintances to support. The letter describes the two main coloured political parties as follows. "(a) The Federal Coloured Peoples' Party's policy is to seek its community's interests through dialogue with the authorities, and to try to achieve consensus. (b) The Labour Party does not follow the path of dialogue, but attempts to achieve its ends through confrontation with the authorities."

The Broederbond's plan again backfired. The Labour Party was returned with an increased majority, winning 31 seats to the Federal Party's eight.

But the organisation's support for the Federal Party faithfully continues. The South African Broadcasting Corporation, which is Broederbond-controlled, gives extensive coverage to the utterances of the current Federal Party leader, Dr W J Bergins, while the demonstrably more representative Labour Party views go virtually unreported on either radio or television in South Africa.

The position of the "brown Afrikaners", as the coloured people are called, has been a source of constant embarrassment to the Nationalist Government which has come under heavy pressure, even from its own ranks, to act on the issue.

Towards the end of the 1976 Parliamentary sitting, the eagerly awaited report of the Erika Theron Commission was tabled.

The commission had been appointed on March 23 1973 to investigate the progress of the coloured people in social, economic, constitutional, sport, cultural and local government matters, to identify points of contention in these spheres, and to investigate any further connected matters that came to the notice of the commission and in its view warranted examination. After hearing evidence for three years, the commission of 12 white and 6 coloured members headed by the prominent Stellenbosch sociologist, Professor Erika Theron, compiled 178 recommendations.

There was a widely held belief that Mr Vorster would use the findings as a basis for dramatic moves towards a new dispensation for coloured people, breaking down barriers that a large number of people, including many Nationalists, no longer thought justified. These hopes were, however, largely dashed. When the commission's report was tabled the Government presented an interim memorandum containing its provisional comments on the inquiry's findings and recommendations. Virtually every recommendation that would hold any meaningful political consequence for the coloured population was rejected.

Among these were recommendations to repeal the Mixed Marriages Act and to repeal Section 16, dealing with prohibition of sex across the colour line, of the Immorality Act; to give coloured people direct representation at all levels of government; to repeal all statutory reservations in the use of labour; and that coloured people should be able to lease or own farming land anywhere in the Republic.

The Government's interim report said recommendations that would amount to abandoning the recognition and development of the identity of the various population groups in the Republic were not conducive to the orderly and evolutionary advancement of the various population groups in the Republic as a whole. For this reason the Government was, for example, not prepared to change its standpoint, in the light of the South African situation, in regard to the Immorality Act and the Prohibition of Mixed Marriages Act.

Any recommendation to the effect that direct representation should be granted to coloured people in the existing Parliamentary, provincial and local institutions was, consequently, not acceptable to the Government. The Government announced that it would table a comprehensive response to the commission's report later, in the form of a White Paper.

Throughout this process the Broederbond was an active presence, intimately involved in the formulation of the Government's provisional comments and in the drawing up of the White Paper. It gives an indication of this in its circular letter 5/76/77 of July 1 1976. "Branches are aware of the first reactions to the release of the report of the Erika Theron Commission on coloured matters. The Executive Council had a special consultation with the relevant responsible friend (Mr Hennie Smit, Minister of Coloured, Rehoboth and Nama Relations) before the report was released. The provisional comments ... of the Government on the report represent the considerations discussed in this consultation.

"There are naturally other contentious proposals as well, apart from those on which the Government has already reacted, which will be handled in later comment: for example, land ownership. Meanwhile, the Executive Council trusts that branches will study the reasonably comprehensive summaries of the commission's recommendations, and the Government's responses, as published by the newspapers (and if possible study the report itself, although that is a big job). The Executive Council's committee for coloured matters will study the report and will shortly transmit its comments to the branches for guidance. With its help, our members should be able to give a lead in public life."

Later, in March 1977, the Executive Council said much progress had been made with the study of the report. "The Executive Council's special committee has worked on this since July 1976 with the help of a panel of expert friends and has already completed its recommendations. It has on a number of occasions discussed its findings in detail with the relevant responsible friends" (Circular 1/7/78 of March 3 1977).

In April of that year the Government tabled its detailed White Paper on the Theron Commission. It confirmed all the worst fears of anyone who had hoped for significant change.

Shock, anger and disappointment met the Government response which was slammed as a "whitewash job" by the *Sunday Times* on April 17 1977. Seven of the commissioners, including Professor Theron, issued a statement publicly condemning the White Paper; the (coloured) Labour Party rejected it as an "apartheid document."[6] Two months later the Broederbond Executive circulated to its members a summary of the report it had passed to the Government. Any doubt that the Broederbond wields enormous influence in the establishment of Government policy is immediately dispelled by the organisation's introduction to this secret report. "As announced last year, a series of panels of friends were appointed to study the Erika Theron report and to prepare comment that could be presented to the Government on behalf of the Executive Council.

"This huge task has been completed and discussions have been held on more than one occasion with friends in responsible circles. The following is a summary of the comment eventually presented on behalf of the organisation to friends in the Government. As will be noticed, much of the comment has been taken up in the White Paper which was tabled in Parliament by the Government during April."

This is, in fact, the case. A large number of the Government's responses to the Theron Commission's recommendations reflect, in revised language, the views expressed in the Broederbond's document. In one section the White Paper reproduces virtually word for word the Broederbond reaction. This deals with the commission's recommendation 85(c) that "colleges of advanced technical education should fall directly under the Department of National Education." To this the Broederbond responded:[7]

"*The limitations in the tuition currently experienced at the college are mainly due to a shortage of laboratory facilities and lecture theatres.* These shortcomings will be overcome with the addition of the facilities provided for in the Administration's building programme with a tender date in April 1977. The anticipated costs of the building project are R1 850 000 and the contract period is 36 months, so the additional accommodation ought to be completed by 1980. *A second college for advanced technical education for the Western Cape within the foreseeable future cannot be justified. Instead, a similar institution is envisaged for Port Elizabeth.*" The Broederbond said the commission's recommendation was in conflict with the current constitutional arrangement under which the education of coloured youth up to college level was one of the functions of the Coloured Peoples' Representative Council.

In the White Paper, the Government responds to the recommendation in the same language: the only difference is that the White Paper shortens and joins into one the sentences not in italics in the Broederbond circular. Generally the Government White Paper faithfully reflects what the Broederbond document suggests, although the above example is the only case where the language has not been substantially modified. The discrepancy might be attributed to the fact that the Broederbond document in the authors' possession is an abridged version of the organisation's actual report to the Government. It may also be the case that when the Broederbond enjoyed the advantage of secrecy it expresses its views more forthrightly while the Government had to consider public opinion, particularly sensitive on this issue, and may consequently have slightly modified the White Paper's language to make the point less bluntly. For example, one recommendation which the Broederbond categorically rejected, the Government accepted with reservations – although to date it has done nothing about implementing it. This was clause 176 of the Theron Report, which recommended that: "Apart from the possibility that certain facilities (within group areas) can be reserved for specific race groups, the gradual derestriction on a selective basis of public places, facilities and certain beaches be accepted as an objective."

The Broederbond gave a flat "no support" for this idea and emphasised the need for the development of facilities "in their own (coloured) areas." It said developers should be restricted when they bought land for development as "white" beaches. It should be established in advance that the land was not in a traditional coloured area. The Broederbond thereafter suggested a remarkable modification to existing legislation, giving an insight into the organisation's obsessional character and its addiction to absolute order.

"Currently all land above the high-water mark is State property. This means that the area between the low-water mark and the high-water mark is no-man's-land, affording free access and movement. In order to do the right thing by the landowners, the determinations (of the Act) must be extended to the low-water mark, so that control over movement can be exercised."

The Government responded to this particular recommendation of the commission by giving conditional approval, as long as it was done on a selective basis, when the need arose or when segregation arrangements had become superfluous – a comfortably vague and noncommittal reaction which leaves the Government ample room for manoeuvre. This is the only recommendation on which there is evidence of any conceptual difference between the Broederbond document and the Government White Paper, and even then it can hardly be described as a traumatic divergence of views.

One of the criticisms of the White Paper by the Theron commissioners was that it gave no guidelines on future policy for the coloured people. This was taken up by other commentators who accused the Government of having in fact no policy on the matter at all.

If this is the case, it is not true for the Broederbond. The organisation has a very clear policy for the coloured community, based on the establishment of coloured economic areas. Although it shies away from the concept of a coloured homeland *per se,* in essence the Broederbond plan amounts to the establishment of a Colouredstan arranged not on geographic lines, although geographically demarcated areas are involved, but on economic grounds.

The arguments behind the Broederbond's policy are that the coloured people in South Africa face enormous economic disadvantages. There is no coloured economy as such. Coloured entrepreneurs run mostly small, one-man businesses, and even on this level the whites are about six times stronger than the coloured people. One of the factors working to the disadvantage of the coloured people is the nature of the coloured market, which spends an average of only 25 per cent of its income at coloured business concerns. Largely as a result of their geographical distribution, coloured consumers spend their money mainly at white outlets.

Secondly, coloured entrepreneurs experience a shortage of capital as a result of the first problem. And thirdly, says the Broederbond scenario, the coloured people are competing in a milieu where the whites have always held the initiative and still do, making it difficult for their own initiative to come into play.

According to the Broederbond plan: "For all three of these problems a better geographic consolidation of the coloured people is of vital importance."[8]

According to the organisation's scenario, there are two alternative methods of developing a group of people, who, within a single population, have an economic disadvantage. The first is active discrimination in favour of such a group through the establishment of special corporations (for example, the Coloured Development Corporation) and of departments and State institutions giving direct support and preference to the education of such a group, and by ensuring that in all commercial contexts the group is given opportunities and receives special advantages. "This method makes political power for coloured people inevitable. If the coloured people shared, for example, white political institutions, they would be able to exert tremendous political pressure through their labour vote and by using this pressure could channel discrimination to their advantage."[9]

The Broederbond is doubtful as to whether this method would offer any long-term policy prospects. Obviously, the Bond would be repelled by the basic requirement here, which is for coloured people ultimately to share political power, and the organisation would make energetic efforts to demonstrate that this was not feasible.

The second method of economic advancement, in the organisation's view, would promote the interests of a population group on a territorial basis. "A diversity in the geographic framework can bring about a measure of separation, although such separation need not necessarily have political division as its final aim or result... An advantage of this method is that there would not need to be so much discrimination and subsidisation in favour of the coloured people, particularly in view of the fact that capital accruing to the coloured people as a result of their own endeavours could be spent at coloured outlets in their own areas. In this way, a certain proliferation factor comes into play which will make an important contribution to the improvement of the coloured people's economic status."[10]

This alternative is clearly much more in line with Broederbond thinking and the organisation comes out firmly in favour of "separate regional economies whereby coloured people can benefit in a geographical context." It says: "At a later stage, when the development has further advanced, it would be possible to make a political choice between general integration and a measure of separation."[11]

The authors of the scenario hasten to emphasise that what they recommend should not be envisaged as a coloured homeland, but as an attempt to achieve economic advancement for the coloured people. "Therefore it is recommended that large coloured centres consolidated at Johannesburg, Port Elizabeth and Cape Town be considered, and that agricultural land be made available to coloured people north of Cape Town on the west coast up to the Orange River. The agricultural areas must be able to support a variety of types of farming. As against the recommendation of the Theron Commission that areas must become available everywhere, we recommend the opening of selected consolidated areas: coloured preference areas."[12]

The Broederbond's coloured policy and the philosophy behind it are spelt out in far greater detail in another secret document entitled *The Coloureds – a view of their future.* The document, remarkable for its meticulous, dogmatic logic, starts by saying that despite legislation South Africa is moving towards economic integration, particularly with regard to the coloured people. It goes on: "Statutory and administrative control . . . alone will not achieve set objectives. Together with these, urban complexes must be planned geographically and socio-economically specifically to achieve the objectives of the State.

"Take Cape Town as an example. The coloured community in the Peninsula lies directly in the path from Cape Town to the white heartland which includes the Strand, Stellenbosch and Paarl . . . Physically, the white development out of the Cape in the direction of the white heartland is being inhibited by the giant coloured residential areas developing on the Cape Flats, and white development will soon have to leapfrog this non-white area and develop around it . . . If whites and blacks are employed in the same development sector, it is difficult to achieve economic parallelism. In the long term, with giant population concentrations the current line of development will force integration.

"The following considerations apply. In the same sector whites and blacks use the same roads, power and water distribution systems, telephone systems, trading services (shops, garages etc). The implication is clear: the same telephone system serves, for example, white and non-white (and the respective communities) and therefore whites alone cannot provide the exchange staffs and maintenance technicians...

"The same happens in all the systems used communally: roads, water, power, trade etc. All these services require clerks, typists and other personnel. Whites cannot attend to it all, and so non-whites take over on a significant scale. The trouble with developments tending towards integration is that advance towards the coloured people's own economic entity is hindered and it is largely absorbed by the white economy. Without territorial structuring on a large scale ... the maintenance of community services alone will to a large extent force functional integraion."

The scenario goes on to emphasise the need for careful town planning, so that parallel white and coloured communities can develop. These are some of the planning considerations. (1) The interface of white and coloured sectors must be developed as industrial and commercial zones "where any necessary, unavoidable and significant contact takes place." (2) The industrial and commercial zones can be so planned that the part of the white sector that borders on the coloured sector can be used for white industries where coloured workers will be limited by job reservation. The reverse, including job reservation against whites, would apply in the coloured sector.

(3) Logistical planning of railway lines and road systems must ensure that the two groups move economically and effectively without using the same routes. (4) Services, including commercial services, must be developed in the coloured area to allow the coloured people to develop their own economy by their own efforts as quickly as possible. (5) Where coloured areas do not have the resources of trained manpower to develop their own services, consideration must be given to authorising white capital and initiative under safeguards. (6) There must be only a few special preference areas for coloured people so that they become focal points for the coloured people's social, economic and political self-realisation.

The most important advantage of this system, so far as the Broederbond is concerned, is that the coloured people become increasingly independent economically and socially. Contacts with the white group, after the organisation of their own community has become so important to them that they do not hanker after what the other races have and are no longer dependent on whites for the maintenance of their own community, will be less complicated. White management of coloured affairs would eventually fall away.

"Economic forces still exercise the most powerful natural effect on desirable socio-political evolutionary patterns. The establishment of preference areas ... provides the best mechanism to achieve, and in a sense to compel, reconstruction of community settlement and the formation of national entities in South Africa – even if local administrative bodies and capital do not always want to underwrite and support the objectives of separate development

"The coloured preference points will eventually develop into coloured conurbations where the glories of first-class citizenship unfold for them... Work opportunities will develop for them in their own municipalities, transport undertakings, industries, large and small businesses, construction and property firms and in other directions characteristic of large conurbations. While a number of coloured cities are being established according to a set plan, all existing coloured areas can be retained. The conurbations need provide only for the 2,7-million additional coloured people to be accommodated by the turn of the century."

At the Cape congress of the ruling National Party held in August this year, striking similarities can be distinguished between the party line and that of the Broederbond as regards the position of the coloured people. The following report appeared in the *Rand Daily Mail:*[13]

"The National Party's Cape congress in East London yesterday reaffirmed that the Western Cape would remain a "coloured preference area" and called for far-reaching measures to keep "illegal blacks" out.

"A controversial *verligte* motion proposed by the Stellenbosch branch calling for an end to restrictions on blacks and the granting of 99-year leasehold rights as in other areas fell away when the Congress overwhelmingly accepted an opposing resolution proposed by the Cape leader, Mr P W Botha.

"Mr Botha's resolution combined three other resolutions which reaffirmed that the Western Cape would remain a "preference area" for whites and coloureds.

"It called for several measures to enforce this, including:

"Prohibitive minimum fines and the withdrawal of the labour allowance from employers of illegal workers;

"The immediate repatriation of blacks found guilty of being in the area illegally, and speedy trials to ensure that this would happen without delay;

"The imposition of levies to make black labour in the area more expensive and the prevention of black labour recruitment if there was unemployment of coloureds.

"Dr Denis Worrall, MP for Gardens, supported the resolution saying the issue went to the heart of Government policy which was working towards a radical form of partition between 'blacks and non-blacks.' 'This resolution is saying we must limit the movements of blacks outside the existing homelands and says we must reduce the number of blacks in this area,' he said.

"Those in favour of the Stellenbosch resolution said they supported the Western Cape remaining a coloured preference area but this could be done by means of influx control and not by indiscriminatory measures that did not apply elsewhere. Another delegate who spoke in favour of the Stellenbosch resolution said coloureds no longer wished to do "cheap work" such as scrubbing floors and mowing lawns.

"A delegate who called for tighter restrictions on blacks in the Western Cape said children of illegal workers should not be allowed to attend school in the area, no illegal blacks should be treated at hospitals or clinics unless they had a certificate from a district surgeon and any worker who broke his employment contract should be repatriated to a homeland within 24 hours.

"Dr Connie Mulder, Minister of Plural Relations, said his department would continue to ensure that the Western Cape remained a 'coloured preference area.'

"Conditions for legal black workers in the area would be made as pleasant as possible, but illegal workers would be repatriated. The Crossroads squatter camp could not be allowed to exist. Legal workers would be rehoused and others sent back to their homelands, he said."

It is therefore shown quite clearly that the Broederbond's proposals for the coloured people have been accepted by the National Party and that their plan for the coloureds which they outlined in such detail in the secret documents is being put into effect. It is not surprising in the light of this information that the Government's new constitutional plan for whites, coloureds and Indians bears the unmistakeable stamp of Broederbond approval. The *Sunday Times*[14] was able to reveal Broederbond involvement when it reported:

"Similarly, the Broederbond was involved deeply in the formulation of the new three-Parliament constitutional system for whites, coloureds and Indians which the Government plans to introduce.

"Circular 7/77/78 dated September 1 1977 told members: "The Executive Council is pleased to say that friends in responsible circles took part in our brainstorming (on the masterplan and its effects on the coloured people) and that there was a healthy exchange of ideas."

"It goes on to say in response to queries from members that it was indeed a party to the discussions that preceded the formulation of the new constitutional proposals and that the Broederbond view was presented to 'responsible friends long before the plans were announced.'"

The fact that the Broederbond's proposals were submitted to and approved by the organisation *before* they came before Parliament once again points to the strength of its influence over policy-making decisions.

1. *Rand Daily Mail,* December 15 1944.
2. October 1 1972.
3. *Standard Encyclopaedia of Southern Africa,* Vol 3, p 331.
4. Immediately after the election, the one successful independent candidate joined the Federal Party.
5. *Die Vaderland,* July 10 1970.
6. *Rand Daily Mail,* April 22 1977.
7. The recommendation dealt specifically with the Peninsula College for Advanced Technical Education.
8. Broederbond document, *Comments in Connection with the Report of the Erika Theron Commission,* p 3.
9. Ibid.
10. Ibid. p 4.
11. Ibid.
12. Ibid. p 5.
13. August 23 1978.
14. January 22 1978.

11 *Division Among Brothers – the HNP Split*

The most traumatic experience for Afrikanerdom in recent years was not Sharpeville nor Soweto, but the split in the National Party which led to the formation of the Herstigte Nasionale Party. It also caused a split in the Broederbond, but once again the organisation played a key role in maintaining unity in Afrikaner ranks – or at least in restricting the split to a minimum.

It could easily have gone the other way. At one stage there were rumours that nearly 40 National Party Members of Parliament would leave the party and, more important, that they would have support from the biggest and most influential part of the Broederbond. How it happened is a story of political intrigue and in-fighting seldom equalled in South African history. It is a subject that could fill a book, as indeed it did fill J H P Serfontein's *Verkrampte Aanslag*. For the purposes of this chapter, not more than a synposis can be given with the emphasis on the role of the Broederbond in the drama.

There were three main characters involved in this test of strength:

- Dr Johannes Albertus Munnik Hertzog, ultra-conservative Afrikaner, son of the former Prime Minister, General Hertzog;
- Dr Piet Meyer, chairman of the Broederbond and of the SABC's Board of Governors.
- Advocate Balthazar Johannes Vorster, South Africa's seventh Prime Minister.

Dr Hertzog qualified as an advocate at Oxford and returned to South Africa in 1929. During his eight-year study period overseas, mainly in Britain, Dr Hertzog was much impressed by the rise of the working class. "There he perceived the political power these workers' groups held. The workers' organisations gripped his interest, and gradually the importance that trade unions for Afrikaners in the cities could hold for the country's politics dawned on him.

"Just before his return to South Africa a young academic, Dr

Dr J A M Hertzog. Suspended by the Bond for his divisive right-wing activities.

Piet Meyer, also came back from Europe. It was destined that the paths of the energetic and inspired Albert Hertzog and the equally inspired Piet Meyer would soon join in South Africa. Together, with a few other young Afrikaners, they would play a decisive role in linking the Afrikaner worker closely with the rest of the Afrikaner nation, thus getting political power into Afrikaner hands."[1]

By organising Afrikaner workers, Dr Hertzog created a strong political powerbase for himself. He secured vast trusts worth millions which served under his control, as the financial backing to carry out his work. From the Pieter Neethling Building in Pretoria he controlled his growing network of cultural and trade union front organisations with the help of his loyal lieutenant, Schalk J Botha, and Gert Beetge. In the Broederbond his power was great, as the longest-serving executive member with 20 years' experience. He swung the Mineworkers' Union behind the National Party in the 1948 election, gaining six marginal seats to give the National Party its sensational victory.

A reward had to follow and he got the Parliamentary nomination for Ermelo, gaining the seat for the National Party. Ten years later Dr Verwoerd promoted him to the Cabinet. Hertzog moved swiftly to extend his influence. He appointed his spiritual brother, Dr Meyer, as chairman of the Board of Governors of the SABC. Dr Hertzog also became active among young Afrikaner politicians, especially MPs. Scores of secret "study meetings" were held under his guidance. As an expert exponent of Christian Nationalism, he was in an ideal position to influence the young men and impress on them the danger of the party's straying from its set course.

But Dr Hertzog's strongest weapon in the battle to strengthen his influence and keep the party to its 1948 policy platform, was the secret *Afrikaner-Orde,* which played a major role in the events leading up to the split.

Dr Hertzog was instrumental in the formation of the *Afrikaner-Orde* in 1929, shortly after his return from overseas (Addendum F to minutes of 1965 annual meeting). The organisation was formed on almost the same lines as the Broederbond with secrecy supreme, and its aim was to take over control of the Pretoria City Council. In the early 1960s trouble developed between the *Afrikaner-Orde*, the Broederbond and the National Party. The Broederbond objected that there was no need for a separate "duplicate" organisation in Pretoria, and that *Afrikaner-Orde* members were infiltrating its ranks without telling the Bond that they were already members of the *Orde.* But Dr Hertzog was not to be so easily outmanoeuvred. He would not sacrifice his highly-organised powerbase. Instead he offered an acceptable compromise: the *Afrikaner-Orde* would be willing to operate under the aegis of the Broederbond. Dr Meyer was chairman of the Bond, and Hertzog was on the Executive, so they could protect the *Orde* from there.

The justification for this step, which was accepted by the Bond, is given fully in the above-quoted addendum. "The *Afrikaner-Orde* has existed since 1929 in Pretoria and it concentrated mainly on the municipal sphere. It is also largely due to the *Orde* that the city council, through the municipal ratepayers' association, fell into the hands of the Afrikaner. The need for a confidential organisation with an effective modus operandi arose early and it was developed and used to great effect. It was, however, inevitable that two confidential organisations operating without proper co-ordination and co-operation in the same area would encounter friction and unrest. Dual membership sometimes created confusion and frustration."

At the *Bondsraad* of 1955 it was decided that Broeders could belong to the *Orde,* but the wish was expressed that other secret Afrikaner organisations be placed under control of the Board. In 1962 co-operation was discussed again in the light of the need for secret action among Afrikaner workers.

The document added: "During this time the people at the head of the *Afrikaner-Orde* (all Broeders) came to the Executive to offer everything they had to the Afrikaner Broederbond for the fulfilment of this task (co-operation). The Executive had the alternatives of destroying this society of more than 400 well-organised men, or using their strength productively. The Executive decided not to reject any available strength. It decided to take over the *Orde,* use it and control it. The management committee *(dagbestuur)* of the Executive became the High Council *(Hoë Raad)* of the *Afrikaner-Orde,* it was stipulated that the chairman of the AO's executive must be a member of the Broederbond Executive, the funds of the *Orde* were absorbed by the Broederbond, and an official of the *Orde* was appointed to the Bond Executive. It was further decided to restrict the *Orde* to Pretoria."

At the head of every *Heemraad* (cell) was a leader who must be a

Broeder. Broeder P M Smith became chairman of the *Orde's* Executive, Broeder Gert Beetge became a Bond official and Broeder Jan Swart became the *Orde's* chief secretary. At that stage there were 420 active *Orde* members. The Broederbond thought it had the *Orde* now firmly under its control – but it was mistaken. It was still run by the Hertzog group, to whom it owed first loyalty. Separate meetings were held as *Orde* members felt they could not trust Broederbond officials. The study groups still continued under Dr Hertzog's guidance, and at one stage his list of associates was impressive: Dr Connie Mulder, Mr S P Botha, Dr Piet Koornhof, Mr Daan van der Merwe, MP, Mr Jaap Marais, MP, Mr Val Volker, MP, Mr Ben Pienaar, MP, Mr Willie Marais, MP, Mr Cas Greyling, MP, Mr Louis Stofberg, MP, Mr Braam Raubenheimer, MP, Mr Wilken Delpoort, MP, Mr Sarel Reinecke, MP, Mr Fanie Herman, MP, Mr N C Sadie, MP, Mr M J van den Bergh, MP, Dr A J Visser, MP, and Mr Gaffie Maree, MP.

The study groups were developing along dangerous lines. They spent their time analysing policies and in many cases came to the conclusion that the National Party was deviating from the 1948 policy and the Broederbond's strict basis of Christian Nationalism. Criticism of Dr Verwoerd came to the fore, although he was so powerful that he was almost untouchable. But some of the Super-Afrikaners criticised him all the same. His increasing English support was seen as holding a danger that Afrikanerdom could become diluted, the immigration policy could have the same effect, completely independent Bantustans could lead to communist infiltration etc.

The voices were muted but they were heard. Young MPs who were approached to join study groups told colleagues about them. Stories kept surfacing of the Hertzog group and the *Afrikaner-Orde* continuing to push their supporters into key positions. The name of Albert Hertzog kept cropping up.

One man alert to what was happening was Mr John Vorster, Minister of Justice. Some security police officers had infiltrated the *Afrikaner-Orde* and had come back with stories of plotting and dissent; now an instruction went out that a number of security men must be introduced into the Broederbond without the customary scrutiny by branches. The list was drawn up by General H J van den Bergh, himself a top Broeder. The pretext given for this extraordinary procedure was that there were not enough policemen in the Bond – every sector of public life had to be well represented.

The widening split in Afrikanerdom's ranks became more apparent when Mr Vorster took over as Prime Minister after Dr Verwoerd's murder in September 1966. Dr Hertzog probably realised his last chance to become Prime Minister had slipped by – not that anybody but his own group gave him a serious chance in the Premiership stakes. His only role now was that of the elder statesman, protecting everything dear to the Afrikaner, sticking to the 1948 policy and implementing the Broederbond's Christian national philosophy.

Whereas Dr Verwoerd could contain differences because of his personal status and by sticking fairly closely to the old party line, Mr Vorster faced a formidable task. He had to follow in the footsteps of a man worshipped by Afrikaners – but, more important, he faced an entirely new set of circumstances, a new world in fact.

A hostile outside world forced him to look anew at South Africa's situation. What he saw was not pleasing. South Africa's increasing isolation demanded a more pragmatic approach than Dr Verwoerd's "granite policies". Terrorism was increasing in Rhodesia; in Mozambique and in Angola the Portuguese were losing ground; South Africa was under strong pressure to relinquish South West Africa; in the sporting field the country stood alone, faced by almost total boycott.

In all the policies he adopted he faced bitter opposition from the Hertzog group, the *Afrikaner-Orde,* and an influential section of the Broederbond. They opposed his "outward policy" of making friends in Africa, his attempts to break sports isolation by making more concessions, his attempts to strengthen the white population through immigration, and his advocacy of close unity between Afrikaans- and English-speaking.

Mr Vorster realised while he was still Minister of Justice that the battle between *verkramptes* and *verligtes* would be won or lost in the powerful Broederbond. Whoever won control of the organisation would win control in the party. It is clear from the documents that he liaised closely with the Broederbond Executive soon after he became Prime Minister, and that he called on them to fulfil their historical role in Afrikanerdom by maintaining peace and unity. The differences between *verkramp* and *verlig* were so evident that the chairman, Dr Meyer, sent out an extraordinary circular less than a year after Mr Vorster had become Prime Minister. It is clear from the circular that Mr Vorster had secured a promise of support from Dr Meyer.

The circular, headed *Us and Our Political leaders* (August 2 1967) stated: "The Chairman of the Executive personally conveyed our organisation's sincere thanks and appreciation to our Brother, the Prime Minister, after the recent session of Parliament, for everything the Government had done in the interests of the country and all its nations." Dr Meyer specifically thanked Mr Vorster for the introduction of a long-standing Broeder aim, the National Education Bill, for his Christian leadership, and for his active interest in Afrikaans cultural affairs.

It may be recalled that at this stage Dr Meyer had already made some speeches (see Chapter 8) especially on Afrikaans-English relations, which closely approached the sentiments of the dissident Hertzog group. The HNP's policy of Afrikaans as the only official language was not so very different from the views expressed by Dr Meyer. Evidently, Mr Vorster saw the danger of Dr Meyer playing a double game and swinging a large part of the Broederbond behind Dr Hertzog in the political battle which he knew was coming. It can therefore be taken that Dr Meyer included the following paragraph in the newsletter at Mr Vorster's urging. "In our discussions with our political leaders, a few cases were mentioned to us where it appeared that some branches of our cultural bodies trespassed on the political area by getting involved in the election of officebearers or representatives of the National Party. The Executive wishes to reiterate that our divisions and committees of cultural bodies in which our members serve, can only act as individual members of the party in the political area.

"As many points of difference have recently emerged between Afrikaners in public life . . . the Executive wants to make an urgent appeal . . . that members refrain from personal attacks . . . Finally, we want to re-state our confidence in the leadership of the Prime Minister, and we make an urgent call on our members to support him and his Government fully."

Dr Meyer's appeal did little to restore unity. In Pretoria, and especially in the *Afrikaner-Orde,* Dr Hertzog's supporters were preparing for the inevitable clash. At the beginning of 1968 they took over control of the Pretoria council of the National Party after active lobbying of delegates. The legal counsel of the party overruled the election on technicalities, but the message was clear to Mr Vorster: he had to watch his back. He now produced evidence that the *Afrikaner-Orde* was interfering in National Party politics and working to undermine his position.

Dr Meyer tried to protect the *Orde* by disclosing that Dr Verwoerd, shortly before his death, had dismissed similar allegations as "rubbish". But Mr Vorster was adamant – the *Afrikaner-Orde* had to be disbanded. The compromise he reached with the Broederbond provided that the *Orde* would disband, but the names of members would be circulated as prospective members of the Broederbond. Mr Vorster won the day under the terms of this arrangement, because only a fraction of the *Orde* members were admitted as members, the rest were blackballed by Broeders who had long viewed the *Afrikaner-Orde* as a rival.

In February 1968 Mr Vorster took the Ministry of Posts and Telegraphs from Dr Hertzog, leaving him only the portfolio of Minister of Health. The Hertzogites were now fighting a battle for political survival, and bitterness increased.

The tension was reflected in the minutes of a meeting of the founder-members of the Broederbond circulated on March 21 1968. It called on Broeders to remember their oath and do everything in their power to heal the split that had widened in spite of appeals from the highest quarters. The founder-members said it would be a sad day if the following year's fiftieth anniversary of the Bond was marred by disunity among Brothers *(Broedertwis)*. "It is painful for us, as founder-members – and strange to an organisation like the Afrikaner Broederbond – that Broeders criticise Broeders sharply in public. The danger cannot be excluded that the dearly bought unity among Afrikaners ... could disintegrate. The AB played an important part in this struggle, and it is not necessary for us to point out the disastrous results such disunity could have on our nation and country ... The Afrikaner Broederbond must once again fulfil its destiny as the cohesive organisation, restoring and guarding peace in Afrikaner ranks."

The battle for power continued unabated, however, and on August 9 1968 Mr Vorster dismissed Dr Hertzog from the Cabinet. The *Bondsraad,* meeting two months later, gave Mr Vorster the opportunity of defending himself and his action in the very heart of the Broederbond. And he met every point on which he was criticised by the *verkramptes*. He put the unity of the party above everything else, and warned that people who wanted to destroy it risked destroying the white man and South Africa. He pointed to the need for Afrikaans-English unity, each protecting his own culture. "I now want to say clearly to you as Broeders what I said to the caucus, that as long as I am Prime Minister and leader of the National Party I will not cheat those English-speakers who support my policy and accept South Africa as fatherland – and nobody must expect it of me."

As long as Afrikaner identity was maintained, the road of co-operation between the two sections was the right one. He found it strange that some said they no longer supported the National Party's policy because English-speakers and even blacks now supported it. He disputed a section in the annual report which stated that the split started after he had been elected Prime Minister. In fact, he said, it already started during the 1966 election. "In 1966 there were already people, and Broeders among them, who talked about a new political party because Dr Verwoerd was too far left."

He also came to the defence of Broeders in business who had been blamed for "selling out to Oppenheimer" during the *Federale Mynbou*-General Mining transaction. "Once you have destroyed them and made them suspect, what remains of your Afrikaner concerns? To whom is the field then left?"

Mr Vorster then defended the sports policy, saying Dr Verwoerd's Cabinet had decided a mixed South African team could participate in the Olympic Games, and Maoris had been allowed to tour South Africa in an All Black team in 1928.

Referring to a statement in the annual report that "questions arose" over his "outward policy" of making friends with African states, Mr Vorster said the National Party's policy did not prohibit this. The National Party had had diplomatic relations with India in the 1920s and India had had an ambassador in South Africa until 1961. "There are people now who are worried about where the children of black diplomats ... will swim. Here too there should be no misunderstanding. There is no such thing as a first class or a second class diplomat. Black diplomats will come to South Africa. I want you to know it, and if you have any objection in principle then you must put it to me because then I cannot be your leader. This is the road I am going to take."

Mr Vorster's strong line clearly made a strong impact on the 800 influential delegates at the *Bondsraad,* and tipped the scales in his favour. The strongest indication of this was that Dr Piet Meyer and Dr Andries Treurnicht did not follow Dr Hertzog, Mr Jaap Marais, Mr Louis Stofberg and Mr Willie Marais when they were forced out of the party and formed the Herstigte Nasionale Party in 1969.

Mr Vorster also attended other Broederbond rallies, taking the same stand against the HNP and swinging more and more Broeders behind him. The shrewd Dr Meyer and Dr Treurnicht soon detected that Mr Vorster now had the majority of Broeders behind him and that it would be foolish to follow Dr Hertzog into the political wilderness.

The mournful tone of Dr Meyer's 1969 address as chairman gave the game away – he was coming out fully on Mr Vorster's side although he still clung to many of his old *verkrampte* beliefs. In 1968 and 1969 Mr Vorster and Dr Meyer met on several occasions, and Mr Vorster must have warned him of the dire consequences should he try to swing the Broederbond behind Dr Hertzog. His position as chairman of the SABC and the Broederbond gave him a strong powerbase which he would have lost if Mr Vorster had turned against him. It is not strange, then, to find Dr Meyer saying in his 1969 chairman's address: "After Dr Verwoerd's tragic death I campaigned personally and actively as a member of the National Party for the election of Broeder John Vorster as Prime Minister and so linked all my other activities to his political leadership. Between Broeder Vorster and myself there has since then been continuous, personal frankness and benevolent co-operation, even in situations when the darkest picture was painted outside by the ill-informed! Broeder John Vorster is a straightforward man who confronts people directly with everything he has heard about them. He puts his case honestly and bluntly and carries on with his work."

Dr Meyer then spoke of the major role he played in trying to restore unity between the Vorster and Hertzog supporters in the Broederbond "behind the scenes," without revealing full details. Dr Meyer's decision to back Mr Vorster proved to be the right one when the HNP did not win a single seat in the 1970 general election. What must be remembered was that they had little time to get off the ground. They had been ousted from the party – something they wanted to avoid at all costs. They wanted to conduct the fight from within, because they realised the difficulties of forming a new party to oppose the powerful National Party machine. As soon as they were out, and forced to form the HNP, Mr Vorster called a snap election and they only had a few months in which to prepare for it. Once it was proved that the HNP did not have as much support at grassroots as even Mr Vorster had feared, the witch-hunt against them in the Broederbond increased in intensity.

Scores of complaints were lodged against HNP leaders who attacked Broeders in the National Party from public platforms. This was regarded as "unbrotherly" but complaints from the HNP on similar lines were apparently never taken seriously. In the circular of June 2 1970 the Executive gave a detailed description of how Broeders should go about laying complaints for "unbrotherly" behaviour. The circular warned that membership of the Bond was earned on personal merit and could, therefore, not be terminated on a group basis. (A few years later the Executive violated its own ruling.)

The Broederbond now started taking action against HNP leaders. The first to be suspended, in early 1971, were Dr Albert Hertzog and Mr Jaap Marais. They and their followers tried to fight back by citing cases where the Executive violated the constitution (Article 88) by supporting a specific political party – the National Party. Their complaints were ignored or deferred.

On February 23 1971 Mr Jan Jooste, Mr W T Marais, Mr P J Malan, Mr G H Beetge and Dr A D Pont wrote to the Broederbond secretary, Mr Naude Botha, to ask for an urgent interview with the Executive to discuss the Hertzog and Marais suspensions. Botha replied on March 4 1971 that the Executive could not grant the request for a meeting, because no action had been taken against Dr Hertzog and Mr Marais "because of their membership of a specific political party."

On March 31 1971 Mr Jooste and his co-signatories sent a lengthy reply to Mr Botha. "Since the political division the Prime Minister has used several meetings of the Broederbond to promote his own party and to attack political opponents who were also members of the Bond. This is in conflict with our constitution," they complained. "No reply has been received to a memorandum on this subject which was handed to the chairman before the previous *Bondsraad.* Circulars have also been used for promoting a specific party. Here the Executive contravened the constitution (Article 6 and Regulation Article 88). The Secretarial Report submitted to the previous *Bondsraad* went even further. It stated: 'The Executive went out of its way to encourage support for the National Party. This is not only in conflict with the constitution but implies indirect actions against Broeders who do not belong to the National Party.' The letter further queried the statement in the report that the Executive held meetings with "individual Broeders and groups of Broeders to prevent a split." Mr

Jooste and the other HNP leaders knew nothing of such discussions.

On May 11 1971 Mr Botha wrote back to say the Executive required a memorandum on the issues Mr Jooste and his group wanted to discuss, and he would then try to arrange a meeting. Mr Jooste replied that there was no need for a new memorandum – the chairman, Dr Meyer, had already received one and his letter of March 31 listed the issues. But Mr Jooste repeated the things they wanted to discuss all the same. However, the delegation did not have the meeting it had requested. Nearly a year later, as Mr Jooste had still not been granted a meeting, he sent copies of the correspondence to Broederbond members whose addresses he had. His membership was suspended. He wrote back on March 8 1972 to say he was prepared to meet the Executive immediately, provided the issues listed by his delegation were dealt with first. These were:

(a) Certain leading Broeders took part in activities of USSALEP (United States South Africa Leadership Exchange Programme) – an organisation repudiated by the Bond.
(b) An Executive member, Dr P E Rosseau, had a prominent post in the SA Foundation which had stated that South Africa should accept liberalism.
(c) No notice was taken of Piet Cillie (editor of *Die Burger*) and Schalk Pienaar (editor of *Beeld*) sowing division in Afrikaner ranks.
(d) Protests against Dr A E Rupert and Dr A J van der Merwe serving on the Abe Bailey Trust – nominated by the Cecil John Rhodes Trust, the "essence of enmity against Afrikanerdom" – had come to nothing.
(e) Advocate Pik Botha, a relatively new Broederbond member, pleaded openly for the acceptance of the humanistic-liberalistic Charter of Human Rights of the United Nations.

Mr Vorster's use of Broederbond platforms for promoting the National Party in conflict with the constitution was outlined again. The Broederbond was blamed for drawing up the new "liberalistic" sports policy for Mr Vorster.

On May 9 1972 Mr Jooste was informed that he was expelled from the Broederbond – without an opportunity for him, or others, to present a defence at an Executive meeting. He made it clear in a letter to the Secretary (July 3 1972) that he no longer felt himself bound by the oath of secrecy. He said he had not taken an oath to an organisation which harboured and protected "liberalistic elements" and promoted their ideals.

On the same day Mr Gert Beetge resigned. "You will notice," he wrote to Mr Naude Botha, "that I no longer address you as Broeder because you stopped a long time ago showing any kind of Brotherliness towards me." He recalled that Mr Botha wanted to take disciplinary steps against him for refusing to give Mr Vorster a standing ovation at a Broederbond meeting when the Prime Minister related how he had persuaded Mr Ian Smith to hold the *HMS Tiger* discussions with Britain.

Mr Beetge listed much the same complaints as Mr Jooste had and wrote: "The Afrikaner Broederbond even leads the party in taking the youth into a world of multiracial sport and social mixing. I refer here to the Broederbond committee which worked out the multiracial sports policy for Mr Vorster – a sports policy which is in conflict with the spirit of the Broederbond as I had known it for more than 20 years. I still remember the day in your office when I protested to you that the Bond was linking itself to the Government party, and you replied that the Broederbond supported Mr Vorster's party because he was implementing Broederbond policy."

Mr Beetge recalled in his letter that Mr Vorster had disbanded the *Afrikaner-Orde* and the security police had infiltrated the Freemasons. He said that although the Bond differed from the Freemasons, they were never regarded as a danger to the State. "If it can happen to the Freemasons, then I must accept it will also happen to the Afrikaner Broederbond," he wrote.

At the HNP congress on October 17 1972 the chairman, Mr Jan Jooste, showed that his threat that he no longer regarded himself as bound by the oath of secrecy was not idle. He revealed the Broederbond's interference in party politics and the names of certain members, and created a stir in the organisation. The Executive was quick off the mark. It decided (circular of October 17 1972) that each branch must immediately hold an urgent extraordinary meeting where members must re-dedicate themselves to the Bond and swear they had no connection with the HNP "through membership or association. If I have been associated (with the HNP) thus far then I undertake to break it off immediately." Two witnesses had to sign the "red oath" as the HNP called it.

Branches were instructed that all members should attend the meeting and reasons for absence should be supplied in writing to the Executive. Members who could not be present must be visited by two committee members before November 3 to get the pledge signed. The circular had to be fetched and delivered by hand to a representative of the Executive and normal postal channels were not to be trusted.

Outside *(buite)* and resting *(rustende)* members had to be approached separately and should not be invited to the meeting. No member was to be allowed to attend any further meetings before he had signed the pledge. The extraordinary meeting should be conducted in a solemn atmosphere and opened with scripture reading and prayer. The induction pledge had to be read again and a two-minute silence given for members to consider their position before signing the pledge.

The exercise was a huge triumph for the Broederbond. On April 4 1973 the Executive reported to the branches that 8 859 of the 9 027 had signed the new pledge that they would have nothing to do with the HNP. Six signed "under protest", 19 refused to sign, 11 resigned for "other reasons", 10 were expelled by the Executive and 33 signed but questioned the Executive's action.

The battle for the Broederbond's support was over, and had been won by Mr Vorster. The HNP had lost a strong powerbase and, as subsequent elections proved, posed no immediate threat to his regime. Mr Vorster's view that the Broederbond held the key to the battle was proved correct. Without the support of the Broederbond no Nationalist can even become Prime Minister, let alone rule the country effectively.

1. Naude, Louis, *Dr Albert Hertzog en die Mynwerkers,* p 10.

12 *The Broederbond and Apartheid*

Advocates of apartheid, or separate development as they prefer to call it today, claim that the roots of the policy can be traced back to the landing at the Cape of Good Hope by Jan van Riebeeck in 1652. One of the first things van Riebeeck did was plant a fence separating the colonists from the Hottentots. As the Boers pushed inland, borders between themselves and black tribes became their main concern.

During the 1830s large organised groups of whites left the colony, mostly because they were dissatisfied with the erratic policy which the British administration followed toward the Xhosa from 1806.[1] Life and possessions along the borders were endangered, and the burghers felt their national aspirations were not fulfilled. The aim of the Trekkers was to establish independent republics in the hinterland.

In Natal, Andries Pretorius and Piet Retief made contact with the Zulus. In the Free State, Andries Hendrik Potgieter, who crossed the Orange River in 1836, met the Barolong, a few Tswana tribes and Zulus who had fled from Natal as well as the Kwena in the north-eastern Free State. Potgieter moved northwards to establish Potchefstroom between the Vet and Vaal rivers. There the Trekkers met the Ndebele and a few Tswana tribes. When Potgieter moved in 1845 to Ohrigstad and Lydenburg, he came across the Pedi, Venda and Tsonga at the Soutpansberg in the north, the Swazi in the east, the Zulu in south-eastern Transvaal and the Ndebele in the central areas.

By the middle of the 19th century whites had been in contact with all the black groups in South Africa. For decades to come, relations between black and white would become the burning central issue of South African politics. The white man's urge to remain separate from blacks was not an invention of the National Party or the Broederbond. It was always there; what they did was formulate a rigid policy and entrench separation in legislation which brought upon South Africa the wrath of the world.

Even General Jan Smuts recognised and supported this historic urge for separation, in a speech he made in the Savoy Hotel in London in 1917. "With us there are certain axioms now in regard to the relations of black and white; and the principal one is intermixture of blood between the two colours. It has now become an accepted axiom in our dealings with the natives that it is dishonourable to mix white and black blood.

"More than 20 years ago an experiment in native self-government was begun by Cecil Rhodes in the old Cape Colony, which gave local institutions to the natives in the Glen Grey Reserve. That principle has been extended over a large part of the old Transkeian territories, and so successful has it been that when we came to framing the Act of Union an appendix was added about the future administration of the protectorates when they should become incorporated into the Union. This appendix laid down that the native territories in South Africa should be governed apart from the parliamentary institutions of the Union, and on different lines which would achieve the principle of native self-government. More and more the trend has hardened in the same direction.

"We have felt more and more that if we are to solve our native question it is useless to try to govern black and white in the same system, to subject them to the same institutions of government and legislation. They are different not only in colour but in minds and in political capacity, and their political institutions should be different, while always proceeding on the basis of self-government.

"Instead of mixing up black and white in the old haphazard way, which instead of lifting up the black degraded the white, we are now trying to lay down a policy of keeping them apart as much as possible in our institutions. Thus in South Africa you will have in the long run large areas cultivated by blacks and governed by blacks, where they will look after themselves in all their forms of living and development, while in the rest of the country you will have your white communities which will govern themselves separately according to the accepted European principles. The natives will, of course, be free to go and to work in the white areas, but as far as possible the administration of white and black areas will be separated, and such that each will be satisfied and developed according to its own proper lives."[2]

The Broederbond devoted its first decade almost wholly to overcoming organisational problems and putting the final stamp on the secret nature of the movement. It also gave attention to cultural affairs aimed at the promotion of Afrikaans. Once the FAK was formed to become its public cultural body, it started giving attention to racial matters. It had noticed the militancy among Afrikaner workers during the 1922 mining strike when their jobs were threatened by the introduction of cheap black labour. Slum conditions developed in Johannesburg for impoverished Afrikaners and blacks in search of work. The Broederbond saw the social and political conditions as a threat to the continued existence of the Afrikaner nation, and was searching for ways and means to overcome it.

W A de Klerk[3] describes the search for a new typical Afrikaner philosophy and outlook. "There was a quieter, more effective and earnest core of people meeting within the innermost *binnekring* of the Broederbond, thinking, talking, into the small hours of the morning.

"This marked the steady driving inwards of the Afrikaners' political thought and sentiment. Afrikaner politics was slowly but fatally being theologised. There was a growing urge to set the South African world aright, once and for all; to reconstruct it and redeem it in terms of a newly-defined Afrikaner *lewens- en wêreldbeskouing* – a world-view."

The first Broederbond-formulated policy on black/white relations was sent out in a secret circular to members as early as 1933. "In some ways this can be seen as the Afrikaner Broederbond's declaration of faith in this regard," said Professor A N Pelzer in his historical review at the golden jubilee *Bondsraad* meeting in 1968.

The 1933 circular read: "Without giving an exposition of different points of view regarding the native question, we want to state our own point of view briefly, and thereafter the basis on which it rests. Total segregation should not be only the ideal, but the immediate practical policy of the State. The purchase and separation of suitable and adequate areas for habitation by natives' families, and tribes living on farms and smaller reserves, should take place at any cost.

"The opportunity should be provided for different tribes to gather in separate areas. Then it should be made compulsory for these groups of natives to return to these areas. Here they can become cooperative or separate landowners. But the land should be purchased by the natives from the State through a form of taxation such as hut tax, or occupied in freehold from the State. In these areas, greater degrees of self-government can be granted after some time. This should be in line as much as possible with the natives' history and traditional form of government. Areas should be under control of specially trained white commissioners directly answerable to the Minister of Native Affairs.

"Here the native can fulfil himself and develop in the political, economic, cultural, religious, educational and other spheres. In these areas whites cannot become landowners, and whites who settle there as traders, missionaries, teachers etc, will have no political rights there.

"A native who has reached a stipulated age will be allowed, with the permission of his tribal chief and the commissioner, to go temporarily to white areas to work on farms and in towns and cities. But he will not be allowed to take his family.

"The detribalised native must as far as posible be encouraged to move to these native areas. Those who cannot do so must be housed in separate locations where they will enjoy no political rights and own no property because they must be viewed as temporary occupants who live in the white area of their own choice and for gain. Unemployed natives should be forced to leave these locations and move to the native areas after having been allowed a reasonable time to obtain work."

Although this was only a brief policy statement, it contained all the cardinal principles on which the Government's policy is still based 45 years later.

Professor Pelzer added in his review: "In order to make a lasting and meaningful contribution to the solution of South Africa's racial problems, the Executive came to the conclusion as early as 1940 that an expert body had to be formed to consider the racial question on behalf of Afrikanerdom. The Executive therefore instructed its Racial Question Committee to consider the establishment of such a body and to advise the Executive about the possibility of holding a *Volkskongres* on these matters. A few months later Broederbond chairman held a meeting with representatives of the *Afrikanerbond vir Rassestudie.* As a result the Executive decided to direct the FAK to appoint a Commission for Race Relations consisting mainly of members of the Executive's own committee and of the *Afrikanerbond vir Rassestudie.*

"This commission was to organise the *Volkskongres,* linking up with a normal FAK congress, during which a permanent institute for race relations (not to be confused with the SA Institute of Race Relations) would be established. Following the establishment of the commission, the Executive transferred responsibility for racial matters to the FAK, disbanded its own Racial Question Committee, and kept complete silence on this matter for seven years.

At the 1947 *Bondsraad* much time and attention was given to racial questions. Because the vastness of the question was seen clearly, and only a glimmer of a solution, it was realised that the time was ripe for positive action on racial questions. The *Bondsraad* therefore asked the Executive to consider the establishment of a study and action body for racial matters. The preparatory work required much consultation because the Executive was aware of similar moves on the part of the Synodal Mission Commission of the *Nederduitse Gereformeerde Kerk* in the Transvaal and some lecturers at the University of Stellenbosch. The Executive managed to coordinate the different attempts, eliminating dissipation of forces and overlapping. The body was formed in September 1948, the South African Bureau for Racial Affairs. SABRA would on the one hand formulate policy, and on the other give attention to "practical aspects of the Bantu question" such as social questions, communism and commerce. Since its inception SABRA has been financed heavily by the Executive of the Afrikaner Broederbond.

"Closely linked to the wish to study racial affairs within the borders of South Africa scientifically, was the realisation that Africa must be the subject of continuous study because of the big changes which had taken place since the end of the Second World War. The need to establish an Africa Institute was mentioned to the Executive as early as May 1952 by Broeder Schumann. Two years later Broeder Hertzog (Albert) returned to the subject and emphasised the necessity of giving urgent attention to events in Central Africa particularly. The Executive gave further attention to the matter on both occasions, but it was not until 1960 that the South African Academy for Science and Arts formed the Africa Institute. Although the Afrikaner Broederbond thus had no direct hand in the eventual establishment of the institute, it did the preparatory work which inspired the inception of such a body."

Professor Pelzer's brief notes did not do justice to the Broederbond's role in the formulation, propagation and implementation of the policy of separate development. It is demonstrable that without the organisation's think-tanks and the fact that it had members in leading positions to implement the policy, apartheid would not have got off the ground. As W A de Klerk[4] describes it: "Meanwhile, in the Koffiehuis in Cape Town, D F Malan and his group of eager, efficient young Nationalist intellectuals – mainly lawyers, journalists from *Die Burger* and professional politicians – sat around their coffee tables. They often listened to the measured tones of *Doktor,* but mostly to each other: discussing not only the form and content of the new nationalism, but also as a necessary corollary, the coming Republic. They regarded the increasingly urgent question of race relations as being of paramount importance, as it formed part of their deepening concept of the Afrikaner nation. They wondered how the other groups, white, brown and black, would fit into the new all-encompassing design. At the Afrikaans universities, similar groups of dedicated academics were labouring in their studies, adding deeper dimensions to the discussions of the men in the marketplaces of politics and journalism. Among the students, the new nationalism was being nurtured by a consecrated bond of the nation-conscious *Afrikaanse Nasionale Studentebond.*"

Dr N Diederichs, Dr P J Meyer and Dr G Cronje, all leading Broederbonders, moved from campus to campus addressing and inspiring the students. Diederichs, then a professor of political philosophy at Grey University College, had just published his study of nationalism as a world-view in 1936.

"It was, in many respects, to form the cornerstone of the great theorising which was to arise from the fundamentals of the nation. At the secret heart of all this activity was the deep inner circle of the Broederbond. Nothing so stirringly spoken by Diederichs, Meyer and Cronje could find public utterance before it had been the subject of intense pondering and discussion by this "Band of Brothers" so completely devoted to the cause of alienated Afrikanerdom. Its members were the true spiritual progenitors of the new idea which had already been born in 1935, somewhat prematurely perhaps but nevertheless lustily enough to provide the promise of vigorous future growth.

"Diederichs's treatise on nationalism as a world-view, as the basis of what would soon become the concept of "apartheid" or "separate development", was the first sustained statement of theologised politics to come from an Afrikaner."[5]

Dr G Cronje published *'n Tuiste vir die Nageslag* (A Home for Posterity) in 1945. "It was closely aligned to what Diederichs, Meyer and some others had written," De Klerk says, "but it was more than that. In its own way it was a remarkable piece of preliminary draughtsmanship for the coming system. Essentially, everything which was to be part of an "unfolding" of the redemptive idea of "apartheid" or "separate development" was contained in these pages."

Cronje's thesis was that it was the will of God that the Afrikaner should promote a policy of racial and cultural variety. "The Boer people have themselves gone through the crucible of imperialist and capitalist domination and exploitation," he wrote. "They still show the wounds and bruises of it all. Their national life and culture have been disrupted. As a nation they almost perished because they served the interests of other people. They know what it means to see their own destroyed, but they also know what it means to promote through their own efforts a national revival and restoration... The Boer national can therefore fully understand the suffering of the Bantu. It is that same imperialism and capitalism, having them believe that the foreign is better than what is their own, which seeks to destroy their tribal life."[6]

Cronje suggested complete separation of the races which would enable the Afrikaner nation to remain racially pure. The same racial policy would apply to all races. A separate homeland had to be given to the coloured people with a Coloured Council to look after their interests. Control had to be vested in white hands, otherwise it would be the end of the whites in Africa. In this way, the Bantu would also survive as a separate race with their own culture. He advocated immediate local racial segregation (later embodied in legislation for separate racial group areas) and dissolution of the mixed trade unions. He foresaw the need for a population register to distinguish between the races, especially between whites and coloureds.

"Cronje's concept was that of total separation, also territorially," says De Klerk. "Basically his total view was a remarkably correct forecast of what was to be attempted. The order which was ultimately to arise on the coming to power of the Afrikaners was not prepared to accept the demand for complete territorial separation. But almost every other detail of Cronje's vision would become a part of the socio-political ideal of apartheid. Even his alternative use of the word "separate development" was, in a sense, prophetic.

"The book formed the subject of intense discussions within the Broederbond. In the cells, Cronje's facts, figures and arguments were thoroughly dissected, critically weighed and basically accepted. What strikes the objective viewer after more than a generation is the assumption and unquestionable belief, in the writings and speeches of Meyer, Cronje and the other members of the new intellectual elite, that a new order would arise in which the Afrikaners would be able to implement the whole new concept of a reconstructed South Africa. On a par with this is their faith that this order would last for so long that the future could, in terms of the new vision, be finally secured."[7]

The *Afrikanerbond vir Rassestudie,* under the leadership of Broederbonders, studied the concept of apartheid from 1935. By 1943 Dr D F Malan had started to use the word in speeches, and in September 1944 a *Volkskongres* in Bloemfontein, organised by the Broederbond, accepted the policy. By 1945 Malan's Herenigde Nasionale Party embraced it as official policy.

Cronje published a second book *Regverdige Ras Apartheid* (A Just Racial Separation) in 1947. This time he was supported by two prominent Broederbonders, Professor E P Groenewald and Dr W Nicol, in their own contributions to the book.

"This was the situation in 1947, with the nationalist Afrikaners meeting in the Broederbond and elsewhere, talking into the small hours and cogitating on the new vision of a policy which would finally put an end to the incohate state of the country. A massive black proletariat was building up in the ghettos of the cities, posing a threat to the survival of the white race and especially to the Afrikaner nation, as lately conceived and described.[8]

"The growth of an intellectual elite out of the new *Burgerstand* was the true power behind the revolutionary idea of the forties. The broad basis was a great variety of "separatist" cultural societies and organisations, all under the aegis of the Broederbond: but with relatively few in the know and ostensibly linked by a strictly culturally concerned co-ordinating organisation."[9]

This was manifested in the National Party's commission to formulate the policy before the May 1948 election. The chairman was a Broeder, Mr Paul Sauer, and his commission supported the concept of apartheid enthusiastically because it was, according to them, based on the Christian principle of right and justice. The races would be separated socially and politically, influx control and labour control would be instituted, Bantu trade unions would not be allowed, in the House of Assembly and Cape Provincial Council "native representation" would be abolished.

"The report could be seen as a statement of the new theologised nationalism with all its corollaries and its conclusive crystallisation after its growth of a decade or more. The students whom Diederichs, Meyer and Cronje had addressed so stirringly in the late thirties, had by this time reached political maturity and were already impatiently hammering at the portals of politics. Among them was B J Vorster, who had been active in the Ossewabrandwag during the war, and had been interned by Smuts for his pains. As a student at Stellenbosch and a leading figure in student politics, he had listened attentively to the speeches by Diederichs, Meyer and Cronje."[10]

Thus the Broederbond had set the scene for the spectacular victory of its political arm, the National Party, in 1948. The concept of apartheid gripped the imagination of the white electorate and ensured victory. They saw it as a policy which would protect them against the black masses and guarantee their survival. Without the painstaking efforts of the Broederbond and its leading members in evolving the policy, the 1948 victory would have been impossible.

Since 1948 the implementation of the apartheid or separate development policy had been firmly in the hands of Broederbonders. All the successive Ministers of Bantu Affairs, Dr E G Jansen, Dr H F Verwoerd, Mr M C de Wet Nel, Mr M C Botha, and now Dr Connie Mulder, as Minister of Plural Relations, were Broederbonders. Dr W Eiselen, also a prominent Broeder, was a driving force in implementing the policy in its early stages as Secretary for Bantu Affairs.

The pivotal figure giving content to and implementing the policy of separate development was Dr H F Verwoerd, former editor of *Die Transvaler,* and an extremely active member of the Broederbond on whose Executive he served. He was defeated in the 1948 general election in Alberton but entered Parliament as a Senator. In his first major speech in the Senate he said: "I want to state here unequivocally now the attitude of this side of the House, that South Africa is a white man's country and that he must remain the master here. In the reserves we are prepared to allow the Natives to be the masters, we are not masters there. But within the European areas, we, the white people in South Africa, are and shall remain the masters. We are prepared to accord to non-Europeans the right to their own opportunities and development, where we bring it about not by means of the sword, but through the benevolent hand of the Europeans who are in the country. Then we do not arouse the suspicion of the world outside ... that there is oppression but show them there is a policy which seeks right and justice toward all."[11]

Verwoerd became Minister of Native Affairs in 1950 and gathered round him officials like Eiselen, fired with Broederbond idealism to save Afrikanerdom from being swamped by blacks in its own country. Even after he became Prime Minister in 1958, Verwoerd still kept African affairs under his control by appointing a faithful follower and Broeder, Daan de Wet Nel, as Minister. All the major moves on black policy were made under his regime as Minister or Prime Minister. He kept in constant contact with the Broederbond by attending their meetings and conferring continuously with the Executive.

The Group Areas Act (1950), forcing people of different colours to live in separate areas, the Resettlement of Natives Act (1954), empowering the Government to remove 100 000 blacks from squatter camps in western Johannesburg to Meadowlands, the Immorality Amendment Act (1950), prohibiting sexual intercourse between black and white, the Population Registration Act (1950), enabling the Government to draw up race registers, the Reservation of Separate Amenities Act (1953), keeping the races apart in public places, the Abolition of Passes and Co-ordination of Documents Act (1952), designed to control the movements of blacks in the country, the Bantu Education Act (1953), the Extension of University Education Act (1959), to enforce university separation, the Bantu Authorities Act (1951) to establish self-government structures in the homelands, the Promotion of Bantu Self-Government Act (1959) and the Urban Councils Act (1961) followed each other in rapid succession.

South African society was being restructured by Verwoerd with a zeal, faith and enthusiasm never seen before.

"Never in history have so few legislated so programmatically, thoroughly and religiously, in such a short time, for so many divergent groups, cultures and traditions, than the nationalist Afrikaners of the second half of the 20th century. Never has such a small minority of all those affected done so much with such a high purpose, vocation and idealism. Never have so few drawn such sharply critical attention from a wondering world."[12]

Race relations is discussed at almost every Broederbond meeting in branches, regional conferences and annual meetings. Execution of the policy of separate development is seen as a prerequisite for the survival of Afrikanerdom, the most important task as far as the Broederbond is concerned. The organisation's chairmen devoted much time to the subject in their addresses to congresses, and there are scores of references to black/white relations in their secret documents.

At the 1968 *Bondsraad* meeting, the chairman, Dr Piet Meyer, once again stressed that the policy of separate development was the Broederbond's brainchild.

"Around 1933, our brotherhood commenced a task which later became one of the main tasks of the national political ideal, namely the arrangement of a healthy relationship between white and non-white to the maintenance advantage of every separate national group.

"In 1935 the *Bondsraad* accepted a policy statement in which our policy of separate development was set out on principled and logical grounds. The implementation of the policy was not only set out in broad terms but ordained and planned in advance with astounding vision of future developments up to the establishment of different self-governing Bantu homeland governments. It also served as guidance for Broeders in the National Party to popularise it as public policy. Later the Afrikaner Broederbond formed SABRA to investigate this policy scientifically and to propagate it. The role that our Brotherhood played in implementing our policy of separate development and at the same time good neighbourliness with the former Protectorates and other African states, can never be overestimated. And with this we have persevered to the present day while the same task still stretches into the far future.

"In our efforts to find a morally defensible Christian way of co-existence between white and non-white in our country and on our borders, the Broederbond came in direct contact with the two biggest and most dangerous present-day forces of the dark bedevilling relations, namely communism and liberalism. These are forces which enter the spirit of the people and can not be stopped by solely political and military defence methods – forces which must be fought on religious, cultural and political grounds. It was therefore the Afrikaans churches and the Afrikaner Broederbond which worked for the closure of the British embassy in Pretoria, started the battle against communism through the formation of well-disposed organisations in the trade union field, especially in the clothing and mining industries, and which alerted the nation and the country to the danger through the church congress on communism and later the *Volkskongres* on communism."

In the same speech, in the prophetic *Brotherhood the next 50 years: 1968–2018,* Dr Meyer said: "Our Brotherhood in action in the coming years demands the further consistent implementation of which and Bantu relations on the basis of our policy of separate development – the self-development of every national group in their own areas. On the same Christian-moral basis we will have to get more clarity on the independent self-development of the coloured and Indian communities in our midst, with or without their own homelands... There are no impersonal, legalistic short cuts to healthy human relations. To carry this message to everybody in our country is a necessity of Brotherhood in the future which we cannot and may not sidestep."

At the same secret meeting the former Prime Minister, Mr Vorster, said: "The basis of the policy of separate development is not a denial of a person's right to be a human being. It is the maintenance of the identity of everyone, the creation of opportunities which did not exist before and which would not exist under any other policy. For the rest it is a practical arrangement to remove friction between races. And it is in this that the world has not succeeded. The English could not do it in Britain, neither could the Americans in the USA."

Mr Vorster said that despite world opinion against South Africa, understanding of the country's policy was growing. "I believe that one day people will come to South Africa not only to enjoy the sunshine and the climate, but to see how it is possible that people of different languages, colours, outlooks and religions can live so calmly and peacefully in the same geographic area as we do here in South Africa."

Another speaker at the *Bondsraad* was Dr Andries Treurnicht who also praised the Broederbond's role in the implementation of the policy. "The Afrikaner Broederbond with its strong accent on the continued existence of the Afrikaner nation – also as a white nation – made no small contribution to the fact that the policy of separation with the view to separate nationhood was accepted and implemented successfully."

Dr Meyer also referred to the policy in his subsequent chairman's addresses.

1969: "For the Afrikaner Broederbond a spineless Afrikanerdom which wants to maintain itself... means the beginning of an increasing white/non-white integration process which will eventually destroy both groups... To think that these relationships will develop healthily and happily through the mere propagation of pleasant, sentimental manners and the removal of so-called 'petty apartheid' is very unrealistic."

1970: Dr Meyer said one of the measures the Nationalist Government undertook after the 1948 victory which could not easily be changed was the introduction of separate development. "They placed the country inexorably on the road of apartheid. On this road there could be no turning back. Hendrik Verwoerd was unquestionably the great architect of the independence of our Bantu nations... It is clear that the postwar South Africa and postwar world have moved in different directions and have become diametrically opposed... We must therefore accept that world animosity against our country in the years to come will increase rather than decrease as long as we continue our policy of separate development unambiguously and undiluted... We must never accede to any demands to scrap or water down our policy of separate development and anti-communism ... all forms of integration in our country must be fought and rejected on all fronts – in the churches, and in the social, cultural, economic and political spheres. After all, integration of any description and involving any non-white nation, means a victory for the antagonistic postwar world in which we live."

1972: Dr Meyer warned that Afrikaner unity was a prerequisite for the successful implementation of all policies. "Our unity programme to be of any concrete help demands therefore that all our Afrikaans cultural powers must be united in, and remain in, one national political party. We dare not go into an election with the Afrikaner national political power divided... It is beyond question that the most important result of decisive Afrikaner political power in conjunction with Afrikaner economic power will be the stable and consistent implementation of our policy of separate development... If the outside world should get the impression that we are beginning to doubt our own policy and are prepared to dilute it, then the independent existence of our Republic as white territory will be seriously jeopardised... Our Afrikaner existence is seriously threatened today as it has been from the beginning. The most critical period was when other nations in this country demanded it for themselves. Oom Paul said clearly 'They do not want to vote, they do not want a share in our country – they want our country.' We are experiencing it again today – many non-white leaders claim our country, South Africa, for the Africans forming a numerical majority there. They are supported by the United Nations, the Russians and Chinese and by almost the whole Western world. They will not be satisfied with the abolition of the Immorality Act and job reservation, with the reduction of the pay-gap between white and non-white, with sports integration, the removal of so-called 'petty apartheid', eliminating social separation between 'civilised' people of all races – no, only the take-over of power by the numerically strong 'Africans' will satisfy them. While we continue with the consistent implementation of our policy of separate development, while we from our side try to remove all unnecessary and avoidable points of friction between us and the non-whites, and while we try to make as many friends as possible for our policy, we must not neglect to strengthen and protect our *Afrikanerskap* and the independent existence of our White South African nature in all ways against the onslaught of our enemies demanding our country for themselves. Let us continue with the fulfilment of our divinely ordained calling in our country and in Africa in the knowledge that it is God's road with and for our nation."

In the approach to the racial question of the new chairman, Professor Gerrit Viljoen, there was a strong shift of emphasis. It is more pragmatic than his predecessors' and more in line with Mr Vorster's thinking. He emphasised the need for more *development* rather than the separation aspect, the need for a new deal for urban blacks, and the removal of discrimination based on colour. At the same time he kept within the framework of separate development, however. In his 1976 chairman's address Professor Viljoen listed the tasks ahead.

Task 3: "Effective and continuous implementation of our homeland policy so that the aim we seek can be achieved – the establishment of existence potential and therefore political homes for the majority of black people in their own homelands or states in order to form the basis of the maintenance of political power by whites in the so-called white country,

Task 4: "For the great number of blacks living in the white area and to remain there for a long time, decent living conditions, effective local self-government and maintenance of law and order must be ensured. The basic rules of human social engineering make it essential that acceptable procedures and structures for local *self-government,* leadership and expression of views should be created. (Here we must bear in mind that the present policy of homeland liaison with urban management entails serious problems for the future when the homelands become independent.) Is local self-government for urban blacks in conflict with the principle of refusing to share power in national government? Can we let them live in the present unprotected way in the black cities?

"Blacks must get a measure of autonomy to maintain law and order and put down gangsterism in the black urban areas. We will have to get away from the old idea that life in locations must be made as uncomfortable as possible to encourage migration to the homelands.

No matter how successful the homelands are, there will still be hundreds of thousands of blacks in white cities' locations and certain *minimum comforts* are essential such as home ownership, a better physical environment, services like lights, water, sanitation, trading facilities, sport and recreation. The cost can be covered by taxes, rents or the money paid for houses and it is not necessary for everything to be given to them."

Task 6: "Giving practical effect to the much-discussed elimination of unnecessary separation measures. Reviewing laws or regulations which benefit ourselves at the expense of others, for instance aspects of the Group Areas Act and job reservation. The urgent necessity for an Afrikaner initiative to make contact through the fence which divides our nations, for example welfare work, educational help, commercial help, advice to workers; the necessity to ensure in future more consultation with black and brown people during policy formulation, instead of a unilateral decision being taken over their heads – a prerequisite for knowing and understanding each other's circumstances to an unusual extent. There is a strong demand among developed blacks for normal acceptance by the *Boer-Baas* and to be addressed and treated as an equal human being.

"In this connection it must however be remembered that an authoritarian structure is at its most vulnerable when it embarks on self-analysis and the correction of its shortcomings. Then precautions must be taken against confusing your own people and undermining their instinct for self-preservation, and also against provoking expectations on a revolutionary scale among those affected by the system. At the same time the necessary corrective measures must be identified and implemented timeously. Too little, too late can be counter-productive and look like concessions made under pressure."

Task 7: "Re-examination of our long-term vision of our *white homeland.* Can we keep the whole of White South Africa for ourselves indefinitely in our exclusive white control, or will we have to be satisfied with a smaller but truly white area? Must we not think again in our inner circle about Dr Eiselen's idea of a neutral or grey area with political power shared by white and non-white, alongside a smaller, exclusive white state?"

It is obvious that the Soweto riots had a profound effect on the Broederbond thinking. A comparison between some of Professor Viljoen's earlier speeches and his 1976 chairman's address delivered in October, about three months after the riots, shows a new awareness that something drastic will have to be done urgently.

One of the practical contributions he made was to follow up his own suggestion of more contact with black leaders. Most of these talks were of a confidential nature, but in August 1978 a series of meetings between him and Dr Motlana, the Committee of Ten chairman, was publicised in the daily Press although statements were not attributed to individuals. The significance of these meetings was that Dr Motlana, who had been jailed without trial only a short while before, was now in a position to talk man to man to the Broederbond chief about the grievances of urban blacks. No doubt the implication would get through to the Broederbond and the Cabinet.

After Professor Viljoen's speech pleading for more contact, the Broederbond sent out guidelines to branches on how such meetings should take place (Circular 3/3/77).

6.1 "Liaison should preferably take place in the national context. The nation-divisions must be respected and increasingly maintained. We are too prone to think as liberally inclined people do in terms of black-white-brown categories.

6.2 "Liaison must be functional and purposeful, and follow a prepared agenda. Objectives must be set which can be followed up, so that liaison does not in practice increase frustration.

6.3 "The personnel for meetings must be selected with a view to effectiveness. They must be knowledgeable people who can act spontaneously and naturally in the situation, and stand their ground without being hostile.

6.4 "Liaison and meetings must always respect the principle of

separate development and work towards its acceptance. Thus liaison with leading teachers must respect the essence of nation-tied education, that with business leaders at the development of an independent economy, with cultural leaders with due regard for the role of culture in national life, with church leaders with regard for that diversity within unity which is professed and striven for.
"The following negative aspects can be considered.
1. "Liaison does not take place in the spirit of 'Bring me a black man, I want to hear what he thinks.'
2. "Liaison is not a pretext for expressing grievances and inducing guilt.
3. "It is not to provide a forum for notorious critics to fulminate against whites, specifically the Afrikaner.
4. "Liaison does not take place because it is the fashion. The black man becomes allergic to worthless talks with whites."

The Broederbond has a watchdog committee for African affairs which keeps the organisation in touch with the latest developments and trends. Over the years it has circulated many newsletters and in-depth research papers. It has urged members to encourage young people to treat people of other colours decently and respectfully, made an appeal to members in leading positions to speak more positively on separate development in public, distributed a booklet on blacks in urban areas, and called on members to co-operate with the Government on homeland consolidation ("One of the most difficult facets of the policy of separate development").

In Circular 3/2/75 members were informed that the Government was taking control of mission hospitals in the homelands. "Almost 40 per cent of the white personnel at these hospitals are recruited overseas. Because of their background and political views some of them are often hostile towards State policy, sometimes in a very subtle way. Recently complaints have been received from several homeland leaders about improper interference by mission hospital personnel in their politics. It is obvious that the Government cannot tolerate this state of affairs... Members are requested to bring the matter pertinently to the attention of well-disposed South Africans to ensure its better understanding. Members are also requested to encourage doctors and paramedical personnel to make their services available. Members who are interested can contact Head Office for more details."

In Circular 5/76/77 members were advised that *Black De-*

velopment in South Africa had been published in Afrikaans, English, German and French. It was based on research by the Bureau for Economic Research on Bantu Development (BENBO) and the Broederbond prepared from it a brochure for members. "Many of the topics considered by our own committee on relationships with the Bantu are dealt with in the book. Some of our members, and members of the above-mentioned committee, played a very important role in the preparation of the book."

From 1972 the Broederbond and the Government became aware that one of the biggest policy weaknesses was legally entrenched colour discrimination. Officials of the department of Foreign Affairs and Information and other government agencies all came back from overseas with the same message: legal discrimination based on colour is indefensible in the eyes of the world. Here too the Broederbond used its massive influence, to get the Government to accept "the elimination of unnecessary discrimination."

In Circular 5/3/75 it told its members: "Recently many leaders stressed that as the implementation of separate development proceeds, we must from time to time consider whether the reasons for certain discriminatory measures have not perhaps lapsed because of changing circumstances and should therefore be reviewed. The Executive is convinced that our organisation can and must play an important role in promoting healthy consideration of this delicate subject. Especially in view of our confidentiality the issue is ideally suited for our productive discussions openly, in brotherhood, with mutual trust in each other...

"The Executive has decided to make this topical matter of the elimination of discrimination the subject of regional meetings. A nation-wide discussion will be held between one or two representatives of each regional council and the Executive on Saturday June 7 1975."

The Executive also included with the newsletter an exposition of the subject and urged the branches to discuss it as soon as possible. The exposition started with a quote from Dr H F Verwoerd, the apostle of apartheid, to prove that elimination of discrimination was not a deviation from basic policy. "The policy of separate development is not a policy on entrenching discrimination, but exactly the opposite. As the policy is implemented, discrimination will be reduced more and more."

Then a long list of "guidelines" is given, showing that the subsequent discussions were arranged merely to *inform* the network of the Executive's decisions – based on the conclusions of its own expert commission – rather than to ask the rank-and-file membership for a decision.

2.1 "Measures necessary to keep political control of the white man's future in his own hands must not disappear. Thus no form of political power-sharing with non-white nations is acceptable.

2.2 "Certain measures are necessary for the maintenance of white identity (for example separate schools, living areas and the Immorality Act).

2.3 "The numerical factor must be considered. In some cases the numerical strength of the non-white might create problems in the absence of adequate separation, while in others the sophistication of the facility will create a natural qualitative and quantitative selection which makes forced suburban trains with the Blue Train or SAA flight, a sophisticated provincial theatre with ordinary popular bioscopes or theatres.

2.4 "Any measure which is necessary to maintain peace and order and eliminate friction between races remains justified.

2.5 "Some measures are necessary, to avoid embarrassment, as a result of different standards of hygiene among the different national groups.

2.6 "The white has, in spite of his willingness to share certain amenities with non-whites, the right to demand privacy and exclusivity in his own area. Therefore, if facilities are opened to other national groups this must not be enforced or in a way that discriminates against the whites. It is, for example, the white's right to reserve certain shows or evenings for his people without being ashamed of it.

2.7 "Discriminatory measures which are hurtful and humiliating without achieving anything positive cannot be justified.

2.8 "The opening of certain amenities for non-whites can be justified if such amenities cannot be duplicated for them in the foreseeable future for economic reasons ... Here precautions must be taken to avoid delaying the cultural development of a national group ... by deferring or cancelling the provision of separate facilities.

2.9 "It must always be clear that the removal of unjust discrimination does not flow from the idea of a multiracial common society, and is not to be used as an argument to combat any differentiating measures related to basic separate development.

2.10 "Appropriate steps must be taken timeously, to avoid the impression that a concession has been made under pressure. Precautions must also be taken against unwholesome feelings of guilt and self-pity which lead to leaning over backwards with ill-considered adaptations mainly constituting plain capitulations."

The newsletter then appealed for proper human relations, the elimination of friction, provision of necessary facilities for blacks in urban areas and along the national roads, places where leading blacks and whites could meet, and restrooms and eating places for blacks working in the cities. Finally, it called for separate development to be speeded up through the reduction of blacks in the cities, establishment of towns, houses and transport in the homelands, more work opportunities in the homelands and border areas, and the consolidation of the homelands. On November 1 1977 branches were sent a questionnaire asking what had been done in their areas regarding the provision of separate facilities in shopping centres and elsewhere, and the removal of unnecessary discrimination as defined in the 1975 circular.

Over the years the Broederbond has sent its branches lengthy study documents after reports from its expert committees. These include *Consolidation of the Homelands, Separate Development and Self-Development, White Entrepreneurs on an Agency Basis in the Bantu Homelands, Measures for the Encouragement of Industrial Development in the Border Areas, Multi-National Liaison of the Scientific Sphere, Independence of the Transkei, Development of the Bantu through Industrial Development in Border Areas* and *Progress with Homeland Development.*

At the beginning of 1976 (circular of May 3 1976) the Executive recalled that it had previously stressed the need for 'a masterplan for white survival'. It went on: "Meanwhile the Executive's expert committee on our relationship with the Bantu has been busy with intensive studies and discussions with Broeders in responsible circles (Cabinet ministers and senior civil servants) and has gathered important material for the masterplan. Some preliminary facts giving an idea of the vastness of this task are given here.

"Population growth, settlement and housing, linked with the cost of express transport, are the basic problems facing us. Scientific studies show that the population for which the 22 Bantu administration boards have to provide housing is increasing by 4 per cent a year and will reach 11 261 167 by the year 2000. This implies an increase of 1 172 818 houses. Assuming an inflation rate of

10 per cent a year, the cost for housing and public buildings in white areas would be R17 381 196 624.

"If the houses were to be built in a Bantu area, important factors enter the calculation.

2.1 "If towns are established on land already belonging to the South African Bantu Trust, the cost of ground is eliminated. There is another aspect. The Bantu buy the house and the plot from the Bantu Trust so that much less State capital is required.

2.2 "The exciting aspect is that capital returned to the State in this way can be used for transport services to homelands... It is possible to build more than 6 000 km of roads for R1 343-million.

1.3 "The committee is therefore working on a national development plan in which all the factors of labour, housing, consolidation, decentralisation and transport services can be co-ordinated. More details will be made available later."

In August and September two parts of this plan were circulated secretly to Broederbond branches.

They make it evident that the Broederbond:

(1) Will consider adaptations only within the framework of separate development;

(2) Will not even contemplate the sharing of power in the white part of South Africa;

(3) Sees the solution to South Africa's racial problem in the faster and more meaningful implementation of separate development through:

(a) Consolidation of the homelands;
(b) Creation of more job opportunities in the homelands;
(c) Establishment of towns in the homelands which will draw Africans from the cities;
(d) Provision of attractive *single* accommodation in urban areas;
(e) Establishing a system of express transport to enable blacks to live in the homelands and work in the "white" cities;
(f) Provision of amenities in urban areas leading to self-government without sharing national political power;
(g) The removal of unnecessary discrimination as defined in the 1975 circular.

The plan (August, Part 2A) makes the Broederbond view quite clear. "It must be said candidly that there is no alternative to the policy of multinational development in South Africa... The will and determination to make it succeed must be not only a slogan but a life philosophy... One stipulation remains paramount and that is that economic co-operation (with the homelands) and economic interdependence can be developed to full advantage only if *political power has been finally divided* and is accepted as such by black and white, especially by those black communities still relatively permanent in the white homeland... Those who do not willingly fall in with this cardinal precept must be compelled to do so in their own interests... Anyone who rejects the highest honour and right of every individual on earth, to be governed by himself and to have his status respected and recognised by others, must be prepared to accept the dishonourable status of enslavement and the conditions accompanying it. It is in any case his own decision.

"... It is the main aim of this plan to let the blacks settle and work as far as is practicable in their respective homelands. Where that is not possible, it is intended to let them live in their own homelands while working on a daily basis in the white areas... The positive encouragement of travelling between homeland and work *(pendelverkeer)* not only on a daily basis, but especially on a weekly and even monthly basis, now deserves urgent attention as an aspect of planning... Employers will be required to change the contracts of monthly commuters to enable them to be at home every month for a long weekend."

The plan also provides for sending to the homelands for development purposes as much as possible of the money earned by blacks in white areas. It suggests consideration of an additional levy on employers who do not use commuter labour. It therefore appears that a big assault must be launched on the 36,3 per cent in commerce and service sector and that it must be regarded in future planning as extremely high priority (because most of the married, settled black labour occur in this category).

The circular summed up: "The few elements whose motives and insidious intentions are not in accordance with these aims, must be identified and gradually neutralised."

The third part of the masterplan, entitled *The Strategy* (September 1976) said the position of the white South African was untenable unless the plan was accepted and implemented. It reiterated that the plan must be imposed to ensure co-ordination of all State departments and statutory bodies. The Prime Minister should establish a Development Council with its own chairman, to include all the departments and bodies dealing with planning and under the direct control of the Prime Minister. "To enable it to call directly upon the Prime Minister, the council must come under his control and then, with the help of a Cabinet committee, ensure that the council's recommendations are enforcible."

The plan suggested that as a quid pro quo encouraging blacks to accept homeland citizenship, there would be no discrimination in white areas against blacks with such citizenship. "Thus acceptance of (homeland) citizenship and the identification of blacks with their own countries, will be given a positive value while the danger will be eliminated of discrimination being abolished to give the Bantu in white areas more rights and privileges."

The masterplan suggested a review of all statutory measures giving permanence to blacks in white areas. The review was to include Article 10 of the Bantu (Urban Areas) Consolidation Act of 1945 – virtually the only basis for permanence for Africans born in the urban area and that applying only to those who had the same employer for more than ten years. Significantly, it suggested a reduction of the number of Bantu administration boards – a "suggestion" promptly followed by the Government. "Every Board should be instructed to implement the masterplan for the Bantu homeland and the white area in which it operates," the document added. It called for prompt "public action" supported by an organisation with the necessary funds and manpower to provide a positive climate for the implementation of the masterplan.

The document envisaged the support of Afrikaans churches, the FAK, SABC, Press, other media, educationists, including the teachers' associations, academic action, the SA Agricultural Union with its provincial and district organisations, the *Afrikaanse Handelsinstituut* and its *sakekamers,* the Federated Chamber of Industries, labour organisations, municipal associations, womens' organisations, youth organisations, Rapportryers, Junior Rapportryers and other organisations to propagate and implement the masterplan. It foresees a commonwealth of southern African states. It calls for a kind of Marshall Plan assisting the development of the homelands, and the holding of a multinational homelands convention on Government level to discuss matters of common concern. "A basis for a commonwealth of South African states can be laid in this way."

Then the Broederbond advises homelands, from its own experience, how to take control of the political situation.

"Just as in the white country, a central body must be established for every homeland to mould public opinion in favour of policy.

In this, the national leader, the mass media and especially the radio will play important parts. The following should be emphasised.

8.1 "Nationalism as the foundation... Every available resource must be thrown into the battle to inculcate a Christian national philosophy among black nations.

8.2 "The key role of the teaching profession.

8.3 "The influence of the leader... These leaders must be recognised not only by their own people but also by the whites.

8.4 "The importance of sport. The value of sport cannot be overestimated. Not only has it cultural value, but it fosters national pride and patriotism. Sportsmen become national heroes... Sports facilities must be established in the homelands (compare Mabanto Freedom Stadium).

8.5 "Concentration on the youth.

8.6 "Attention to economic leaders.

8.7 "Power of the mass media. The radio services for the respective black nations must play a giant role here. Public opinion in sympathy with the homelands must be built up... it must culminate in a *volksbeweging*."

The question of whether SABRA should be the co-ordinating body is left open.

It is a Broederbond blueprint for the blacks. The comprehensive formula which brought the Bond to power was now being handed over to the individual ethnic groups. The circular ended chillingly: "Events in the past weeks have spelt out in flames and blood that the status quo can no longer last..."

In Groote Schuur, Cape Town, somebody else was pondering the bloodshed and violence in the townships. He too came back to the original concept – separate development. In the circular of November 22 1976 the Executive reported on its meeting with the Prime Minister, B J Vorster. "The Executive was riveted by the declaration of faith with which the Prime Minister recently concluded a frank discussion. He stressed with great determination that his profound analysis of the recent trying months and weeks had convinced him anew that there is no way to handle race relations but the way of separate development. He added that the greatest legacy of Dr Verwoerd was his vision of separate homelands which could be developed to full independence. Without the homeland policy, he said, we would now have been in the same position as Rhodesia. He called on the AB to take stock and throw everything into the battle to maintain and promote this policy."

1. Tomlinson Commission report, p 23.
2. *The Speeches of General the Rt Hon J C Smuts,* pp 17–18.
3. De Klerk, W A, *The Puritans in Africa,* p 199.
4. Ibid. pp 202–203.
5. Ibid. pp 203–204.
6. Cronje, G, *A Home for Prosperity,* p 24.
7. De Klerk, W A, *The Puritans in Africa,* p 219.
8. Ibid. p 223.
9. Ibid. p 229.
10 Ibid. pp 231–2.
11 Pelzer, A N, *Verwoerd aan die Woord,* p 16.
12. De Klerk, W A, *The Puritans in Africa,* p 241.

13 *Soweto – June 16*

June 16 1976 will forever remain memorable in South African history. It was a day that shook South Africa, and further undermined its already weak international position. It was the day Soweto exploded. For months afterwards, rioting continued in the vast dormitory township of about a million black people – Johannesburg's labour reservoir.

Most of the clashes took place between riot police and pupils at the black schools. The first major confrontation began when black and white police in a car from Orlando police station intercepted marching children and attempted to remove posters protesting the compulsory use of Afrikaans in black schools. Between four and five thousand children were going from school to school, urging pupils to join a mass boycott of classes.

It is difficult to establish exactly what happened in the melee that followed. Pupils would claim the police fired first – the police version was that they were stoned and were forced to retaliate by opening fire. The first victim, Hector Peterson aged 16, was carried off by his crying schoolmates when the crowd dispersed. The rioting continued and 23 people, including three whites, died on the first day in Soweto. Among them was Dr Melville Edelstein who had devoted his life to social welfare among blacks. He was stoned to death by the mob. Millions of rands worth of damage was done in the ensuing days as schools, buses, beerhalls and bottlestores were set alight by pupils. These places were seen as symbols of "the white man's system". Buses were withdrawn and clinics closed.

Violence spread to the East and West Rand, northern Natal and Cape Town. Army and other defence force units were on standby as the townships were gripped by mob violence. Gangsters made the most of the situation, intimidating and robbing people and looting shops. Sporadic violence lasted several weeks. On June 18 *The Star's* banner headline said: "Townships ablaze all over Reef." At the end of 1976 the death toll stood at 499.

What caused the riots among schoolchildren?

There can be no doubt that there can be many reasons, the strongest probably their hatred of the system of apartheid which relegated them to a position of inferiority and poverty throughout the whole South African structure. Shortly before, they had witnessed a dispirited and virtually defeated Portugal withdrawing from Mozambique and Angola and handing over control to black guerilla movements. This had a profound effect on black South Africans striving for a better deal, but the young blacks also felt strongly that salvation did not lie with their elders. They were regarded as too timid, intimidated by the white man. They had drifted along like Uncle Toms, so dependent on their jobs that they were scared to move.

National Party commentators later blamed "agitators" for inciting the young people to riot. The truth is, of course, that people do not lightly riot and take their lives into their own hands. Agitators can be successful only if the audience is responsive, the people unhappy and discontented. This was so in Soweto.

And while one can find many general reasons for the riots, the straw that broke the camel's back was the issue of Afrikaans in black schools. This produced the boycotts and was the immediate cause of the first riots. It is extremely unlikely that the violence would have taken place at all if the Government, under pressure from the Broederbond, had not provided this spark. *The Star* summed up on June 18: "The Afrikaans teaching issue was certainly the spark but there are other things behind the riots, other factors which edged Soweto towards violence." It is ironical that the Broederbond, born out of the frustration caused by Lord Milner's policy of anglicising Afrikaners, should blunder a few decades later by trying to force its own language on blacks. That they of all people did not learn the lessons of their own history will remain one of the most inexplicable aspects of the organisation.

Their fanatical determination to inculcate Afrikaans did not stop with Afrikaners and mother-tongue education. Their drive to Afrikanerise English-speakers and immigrants (see Chapter 8) spread to other groups. Through the years they repeatedly discussed at secret meetings with Cabinet Ministers how they could get blacks to accept Afrikaans as a second language, instead of English.

The Department of Bantu Education became a powerful means to this end. Loaded with Broeders, from the Minister downwards, the department was instructed to ensure that Afrikaans became a compulsory teaching language in black schools. The Broederbond issued an extensive circular with details of employment opportunities in the department. The minutes of an Executive Council meeting held on March 21 1968 stated: "(P) AFRIKAANS AND BANTU EDUCATION. The Babanango division is of the opinion that Afrikaans as spoken word is neglected in Bantu education. Broeders in responsible circles (Cabinet) have confirmed that much has already been done to give Afrikaans its rightful place, but that there were many problems. It is recommended that the Executive refer this issue to Broeders in the department with the request that serious attention should be paid continuously to the use of Afrikaans in Bantu education."

Two years before the Soweto riots, the Department of Bantu Education sent out a circular stating that half the subjects in secondary schools had to be taught in Afrikaans. The circular, issued by Bantu Education's regional director in the Southern Transvaal, Mr W C Ackerman, was clear: arithmetic, mathematics and social studies had to be taught in Afrikaans; science, woodwork, arts and crafts in English. Headmasters in Soweto schools protested, and representations were made to Mr M C Botha, a leading Broeder and Minister of Bantu Education. The pleas were turned down. Shortly after the outbreak of the riots, blacks identified the Afrikaans issue as the cause. Mr Ernest Mchunu, a head messenger, told the *Rand Daily Mail* on June 19: "They come home after school saying how much they hate Afrikaans, but it is only because they are forced to study it." Black teachers were adamant that Afrikaans was at the root of the rioting.[1] Mr Wilkie Kambule, headmaster of Soweto's biggest school, said: "The main reason is that young blacks these days tend to be radical and they see Afrikaans as part of the people in authority."

There was ample warning that tension would build up over the language issue. Mr Ackerman's circular provoked a series of protests. The African Teachers' Association wrote to the Minister of Bantu Education "that it is cruel and shortsighted."[2] The joint school and committee boards of the southern and northern Transvaal regions met officials from Bantu Education. Homeland leaders requested the Prime Minister that "the medium of instruction in Bantu schools in the white areas should be the same as that in schools in the corresponding homeland.[3]" The Deputy Minister, Mr Punt Jansen, said in Parliament he had not consulted blacks "and I am not going to consult them" on the language issue.[4]

The South African Institute of Race Relations drew up a calendar of events from January 1 1976, disclosing the growing anger over the enforcement of Afrikaans in black schools, as part of its testimony to the Cillie Commission of Inquiry into the riots. The institute subsequently published a book entitled *South Africa in Travail: Disturbances of 1976/77* in which this calendar appears.

EVENTS OF 1976 WHICH CULMINATED IN THE DISTURBANCES OF JUNE 1976

(This chronology is based largely on newspaper reports)

JANUARY

20 January: A meeting of the Meadowlands Tswana Board at the Moruto-Thuto Lower Primary School. Minutes of the meeting read: "The circuit inspector told the board that the Secretary for Bantu Education has stated that all direct taxes paid by the black population of South Africa are being sent to the various homelands for educational purposes there.

"In urban areas the education of a black child is being paid for by the white population, that is English and Afrikaans-speaking groups. Therefore the Secretary for Bantu Education has the responsibility towards satisfying the English- and Afrikaans-speaking people.

"Consequently, the only way of satisfying both groups, the medium of instruction in all schools shall be on a 50-50 basis.

"The circuit inspector further stated that where there was difficulty in instruction in the medium of Afrikaans an application for exemption can be made. He stated that if such an exemption is granted by the Department of Bantu Education, it shall be applicable for one year only.

"In future, if schools teach through a medium not prescribed by the department for a particular subject, examination question papers will only be set in the prescribed medium with no option of the other language. The circuit inspector stated that social studies (history and geography) and mathematics shall be taught through the medium of Afrikaans, physical science and the rest through the medium of English.

"Asked whether the circuit inspector should not be speaking at the meeting in an advisory capacity, the inspector stated that he was representing the Department of Bantu Education directly.

"The board stated that they were not opposed to the 50-50 basis medium of instruction but that they wanted to be given the chance of choosing the language for each subject.

"The circuit inspector stated that the board has no right to choose for itself, but should do what the department wants. He suggested that the board could write to the department via himself and the regional director on this matter. At this juncture the circuit inspector excused himself and left the meeting.

"The board was not happy about the statements of the circuit inspector and stated that to write a letter would not offer any favourable reply.

"The board unanimously accepted a motion moved by Mr K Nkamela and seconded by Mr S G Thwane, that the medium of instruction in schools under the jurisdiction of the Meadowlands Tswana School Board from Standards 3 to 8 should be in English. The meeting further resolved that the principals be informed about the decision."

FEBRUARY

Early in February two members of the Meadowlands Tswana School Board, Mr Letlape and Mr Peele, were dismissed. In the Assembly on 27 February the Deputy Minister stated that they were dismissed in terms of regulation 41(1) of Government Notice R429 dated 19 March 1966, which states that the regional director may, "if he is of the opinion that the continued existence of any school board or the membership of any member of any school board is, for whatever reason not in the interest of the Bantu community or the education of Bantu, at any time dissolve such school board and order the constitution of a new school board or terminate the membership of such member of any school board."

The regional director gave no reasons for the dismissals, but it was believed that they were due to the board's refusal to use Afrikaans as a medium of instruction in their schools.

6 February: The remaining seven members of the board resigned in protest at the dismissal of Messrs Peele and Letlape.

Mr W C Ackerman, regional director of Bantu Education for the Southern Transvaal, refused to comment on the matter. Mr M A N Engelbrecht, chief inspector of schools, in a statement to the *Rand Daily Mail,* said that black schools were entitled to choose between English and Afrikaans as a medium of instruction depending on proficiency, that the choice was made through an application by the principal of the school which is considered by the Secretary of the Department of Bantu Education, and that it was a professional matter that fell outside the jurisdiction of the school boards.

Chief Lucas Mangope took up the matter with the Central Government and subsequently reported that the school boards were free to choose the medium of instruction to be used in their schools.

24 February: Junior Certificate students at Thomas Mofolo Secondary School clashed verbally with their principal over the medium of instruction and police were called in.

27 February: In the Assembly the Deputy Minister of Bantu Education, Dr Treurnicht, said that applications for exemption from the language ruling had been received from school principals, but that no statistics were kept of such applications. He went on to say, "The change-over to the twelve year structure has entailed that the principle in respect of the medium of instruction applicable in the case of secondary schools also becomes applicable in the case of Standard 5. Applications to deviate in these cases are considered in the light of: the availability of teachers proficient to teach through the medium of one of the official languages, the fact that textbooks in a certain language have already been supplied to the senior classes of the schools which the pupils will eventually attend."[5]

MARCH

Members of the Meadowlands Tswana School Board said they had been informed that they would only be reinstated if they withdrew a circular saying that schools under them should be instructed in English.

14 March: Parents at Donaldson Higher Primary School unanimously rejected the use of Afrikaans as medium of instruction.

APRIL

26 April: A delegation from the African Teachers' Association of South Africa met the Secretary for Bantu Education, to whom they presented a memorandum concerning medium of in-

struction, and reported that the problem was to be reviewed by the Department.
30 April: Opposition speakers in the House of Assembly called on the Government to allow black pupils to choose the official language in which they wished to be educated.

MAY

17 May: Students at Orlando West Junior Secondary School went on strike in protest against the enforced use of Afrikaans as medium of instruction. They demanded to see the inspector, Mr de Beer, but he refused to meet the pupils.
19 May: A committee of students from Orlando West presented a 5-point memorandum protesting against the use of Afrikaans as medium of instruction to their principal, Mr Mpulo. After several meetings with the principal and staff the students drafted a letter, stating their grievances, to the regional director.
Students at Belle Higher Primary School also went on strike.
20 May: Emthonjeni Higher Primary and Thulasizwe Higher Primary schools joined the strike.
21 May: Mr M C de Beer, circuit inspector for the striking schools, stated that the Department was "doing nothing about the matter."
22 May: A meeting of parents, school board members from various areas and Inkatha Yesizwe members was held and it was decided that students should return to school while the matter received attention.
24 May: Striking pupils ignored pleas by the Orlando-Diepkloof School Board to return to school.
Pimville Higher Primary and Khulangolwazi Higher Primary schools joined the strike.
25 May: The Director of the SAIRR[6] sent the following telegram to Mr R de Villiers, MP (a member of the Executive Committee of the Institute): "Deeply concerned Afrikaans medium controversy black schools x Position Soweto very serious x Could you discuss matter with Minister concerned." Mr de Villiers conveyed the contents of the telegram to the Deputy Minister of Bantu Administration, Dr Andries Treurnicht, who said he was not aware of any real problem, but would enquire about the matter. A day or so later Dr Treurnicht sent the following note to Mr de Villiers: "The problem with regard to the strike of pupils in Soweto is

being dealt with on a low level at the moment, and negotiations have not yet reached a point of deadlock. Nor has the matter been referred to the Secretary of the Department, although this might happen later. We will determine what the contributory causes are, but at the moment it is said that the pupils are striking because the teachers (according to the children?) are not capable of teaching subjects in Afrikaans! Possible the matter is not as simple as that" *(translation from the Afrikaans).*

26 May: Members of the SAIRR staff spoke to Mr T W Kambule, principal of Orlando High School. Mr Kambule stated that there was no doubt that principals and teachers at the striking schools were being intimidated by the circuit inspector, Mr de Beer. Apparently teachers, having been asked whether they could speak Afrikaans, to which they answered "Yes" for fear of losing their jobs, were then told that they could therefore teach through the medium of this language. (It should be borne in mind that African teachers have no language endorsement on their professional certificates, and that most teacher training colleges for Africans use English as medium of instruction.) Mr Kambule said that Mr Ackerman, Regional Director, had asked him to help mediate between the Department and the striking schools. He attended a meeting between Mr Ackerman and the principals of the schools and although he (Mr Kambule) *knew* that the schools did not have staff qualified to use Afrikaans as medium of instruction, when Mr Ackerman put the question to the principals, they all said that they did have the staff, undoubtedly because they were afraid of victimisation.

27 May: The first violent incident was recorded when Mr K Tshabalana, a teacher of Afrikaans at Pimville Higher Primary School, was stabbed with a screwdriver by a student. Students stoned police who came to make an arrest in connection with the stabbing.

According to various newspaper reports, Mr de Beer had threatened during May to expel pupils who stayed away from school for more than two weeks.

JUNE

1 June: Pupils at Senaoane Junior Secondary School went on strike.

3 June: Pupils at Emthonjene, Belle, Thulasizwe and Pimville

started returning to classes. Pupils were apparently told that lessons in mathematics and social studies – the subjects taught in Afrikaans – would be suspended for the time being.
5 June: Pupils at Belle Higher Primary School stoned the school buildings and other children who had returned to classes during the lull in the strike.
7 June: A pupil was arrested at Belle Higher Primary following the stoning incident on the 5th.

A five-man deputation from UBC[7], accompanied by Mr N P Wilsenach, the WRAB[8] director for housing, met Mr M C Ackerman, to discuss the school strikes. Mr Makhaya, chairman of the UBC, said the deputation had requested Mr Wilsenach to accompany them to speed up the appointment with Mr Ackerman. At the meeting Mr Ackerman said there was nothing he could do about the issue.
8 June: Police went to Naledi High School "to make some enquiries about the matter." Students stoned the police and burnt their car.

Fifteen pupils from Thulasizwe Higher Primary were detained, and released after questioning.
9 June: Pupils at Naledi High School again stoned policemen who had come to the school to investigate the previous day's disturbance.
10 June: Pupils at Emthonjeni refused to write their social studies exam in Afrikaans.
11 June: Pupils at Morris Isaacson High School posted a placard at the main gate reading "NO SB's allowed. Enter at the risk of your skin." According to a teacher, antagonism towards the police was running high at the school.

Students at Orlando West Junior Secondary refused to write their June exams.

The Deputy Minister of Bantu Education, in reply to a question in the Assembly, stated that this Department had no knowledge of the incident in which police were stoned at Naledi High School.[9] The SAIRR sent a further telegram to Mr de Villiers:

"Situation in Soweto schools re Afrikaans as a medium deteriorating daily x Violence already appeared and could easily be repeated. Trust Dr Treurnicht aware of situation."

Dr Treurnicht, on being informed of the contents of the telegram, said that he did not think there had been an escalation of the dispute, but would make further enquiries. Later he told Mr de

Villiers that he had spoken to his officials and had reason to believe that the matter would be amicably settled.

At a Press conference Dr Mathlare announced the inauguration on 4 July of the Soweto Residents' Association and said that a committee would be elected to "fully represent Soweto parents in matters concerning the recent school strikes," as many parents had agreed that school boards and committees were not representing them properly. He also said, "We reject Afrikaans as a medium of instruction because it is the language of the oppressor."

13 June: In an article in *Weekend World,* Mr T W Kambule, principal of Orlando High School, was quoted: "If teachers in the junior high schools accept or are forced to use Afrikaans, then the Government will have a good case in forcing Afrikaans as the medium of instruction in high schools. Schoolchildren are doing exactly what the parents and everybody feels about Afrikaans – only they have the courage to stand up against it."

14 June: Councillor Leonard Mosala warned that the enforcing of Afrikaans in schools could result in another Sharpeville. Speaking of the children, he said, "They won't take anything we say because they think we have neglected them. We have failed to help them in their struggle for change in schools. They are now angry and prepared to fight and we are afraid the situation may become chaotic at any time." He also said that police interference in the schools should be avoided at all costs, as the children might become aggressive at the sight of the police.

16 June: A march in protest against the use of Afrikaans as medium of instruction, apparently initiated by pupils of Naledi High School, moved through Soweto and converged on Orlando West Junior Secondary School, where the strikes had first started a month before. There was an incident where police tried to remove placards from the marchers. The 10 000 marchers were confronted by the police as they gathered in front of the school and tension increased, especially when police fired teargas into the crowd. The children retaliated by throwing stones at the police who opened fire, apparently first firing warning shots and then into the advancing children, killing at least one child, Hector Petersen.

Later, Dr Melville Edelstein was killed at Morris Isaacson High School and Mr N Esterhuizen, a WRAB official, was also beaten to death.

Police reinforcements were brought into Soweto and army

troops were placed on standby as rioting spread throughout Soweto and buildings and vehicles were burnt.

All schools were closed by the order of Mr M C Botha. In a statement in Parliament Mr Kruger, Minister of Justice and of Police, said: "Student unrest over dissatisfaction with their curriculum was brewing in Soweto for the past 10 days" (this was four weeks after the first school had gone on strike).

The Director of the SAIRR issued the following Press statement: "The tragic situation which has arisen in Soweto was entirely preventable. First, the enforced use of two new media of instruction in secondary education at the same time is educationally unsound, and the Bantu Education Department knows this. For months representations have been made by homeland leaders, school boards and other bodies. The African Teachers' Association saw the Secretary for Bantu Education on this issue late in April. Yet no conciliatory statement was issued by the Minister of Bantu Education who has now closed Soweto schools.

"Secondly, the pupil strikes in one area which preceded yesterday's more widespread demonstrations and subsequent rioting were due largely to inept handling of the language medium issue in one limited Soweto area. Here again warning signs and repeated requests for action were ignored, thus causing rising tension.

"Failure to act wisely in time is the prime cause of the deaths and injuries, of destruction of property and a tragic disturbance of public order and race relations.

"We appeal for wise and responsible guidance from the country's leaders."

17 June: Many pupils, apparently unaware of the suspension of classes, returned to school.

Rioting continued, apparently now led by *tsotsis*[10] who had taken advantage of the previous day's violence and had started looting.

Putco suspended bus services and all clinics in Soweto were closed.

Pupils in Tembisa demonstrated in sympathy with Soweto scholars and rioting broke out in Krugersdorp's Kagiso township.

In a statement in *Beeld* Dr Treurnicht said that in the white areas of South Africa the Government should have the right to decide the medium of instruction, as the Government supplies the buildings and subsidises the schools.

In the Assembly Mr Kruger, Minister of Police, said that the

Government had not expected the riots in Soweto to result from the school strikes against Afrikaans as medium of instruction, and that the language question was not really the cause of the riots. The Minister also announced the appointment of Mr Justice Cillie as a one-man commission of inquiry into the causes of the riots.

Mr M C Botha, Minister of Bantu Administration and Education, stated that at seven of the senior secondary schools involved in the demonstrations subjects were taught in English only, and that at one high school only one subject was offered in Afrikaans. (It should be borne in mind that although not directly affected by the ruling at present, senior secondary and high schools would eventually be affected as the children at present at higher primary schools progress. In addition, many high school pupils have brothers and sisters in the lower classes, which were affected by the ruling, and sympathised with and wished to support them over this issue). According to Mr Botha the equal treatment of the two official languages as entrenched in the constitution had to be considered and teachers were employed under the explicit assumption that they were proficient in both languages.

Opposition members called for the resignation of the Minister and Deputy Minister of Bantu Administration because of their inept handling of the matter.

Chief Buthelezi called for a conference of leaders to resolve the crisis.

18 June: Rioting occurred at Alexandra township, Vosloorus at Boksburg and Kathlehong near Germiston, Mahlakeng in Randfontein, and again at Kagiso. Students at Turfloop protested at the shootings in Soweto, but there was no damage to the university. At Ngoye[11] the administration buildings and library were burnt down by protesting students.

Students at the University of the Witwatersrand and the medical faculty of the University of Natal held protest marches. In Durban 87 black students were arrested.

Mr John Rees and Dr Beyers Naude received orders warning them to dissociate themselves completely from the "situation of unrest" and public gatherings were prohibited until 29 June in terms of the Riotous Assemblies Act.

In a statement in Parliament Mr Vorster said that law and order were to be preserved at any cost.

Homeland leaders called for calm and an end to rioting.

Soweto leaders demanded that Afrikaans be dropped as medium

of instruction before they would co-operate in the setting up of a reconstruction committee.

The following letter was sent to the Prime Minister and the Minister of Bantu Administration, Development and Education, by the Assistant Director of the SAIRR: "The South African Institute of Race Relations, deeply concerned about the violence that has taken place in Soweto, has instructed me to appeal to you to accept the reasonable request of the African people that their children should be educated through one medium chosen by their parents. We believe that such a decision would help significantly in present conditions, since it would show that reasonable requests made by responsible African people are not rejected out of hand by those with the power to make decisions.

"We realise, however, that this request must be considered in an educational context, and we therefore take the liberty of suggesting how it might be framed on educational grounds.

"We respectfully submit that the following principles could form the basis of an acceptable policy:

1. It is desirable that children begin their education in their mother-tongue.
2. In a multilingual country such as South Africa, it is necessary that children switch to one of the official languages as a medium of instruction at some stage of their schooling if that language is not their mother-tongue.
3. The point at which such switch should be made, and the language medium through which such children should be educated, are matters which, in principle, should be decided by the parents or communities involved.
4. Both official languages should be taught as subjects to all children in South Africa.
5. It is accepted that in teaching any language, that language should be the medium of instruction.

"The above principles are educationally sound and accord with the historic experience of Afrikaans-speaking South Africans. Their acceptance should therefore be seriously and urgently considered by the Cabinet.

"In making our request, we are as concerned as all other responsible South Africans to contribute to the restoration of peace, public order and goodwill in our area.

"I am taking the liberty of sending a copy of this letter to the

Hon. the Minister of Bantu Administration, Development and Eduction."

19 June: Rioting in the townships of the Rand died down, except for sporadic outbursts.

Dr Selma Browde was served with a warning order similar to those served on the Rev Beyers Naude and Mr Rees.

Mr M C Botha met black leaders in Pretoria. A joint statement was issued saying that the "tragic occurrences in Soweto were caused by misunderstanding and confusion." A meeting between Mr Rousseau, Secretary for Bantu Education and black leaders was scheduled for Friday 25 June.

21 June: There were fresh outbreaks of rioting at Mamelodi, Atteridgeville, Hammanskraal and Mabopane, near Pretoria, and at Kwa Thema, Daveyton, Duduza and Wattville on the East Rand, near Pietersburg and Potgietersrus and at Sibasa and Witsieshoek.

A meeting of Soweto school principals was held after which a statement was issued calling for the immediate scrapping of Afrikaans as medium of instruction, and stating that it was the language issue which was the real cause of the riots and other grievances were secondary.

Mr M C Botha issued a statement in which he said that there would be regular consultation between black urban leaders and white authorities at which various grievances would be discussed.

22 June: Disturbances in Mamelodi led to further deaths, and there was unrest in GaRankuwa, where high school students demonstrated "in sympathy with those killed in the struggle."

In the Assembly Mr M C Botha stated that the Government intended to decide whether to repeal or amend the language ruling before schools reopened. He reiterated the previous statement that the four senior secondary schools which had started the protest march, did not use Afrikaans as medium of instruction.

Mr Kruger, Minister of Police, praised police action in the riots and attacked the PRP,[12] accusing them of becoming identified with Black Power movements.

In the United Nations Security Council, Mr David Sibeko, Director of Foreign Affairs of the Pan African Congress of South Africa, suggested that blacks killed by fellow blacks in the riots were those suspected of being Government informers.

23 June: All remained quiet in the main trouble spots, although there were cases of arson in Kwa Thema and near Nelspruit (where a building at Ngwenya Teachers Training College was fired). There was a minor outbreak of rioting at Jouberton near Klerksdorp, involving schoolchildren.

Chief Kaizer Matanzima condemned the use of guns on students, and called for the repeal of all discriminatory laws by the South African Government.

24 June: In Jouberton two buses were stoned by *tsotsis* and in Langa, Cape Town, police were called in after a crowd surrounded the vehicle of two Bantu Board officials.

25 June: Thirty black leaders and educationists from Soweto met Mr G J Rousseau, Secretary for Bantu Education, to discuss the language issue. Mr W C Ackerman, regional director, was not present at the meeting. A memorandum on the matter, originally drawn up by ATASA[13] was presented by the joint committee. After the meeting the view was expressed that the Government was expected to soften its attitude on the enforcement of Afrikaans as medium of instruction

(In a subsequent meeting with members of the SAIRR staff, Mr Dlamlense, secretary of ATASA, said that at this meeting the following requests were made:

1. That all five circuit inspectors and Mr Ackerman should be removed from their present posts.
2. That elected members of the school boards who had been dismissed should be reinstated.
3. That a single medium of instruction should be introduced immediately.

Mr Dlamlense said that ATASA totally dismissed the Minister's earlier statements about "confusion" over the language issue. He said that the matter had been forced and referred to the department circulars of 1974, which stated that social studies and arithmetic *must* be taught through the medium of Afrikaans.)

25 June: Major outbreaks of arson and rioting continued to occur in various parts of the country.

The Broederbond's policy of getting more blacks to use Afrikaans is set out at length in the secret circular of September 1968 headed: *Afrikaans as a Second Language for the Bantu*. "Two years ago in our monthly circular we drew the attention of members to the importance of using Afrikaans to Bantu. That idea and the hints given with it created widespread interest and have borne fruit. As a result most right-thinking Afrikaans-speakers today concentrate on addressing Bantu in Afrikaans wherever they meet them."

The circular added that blacks used seven ethnic languages and that after 100 years of contact with Afrikaans and English these languages were still grammatically pure. The Government's aim and policy is to see that the Bantu language retains its place of honour in its own community and plays an increasing role in the maintenance of a specific national character. Where the promotion of Afrikaans is advocated, therefore, it must in no circumstances be seen as a move to replace the Bantu language with Afrikaans. Because of the requirements of the national economy, Bantu are in continuous contact with white employers and co-workers. A knowledge of one or both the official languages is therefore a requirement and both these languages are learnt in the following two ways: (a) by using it in contact with whites, (b) through instruction at school from the first school year.

"The contention is that the Bantu must learn one of the official languages as *second language*. The other official language can be a *third* language which he does not necessarily have to know as well as the second language. This second language must be *Afrikaans* and the following arguments are given for this:

"(a) By far the majority of people in the Republic speak Afrikaans (2¼ million whites plus 1½ million Coloureds, that is ±4 million against the 1¼ million English-speakers).

(b) Bantu workers make far more contact with Afrikaans-speakers, for example in the mines, industry, farming, commerce etc.

(c) Bantu officials and teachers mainly come in contact with Afrikaans-speaking officials and principals.

(d) Experience has shown that Bantu find it much easier to learn Afrikaans than English and that they succeed in speaking the language purely, faultlessly and without an accent. There are even a few small Afrikaans-speaking Bantu communities.

(e) Both the lecturing and administrative personnel at the three Bantu universities are almost 100% Afrikaans-speaking.

(f) Afrikaans is a language true to South Africa which for many reasons can serve the peculiar requirements of this country.

(g) White hospital personnel are mainly Afrikaans-speaking.

(h) The police, with whom the Bantu make a lot of contact, are almost all Afrikaans-speaking.

(i) The white personnel of the Railways are predominantly Afrikaans-speaking."

The circular then listed the progress already made towards establishing Afrikaans as a second language among blacks:

"(a) According to available figures about 3½ million Bantu live on white farms. It can be accepted that a minimum of 3 million ... use Afrikaans in contact with their employers. English is seldom used on farms.
(b) A further 4 million Bantu live in urban areas where a majority of the workers have a good or reasonable knowledge of Afrikaans. The ordinary Bantu worker's knowledge of English is poor. It is only domestic servants in English households that develop without Afrikaans.
(c) There are presently about 38 000 Bantu teachers in the employ of the Department of Bantu Education. Of this large number it can be said that:
(i) Almost all can read Afrikaans.
(ii) About 80% can also write it and teach it as school subject in primary school.
(iii) About 15 000 had Afrikaans as language up to Standard 8 and speak and write at a fairly cultivated level.
(iv) About 5 000 teachers speak Afrikaans almost faultlessly.
(v) About 500 Bantu teachers teach Afrikaans as a subject in secondary school up to Standard 8 and matric.
(vi) While the majority of Bantu teachers speak English well, a good knowledge of Afrikaans has become a status symbol to them.
Unwittingly they make a contribution to the promotion of Afrikaans among their own people.
(d) There are presently about 2 million Bantu pupils taking Afrikaans as a school subject from Sub-standard A to Standard VI. The quality of teaching depends on the teacher's knowledge of the language and ranges from good to poor. At the end of 1967 about 80 000 pupils wrote Afrikaans as an examination subject for the Standard VI public exams and about 90% passed; the standard is about the same as for Afrikaans lower in English-medium schools.
(e) There are about 70 000 Bantu pupils taking Afrikaans as a high school subject and in 1967 21 000 wrote it as examination subject for the Junior Certificate public exam and 70% passed. About 2 000 wrote it as a matric subject and 50% passed. At secondary levels the standard throughout is like Afrikaans lower in white schools.
(f) In all primary schools Bantu pupils learn, wherever possible, two subjects through Afrikaans medium.
(g) Throughout school, Afrikaans is a compulsory subject.

"From the foregoing we can deduce that because of the Government's Bantu education policy, Afrikaans is slowly but surely gaining an important place."

Under the heading *What the Afrikaner should do to get Afrikaans into first place after the mother-tongue (Bantu language)* the circular stated:

"(a) It must be stressed again that we must speak Afrikaans to Bantu servants, messengers, waiters, teachers, officials and everybody we contact. We can switch to English with the battling Greek or shop assistant, but not with the Bantu at the petrol pump or hotel. It is not necessary for him to maintain English.

(b) Officials who communicate with Bantu through an interpreter must use mainly Afrikaans. For the purpose of equal use English can also be used, but mainly Afrikaans.

(c) In all circumstances use *pure correct Afrikaans.*

(d) Provide simple pieces in Afrikaans for your employees to read.

(e) Let the Bantu understand in all circumstances that Afrikaans is the language of *most* whites and also the *most important* whites."

In Circular 3/70/71 Broeders were once again urged to make Afrikaans the second language of blacks: "It must be our aim to establish Afrikaans as second language among as many Bantu as possible." The following year (Circular 3/71/72) a call went out to all Broeders to donate books to black schools. "A good number" of Afrikaans books were received. "If there are any more donations the nearest inspector of Bantu education must be contacted. Members are also requested to use their influence to persuade employers to make Afrikaans reading matter like newspapers and magazines available to their employees. The Bantu are increasingly becoming readers of English newspapers and magazines, and we can make a contribution to change this pattern."

It is clear from these circulars that the Broederbond was determined to establish Afrikaans among blacks. Every avenue was to be used. The schools were of course the most important means, especially as the Department of Bantu Education with so many Broeders in its ranks was a willing partner in the exercise. The process of enforcing Afrikaans in schools, which started slowly, was accelerated in the mid-1970s and the scene was set for the clashes which followed. No wonder an almost panicky atmosphere existed in Broederbond ranks during the long-drawn-out riots.

The petrol bombs which destroyed part of Jan van Riebeeck primary school on September 9 – the oldest Afrikaans school in the country – gave the message loud and clear. The Broederbond Executive discussed the riots at several meetings. Meetings between the Executive and Cabinet Ministers were held on a regular basis to keep the members informed. A meeting between the Broederbond Executive and Broederbonders who were chairmen and officials of Bantu Administration Boards also took place (Circular 1/9/76). "The Executive wishes to thank members who work in the Bantu administration boards.

"It is clear that their work and that of other people during the riots was done in difficult circumstances and that more understanding is needed. Reports, letters and comment in the Press seek to put the blame for the riots on the shoulders of the Bantu Administration Boards. The Executive is certain that this is not the case. The Executive makes an appeal to members not to erode the image of the Boards, but rather to improve that image."

The first step was to try to dispel the notion that Afrikaans was the main issue sparking off the riots. This was essential from their own point of view because neither the Broederbond nor the Government could afford to carry the blame. On July 1 1976 the Broederbond Executive reported to members: "The Executive is deliberating with friends in responsible circles (Cabinet Ministers) and therefore no final comment or information can be given at this stage. Apart from information in later newsletters the Executive wishes to make these points.

"The Minister of Bantu Education's statement on Afrikaans as teaching medium, issued on Friday June 18, must be thoroughly considered. Among other things he said the policy on the medium of teaching has remained unchanged since 1955, namely mother-tongue education in primary schools and the two official languages on a 50-50 basis in secondary schools. Recently new curricula were introduced as a result of which Standard 5 becomes the first year of secondary school, with the instruction in the two official languages in subject-teaching.

"In practice the state of affairs regarding the use of English and Afrikaans is far removed from the principle of equality. On secondary level the average is close to 95% in favour of English. The only subject which comes near equality is mathematics in Form Three. The permission of the department is necessary where people want to deviate from the principle of equality. This is in cases of non-availability or lack of qualifications of teachers. The department has certain responsibilities in its approach to the matter and cannot simply grant any request. The equal treatment of the two official languages is entrenched in the South African Constitution.

"The alleged feeling against Afrikaans can hardly be the only reason for the demonstrations. At seven of the schools which took part in the demonstrations, subjects are taught only in English."

On September 1 1976 a circular was sent to branches, based on information received from the Minister of Bantu Education and other officials. It stated emphatically: "The relative unimportance of resistance to a teaching medium in two subjects, restricted to one Bantu area, must not be judged without considering the systematic and determined creation of a Black Power climate which has been in progress for a considerable time throughout the country." But later in the circular the Executive admits that the first phase of the riots took place when the 50-50 language policy "could be exploited to mobilise students, pupils and parents to take action."

The Broederbond action in washing its hands of responsibility for the language issue was followed slavishly by its members in influential positions all over the country. From the Minister and his deputy came denials that Afrikaans was the cause of the riots. This line was followed by the Broederbond-controlled South African Broadcasting Corporation, Bantu Administration Boards and Sections of the Afrikaans Press.

The fact of the matter is, however, that virtually all the demands that pupils, parents and teachers made on the issue of Afrikaans had to be met by the authorities in order to defuse the issue. Mr Ackerman, the man who sent out the circular enforcing Afrikaans, had to be transferred with almost his entire staff of circuit inspectors, and the rigorous enforcement of Afrikaans in black schools had to be dropped.

Once that was settled, the Broederbond Executive notified members that strong police action would be taken to restore law and order. In the circular of September 11 it reported: "During a recent meeting with a friend in a responsible position it became clear that, depending on the development of foreign relations, considerably increased action can be expected in the interests of the restoration of law and order in black townships, especially in Soweto. In this connection the Executive wants to stress that our black population is substantially different from the white Westerner, especially in terms of respect for power, violence and strong action. It has become urgently necessary to give conclusive proof to the vast majority of non-rioting blacks of the Government's *will* and its *power* to maintain law and order in everybody's interest. The unruly element will have to be struck down hard and effectively before a long-term programme of peaceful adjustments can be executed. Such adjustments include effective responsibility for local self-government in black communities and especially for the maintenance of law and order in their own townships. We must accept that the routines and methods which their own police will use among their own people will sometimes be different from those of a white community. We will not always force our norms on them. We want to call on our members to cultivate an understanding that the average African is different from whites in his view of violence and power and this must be kept prominently in mind. It will be self-defeating in the present situation to keep on using rules which can be applied to a homogeneous Western community where they are generally respected." The Broederbond was thus preparing its members for action which could not be reconciled with Western democratic behaviour.

Hundreds of people were detained without trial, and on October 19 1977 the daily *The World* and *Weekend World,* mass circulation black newspapers, were banned. Their editor, Percy Qoboza, was detained with members of the Committee of Ten, including its chairman, Dr Motlana. After months in jail they were released without being charged.

The position of *The World* had often been discussed at Broederbond meetings and in circulars. They were watching its progress and direction very carefully, fully aware that it was a powerful vehicle for anti-Government propaganda. The Broederbond was also concerned about the fact that it was an English-language newspaper, teaching blacks English instead of Afrikaans. In the September 1968 circular the Broederbond Executive showed itself more worried about the language issue because it classed *The World* then as "a moderate newspaper which is not antagonistic towards the Government." The editor then was the moderate Mr Monasse Moerane, later replaced by the outspoken Mr Qoboza who gave more space to political news. This development disturbed the Broederbond and the Government and led to the banning order.

The circular stated that *The World's* increasing circulation could result in:
(a) An English-reading black community in urban areas.
(b) A majority of developed blacks accepting English as second language.
(c) The habit of reading newspapers, followed by an increased interest in English books.
(d) English once again rising as a powerful language in South Africa, with Afrikaans as a minor and less significant language.

It listed the following details of the circulation growth of *The World:*
"(a) Six years ago it was *The Bantu World* with two editions a week at one cent a copy and a circulation of 22 000.
(b) Six years ago the name was changed to *The World* and it became a daily (small format) of 16 pages. Since then the circulation has grown to 90 000 *a day* (*Transvaler* 35 000, *Vaderland* 60 000, *Die Burger* 50 000 – round figures).
(c) Today *The World* is the fourth biggest English daily behind *The Cape Argus*, the *Rand Daily Mail* and *The Star*.
(d) Shortly *The World* will also start a Sunday edition called *Weekend World* and it will probably start with a circulation of 100 000 and the readers will all be Bantu."

The banning of *The World,* therefore, did not come out of the blue. The newspaper's progress, influence and political line were carefully studied not only by the Minister of Justice, Mr Jimmy Kruger, and the security police but also by the Broederbond.

The international effect of a possible banning was carefully contemplated and weighed. In the end the hope that taking *The World* off the streets would help to restore law and order was the clincher. The international and internal outcry was fierce but once the Government crossed the bridge there was no going back.

1. *Sunday Express,* June 20 1976.
2. *The World,* January 3 1975.
3. *Hansard,* May 5.
4. Ibid. May 6
5. Ibid., No 5, Col 401.
6. South African Institute of Race Relations.
7. Urban Bantu Council.

8. West Rand Administration Board.
9. *Hansard,* No 19, Col 1185.
10 Gangsters.
11. University of Zululand campus.
12. The Progressive Reform Party.
13. African Teachers' Association of South Africa.

14 *Sports Policy*

The South African Government's new sports policy announced in 1971 is an outstanding example of how the Broederbond influences Government policy. It is also an example of how the organisation can operate beneficially, finding solutions through its think-tanks and enabling its influential membership to enlighten Afrikanerdom as a whole.

The present sports policy represents a complete somersault from what it was from 1948 to 1971. Rigid sports apartheid had been applied since the Nationalists came to power. As in all other spheres of life, segregation applied in sportsfields, seating and clubs. All over the world boycotts of South African sportsmen started to mushroom until even rugby – the Afrikaner's favourite game – was hit by boycotts and protests. The situation reached a critical point when on September 4 1965 Dr Verwoerd, addressing a meeting at Loskop Dam, closed the door firmly on a visit by an All Black team (New Zealand) which included Maoris.

He said: "Our standpoint is that just as we subject ourselves to another country's customs and traditions without flinching, without any criticism and cheerfully, so do we expect that when another country sends representatives to us they will behave in the same way, namely not involving themselves in our affairs, and that they will adapt themselves to our customs."

Any doubts about the speech in Nationalist ranks were removed three days later when the Minister of the Interior, Senator Jan de Klerk, issued a lengthy clarifying statement. A mixed New Zealand team would not be allowed.

It was like fuel on the fire of international sports boycotts against South Africa and although the country's isolation in this field grew almost daily the then Minister of the Interior, Mr P K le Roux, said the Government would remain "inflexible and immovable" in enforcing the principle of no mixed sport in South Africa.[1]

A new Department of Sport was created with a former rugby

Springbok centre, the rather inept politician, Mr Frank Waring, as its first Minister. The hope that such a department could overcome the isolation was idle, however, because there was no political change.

Although the new Prime Minister, Mr Vorster, reviewed Dr Verwoerd's policy of "No Maoris," he was adamant on local sport – each colour group's sport had to be practised and administered separately.[2] A few weeks later he told Parliament: "Inside South Africa there will not be mixed sporting events, irrespective of the proficiency of the participants. On this there can be no compromise, negotiations or abandonment of principle."[3]

Mr Vorster defended his green light for the inclusion of Maoris in the All Black side by stating: "Our standpoint has all along been that as far as the Springbok side is concerned it is a white side. It has always been one ... and the fact is that when the first New Zealand team came out to South Africa in 1928, I am reliably told that there were three players in that side of Maori blood. They came out to South Africa, they were accepted, the same as all the other players were accepted."

The backlash from his own Parliamentary caucus and right-wing Afrikaners was strong. They saw it as a deviation from Dr Verwoerd's granite policy and a step towards sport integration. But there was also confusion – some thought Maoris would not be allowed and others that they would. According to J H P Serfontein[4] the first confrontation between Mr Vorster and the Hertzog group, who were strongly opposed to the inclusion of Maoris, took place in the caucus in February 1967. After the meeting Mr Vorster summoned to his office Mr Jaap Marais and Mr Willem Delport, a former Springbok rugby player, both staunch Broeders. He wanted to know if there would be any objection in principle against holding the Olympic Games in South Africa and, if not, what would be the objection to Maoris in the All Black team. Serfontein[5] says Mr Marais expressed some concern but said he would give his objections in writing. But Mr Vorster decided to discuss the matter again in the caucus and he addressed them for an hour. Mr Marais and Mr Basie van Rensburg opposed the new policy while Dr Piet Koornhof and others supported it. Here, for the first time, was a deep division in the Broederbond ranks.

A deputation of 13 MPs went to see Mr Vorster. They were Dr Connie Mulder, Dr Johannes Otto, Messrs Jaap Marais, Jannie de Wet, Joos le Roux, Willem Cruywagen, Johan Engelbrecht, Ben

Pienaar, Bret van Wyk, Jan van Zyl, Willem Delport, Chris Sadie and Advocate Jimmy Kruger. According to Mr Marais, Mr Vorster said neither Basil D'Oliveira nor the Maoris would be allowed to visit South Africa in sporting teams but the others, with the exception of Mr van Zyl, denied it. Mr Vorster rode out the storm and at the next caucus meeting his policy was accepted. But it was one of the direct reasons for the HNP split which also shook the Broederbond (see Chapter 11).

The divisions in the party and the Bond were probably the reason Mr Vorster decided to "sacrifice" cricket the next year, as a commentator put it. By trying to save rugby – mainly an Afrikaner game – by allowing the Maoris to tour, he created a storm in rightwing circles. He probably felt he had to balance it with some strong-arm action in another direction, hence a blunder which cost South Africa its international cricket ties. Basil D'Oliveira, a coloured cricketer who left South Africa because in terms of the policy he could never play for his fatherland, was included in the MCC team to tour South Africa. To a cheering Free State Nationalist Congress Mr Vorster announced that D'Oliveira's selection was political and not acceptable. The MCC immediately cancelled the tour and in 1970 stated that no further test matches would be played between England and South Africa until cricket in the Republic was played multiracially and teams were selected on merit.

South Africa's sportsmen were now almost totally isolated. The competitive spirit so essential for good performances was dying a slow death in many sports. Brilliant sportsmen, capable of performances which could bring international fame to South Africa, had to remain home or return home from abroad unable to compete because of the boycotts. Another link with the outside world was cut – and the youth of South Africa lost a dimension in their lives – not being able to strive for the highest reward in South African sport, the coveted green and gold Springbok blazer. In the long run the effect on the youth, politically as well, could be staggering. Something had to be done.

Enter the Afrikaner Broederbond.

The Broederbond, always alert and sensitive to issues, was picking up signals from its vast network of branches that sports stagnation could have vast social and political implications. But it was in a dilemma because, more than any other body, it was responsible for the apartheid policy which had led the country into a sport dead-end. Its first effort was merely an attempt to boost morale of (circular June 2 1970). "The latest developments in international sport show clearly that there is a persistent campaign to isolate our country as much as possible. It is also clear that the issue is not mixed teams and participation, but the destruction of the existing order in South Africa. It can easily happen that our young people will get the wrong impression of the events because they do not realise the full implications or perhaps attach an exaggerated value to sport. Therefore anybody who has anything to do with youth must try to bring the true issue before them. Teachers, school principals, lecturers, youth leaders, sport administrators etc, must especially give attention to this. The Executive's sport committee will in due course make a memorandum available to branches, but meanwhile you must consider what you can do in this connection."

Mr Vorster now felt freer to move. The 1970 All Black tour was a spectacular success and the Maori players in the team became some of the most popular. Nothing came of the threatened boycott by rightwingers. In the 1970 general election the new Herstigte Nasionale Party was routed and all four of its MPs were defeated. Many HNP candidates lost their deposits despite their having exploited "sport integration" to the maximum. Clearly the electorate was far more ready to accept change than even Mr Vorster had suspected. The Broederbond also survived the split among its stalwarts. The leadership managed to keep the organisation intact.

It was in this climate that Mr Vorster and the Broederbond got together to discuss a new sports policy. It was a clever move on his part, because by using the organisation to draw up the new policy he also tied it to the consequences and staved off the expected backlash from the right. Basically the Broederbond choice was between total sports isolation – which the country could not afford – and opening the doors for multiracial sport which could spark off a rightwing result. The latter road was dangerous but a calculated risk had to be taken. Its first step was to call a two-day conference of all Broeders involved in sport. The only way out of an impasse was to try to devise a system of merit selection – but one arguably based on separate development.

The result of the deliberations was then discussed and reformulated by the Broederbond's expert committee on sport on which the rightwing Dr Andries Treurnicht was chosen to serve so as to tie him to the decisions. The Broederbond Executive further loaned the new policy and sent it to Mr Vorster for approval.

The Broederbond's biggest task was now to get rank-and-file backing from the membership for the revolutionary new policy in terms of National Party thinking. On April 1 1971 it sent out a series of newsletters. The first was designed to make the Broeders realise how serious the onslaught was.

"Sport and the Present Onslaught against South Africa"

A study document on this subject is hereby sent to divisions. It has been made available by the Sport Committee. You are requested to consider how its contents can be made public in your area. A talk by school principals or teachers in primary and high schools, a talk to Rapportryers or other public bodies (youth organisations, sports clubs, etc) are methods that can be used. You should not mention the study document. The contents can be rephrased and given as the speaker's own thoughts. Please do not read the document in public. (It will seem very strange if people all over the country suddenly appear in public with the same document!)

"It has been arranged that a series of articles on different aspects of sport will appear over the next months in *Handhaaf*. The contents of the present paper will be enlarged upon in those articles. You are requested to read the series and bring it to the attention of interested parties." Under the heading *Sport and Politics* the first circular stated: "We have always believed that sport should not be mixed with politics, and politics must be kept out of sport. Throughout the world, however, the importance of sport in international affairs, for the prestige of countries and the promotion of a cause, has come strongly to the forefront and politics are drawn more and more into sport.

"That the two issues can no longer be separated is obvious from recent developments on the international and the national level... It is very clear that our enemies have gained much courage from their success (in isolating South Africa)... They are full of confidence that sports isolation will help to bring the whites to their knees ...

"... a total of 500 million people participate in sport ... and sport has indeed become a world power."

The newsletter made it clear that sport could be of much value to the youth in strengthening national and international ties, creating fitness and a healthy nation – necessary for national preparedness leading to the useful spending of free time and a spirit of competitiveness. But there was also the inevitable warning to appease the *verkramptes*. "There can be no deviation from our traditional policy of separate development. The maintenance of identity of each nation must be preserved... No concession or compromise which can lead to mixed sport internally may be made."

These points are also stressed in the document entitled *Sports Policy* circulated at the same time, but it must have been clear that the new policy was opening the door to mixed sport, no matter how much emphasis was given to the "multinational" aspect.

The document stated: "The Executive has given much attention in recent months to sports policy, especially the relations between white and non-white. Memoranda from divisions and members in sports bodies have been received and studied. A fruitful two-day meeting between a great number of members in different sports controlling bodies over the whole country was held recently, and committees from their ranks submitted to the Executive a number of fundamental policy formulations for consideration."

And then the Executive told the members that the Cabinet had accepted the Broederbond policy and that a statement could be expected soon. "The Executive has considered these policy formulations and submitted them to friends in responsible circles (Cabinet) and it is expected that the formulations will be contained in official Government statements in the coming days or weeks. Through this document the Executive wants to inform members about the policy which it submitted to these friends.

"The principal formulation ... is a signpost rather than a map. It does not have to be made public or implemented in all its aspcts. In many cases the maximum delay, in accordance with our eventual aims, is desirable. As soon as the policy has been decided on, no concession or compromise should be made." The first aim of the sports policy is given as "the maintenance of the white population in South Africa through and within the policy of separate development."

The principle of the sports policy was based on the "nations" approach allowing for the different ethnic groups to compete against each other – the so-called multinational approach. At the international level South Africa would not prescribe the composition of overseas teams; in other words these teams could be multiracial. There would, however, be no mixing on club or provincial level. The plan envisaged the establishment of a sports council to co-ordinate all sport in South Africa and implement the new policy. It clearly aimed at putting control in the hands of the Broeders. "Where the control of most sports is not in the hands of well-disposed people, abuses and embarrassment can be created." The council would consist of a full-time executive of not more than five people; in order to secure control of the council the executive would be *nominated* and not elected. Clearly, the Minister would nominate a council of "well-disposed" people. An international sports complex would be built in the white area in such a way that "friction" between the races could be eliminated.

When the former Prime Minister, Mr Vorster, disclosed the new sports policy towards the end of April 1971 in Parliament, it followed almost to the letter the Broederbond plan. Some of the phrases he used were almost exactly the same as in the secret Broederbond document.

The Broederbonders meanwhile moved swiftly to get control of as many sporting bodies as possible. Professor Hannes Botha became chairman of the South African Amateur Athletics Union, and Mr Rudolph Opperman chairman of the South African Olympic Council. A few years earlier another Broeder, Mr Jannie le Roux, had become president of the Transvaal Rugby Board and Dr Danie Craven had to stave off a challenge from Broeder Kobus Louw. In sports adminstration, Broeders like former Springbok rugby captains, Avril Malan, Johan Claassen, Dawie de Villiers, MP, and Hannes Marais made their presence felt. Former Springboks Butch Lochner, Piet (Spiere) du Toit, Mannetjies Roux and Willem Delport, MP, are also members. So are Professor Fritz Eloff, president of the Northern Transvaal Rugby Union, Mr Steve Strydom, Free State rugby boss, Sid Kingsley, former Northern Transvaal rugby president, and Professor Charles Nieuwoudt, new athletics chief. At one stage there was a Broederbond move to oust Morné du Plessis as Springbok rugby captain because he had been "anglicised" and was not a Nationalist, but newspaper publicity frustrated this.

The Minister of Sport, Mr Frank Waring, of course not a Broeder, was extremely uncomfortable trying to explain the new policy in Parliament. At one stage Mr Vorster had to intervene personally because Mr Waring made a mess of it. Mr Waring left the Chamber in a huff. The whole concept on which the policy was based was foreign to him, and he clearly did not understand the intricacies of the Nationalists' "multinationalism". Worse still was that the policy had already been accepted by the Broederbond and Broeder Cabinet Ministers by the time he was presented with it. When Mr Waring gracefully retired, a top Broeder, Dr Piet Koornhof, was made Minister of Sport. The secretary of the department is Mr Beyers Hoek, also a Broeder.

In June 1973 the two Broeder sports chiefs, Professor Hannes Botha and Mr Rudolph Opperman, persuaded the South African Olympic and National Games Association to appoint a committee to investigate the establishment of a sports council as spelled out in the Broederbond sports policy. The other requirement in the secret circular – the establishment of a national sports complex – is still very much on the cards as far as the Government is concerned and will probably be implemented as soon as finance is available.

The Broederbond plan as outlined by Mr Vorster was not passed without resistance. Rightwingers in the organisation saw it as the first step towards multiracial sport. Dr Piet Koornhof and Dr Andries Treurnicht addressed a series of regional Broederbond meetings to allay these fears. From the secret circular of October 1971 it is clear that some branches were very unhappy. "Some divisions did not comment because they regarded it as unnecessary in the light of the fact that the policy was publicly stated before they received the study document and they were not consulted prior to the announcement.

"Although almost all the divisions which commented supported the policy, they especially emphasised the following:

"4.1 Concern over the correct implementation of the "nation basis" of the policy.

4.2 Anxiety that the policy of separate development might become diluted because of sports "concessions".

4.3 Vigilance must be strong against mixing after sports games, mixed audiences, integration, conditioning of whites towards integration, mixed participation on the local level etc.

4.4 The fear that the sports policy opened the door slightly and might be the thin end of the wedge.

4.5 The urgent necessity of strong control by a nominated sports council."

The Executive then stressed that it did not draw up the policy under pressure, that no concessions were made and that the policy was "the logical consequence" of the policy of separate development on the sports level. A consistent policy had to be drawn up to eliminate ad hoc decisions which created problems. "Because the administration of most sports is in the hands of people not well-disposed towards the Afrikaner ideal and Government policy, they could often create problem situations and cause embarrassment." It advised Broeders to refer to "multinational" instead of "mixed" sport.

The Executive also sent all branches a National Party document on its sports policy, evidently to reassure them that the party was obediently following the Broeder plan.

In the administrative report to the 1972 *Bondsraad* meeting the issue was once again discussed. "The fact that control of most sports is still in non-Afrikaner hands has resulted in our not being able to have a positive influence in all places. The Executive once again wants to appeal to Broeders to exert themselves to place well-disposed Afrikaners in control of sport. Sport exerts an important influence on competitors . . . and it is our duty in this way to eliminate wrong influences on young Afrikaner competitors."

This appeal is repeated in the September 1 1973 secret circular. "We as Afrikaners must accept our responsibility to take a greater share in the management and organisation of the different sports. The correct implementation of our sports policy is endangered by the foreign control of several kinds of sport." Lists of sports clubs controlled by "Afrikaners and/or well-disposed people" were included to enable Broeders to support them. "In this way we can help friends (Broeders) to advise young Afrikaners who come to the city on where they should link up."

Among the clubs were *Kimberley,* tennis, Police Club and South African Railways Club, Pirates and Police (open club); *Port Elizabeth,* rugby, tennis, baseball, Park Club, and tennis, Diaz Club; *Florida,* tennis, Van der hoven Park; *Pretoria,* Lynnwood Tennis Club, Pretoria Sports Federation (Pretoria rugby club included), Oudstudente Sport Union (including Oostelikes rugby club), Sonop Tennis Club, Capital Park Bowls Club, Pretoria North Bowls Club; *Bellville,* Bellville Rugby Club, Bellville Athletics Club and Bellville Tennis Club.

The need for Broederbond and "well-disposed" Afrikaner control of sport organisations is a recurring theme in the secret documents. June 26 1976: "A survey just completed among divisions shows that our members and right-thinking Afrikaners are fairly thin on the ground in the administration of the various sports. Your own survey would have shown this weakness. What is your division going to do to ensure that young Afrikaner sportsmen do not come under the wrong influence, and that right-thinking Afrikaners (not necessarily members of our organisation, the youth organisation or Rapportryers) get the support they deserve?" February 2 1977: "From an investigation it appears that there is not enough interest among members in the teaching profession in the action of the schools rugby adminstrators in their respective areas. The result is that few members (Broeders) are elected on the committees of their schools rugby councils. This was the reason why only one of our members was elected to the committeee of the South African Schools Rugby Union. The SA Schools representative may shortly become a full member of the SA Rugby Board with voting powers. At the present time it is essential that as many well-disposed people as possible be put in executive posts."

The same circular complains that delegates often fail to vote according to instructions. "It also happens that with the election of the SA Schools Committee during Craven Week instructions are given to anybody, say a manager, to go and vote. Such a delegate does not vote according to instructions. It is our duty to see that the SA Schools Committee is manned by well-disposed people so that the schools can also exercise their voting power on a higher level. Divisions are therefore requested urgently to give attention to this matter and to see to it that delegates to the annual meeting are well-disposed people."

March 3 1977: "An urgent appeal is once again made to all members and divisions to do everything possible in their power to exercise a positive influence in local sports clubs. This will mean that more members and other well-disposed Afrikaners should become directly involved in the administration of clubs. Divisions will have to report on this at the end of the present book year."

It is clear from the developments in the sports policy, and data in the secret documents, that the fears of conservative Broeders were fully justified – the new policy was indeed the thin end of the wedge preparing the way for fully integrated sport.

The Broederbond Executive was to some extent outwitted – or quietly went along with the Government while protesting at meetings against any concessions. Mr Vorster's strategy was to let the policy develop, and take the Broederbond along with him. The man he chose for this difficult tightrope exercise was Dr Piet Koornhof, who through his own kind of "double-talk" had to confuse the issue by using jargon like "multinational". All along he protested that the new policy did not deviate from the policy of separate development.

As a former secretary of the Broederbond, Dr Koornhof's credentials were impeccable – nobody could accuse him of not being a "good Afrikaner". He also knew from within exactly how the Broederbond operated, how he could nudge it along by lobbying, addressing secret meetings in various parts of the country and by other tactics. He realised the danger if the Broederbond blocked any further concessions. It was for this reason that he canvassed actively for the election of Professor Gerrit Viljoen as chairman of the Bond in 1974. The rightwing Dr Andries Treurnicht had to be blocked to enable the more pragmatic Professor Viljoen to take over. In this Dr Koornhof was successful; the formidable Dr Treurnicht, who had threatened to resign as member of Parliament if more sport concessions were made, lost the most powerful and best organised powerbase in Afrikanerdom and was to a degree neutralised.

Dr Koornhof also largely neutralised another powerful agency – the Press. On several occasions he pleaded with editors and sports writers not to "embarrass" the Government by publishing stories on the sports policy which could provide ammunition to the *verkramptes*. He always knew that all discrimination in sport would have to go before South Africa would become internationally acceptable again. But through semantic acrobatics he had to allay the fears of rightwingers. It can be predicted now that in about two years all races will play together on club, provincial or national level, will sit together on stands, will use all the club facilities such as bars and toilets and that no more applications for permits will be needed.

It was quite an achievement, considering the constant concern in the Broederbond. A 1974 survey among members shows 92,7% accepted the inclusion of non-white athletes in a South African team for the Olympic Games as an interim measure only, 92,1% said such an extension of this principle (mixed teams) to other sports like rugby, cricket and soccer should be prevented, and 97,4% said the establishment of national sporting bodies for every separate "nation" and their affiliation with world sporting bodies must be expedited. The circular (June 5 1974) concluded: "As a result of this survey, meetings with friends in influential circles (Cabinet) have been held."

In 1975, after Dr Treurnicht had failed in his bid to become chairman, the Broederbond Executive made an important change in the sports policy by accepting mixed South African teams for international competitions. The justification for this was that separate teams were accepted for international competitions only if they represented separate *independent* countries. Until the homelands all became independent, South Africa would therefore have to provide a place for black sportsmen in her teams if she wanted to retain international ties. Moreover, in terms of the separate development policy no independent homelands for Indians and coloured people were foreseen and room had to be made for them in sports teams. A series of meetings with Cabinet Ministers and sports administrators once again took place and the Executive said it had "come to the conclusion that we have come up against a wall because of changing circumstances" (March 3 1975).

The Executive thereupon informed the Broeders in the Cabinet that the policy could not be changed. One of the reasons, it told members, was that it had received confidential information convincing it "that international sporting ties, especially in rugby and cricket, have serious implications at this critical stage for our country, regarding international trade, national trade, military relationships and armaments and strategic industrial development."

But once again they tried to reassure members. "In conclusion the Executive restates its existing policy – which is also that of the Government – of no mixed teams on club, local, provincial or national level. The Executive is deeply aware that there is strong division of opinion over this matter. It took the above decision in the light of all considerations at its disposal and after lengthy, serious deliberations in the best interests of our country and our nation. Members are asked to study this circular seriously and to formulate their point of view with great responsibility and understanding."

The next year (April 1 1976) the Executive had to reiterate that mixed sport on club level was unacceptable, after inquiries had been received from branches. The Cabinet had been asked to introduce legislation to prevent mixed club teams. On September 1 1976 it once again came out against mixed sport on provincial and club level – but only two days later a hurried meeting took place where Cabinet Broeders told the Executive that the Government was considering a change of policy to allow mixing at club level. The National Party congresses and its Federal Council had to accept the changes, and once again the Broederbond was informed before the party's rank-and-file membership. In fact, it appears from the secret documents that the Broederbond had set the scene for the changes as early as 1975 and was now simply using the excuse that the Government had to make a hurried change to avoid making its own membership unhappy.

Circular of October 5 1976: "The Executive conveyed the following to friends in responsible circles (Cabinet). 2.1 The Executive confirms the point of view it took in 1975 during meetings on the elimination of unnecessary separation measures, that contact and/or liaison between the different nations/national groups of the Republic must take place not only on national level but also on local levels, provided it does not endanger the identity of the different nations." The Executive thus accepted the change and the fact that "it was not possible to inform it prior to the changes."

In considering the matter the Executive was influenced by "the recent drastic changes in the internal security situation which make the promotion of internal peace and good relations between whites and non-whites essential. The policy change is seen as an important step to prevent or decrease tension and promote goodwill among large sectors of the population."

By 1977 the Broederbond Executive had again received a number of inquiries from branches which expressed concern about mixing in sport on club and provincial level – mixed teams as opposed to teams of different colours playing against each other which were approved in the October 1976 circular. Once again the Executive saw Dr Koornhof and he gave the assurance that the Government stood firm on the principle of separate club teams for different racial groups. He prefers, however, to persuade people who contravene the policy on a personal level, rather than to confront them with strong-arm tactics. But as they did not want to listen, he would act against them (March 3 1977).

And then came a strong reassurance from the Executive to the Broederbond membership. "The Executive accepts that the Government stands by its policy of no mixed sports clubs, and divisions are requested to act locally to prevent any deviations from this policy. Our organisation is not prepared to go further with the sports policy than what was approved by party congresses."

And that is where the situation rests at the moment. The Broederbond is determined to prevent mixed clubs, while Dr Koornhof knows he has to surmount this hurdle before he can persuade the world that sport has been fully integrated in South Africa. He is up against formidable odds and whether he can succeed in his usual weaving and bobbing style remains to be seen. He has already lost considerable credibility among the Super-Afrikaners whose adminstration he once headed. He can only hope that the climate for mixing improves as people get used to the idea, made more acceptable through the medium of television.

Leading Broeders in sport have already been working on a way out of the impasse so that both the Broederbond and the Government can save face when clubs become mixed. In July 1978 Mr Rudolph Opperman, president of the SA Olympic and National Games Association, suggested that South African sport had reached the stage where an official sports policy was no longer necessary – sportsmen should run their own affairs and, obviously by implication, form mixed clubs if they wanted to. The Minister of Sport should serve sportsmen of all colours, Opperman said, and sport should be exempted from the Group Areas and Liquor Acts which require permits for mixing. Opperman must have acted with strong support from sports administrators in the Broederbond and may have indicated a way out of the deadlock.

1. *Cape Times*, February 9.
2. Ibid. March 6 1967.
3. Ibid. April 12 1967.
4. Serfontein, J H P, *Die Verkrampte Aanslag*, p 119.
5. Ibid. p 120.

15 *Education*

South Africa's present highly compartmentalised education system is a living monument to the Broederbond's pervasive influence, and its driving determination to promote its cause of an exclusive sectional Afrikaner *volk* in the country. In the orgy of self-glorification the organisation allowed itself at its 50th anniversary in 1968, the chairman, Dr Piet Meyer, rated the Broederbond's activities with the youth as the "most important form and content of Brotherhood in the past 50 years.

"The Christian national education of our Afrikaner youth in and by own mother-tongue institutions from kindergarten and primary school to university and other institutions of tertiary education, was one of the primary objectives of our Brotherhood from the beginning," he said in the particular brand of tortuous Afrikaans for which he is noted. "Our participation," he continued, "in the establishment of mother-tongue schools and the Afrikanerisation of our universities is the golden thread that runs through all our activities... It is also our Brotherhood that, with unstinting labour at Bond councils, in study committees and in consultation with education heads at provincial and national levels – who were and are Broeders – has been able to formulate the ideal of a national education policy for our nation and country. We have carried it through to its present stage and will continue to do so in the years that lie ahead."

In this memorial to the Broederbond's consummate role in framing the education systems of South Africa, Dr Meyer passed easily over nearly half a century of bitterness and suspicion on the part of non-Afrikaners that accompanied each Broederbond triumph. In the lasting divisions which have been created in South Africa, and which are perpetuated through its education systems, the Broederbond has much to answer for.

The ringing calls for white unity currently popular among Nationalist politicians sound hollow when examined against the background of the education systems they have created and the sectional motives that lie behind it all. Calls for national unity of all races in South Africa border on fantasy when viewed against the backdrop of deliberate barriers which have been consistently thrown up against common education. The Soweto riots of 1976 demonstrated in tragically clear terms the burning hatred young blacks have for the system of education imposed on them. The Nationalist Government's insistence on Afrikaans as a medium of instruction was listed by the Institute of Race Relations in its evidence to the Cillie Commission investigating black unrest as the major contributory factor to the riots, which exploded into injury and death on June 16 that year.[1] Again, the Broederbond must look to its conscience for what happened in those riots (see Chapter 13). Its zealous pursuit of division and ruthless passion for "order" in South African society are faithfully reflected in the education systems it helped create for the various race groups in South Africa.

It all started in the bitter aftermath of the Second Anglo-Boer War. In the smouldering, resentful defeat of the ragged band of Afrikaners who had fought so bravely against such overwhelming odds, the greatest resentment was against Lord Milner's policy of anglicisation. Milner insisted that English was to be the medium of instruction in all public schools in the Orange Free State and the Transvaal and, he added arrogantly, "damn the consequences." One of the consequences was that Dutch leaders set up private schools to teach Afrikaans and the tenets of Calvinist doctrine.

The Dutch Reformed churches played a leading role in this move and many predikants were active in school committees and the struggle for Christian national education.[2] Dr A P Treurnicht, at present Deputy Minister of Education and Training, and responsible for black education, summed up the mood at the time in a speech at the Broederbond's 50th anniversary celebration in October 1968. "For too long," he said, "... the Afrikaner had to suffer the insult of an alien cultural stamp being forced on to the education of his children in the persistent anglicisation process. It became the logical and compelling demand of his own nationalism that his education should be in his own language and should form young lives for the Afrikaner community. And because the nation's origins and growth were so closely connected with the work, doctrine and activities of the church, it was obvious that the national life should be Christian in its education."

That was the ideal. After the two former Boer republics were

Dr A P Treuernicht. Deputy Minister and ex-Broederbond chairman.

granted self-government, however, the ardent pursuit of the Christian national ideal waned somewhat. Afrikaans was officially recognised in the schools and Generals Smuts and Hertzog, to varying degrees, pursued a policy of dual-medium instruction.

The Anglican and Catholic churches sponsored a number of English schools, which attracted a large number of Afrikaans children. Many Afrikaans families, without sacrificing their own cultural and national identities, recognised that Afrikaans would always have limited use, while English was a lingua franca and at that time almost exclusively the language of business and politics in South Africa.

But the disciples and advocates of the new spirit of Afrikaner nationalism sweeping across South Africa were not satisfied with this arrangement. Theirs was a more exclusive ideal. The Broederbond regards May 17 1921 as the first important milestone when it committed itself categorically to strive for the establishment of mother-tongue education in South Africa.[3]

With an unsympathetic government in power, however, progress towards this aim was slow until on July 6 and 7 1939 the Federasie van Afrikaanse Kultuurverenigings (FAK), operating under the auspices and direction of the Broederbond, arranged a Christian national education conference in Bloemfontein. Out of this conference an important agent in the fight for the Afrikaner education dream was born: the Nasionale Instituut vir Onderwys en Opvoeding (National Institute for Teaching and Education), NIOO. This was controlled by the Broederbond's chief secretary, the ubiquitous I M Lombard.

Meanwhile, the campaign to secure an exclusively Afrikaans education system had been proceeding on a broad front. In 1933, on a motion proposed by Dr Piet Meyer, already a rising star in the Broederbond, the National Union of South African Students (NUSAS) was split along English-Afrikaans lines by 147 votes to 118.[4] The Afrikaanse Nasionale Studentebond (ANS) came into being as a result, with Dr Hans van Rensburg, later to become leader of the Ossewabrandwag, as honorary president.

The following year the first national congress of the ANS was held under the chairmanship of Dr Diederichs (just back from studying Nazi methods in Germany). The constitution accepted at the congress specified its aims: "The Bond rests on a Protestant-Christian and cultural nationalism basis and acknowledges the leadership of God in the sphere of culture as in every other sphere of life concerning the Afrikaner people's traditions as embodied in history."

During the war the ANS issued a *Freedom Manifesto* (July 1 1940) that enunciated the republican ideal and reflected the oganisation's sympathies for Hitler's national socialist philosophy. Four points of major significance in the manifesto were: (1) The Union of South Africa is to be changed into a republican state in which the President, chosen by the people for a fixed period and responsible to God alone, will conduct an authoritarian government, with the assistance of an executive council and regional and vocational representatives; (2) Within a Christian national education system, teaching will be thoroughly adjusted to the requirements of our commercial life through the establishment of technical, professional and effective academic educational facilities; (3) The State will employ the Press, radio, film and library media, as well as other means, for a healthy popular education; (4) Afrikaans will be the official language of the country and English will enjoy full rights as the second language.[5]

The end of the war and Hitler's defeat spelled the demise of the ANS. But, in effect, it was reconstituted in the form of the Afrikaanse Studentebond (ASB) in 1948. Entrenched in its constitution is a commitment to a "Christian national basis as embodied in the Afrikaner people's tradition." The ASB today remains a Broederbond organ, although many Afrikaans student members are unaware of this. The ASB is officially affiliated to the Broederbond's cultural wing, the FAK, and has its headquarters at the Broederbond headquarters at Auckland Park, Johannesburg.

The late 1930s and early 1940s saw a surge of Broederbond activism in the language-medium struggle. Following the FAK's Christian national and *moedertaal* (mother-tongue) congress in 1939, the issue blew up into a major political debating point. Smuts's United Party wanted to keep children of both language groups together, while the Nationalists under Malan believed children of the two language groups should be segregated. The UP advocated dual-medium instruction in secondary school, while the National Party argued for mother-tongue education throughout. The second language should be taught as a separate subject, in the form of a foreign language, it argued.

Determined to prevent school integration at all costs, the Broederbond and National Party started a major offensive. A leading figure in this campaign was the Rev. William Nicol, Moderator of the Dutch Reformed Church, a top-level Broeder and later to become Administrator of the Transvaal. Nicol believed that when two language groups were together in one school "one culture would be swamped by the other."[6]

Nicol also played a leading role in mobilising the "Christian" aspect of the policy. He wrote prolific articles in church journals, spurring Afrikaner emotions to support the cause. The church's prodigious weight was thrown into the campaign. Nicol wrote that language mixing "would be fatal to religion and it cannot be tolerated by us ... To have children of the Afrikaans churches under the same roof as the children of other churches cannot be tolerated."[7] As Malherbe drily comments: "Presumably the Afrikaans-speaking child, by associating with an English-speaking child, would be contaminated and lose his pure Afrikaner character."

Dr E Greyling, also a Dutch Reformed minister and Broeder, added his voice: "God has willed that there shall be separate nations each with its own language and that mother-tongue education is accordingly the will of God. The parent should, accordingly, have no choice in this case."[8]

In the March 5 1941 edition of *Kerkbode,* the official Dutch Reformed mouthpiece, Nicol wrote: "It is the firm policy of our church, reiterated with emphasis at our last synod, that our children must be educated in separate schools with Afrikaans as the medium ... Not only the salvation of our *volk,* but the preservation of our church depends in large measure on separate schools."

According to Malherbe, "Here we find the reason why so many ministers of the Dutch Reformed Church became members of the Afrikaner Broederbond, whose primary educational objective was the development of separate unilingual Afrikaans-medium schools. What they really wanted was a revived form of Christian national education schools which would be parochial Dutch Reformed."[9]

Clearly, the idea was that a system of separate Afrikaans schools would provide the purveyors of Afrikaner Nationalism with a system which would more conveniently lend itself to the cultivation of the spirit of exclusivity. Once the children were herded into their separate schoolrooms, the Afrikaner children could be nurtured on the philosophy of republicanism, based mainly on glorious memories of the past. In the course of time, they would become the ruling political force in South Africa.

The purpose was succinctly expressed at the Broederbond-inspired *Moedertaalkongres* (mother tongue congress) in Bloemfontein in December 1943. A Free State school inspector told the congress: "The Afrikaner teachers will then demonstrate to Afrikanerdom what a power they possess in their teachers' organisations for building up the youth for the future republic. I know of no more powerful instrument. They handle the children for five or more hours daily, for five days each week, while at hostels and boarding schools the contact is continuous for longer periods. A nation is made through its youth being taught and influenced at school in the tradition, customs, habits and ultimate destination of its *volk.*"

A more concise appraisal of the Broederbond's attitude to education would be hard to find. This statement contains all the relevant clues to the obsession the organisation had, and continues to have, about education.

The NIOO, the FAK-Broederbond offspring, threw itself energetically into the mother-tongue campaign and joined the propaganda war with gusto. Operating through the Broederbond's extensive secret cell network, Lombard was able to manufacture an effective illusion of spontaneous response to major issues, particularly the language question. Every time the matter came to the fore, Broeders throughout the country would deluge Parliament and the provincial councils with telegrams expressing what was supposed to be the gut reaction of the people.

Natal, ever a thorn in the republican side, provided the Broeders with an emotive cause to exploit. In Pietermaritzburg, the Voortrekker Afrikaans (primary) school became overcrowded, so the provincial authorities arranged for the surplus Afrikaner children to go to an English-medium school where they would be taught in Afrikaans in parallel classes. The Broederbond and its campaigners immediately saw the emotive potential of the situation and seized on the issue. Professor van Rooy, chairman of the Broederbond, issued a nation-wide appeal for funds to build an exclusively Afrikaans school and eventually in 1945, the Christian-National Voortrekker Infants' School, popularly known as the "Protest School", was opened. The FAK, which played a major role later, said jubilantly that the event would "in future bear witness as a monument to Afrikaner determination and purposeful action on behalf of its cultural heritage."[10]

The Broederbond, under the cloak of its front organisations, also organised a strike of Afrikaner schoolchildren to protest against dual-medium instruction. The arrangements were in the hands of Mr M C Botha, honorary secretary of the Afrikaanse

Kultuurraad in Pretoria, later to become Minister of Bantu Administration and Development and of Bantu Education, ironically the position he still held at the time of the Soweto riots of 1976 one of the causes of which was given as protest against a medium of education – this time Afrikaans.

According to Mr Botha's plan, the churches, members of Parliament and of the provincial councils, school committees, even teachers and principals were to be harnessed to the strike which was to last long enough "to bring the Government to its senses." The plan had to be aborted, however, when it was exposed in public.

On and on, through all forums of South Africa, the language-medium debate raged. It resulted in a heated and protracted debate in Parliament. Inevitably, the matter became a major issue in the 1943 Parliamentary and, perhaps more particularly, provincial council elections.

In the provincial elections, where the subject had become the main issue, the UP won by large majorities in three of the four provinces and gained four seats in the Nationalist stronghold of the Orange Free State. It read the election results as an endorsement of its educational policy.

The UP took as a further pointer to the desires of the people at the time a survey of soldiers' opinions during the war. Published as *What the Soldier Thinks* (1944), a Union Defence Force official publication in English and Afrikaans, it was said to be representative of the thinking in the forces. The survey consisted of a sample of 7 000 soldiers in more than 200 units. It included officers, other ranks, men and women, army and air force, men in the Union and outside.

The following percentages show how the soldiers responded:

1. We shall have more national unity if English- and Afrikaans-speaking children go to the same schools: 93.
2. It is better for English-speaking and Afrikaans-speaking children to go to separate schools: 6.
3. Don't know, or no reply: 1.

On the language-medium question, the answers were as follows:

1. Children should be taught only through the medium of their home language; the other language should be taught merely as a subject: 13.
2. Children should be taught mainly through the medium of their home language, but it is a good thing for them to learn some

subjects through the medium of the other language: 81.
3. Don't know, or no reply: 6.
But this was not acceptable to the ardent band of brothers seeking their own ends. The ferment continued. At last, in 1948, the Nationalists came to power and the way was opened for the Broederbond-Nationalist ideal of Christian National education. In November 1948 the National Party congress accepted a motion that the country's education system should conform to their version of a Christian National education policy. The policy had been formulated by a group of university professors and National Party politicians, including two Cabinet Ministers. They were Dr T E Dönges, Dr E G Jansen MP, Professors J Chris Coetzee, J E Meiring and H P Wolmarans, Dr E Greyling, the Rev G Worst, Advocate G F Hugo and Mr J H Greybe. All of them were members of the Broederbond.[12]

The policy contained some strictly fundamentalist Calvinist doctrine. For example, the theory of evolution was completely rejected in favour of predestination. *Blackout* journal commented: "Creation took place in six calendar days and fossils must be explained presumably ... as 'examples of degeneration since the flood'.[13] History and geography were to be taught as divinely inspired in the narrow sense of the word. God had given to each people a country and a task. It was the Afrikaner's task to rule South Africa, and nobody had the right to question what was divinely ordained. Teachers who refused to subscribe to these doctrines would simply not be appointed.[14]

The policy caused such an outcry that it had to be shelved, but it was revived in more refined terms in the Education Advisory Council Act of 1960 and the National Education Policy Act of 1967, in which the Broederbond's pervasive hand played a leading part.

In 1959 the organisation had appointed an education task group under the chairmanship of Professor H J J Bingle, Rector of the University of Potchefstroom. By 1963 its report was ready and Professor Bingle, Dr J S Gericke, Moderator of the Nederduitse Gereformeerde Kerk, J H Stander, Director of Education in Natal, and Dr A P Treurnicht, at that time a dominee-turned-editor were delegated to present their national education policy blueprint to Brothers in responsible circles – the Cabinet.[15]

In the following two years, the Broederbond held two major conferences to thrash out the details of its policy. Dr Meyer's claim (above) that the Broederbond formulated the National education policy is supported by an examination of details of the organisation's education blueprint contained particularly in two of its secret documents. In a comprehensive document *Dringende Take (Urgent Tasks)* the following points were emphasised.

(A) The organisation should help ensure that the Department of Education, Arts and Science be divided so that education could exist as an independent department. Under this department should fall:

(i) The universities, including technical training and teacher training. While this would mean that teacher training would be removed from provincial jurisdiction, provincial governments would still be involved via the National Education Advisory Board and the professional Education Council;
(ii) Adult education;
(iii) The Bureau for Educational and Social Research;
(iv) The co-ordination of all educational services in the provinces; psychological, preparational, health, special, remedial, etc;
(v) The co-ordination of library services;
(vi) Liaison with State departments, such as Labour, Trade and Industry, Agriculture and with the trade unions;
(vii) Supervision of the execution of the policy of the National Educational Advisory Board through the provincial authorities, which in broad terms are concerned with the system of education, the education itself, and the profession;
(viii) Financing of education as a whole, including the provinces.

(B) The provincial education departments should remain in existence. Under their control would come:

(i) Nursery school education, which should be organised as a specific facet of education;
(ii) Primary education;
(iii) Secondary education, including academic, technical, trade, agricultural, and domestic science education;
(iv) Special education in all its aspects;
(v) Compulsory post-school education;
(vi) Apprenticeships.

(C) A professional teachers' council should be introduced soon so that the teacher corps can be involved in all facets of education at a level appropriate to a profession.

(D) A national parents' council should be established.

(E) Education should be financed by the State so that no child would have less opportunity than another for financial reasons.

(F) The Executive Council unequivocally demands that the spirit and direction of the education of the Afrikaans-speaking child will be Christian in accordance with the Afrikaans creed and in national conformity with the history and culture of the Afrikaner nation. "The Executive Council is convinced that in this way the first steps will be taken towards a national education system in line with our history and our current requirements for national cohesion within the boundaries of the Republic of South Africa."

Another document, *Memorandum 1/S Die Noodsaaklikheid van Beroepsgerigte Onderwys Dom-Normale Leerlinge in Provinsiale Skole (Memorandum in connection with the necessity for vocation-oriented education for backward children in provincial schools)* advocates that vocational schools be expanded to accommodate children who for various reasons are not emotionally or intellectually equipped for a standard academic education.

In every material detail, all these aspects of the Broederbond's education blueprint are incorporated in the system of education provided for whites in South Africa today. The latest developments in education have clinched the plan. The organisation's concern for backward children has been implemented in the form of a parallel education course known as the Practical Matric. In 1977 the professional teachers' body came into being in the form of the South African Teachers' Council for whites. Its first chairman is, appropriately, a Broederbonder, J D V Terblanche, Rector of the Pretoria Teachers' Training College.

On June 5 1968, the 50th birthday of the Broederbond, celebrations were held in the organisation's branches throughout South Africa. The occasion was commemorated by an oath-swearing ceremony, rededicating the Broeders to the oganisation's ideals. As part of this oath, they renewed their commitment to a Christian National outlook and a mother-tongue education system.[16]

In October that year a national congress of the Broederbond was held. Among the speakers was Dr Treurnicht, who had been a member of the education task force. He said it was "in a sense epoch-making that our Government placed a law of Christian National education on the statute book last year." He added: "Nobody will fail to appreciate the role of the Afrikaner Broederbond in the achievement of this ideal. It will also remain a serious matter for the Afrikaner Broederbond to help ensure, in the interests of the Afrikaner, that this law is executed effectively for the sake of the generations to come."[17]

Four years later, the chairman of the Broederbond reaffirmed the Bond's commitment to the principles in education for which it had fought so ardently through the years. "The heart of the successful programme of action to achieve Afrikaner unity on the basis of our own distinctive Afrikanerdom," he said, "is naturally how we educate and train our children and youth. As Christian Afrikaners we undertake, when our children are christened to educate and have them educated in Christian faith and to the honour of our Creator. This education process begins in the family life and must be continued in our schools and institutions of higher education.

"At the same time, we teach our children Afrikaans as their mother-tongue in our homes and adjust them in this way to their own Afrikaner cultural assets, a process which is also continued in and through our educational institutions. To achieve one's own mother-tongue, and thus one's own culture is at the same time to achieve awareness of one's own distinct Afrikanerdom. Education whereby one's own Christian Afrikanerdom is achieved and enriched is the key to Afrikaner unity. If Afrikaner parents, teachers and lecturers fail in this task, or carry it out defectively, Afrikaner unity will suffer irreparable damage."[18]

The Broederbond, through its secret distribution of members, is in a very powerful position to safeguard its education system. Of the organisation's total membership of nearly 12 000, the largest single group by profession is teachers and lecturers. They number 2 424 or 20,36 per cent of the total. The spread of this group is impressive in its scope. They range from the Minister of National Education himself, Dr Piet Koornhof and senior members of his staff including the Director of National Education, S C M Naude, the Director of University Affairs, Dr H S Steyn, and the Deputy Secretary of the department, C J Orrfer. It spreads down through the principals and chancellors of the Afrikaans universities (see A Profile of Power), in the provincial departments of education and down to individual teachers and lecturers at schools and educational institutions throughout South Africa. The guardians of the Broederbond's Christian National ideal are immovably instituted within and throughout the country's educational structure.

Two universities in South Africa owe their existence largely to Broederbond efforts. In Johannesburg a need was felt to counter the liberal traditions of the English-language University of the Witwatersrand, where, in the 1960s, NUSAS was at the height of its anti-government activities. In the early 1960s the Executive Council of the Broederbond started working in earnest for the creation of an Afrikaner university in the city. Thus one finds in the secret minutes of an Executive Council meeting held at the Volkskas Building in Johannesburg on December 1 1965, "Brother chairman (Dr Piet Meyer) sketched the whole background of the representations which led to the establishment of an Afrikaans university on the Rand. He disclosed the role of the relevant committee in connection with the character of the univer-

The 1975 opening of the Broederbond controlled Rand Afrikaans University.

sity, the conscience clause, the grounds, the collection of funds etc. The Executive Council held an open-hearted discussion about the matter during which various standpoints were expressed in connection with the entrenchment of the character of the university in its Act."

The close involvement of the Broederbond in the establishment of this prestige university, the Rand Afrikaans University – situated in the Broederbond stronghold of Auckland Park, Johannesburg – is reflected in its hierarchy. The late Dr Nico Diederichs became the chancellor; the Rector, Professor Gerrit Viljoen, is currently chairman of the Broederbond; the chairman of the University Council is Dr Piet Meyer himself.

The other university was in Port Elizabeth. Rhodes University in Grahamstown, a traditionally English-speaking campus, had decided to establish a satellite campus in Port Elizabeth. To counter the spread of English-speaking influence, the Broederbond initiated moves to establish a university it could control in the seaport. As a result, the University of Port Elizabeth came into being under the rectorship of a senior Broeder, Professor E J Marais. Having established the university, which is bilingual in character, the Broederbond made strenuous efforts to ensure that the bias of the campus was towards Afrikaans. It launched a campaign to fill the university as far as possible with Afrikaners. An instruction was sent to members in the monthly circular letter number 4/64/65 dated June 2 1964: "With the establishment of a university in Port Elizabeth in mind, it is cordially requested that in particular friends (members) in the area will use their influence to ensure that as many Afrikaner students as possible register there. Friends across the whole country can naturally assist in this matter."

The Broederbond-Nationalist compulsion to separate all aspects of education naturally extended to colour compartmentalisation in South Africa. The original Christian National education policy, drafted by the Broederbond in 1948, caters for black and coloured people as well as whites.

Article 14 deals with the coloured people. "We accept the principle of trusteeship of the non-European by the European, and particularly by the Afrikaners. This trusteeship imposes on the Afrikaner the solemn duty of seeing that the coloured people are educated in accordance with Christian and national principles... We believe that the coloured man can only be truly happy when he has been Christianised ... We believe that the welfare and happiness of the coloured man rest upon his realising that he belongs to a separate racial group ... The financing of coloured education must be placed on such a basis that it is not provided at the cost of European education."[19]

Article 15 deals with African education. "We believe that the role of white South Africa with respect to the native is to Christianise him and help him on culturally, and this vocation and duty has found its immediate application and task in the principles of trusteeship, distinguishing the native status from that of the white, and in segregation ... that instruction and education for natives must lead to the development of the native community on Christian National lines, which is self-supporting and provides for itself in every respect."[20]

The Bantu Education Act of 1953 placed its supervision under the Department of Native Affairs; in 1958 a new Department of Bantu Education was established. The Minister and Deputy Minister of its current version, Willem Cruywagen and Dr A P Treurnicht, are both Broeders.

In 1959 the separation process was completed with the passing of the Extension of University Education Act, which effectively segregated the universities, ending the enrolment of "non-whites" at the universities of the Witwatersrand and Cape Town, which had been open. Provision was made for ethnic universities to be established. This is now reality in the form of the Universities of Zululand (Ngoye), of the North (Turfloop) and of Fort Hare, all of which had Broederbond principals until they were gradually replaced by blacks in accordance with the concept of evolving autonomy for the homelands.

Similarly with the University of the Western Cape, for coloured students, and of Durban-Westville, for Indian students. The latter still has a Broederbond rector, Professor S P Olivier, a former member of the organisation's Executive Council.

The Broederbond-Nationalist obsession with separation has bred countless personal tragedies in South African history. Schoolchildren have not escaped the traumas this obsession has imposed. One of the most moving and publicised cases of this kind is that of Sandra Laing. Born of white, Afrikaner parents, she had dark skin and tightly curled hair, the physical characteristics usually associated with negroid or coloured (mixed race) people. She attended a "white" school in the platteland town of Piet

Retief, where she was completely accepted by her contemporaries. All appeared to be well until in 1964 two Broederbonders, the Administrator of the Transvaal, Mr Sybrand van Niekerk, and the local Member of the provincial council, Mr Theo Martins, told her parents there had been complaints.

Two years later, Sandra Laing was classifid "coloured". Her parents, who in the eyes of the law remained "white", received a letter from the principal of the school asking them to remove their daughter in terms of a request by the Transvaal Department of Education, whose director was a Broederbonder. Her father refused to comply. Two weeks later uniformed police arrived at the school and took Sandra away. Eventually, after protracted legal action, Sandra Laing was re-classified "white" again.

The end of the story has a strange irony. Sandra Laing never fitted comfortably again into the "white" box from which she had been rejected and then grudgingly readmitted. She finally married an African and settled into a happy but simple existence with him in a rural township in the Transvaal.

Malherbe[21] has assessed the effect of South Africa's system in these terms: "The Broederbond knew that by separation, the future of Nationalist policies would be assured."[22]

(Their means of doing this was attacked by Mr S J V Geldenhuys, MPC for Pretoria District, who claimed that Nationalist indoctrination had been going on for years in Afrikaans schools and stated in the Provincial Council debate: "If it were not for the Afrikaner teacher and predikant, I doubt whether the National Party would ever have come to power."

A member: "Through indoctrination?"

Mr Geldenhuys: "Yes, through indoctrination.")[22]

"This isolationist view of the function of the school," continues Malherbe, "ignored the fact that South Africa was a bilingual country and that its children, no matter what their home language might be to start with,were destined to associate with one another when they became adults in nearly every kind of political, social and economic activity. As this view gained ground the State school, instead of being regarded as virtually a replica of the South African community in miniature, became more and more designed to preserve the identity of the Afrikaner majority and thus to consolidate its political power.

"This exclusiveness of the school in course of time served to generate stereotype attitudes not only in regard to English-

Afrikaans relationships, but also on ideological issues involving black-white relationships as reflected by the party in power.

"The fact that young people, during the most impressionable years of their lives, were, by deliberate segregation, deprived of the normal opportunities of rubbing shoulders with persons holding different views from their own, tended to make them less adaptable in meeting new challenges due to changing circumstances. The same would also to a large extent apply to the teachers in these separate schools.

"It is, therefore, not surprising that a nation-wide survey, conducted early in 1974 by Professor Lawrence Schlemmer, Director of the Institute of Social Research at Natal University,[23] revealed that the political opinions of Afrikaners under 25 years of age 'offered scant encouragement to those who hoped for more enlightened and forward-looking policies. Their apathetic attitude (I'm all right, Jack) showed no sense of urgency to come to terms with our basic racial conflict, and it differs little from that of their elders.'"

Apart from its formal education systems, the Broederbond has at its disposal an impressive party of bodies and oganisations to carry out its propaganda functions. The two most notable of these are the Federasie van Afrikaanse Kultuurverenigings (FAK) and the Suid Afrikaanse Buro vir Rasse Aangeleenthede (SABRA). The FAK is referred to by the Broederbond as its public cultural wing. General Hertzog quoted a Broederbond document during his Smithfield address which described the FAK as "our so-much-bigger son" (see Chapter 2).

One of the first major actions of the Broederbond was the establishment of this open, cultural wing. It was created on December 18 1929 to undertake various Afrikaner programmes and co-ordinate and stimulate others. Its first chairman was the ever-present Lombard, also chief secretary of the Broederbond. The FAK is housed at the Broederbond's Auckland Park headquarters and receives regular appropriations from the Broederbond.

One especially interesting instance in which the Broederbond used the organisation, and which has been referred to elsewhere, is revealed in a special circular to all Broeders dated August 1 1962. "The Executive Council of the Broederbond announces that friend Dr Piet Koornhof, formerly deputy secretary of the National Party of the Transvaal, has been appointed chief secretary of our organisation as from the beginning of the new *Bond-*

sjaar... To the outside he is known as the Director of Cultural Information of the FAK and in that capacity will serve as a link with affiliated bodies of the FAK and will, when necessary, act as mouthpiece of the FAK...

"The Executive Council is grateful that arrangements could be made with the FAK to link the post of our chief secretary with the public post as it enables friend Piet Koornhof to carry out our activities tactfully in the open."

Secret Broederbond Circular 2/63/64 of June 12 1963 provides another example. It deals with a *volkskongres* on education matters and adds: "It is being publicly organised by the FAK in collaboration with the inter-church Commission on Education." Planned topics for discussion included the role of the State in education, the National Educational Council and the national education policy. In this way the FAK ensures the public expression of the Broederbond's secret deliberations.

The FAK's influence in South African affairs has been a constant presence, running parallel to and coinciding with the activities of the Broederbond. In 1938 the FAK organised the highly successful and emotional oxwagon trek, which commemorated the Great Trek of 100 years before, and essentially marked the beginning of national awareness among Afrikaners. The organisation was closely involved in the language-medium struggle and the formulation of the Christian National education policy. It was a leading factor in the economic *Reddingsdaadbond* and *Helpmekaar* movements. In all these ventures it was acting as the Broederbond's public agent.

The FAK's main function is the co-ordination of Afrikaner cultural activities throughout South Africa. To this end it has built up a huge range of members, affiliated bodies and co-operating bodies. Apart from cultural organisations per se it includes teachers' organisations, youth organisations, church organisations, student organisations and women's organisations. "In fact," says Malherbe[24] "it involved the whole Afrikaans body politic. At the centre there was the Afrikaanse Nasionale Kultuurraad (ANK). This was described by its first chairman, Dr N J van der Merwe (a Broeder) as a 'concentrated focal point where all the rays of the Afrikaans life are kindled through the FAK as with a magnifying glass'." According to a report in the *Sunday Times*, January 28 1973, the FAK had more than 2 000 cultural, religious and youth bodies affiliated to it.

Among the more important of these are the three main Afrikaans churches, the Voortrekkers (the Afrikaans equivalent of the Boy Scouts movement) the Afrikaanse Studentebond (ASB), the Afrikaanse Taal en Kultuurvereniging (ATKV) an organisation for railways employees, the Afrikaanse Taal en Kultuurbond (ATKB) for postal employees, the Afrikaanse Kultuurvereniging Volk en Verdediging (AKVV) for Defence Force personnel, the Afrikaanse Kultuurvereniging van die Suid-Afrikaanse Polisie (AKPOL) for the police, and the Afrikaanse Verpleegbond (AVB) for nurses. There is also a national association for Afrikaner folk music and dance.[25] The Afrikaner service organisations, Junior Rapportryers and Rapportryers, are also connected in this way.

The FAK keeps in regular touch with its members through its newsletter *Handhaaf* (literally, Maintain or Preserve) which acts as an open conduit for Broederbond ideas. It also publishes booklets and study papers.

Apart from its purely Afrikaner cultural functions in South African society, the FAK performs an important role in Afrikaner and national politics. It is the central organising body for the many *volksfeeste* (national celebrations) on the South African calendar. These, particularly Republic Day on May 31 and the Day of the Covenant on December 16, give Nationalist politicians valuable platforms where they regenerate enthusiasm and support for their ideals, largely by capitalising on the emotions associated with past Afrikaner triumphs.

Vatcher[26] describes the nature and scope of the FAK's activities thus: "The FAK has been singularly aware of the value of music, opera, plays, literature, monuments and language in inculcating and maintaining a strong nationalism and a feeling of unity within a group. From time to time, the FAK sponsors massive rallies and festivals, which have the effect of infusing and renewing pride in *ons eie*. . .

"Thus the FAK stresses all things Afrikaner: language, music, song, literature, dress, customs, experiences. For example, the concentration camps established by the English in the Boer War are constantly recalled to bolster nationalistic feelings. The FAK has even purchased one of these camps to serve as physical evidence of Afrikaner grievances.

"The Voortrekkers, who represented die-hard resistance to British suzerainty, are brandished before *die volk* like a cloth before a bull. Van Riebeeck has been all but deified. His statue at Cape

Town greets the visitor to South Africa and reminds the Briton that the Dutch were there first."

The Broederbond's other major public propaganda arm, SABRA, which is based in Pretoria, is basically a study organisation which examines aspects of South African politics. It seeks good race relations, but works strictly on the premise that separate development, or apartheid, is the only viable method of achieving this. A Broederbond document about the organisation, circulated to members in 1974, said: "It is our only public arm in connection with relations matters, homeland development and connected affairs. With one or two exceptions, the members of SABRA's controlling council are all members of our organisation."[27]

SABRA has about 3 000 members and affiliated bodies that promote its aims locally. It is regionally divided into provincial committees.

SABRA, which was founded in 1948 by a group which included such prominent Broeders as Dr T E Dönges, Professor H B Thom, Dr W W M Eiselen, Dr M C de Wet Nel, and Dr Nico Diederichs, receives regular financial donations from the Broederbond. Its current chairman, Professor C W H Boshoff, Verwoerd's son-in-law, is a prominent Broeder.

The organisation lists its activities as youth programmes for black and white children; arranging congresses for adults; establishing contact between white and black leaders – "teachers, who play a key role in cultivating good dispositions among the youth, have received particular attention recently" – the publication of a quarterly magazine, a yearbook and a newsletter to members; and research, particularly into the problem of homeland consolidation.

Between them, the FAK and SABRA campaign energetically to win the minds of the youth over to the concepts of Nationalist philosophy, their most important function. The FAK's youth organisation is the *Nasionale Jeugraad* (National Youth Council) which holds camps and conferences for young Afrikaners. SABRA holds similar courses and conferences, usually during school holidays. The Voortrekkers play a similar role.

The seriousness with which the adult Afrikaners view this work for the *volk* is reflected in the stature of the people appointed to address the gatherings. For example, the 1968 report of the liaison secretary between the Broederbond and the FAK's *Jeugraad,* Broeder Francois Retief, shows that at the national youth congress the organisation staged that year, the former Prime Minister, Mr

Vorster, spoke along with his Cabinet colleague, Dr Piet Koornhof.

At youth meetings that year, prominent Broeders who addressed their young compatriots included the Minister of Agriculture, Mr Hendrik Schoeman *(The Youth's Task and Calling)* Mr H D K van der Merwe, MP, *(Youth in Action – Constitutional),* Dr R McLachlan MP, *(The Youth Leader's Task in the City),* Professor W J de Klerk of Potchefstroom, later to become editor of *Die Transvaler,* official National Party mouthpiece in the Transvaal *(The Youth's Share in the Perpetuation of the Christian and White Civilisation in Southern Africa)* and Dr A P Treurnicht *(The Christian-National Outlook of the Afrikaner).*

The Jeugraad also has an advanced offshoot in the form of the *Nasionale Jeugleiersinstituut* (National Youth Leaders' Institute) which holds regular camps and conferences for senior pupils and students.

A report by Hennie Serfontein in the *Sunday Times* of February 4 1973 dealt with a FAK camp in the Western Cape: "The FAK, the official 'cultural' front of the secret Broederbond, has now openly entered the party political arena. It is opposing attempts to bring whites and coloureds closer together and is taking a pro-homeland (for coloureds) line. The Afrikaanse Nasionale Jeugraad ... has embarked on a series of 30 leadership conferences in the Western Cape for high school youths.

"Two years ago a junior Sabra conference in the Cape was used to push the homeland idea when it was addressed by its chairman, Professor Gerrit Viljoen, Rector of the Rand Afrikaans University.

"It is significant that the decision to launch a youth action campaign through the FAK was taken some years ago by the Broederbond executive. It was decided to concentrate on high-school children, especially prefects, influencing them with a *verkrampte,* narrow Afrikaans ideology under the smokescreen of leadership conferences. By creating an innocent body, such as the Jeugraad, the help of the Department of Education, which is completely Broederbond-controlled, would be obtained."

Yet another important arm of propaganda work for the Broederbond is the *Maatskappy vir Europierse Immigrasie* (Society for European Immigration) which has as its main task the Afrikanerisation of immigrants to South Africa. In a document circulated to Broeders, *Inskakeling van Immigrante* (Absorption of Immigrants) the MEI urged Afrikaners to set up a chain of concerns for new immigrants, "many of whom have doubts about the policy of apartheid," to win immigrants over to the Afrikaner cause.

The MEI also devotes a large part of its activities to immigrant children as shown by extracts from a Press report on an MEI youth camp. "Sponsor of the seven-day *Praat Afrikaans* (Talk Afrikaans) holiday camp on the south coast was the Division for Cultural Advancement of the Department of National Education. The children paid only R10 each, and the Government R1 400." Activities included singing the national anthem, flag-raising ceremonies, games, handicraft lessons and talks.

"On Saturday it was *The Habits and Customs of the Bantu.* On Monday the children were told about C J Langenhoven, composer of the National Anthem, and *How South Africa is Governed.* On Tuesday it was *Our Flag and Anthem* and *The Population Groups of South Africa.* The last lecture on Wednesday was *South Africa – Yesterday and Today.*

"After lectures the children had an hour of Afrikaans followed by Afrikaner games. Just before supper the flag was lowered while the children sang *Die Stem.* In the evening they practised for the end of camp concert, had *volkspele* and saw films provided by the Department of Tourism and of Information."[28]

Afrikaans newspapers in South Africa form an important part of the Broederbond's propaganda machine. The two giant Afrikaans Press groups, Perskor and Nasionale Pers, are Broederbond-dominated. Perskor's board of directors includes at least nine Broeders out of a total of 12. They are the chairman, Mr Marius Jooste, Mr M C Botha, Senator Jan de Klerk, Dr C P "Connie" Mulder (Minister of Plural Relations), Mr Marais Viljoen (President of the Senate), Senator J H Steyl, Transvaal secretary of the National Party, Professor Gerrit Viljoen, Dr T F Muller, head of the semi-State corporation Iscor, and W van Heerden.

The editor of the company's flagship newspaper, Dr "Wimpie" de Klerk of *Die Transvaler,* is an executive member of the Broederbond. Perskor has 10 newspapers on its portfolio, two financial weekly magazines, a magazine for blacks, 14 general magazines and 26 "mini-magazines". It also has a huge publishing business which handles a great many Government contracts and has cornered the major slice of the school textbook market, both in South Africa and in the homelands.

Nasionale Pers' board of directors has a similar Broederbond loading. Its Broeders include the chairman, P A Weber, W J Pretorius, P W Botha, Minister of Defence and current Prime Minister, Louis le Grange, Minister of Public Works and of Tourism, C V van der Merwe, A D Wassenaar, S P Botha, Minister of Labour, Dr Piet Koornhof, Minister of National Education and of Sport, and the managing director, D P de Villiers.

Its portfolio includes the highly respected Cape newpaper *Die Burger,* and four other newspapers and six magazines.

The Afrikaans newspapers are all, in varying degrees, Government supporters.

It has long been a source of anxiety for the Broederbond that the Afrikaans Press in South Africa is not nearly as widely read as the generally anti-Government English-language press. In the early 1960s the oganisation conducted an investigation into what it called the "disturbing" lack of readership of Afrikaans newspapers as compared with the English-language competitors. Using detailed breakdowns of the official circulation figures of the various newspapers, the investigation paid particular attention to the effects of school-leavers on the circulation figures.

Taking a five-year period from 1953 to 1958, it found that 141 000 Afrikaner pupils left school in that time. The circulation of Afrikaans newspapers in the corresponding period rose by 22 500. The corresponding figures for the English sector were 82 000 school-leavers and a circulation increase of 69 000. "This enormous rise in the circulation of English dailies was caused in the first place by the newspaper-conscious English-speaking population itself, and in the second place by many thousands of Afrikaans-speaking readers," was the gloomy conclusion of the investigators.

This trend has continued into the 1970s. A survey in 1977 by a Rand Afrikaans University academic, Dr C R Swart, senior researcher for the university's Institute for Urban Studies, found that, because of readership trends, in terms of acculturisation the English-language Press would have a greater influence on Afrikaans-speakers than the other way around. Considerably more Afrikaans-speakers read English-language newspapers than there were English-speakers reading Afrikaans newspapers.[29]

All this gave cause for grave concern to the Broederbond which started agitating for a "well-disposed" English-language newspaper. An item in the report of the chief secretary (Dr Koornhof) for the period from August 24 to December 5 1963 says: "Press task group: the following recommendations are presented.

(a) That an English-language newspaper be established which is equipped to reach the top level of English-speakers and by that means exercise influence."

Whether or not the Broederbond played any part, their wishes as expressed by Dr Koornhof were realised in 1976 with the establishment of a pro-Nationalist daily newspaper, *The Citizen.* It may or may not be pure coincidence, but the founder of that newspaper, South Africa's genial fertiliser king, Mr Louis Luyt, is a close associate of Dr Koornhof. Mr Luyt is not, however, a member of the Broederbond.

In the same Koornhof report, it was recommended that there should be no form of censorship of the Press, but that the Press Council should be retained to exercise a "dampening effect on the venom in the English-language Press."

Another secret Broederbond document, *Ons Taak Vorentoe (Our Task Ahead)* published the same year alleges that the "Oppenheimer group," having achieved control of the Argus Company[30] was using the English Press in South Africa and elsewhere in Africa to propagate multiracial states to protect its financial interests. "Our future," says the document, "demands that a large and important portion of the English-language Press in our country is not controlled by a powerful inter-Africa and international money group for the promotion of multiracialism. This monopolistic stranglehold on our future must be ended as soon as possible by state intervention."

The Government did not step in to strip the Argus Company shareholdings from the "Oppenheimer group." But it did leap in to prevent a merger between the Argus Company and South African Associated Newspapers in 1972. If the merger had taken place, the entire English Press empire in South Africa would have been under one group.

A fascinating feature of the Afrikaans Press is the manner in which it has reported disclosures about the Broederbond. In 1963, when the *Sunday Times* broke the first major exposure of the organisation since Hertzog's Smithfield Address, South Africa was agog. But not a word of the raging controversy was reported in the Afrikaans newspapers.[31] More recently, the Afrikaans newspapers have stopped treating the Broederbond like a sacred cow, but are very careful in the way in which they report on the organisation. They never initiate news about it and usually react to other news items on the organisation in a highly defensive tone.

What was even more remarkable about the 1963 disclosures was that while the Afrikaans papers kept mum, the South African Broadcasting Corporation, under the chairmanship of the Broederbond chairman, Dr Meyer, took it upon itself to interrupt its regular radio programmes on several occasions to defend the Broederbond. In the ensuing outcry, even *Die Burger* expressed some surprise at this.

While interrupting radio programmes to defend something like the Broederbond might be surprising in its lack of finesse, the underlying sentiments are not in the least surprising. The SABC is a valuable Nationalist-Broederbond asset. As we have seen in Profile of Power the SABC's hierarchy is heavily laden with Broeders. There have been suggestions that top jobs in the State-controlled corporation have been rewards for political favours in the past.

In any event the sprawling bureaucracy that controls the radio and TV networks of South Africa is assuredly in the grip of the Broederbond and as such the service must count as one of its strongest propaganda weapons. And it is a weapon that brooks no competition. The Government maintains a jealous guard over its monopoly control of the service. During the early 1970s an application by the Argus Company to run a commercial television channel was turned down flat.

Apart from the blatant use of the SABC's radio services for the defence of the organisation, perhaps the closest links that have been drawn came during the late 1960s when South Africa was embroiled in debate about whether or not to introduce a television service. In 1968 the logjam keeping out television was breached when Vorster sacked Dr Albert Hertzog as Minister of Posts and Telegraphs. The arch-conservative Dr Hertzog had long resisted television, or, as he called it, *klein bioskoop* (little cinema). He regarded it with deep suspicion and said it was the instrument of the devil. In a debate on the issue in the Assembly in May 1967 he accused the Opposition of nefarious motives in agitating for a television service.

They were interested only because a group of their friends were out to make a profit, because South Africa would be forced to import TV films propagating mixing across the colour line and because advertising would engender a sense of dissatisfaction among the country's non-whites and so inflame race relations.[32]

With Dr Hertzog stripped of the Posts and Telegraphs portfolio, the clamour for television increased and pressure mounted on the Government to appoint a Commission of Inquiry into television.

In December 1969 the Government gave in to the pressure and announced the appointment of such a commission. Mr Etienne Malan, the United Party's spokesman on communications was unimpressed and told the Assembly: "Nine commissioners (out of 12) were Afrikaans-speaking and the remainder English-speaking. When one looks at the names of the Afrikaans-speaking members, I am sure that if the majority of them were ever to get together it would be like an old home week of the Broederbond, with cabalistic rites, secret handgrip and all."[33]

Dr Piet Meyer. Ex-Broederbond chairman and present head of the SABC.

He was absolutely right. The commission was headed by Dr Piet Meyer, who was simultaneously head of the Broederbond and of the SABC. Along with him on the commission were Broeders Dr J S Gericke, Moderator of the synod of the Nederduitse Gereformeerde Kerk; Professor H B Thom, rector of the University of Stellenbosch and a former Broederbond chairman; Dr P J Riekert, economic adviser to the Prime Minister; Dr S M Naude, President of the Council for Scientific and Industrial Research; Dr G Beukes, head of the Department of Afrikaans at the University of the Orange Free State; Dr S J Naude, financial adviser to the Nederduitse Gereformeerde Kerk; Dr Jan Schutte, assistant director of the English, Afrikaans and Special Services of the SABC.

It has not been established whether or not the remaining Afrikaner, Dr P A W Cook, under-secretary in the Department of Bantu Education, was a Broeder at the time. It is more than likely that he was. The remaining English-speakers were hardly noted for their lack of sympathy to the Nationalist cause. Professor Owen Horwood had just given up his job as Principal of the University of Natal to become a Nationalist Senator; Professor S M Leighton was professor of English at the Broederbond stronghold, Rand Afrikaans University. The remaining English-speaker was Bishop R Cowdrey, assistant bishop of the Anglican Church in Cape Town.

The Broederbond was quick to move in on the act. The Minister of Posts and Telegraphs, Mr M C van Rensburg, announced the commission on December 3 1969. Two days later the Broederbond sent out a secret special circular to all its members. "Dear friends," it said, "now that our friend, the Minister of Posts and Telegraphs, has announced a commission of inquiry into the desirability and possibility of a distinctive television service for our country, under the leadership of the Executive Council chairman, we are pleased to announce that this matter was discussed beforehand, at the request of our Prime Minister, at the previous Executive Council meeting. Brother Meyer informed the Executive Council about the basic specifications the Minister had set, with which a possible television service would have to comply before it would be considered by the Government.

"These requirements are that:

(a) It must be integrated into the existing services of the SABC and there will be no continuous, parallel service.

(b) As a statutorily-controlled service it will be subject to strict programme control arrangements.
(c) It will not, as is the case abroad, degenerate to a medium for play-films of all sorts, and also that it will not try to take over or limit the functions of the Press, the film and entertainment industry.
(d) The service will aim mainly at informing and educating in the interests of our country and all its nations.
(e) In no circumstances may it be a commercialised service in search of profit, as is the case particularly in America.
(f) It must provide, as soon as possible, separate cultural services for the Afrikaans-, English-, and Bantu-speaking national communities in our country.

"The Executive Council, after discussing the matter, decided to give its support to a distinctive South African television service that will comply with all these high and important requirements. It will thus not be a service that will be a pure replica of overseas services, but one that will by definition prevent all the excessive and undesirable effects of overseas systems on particularly the morals of the population and particularly of the youth of the country.

"The Executive Council requests all branches and members that are interested ... urgently to send their opinions and thoughts to the Chief Secretary for personal presentation to the chairman of the commission (Broeder Meyer).

"You are cordially, but urgently, requested to handle this communication with the highest degree of confidentiality, but also to inform members of your branch about this in a discreet way before your next meeting."

It was, therefore, a foregone conclusion. The Broederbond had decided there would be a television service. The commission of inquiry was totally Broederbond-dominated, *ergo* there would be a television service. While the commission was busy with its "investigation", the Broederbond sent out the following communication to its members in Circular letter 5/70/71, dated August 3 1970. "The Executive Council would like to thank heartily the branches for their opinions and recommendations about the possible introduction of television in our country ... Of the 104 branches that commented, 101 expressed themselves in favour of the introduction of television on the basis which was set out. Throughout, it was emphasised that the crux of the matter is effective control and the greatest possible insurance against any misuse of the medium now or later to the damage and disadvantage of our Christian National outlook and lifestyle. Along with this it is emphasised that no good or evil lurks in a technology as such, but very much so in the manner in which it is used and that it is better if a sympathetic Nationalist Government introduces such a service than to leave it over for a possible, later non-National Government ...

"The Executive Council chairman has carefully summed up all the points and comments that the branches sent in. He personally ensured that the commission of inquiry gave the necessary attention to them. Our organisation can rest assured not only that the real and correct data will appear in the report, but thorough consideration and well-motivated recommendations will also be given.

"The Executive Council chairman has undertaken to inform the Executive Council fully about the effective methods that are recommended to control television in our country, if it is introduced, to the advantage of our nation and country *before the report (of the Commission) is handed in* (own emphasis)."

In other words, in a flagrant breach of Parliamentary procedure, the chairman of the commission of inquiry, who was also the chairman of the Broederbond, was calmly undertaking to reveal the contents of his report to the organisation before he revealed it to the Government or Parliament. Apart from the morality of such a practice, other questions also arise.

At the time of the announcement of the commission of inquiry into the feasibility of setting up a television service there was intense activity in the electronic world in South Africa. One of the more active firms was Teljoy. This report appeared in the *Rand Daily Mail* on December 23 1969. "A television leasing company, which has taken several full-page advertisements and advertised widely in the Press, is to begin installing TV sets in South African homes early next year. The sets ... will be imported from Europe, according to the company managing director, Mr Theo Rutstein ... More than 7 000 people had approached him about leasing sets since the Government appointed its commission of inquiry ... he said. Altogether more than 25 000 people had leased sets with this company ..."

The Star followed up the report the following day. Mr Theo Rutstein of Teljoy told the newspaper: "I want to make it clear that we have absolutely no inside information on television's arrival." The newspaper added: "A number of Nationalist Senators are directors of Teljoy."

At least one of them was a member of the Broederbond, and had thus been told that the commission's chairman and the majority of its members were going to support the introduction of television in South Africa. Teljoy became one of the biggest television rental companies in South Africa.

Needless to say, the SABC's television service is no less pro-Government than its radio service. An article by John van Zyl, a former lecturer in communications at the University of the Witwatersrand and TV critic observed in the magazine *Reality* of July 1978: "TV news has several built-in features that comment visually on the words spoken by the newsreader. The use of lurid or emotive graphics can slant the news. The map used by SABC-TV depicting South West Africa and Angola has an arrow pointing south, with a hammer and sickle at the northern end. Other local examples are the use of crude caricatures of Carter or Castro, contrasted with the usual slide of a smiling, benign Vorster. When we look closely at SABC-TV news some depressing features emerge.

"The absence of overseas news on some evenings, the fact that the SABC has only one representative overseas, and the excessive use of certain news commentators gives the news a bias which is always noticeable and sometimes is downright crude. I cannot imagine another television service in the 'free world' (that concept so assiduously bandied about by SABC-TV) that would tolerate so many eager pre-digestors, or masticators, of the news.

"It is common knowledge that television programmes that offend the sensibilites of SABC-TV are summarily banned . . .

"Two surveys conducted by *The Star* and the Department of Journalism of Rhodes University respectively have revealed some interesting statistics. *The Star* reported on June 12 1976 that Cabinet Ministers were getting nearly 10 times as much exposure on television as spokesmen for all the country's opposition parties combined . . .

"This is, of course, not the whole picture. The featuring of Cabinet Ministers for the promotion of Government viewpoints uncritically can by no means be regarded as news. The only place where this might take place is within a discussion programme, and then hopefully, with a critical interviewer, or an opposition spokesman to test the validity of the viewpoint.

"Apart from the Cabinet Ministers, there is a series of familiar faces of pro-Government black spokesmen and white spokesmen belonging to the 'pyramid of access' that can be relied upon to trot out obligingly the familiar bogeymen of communism, corrupt black governments and 'hypocritical' Western politicians.

"The Rhodes survey . . . investigated the news broadcasts over a month during the period September-October 1977. Although the findings were not totally conclusive, some of the results are significant. It was found that 32 per cent of the news times was given to political representation, i.e. reports pertaining to the policies or principles of political parties in South Africa. This is already significant in terms of the proportion of 'hard news' and 'purportive news'.

"Of this time, 47 per cent was devoted to showing and hearing of Government officials and National Party officials. Thirty-four per cent of the political time consisted of hearing statements from or news about Government and National Party officials. When these figures are combined, it may be seen that 81 per cent of political news was centred on Government or National party officials. The rest of the statistics are depressingly predictable.

"It is obvious that the party in power will always have an advantage of newsmaking and newsworthiness, but it is only a television service which is overwhelmingly an official service which will provide such an accessible platform for Government views which are not tested or probed by informed interviewers. It is this, finally, which makes our television service an official one rather than a national service."

Shortly after a report of this survey appeared in the *Sunday Times,* SABC-TV devoted the bulk of one of its programmes[34] to denouncing the surveys and denying the conclusions reached by them.

Among the most influential propaganda agencies for Broederbond-Nationalist ideals are the three main Afrikaans churches, particularly the two largest, the Nederduitse Gereformeerde Kerk and the Nederduitsche Hervormde Kerk. The smallest, although it believes in separation of the races, has lately become quite outspoken in its questioning of anomalies, inconsistencies and lack of morality in major aspects of Government policy, for example the cornerstone legislation embodied in the Immorality and Mixed Marriages Acts. But the two main churches are, as institutions, committed disciples and in this context more relevantly, advocates of the tenets of apartheid.

The churches are a highly influential force in Afrikaner society. The Dutch Reformed churches are virtually synonymous with Afrikanerdom. All National Party leaders are staunch Calvinists from one of the three churches. Sir de Villiers Graaff, former Leader of the Opposition, once reported that when he visited Dr Verwoerd after the attempt on his life in 1960, the Prime Minister referred to God more than a dozen times in the course of a two-hour conversation, and insisted that the fact of his survival was proof of divine acceptance of Nationalist policy.[35] It has also been reported that members of the Government frequently consult *dominees* on matters of State.[35] Not surprisingly, then, the *dominee* enjoys high status in the traditional Afrikaner social hierarchy. A strongly Godfearing people in general, the Afrikaners place great store on the statements and attitudes of their church and tend to follow its lead unquestioningly.

As we have seen earlier in this chapter, the church plays an important role in the political life of South Africa. Its involvement, for example, in the language-medium struggle was considerable. Many *dominees* have stepped from their pulpits into national politics, the most obvious example being the first National Party Prime Minister, Dr D F Malan. According to Vatcher[37] the Dutch Reformed Church in South Africa is the only body that rivals the National Party in influence. Apart from its influence on policy, its principal importance for Afrikaner nationalism is that it is largely responsible for the closeness of the Afrikaner community. It has certainly been a rallying force behind nationalism. The Nederduitse Gereformeerde Kerk in particular continues to play a paramount role in the political life of South Africa. Its synods each year are watched with keen interest in South Africa because it then formally pronounces on cardinal political aspects.

The fifth most numerous group of Broederbond members by profession are the *dominees*. There are 848 of them. Following a power struggle in the 1960s (see Chapter 16) the Broeder *dominees* have secured control of the top positions in the Dutch Reformed Church family. The Moderator of the Nederduitse Gereformeerde Kerk of SA, Dr D P M Beukes, is a member of the Broederbond's supreme Executive Council. The Western Cape Moderator, Dr J D "Koot" Vorster, the Prime Minister's brother, is a Broeder, as is the Eastern Cape Moderator, Dr D T du P Moolman. The powerful Northern and Southern Transvaal Moderatures are in the hands of Broeders, Dr J E Potgieter and Dr D P M Beukes respectively. The *skriba* of the Hervormde Kerk, Dr P M Smit, is also a Broeder.

From here, through the provincial formations of the church, into the parish pulpits and the church's various publications, the Broederbond leaves a trail of important representatives and evangelical agents. If it is a truism that the Dutch Reformed Church is the National Party at prayer, then it is equally true that superimposed on this image is the ever-present spectre of the Broederbond.

In an imposingly comprehensive secret document, *Masterplan for a White Country: The Strategy,* the Broederbond reveals just how much it can rely on the support of all its propaganda agencies when it frames its plans. The document was drafted in the wake of the 1976 disturbances among South Africa's blacks and urges drastic action to settle the country's racial problems, mainly by means of an accelerated programme of action taking Verwoerd's original Bantustan policy to its logical conclusion. Linchpin of the masterplan is that blacks must be moved out of the "white" areas and into their bantustans as fast as possible. From there they could provide South Africa's labour requirements as migratory workers, preferably on a daily basis.

A major part of the plan is devoted to propaganda. Under the sub-heading *The Strategy aimed at the Private Sector and the General Population of the White Country,* the document says "In the strategic planning of South Africa it is accepted that in the defence of the country, only 20 per cent can be achieved by military preparedness; the other 80 per cent depends on spiritual preparedness ... A popular movement fed and supported by an organisation with the means and manpower to give effective leadership throughout the country, on the one hand to establish a positive climate for the execution of the masterplan, and on the other hand to play a direct part in combating radical ideas, must be created immediately.

"Just as radicalism has abandoned the use of political methods to achieve its goal, so will a counter-action have to parallel politics and be less dependent on politics. In practice politics will have to rely on and exploit the climate that the counter-action establishes, to enable it to achieve its objectives.

"An unwilling and unmotivated public opinion that is constantly urged to make concessions and change can eventually become such a hindrance to the Government that it cannot achieve its objectives. That must be prevented.

"Such an effective counter-action will of necessity have to be defensive, disseminating knowledge about the objectives and methods of radicalism in South Africa and about its specific characteristics. Radical action will have to be stigmatised in the same way that actions to put it in jeopardy are currently stigmatised.

"Resistance to radicalism must be engendered on a broad front and there must be co-ordination on the various aspects of life. The calculated manner in which target groups or individuals are isolated and estranged from their accepted values must be countered by calling for a healthy balance between the values of the individual and the values of family, nation, church and other connections and, as far as the youth is concerned, for at least one generation to place the emphasis firmly on group connections. By emphasising the value of group connections, the process of 'detribalisation' can be fought at source.

"Just as the youth is currently being encouraged to resist discipline, parental authority, school authority etc, so can they be brought into revolt against what is decadent and destructive. Against the instability, confusion and disintegration that characterises the radical attack, there must be one fundamental creed *(gelofsgrondslag)* upon which a life and world view can be developed and according to which thought and progress can burgeon in all areas of life ...

"The positive side of the counter-action is to spread reliable and relevant information continuously and to disseminate it through the mass media. Incomplete knowledge of the principle basis of the policy, and especially the progress being made with its implementation, favour the radical contentions that the policy is ultimately ineffectual. Ignorance about the moral foundation supports the allegation that the policy is a breach of human values and of Christian norms.

"To make the information and preparation strategy succeed and to get the masterplan accepted as a national priority in all spheres will require large scale and broad-fronted action, so that the initiative can be wrested from the radicals and come into the hands of those who carry out the policy. Liaison and co-ordination with all bodies and media that affect public life and give it direction must be brought into being. Bodies whose co-operation must be won are the following: the Afrikaans churches, the FAK, the SABC and other media (including the Press), teaching and education, including teachers' organisations, the South African Agricultural Union (many of whose senior officials are Broeders) with its provincial and district organisations, the *Afrikaanse Handelsinstituut,* the Federated Chamber of Industries, labour organisations, municipal associations, women's organisations, youth organisations, Rapportryers, Junior Rapportryers and other cultural bodies not named above, and new channels will have to be established to give effect to our ideas...

"Just as for the white country, a central body must be established for every homeland to help form public opinion in favour of the policy. The national leaders and the public media, particularly the radio, will play an important role in this regard."

In order to implement this, the plan says nationalism must be inculcated in the black groups along with sympathy with the Christian National outlook; within the framework of a comprehensive strategy, Afrikaans education organisations must help establish similar organisations in the Bantustans, a project which the Broederbond-controlled Transvaal *Onderwysvereniging* has already begun; sport must be used to foster this spirit of nationalism. The masterplan also calls for considerable concentration on the black youth. "The youth must be inspired to respect their leaders, their country and their future. Essay competitions, debating contests and youth congresses, where they learn to know their own leaders, must be held."

Finally it comes again to the public media. "The daily newspapers' contribution cannot be overestimated, nor the damage they do if they undermine the policy. It is, however, the separate radio services for the black nations and the coming television service (for blacks) that must play an enormous role here. A public opinion sympathetic with the homelands must be built up. Cultural organisations and social services must be stimulated on this basis ..."

The document argues that SABRA, the Broederbond's creation, should be developed into the national co-ordinating body for the implementation of the masterplan.

Although this plan, at least as far as the public is aware, is not yet in operation on the scale envisaged in the Broederbond document, definite features of it are recognisable in present practice in South Africa. As we have seen above, for instance, SABRA is busy with congresses for black children and liaison with homeland personalities, and is concentrating much of its attention on the teachers. The SABC regales its listeners/viewers constantly with propaganda in favour of the Government's apartheid policy and emphasises matters that put the homelands in a favourable light. One interesting factor in their presentation is that SABC maps of Southern Africa always show the Transkei as an independent country, but never the equally independent Bophuthatswana (at the time of writing it had been independent nine months). One of the major arguments against the Bantustan policy is that without proper consolidation at least, the so-called homelands can never be viable. Bophutatswana is cut into six widely scattered chunks, which hardly makes impressive viewing on a map.

The main facets of the strategy, the combating of "radicalism", is being implemented with a vengeance in South Africa. Heavy censorship has been imposed, including onslaughts on the progressive Afrikaans writers. Bannings and detentions are a common feature inhibiting potential "radicals" from active opposition. In short, a formidable arsenal of authoritarian weaponry is in operation, covering every aspect of South African life.

Many or most of these features were operating to a greater or lesser extent at the time the masterplan was drafted, but there have been marked clampdowns since. Most notable of these, perhaps, was the security putsch of October 19 1977 when widespread action included the banning of the black newspaper *The World,* the detention without trial of its editor, Mr Percy Qoboza, the banning of the editor of the *Daily Despatch,* Mr Donald Woods, the banning of the Christian Institute and its leaders Dr Beyers Naude and Rev Theo Kotze and its publication *Pro Veritate.* According to figures compiled by the South African Institute of Race Relations[38] by June 1978 there were 306 people being held in detention under South Africa's various security laws. At the end of May that year at least 115 people were under banning orders.

1. *South Africa in Travail,* p 33, SA Institute of Race Relations, 1978.
2. Vatcher, W H, *White Laager,* p 100.
3. Secret Broederbond document, *Die Afrikaner-Broederbond: 'n Historiese Oorsig,* October 1968.
4. *Student Perspectives in South Africa,* p 65.
5. Vatcher, W H, *White Laager,* p 107.
6. Malherbe, E G, *Education in South Africa,* Vol 2, p 40.
7. Ibid. p 44.
8. Ibid. p 101.
9. Ibid. p 45.

10. FAK Silwer Jubilee 1929–1954: *Die Stryd om Moedertaal Onderwys.*
11. Malherbe, E G, *Education in South Africa,* Vol 2, p 43.
12. Ibid. p 106.
13. Vatcher, W H, *White Laager,* p 105.
14. Malherbe, E G, *Education in South Africa,* Vol 2, p 106.
15. *Die AB: 'n Historiese Oorsig,* Halfeeufees Oktober 1968.
16. Secret Broederbond document in the form of a commemoration programme, dated June 5 1968, p 5.
17. Secret Broederbond document, *Die AB in die Hede,* Oktober 1 1968, p 4.
18. Secret Broederbond document, *Afrikanerskap Een en Verdeeld,* chairman's address, 1972.
19. Vatcher, W H, *White Laager,* p 103.
20. Ibid. p 104.
21. Malherbe, E G, *Education in South Africa,* Vol 2, pp 47, 48.
22. *Sunday Times,* August 28 1966.
23. Market Research Africa Survey on behalf of the 1820 Settlers National Monument Foundation, and quoted by H L Watts in a paper, *A Social and Demographic Portrait of English-speaking White South Africans,* 1974.
24. Malherbe, E G, *Education in South Africa,* Vol. 2, p 49.
25. Vatcher, W H, *White Laager,* p 90.
26. Ibid, p 98.
27. Secret Broederbond document, *Sabra,* p 1.
28. *Sunday Tribune,* April 22 1973.
29. Swart, C F, *Politieke Profiele ten opsigte van Kontemporêre Aangeleenthede van die Blanke Grootstedelike Bevolking van die Witwatersrand,* Rand Afrikaans University 1977, pp 63–6.
30. The biggest English-language Press group.
31. Malherbe, E G, *Education in South Africa,* Vol 2, p 681.
32. *Rand Daily Mail,* May 4 1967.
33. Ibid., April 21 1970.
34. *TV Topics,* August 14 1978.
35. Vatcher, W H, *White Laager,* p 110.
36. Ibid. p 110.
37. Ibid. p 114.
38. *Rand Daily Mail,* June 29 1978.

16 *The Struggle for the Churches*

"A faith," wrote Arthur Koestler in his essay on communism, "is not acquired by reasoning. One does not fall in love with a woman, or enter the womb of a church as a result of logical persuasion. Reason may defend an act of faith – but only after the act has been committed, and the man committed to the act. Persuasion may play a part in a man's conversion; but only the part of bringing to its full and conscious climax a process which has been maturing in regions where no persuasion can penetrate. A faith is not acquired; it grows like a tree. Its crown points to the sky; its roots grow downward into the past and are nourished by the dark sap of the ancestral humus."

Such is the stuff of which the Broederbond's deeply rooted faith in the God-sanctioned righteousness of its cause is made; it is not a belief acquired by reasoning. That the organisation, and generally-speaking Afrikanerdom at large, does have an unshakeable faith in itself and in God's blessing for all it does, is indeed a fact. This faith goes to the essence of all that the organisation embodies. One may argue the merits of the belief, but there is no arguing the fact of the belief.

The organisation takes as its *uitgangspunt* (premise) the conviction that Afrikaners were placed by God on the southern tip of Africa to fulfil a spiritual, religious calling. With missionary zeal it believes that its actions and thoughts are, in fact, ordained by God. So solid is this belief that the organisation perceives in attacks on its credo and existence sacrilegious assaults on the Kingdom of Heaven and its plans for the arrangement of earthly affairs.

Just as, in Koestler's terms, "one does not fall in love . . . as a result of logical persuasion," so is logical persuasion a poor tool with which to question the Afrikaner/Broederbond faith. For all the characteristics which the Afrikaner has taken as his own, he has found supportive Biblical rationale. Apartheid, for example, is held to be the manifestation of God's express intention for South Africa. Attempts to shake that belief by logical persuasion are met with an impenetrable wall of dogma. The dark sap of ancestral humus has so nourished the tree of Afrikaner faith in its particular historical course and development that it has become his very core and essence. He wears that conviction like an armour which is impervious to assaults of criticism and reasoned attack. To allege that this armour is the stuff of expediency is to underrate the quality of its mettle: the belief, however shaky its foundation, is absolutely sincere. And it is all-pervasive; it permeates the strata of Afrikanerdom's hierarchy and the State in a relationship of inseparable intimacy.

It is the intimacy of long association. As the Broederbond said in a document to members at its 1972 *Bondsraad:* "The history of the Afrikaner nation cannot be written without the history of the Afrikaans churches."[1] The document goes on to point out that the Afrikaner nation was never in its existence without the Church. When official institutions condemned the Great Trek, the trekkers did not dissociate themselves from the Church and form their own religion. When British imperialism intruded on the freedom of the Boer nation in the two "Freedom Wars," Church officials and *predikante* joined the fighting forces in the field. During the exile and awful days of degradation, the Church sent dozens of *predikante* to its people in the wilderness; it defended its people against foreign allegations of all sorts of crimes and un-Christian attitudes during the Second Boer War.

In the years of reconstruction, when the imperialist laid his hands on education to anglicise the Afrikaner children, churchmen joined ranks with educationists and others in the struggle against Milner and his cohorts. The Church was a constant, faithful presence during the dreadful years of the Poor Whites crisis.

"Consider," urges the document, "the Church's missionary policy and action on the basis of separate ecclesiastical organisations for various national, language and cultural communities. Consider also the meaning that the Church's deliberations about our race relations in the light of scripture had for our political, social, and constitutional arrangement. The fact that the Afrikaans Churches clearly declared themselves against integration and blood mixing between white and non-white gave the Afrikaner nation incalculable moral support." This close union of Church and nation has inevitably spawned clerics who became national leaders in other spheres, notably politics. Equally inevitably, the church and its affairs became the affairs of the Broederbond. In the scheme of things Afrikaner, spiritual comfort is a vital ingredient. Accordingly control of the churches became a vital ingredient of Broederbond power. From the time of the organisation's founding in the Johannesburg hills in 1918, that factor was recognised and given personification in the form of Rev J F Naude, who blessed the birth.

It is not surprising, given the Church's political significance, that the peculiar organisation of South African society has been given the stamp of spiritual approval. A commission of the *Nederduitse Gereformeerde Kerk* in the 1950s expressed the view that "every nation and race will be able to perform the greatest service to God and the world if it keeps its own national attributes, received from God's own hand, pure with honour and gratitude...

"God divided humanity into races, languages and nations. Differences are not only willed by God but are perpetuated by Him. Equality between Natives, Coloureds and Europeans includes a misappreciation of the fact that God, in His providence, made people into different races and nations... Far from the word of God encouraging equality, it is an established scriptural principle that in every community ordination, there is a fixed relationship between authorities... Those who are culturally and spiritually advanced have a mission to leadership and protection of the less advanced... The Natives must be led and formed towards independence so that eventually they will be equal to the Europeans, but each on his own territory and each serving God in his own fatherland."

The whole basis of Afrikaner religion is a strict form of Calvinism. John Calvin was born to French parents in 1509, but lived most of his life in Switzerland. A man of austere intellect and belief, he was a reformer who sought ardently to purify the individual. According to his belief, all life's compartments should be permeated with religion. Central to his doctrine was a belief that God had fore-ordained certain of mankind, the Elect, to eternal life and others to damnation. He taught his followers that they were a chosen people with a great destiny in the providential scheme. In seeking to restore the religious form of early Christian life, he introduced a large measure of lay participation in Church government. He also followed early Christian practice in barring the unworthy from the sacraments. This required an inquisition which worked through a mixed council of clergymen and laymen. The council had frightening power to penalise private lives and was the cause of terrible cruelty and suffering. Adultery, blasphemy and heresy were all crimes punishable by burning at the stake.

Calvin himself was party to the fiery execution of his friend, Servitus, for heresy. Calvin's doctrine spread through Europe, taking its firmest hold in Holland, whence it was imported to the empty shores of South Africa in the seventeenth century by the early settlers, whose baggage always included the much-consulted and treasured family Bible.[2]

The primary element of Afrikaner belief is that the State is divinely ordained and created. It is regarded as completely independent of its citizens as it is a manifestation of God's will. The State, therefore, has exclusive powers over the citizens. Accordingly, the rulers of the country are really responsible only to God. "They, in effect, are God's earthly agents, acting in His name.[3]

"Given this belief, the frequency with which government leaders seek the guidance of Dutch Reformed Church ministers is readily understandable. The doctrine strongly rejects the concepts of popular sovereignty, the quality of all men, and the origin of sovereignty in the mass of the people... For the theologians of the DRC and the National Party, the vote is merely the symbol of divine authority, for use only by the Christian and by those who are 'politically mature.' But possession of the vote, in any case, conveys no authority to make laws. Laws are God-given. If a government does not act in accordance with God's will, it loses the mandate of heaven and can legitimately be replaced."

Not only does the church give spiritual sanction to the apartheid structure of South African society, but reflects it in its own composition. The three main Afrikaans churches are all separated into segregated white, Indian, coloured, and African entities, a situation which is causing considerable tension. Within the Dutch Reformed Church "family", the "non-white" churches are referred to as the "daughter churches". In the realities of the 1970s, the "mother church" is facing angry revolt from its rebellious offspring.

The dissenting progeny is waging a strong campaign for the unification of the church – presenting a strong, Biblically-based challenge to the also (allegedly) Biblically-based approval by the parent church of apartheid and all its ramifications.

Trevor Huddlestone, the well-known Anglican priest who was expelled from South Africa, has eloquently attacked this separatist, racial rationale by the Afrikaans Church in his book *Naught for*

Your Comfort.[4] "It carries with it the implication that all racial differences are not only willed by God in His act of creation, but are to be sustained by Him to the end of time. It further involves the assumption that there has been no intermingling of races through the centuries without loss and, presumably, sin – since such intermingling must be, *ipso facto,* contrary to the Divine Will. And it makes no mention whatever of the intervention of God in the world in the Person of His Son. In other words, the view here expressed (and I am convinced that with some modifications and differences, it is the view of most DRC members) is sub-Christian. I say sub-Christian rather than 'Old Testament,' because I suppose that somewhere behind the obscure and murky twilight theology it represents, there are remembrances of the Gospel message. I cannot find them.

"The truth is that the Calvinistic doctrines upon which the faith of the Afrikaner is nourished contain within themselves ... exaggerations so distorting and so powerful that it is very hard indeed to recognise the Christian faith they are supposed to enshrine. Here, in this fantastic notion of the immutability of race, is present in a different form, the predestination idea: the concept of an elect people of God, characteristic above all else of John Calvin. And, like so many other ideas transplanted from their European context, it has been, subconsciously perhaps but most really, narrowed still further to meet South African preconceptions and prejudices.

"It fits exactly the meaning which the Afrikaner likes to give to the Great Trek. Just as the children of Israel had their Exodus and their journeyings through the wilderness to the Promised Land – so the *Voortrekkers* had to escape from the Egypt of British domination and to fight their way through the onslaughts of the heathen ... Just as the Children of Israel had a divine mission, a divinely-given leadership which set them apart from and over ... the indigenous peoples, the tribes they had met with and conquered – so the *'Afrikaner volk'* also had its unique destiny on the continent of Africa. It is to be, for all time, the nation representing purity of race: whiteness, divinely-ordained and given. Logically, therefore, the native peoples are also part of a divine plan. They are in South Africa by right also ... But they must know their place. They are to be led, to be guided, to be governed by the chosen people. That is their destiny. It is written in the Book. Or if it isn't, ought to be. Calvinism, with its great insistence on 'election' is the ideally suitable religious doctrine for white South Africa. It provides at the same moment a moral justification for white supremacy and an actual day to day reason for asserting it."

The Afrikaans churches in South Africa suffer such attacks with indignation. It is interesting that a Broederbond document of April 6 1972, *Ons Taak: Kerklik Godsdienstig* (Our Task: Clerical Religious) contains a list of the common allegations made against the Dutch Reformed Churches, including most of those covered by Father Huddleston. It refers to Huddleston's type of faith as "liberal pink religion"[5] and warns its members to expect and be able to identify the religious "intimidation" from such quarters. It acknowledges that the allegation is made that the apartheid policy is un-Christian, along with other Afrikaner Nationalist hallmarks, like Christian-National Education (the accusation being that the latter two are mutually exclusive). However, it does not attempt to give Biblical justification for any of its rebuttals of the accusations. A faith "nourished by the dark sap of ancestral humus," the absolute righteousness of the cause is so ingrained that justification presumably has become tedious and obvious.

But that is not to say that the churches do not take such attacks seriously. Again, without substantiating its own cause, it urges its supporters to be on the defensive and look out for such assaults. Ensure that the walls of the *laager* will hold against attack, without examining first whether the contents of the *laager* are worthy of defence. In another secret Broederbond document, the nature and tactics of the "enemy" are explained in detail. The document, *Die Christen-Afrikaner – Sy Toets en Krag* (The Christian Afrikaner – His Test and Strength), says: "The opponents and enemies of the Afrikaner are realising with more clarity that his political convictions and general life and world attitude have a deep religious basis, and that his association with the Bible and his attachment to his church are of fundamental meaning.

"Therefore, there are attempts to so erode the religious and Christian world view of the Afrikaner and provide it with a new content that an attitude, whereby he disparages or denounces his national bonds, can also be regarded as Christian – actually as more Christian than the attitude of the Afrikaner who strives for the maintenance of his national connection." The Christian Afrikaner, continues the document, has a clear awareness of his calling. "The knowledge of God does not lie watertight within his own national existence, but he does accept responsibility for the conversion of the nations in his midst and round about.

"The pattern is clear: for the Christian Afrikaner, the voice of the Church of Christ carries great weight. The Church is associated with the words: So speaks the Lord. The enemies of the Afrikaner realise this. Therefore, ecclesiastical declarations whereby multiracialism is presented as the real life pattern and separate freedom and independent development is branded as immoral and anti-Christian are welcomed and exploited, even by the non-ecclesiastical opponents of the Afrikaner. The intention is to make as many churches as possible declare themselves against apartheid to make the Christian Afrikaner doubt the honesty and scriptural basis and Christ-obedience of his own church. And if the Afrikaner should begin to feel that his church is presenting him with a false moral standard, by approving of independent development or separate freedom for the nation – while this is actually un-Christian and immoral – then to remain as a separate nation with separate freedom would be like Ichabod with his struggle and strife. If the Christian Afrikaner had to believe that his striving for a separate freedom for himself, as distinct from that of the non-white, was immoral, the politicians could just as well drop apartheid; they would not be able to maintain it."

Significantly, the document does not then defend its stand in favour of apartheid on scriptural or religious grounds, but in terms of the survival of the Afrikaner. It is a clear, documented admission that the Broederbond at least regards the religious content of its policy in political terms; in sectional Afrikaner terms at that. It says: "False tolerance cripples the nation's will to fulfil his own calling. And where the own calling of the Christian Afrikaner prescribes an independent separate existence, it is clear why he does not trust the peace and tolerance of the liberals. The latter want the Afrikaner to be so Christian-tolerant that he can be swallowed up or dominated by other race groups *(volksgroepe)*."

Elsewhere in the same document it is stated: "... the ecclesiastical agitation thus assumes the colour of hostile politics; our nation is in the path of multiracialism in South Africa. And furthermore, if these churches succeed, South Africa with its riches will fall into the hands of other powers – foreign powers!"

It is bad enough when the Church has to endure such onslaughts from "alien" organisations and faiths such as, for example, the Anglican, Methodist and, more particularly, Roman Catholic churches. But when it comes from within, from Afrikaner churchmen, the establishment church acts fast and ruthlessly to stamp it out. The Broederbond, which permeates the Church at all levels, is usually the agent and catalyst of such action.

Probably the best example of this is the astonishing story of Professor Albert Geyser. Born into a deeply religious family – his grandfather and great grandfather had founded the *Nederduitsche Hervormde Kerk* – he grew up in a pious, but humble home. His father, Petrus, was a railway worker; his mother, Nina, a typical Afrikaner housewife.

Albert and his brother were the pride of their home when they became ordained as ministers of the *Hervormde Kerk,* second largest of the three main Dutch Reformed Churches. Albert was a brilliant student and went on with his studies until he became a young professor of theology at the University of Pretoria. He was an ardent Nationalist and conformed in every possible way with the Afrikaner stereotype from which he had emerged, even to the point where he was a member of the fervently nationalistic youth organisation that sprouted in South Africa during the 1930s, largely as a result of the Broederbond's flirtation with, and admiration for, the ascendency of Hitler in Germany.

A logical step from here would have been to become a member of the Broederbond, and he was, in fact, twice invited to join. However, he refused on both occasions, heeding the advice of his father, himself a Broeder, that: "If you put store by the freedom of your conscience, beware what organisations you join." The aberration apart, Albert Geyser was smiled upon fondly as a true Afrikaner son with a promising, possibly great, future ahead of him.

The early clouds of impending conflict began smudging this hopeful horizon in 1954. The Moderator of the *Hervormde Kerk,* Dr A G J Oosthuizen, returned to South Africa from a World Council of Churches meeting with a serious problem: he had been challenged to provide Biblical justification for apartheid and found himself in the humiliating position of being unable to provide a convincing reply. A Church commission was duly appointed at the first opportunity to seek and find scriptural justification for the policy, to which the Church faithfully subscribed. In fact, the policy was reflected in the Church's own constitution, Article Three of which stipulated (and continues to stipulate) strict segregation on racial grounds. The commission was to consist of two members: Professor B Gemsar of the University of Pretoria, an Old

Testament expert; and Professor Albert Geyser, the New Testament expert.

Professor Gemsar, an elderly man, withdrew from the commission and was replaced by another Old Testament specialist, Dr Egges Mulder. Professor Geyser recalls entering his task with absolutely no doubt that he could fulfil it to the Church's satisfaction. It was not, however, a lasting conviction. The more he searched, the more his doubts grew until at last, after exhaustive research, he came to the personally shattering conclusion that there was no scriptural justification for apartheid. Dr Mulder was confronting a similar torment. After independently scouring the Old Testament, he came to the same conclusion.

With trepidation the two theologians faced their Church, and read their reports. There was pandemonium. The synod erupted into incensed argument: this was contrary to every tradition of the Afrikaner; if it was true, the Afrikaner forefathers had lived under a terrible misconception; it would be a betrayal of the Voortrekkers and their struggle if these outrageous findings were to be accepted. The Church refused to suffer this humiliation and both reports were quickly plucked from view and have never been seen since.

But Professor Geyser had involuntarily launched himself on a course from which he could not be diverted; his study and integrity had placed him on a collision course with his own establishment which was eventually to lead to a national and international issue. His next step along this course was when Dr Verwoerd, at the time Minister of Native Affairs, introduced a Government White Paper proposing that blacks be prevented from entering churches in "white" areas. There was an outcry, during which the pro-Nationalist newspaper, *Die Vaderland,* published an editorial appealing to the Prime Minister, Mr Strijdom, to take such a delicate matter out of the hands of the Minister. Professor Geyser wrote a letter of support to the newspaper, which was published as a follow-up editorial.

This landed him in the dock at the next synod of his church, where he was charged with contravening Article Three of the constitution. He adroitly persuaded the synod, however, that criticism of a Church law could never be construed as transgression of the law. He was acquitted, but as a precaution the Church passed a ruling that no contentious statements could be published or issued from the pulpit without approval from the Church's General

Commission. Professor Geyser ignored the injunction and used every opportunity to proclaim that the Afrikaner and his Church were heading in the wrong direction and that the ultimate victim would be Afrikanerdom itself. The Church would not tolerate this and started introducing measures to stop it. One of these was the introduction of a heresy clause into the constitution. Recalls Professor Geyser: "I was so naive. I felt so sure that all this had nothing to do with me and I in fact voted with the crowd. I assisted the smithy as he forged the irons to clamp me down."

In 1960 Sharpeville occurred: that tragic explosion of violence and death in which South African police opened fire on African marchers, led by Pan Africanist Robert Sobukwe. The marchers were protesting against influx control and the indignity of having to carry "pass books", the hated identity documents which dominate black lives in South Africa and have come to symbolise all the ramifications of apartheid. The shockwaves of Sharpeville reverberated throughout South Africa and the world. Among those deeply moved by what had happened was Professor Geyser, whose conviction that apartheid was evil was strengthened and nourished. It led him later to edit a highly controversial book, *Delayed Action,* in which he and 10 other Afrikaans theologians attacked race discrimination and apartheid.

The book coincided with the equally controversial Cottesloe conference of the World Council of Churches in Johannesburg, in which major aspects of apartheid were roundly condemned and which marked the end of Afrikaans church participation in WCC affairs. Cottesloe presented the Broederbond with a major setback. In a time when a clerical revolt against apartheid was gaining momentum, the hardline attitude of the WCC against its policies could hardly have come at a worse period. Dr Verwoerd, anxious to contain the damage, made placatory noises in an address in the New Year of 1961, reminding the electorate that the decisions of Cottesloe remained to be ratified by the individual church synods. The Broederbond immediately set to work to mobilise church opinion to make the "correct" decisions at the coming synods. On January 9 1961 it sent out a special circular to its members. It announced that the Executive Council had held a special meeting in Pretoria to discuss the Cottesloe decisions and wanted to report to its members "to prevent any serious detrimental effects on our nation as a result of this conference." It repeated Dr Verwoerd's reminder that all decisions had to be ratified by the synods and immediately followed with its own standpoint on the decisions. It was opposed to the conference's view that coloured people should be represented by coloureds in Parliament and that "domiciled Bantu in the white area" should have political and other rights. "On the question of mixed marriages, our standpoint was and remains to support the existing leglislation."

One by one the three main Afrikaans church synods dissociated themselves from the decisions of Cottesloe and withdrew from the World Council of Churches. But all of the churches have remained uneasy about Cottesloe ever since and even today, eighteen years later, a divisive debate on the issue persists within their circles.

Afterwards, reviewing the Cottesloe crisis, the Executive Council of the Broederbond reported: "It was necessary from time to time to have serious discussions about the effects these upheavals were having on the national life. By mutual consultation with Broeders in the leadership of the various churches, the Executive Council did everything in its power to prevent a split in the *volk* on this terrain. The Executive Council regards it necessary to urge all Broeders in the leadership of the various churches, and every Broeder as a member of his church, to combat the spread of liberal ideas through the church. For the positive action of Broeders in the editorials of church magazines, synodal commissions, moderatures, other church bodies etc in maintaining the unity of the Afrikaner in the church field, the Executive Council has only the highest appreciation.[6]

Meanwhile, Professor Geyser continued to be a thorn in the flesh. The final straw came when, writing in the journal *Inspan,* he openly crossed swords with the Broederbond, which he described as a "malignant growth" that was promoting disunity between English- and Afrikaans-speaking South Africans. Discussing obstacles to national unity, he warned that the Broederbond was operating like a cancer in the fibres of unity and compared it with the Mau Mau, Jomo Kenyatta's guerillas who were terrorising whites in Kenya at the time. It was a terrible accusation, particularly from an Afrikaner, when white South African feeling was running high against the harbingers of *Uhuru* further to the north. "Instead of binding the nation to a unity," wrote Professor Geyser, "the Broederbond is busy flourishing in secret and in the darkness of that body. There is only one body which can grow in secret inside another . . . and that is a cancer.

"One gathers that the Broederbond is the darkroom assistant of the ruling party and even dominates the *baasskap* people. Everyone in this country who honestly desires unity must shun this malignant growth. It percolates into every fibre of our national unity. Its morals are the morals of the dark and murky night. The destruction and elimination of the secret organisation, root and branch, is one of the first conditions for unity in South Africa."

Meanwhile, he continued to teach theology at the University of Pretoria. The church and its ever-watchful agent, the Broederbond, became increasingly aware that something would have to be done to check this erosion in their midst. If it was allowed to continue, the very soul and spiritual content of all that the Afrikaner was striving for politically might be terribly undermined. Young aspirant *predikante* were dangerously under the influence of a man so radical that he disputed the God-sanctioned righteousness of the apartheid cause, and even challenged the Church's Biblical right to remain a segregated institution.

The final move against Professor Geyser was plotted at a Broederbond meeting in Pretoria at the home of Professor F J van Zyl, a colleague in the theology faculty. There it was decided that three of Professor Geyser's students should take comprehensive notes during his lectures, seeking material which might be contrary to the teachings of the *Hervormde* church.

The three students, H G van der Westhuizen, W C M de Beer, and E Engelbrecht eventually drew up an indictment and on October 5 1961, it was announced that "Professor A S Geyser, outspoken critic of racial discrimination in the Church, has been charged with heresy against the doctrine of the *Nederduitsch Hervormde Kerk.*[7] A second charge was also brought against him, namely that he had failed to observe an order prohibiting criticism of Church laws or decisions.

On October 24, 15 black-clad, white-collared church commissioners assembled at the *Hervormde Kerk* headquarters in the Dirk van der Hoff Building in Pretoria to try their contemporary. The trial, already a controversial affair, opened inauspiciously when the commissioners ruled that it would be held in camera, which at least one theologian at the time commented was contrary to church law.[8] The Church further antagonised observers by refusing a request by Professor Geyser to have a stenographer keep a record for him of the proceedings, and to use a tape recorder for the same purpose.

While local members of the Church – the only people allowed to attend the hearing – drove miles to watch the case unfold, churchmen in Holland became incensed at what was taking place in one of their affiliate churches. "Such action is contrary to church custom," said Dr P A Stempvoort, Professor of New Testament Theology at the University of Groningen. "It seems to confirm the impression that there is a virtual dictatorial authority at the back of the whole thing."[9]

As the trial got under way, news leaked to the Press indicated that the charges were of a technical nature.The objection appeared to be that Professor Geyser taught heretical tenets of Arianism, one of the ancient heresies in church history. The doctrine taught by Arius of Alexandria in the fourth century denied the consubstantiality of Christ and said the Son was inferior to the Father.[10] Observers believed, however, that at the back of it all lay the much more obvious complaint that Professor Geyser had preached against the doctrine of apartheid.[11]

Inside that remarkable courtroom an amazing battle of wits unfolded in which Professor Geyser, described as "one of the most brilliant theologians in South Africa,"[12] more than held his own. Assisted by an outstanding colleague, Professor A van Selms, professor of Semitic Languages at Pretoria University, he often put his student accusers into difficulty with his highly informed scriptural arguments, which he conducted in Afrikaans, English, Greek, German, French and Latin, quoting authoritative commentaries and theologians to support his case.[13]

The shabby trial continued amidst deepening controversy. Many of the members of the *Hervormde Kerk* were embarrassed by what was taking place. Suspicions were further aroused when it became apparent that there was much more involved than just three students taking on their mentor. It emerged in an affidavit at the trial that three Pretoria University colleagues of Professor Geyser were central figures in the affair. One of them, Professor S P Engelbrecht, was a member of the synodal commission before which Professor Geyser was appearing. The other two were Professor A D Pont, and Professor E S Mulder, who, since dropping the no-justification-for-apartheid bombshell with Professor Geyser at the *Hervormde Kerk* synod years before, had been pulled back into line and forgiven his earlier indiscretion. They were called to the trial as expert witnesses against their accused colleague. All three had been openly hostile to Professor Geyser before the trial. All three were members of the Broederbond.

The affidavit, submitted by a theology student who had quit his course because of threats and intimidation by professors, said: "Before I even met Professor Geyser, I believed him to be the biggest crook alive." The student, Mr E Nagy, an Hungarian refugee, said in his sworn statement that Professor Engelbrecht had told him he hoped he would not come to "like Professor Geyser too much," because Professor Geyser wanted to eradicate the whites in Africa. He was also told that Professor Geyser wanted to allow "natives" in the Church, thus driving away the Europeans. Professor Pont, according to the affidavit, had warned Mr Nagy that his financial aid could be withdrawn if he became "too friendly" with Professor Geyser. A similar accusation was made against Professor Mulder.

Handing the affidavit to the trial, Professor Geyser accused the three professors named in it of collusion with the students who had laid the charges against him. He said they were often to be found in consultation with each other during intervals at the hearing. There was a further stir, and more anxiety, when Professor Engelbrecht admitted that the 13-page indictment, ostensibly drawn up independently by the three students, had, in fact, been typed in the Pretoria offices of the *Hervormde Kerk* on the church's typewriter. At the time, the general commission of the church, which was sitting in judgement on Professor Geyser, had been meeting at the same building.There were also moments of personal drama. For Professor Geyser a triumph was scored when the Reverend J Dreyer, vice-chairman of the commission, paled visibly when letters from his son were read out at the trial. They were full of praise and support for Professor Geyser. One of the student accusers had just charged that Professor Geyser tried to indoctrinate his classes. Professor Geyser produced two letters from Reverend Dreyer's son, André, who at the time was studying in Utrecht, Holland.

In the first, André wrote that he would like to complete his degree under Professor Geyser, whom he described as the only professor he had come across so far who allowed his students to draw their own conclusions. In the second, he said that after reading in the Dutch Press about the heresy trial, he wished to express his disapproval of the charges.[14]

One of the favourite tactics employed by the Broederbond against its opponents is smear campaigns among other activities

From left: Mrs Naude, Dr Beyers Naude, Mrs Geyser, Prof Geyser and daughter.

designed to isolate its enemies from their associates and friends. The organisation did this to General Hertzog by way of the Freemason letters. It used the same tactics to hit at Professor Geyser. On November 12 1961, *The Sunday Times* carried the following report: "The Broederbond has told 69-year-old Mr Petrus Geyser to withdraw from the organisation. Mr Petrus Geyser is the father of Professor A S Geyser, who is appearing in the Heresy Trial in Pretoria. A representative of the Broederbond called secretly on Mr Petrus Geyser to give him his instruction to quit. One of the reasons given for the Broederbond's expulsion order was that Mr Geyser, a railway pensioner in excellent health was 'getting old.' (This was patently a ploy. The Broederbond does not tell its members to quit because of age. On the contrary, they have to seek dispensation from the organisation to stop attending meetings when they become too old or infirm to carry on.) But it was made clear to him that the real reason was the fact that the Broederbond disapproved of his son, Professor ... Geyser, who is accused of heresy and insubordination before the Synod Commission of the *Nederduitsch Hervormde Kerk* in Pretoria. The Broeder who called on Mr Geyser told him that (his son) was *persona non grata* with the Broederbond.

"When I put these facts to Mr Petrus Geyser at his home in

Naboomspruit ... he said: 'I am under oath to the Broederbond. Therefore, I have nothing to say on the subject of the Broederbond.'"

Oom Petrus and his wife, Tant Nina, refused to discuss the organisation at all, but were prepared to talk about the trial of their son. "We are humbly and deeply grateful and proud to be the parents of a man whom we do not only believe, but whom we know, to be following in the steps and teaching of his Master with a clear heart and a clear mind," they told the reporter concerned, who continued his account: "The trial in Pretoria lies like a heavy shadow over the gentle lives of the ageing couple. (Said Tant Nina:) 'Sometimes I wonder if the Bible has not become just a *toor-boekie* (a book of spells and incantations) to be opened by some of my Afrikaner people at political meetings – then put aside and forgotten... So many of the things that are happening are so far from the spirit and teachings of Christ. How long will He suffer them to happen?' In the Geyser household, the old Afrikaner custom of daily worship with the servants, and all who happen to be under the roof is carried on. Oom Petrus was more bitter. 'Among the things which make me unhappy,' he said, 'is the fact that when the State President was sworn in, there were 30 non-whites allowed in the church. Yet, when it is for the sake of Christ, they are debarred from the church.' In English, and without hesitation, he quoted the 17th Verse of the Book of Kings II, chapter 6, to me: '*And Elisha prayed and said: Lord, I pray thee open his eyes that he may see. And the Lord opened the eyes of the young man and he saw, and behold the mountain was full of horses and chariots of fire around Elisha.* My son is not alone,' said Oom Petrus." The report ended: "Three times a day the old couple phone their son. But Professor Geyser, and others in communiction with him, believe that his telephone is tapped."

Meanwhile, in Pretoria, the Heresy Trial ground on through hours and days of complex scriptural argument. The tension wore heavily on Professor Geyser, who came under doctor's orders. He had been suspended from his teaching post at the university and from performing his functions as a minister of the Church. For six months the hearings dragged on until at last, on May 8 1962, the verdict of the commission was announced. Professor Geyser was guilty of heresy, but acquitted "on the benefit of the doubt" of insubordination. He was defrocked; his three student accusers by that time had all been accepted as Ministers.

In its judgement, the commission stated it was "grieved that one of our brother professors has been found guilty of heresy and we call him back from the path on which he has strayed. The commission wishes to assure him of its prayers on his account and they will call the Church to do the same so that it may please the Lord of the Church to lead him back."

The 15 members of the commission that convicted Professor Geyser were the Reverend A G J Oosthuizen (chairman), the Reverend J G N Dreyer (vice-chairman), the Reverend T F J Dreyer (secretary), Professor P S Dreyer, Professor S P Engelbrecht, the Reverend P M Smith, Reverend C L van den Bergh, the Reverend A J Nolte, Mr D P J van Schalkwyk, Mr J H Lotz, Mr H A Smit, Mr G W T Oosthuizen, Mr C H Buitendag, Mr F H Ras and Mr J H H Janson. The conviction was not a unanimous decision. Two of the 15 voted against it. They were Mr Janson and Mr Ras. Mr Janson and Mr Ras were the only members of the commission who were not members of the Broederbond.[14]

After the trial, Professor Geyser said: "Although I had prepared myself for a verdict of this kind, the realisation came as a shock." He said South Africa would be overtaken by a "terrible calamity" unless human relations were motivated by true Christian values and principles. The erosion of Christian values would have to be stopped if the people of South Africa were to live at peace with their consciences and in harmony with the rest of the world. Too many people, he said, were closing their minds to this erosion which was going on before their eyes. The only hope of a peaceful and orderly life in South Africa was to be found in a common conscience with a common content of moral values. "That is why the forces of Christianity must be marshalled to see that our way of life is in accord with the Christian conscience."[16]

Professor Geyser, who had vowed to fight his case to the "bitter end," proceeded to do just that. He took his heresy conviction on appeal to the South African Supreme Court. In his declaration to the court, he alleged that at all relevant times, the 15 members of the commission, or some of them, were so biased and (or) hostile towards him as to render them incapable of hearing the charge against him in an unprejudiced manner.

Theologians and lay people packed the gallery of the Old Synagogue Court in Pretoria as the appeal began. Then on the eighth day, a dramatic turn of events forced an adjournment. Watched by a crowded court, Professor Geyser took the witness stand and sketched his studies. Relating his heresy trial, he told the court he had hoped against hope that the finding of the church would be different. But it was a remote hope and he had met the final verdict with the "spiritual callouses" which he had acquired.

It was as he started his description of the proceedings at his heresy trial that the turning point came. He said: "I pleaded not guilty and said I believed that Jesus Christ is the Son of God and one of substance with the Father, which is my belief now and always has been." At this point, Mr M R de Kock, appearing for the Church, rose. Professor Geyser carried on speaking until he was stopped by his own counsel, Mr G P C Kotzé. Mr de Kock asked Mr Justice Ludorf if there could be a short adjournment for discussion between counsel, in view of what Professor Geyser had just said.

When the court resumed nearly 40 minutes later, Mr Kotzé asked Professor Geyser whether he subscribed to the Articles of Faith of the *Hervormde Kerk,* including Article 28. When Professor Geyser said he did, Mr Kotzé asked him to read Article 28 to the court and affirm it as his own belief. Professor Geyser read the Article, which states in effect that there is only one Father, one Son and one Holy Ghost in the Holy Trinity, and that they are all equal to one another, none being superior or inferior. He added: "This is the creed of my Church and my creed."

There was a buzz of conversation in the court as Mr Kotzé asked him to read a section, substantially the same, from the Church Hymnal, first silently to himself and then aloud, if those were the tenets of faith to which he subscribed. After reading the section aloud, Professor Geyser again said: "These are the tenets of my belief."

Then followed another adjournment, during which 12 or 15 members of the Church went to the Church counsel's table and consulted, all deferring to Reverend A G J Oosthuizen. Professor S P Engelbrecht, who was one of the main figures behind the original heresy trial, did not join in the discussion, but remained in the public gallery. The three advocates representing Professor Geyser conferred with him outside the court. In the public gallery, partisan groups formed and speculated.

When the court resumed, Mr de Kock successfully applied for an adjournment.[17] What had happened was that the Church's counsel had seen in Professor Geyser's statement of belief in the doctrine of the Church a way out of what was shaping up to be an embarrassing episode in the Church's affairs. During the ensuing adjournment, the Church settled with Professor Geyser, agreeing to pay all costs, which amounted to about R100 000. It might have been able to save face in this way had it not been for Professor Van Stempvoort, the world New Testament authority who had come to South Africa from the Netherlands to testify for Professor Geyser.

On his way back to Holland, he issued a statement criticising the terms of the settlement as "not exactly the truth." He said the settlement was framed in Church language to give an innocent appearance. "In fact," he continued, "Professor Geyser has won the action completely. The Church was afraid of the consequences and did not go on with the proceedings. My opinion of the General Committee of the *Nederduitsch Hervormde Kerk* is a very bad one. People in the *Hervormde Kerk* ought to know the exact facts of what happened in the whole case, so there can be difficulties for the General Committee."

Professor Geyser, he said, had always believed in the faith of the Church. His reaffirmation during the appeal in Pretoria, which led to the settlement, was nothing new. Professor Geyser had made the same affirmation 16 times during the heresy trial the previous year. "The General Committee of the Church wants to cover up its own great faults of the heresy hearing," he said. "I hope that the General Committee has great difficulties – that people in the General Assembly ask why it is that the Church must pay R100 000 in costs."

Pressing his scathing attack, he said the original heresy charge had been "nonsense." "They made it a case of heresy because they had the political feeling that he was an attacker of Article Three, which is very bad on scriptural grounds. The Church has no right to exclude non-whites."[18]

The Church, which had prepared for publication a supplement on the entire Geyser affair, suddenly withdrew it and said it wanted no more publicity on the matter. In the way of all scandals the episode eventually faded into the past. But it remains a sorry period in the history of the *Hervormde Kerk,* and one which cost it dearly. A number of its members left the church in bitterness and disgust over what had taken place and in all respects the Church emerged in shame.

In the aftermath of the affair, Professor Geyser accused the Broederbond of playing a leading role. This brought a swift denial from Broeder-Reverend T F H Dreyer. Later, the Church appointed Mr J C Oelofse to investigate the Broederbond's alleged role in the heresy trial and subsequent events. He reported that he did not "find the hand of the Afrikaner Broederbond anywhere in the whole matter."

The final break between Professor Geyser and the Church came during the General Synod of the *Hervormde Kerk* in Pretoria in May 1964, when he asked for a second hearing. He walked out in disgust when it was denied. After his departure, the meeting adopted a motion thanking the General Commission of the Church for its action in the affair. The motion congratulated the commission and the executive body of the Church for the "brotherly agreement" it had reached with the professor after the Supreme Court case.

A further motion noted the "deep disappointment" of the Church on his attitude subsequently. In an astonishing act of sheer effrontery, the administrator of the Church, Mr A B Herbst, admitted that he had approached Professor Geyser to make a financial contribution to the Church's costs in the Supreme Court action. Professor Geyser, now a Professor of Divinity at the University of the Witwatersrand in Johannesburg, has had nothing to do with any of the Afrikaans churches every since. Even recalling his treatment at the hands of the Church, clearly still affects him badly 15 years later.

Running parallel with the unfolding of the Geyser story was an increasing disquiet about the Broederbond in the broad family of the Dutch Reformed Churches. There was growing concern among Afrikaans theologians about the interference of the Broederbond in Church affairs. One prominent minister told the *Sunday Times*[19]: "The Broederbond is a canker in the body of the Church. Its influence has undermined the independence of the Church from party politics." Another told the newspaper: "The Church is one body scripturally and cannot allow itself to be infiltrated by any other organisation of whatever description. Membership of the Church is wholly incompatible with membership of the Broederbond... The Church is called upon to testify on the righteousness of the State; it must even be free to criticise the Government. But if the Church is controlled, as is the Government, by the Broederbond, it is in no position to discharge this duty. This is, in fact, what is happening. The gravest danger facing the Church today is that it may be prevented from being a universal testimony to a universal God, through involvement in local Nationalist or party political aims. The Broederbond's claim to Christian nationalism is sacrilegious: Christ and nationalism are not compatible."

The clerical revolt grew and found avenues of expression in books like *Delayed Action* and in a remarkable ecumenical journal *Pro Veritate,* edited by the prominent *Nederduitse Gereformeerde Kerk dominee,* Beyers Naude. Clearly deeply concerned at this growing dissension from such an influential and, particularly in Afrikaner terms, important quarter, the Broederbond launched a campaign to stamp out "independent" thinking in Afrikaans and nationalist controlled bodies.[20] Orders went out to Broeders in all public bodies, including several hundred leading Afrikaans churchmen, to eliminate dissident viewpoints.

The Executive Council issued a special three-page memorandum to members to counter growing moves against the organisation and against the morality of apartheid. These views, which it identified with communism and liberalism, were "one of the most dangerous attacks" on Afrikanerdom. "Even within our own circles," it warned, "it is sometimes argued with a great measure of fanaticism that our policy of apartheid is not Biblical. The Executive Council solemnly calls on our Church leaders to combat this liberalistic attack on our Christian spiritual convictions and on the Christian-National philosophy on which our national struggle on the cultural, social, economic and educational front is founded, and to expose it firmly and clearly..."[21] This directive galvanised into action Broeders in Church councils, Rings, moderatures and the editorial boards of Dutch Reformed Church publications. A "spontaneous" campaign suddenly erupted on a national scale against *Pro Veritate.*

One such public move came from Professor A B du Preez, a senior Broederbonder in the theological faculty of the University of Pretoria. Writing in the *Kerkbode,* official journal of the *Nederduitse Gereformeerde Kerk,* in September 1962, he attacked unnamed churchmen for "disloyalty" and urged a clampdown on criticism of synod decisions in the current "national crisis." These proposals caused an unroar and were seen as an attempt to crush any Dutch Reformed Church deviation from Government race policy. As opposition swelled, the Executive Council issued orders for pressure on the Church as a whole to toe the line. Urging the silencing of dissident churchmen, it stated in October 1962: "The Afrikaans churches decidedly cannot allow the formation of groups outside or within the Church to continue."[22] In thinly-veiled terms it called for a stepping up of the assault on *Pro Veritate,* and for a "no public criticism" gag on churchmen. "Everyone is surely aware," declared the directive, "of the fact that in each of the churches there exist groups who are not only acting disloyally to the Church but are also busy with the formation of groups alongside or against the Church."[22] These elements should be forced to express their view through "official channels" in the Church.

The Broederbond, ever-watchful and quick to attack the Freemasons, presumed that behind the revolt in Afrikaner ranks was the work of its rival secret organisation. In November 1962, the *Nederduitse Gereformeerde Kerk* issued a ban on Freemasons; a call went out to all *Nederduitse Gereformeerde* members to resign from Freemason bodies and a ban was imposed on Freemasons joining the Church or holding official posts. This unleashed opposition, particularly from church councils in the Orange Free State, where thousands of Afrikaners were members of the Freemasons. Church councils started urging that the ban be extended to the Broederbond as well.[24]

The anti-Broeder drive extended to the Transvaal, and the Southern Transvaal synod of the *Nederduitse Gereformeerde Kerk* was asked in two motions to investigate the activities of the organisation. A special committee under the chairmanship of Dr A C Barnard studied the resolutions at the synod and strongly urged a probe in the light of the Church's stand against Freemasonry. The committee said that "rightly or wrongly, there are doubts in many hearts in the Church" about the secret society. It expressed the hope that the organisation "will not only welcome such an investigation, but will facilitate it." Introducing the proposal, Dr Barnard said: "If the Broederbond has nothing to hide, let it welcome an investigation . . . I fully realise how very sensitive this matter is, for quite a number of ministers here belong to the Broederbond. (An earlier report claimed that more than 40 per cent of Afrikaans *predikante* were Broeders.) I realise too that in asking for an inquiry I might expose myself to criticism. Yet I feel, in all honesty, that we must examine the Broederbond in the light of God's word."

For the first time in 20 years, since the purge by General Smuts, the organisation came out into the open in the form of an official statement. The statement was delivered at the synod by Dominee D P M Beukes of Linden, Johannesburg. Putting up a spirited defence of the organisation, Broeder Beukes said "such an investigation will only cause suspicion and uncertainty at a time when we cannot afford to divide Afrikaner forces." Points made in his declaration were that the Broedebond's secrecy was merely a practical way of achieving its aims and not a matter of principle. "In itself secrecy is neither good, nor evil," he said.

Other bodies, like the Church, State, societies and companies found it practical "to use secrecy for the fulfilment of their own functions and tasks." Broeders were Afrikaners who had satisfied the "highest and most difficult demands of religious conviction, leadership, character, temperament and selfless service to the community without expecting reward." Disclosure of their names could cause "unnecessary subjective feelings" among other Afrikaners who, on comparing themselves with individual Broeders, might feel that their capabilities and devotion to their people had been undervalued. Often, however, prominent Afrikaners were overlooked for "purely incidental factors of a practical and fleeting character." The Broederbond was a "democratic" body and any improper conduct within its ranks would be censured at the annual congress. If any organisation abused its secrecy in order to injure or undermine other bodies or persons, the State should act against it. Dealing with its Christian-National ideology, Dominee Beukes said: "The Bond supports the Christian Afrikaans churches in order to perpetuate and strengthen the Afrikaner *volk* as a Protestant Christian community and combats in particular any Roman Catholic attack on the Protestant Christian make-up and character of the Afrikaner *volk*." While the organisation operated only in the sphere of national affairs, it also sought to promote the Church wherever possible. The Broederbond believed that "the Afrikaner *volk* has been called into existence by God in the southern corner of Africa with its own Christian mission to bring honour to His name."[25]

The concerted underground campaign the organisation had been waging inside church organs for several months previously paid dividends at the synod. Broeder Beukes won the day and the motion to investigate the organisation was defeated by a majority of about three to two. In defeating the motion, the *Nederduitse Gereformeerde Kerk* reaffirmed the findings of a previous investigation in 1951, which found the Broederbond to be "wholesome and healthy, seeking only the progress and best interests of the Afrikaner nation ... not inimical to anyone."

The very *dominee,* Broeder Beukes, who in 1963 was in a tight spot defending the organisation from his clerical colleagues, is today supreme head of the *Nederduitse Gereformeerde Kerk* in South Africa. He is moderator of the General Synod. He is also a member of the Executive Council of the Broederbond.

The same synod also marked other coups for the organisation. It passed a ban on public criticism of Church policies and there was much agitation against *Pro Veritate.* It did not all go the organisation's way, however. In a surprising development, Reverend Beyers Naude, the outspoken editor of *Pro Veritate,* was elected moderator of the Southern Transvaal region by 209 votes to the 167 polled by the Broederbond favourite, Reverend H J C Snijders. A further setback for the organisation was soon to follow when Dr F E O'Brien Geldenhuys, who shortly before had quit the Broederbond amidst the clerical revolt, was elected moderator of the Northern Transvaal synod. He narrowly defeated the Broederbond-backed candidate, Dr A M Meiring by nine votes.[26]

But the conscience of the Church continued to stir uneasily at what was occurring secretly and insidiously in its midst. One minister reported: "The Broederbond's activities are causing tension, suspicion and division in the Church. Church members cannot serve God and belong to the Broederbond: the two are incompatible. While the whole tenor of the Bible is to reveal, the Broederbond's is to conceal. Jesus said that he never did or said anything in secret ... Those ministers who belong to any secret society are flagrantly disobeying the Lord of the Church."[27]

In the continuing ferment, Afrikaans *dominees* redoubled their efforts to have the Broederbond investigated by the Church, arguing that the 1951 inquiry had been "superficial" and was now outdated. Said one of them: "If the Church is going to ban Freemasonry on the grounds of its secret nature, why should the Broederbond, with its similar nature, be exempt from any ban?"[28]

Then came a punishing attack on the organisation in the form of a pamphlet issued by the Pretoria theologian, Professor A van Selms, who had defended Professor Geyser. Entitled *Church and Secret Organisation, with reference to the Freemasons and the Broederbond,* it was an eloquent treatise against any secret organisations acting in the body of the Church. The section on the Broederbond was particularly damning. Professor van Selms said Broederbond members of the Church were hypocrites. At meetings they prayed for divine guidance, but they were compelled to ignore the arguments of their colleagues because they were committed to vote or argue the way the Broederbond had ordered them to. "I declare openly that I regard the continuance of membership of the Broederbond by somebody who calls himself a Christian as a lack of moral judgement," he wrote.

Professor van Selms accused the Broederbond of employing communist tactics of infiltration. "It is known that a minority of 10 per cent which comes well organised and thoroughly prepared to a meeting usually succeeds in turning the meeting its way and obtains control of the key positions by filling them with its supporters. The communists in the past played this game with fervency and competence in several countries. Today, however, it is not only the communists who do this. They find good imitators in opposite camps. Should these tricks be known to the other members of the meeting, they could resist them, but the other members do not know that a secret scheme is, in fact, being operated. They do not know that two speakers, who apparently support the same idea because of their own convictions, have in fact been nominated by the secret organisation to talk this way... They think it is spontaneous support which the one gives to the other and have no suspicion that everything has been pre-arranged... There is no point in arguing or deliberating with them at the meeting ... they cannot talk and act in accordance with their own insight and conscience. They are bound before they come to the meeting."

The anti-Broederbond sentiment moved through the *Hervormde Kerk,* was taken up in the *Nederduitse Gereformeerde Kerk* and eventually was mirrored in the ranks of the smallest of the Dutch Reformed Churches, the *Gereformeerde Kerk.* Members of this Potchefstroom-based "Dopper" church drew up a five-page petition against the activities of secret societies in the church, disclosing that "more than half of the predikante of our Gereformeerde Kerk are members of the Broederbond."[29] It, like the *Nederduitse Gereformeerde Kerk* petition, argued that it was inconsistent to ban the Freemasons and not the Broederbond. Basing their argument on a decision of a synod in 1897, the petitioners contended that the Church had expressed itself strongly against any secret society.

Article 155 of the decisions of the 1897 synod declared that "somebody who becomes a member of a secret society, as for example the Freemasons, (the Broederbond had not come into existence at that stage) cannot be a member of the Gereformeerde Kerk, as the Christian Church is a spiritual public society which cannot associate with organisations or societies which stand outside it and which are strange to its spiritual and heavenly origin."[30]

Meanwhile, outside the clerical field, an extraordinary movement was coming into being. Incensed by the publicity that had surrounded the Broederbond for several months, a band of Afrikaners, staunch Nationalists one and all, formed in opposition to the Broederbond. Based mainly in the Orange Free State, the *Nasionalistebond,* as it was called, had a short, but spirited existence. Among the aims listed in its constitution were the maintenance of the pure application of the policy and principles of the National Party as contained in its constitution; to be vigilant in respect of the rights of Nationalists inside the party as well as in society and, above all, to fight injustice towards Nationalists in the social and economic spheres; to oppose the Broederbond inside the National Party. It also sought to bind Nationalists together and organise them properly; arrange mutual help and practical uplifting of Nationalists; protect them against unreasonable and unfair treatment; to checkmate all underhandedness, abuse and graft in respect of Nationalists; to fight with every available smearing of Nationalists by Broederbonders; to ensure that Nationalists were represented in the provincial councils and Parliament and not Broederbonders; to ensure that the organisation of the party rested in the hands of genuine Nationalists and not Broederbonders and their tools.[31]

After a flurry of recruitment and organisation, the *Nasionalistebond* faltered and eventually died; it was no match for the bond it had come to fight. In any event, it was really only a diversion from the real fight that continued to rage within the churches.

The Broederbond, realising that its blockbuster methods of trying to cope with the revolt in the Church were failing, decided on a more subtle approach. In October that year it sent out a circular to members containing the following advice: "If the Broederbond is discussed in church council meetings, do not attempt to stop the discussion. Allow (it) to run its full course. Then propose that the matter be referred to the synod for action."[32] The Broederbond was well aware that, in this way, it could contain the attacks. Justifiably, it was confident that it had the synods sufficiently under control to prevent any investigation of its affairs.

Slowly the indomitable purpose of the organisation was bringing the clerical crisis under control. Slowly, it was enfolding the revolt in its smothering embrace. One by one, it was extinguishing the fires of criticism and attack. The onslaught was dwindling, losing direction and power. But, on another level, the organisation was involved in a feverish witch-hunt. Each step in its campaign against the churches, and in other areas, had been mysteriously reported in the *Sunday Times*. Week after week the newspaper reported sensational disclosures about the organisation, bathing it in the harsh glare of publicity it always energetically seeks to avoid. The whole affair plunged the organisation into panic. Names of members were being revealed holus bolus, causing tremendous embarrassment.

The organisation's documents throughout 1963 reflect its concern at what was taking place. The leaks to the Press began in April. The next circular letter to members, Number 1/63/64 dated May 4 1963, had as its first item *The New Challenge*. In it it told members that the latest onslaught on the organisation carried clearly the "communist pattern of sowing suspicion and undermining the Afrikaner and his most spiritual traits." It assured members, however, that at the latest meeting of the Executive Council, it was decided that the Broederbond would continue its work with "determination and strength."

The following circular letter, Number 2/63/64 dated June 12 1963, contained, under the heading *Press Reports*, this item: "On behalf of the Executive Council the assurance is given that the recent press reports are receiving serious attention. The Executive Council is aware that exceptional local problems may have arisen as a result. You are requested to overcome such problems with the greatest deliberation and calm. Please consult the Executive Council whenever there is any uncertainty about behaviour. The Executive Council assures you that everything possible is being done to clear up this problem."

Among the steps being taken at this stage was that the help of "expert friends" had been called in to investigate the leak. The expert friends were the Security Police. The investigation was placed under the head of the Security Police, then Colonel Hendrik van den Bergh.

Contrary to the placatory tones it adopted in its communications with members, the organisation was really beside itself with worry. It took extraordinary measures to protect itself from further security breaches. One of the first things it did was abandon, at the last minute, the *Bondsraad* meeting which had been scheduled for the 9th and 10th April, because "we received confidential information that the date and venue of the meeting was known to the hostile press and other persons. That apart, information was received that irresponsible deeds by hostile persons were not ruled out. The Executive Council therefore had to postpone the meeting post haste and notices had to be sent to all corners of the land by express post and in some cases by telegrams . . . "[33]

Later, as an exercise in morale boosting, the organisation decided to hold as big a *Bondsraad* meeting as possible. In the circumstances, the greatest measure of secrecy had to be observed. It was a one-day meeting on the farm *Tweefontein* near Bapsfontein on the East Rand. Cells and delegates were informed of the congress by hand-delivered letters. The letters did not disclose the venue of the meeting, but instructed members to head for various rendezvous points, from were they were guided, under the strictest security, to the farm itself.[34]

At the congress, the chairman, Dr Piet Meyer, delivered an emotional welcoming address reminding his audience of exceptional circumstances under which the *volk* had had to gather from time to time.

Starting with the Covenant taken before the Battle of Blood River in 1838 he traced periods when the Afrikaner had gathered as a beleagured *volk* to muster its resources against hostile forces: the gathering of a number of Transvaal burghers at Wonderfontein in 1879 when the return of the freedom of the republic was demanded; its confirmation at Paardekraal; the unity meeting at Monument Koppie in 1938 after the oxwagon trek; and the Republican referendum in 1960. All of these occasions have enormous emotional and religious content for the Afrikaner. Bringing his audience to its current situation he said the new threat was from communists and "leftists" throughout the world. "The struggle against South Africa is aimed at rooting out the last vestige of white Christendom. We have accepted it thus: we want to be a Christian nation. In that spirit we stand here. Christ is the highest, the most powerful weapon against communism. As a nation, we want to be an instrument in the hands of God to take on the struggle against communism," he said. After a highly emotional congress, filled with religious exhortations and fervour, the Broeders solemnly left the farm, one by one piling rocks into a symbolic cairn to commemorate the historic occasion.[35]

The *Bondsraad* may have done much to boost the flagging morale of the organisation, but it did nothing to stop the infuriating reports in the *Sunday Times*. Driven to complete distraction, it distrusted everything around it. Nothing of importance was discussed on the telephone and even the postal service was suspect. This created tremendous problems for the organisation. More than ever, it had to continue communicating with its members, but had cut itself off from its channels of communication. Normally its links with the nation-wide network of cells were maintained by post. Now new arrangements had to be made.

The problem was overcome by sending a courier by car to every branch throughout the country month after month. He was accompanied by an armed guard as he tore across the country on his massive delivery round.[36] At the end of that year an exhausted "travelling secretary," Mr J H Swart, reported to the Executive Council that for a week at a time for four months he had scurried about delivering circular letters. "These journeys, which in the nature of affairs had to be completed in limited time, were an experience never to be forgotten. In the process heavy demands were made on the car I used, especially because of bad roads; about 12 000 miles were covered in shifts of between 450 and 700 miles a day. With great thankfulness it can be reported that there was seldom a delay and never an accident."[37]

The organisation also believed its offices would be burgled and had to "make arrangements to guard them every night." The arrangements were that Broeder G F Rautenbach of the Johannesburg cell, Gerrit Maritz, for more than 10 months slept every night in the organisation's offices. "Despite the inconvenience it involved him in personally, he was constantly at his post and the offices could be shut every night with a peaceful heart,"[38] the organisation noted gratefully later.

Meanwhile, the Security Police, pursuing the elusive leak with firm resolve, were drawing close to success. They raided the offices of the *Sunday Times* in Main Street, Johannesburg. Claiming they were investigating a charge of theft they removed photocopies of seven Broederbond documents and spent almost two hours in the offices taking statements from editorial staff.

They moved quickly from there and the dissident theologian Beyers Naude was interrogated by Colonel Van Den Bergh. He had been a member of the Broederbond for 22 years, a fact which on disclosure caused amazement to outsiders, because he was known to be a man to whom the organisation was implacably opposed because of his outspoken criticism of all that it stood for. He

Dr Beyers Naude. The Broederbond's first defector.

resigned from the organisation in March that year. It transpired that the documents which had been published in the *Sunday Times* had been in his possession and that he had shown them to a fellow theologian, who was not a member of the Broederbond. His colleague had photographed the documents and passed the negatives to a newspaperman. The colleague was none other than Professor Geyser.[39]

He too was visited by the Security Police, who again claimed to be investigating a theft charge. In a statement to the Press, Professor Geyser said the Reverend Naude had shown him the documents when asking him for advice in deciding between conflicting loyalties. Reverend Naude had not given the documents to the Press, he said. "Reverend Naude visited me about seven months ago in some distress. He felt himself bound by his word to the Broederbond, while at the same time he had a severe battle of conscience over the menace that organisation had for the Christian church in South Africa. He gave me a number of the Broederbond documents so that I could form my own judgement on the problem."

Professor Geyser said that portions of the documents plainly indicated the use of the Church for the political goals of the Broederbond. He saw in the documents the type of quasi-Biblical argument which he had come to know in the hearing of the heresy charge against him. "For this reason, I decided that the only way to frustrate these views would be to make them public." Professor Geyser accordingly took the documents to his offices at the University of the Witwatersrand and, using his Leica camera, painstakingly photographed each page. Then he gave the negatives to a *Sunday Times* journalist, whom he knew, Mr Charles Bloomberg.

He ended his statement: "Two officers, one from the Security Police, visited me on November 11. I answered their questions and in turn asked them if they were members of the Broederbond, which they denied. I asked them how a member of the Security Police fitted in with an investigation of a complaint of theft and burglary. They gave an evasive reply."[40]

All in all, the Security Police's involvement in something so mundane as a theft investigation caused many raised eyebrows. The Commissioner of Police, Lieutenant General J M Keevy (who has the dubious record of being the man who was rejected by the Broederbond most times before becoming a member) issued a statement that there was nothing strange in this at all. If a member of the force was considered best for a particular job, he was assigned to it, he said. He destroyed the logic of his own statement, however, by adding that it was "possible" that Colonel van den Bergh had interrogated the Reverend Naude. "He questions a lot of people that I don't know about."[41]

There remained only one more link to be identified and the whole chain of events would be secured. Mr Bloomberg had left for London to pursue his studies, but the articles had continued after his departure. The man who took over the major part of the reporting was Mr Hennie Serfontein, 30 year old public relations officer for the opposition Progressive Party. After he had been visited by a captain in the Criminal Investigation Department, he said: "I refused to give any statement because I regarded the police action as political intimidation and because I had no knowledge of any theft or any criminal matter... I have been a freelance journalist writing political as well as non-political articles for about a year. As such, I was asked to assist in the translation of Broederbond documents which had come into the possession of the *Sunday Times* and to help in the preparation of the reports which subsequently appeared in the newspaper..."[42]

The night before, as Mr Serfontein was issuing his statement, an astonishing event took place. The South African Broadcasting Corporation, under the chairmanship of the Broederbond chief, Dr Piet Meyer, interrupted its regular radio programmes to give two fifteen-minute nation-wide statements on the Broederbond affair, one from the Reverend Naude and the second from the organisation's Chief Secretary, Dr Piet Koornhof.

In the normal course of events, it would be a requirement here at least to summarise both points of view expressed during those broadcasts and in subsequent developments, when certain allegations and counter-allegations were made. However, the situation under which Dr Naude now finds himself is far from normal. It must have been a matter of heartfelt satisfaction to the Broederbond when one of its senior members, the Minister of Justice, Mr Kruger, banned Dr Naude, the Christian Institute of which he was director, and the magazine *Pro Veritate,* of which he was formerly editor, in the massive and controversial security swoop of October 19 1977.

Apart from the fact that one of the organisation's members executed this task, the Broederbond itself can claim some of the credit at least for this consummate act of revenge. It was the Broederbond that initiated the line that clerical action like Dr Naude's opposition to apartheid and other aspects of latter day Afrikaner nationalism were linked with the communist onslaught against South Africa. Those who know Dr Naude, a devout and deeply committed Christian, scoff at the absurdity of such an allegation. Be that as it may, the life to which Dr Naude has been committted, without any judicial process, means that he may not be quoted; statements he made prior to the application of his five-year gag, which can be renewed arbitrarily by ministerial decree, are likewise muzzled. This banning, which has been the fate of hundreds of South Africans, carries wider implications: among other limitations, he may never be in the presence of more than one person at a time; he may not leave the magisterial district of Johannesburg without permission; and may not prepare any material, or assist in the preparation of any material for publication. The fundamental implication and intention of banning is, therefore, to silence Government opponents. In the circumstances, as Dr Naude is denied the right of defending himself, the Broederbond must here suffer the same arbitrary fate and its allegations accordingly go unrecorded. Suffice it to say that in the end the charge of theft was never pursued.

There is no doubt that to date the "treachery" of Dr Naude was the most traumatic event in the organisation's history, far more serious in its implications than General Hertzog's Smithfield Address, or General Smuts's purge of the civil service. What made the event even more traumatic than the mere horror of seeing its precious secrets paraded in the "hostile Press" was the fact that Dr Naude was recognised as an outstanding Afrikaner.

His eloquent denunciation of the Broederbond and all it stood for was the worse for the fact that he came from within the organisation and in fact had been a branch chairman. Worse still was the fact that Naude was a revered man in the Broederbond's history. The Dominee Naude that had provided the vital spiritual dimension to the organisation's founding in 1918, was the father of Beyers. It was thus a "family affair" and Dr Naude's stinging rejection was all the more keenly felt by the organisation as a result. It retaliated with awesome vengeance.

According to Professor Geyser both he and Naude were subjected to a concerted campaign of intimidation and abuse. They both received a number of death threats by telephone and by letter, which were duly reported to the police, but to no avail. Perhaps a worse form of retaliation was the resolute wall of silence that was erected between them and their *volk.* Both men and their families are Afrikaners, albeit unusual ones, in the sense of their deep emotional attachment and tribal links with their own people. Their actions in defiance of the popular course of their people carry the heavy penalty of total ostracisation from them. Former friends, associates and acquaintances now have nothing to do with them. They have become pariahs, islands of firm principles in a sea of opposing, but equally firm principle.

For Professor Geyser, the price of his defiance of the Establishment Church exacted terrible personal suffering on a personal level. The tension, strain and awful pressure became unbearable for his wife Celia and ravaged her health completely, forcing her to live a life in and out of medical institutions. He, a vital, lively man with a twinkling, mischievous humour, retains the strength of his conviction, but has withdrawn from public prominence. Tragically, but understandably, the Geyser affair is, to all intents and purposes, dead and buried as far as the Afrikaner is concerned. At a recent congress of the *Afrikaanse Studentebond* (ASB), there was opportunity to ask numerous Afrikaans students, including several senior theological students, if they knew anything about the matter. Not one had heard of it.

Beyers Naude, shortly after it became known that he was responsible for the 1963 exposure of the Broederbond, was offered the position of Director of the Christian Institute, a non-denomination ecumenical institute of research and Christian study. According to Mrs Naude, he applied to the *Nederduitse Gereformeerde Kerk* for permission to take the position. It was refused without reasons.

Shortly afterwards he joined the C.I., an action which declared his preparedness to forfeit his cloth. He duly moved to a suburban home in Greenside, Johannesburg and joined the local congregation of the *Nederduitse Gereformeerde Kerk,* where he was invited to become a church elder. He accepted, but objections were immediately raised from outside the community. The objections, piloted by the Reverend N J Loggerenberg, a Broeder from nearby Benoni, were rejected through the various bodies of the Church, until he took them finally to the synod of the Southern Transvaal, where they were upheld. Beyers Naude was debarred from serving in any office in the Church even as an elder.

He subsequently threw himself into his work as Director of the Christian Institute, which became an internationally regarded organisation. It also became a formidable political voice in South Africa, pronouncing itself unequivocally whenever injustice prevailed. Its voice was often heard. He himself became an international figure, whose opinions and counsel about South African affairs, were constantly sought by people from all quarters of the world.

Now he is banned and his voice and that of the institute and its publication, *Pro Veritate,* is silenced. He lives at home in Greenside with his wife Ilse, a diminutive woman of towering strength. Most of his time is spent in his book-lined study at home where he receives a stream of visitors and friends, one by one. Each time a guest arrives, Mrs Naude quietly rises and leaves the room; a conversation of three constitutes a "gathering" in terms of the banning order and would be a criminal offence. Their Greenside home, which has chairs side by side lining the walls of the lounge used to reverberate with intense discussion and vibrant debate. Now it is quiet and the chairs along the walls are empty. But there is in that home an atmosphere of strength and courage that remains unbowed.

The two men, Geyser and Naude, who in their ways are like latter-day Afrikaner Thomas Mores, sadly achieved little in terms of institutional reform in their respective churches. The controversial segregation clause, Article Three, remains firmly entrenched in the constitution of the *Hervormde Kerk;* the *Nederduitse Gereformeerde Kerk* continues to reflect divided South Africa in its formal structure and the Dutch Reformed Church as a whole, in varying degrees, continues to give spiritual blessing to the grand design of apartheid. Unassailable, stronger than ever, the Broederbond remains an inherent, powerful and abiding presence within the soul of the Afrikaans Church, which, in turn remains the soul of the South African State.

1. *Ons Taak: Kerklike-Godsdienstig.*
2. Troup, Freda, *South Africa: an Historical Introduction,* p 48.
3. Vatcher, W H, *White Laager,* p 110.
4. p 63 foll.
5. Ibid. p 5.
6. Sekretariele Verslag van die Uitvoerende Raad oor die tydperk 1 Maart 1963 tot 28 Februarie 1965, p 13.
7. *Rand Daily Mail,* October 5 1961.
8. *The Star,* October 24 1961.
9. *Rand Daily Mail,* October 25 1961.
10. Ibid.
11. *The Star,* October 24 1961.
12. *Rand Daily Mail,* October 24 1961.
13. Ibid., October 26 1961.
14. *Sunday Times,* November 5 1961
15. Ibid., September 1 1963.
16. *Rand Daily Mail,* May 11 1962.
17. Ibid., May 10 1963.

18. Ibid., May 17 1963.
19. *Sunday Times,* May 22 1960.
20. Ibid., December 2 1962.
21. Ibid., April 21 1963.
22. Ibid.
23. Ibid.
24. *Sunday Times,* December 9 1962.
25. Uittreksel uit Acta van die Sinode van die Suid-Transvaalse NG Kerk, April 1963.
26. *Sunday Times,* April 21 1963.
27. Ibid.
28. Ibid., May 12 1963.
29. Ibid., September 8 1963.
30. Ibid.
31. *Sunday Times,* October 20 1963.
32. *Sunday Times,* October 6 1963.
33. Sekretariele Verslag van die Uitvoerende Raad oor die tydperk 1 Maart 1963 tot 28 Februarie 1965, p 4.
34. Ibid. p 7.
35. Notule van die Een-en-Veertigste gewone Jaarvergadering gehou op 21 Mei 1963, pp 1, 2 and 9.
36. *Sunday Times,* November 10 1963.
37. Verslag van Reisende Sekretaris J H Swart vir die jaar 1963, p 1.
38. Sekretariele Verslag van die Uitvoerende Raad oor die tydperk 1 Maart 1963 tot 28 Februarie 1965, p 6.
39. *Rand Daily Mail,* November 20 1963.
40. *The Star,* November 21 1963.
41. *Rand Daily Mail,* November 20 1963.
42. Ibid., November 22 1963.

17 *The Commission of Inquiry*

In the aftermath of the Beyers Naude "treachery", with all the trauma it involved for the Broederbond, pressure mounted on the Prime Minister, Dr Verwoerd, to appoint a Commission of Inquiry into the organisation. While the Broederbond desperately struggled to heal its shattered defences, forces were growing outside to delve into the heart of the organisation. Its opponents sensed it was reeling from a devastating blow and wanted to use the resultant vulnerability to maximum effect.

Once again, the Broederbond and its activities were the subject of intense debate in Parliament. The United Party opposition, led by Sir de Villiers Graaff, demanded an inquiry and pressed an inexorable attack until at last, on January 24 1964 Dr Verwoerd interrupted a speech by the Opposition leader to demand: "Are you proposing a judicial commission to inquire into any subversive acts which may be done by the Broederbond, the Freemasons, or any other body which may possibly interfere in politics secretly?"

"The Hon the Prime Minister," replied Sir de Villiers, "has practically formulated the terms of reference now. As far as I am concerned, my proposal is that an investigation be instituted into the actions of the Broederbond itself. If the Hon the Prime Minister considers it necessary to have any other alliance, organisation, company or body investigated, then I am satisfied." The inquiry, he added, should meet four conditions: he and Dr Verwoerd should agree on the commissioners, the terms of reference, that evidence should be given under oath and that the inquiry should be public.[1]

Three months later, on April 28, Dr Verwoerd announced that he was prepared to appoint a Commission of Inquiry to investigate secret organisations, including the Broederbond, the Freemasons and the Sons of England. The Broederbond reacted instantly. Its chief secretary, Dr Piet Koornhof, issued a statement the same day. In it, Dr Koornhof, who suffered the indignity of being photographed delivering the statement at the offices of the

Rand Daily Mail in Main Street, Johanesburg, said: "The Afrikaner Broederbond would welcome a Commission of Inquiry into its activities if the Prime Minister should so decide. It will give the Broederbond the opportunity ... to inform the public, through the report of such a commission, about its own activities in the interest of South Africa and all its population groups.

"The Broederbond will be prepared to give evidence before such a commission to put the nation in a position to judge for itself about the accusations made against the Broederbond. This evidence can then be judged in the light of the activities of other secret organisations."

Given the intimate relationship between Dr Verwoerd and the Broederbond, it is inconceivable that in the time available he had not discussed the prospects of an inquiry with members of the Executive Council before going to Parliament with his announcement. There was certainly a precedent for this line of action, however unethical it might be in Parliamentary terms, as the Executive Council itself pointed out in its monthly circular to members, No 3/64/65 dated May 5 1964: "It should be remembered that Dr Malan also previously made such an offer of an investigation, with the knowledge of the Executive Council..."

In the same circular, the Executive Council expresses pleasure at Dr Verwoerd's insistence that the Freemasons and Sons of England be included in the probe and says the Opposition had only itself to blame that their own secret organisations would also be investigated. Significantly, it went on to perceive in the attack on the Broederbond an attack on the Prime Minister himself. The Executive Council told its members in the circular: "The conflict in the first place is not against the Afrikaner Broederbond as such – they naturally want to destroy it – but it is an attempt to break Afrikanerdom, to cause the fall of the National Party Government and Dr Verwoerd. The Afrikaner Broederbond is now being used as an instrument in this (attempt).

"The merciless fight that will result from this will do the organisation and Afrikanerdom, yes the whole of South Africa, the world of good, because the Afrikaner Broederbond has only the welfare of South Africa as its intent and therefore nothing warrants the attacks. The end, therefore, can only be that the protracted feud will collapse...

"It is clear that our national enemies are seizing the possible investigation as a method to subvert the resistance of our nation against subtle attacks on our spiritual heritage. They want to do this by insisting on a public investigation in which the membership of our organisation must be revealed so that they can sow suspicion and undermine the power of the activities of recognised national leaders in all areas of our national life by personal attacks and abuse. The Executive Council will not permit the destruction of our organisation or the debilitation of its influence. The Executive Council will be able to co-operate in an inquiry in the interests of our nation *(volk)* and that does not need to undermine our nation, nor divide or weaken it.

"The Executive Council feels that an investigation into the activities and objectives of the organisation does not mean that membership must be revealed. The Executive Council regards itself bound by the promise made in the induction ceremony, that the membership of a person will not be revealed without his permission." The Broederbond leaders thus gave an unequivocal undertaking to the members that they would not reveal their names and gave an instruction that no member should give evidence before the commission without the Executive Council's permission.

They then gave a remarkably confident declaration to their Broeder colleagues: "The Executive Council places on record its conviction that the Prime Minister will only allow an inquiry under such conditions that will be to the advantage of our country in the current difficult world circumstances. *He will not do something that will lead to the destruction and impotence of the organisation and our nation* (own emphasis).

The Executive Council further urged its members to guard against attempts to drive a wedge between the Broederbond and the Government. "We make an urgent appeal to all members to be calm and to place the necessary trust in the Executive Council *and the Prime Minister . . .*" (own emphasis).

Their confidence in Dr Verwoerd's protection was understandable, as a brief examination of the political developments at the time will indicate. Three years previously, South Africa had become a Republic free from the shackles of the British Commonwealth, a momentous achievement for the Afrikaner and a huge boost to Dr Verwoerd's personal stature and support. He knew only too well that he owed the Broederbond an enormous debt in the achievement of that ideal (see Chapter 5). Following this vital triumph, Dr Verwoerd turned his attention to the implementation of the Bantustan policy. 1964 was the year of the Transkei Act, that crucial beacon pointing the way to Afrikaner nationalism's apartheid solution to the race question in South Africa. Again, Dr Verwoerd could hardly escape the fact that the spectre of the Broederbond and its enormous influence loomed large in the achievment of the Bantustan experiment, and in fact in the formulation of the whole apartheid concept.

A more straightforward, but no less compelling factor in the Broederbond's confidence was the fact that Dr Verwoerd himself was a member. He was hardly likely to allow an investigation that could damage him and, thereby, the ideals in which he so ardently believed.

Dr Verwoerd demonstrated that the trust of his fellow Broeders was not misplaced when, on Tuesday June 9 1964, he announced to Parliament that a one-man commission of inquiry, under Appeal Court Judge D H Botha, would investigate aspects of "Secret and Other Organisations." He enraged the opposition by declaring that the commission would collect is evidence in camera, a measure that required the Commission Act of 1947 to be amended specially for the inquiry at hand. (This paved the way for subsequent secret commissions, notably the notorious Schlebusch Commission of 1974, which included in its ranks commissioners from the United Party. It investigated bodies such as the National Union of South African Students, which was declared an Affected Organisation as a result. Eight student leaders were banned. Mr Vorster, the former Prime Minister, then Minister of Justice, played a leading role in the debate and in the amendment of the Act. It was a busy session for him. He also piloted the infamous 90-day detention clause through Parliament that year, opening the way for the use, now a common feature, of detention without trial in South Africa).

Dr Verwoerd somewhat spuriously explained this extraordinary step in the following terms:

(a) There is no indication of the commission of any crime or offence, which should have been heard in public. It is only as a result of so much comment of a particular kind, both in the Press and Parliament, that, although akin to slander, it was considered wise to investigate in an impartial manner whether grounds for suspicion existed in order to clear the atmosphere of our national life. Should any offence be disclosed, a public hearing would then take place. If not, the persons or bodies concerned are entitled to their privacy.

(b) The bodies already mentioned in debates have voluntarily made themselves available for investigation. It would be unjust to them to take unfair advantage of this offer and allow matters to be disclosed as well which they regard as their private affairs and in which nothing wrong is found. Normally any use by the State of its power to interfere without sufficient reason in the private affairs of individuals, undertakings or organisations, even by means of a confidential inquiry, would be condemned.
(c) A public hearing would possibly involve bodies and persons not accused of any offence in great expenditure on legal representation which would not be recoverable for complaints. This could happen should it suit others to make ample use of the services of lawyers, for example a newspaper or periodical seeking financial advantage from the publicity which a lengthy inquiry would provide and which they could attempt to convert into a cause célèbre.
(d) A public hearing would also provide the opportunity for a heresy-hunt by opponents of any body, organisation or business undertaking under investigation. This could be done by laying bare confidential matters or business secrets to which it is entitled and which are innocent in order to destroy the organisation or undertaking against which the vendetta is directed, or which is a competitor.
(e) It is not in the public interest that peace and order in South Africa should be disturbed, perhaps for months, and that doubt and suspicion about life in South Africa should be sown abroad through a slow and perhaps deliberately extended process of accusation and refutation. The damage done would not disappear even though the inquiry resulted in the complete justification of the organisations concerned. Such a finding would be news for just one day, and perhaps even reach only a back page as not being sensational enough in comparison with the continuous sensational reports which could be extracted from the public hearing.
(f) On the positive side, for the kind of case now being dealt with, a personal inquiry by such a commission, guided by clearly defined terms of reference, is the best procedure. It can meet and interrogate witnesses in an unconstrained and even informal manner, visit offices and inspect documents there, and be taken fully into confidence, which does not happen in a public hearing where hostile elements are present.

Because of Dr Verwoerd's insistence on a secret inquiry, the leader of the Opposition, Sir de Villiers Graaff, refused to consult on the nature of the commission and so forfeited his right to have a say in the constitution of the inquiry or its terms of reference. Whether or not Dr Verwoerd had counted on this, it certainly suited the Broederbond. When Appeal Court Judge D H Botha was appointed to conduct the one-man inquiry, the terms of reference posed scant threat to the security of the Broederbond, or for that matter, the Freemasons and Sons of England.

Judge Botha, who was not a member of any secret organisation, was full of praise for the complete co-operation he received from the three organisations, whose conduct he was charged to investigate "in respect of anything which renders such an organisation guilty of:"

(a) *Any form of treason or intrigue, or of attempts to obtain for itself domination of, or of harmful or unlawful influencing of, or of subversive activities against, the people or the State or any of its organs such as the Central Government, the Provincial authorities or the Administration of Justice.*

Obvious evidence in connection with "domination" is that chillingly ambitious objective set by the then chairman, Professor J C van Rooy, in 1934: "... the primary consideration is whether Afrikanerdom will reach its ultimate destiny of domination *(baasskap)* in South Africa. Brothers, our solution to South Africa's ailments is not whether one party or another shall obtain the whiphand, but that the Afrikaner Broederbond shall govern South Africa."

The Broederbond has never publicly denied that aim; whether or not it did so in the secrecy of the Botha Commission is not known. By 1964, Professor van Rooy's ideal was virtually reality, consequently there is no question that the Broederbond would occupy itself in subverting the State. Effectively it was, and is, the State.

(b) *Anything which may weaken the determination and will of the people of South Africa to fight for their survival.*

This depends on one's definition of "the people of South Africa." Certainly the Broederbond aims to strengthen the determination of the white people of South Africa, and more particularly the Afrikaners, to fight for their survival.

(c) *The acquisition of funds from hostile sources, or the use of its own funds, for the financing of subversive action against the authority of the State or of threats to the security, peace and order of the population, or for the overthrow of the Government by impermissable and undemocratic methods.*

As far as the State is concerned, the same criteria apply in (a). Again, in the case of "threats to the security, peace and order of the population," it depends on the definition of "population." If this means the "white" population, there is clearly no charge against the Broederbond, but black people could probably argue that the policies pursued by the Broederbond contained such a threat to them. In fact they did argue thus, with stones in their hands, in the 1976 unrest. However, in 1964, these broad terms were probably intended to describe only the white population.

(d) *Nepotism or interference with appointments and promotions in the Public Service, the Defence Force or the Police Service so that persons are appointed or promoted for reasons other than merit.*

Dr Verwoerd himself provides ample evidence of the intention to do just this in his speech in Bloemfontein in 1943 when he said: "The Afrikaner Broederbond must gain control of everything it can lay its hands on in every walk of life in South Africa. Members must help each other to gain promotion in the civil service or any other field of activity in which they work with a view to working themselves into important administrative positions."

The organisation as a whole, as defined in its constitution, would condemn such practice. However, the very nature of the organisation and its determined and concerted efforts to win for itself top positions throughout the State structure makes nepotism virtually an unavoidable malaise. Judge Botha conceded[2] that individual cases of abuse of position probably did take place.

(e) *Attempts to subvert the relations between the English and Afrikaans-speaking people with the object of bringing about strife and national discord and of undermining national unity.*

That the sectional interests of the Broederbond could promote division between the English and Afrikaans sections of the population was the major objection expressed by General Hertzog in his Smithfield Address (see Chapter 2). But it is improbable that the Broederbond's object is to sow strife in this regard. It is more likely that its arrogance and single-mindedness ignore the fact that this could be the result of its exclusive sectionalism.

(f) *Improper or objectionable activities which harm, prejudice or undermine the right, liberties or interests of persons or groups or which aim at controlling other organisations in an irregular manner.*

Again, in white terms it would be difficult, but not impossible to prove a case against the Broederbond. Its aims and objectives state clearly that it is concerned first and foremost with the Afrikaner cause. The Broederbond-State relationship could give rise to a strong case of English-speakers being prejudiced in certain respects.

When it comes to blacks, however, the entire fabric of South African society, framed with the active assistance of the Broederbond, demonstrably prejudices and undermines "the rights, liberties or interests of persons or groups." However, it is unlikely that a commission appointed by the Government that so ordered the society would find this "improper or objectionable."

(g) *Subversion in any form of the morals, customs and way of life of the people of South Africa by circumventing or transgressing the country's laws or by any other means.*

Here again (f)'s criteria apply. Blacks could argue that the country's laws themselves subvert their customs and way of life.

(h) *Becoming a serious danger to peace and order in the body politic by exerting influence in an impermissable manner in the economic and cultural spheres.*

Yet again, in white terms a difficult proposition, but not so in regard to blacks. The policies of influx control, job reservation and differential education for blacks have all at one time or another resulted in threats to peace in South Africa. The Broederbond, by nature of its inextricable links with the Nationalist Government, has to share responsibility for this.

(i) *Attempts to dominate the Prime Minister, Ministers, Administrators or any other persons in authority in an effort to use him or them in the service of an organisation in such a manner that, as far as the performance of his or their official duties is concerned, loyalty is in the first place shown to the organisation and not to the State.* See comments on (a).

The Broederbond dutifully submitted to the inquiry and gave both formal and oral evidence. Extracts of the formal evidence were contained in two monthly circular letters to members, 6/64/65 and 8/64/65, dated September 2 1964 and November 3 1964 respectively. Among the claims made in these submissions were the following: "Our organisation does not give instructions to its members, but expects that each one in his profession and in all his activities will not serve himself, but his country according to the principles and objectives to which every member binds himself with a solemn promise at induction. Because this is so, and because of its relatively small number of members, the organisation never attempts to take over executives *(besture)* by trying to gain a majority in them – that is in any case practically impossible – but it and its members work by persuasion, through ideas that can be accepted if they are good, or rejected if they are judged as no good by non-members. The organisation does not coerce – it convinces by study, by quality, by inspiration because it works infused with ideals in the interests of a nation.

"The allegation that the organisation promotes or benefits its members at the expense of other Afrikaners is absolutely untrue. That this may have occurred in sporadic and individual cases, because of human weaknesses, is probably true, but that this is a pattern or aim of the organisation is untrue and goes against the very nature and being thereof. More examples of good Afrikaners that are not members and that were placed in responsible positions as a result of their attempts to seek the best for their country and nation could be named than of members that have been promoted or favoured by fellow members, chiefly or among other things because of their membership.

"An Afrikaner does not achieve high positions as a result of his membership of the organisation, but becomes a member thereof as a result of his inherent talents and traits as a consequence of which he would reach those positions himself in any case. He often becomes a member of our organisation as a result of the positions he has achieved in public, because he thereby gets the opportunity to prove that he possessed the qualities that are sought in potential members. The reward of membership is the pleasure which is derived from unadulterated service...

"Where the activities of the Afrikaner Broederbond in the national domain are closely connected with the spheres and responsibilities of the individual, the family, the State and the church, it is obvious that the Afrikaner Broederbond refrains from any actions which really belong in other areas. The Broederbond has thus never limited, and never wants to limit the conscience and freedom of the individual from making his own contribution to the welfare of his nation and of others; it also never wants to take upon itself, or illicitly interfere in, the functions of a political party which strives to capture executive power by public actions for the achievements of set objectives.

"It is the policy of both the Broederbond and Government people that there must not be the slightest reason for even the unjustified suspicion that influencing or interference exists, or that the National Party organisation does not have authority over the Government and its policy, but is manipulated by others. The Broederbond never does this in any circumstances and condemns any attempts in this direction.

"All that the Broederbond does, and always will do, is to support and promote, in so far as it is able, activities in other spheres that lead to the spiritualisation, strengthening and refinement of the Afrikaner nation as a Protestant-Christian language and cultural community; but also at the same time to expose and oppose all phenomena and trends in all spheres of life which are calculated to damage or destroy this nation, first of all by means of appeals to our leaders in those areas, and if these appeals fall on deaf ears, to awaken and organise action on the broad national front to oppose it.

"Philosophies like communism, liberalism, individualism, humanism, evolutionism serve as examples of this as well as other associated beliefs which could lead to the destruction of the Afrikaner nation in all areas of life. These trends do not only lead to the suicide of our nation, but to the destruction of all the independent life connections and domains which distinguish us, or at least to the subjection of the function of one to those of the rest.

"The Broederbond does not apply itself to the survival of the Afrikaner nation because it places this nation above all others or as an end in itself, but because it accepts this nation has intrinsic value, as a God-given institution and therefore does not want to and cannot unconcernedly allow that this nation be destroyed or recklessly commit suicide.

"We do not know how much time God will grant the Afrikaner nation to survive on earth for the fulfilment of its calling – what we do know, however, is that no force from outside can destroy us during that time."

All things considered, it was not surprising that Judge Botha exonerated the Broederbond, the Freemasons and the Sons of England of any guilt in terms of the inquiry.

Whether or not he was informed of the evidence against the Broederbond, such as the statements outlined in (a) and (d) above, is not known. It may be that in giving evidence in secret, the Broederbond convinced him that these sentiments no longer applied. This was never disclosed, because, as Judge Botha explained in his report: "If I were to give full reasons for my finding that an organisation is not guilty of any particular conduct, I should also have to rely on confidential information furnished to me by the organisation. This would not only be unfair to the organisation concerned, but also in conflict with the explicit request in the commission's terms of reference (that the confidentiality of innocent information be maintained). Were I to omit only such confidential information from the grounds for my finding, it would in turn mean that these grounds would be incomplete and, on the face of things, perhaps not even support my finding.

"Under the circumstances, I came to the conclusion that, where I could make no finding against an organisation, the fairest course for me would be, where necessary, merely to set out my conclusions drawn from all the evidence without my mentioning and analysing such evidence."

In other words, two remarkable features of the Botha Commission of Inquiry were that it heard evidence in secret, the first such case in South African history, and was able to give unsubstantiated findings. The public was expected to take everything the commission said on trust.

But this is not what spared the Broederbond any serious anxiety in the inquiry. Dr Verwoerd had seen to that aspect in the terms of reference of the inquiry. If they had included the clause contained in Dr Verwoerd's original offer of an inquiry, namely "which may interfere in politics secretly," it would have been a totally different story. Throughout this book and elsewhere there is ample evidence of the organisation's secret involvement in political matters. The commission could not have failed to judge against the Broederbond had this clause been retained.

However, as it happened, the terms of reference were so framed that they skirted around the cardinal issue. This is not whether the Broederbond in any way threatened to subvert the State, but on the contrary, that the State and the Broederbond have become indistinguishable. After the Nationalists came to power in 1948, the State was in no danger from the Broederbond. Since then, critics of the organisation have been concerned at the close links, which finally blur into one whole, between the State and a secret organisation which aims for the advancement of the exclusive interests of only one section of a heterogenous society.

Judge Botha may have been hinting at some private concern for this aspect when he said in his report: "The commission's terms of reference, as I understand them, do not order a general inquiry into the organisations mentioned, but only an investigation of the question whether these organisations, or any of them, were guilty of any conduct referred to in the terms of reference. Although I undertook a wider inquiry than was necessary for the purposes of the terms of reference ... I must confine myself in this report to the question whether any of the organisations is in fact guilty of such conduct."[4]

In any event, whatever misgivings there might be, or have been, it was over. For the Broederbond in particular, the crisis, which on critical examination was no crisis after all, had passed.

The epitaph of the commission has some interesting features. In his report, Judge Botha praised the "extremely competent" manner in which he had been assisted by Mr J P J Coetzer, who had led the evidence before the commission, and by Mr C M van Niekerk, the secretary of the commission. "The officers," wrote Judge Botha, "displayed exceptional initiative in obtaining evidence relating to the commission's terms of reference. Without their assistance, it would not have been possible to complete the inquiry in the manner in which, and the time within which, it was carried out."

At the time of writing, the two gentlemen in question were Secretary and Under Secretary of Justice respectively. More important, both had become members of the Broederbond...

Another happy spinoff for the organisation was that it was strengthened in its ability to integrate itself further in the political affairs of South Africa. At the *Bondsraad* the following year, the chairman, Dr Meyer, said: "This brings me to my most important observation that follows on the fact that the Afrikaner Broederbond had been exonerated of any boundary transgressions or damaging behaviour by commissions of inquiry of the church and the State: namely that the Afrikaner Broederbond has been placed in a favourable position to bind all the forces of the Afrikaans national domain into a unit, and will do that by continuing to bring together within its ranks all the real leaders of our national activities. In this way, the separate functions of church, State and nation can be practised in the Afrikaans context in a manner which effectively will complement each other, particularly at a time when we are threatened from within and without as never before in our history."[5]

In short, the Commission of Inquiry initiated by Broeder Verwoerd provided the organisation with an invaluable smokescreen, behind which it could continue the very practices to which its opponents objected: political intrigue and manipulation. It is small wonder, therefore, that when one talks with the Broeder faithful, they innocently refer one to the commission's report.

Mr Vorster, the former Prime Minister, for example, did just that during the 1970 Klip River by-election. He surprised Parliament by informing it that he had submitted articles about the Broederbond to Judge Botha.

Mr Vorster charged that the articles, published in the Durban-based *Sunday Tribune*, deliberately attempted to incite the English and Afrikaans-speaking people against each other. The Prime Minister told Parliament that Judge Botha had authorised him to say that every allegation and charge contained in the articles was the same as those which were placed before his commission six years previously. Each and every one of them, he said, had been found to be "totally untrue."[6]

1. *Hansard,* January 24 1964, Col 311.
2. Report of the Commission of Inquiry into Secret Organisations, p 8.
3. Ibid. p 2.
4. Ibid.
5. Secret Broederbond document *Organisiering van die Derde Terrein in ons Land,* chairman's address 1965, p 2.
6. *Rand Daily Mail,* September 19 1970.

Part three
The mechanics of power

18 *The Broederbond – As seen by the Broeders*

Whatever the outsider's view of the Broederbond, those on the inside see it as a noble organisation. They claim credit for dramatically improving the Afrikaner's economic position and putting him in political control. The exclusivity, the strict secrecy, are explained away as necessary to the salvation of Afrikanerdom and indeed of all the people in South Africa.

These rationalisations are not, of course, voiced in public. They are discussed at secret meetings in order to inspire and strengthen Broeders against attacks from the outside. In the secret documents, four important speeches were uncovered which show clearly how the Broeders see the Broederbond. In the interests of showing objectively how the members of the Bond are motivated, fairly long parts of the speeches have been reproduced here.

In the address he gave at the 50th anniversary of the Broederbond in 1968, the chairman, Dr Piet Meyer, asked: "What is Brotherhood *(Broerskap)?* What is there in its crux and soul that every month brings together mature, serious-minded, businesslike, busy, practical leaders in every sphere – over long distances, and in difficult circumstances – drawing them together to discuss matters of concern to their nation; and compelling them to seek responsibilities or accept duties fostering those interests?" Dr Meyer went on to give his own vision of Brotherhood. "The secret of the Afrikaner Broederbond's 50 years of good and faithful service to our *volk* and country, is *Broerskap.*

"Members of the Afrikaner Broederbond know what *Broerskap* is. It is the secret power which ties together in earnest endeavour 8 000 Afrikaner leaders closely united in service to our *volk* and country, and to the honour of the God of our fathers." Dr Meyer said the Broeders had picked each other "one by one" for their Brotherhood. They had done so in circumstances kept confidential because otherwise there would have been publicity and criticism. "A shared Brotherhood which does not seek personal honours and advantage, can never be anything but secret Brotherhood. Forgoing the secrecy of Brotherhood means forgoing the Afrikaner Broederbond itself.

"Brotherhood is not only voluntary and selfless co-operation in the service of our *volk* and country, nor is it only unseen comradeship — but also leadership. In the Afrikaner Broederbond there are not leaders and followers, but only leaders. The Afrikaner Broederbond does not make leaders of Broeders but Broeders of leaders.

"Brotherhood permits open differences, but nothing is more unbrotherly than the carrying of tales and gossip. Without discipline and punishment the Broederbond could not survive. If Broeders have the right to select each other one by one to work in the interest of the *volk,* then there is an implicit right to reject those who differ in matters of principle or behave unworthily.

"Brotherhood is selective, confidential leadership continuously extended as the inner-mechanism, the heartbeat of the *Afrikanervolk.* It is not leadership which arrogantly prescribes to our *volk* and country from outside. It does not impose policies from great intellectual heights on our *volk* and their organisations. Broeders are not people who dictate tasks from above or from a distance. No, Brotherhood means fully considering and digesting the problems facing our *volk* from time to time, studying the facts to ensure clarity and effective solutions."

Dr Meyer said the Broederbond was formed as "a different kind of answer" to long-standing problems facing the Afrikaner: subservience to the English and Britain, a feeling of national inferiority, impotence, bondage, exploitation and poverty. The Broederbond's response was: "Your honour is in your name, your Afrikaner name; your Afrikaner ancestors, their faith, ideals and sacrifices, their language and history. Your honour is in your faith, your ideals, your mother-tongue and your fatherland's history – betray that and there is nothing left."

In the early years of the Broederbond, action was aimed at securing equality for Afrikaners in "English and Jewish" shops, according to Dr Meyer. But the economic plight of the Afrikaner was grave in the poverty-stricken platteland and the growing urban areas under "British-Jewish" domination. The Broederbond arranged the *Ekonomiese Volkskongres* to plan ways to advance the Afrikaner economically, and later fought for the Republic and separate developmet.

Dr Meyer devoted his peroration to the Broederbond in the

next 50 years, 1968 to 2018. "Neither you nor I can know if we will be granted another 50 years of *Broederskap*. What we do know is that as long as it is God's will that we remain a separate *Afrikanervolk,* the Afrikaner Broederbond will have a task to fulfil. Only if we as a nation, or the Afrikaner Broederbond as central power of our cultural ideal, commit suicide will that alter." He saw the Broederbond's task as furthering the Afrikaans language and the Christian national outlook, preventing the establishment of an integrated Afrikaans-English culture, improving the Afrikaner's economic position, intensifying the Christian-Afrikaner nature of the Republic, and expanding separate development.

"A brotherhood and a Broederbond vain enough to look down on its own society would be busy rendering itself superfluous. The Brotherhood is greater than that – it is an organised Brotherhood which has developed its own methods of co-operation, organisation and operation to carry out most economically and effectively, essential tasks in changing circumstances. Brotherhood develops to cover every aspect of the life of the *volk*, and devise suitable organisational methods to discharge what it undertakes."

Dr Meyer said the Broederbond should not become obsessed with organisation, recruiting for Afrikaner bodies, arranging *volksfeeste* and collecting money for public projects.

"The essence of Brotherhood-in-action is defining problems facing the *volk,* solving them, and giving uniform policies to all the public bodies on which Broeders serve. The essence of Brotherhood-in-action is to confront problems facing the *volk* without consulting one's own interests, without seeking credit or personal advantage."

Dr Meyer then referred to the "divine mission" of the Broederbond – something that all its members believe in with evident fervour. "Broederbond membership, *broerskap,* is that and much more. This 'more' is not something from us and by us. It comes from outside us and above us. It is something which God established Himself; otherwise it remains inexplicable and inconceivable. It is something which we as Broeders have in common with all Christians on earth. *Broerskap* – the Afrikaner Broederbond – is a gift from God to our *volk* . . . to strive and realise its separate destiny to the greater glory of His name."

Dr Meyer added: "And that brings us to the last aspect of our Brotherhood in the coming years. Is Afrikaner *broerskap* still necessary for the fulfilment of the tasks I have mentioned? Has the time not arrived to replace it with a 'white' *broerskap?*

"The Afrikaner Broederbond has already given the answer to this question over the last 50 years. While it is logical on the one hand to say that the safety of the white future in South Africa also ensures the future of the Afrikaner, it is an historical fact that the future of the white and non-white nations of our country depends on the independent future of the Afrikaner. If Christian Afrikanerdom did not remain true to itself in all respects, British liberal politics in our country would inexorably have pushed through integration of white and non-white which had already gone a long way. No one can doubt that this would have ended in so-called majority rule, as everywhere else in former British colonies in Africa. And that would not only have been the end of an independent white nation; it would have permanently damaged the independent national future of the non-whites.

"What is historically true in this connection will remain true in future: the only alternative is revolution. What I have to say about Brotherhood in the next 50 years rests on the unambiguous premise that the future of white and non-white nations of our country depends primarily on ensuring the future of the Afrikaner nation as an independent Christian national nation at the southern tip of Africa... If we do not accept this as fundamental, then we forfeit the Afrikaner Broederbond's right to exist.

"If a Broeder asks whether the Afrikaner Broederbond still has a task for the future, then he questions his own right as a Christian Afrikaner to complete his task in South Africa. Those who doubt, those who have lost their certainty, must make way for those who after 50 years of Brotherhood have not started counting the years."

Broederbonder fanaticism about their organisation is also illustrated by the emotional speech made by one of the founder members, Mr Henning Klopper, at the 50th anniversary of the Bond. "On an occasion like this, celebrating the Afrikaner Broederbond's half-century, one feels very small. You recognise your own insignificance. You realise that but for the grace of God, you would have been nothing.

"The years 1914 to 1917 which culminated in the establishment of the Afrikaner Broederbond in 1918 were years of struggle, division, bitterness; years of frustration for the Afrikaner. It was a decade after the Boer War in which we were destroyed. But we felt we couldn't lie down. With the grace of God we had to arise. And we arose in our faith.

"I speak on behalf of all my colleagues here when I say it is a matter of what we received from God. We who have reached this point are only instruments in His hands. To say it was our cleverness, our determination or our wisdom would be stupid, because we were only children who joined battle. We started when we were young, lately out of school. We continued the struggle, and so far it has been one long struggle.

"Earlier today a question was asked that was in many minds – did not the Broederbond achieve its purpose with the attainment of the Republic? Has the time not arrived for us to dissolve? If that is so, Broeders, then we must ask: who will give us the Government of the country? Who will give us our future Prime Ministers? Who is to mould them? Where are they to come from? Where will they be found?

"Since the Afrikaner Broederbond got into its stride it has given the country its governments. It has given the country every Nationalist Prime Minister since 1948. It has given us the Republic, even though indirectly. It has given us two State Presidents. What would have happened to the Afrikaner *volk* if the Broederbond had ceased to exist? Our nation depends on the Broederbond.

"The Broederbond was small and the members were few but they were very active and worked day and night. I want to give these people credit, these men who stood here in front of you (founder members) – Broeders H W van der Merwe, H le R Jooste, N F Botha, P V Conradie, G J Retief, D H C du Plessis, Iwan Lombard – every one of them was at his post. Day and night they slept,dreamt and thought Broederbond. They gave the ideal momentum and then the nation took over.

"The *volk* brought it to where it is tonight. It is the will of the *volk*. It is in the interest of the *volk*. It is in the interest of the Kingdom of God that the Afrikaner Broederbond shall be there.

". . . out of the Afrikaner Broederbond were born the best and most beautiful things of our nation. The FAK, the economic ideal, the rehabilitation of the Afrikaner, are born out of the Broederbond. In each sphere the Broederbond played its role, as in 1934 with the *Volkskongres* on the poor-white problem when we had 300 000 to 400 000 poor whites.

"When the *volk* was depressed again after the 1938 election, with only 27 out of 140 members of Parliament, God gave us the Oxwagon Trek. It was the Broeders who organised it. It was the Broeders who took the initiative. Through the grace of God the Broeders executed it. It was not that the Broeders sought to become big and powerful in the nation. God used them in this instance too. They planned it, but God used them as instruments to make the trek what it was. Many people told us in places where the trek arrived, 'It is wonderful, it is from God.' The Afrikaner Broederbond is just as wonderful,and it also is from God.

"Do you realise what a powerful force is assembled here tonight between these four walls? Show me a greater force on the whole continent of Africa! Show me a greater force anywhere else (in the world), even in your so-called civilised nations. We support the State, we support the Church, we support every big movement born from the nation. We make our contribution unobtrusively, we carry it through and so we have brought our nation to where it is today.

"We have supplied the leaders to our nation. Pity the nation without a leader! Every time, a leader could be chosen for the nation from the ranks of the Afrikaner Broederbond. When we lost Dr Malan, we had Advocate Strijdom. When death claimed him we had Dr Verwoerd. When he died so tragically, God had another man ready for us.

"The nation has been through terrible crises in the last 50 years. The crisis of the depression, the political developments that started then, the crisis after the symbolic trek, the crisis of the Second World War.

"But from the beginning our Broeders believed that the spirit of *Broederskap* must be planted in the heart of every Broeder. The ties of *Broederskap* must be so strong that they cannot be broken. If we look back now, we can thank God that there were so few occasions when the ties failed. The ties of *Broederskap* brought us to where we are today, surviving all the storms. We who were involved from the beginning, thank God for this. It is far more than we had hoped for, and for that the few of us who are left want to give honour to God to Whom it is due.

"A foreign journalist who visited the country said all he could say about the Afrikaner nation was that it was a miracle. That is because we accepted God our Father as our Saviour in every crisis. In those dark days when it was difficult, we went on our knees with all our problems and God gave us a solution. That is why we were adamant that the Afrikaner Broederbond should retain its Christian character. That must never be lost, and I thank God tonight that this is the case.

"Broeder Chairman, you cannot think how pleasing it is to us that you are such a devoted child of God, that the Broeders on the Executive Council are such devoted Christians. We want you to realise that you have the love not only of the Afrikaner Broederbond, but of the whole Afrikaner nation. When you are serving in the frontline, at the South African Broadcasting Corporation, we want you to know that we are with you in spirit. We remember you in our prayers and we thank God that we have a man like Piet Meyer to serve Afrikanerdom at this stage. May God spare you for many years to serve His cause in the Afrikaner nation.

"Looking at public life in South Africa, we are glad that the Afrikaner Broederbond gives leadership in every facet and sphere and is indispensable there. Everywhere Broeders are manning the front lines.

"Dare anybody still ask whether the Afrikaner Broederbond's time has expired? He dare not ask such a question! Take the Afrikaner Broederbond out of Afrikanerdom, and what remains? Take Afrikanerdom out of Africa, and what remains for the Kingdom of God? Who is going to serve the cause if Afrikanerdom is no longer there? Ask the people of Rhodesia, 'What is at the end of your road?' Nobody can tell you. All they say is, 'We know the Republic is behind us.' And who is the Republic? It is the Broeders of the Afrikaner Broederbond.

"When will our task be completed? When God calls us to a higher duty. Only then is a man's task finished. Your task never ends here. You are called to it until the last minute of your life and there is a challenge for every one of us. A man who puts his hand to the plough should not look back. There is only one yardstick for a member of the Afrikaner Broederbond: service. Not what you can get from the Afrikaner Broederbond, but what you can give. Not what you can get from the *volk*, but what service you can render to the *volk*.

"I was pleased by the reception the Prime Minister was accorded here this afternoon. He needs your prayers, your love, your *Broerskap*. He is called from time to time to take decisions which are unpopular but necessary. I was pleased, therefore, by the reception and by the confidence you have given him. It is our duty to sustain him, our duty, when he is no longer there, to supply his successor. Life must continue. If he is no longer there, somebody else must take his place. In that way our work never ends.

"God help us to continue to the end! In the name of the old Broeders, thank you very much for this wonderful opportunity. God's blessing be with you for the next 50, 150, 250 years, into the most distant future."

Equally rousing was the speech made by Dr A P Treurnicht. Since the days when he was editor of the *Kerkbode,* official organ of the Nederduitse Gereformeerde Kerk, largest of the Afrikaans churches, he was regarded as the coming spiritual leader of the *verkrampte* (conservative) faction in the National Party. When Dr Treurnicht became editor of *Hoofstad* in Pretoria, he was drawn into the rightwing group led by Dr Albert Hertzog, who formed the Herstigte Nasionale Party. For a while it appeared that he might go along with the HNP, and what persuaded him otherwise was Mr Vorster's decisive victory in the battle in the Broederbond (dealt with in another chapter). Dr Treurnicht instead fought a by-election in Waterberg, the former seat of Advocate Hans Strijdom, 'Lion of the North', who at one stage was the only National Party MP in the Transvaal and later became Prime Minister. Dr Treurnicht was soon made a deputy Minister, obviously a clever Vorster tactic to keep him under control.

Treurnicht would have been a great danger outside the National Party as leader of a rightwing group. He has all the potential to become a forceful Afrikaner leader, and Vorster realised it. Bringing him into the Cabinet clipped his wings by making him party to the decision-making body. In practice deputy Ministers do not attend Cabinet meetings where decisions are taken by consensus: they are required to carry out policy without really having a say in it at Cabinet level. In this way Dr Treurnicht became a captive of Mr Vorster's so-called "move to the left".

It was no surprise when Dr Treurnicht succeeded Dr Meyer as head of the Broederbond in 1972. The speech he made at the secret *Bondsraad* meeting in 1968 shows he had ideal qualifications to lead the Broederbond. His views on Afrikaner-English relationships are particularly interesting.

Dr Treurnicht began his speech with a stirring message which Dr A M Moll, one of the original Broeders, had delivered from his deathbed. "Broeders, I don't envy you life, but only the privilege to continue the battle for our nationhood. In the world struggle there is no end, we are all still Voortrekkers on the road of our beloved South Africa. It is too early to unsaddle..." Dr Treurnicht commented: "Struggle for our nationhood!... It is too early to unsaddle! These words came to me like a refrain when I thought about the Afrikaner Broederbond in the past and present. It has been worrying me the last few years that within our own ranks the question is raised of whether the Afrikaner Broederbond still has a task. It has also been suggested that rightwing English-speakers might be accepted into our movement on the basis of South Africa first and then the acceptance of the policy of separate development between white and non-white.

"These suggestions must be viewed in the light of these questions:

"Is the Afrikaner, and is he to remain, a definable national group within the broad white South African entity?

"Has he fulfilled his destiny, and could he therefore disappear?

"Has not the attainment of the Republic meant putting a full stop to his separate existence and individual national awareness?

"I should like to quote from the minutes of June 5 1918 (at the formation of the Broederbond). The chairman, Broeder H J Klopper, stated this aim. 'Our main aim is a brotherhood of Afrikaners, now scattered over South Africa and mainly opposed to each other without the slightest cohesion. The salvation of our nation lies in our striving together in love for its wellbeing. We must bring our nation to consciousness.'

"On July 2 1918 the following aims were formulated. 'Melting together of Afrikaners... Eliminating the differences of opinion over national problems and creating a healthy, forward-looking generation and uniformity. Serving the interests of Afrikaners at all times ... bringing Afrikaners to awareness, creating self-respect and love for the Afrikaner's language, history, country, *volk*. Promoting true, original South African culture and art in every respect. Enhancing our society through the restoration of its traditional beautiful characteristics and customs such as hospitality, democratic friendliness and readiness to support each other in need or distress. We build our future on the Rock, Christ."

Dr Treurnicht went on: "Those were concepts crystallised in the constitution of the Afrikaner Broederbond and formulated as follows. (a) The Creation of a healthy and forward-looking Afrikaner unity to seek the welfare of the Afrikaner nation. (b) The stimulation of national consciousness among Afrikaners, inspiring them with love for their language, faith, traditions, country and *volk*. (c) Promotion of all the interests of the Afrikaner nation.

"The reason I quote at such length is that the Afrikaner Broederbond can be rightly understood today only if we know the roots from which it grows. When we no longer grow from these roots, we lose our identity. And if we no longer want to grow from the Afrikaner roots, but want to be grafted on to a kind of South African root which is not essentially Afrikaner, then we must admit it openly to each other because then the Afrikaner Broederbond's right to existence has expired.

"But that is not the case. The Afrikaner is not prepared to be regarded as ephemeral in the history of nations. He does not believe in a destiny requiring nations to disappear in due time. He does not believe that his right to existence is automatic, regardless of whether he had fulfilled his calling: but he also does not believe that it is praiseworthy to be weakened and to commit suicide. If ever there was a period in our history imposing a duty to resist attacks, then it is now!

"If ever vigilance was necessary to the Afrikaner's interests, and specifically the Afrikaner's, then it is now when some think we have made the transition from inferiority to independence and domination. Our meaningful existence as an Afrikaner nation is not a matter of course – just as our bodies cannot remain strong without food, shelter and care, just as our spiritual life cannot remain healthy as a matter of course without vigilance.

"This meaningful existence has a deep positive content. We are dealing with nothing less than a comprehensive national Afrikaner movement entailing continuous action by the Afrikaner to make an impact as a nation, to contribute and play his role as an equal in every aspect of life: social, economic, scientific, cultural, religious and political. It is more than a political movement. It is the desire of a nation to act independently in every sphere.

"Of course nobody wants to claim the credit for these achievements exclusively for the Afrikaner Broederbond. The Afrikaner Broederbond would not be so presumptuous. But it cannot be denied that from the Afrikaner Broederbond's ranks came a stimulating and fertile influence on the rest of the Afrikaner nation. It is a fact that the Afrikaner Broederbond musters some of the best and most knowledgeable members of Afrikaner society. It is representative of the Afrikaner national movement at its broadest.

"Almost every matter affecting the existence and calling of the Afrikaner nation has been considered deeply by the Afrikaner Broederbond's members. The results of these reflections were passed on systematically to the Afrikaner nation. Matters which were considered confidentially were indirectly submitted to the nation for consideration ...

"I make bold to say that the Afrikaner Broederbond, strongly emphasising the continuation of the Afrikaner nation – also as a white nation – made no small contribution to the acceptance of the separate nationhood policy which has been successfully applied ...

"On the economic front the Broederbond and other organisations of the Afrikaner nation were concerned in the 1930s over the Afrikaner's subjection. It was agreed that something must be done to give the Afrikaner status in commerce and industry. It cannot be denied that we have made great progress.

"The fact remains, however, that a large percentage of the country's commerce and industry is still in foreign hands. If there is one thing making the Broederbond necessary in the ranks of the Afrikaner nation, now and in future, it is that full status cannot be obtained by the Afrikaner if he does not get the greatest possible economic control. Especially now that we put so much emphasis on necessary co-operation between the Afrikaner and English we must make certain – even if it must be done discreetly – that the Afrikaner is the stronger partner. Without that there is still something missing from our full status and independence. This is therefore, what the Afrikaner Broederbond should give urgent attention to now."

After dealing at length with the Broederbond's role in religion and education, Dr Treurnicht returned to the cultural area and Afrikaner-English relations. "It is strange to hear, even among Afrikaners, as well as from part of the English Press, references to Afrikaner jingoism, applied to people who want to maintain the Afrikaans culture, alongside English and other cultures. There are even those who propose to tell us that the *Afrikanerskap* we talk about does not exist. They appear to argue that co-operation between the two language groups on matters of political policy entails repudiation of the Afrikaner culture. That we can never tolerate!

"Let there be no misunderstanding. There are many objectives for which our two white cultural groups should and will fight shoulder to shoulder. We must cultivate a common patriotism.

On cardinal points of political policy we should try to reach agreement in the interest of both groups' preservation. But there is one stipulation that the Broederbond must make clear, and this is that co-operation with our English-speaking co-citizens cannot lead to a reduction in our national pride. One thing we have learnt from our history is that Afrikaner unity is precious and must not be meddled with. We have learnt that you cannot have meaningful unity in South Africa if Afrikanerdom is divided.

"The Afrikaner is not seeking a unity in which Afrikaner unity is not the cornerstone, or in which the unity with his own people is slighted or threatened. If we are going to talk about unity between our two cultural groups, then we must recognise the differences, and the right to differ. We must recognise an intrinsic Afrikaner culture and an Afrikaner nation and culture that we extend the hand of co-operation to our English-speaking co-citizens. Our Afrikaner identity is no stumbling-block, but the very component which is indispensable to meaningful co-operation."

After dealing with the need for the Broederbond to inspire the youth, Dr Treurnicht concluded: "I believe that the Afrikaner nation and the Broederbond must again be called on to resist the blurring of the Afrikaner consciousness in a kind of white unity which will be neither Afrikaans nor English; the overwhelming of our beliefs by liberalistic ideas; a temptation to yield as the tide is turning against us.

"If there is a message for Broederbond members on this 50th anniversary it is:

"We will not tolerate being undermined as Afrikaners,

"We will not tolerate being diverted from our course as a nation,

"We do not want to be liberalised,

"We do not want to split,

"We want to remain one and together on the basis of a Christian nationalism which has become part of us through our years of becoming a nation.

"The Afrikaner nation is called to be spiritual pioneers of our time."

The minutes show that Dr Treurnicht's speech was received "with acclamation" at the *Bondsraad.* It appeared, however, that Mr Vorster did not see the matter of unity between Afrikaner and English in such narrow terms. Although the two speeches appeared superficially to take very much the same line, the emphasis

B J Vorster. Prominent Broeder, now State President of South Africa.

differed. In fact Mr Vorster said he was not prepared to "trick" the English – a clear repudiation of the rightwingers who wanted to use national unity as a front, while working hard behind the scenes for Afrikaner domination.

Mr Vorster started his speech by congratulating Broeder Chairman, Broeder Deputy Chairman and the Executive Council. "The Broeders have put their trust in you and appointed you to those positions. It is not necessary for me, after 50 years of the existence of the Afrkaner Broederbond and everything it has meant and created, to tell you how great is the responsibility on your shoulders. We live in a complicated world. The position in which I find myself does not always make it easy to give all the answers, but the answers must be given in our time. You help with this and I appreciate the co-operation from your side...

"During the past two years I have come to think that we are not here just to live and work and enjoy what South Africa offers in abundance, but that we have been called to fulfil a task, not only in South Africa but in the whole of Africa. We have heard that call so often in the past two years that nobody can doubt it.

"We heard it when depression descended upon us. Every time we were close to succumbing a door opened for us which we as human beings could not have opened. It was done for us by the God who called us to be here in South Africa and to our work. If we look at the situation today in the global context, it is a matter for wonder that numbers, the weight of world opinion, ignorance, and the antipathy in the rest of the world, has not overwhelmed us already. Therein lies the wonder of our existence.

"One thing we must realise very clearly: the future of South Africa does not lie only with the Afrikaner. The future depends on the white man in South Africa and southern Africa fighting for his existence. The attainment of the Republic affected all of us, Afrikaner and English-speaker.

"There are two things we as Afrikaners should not do. We must not overestimate the English-speaking South African: that would be a mistake. But we must also not underestimate him: that would be an even bigger mistake. Because the coming of the Republic has given a message to the English-speaking South African and has brought about a change in spirit which we must evaluate correctly and mobilise in the interests of South Africa.

"The question is how should I co-operate as an Afrikaner with the English-speaking South African? Every one of my predecessors was confronted with that question. I remember well how I as a boy became interested in politics and came across the word "conciliation" used by General Botha. I did not understand it and asked my father, who was not an educated man, 'Father, what does this word "conciliation" mean which is General Botha's policy?' And he replied, 'My son, General Botha wants us to apologise for making the English come and fight us.'

"Later we came to the point of view that the United Party as formulated by Mr Wolfie Swart who said, 'I want my children to be neither English nor Afrikaner.'

"By contrast, we Afrikaners held the view from the days of General Hertzog that permanent co-operation between Afrikaner and English-speaker could only succeed along the lines of the two-stream policy – that I as Afrikaner and everything that is my own, my language, customs, traditions, thoughts, outlook on life, must be prepared to co-exist with an English speaker with respect for his language, customs and traditions.

"The one thing that should bind us together is common loyalty and love for South Africa, our common fatherland. That loyalty and love have not always been there, because there was a double heart and a divided loyalty. The Republic brought about common loyalty and love."

After dealing at length with the attack from rightwing Nationalists on his leadership (see Chapter 11) Mr Vorster indicated what a strong role the Broederbond was playing in his life and his regime. "I am grateful, Broeder Chairman, for what you have said about me. I am grateful for the co-operation I get from you, the Executive Council and the Broeders.

"It is heartening to know there is sympathy and understanding for my task. But I want to repeat, Broeder Chairman: what appears in public is only a small part of what is really done. One could not continue with the task without awareness of our people's trust – given even when they cannot be told what is being done. I am grateful to those who give me this trust. I am intensely thankful, because it enables me to do an almost impossible job. For that I am prepared to sacrifice myself, especially if I know that I can rely on the support, trust and prayers of my Broeders in this organisation."

The Broeders absolute faith that God is protecting their organisation is nowhere better illustrated than in the 1963 minutes of the annual general meeting when the vice-chairman thanked Dr Piet Meyer for his address. "The chairman is a gift from God. God has always given us a leader. God has given our organisation this chairman."

Also clear from the secret Broederbond minutes is a change of tone which has occurred over the years and in turn the Bond's influence on the Government is seen from this. The Government's hard-line attitude on racial matters in the first 15 to 17 years of power was indeed the attitude of the Broederbond. But in later years, when pressure on the country increased and the moral standpoint on racial questions became politically dominant, the

Broederbond mellowed – to be followed by the Government which then publicly declared for the first time that discrimination based on colour must be removed. The difference in tone can be seen by comparing the annual reports of Dr Piet Meyer and Dr Andries Treurnicht when they were chairmen with that of Professor Gerrit Viljoen, the present chairman.

His emphasis on certain aspects of the role of the Broederbond in the present situation differs clearly from those of his predecessors. In place of blind faith in an organisation believed to be guided by God, Professor Viljoen wants more open discussions. "In contrast to the debate five to 10 years ago on whether the Broederbond still had a role after securing stable political control for the Afrikaner, we can frankly state that the Afrikaner has never needed an organisation like the Broederbond more than he does today.

"But then we must ensure that the machine runs smoothly without friction. This demands increased discipline; fraternal candour in seeking solutions to extensive problems aggravated by the radical changes around us; planned progress instead of ill-prepared uncoordinated activity; deliberate, consistent action on all levels; evaluation of results; and the allocation of enough time for thorough and dedicated work for the Afrikaner Broederbond.

"Our primary task is to activate, motivate and guide our members, many of whom carry high-level responsibility for making and directing policy and thus are busy every day 'about the Afrikaner Broederbond's business.' The Afrikaner Broederbond does not achieve its biggest successes by acting organisationally as the AB, but much more through the thorough work of its network of responsible, informed and motivated members. When committees of experts are to be made up of Broederbond members to deal with a national problem, we find that most of the key figures in that particular field already are our people, giving leadership and carrying responsibility.

"The Broederbond's function then is to form committees of experts and interest groups, to bring together members viewing the same problem from different angles, in order to stimulate and coordinate. It is especially valuable to bring together official and private instutitions, experts and amateurs. Productive circumstances ensue on the basis of frank brotherhood for stimulation, cross-pollination and the juxtaposition of new or different ideas."

19 *The Constitution, Administration and Finance*

The membership requirements, aims and objectives of the Afrikaner Broederbond establish clearly its exclusivist character. According to the organisation's constitution, the aims are:

1. The establishment of a healthy and progressive accord among all Afrikaners who strive for the welfare of the Afrikaner nation;
2. The awakening of a national self-consciousness in the Afrikaner and the inculcation of love for his language, religion, traditions, country and nation;
3. The promotion of all Afrikaner interests.

Compared with previous constitutions, these rather general aims reflect the achievement of the Broederbond to date.

As the organisation has watched its stated objectives achieved in South Africa it has removed them from the constitution.

In 1944, for example, the constitutional "check list" was far more formidable than it is today. According to a report, the then Chapter VI of the constitution said:

"The Broederbond desires that all Broeders in their political action will strive for the following sevenfold ideals:

1. Removal of everything which is in conflict with the full independence of South Africa;
2. Termination of the inferiority of the Afrikaans-speakers and their language in the organisation of the State;
3. Segregation of all coloured races domiciled in South Africa with provision for their independent development under the trusteeship of whites.
4. Stopping the exploitation of the natural resources and the population by *uitlanders* (foreigners) including more intensive industrial development;
5. Rehabilitation of the farmers and ensuring a civilised living standard through work for all white *burgers* (citizens);
6. Nationalisation of credit and currency and planned co-ordination of eonomic politics;

ORGANISATIONAL STRUCTURE OF THE AFRIKANER BROEDERBOND

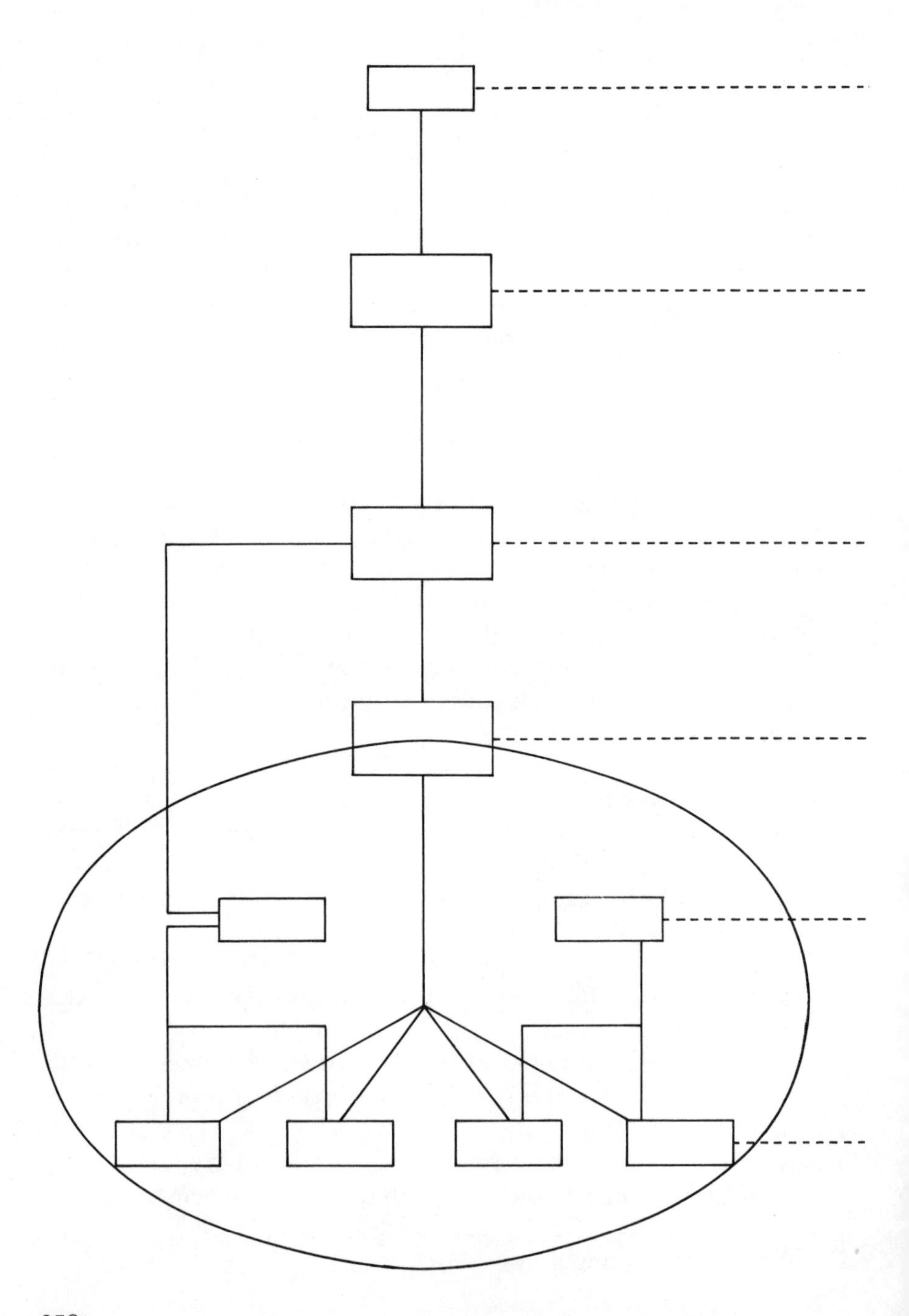

--- *Chairman:* Elected by majority vote in the National Congress's election of Executive Council.

--- *Executive Council:* Highest executive authority. Serves for 2 years and comprises 10 members elected by National Congress and 5 co-opted from remaining Congress nominees. Meets as often as work demands. Has full-time Secretariat to administer organisational affairs. Also elects 6-man management committee of its own members to act on its behalf when necessary.

--- *National Congress:* Highest authority in Broederbond. Meets every 2 years to elect Executive Council, pass budget and, by resolution, frame general policy. Comprises members of Executive Council and 1 delegate from each branch. In the year Congress does not sit, regional conferences are held.

--- *Regional Council:* A number of branches can be bound together by EC to co-ordinate regional activities. Comprises delegates elected by branches.

--- *Central Committee:* In towns/cities where there is more than 1 branch EC may determine that Central Committee be formed to co-ordinate local activities. Comprises delegates elected by branches.

--- *Branches:* Consist of not less than 5, generally not more than 20 Broers. Meet once a month. Must draw up plan of positive action each year to promote aims of the organisation. Each branch has executive of not less than 3 (chairman, secretary, treasurer) and not more than 8 elected annually.

7. Afrikanerising of our public life and education in the Christian national sense with the development of all national groups left free in so far as this is not dangerous to the State.[1]

Almost unnecessarily today, the constitution has a clause proclaiming its language to be Afrikaans.

Chauvinist in its language and nationalist exclusivity, the organisation is also chauvinist in its male exclusivity. Apart from a brief venture into the possibility of establishing a sister organisation, an idea which was decidedly stillborn, the Afrikaner Broederbond is an all-male preserve. Women play a role only in that they must be acceptable as suitable wives for members and must concede to the strict code of secrecy the organisation demands; this is the one area of their husbands' lives they must accept they will know nothing about.

The Broederbond consists of *"Broers"* (Brothers). Admission to this secret circle of privilege and influence is open only to a white male of 25 years or older, provided he is Afrikaans, subscribes to the Protestant faith, is clean of character and firm of principle, particularly in the maintenance of his Afrikaner identity, and accepts South Africa as his only fatherland.

"Be Strong" is the organisation's motto and its credo is Christian-Nationalism, the Calvinist doctrine that lies at the heart of all that the Afrikaner nationalist holds dear in South Africa: his education system, his religion, his traditions, his outlook and his way of life.

The preamble to the constitution says categorically that party politics is excluded from the organisation's activities, although this is a provision which is regularly overlooked, as has been demonstrated elsewhere in this book.

Organisationally, the Broederbond is structured much along the lines of a political party. It consists of branches, linked in urban areas under central committees and further linked under a wider co-ordinating umbrella of regional councils.

Highest authority resolves with the National Congress (*Bondsraad*), which is the general policy-making body. It has the power to amend the constitution (after at least half the delegates present have given written support for the amendment and at least three-quarters have voted for it), makes resolutions, passes the budget and elects the Executive Council. It meets every two years.

The National Congress consists of the serving members of the Executive Council and one delegate from each branch. When the

National Congress is in recess, its power is delegated to the Executive Council, which comprises 10 elected and five co-opted members.

The Executive Council is the highest level of the Broederbond and operates in a rarified atmosphere of power that is distinct even from the general membership. It is at this level that regular contact is maintained with the Cabinet and that major policy matters are negotiated. The Executive Council is elected every two years by a secret ballot in the National Congress. Before the National Congress meets a candidates list is drawn up from nominations submitted by the branches. Each branch may submit a maximum of two nominations.

To become an eligible candidate each nominee must be nominated by at least two branches or by the existing Executive Council, must give written consent to his nomination, must have been a member for a minimum of four years, at least one of which must have been as a branch executive member, and must have completely discharged his financial obligations to the organisation. The Broederbond chairman is the candidate who receives the absolute majority vote in the National Congress ballot. Thereafter up to three existing Executive Councillors with the longest unbroken service of over six years are culled from the list of candidates in declining seniority. The chairman is not affected by this requirement. Consequently, a chairman has served up to 12 years continuously.[2]

From the remaining list of candidates, nine members are elected to the Executive Council by ordinary majorities, with the understanding that a maximum of five can be elected from one province. If it happens that more than five are elected from one province, the excess members are removed from the list in order of their electoral support. A re-vote is then taken from the remaining unsuccessful Executive Council candidates. The 10 elected members of the Executive Council then co-opt five further members from the candidates list to achieve a better group or regional balance on the Council. The Executive Council elects from its ranks a vice-chairman and an executive of six, which acts on behalf of the full Executive Council in urgent matters.

The Executive Council meets about five times a year, usually in Johannesburg or Pretoria for one or two days (3/70/71). The Executive's management committee *(dagbestuur)* meets about 12 times a year.

To administer the organisation there is a full-time Secretariat at the Broederbond headquarters, Die Eike, in Auckland Park, Johannesburg. Top positions in the Secretariat are the Chief Secretary, the Administrative Secretary, the Liaison Secretary and the Youth Secretary. The Broederbond's present Chief Secretary is Mr T J N (Naude) Botha, No 6159. He lives at 69 St Aubyn Road, New Redruth, Alberton. His predecessors were Dr Piet Koornhof, Minister of Sport and Recreation, and Senator Johan van der Spuy, retired Minister of Posts and Telegraphs. Also employed full-time in the Broederbond offices in recent years were J H Swart (No 1843), F P le R Retief (4071), H S Hattingh (7231), S P Boshoff (6837), Mr J Kruger (6086), A J O Herbst (7663), A van Tonder (11946), R C Botha (11556), Izan Meyer (son of Dr Piet Meyer) and Mr C du P Kuun, now in a top position at Saambou-Nasionaal.

There are also a number of female assistants in the Broederbond headquarters in Die Eike. Some are married to members, the others have been sworn to secrecy and proved to be very reliable. Some have served the Broederbond for more than 20 years.

The branches meet more than 10 times a year on average, for about 2½ hours. As there are 800 cells, there are 8 000 Broederbond meetings in South Africa every year. They meet for 20 000 hours, or 2 500 working days of eight hours each. This does not include Executive, *Bondsraad* or regional meetings or those of special interest groups.

The Broederbond's records are so detailed that at any given time they can disclose such data as the average age of members and the average age of those who died the previous year. For example: "The average age of new members during 1974/5 was 36,86 as against 36,11 in 1973/74, 35,35 in 1972/73, 36,24 in 1971/72 and 37,76 in 1970/71. The new members represent a net growth rate of 4,4 percent, as against 4,5 percent, 4,6 percent, six percent and 4,7 percent in the previous four years."[3]

Over a number of years, the Broederbond considered how to group the branches in administrative regions whose councils confer regularly. The following table of regional councils approved in October 1976 shows the even distribution of membership throughout South Africa, not excepting the remotest small town. The omission of some towns from the table does not mean there are no members there: if there are too few members to form a branch they link up with a nearby group.

BANKEVELD DIVISION: Wolmaransstad, Ventersdorp (2), Stilfontein, Orkney, Leeudoringstad, Klerksdorp (6), Hartbeesfontein.

LOWER ORANGE DIVISION: Upington (2), Pofadder, Kenhardt, Keimoes, Kakamas, Groblershoop.

UPPER KAROO: Victoria-West, Prieska, Philipstown, Petrusville, Niekerkshoop, Hopetown, Griekwastad, Douglas, De Aar, Britstown.

BOLAND DIVISION: Wellington (4), Strand (4), Stellenbosch (10), Somerset West (2), Paarl (8), Malmesbury (2), Franschhoek, Darling.

BORDER DIVISION: Umtata, Queenstown, East London (4), Komga, King William's Town.

GRIQUALAND WEST DIVISION: Warrenton, Vaalharts, Kimberley (4), Hartswater, Barkly West.

HOOGLAND-A DIVISION: Steynsrus, Senekal (2), Reitz, Petrus Steyn, Paul Roux, Lindley.

HOOGLAND-B DIVISION: Witsieshoek, Kestell, Harrismith (2), Fouriesburg, Bethlehem (5).

JOHANNESBURG DIVISION: Randburg (12), Eikenhof, Johannesburg (27).

CAPE MIDLAND DIVISION: Tarkastad, Somerset East, Hofmeyr, Fort Beaufort, Cradock, Bedford, Alice, Adelaide.

CAPE PENINSULA DIVISION: Thornton, Parow (7), Kuilsriver (2), Koeberg, Cape Town (10), Goodwood (2), Durbanville (5), Blouberg, Bellville (11).

KAROO DIVISION: Willowmore, Steytlerville, Rietbron, Richmond, Pearston, Murraysburg, Jansenville, Graaff-Reinet (2), Aberdeen.

LOWVELD DIVISION: White River (2), Sabie, Nelspruit (5), Malelane, Lydenburg (3), Komati, Graskop, Barberton.

MIDDLE ORANGE DIVISION: Venterstad, Steynsburg, Noupoort, Middelburg, CP, Colesberg, Burgersdorp.

MIDDELVELD DIVISION: Premiermyn, Ogies, Devon, Delmas (2), Bronkhorstspruit (2).

NAMAQUALAND DIVISION: Wilgenhoutskloof, Springbok (2), Port Nolloth, Nababeep, Alexander Bay.

NATAL DIVISION: All cells within Natal provincial borders, plus Cedarville and Kokstad.

NORTHERN BOLAND DIVISION: Worcester (5), Wolseley, Tulbagh, Touwsrivier, Robertson (2), Montague, Laingsburg, Gydo, De Doorns, Ceres, Bonnievale, Ashton.

NORTHERN CAPE DIVISION: Vryburg, Vanzylsrus, Stella, Reivile, Postmasburg, Olifantshoek, Kuruman, Danielskuil, Bray.
NORTHERN FREE STATE DIVISION: Vredefort, Sasolburg (4), Parys (3), Oranjeville (Vastrap), Heilbron (3).
NORTH EASTERN CAPE DIVISION: Ugie, Sterkstroom, Molteno, Lady Grey, Jamestown, Elliot, Dordrecht, Barkly East.
NORTH EASTERN FREE STATE DIVISION: Warden, Vrede (2), Villiers, Tweeling, Memel, Frankfort, Cornelia.
NORTH WESTERN FREE STATE A DIVISION: Winburg, Viljoenskroon, Vierfontein, Ventersburg, Kroonstad (5), Koppies, Edenville, Bothaville.
NORTH WESTERN FREE STATE B DIVISION: Wesselsbron, Welkom (4), Virginia, Theunissen, Odendaalsrus (2), Hennenman, Bultfontein, Brandfort (2).
NUWEVELD DIVISION: Williston, Sutherland, Prince Albert, Merweville, Fraserburg, Carnarvon, Beaufort West.
OLIFANTS RIVER A DIVISION: Vredenburg, Saldanha, Sandveld, Riebeeck West, Porterville, Piketberg, Moorreesburg, Citrusdal.
OLIFANTS RIVER B DIVISION: Vredendal, Van Rhynsdorp, Nieuwoudtville, Loeriesfontein, Graafwater, Clanwilliam, Calvinia.
EAST RAND DIVISION: Springs (3), Nigel (2), Kempton Park (7), Heidelberg (Tvl) (3), Germiston (4), Elsburg, Elandsfontein, Edenvale, Brakpan (3), Boksburg (4), Benoni (4), Alberton (3).
EASTERN FREE STATE DIVISION: Verkeerdevlei, Thaba 'Nchu-Tweespruit, Marquard, Ladybrand (2), Ficksburg (2), Excelsior, Clocelan.
OVERBERG DIVISION: Villiersdorp, Swellendam, Riviersonderend, Napier, Hermanus, Kleinmond, Grabouw, Caledon, Bredasdorp, Barrydale.
PAUL KRUGER DIVISION: Witbank (3), Stoffberg, Middelburg (Tvl) (3), Marble Hall, Groblersdal, Belfast (2).
PIET JOUBERT DIVISION: Wakkerstroom, Volksrust, Standerton (2), Morgenzon, Evander, Eendracht, Bethal (3), Balfour.
PORT ELIZABETH DIVISION: Uitenhage (2), Port Elizabeth (10), Patensie, Kirkwood, Kareedouw, Humansdorp (2), Grahamstown, Despatch, Alexandria.
POTCHEFSTROOM DIVISION: All Potchefstroom cells (14).
PRETORIA DIVISION: All cells in Pretoria (91) plus Brits (4).
RHODESIA DIVISION: All cells within Rhodesia boundaries.
RUSTENBURG DIVISION: Zeerust, Thabazimbi (2), Swartruggens, Rustenburg (4), Northam, Koster (2), Groot Marico.

SAAMWERK DIVISION: Pongola, Piet Retief (2), Hendrina, Ermelo (3), Chrissiesmeer, Carolina.

CENTRAL FREE STATE DIVISION: Bloemfontein (26).

Warmbaths (2), Roedtan, Potgietersrus (3), Nylstroom (3), Naboomspruit, Mogel, Koedoesrand, Ellisras (2).

SOUTH CAPE A DIVISION: Uniondale, Oudtshoorn (4), Langkloof, Ladismith, De Rust, Calitzdorp.

SOUTH CAPE B DIVISION: Heidelberg, CP, Riversdale, Hartenbos, Mossel Bay, Knysna, George (2), Albertina.

SOUTHERN TRANSVAAL DIVISION: Vereeniging (6), Vanderbijlpark (5), Meyerton, De Deur.

SOUTHERN FREE STATE DIVISION: Trompsburg, Springfontein, Phillippolis, Petrusburg, Luckhoff, Koffiefontein, Jagersfontein, Jacobsdal, Fauresmith, Edenburg.

SOUTH EASTERN FREE STATE DIVISION: Zastron, Wepener, Smithfield, Rouxville, Reddersburg, Hobhouse, Dewetsdorp, Bethulie, Aliwal North.

SWA-NORTH DIVISION: Tsumeb, Outje, Otjiwarongo, Oshakati, Grootfontein.

SWA-CENTRAL DIVISION: Windhoek (5), Walvisbaai, Usakos, Gobabis.

SWA-SOUTH DIVISION: Mariental, Keetmanshoop, Karas, Aranos.

FAR WEST RAND DIVISION: Venterspos, Gatsrand, Fochville, Carletonville (2).

H F VERWOERD DIVISION: Waterpoort, Vive, Soutpansberg, Pietersburg (6), Messina, Louis Trichardt, Dendron.

VERWOERDBURG DIVISION: All cells coming under the two Verwoerdburg central committees (14) plus Olifantsfontein.

WEST RAND DIVISION: Roodepoort (4), Randfontein (2), Ontdekkers (2), Muldersdrif (J Fouche), Maraisburg (L Wildenboer), Magaliesburg, Krugersdorp (6), Florida (4).

WESTERN TRANSVAAL DIVISION: Schweizer-Reneke (2), Sannieshof, Ottosdal, Mafeking (2), Lichtenburg (3), Delareyville, Celigny, Bospoort, Biesiesvlei.

WESTERN FREE STATE AND SOUTH WESTERN TRANSVAAL DIVISION: Hoopstad, Hertzogville, Bealesville, Christiana, Boshof, Bloemhof.

WOLKBERG DIVISION: Tzaneen (2), Phalaborwa, Letsitele, Duiwelskloof, Blyderivier.

Nineteen new divisions (cells) were added in the course of 1977:

Kempton Park (Thys Marais); Kempton Park (Witfontein); Kempton Park (Ysterhout); Bloemfontein (Olienhout); Ermelo (Nooitgedacht); Pretoria (Hartbeespoort); Springs (Presidentsdam); Brits (Die Kareeboom); Pretoria (Concordia); Standerton-Suid; Katimo Mulilo; Durbanville (Door de Kraal); Rustenburg (Olifantsnek); Rustenburg (Wildevy); Upington (de Wet Strauss); Lutzville; Badplaas; Brakpan (Gert Bezuidenhout); Secunda (Carolus Trichardt).

The Super-Afrikaners try to reach as many top people as they can. The latest breakdown of membership shows this.

Even more impressive are the members' positions in their occupations. The Broederbond circulated the most recent information in 1977. Membership then was 11 910. Farmers were the second largest group numbering 2 240 or 18,81 percent.

In the professions exerting the greatest influence on public opinion, such as education and religion, Broeders hold almost all the top positions. The teaching profession constituted the largest group – 20,36 percent (2 424), clergymen 7,12 percent (848) and the public service 4,35 percent (518) of Bond membership. Obviously there are many more Broeders in the teaching profession today but in 1968 they included 24 rectors of universities and teachers training colleges, 171 professors, 176 lecturers, 468 headmasters, 121 school inspectors and 647 teachers.

Sixteen managers of newspaper groups and 22 editors were members. Of the 419 public servants in 1968, 59 were secretaries or assistant secretaries of departments. In the legal profession there were 16 judges, 13 advocates, 156 attorneys and 67 magistrates who were Broederbond members. In banking 154 were managers, 22 accountants and 22 other executives.

It is easy to see from these figures what has happened. By roping the best talent in Afrikanerdom into the ranks of the Super-Afrikaners and pushing them to the top, the Bond has seized control of some of the most important professions. Should a very capable man not be spotted by the organisation, and yet manage to get to the top, the Broederbond will almost certainly consider him for membership provided his credentials are right and provided he is not too old. In this way the organisation's influence is guaranteed to grow all the time.

All the fixed assets of the Broederbond are registered in the name of the Uniediensburo (Pty) Ltd., whose shares are at all times exclusively held by members of the Executive Council, who act as trustees for the organisation.

The appointed trustees must at all times deposit the relevant share certificates and/or blank transfer forms with the secretary of the Executive Council. Control over the organisation's assets is wielded by directors of the Uniediensburo, who follow the Executive Council's instructions in accordance with the procedures laid down in the administration of the affairs of a company.

The Broederbond is financed by membership fees, donations and legacies. The entrance fee is R40 for Broeders under 45 years old, with a loading of R4 for every year above that. The annual membership fee is R20, giving the organisation a guaranteed annual income of about R240 000 from 12 000 members. All finances are handled through Uniediensburo (Pty) Ltd, with the chairman and secretary as the "directors".

At annual meetings, statements of accounts are submitted by the Broederbond's auditors, Meyer, Nel & Co of 511 Volkskas Building, 76 Market Street, Johannesburg. The senior partner of the firm, Mr R Nagel, usually signs the Broederbond accounts personally. He is of course a Broeder himself. The other big fund controlled by the Broederbond, the Christiaan de Wet Fund, now totals more than R2-million. This fund is audited by Meintjies, Vermooten and Partners of 505 Rentmeester Building, Pretoria. Mr JJ Vermooten, a prominent Broeder, signs the audited accounts.

The origin of the Christiaan de Wet Fund was explained by Professor A N Pelzer at the *Bondsraad* of 1968 when he presented an historical review: "The income of the Afrikaner Broederbond has been restricted over the years to the fees established in the articles. Apart from that there was incidental income, but that did not amount to much. From this income the growing internal expenses had to be covered, and where possible help had to be given to deserving activities of the Afrikaner Broederbond or other well-disposed Afrikaner organisations. In this way the Bond made R71 600 available up to June 30 1954 to worthy causes. Because this was only a fraction of what was really needed, the necessity for a substantial reserve fund was strongly felt. Broeder JJ Bosman, first general manager of Volkskas, faced this challenge and submitted a scheme to the Executive Council for the launching of a powerful reserve fund. In accordance with this a non-profit making company with the name 'Christiaan de Wet Fund' was registered in 1949 with its first target to collect R100 000. When this target was reached in 1956 the *Bondsraad* decided to reach a second target of R100 000.

"When the fund had reached R250 000 in 1963, the Afrikaner Broederbond faced an exceptional challenge when deliberate treason put the *Sunday Times* in possession of secret documents. To the AB it was more a challenge than a punishment and therefore the *Bondsraad* decided on May 21, 1963 to increase the Christiaan de Wet Fund to R1 000 000. The favourable reaction from Broeders resulted in the aim to announce during the celebrations of the *Bondsraad* in 1968 that the fund had reached R1 000 000. (This amount had in fact been reached even before the *Bondsraad* meeting)."[4]

The Christiaan de Wet fund cannot use ordinary Broederbond funds like membership fees etc. Neither can the capital be used for any purpose. Broederbond activities, covert or overt, are funded from the interest on the capital only. When the fund was launched members were asked to make donations on top of their subscriptions. When the fund aimed at R1-million, Broeders were asked to contribute R50 over a three year period. Such targets are set and branches are reminded regularly to see that the pledges are contributed.

The latest balance sheet (February 28 1977) shows the fund's total as R2 129 365,75. It is made up as follows:

Capital fund	R1 328 266,23
Investment Reserve	532 988,82
Federal fund	267 288,70
Road building fund (to the Hartbeesjeugterrein)	822,00

The capital fund is made up as follows:
Fixed assets of R974 239,68 comprising:

Office block, Die Eike, (administrative headquarters)	655 353,60
Hartbeesjeugterrein (meeting place for *Bondsraad*, annual meetings etc,)	318 886,08

The investments total 1 084 827,57 comprising:

Listed shares	642 246,75
Unlisted shares	86 656,69
Short term investments	355 924,13
Housing loans	140 031,35

It is noted in the accounts that the administration of the funds and other costs amounted to R70 281,01 and the income from the Hartbeesjeugterrein was R548,16, giving the fund a balance of R2 129 365,75. During 1976 the fund received donations of R123 134 but an amount of R63 387 had to be deducted from the assets because the farm Strydhoek was given back to the donor who had stipulated that it was to be used for a Broederbond holiday resort. After investigating the implications for many years the Executive decided it was not feasible and gave the farm back. (The farm was originally donated, according to Circular 8/63/64, by Broeder S A Maree. It comprised 3 000 morgen "conservatively" valued at R100 000 and was situated in the Drakensberg between Harrismith and Bergville.)

The healthy investment reserve fund of more than R500 000 is accounted for in Circular 5/75/76 which ascribes it to profits on share transactions. (It is interesting to note that while the share market was so depressed the Broederbond managed to make R512 447 on share transactions.) It is the policy of the trustees of the funds to use only the interest.

In the financial year 1976/1977 interest of R112 613,00 on the Christiaan de Wet Fund became available for Broederbond activities. It was spent as follows: FAK R3 100, *Nasionale Jeugraad* R27 014, *Ruiterwag* R10 037, *Afrikaanse Studentebond* R4 359, *Genootskap van Rhodesiese Afrikaners* R1 109, travelling expenses of study committees (watchdog committees) R10 542, student dialogue R9 000, student affairs R322, administration of funds R4 321, microfilming of documents R2 738, secretary for liaison work R12 543, African youth action (SABRA) R15 000, office rent R5 334. It is noted in the accounts that the fund would have to increase by about 10 percent to meet its present commitments if inflation is taken into consideration.

The importance the Broederbond attaches to the Christiaan de Wet Fund and its role is clearly illustrated in many of the secret documents. "The Afrikaner Broederbond is entering a very important new phase of its existence, one which concerns the protection and development of our Christian white man's republic in the life-and-death struggle against the forces seeking to destroy it." Because the organisation cannot face this mighty challenge without the necessary funds, "the *Bondsraad* decided unanimously that the Christiaan de Wet Fund must grow to R1-million in the next three years" (Extraordinary circular to branch chairmen, June 12 1963).

An important aspect of the de Wet Fund's expenditure is the work of the Broederbond's watchdog committees (see Chapter 23). There are 14 of these committees whose 156 members represent "the best brainpower in almost every sphere, not only in South Africa, but probably in the whole world" (circular of June 12 1963.) These committees investigate aspects of Government policy and South African problems and propose solutions.

Large amounts were also allocated from this fund to attain republican status for South Africa. The Broederbond played a decisive role in the referendum narrowly won by the pro-republicans. Their members campaigned actively. As one put it: "Every member (there were about 8 000 then) became an organiser, knocking on doors, persuading people to vote for the Republic." But money plays an important part in such a campaign and the taps of the Christiaan de Wet Fund were turned wide open. "We also helped formulate, disseminate and promote the acceptance of our traditional policy of separate development," according to a secret circular of June 12 1963. "The promotion of the ideals of our nation and the co-ordination of youth, sporting, social and other activities were also made possible by the fund. In these spheres we mostly gave financial support to our organisations acting as our public fronts, to facilitate attainment of our ideals."

The Christiaan de Wet Fund also ploughed thousands of rands into the Coloured Federal Party which, in its early years, supported the Government's separate development policy. It bought more than a dozen Land-rovers with loudspeakers for Chief Leabua Jonathan's Lesotho National Party. It must have been a sad day for the Broederbond when he turned his back on South Africa, a few years after the secret organisation's magnificent gift had helped him come to power. The transaction was so discreetly handled that only a few Broeders were privy to it and it is not certain that even Chief Jonathan knew where the Land-rovers came from.

The Broederbond fund for day-to-day administration amounted to R192 034,57 in 1974. It appears from the balance sheets that the annual administration costs including salaries were R122 939,56 and income from membership fees was R126 271,05. The Bond paid only R64,15 income tax on the fund that year.

Branches retain two-fifths of the membership fees to finance their own activities. It appears that at any given time they have about R150 000 at their disposal. To boost the Christiaan de Wet

Fund, head office called on them to hand over their "surplus". The argument was that money lying idle in branch accounts could be used productively by the de Wet Fund.

Branches have their own accounts at banks or building societies under all kinds of names, making no mention of the Broederbond and approved by the Executive Council. It goes without saying that the accounts are all with Afrikaner banks such as Volkskas and Afrikaner building societies such as Saambou-Nasionaal.

Members paying their subscriptions by stop order are assured in circulars that this will not jeopardise secrecy. In Circular 3/63/64 the Executive said the matter had been discussed with bank managements and that the officials dealing with the stop orders had been sworn to secrecy.

In Circular 4/76/77, members who queried the bank charges on stop orders paid to the Christiaan de Wet Fund through Volkskas, the bank started by the Broederbond, were reassured. "In terms of inter-bank agreements, none of the members' banks can give that kind of service without financial reward. The Volkskas solution is to make regular payments to the de Wet Fund. In this respect, a gift of R3 500 was made recently to the fund." Special wording is used in wills making legacies to the Bond, once again for reasons of secrecy, and the Bond has a fund from which members' wives or relatives get R150 for funeral costs.

The Christiaan de Wet Fund operates in almost total secrecy. The Executive Council is not even prepared to discuss it in a circular in spite of many requests to do so (4/63/64). "Unfortunately, the details are of such a nature that they can only be given personally."

The Broederbond is entrenched in South Africa until nine-tenths of the members request the Executive Council, in writing to disband. In this (unlikely) event, the balance of the assets would go to Afrikaans cultural organisations after the "estate" had been wound up.

1. *Rand Daily Mail,* December 15 1944.
2. Dr Piet Meyer.
3. Statistics for 1974/75.
4. Minutes of the *Bondsraad* meeting, 1968.

20 *Recruitment*

Gaining membership of Afrikanerdom's most exclusive organisation involves a long and complicated process of checks and cross-checks during which all members can have their say. By the time a candidate stands at the threshold of membership he has had to survive a sophisticated surveillance in which every facet of his life has been carefully examined. The organisation knows his background, his habits, his strengths, his weaknesses, his affiliations, and every detail of his family life and working life.

For the greater part of the process – which can take three years – the prospective member has no idea he is the focus of close scrutiny by the Broederbond machine. Again the preservation of the organisation's strict code of secrecy is paramount, and it is ensured by a system of cut-off points at which the Broederbond can abandon his recruitment without having endangered any of its jealously guarded secrets. The process has five formal stages.

1. A Broeder gives notice to his branch that he is going to nominate a candidate. 2. The branch is informed of the personal details of the target recruit. 3. The target recruit is approved by the branch members, the general membership and the Executive Council. 4. He is discreetly approached to discover whether he would be willing to join. 5. The recruit is inducted.

Strict guidelines are laid down in the standing orders for all these processes. No Broeder may be directly or indirectly involved in the proposal or seconding of any candidate until he has been a member for a year. A Broeder may not propose or second a blood relative, or a relative by marriage, nor may he be present when the branch discusses the nomination of a relative. It is absolutely essential that the proposer and seconder know the target recruit well.

They must both be convinced that he strives for the perpetuation of a separate Afrikaner nation with its own language and culture; that he gives preference to Afrikaners and other well-disposed people and companies in the economic, public and professional fields; that he upholds the Afrikaans language at home, in his job and his community at large; that he is a Protestant; that there is nothing in his personality, character or behaviour that would make him unsuitable for membership; that he is exceptionally trustworthy, principled and prudent; that he can meet the financial implications of membership; that he is able and willing to take an active, regular and loyal part in all the organisation's activities; and that he does not belong to any other secret or semi-secret oganisations.

If the target recruit has lived in the branch area for less than two years, or has been known to his sponsors for less than two years, the permission of the Executive Council must be obtained before he can be nominated. If he lives in an urban area where there is more than one branch, and is known to fewer than half the members of the sponsoring branch, his nomination form must be accompanied by a "satisfactory list" of local Broeders who know him well.

A target recruit must not be nominated unless there is a good chance that he will accept membership. The branch executive must satisfy itself completely that the candidate's admission is really desirable, and at least two members of the executive must underwrite the nomination before it is put to the branch for approval.

The Broederbond specifies exacting cultural, family, moral, religious and political characteristics in its recruits. The slightest deviation from strict Afrikaner norms can jeopardise membership. If a target recruit's credentials are tainted, however slightly, he has little chance of being invited to join. For example, scores of otherwise eminently eligible Afrikaners have been rejected because they married English-speaking women. Others have been turned down because they were sent to English-medium schools; others, again, because they belonged to sports clubs whose members were mainly English-speaking.

Irregularity in church attendance is a definite handicap – and the church he attends must be one of the Afrikaner Establishment denominations: the *Nederduitse Gereformeerde Kerk, Nederduitsch Hervormde Kerk, Gereformeerde Kerk,* or the more recently acceptable *Apostoliese Geloofsending van Suid-Afrika.* Divorce puts an end to any chance of membership, and unless under exceptional circumstances is grounds for expulsion. Involvement in court actions is distincly frowned upon and could wreck chances of acceptance.

Participation in any form of Sunday sport or recreation would immediately raise the puritan hackles of the organisation and hamper admission.

Despite a clause to the contrary in the constitution, the "wrong" party political affiliations will prevent membership. This applies particularly to members of the Herstigte Nasionale Party which in the early 1970s shook the Broederbond with its worst crisis and came very close to tearing it apart. The crisis was resolved when the organisation expelled all HNP members. Membership of any of South Africa's opposition parties (the Progressive Federal Party, the New Republic Party, or the South African Party) would be regarded as an aberration militating against acceptance.

If the target recruit is able to emerge unscathed from this obstacle course, the five-phase process of recruitment may continue. The sponsoring Broeder gives verbal notice at an ordinary branch meeting that he intends to make a nomination. At the following monthly meeting, after ensuring that none of the target recruit's relatives is present, the branch discusses his prospects. Unless it is clear that the branch supports the nomination, the process stops here. If, however, there appears to be general support for the nomination, the target recruit is proposed and seconded by the two sponsoring Broeders. This is a formal, written nomination on a prescribed form which contains full details of his personal circumstances.

At the following monthly meeting the target recruit's full personal details are read out to the meeting and a vote is taken. All the branch members must participate by indicating on their ballot forms "Yes," or "No," or "Abstain." Two votes against the nomination are enough to squash it. If the ballot is unanimously in favour, or there is only one vote against, the proposal form is sent to head office. A member casting a negative vote has 14 days to explain it in writing to head office. Failure to do this causes his objection to lapse, and it will be disregarded by the Executive Council. At head office the chief secretary draws up a list of nominations received from all the branches. The list is sent to the branches with the regular monthly circular letter so that members throughout the country can register objections to the candidacy. If there are objections they must be sent with written explanations to head office for consideration by the Executive Council. Although it is not stipulated in the standing orders, it is generally accepted in Broederbond lore that even one objection can block membership.

According to Broederbond sources, the selection process is often abused by members and candidates are often turned down on spurious grounds. It is common for members to raise objections for reasons of commercial or personal rivalry. It appears that once they are on the "inside", members are reluctant to share with newcomers their privileged and exclusive status. In any case the growth of the Broederbond is limited both by the strict and highly sectional membership requirements, and by each branch being limited to a quota of two new members a year, one under 35 years old and the other under 45.

Final say in the selection process rests with the Executive Council. Nomination to the Broederbond is not a one-chance affair. If the nomination fails at the branch or general membership level, the sponsors can renew the nomination after a year. If it fails a second time, they must wait two years before bidding again. The Executive Council has the power to suspend a nomination, even after the candidate has survived the selection process at branch and general level. In this case, six months must pass before a second nomination can be made.

Once the Executive Council has approved a nomination, the actual recruiting process must begin within six months or the whole procedure must start from the beginning again. Recruitment takes place under the direction of an information committee comprising at least two Broeders elected annually by each branch. The first step is taken by a Broeder who knows the target recruit well – in all likelihood one of the two sponsors – who approaches him and puts out discreet feelers to test his attitude towards organisations of the Broederbond's nature. No details of the organisation are revealed.

If the reaction is favourable, the target recruit is put in touch with the information committee which then takes over the recruitment procedure. The committee members can halt this at any stage where they feel the target recruit does not comply fully with all the organisation's requirements. He must give an undertaking that the discussions to follow will be kept utterly confidential – whether or not he finally decides to apply for membership. The standing orders say: "Because the Broederbond is secret, the recruiters must work very carefully. Neither the internal workings, such as the selection system, nor the names of members, may be mentioned without express permission. The standing orders and other documents of the organisation may not be disclosed."

What can be revealed to the target recruit are the following: that admission to the organisation is by invitation only; the contents of the constitution; the existence of a programme of action; the variety of people that belong to the organisation, such as ministers, doctors, professors, farmers, artisans, lawyers, advocates, teachers, officers and merchants; the financial commitments of R40 on admission and R20 annual subscriptions as well as any levies which the Executive Council may impose; that at the annual congress a budget is presented; that a reserve fund exists; and that the Broederbond is strictly selective in its membership.

If the target recruit agrees to join, he must fill in a formal application form which is sent on to the chief secretary at head office. He in turn notifies the branch secretary if the Executive Council approves the nomination, and gives the green light for induction.

21 *Induction*

The Broederbond's induction ceremony is a darkly dramatic affair that culminates in a sacred oath before God to carry the secrets of the organisation to the grave. As the new recruit stands on the threshold of admission to the ranks of the Super-Afrikaners, his knowledge of them is scant and vague. They have framed the ceremony with a caution which is typical of all their activities. Like the recruitment process, it has several cut-off points so that the recruit is exposed gradually to revelations of the organisation's inner secrets. At each of these points he must acknowledge that he is in accord with everything he has heard so far and wishes the induction to proceed to the next phase.

The version of the ceremony which was approved in 1974 may be considered refined, compared with the bizarre, ritualistic enrolment procedure of the Broederbond's early days. Then, according to reports, there was a dramatic rite with a "body" on a bier, transfixed with a dagger. The dummy's winding sheet was embroidered in blood red, with the word *Verraad* (Treason). Every member had to stab it with a dagger, symbolically indicating the penalty of betrayal. The "chaplain" conducting the ceremony intoned: "He who betrays the Bond will be destroyed by the Bond. The Bond never forgets. Its vengeance is swift and sure. Never yet has a traitor escaped his just punishment."[1]

The constitution, standing orders and induction rubric now contain no description of this macabre ritual. But even in its modified form the induction ceremony remains a chilling affair that could come straight from the pages of fiction.

It takes place at night in a darkened room. Two candles give the only illumination. The venue is usually a member's home, or a regular branch meeting-place. The windows are shrouded and all sources of light masked. At the top of the room is a table draped with the South African flag. As a symbol of Afrikaner exclusivity and rejection of the British, whose oppression of the Afrikaners was the original *raison d'etre* of the Broederbond, the Union Jack in the flag is covered, otherwise flags of the former Boer republics are used.[2]

There is a flickering candle at each end of the table. Standing behind it is the Broeder who will conduct the induction ceremony, usually the chairman of the branch. The recruit is escorted into the room by his sponsors and stands facing the table. Silently, the branch members – who are not known by him to be Broeders – file into the room and stand, unseen, behind him. Those who will contribute to the ceremony have torches to read their passages from the induction handbook. Now the emotional and psychological preparation for the induction begins.

There may be a hymn, the only optional part of the ceremony, and then the chairman instructs the branch members that "in these moments of deep seriousness" they must recall their own induction and treat the ceremony as a reaffirmation of their commitment to the organisation. This is followed by a scripture reading and a prayer. Then the induction itself begins.

CHAIRMAN – *reads the full name of the recruit and says:* Your fellow-Afrikaners who are members of the Afrikaner Broederbond have, after careful consideration, decided to invite you to become a member of this organisation.

For this reason, you have been called here to learn what the principles and ideals of the Afrikaner Broederbond are and, after you have heard and accepted what will be expected of you as a member, to make a solemn and binding promise of trust.

But first it is necessary that you comply with two conditions.

Firstly, nobody who is a member of any secret or semi-secret organisation, or is in any way connected with such an organisation apart from the Ruiterwag (the Broederbond's junior organisation) may be a member of the Afrikaner Broederbond, except with the approval of the Executive Council.

CHAIRMAN – *reads the full name of the recruit and says:* Do you solemnly declare, in the presence of the witnesses here gathered, that you are not a member of, or in any way connected with, any secret or semi-secret organisation?

What is your answer?

RECRUIT – *replies:* Yes.

CHAIRMAN – Secondly, you must know that the confidentiality of the Afrikaner Broederbond and its activities is one of the most important characteristics, and that the strictest protection of that confidentiality is demanded in the interests of the Bond and its

members, and in your own interests – *reads the full name of the recruit and says:* Do you then solemnly declare, in all seriousness and sincerity, before these gathered witnesses, that you will reveal nothing of what you are told, or of what you learn here, about the Afrikaner Broederbond and its members?
RECRUIT – *replies:* Yes.
CHAIRMAN – Now that you have complied with these conditions, the following can be revealed to you.

The Afrikaner Broederbond is born from a deep conviction that the Afrikaner nation, with its own characteristics and destiny, was placed in this country by God the Three-in-One, and that this nation has been called to remain in existence as long as it pleases God.

The members of the Afrikaner Broederbond are Afrikaners, aware of their calling, who strive to live out the best in our nation, and to serve.

The Afrikaner Broederbond is wholly devoted to the service of the Afrikaner nation and does not exist to serve or promote the personal interests of its members. Those who join do so to give, not to receive; to serve, not to be served or personally advantaged.

On the basis of our belief in God, and in His service and honour, the Afrikaner Broederbond aims to unite its members in a strong bond of mutual trust and love of their nation; to bind them in love, despite their differences; to work selflessly for the establishment of a healthy common purpose among all Afrikaners who strive for the welfare and advancement of all interests of the Afrikaner nation.

Because membership of the Afrikaner Broederbond entails great responsbility, it is necessary that you carefully consider what will be expected of you. Therefore, I call upon a number of experienced Broeders to inform you about this. *At this point a number of branch members will, with the aid of their torches, read the following passages:*
FIRST BROEDER — It will be expected of you that you will live and work in the firm belief that the Almighty God determines the destiny of nations; and it will be expected of you that you will cling to the Christian national viewpoint of the Afrikaner, as prescribed by the Word of God and the traditions of the Afrikaner nation.
SECOND BROEDER — It will be expected of you that you will always remain true to yourself and your conscience, but that you

will also respect the right of your fellow Broeders to be different; that you will always remember that we are irrevocably bound together in our faith in the Afrikaner Broederbond, of one heart, one outlook, one struggle, but not the same.

FIRST BROEDER — It will be expected of you that you will do all in your power to establish and promote a common purpose among all motivated Afrikaners; to strengthen and develop the Afrikaner nation; and, in particular, to promote its culture and extend its role in the national economy.

SECOND BROEDER – It will be expected of you that you will steadfastly fulfil your duties as a member and that you will faithfully attend the monthly branch meetings.

FIRST BROEDER – It will be expected of you that you will strive for the achievement of the Bond's ideals, not only through co-operation in organised endeavours, but also through individual action in your own work circle, family life and sphere of influence, inspired and strengthened by your fellow Broeders and guided by the Bond's principles and ideals; and that you will co-operate actively and faithfully with your fellow Broeders in a spirit of true common purpose and sincere brotherhood.

SECOND BROEDER – It will be expected of you that you will at all times in your behaviour uphold the honour, value and good name of the Afrikaner Broederbond.

CHAIRMAN – Brotherhood demands of you work and rugged perseverance.

At times it demands conflict and unpleasantness. It not only demands the combating of that which is evil, but more especially obedience to and the practice of Christian principles.

CHAIRMAN – *reads the full name of the recruit and says:* Do you understand the purpose that we have in mind, and the spirit that the Afrikaner Broederbond embodies? From your heart, do you subscribe to the basis and objectives of our struggle as presented to you? Are you now ready to accept the demands of membership and to undertake an irrevocable union?

RECRUIT – *replies:* Yes.

CHAIRMAN – I ask you then, in the presence of the Broeders here gathered who have been called as witnesses if, in full awareness of the seriousness of your promise and the responsibility you are taking upon yourself, you solemnly undertake:

1. faithfully and sincerely to serve the Afrikaner nation through the Afrikaner Broederbond in all that it stands for;

2. never in your life to reveal to any outsider anything you learn about the Afrikaner Broederbond and its members, particularly the membership of a fellow Broeder, even if your own membership is ended, unless you have received prior permission from the Executive Council of the Afrikaner Broederbond;
3. never to reveal your own membership of the Afrikaner Broederbond, without the permission of the Executive Council of the Afrikaner Broederbond;
4. never to become a member of any secret or semi-secret organisation, or to involve yourself by co-operation with any such organisation, without the permission of the Executive Council of the Afrikaner Broederbond;
5. to subject yourself to the conditions of the constitution and standing orders, to fulfil the duties that the Bond Executive may lay down according to the standing orders, and to subject yourself readily to the brotherly discipline that the Bond Executive may apply according to the standing orders;
6. unconditionally to comply if the Executive Council, after consideration, thinks fit to terminate your membership;
7. to subject yourself to immediate expulsion from the Broeders, if you in any way break this undertaking.

Before you are asked to reply, you are now given a few moments to reflect.
CHAIRMAN – *reads the full name of the recruit and says:* What is your reply?
RECRUIT – *replies:* Yes.
CHAIRMAN – In the name of the Afrikaner Broederbond, and in the presence of the other Broeders who stand here as witnesses of the irrevocable union you have forged, I accept your promise of faith and declare you a Broeder.

In the words of our motto, I wish you strength.

Be strong in the practice of your brotherhood.

Be strong in faith if the struggle becomes onerous.

Be strong in your love of your nation.

Be strong in the service of your nation.

With a hearty handshake I, and after that the other Broeders, want to assure you that we accept you from now on as a fellow Broeder.

Hearty congratulations and welcome.

The induction ceremony ends as the lights are switched on and the new member turns to be greeted one by one by his fellow-Broeders. All that remains is for him to pay his admission fee of R40, and he will have crossed the threshold into the ranks of the Super-Afrikaners.

1. Troup, Freda, *South Africa: An Historial Introduction,* p. 237.
2. Since South Africa became a Republic in 1961 the Broederbond has worked strenuously for the flag to be revised.

22 *Secrecy*

"Our strength lies in secrecy." This slogan (Circular 3/9/68) permeates all Broederbond documents. The need for secrecy is stressed in every document and at all meetings. The outstanding single characteristic of the Broederbond is, indeed, the tight discipline and secrecy it has been able to enforce on members since the early 1920s. There have been leaks, but they have been remarkably few considering there are now 12 000 members and the organisation is 60 years old.

Broederbond operations are more secret than those of the Security Police, or even the Department of National Security[1] whose activities can sometimes be glimpsed in court, and whose telephone numbers are listed in the directory. In the Broederbond everything is secret: membership, office bearers, activities. It was not started as a secret organisation. In 1918 membership was open, but the young men who inaugurated it soon realised the power of secrecy and changed the constitution accordingly three years later.

The justification was their belief that the Afrikaner on the Witwatersrand was persecuted at that time. They claimed they would have been hounded from pillar to post for belonging openly to a pro-Afrikaans organisation. This argument fell away after 1948 when the Nationalists came to power. It would have been absurd to suggest then that Afrikaners were "hounded."

Breaking the oath of secrecy that members take on induction is the supreme offence, as far as the Bond is concerned. It is regarded as treason to fellow-members and the organisation. In the early years a gruesome ceremony was performed to emphasize the gravity of the offence. Loose talk, even between father and son or husband and wife, is strictly forbidden.

A good example of the obsession with secrecy emerges from Newsletter 3/76/77 which informed members of the Broederbond's move from the Christiaan de Wet building to their new headquarters. "Our office is now in the new building, Die Eike, 1 Cedar Avenue, Auckland Park, Johannesburg. Our telephone

Die Eike, the secret Broederbond HQ in Auckland Park, Johannesburg.

number is 31-4161. (This was changed to 726-4345 on August 6 1977 when the new automatic exchange at Auckland Park came into operation.) This must not be disclosed to non-members, and friends (members) are requested to phone personally and not to give the number to their secretaries.

"Although we can be reached through the switchboard of the FAK *(Federasie van Afrikaanse Kultuurverenigings)* avoid doing this because the switchboard operator there is not informed of our affairs.

"Our office is on the first floor, listed as Uniediensburo (Edms) Bpk. Visiting friends (members) should take the stairs or lift to the first floor and ask at the office for the official they want to see. Inquiries should definitely not be made on the first floor occupied by the FAK and Rapportryers. Although the male personnel of the FAK are friends (members) the women there are not all married to members. Indiscreet inquiries, therefore, can create embarrassment. Remember also that the second floor is occupied by our youth organisations, Junior Rapportryers, Jeugraad and ASB (Afrikaanse Studentebond). The ASB organiser is not a member." The newsletter warned that casual visitors, friends of Broederbond members or other people might be in the building at any time and members must never assume that anyone encountered in the building was a Broeder. A few months later (July 1 1976) members were again reminded to inquire only at the correct floor; some had made indiscreet inquiries on the ground or second floor.

To complete these security arrangements the Broederbond employed Mr J J Schoeman, a retired member from Vereeniging, as caretaker. He lives in a flat on the top of the building. All documents are locked away in strongrooms with massive doors. The Bond has scores of postboxes and gives strict instructions for members writing to it. These include the use of bogus names of individuals or businesses. The procedures are changed regularly.

In Circular 4/3/64 the Executive Council said: "Documents and letters which are not of an extremely confidential nature we send by post. Normally, officials will not sign them but the designation Chief Secretary will be written or typed in place of a signature. Letters from branches or individual members to head office must carry only the membership number of the sender. Branch secretaries have the addresses to be used. The wording on envelopes must be carefully checked before the letters are posted. A safe method would be for members to give their letters to the branch secretary for posting to head office.

"Where letters, circulars and other documents are of a highly confidential nature they will be delivered by hand to branches. This is costly and cannot happen monthly, but at the outside quarterly. In this connection we would like to use friends who are travelling from here to other parts of the country, or friends returning after visiting the city. It would be appreciated, therefore, if friends would ask the office when they are in the city if there is any post to take with them. Friends are requested to notify the office in advance of a visit."

Each branch secretary is issued with a letter book recording addresses and postal instructions. The standard forms are drawn up in such a way that non-members getting hold of them would not know they were Broederbond documents. Still no chances are taken and the utmost security is prescribed for handling them. "Letters and other documents which would reveal confidential information if seen by non-members must be put in a strong envelope and posted to Mr M Kruger, Box 7714, Johanesburg (circular May 30 1973). This instruction applies to application forms (Form A), nomination forms (Form D), statement at induction (Form G), application for transfer to Outside or Resting membership (Form M), application for forming a new branch (Form J), exemption from attendance (Form B).

"Form C (monthly report), Form L (acknowledgement of receipt of circulars), letters concerning routine matters, and other communications must be sent to these addresses: Cape branches: Mr J Botha, Box 5634, Johannesburg; Transvaal branches: Mr F P Retief, Box 4966, Johannesburg: Natal and South West Africa branches: Mr F v Z Lubbe, Senior, Box 8576, Johannesburg; Orange Free State branches: Mr A Strydom, Senior, Box 6732, Johannesburg.

"All letters, promissory notes, contributions and correspondence to the Christiaan de Wet Fund must be sent by registered mail to Mr M Kruger, Box 7714, Johannesburg. Please note: postal orders and cheques for branch contributions must be made out to Uniespaarklub and sent to J Botha, Box 5634, Johannesburg. Please inform your treasurer of this.

"Names such as Uniespaarklub, C de Wet Fonds, Chief Secretary, must not be written on the envelope. Always use strong envelopes of good quality. Use two, one inside the other, if the contents are heavy, and use registered mail when the contents warrant it. Make sure the correct post box number is written on the envelope and that the envelope is properly sealed. Use 'safe' wording in your letters. Our normal way of addressing each other *(Broer)* must not be used, but rather 'friend'. Use membership numbers instead of names. Addresses to be used on envelopes are supplied to divisional secretaries and treasurers. These addresses must not be used when writing to head office. The addresses in this circular should be used until further notice. The names used do not necessarily refer to officials handling these matters."

The Broederbond offices close for Christmas and the New Year. To avoid security risks such as postboxes spilling over, members are instructed not to write to the office during that period. Secretaries and treasurers who go on leave during December must arrange for the safekeeping of all Broederbond documents (July 1 1977). They must also tell head office where circulars should be sent in their absence, to obviate the security risk of unclaimed letters. Secretaries who move from their areas must give head office without delay the alternative address for circulars.

A secretary must keep careful control of all documents in his possession. He must complete a standard form (R) at regular intervals and send it to head office to ensure that the Bond knows exactly which documents each branch has. Every effort must be made to trace missing documents. Circulars more than a year old must be burnt. But not even the secretary is trusted on his own with this responsibility. Branch committees must nominate somebody to go through the documents with the secretary and burn the old ones (Circular 11/76/77). A list of documents they have destroyed must be attached to Form R. "As a general rule all circulars and membership nomination lists more than a year old, agendas and minutes of annual meetings more than two years old, all letters, forms etc, which have served their purpose, and study documents which are no longer read, can be destroyed. Documents listed on Form R must be kept. A report on this must reach the office before March 15."

The documents to be retained by branches listed on Form R are numbered. Should any of them be leaked to outsiders, the offending branch can easily be identified. As a more frequent check head office, out of the blue, can demand particular documents from a branch. Branches which do not respond to these demands are punished: the monthly newsletter is withheld. Obviously the secretary then comes under pressure from members to do his work properly. In a number of cases head office has instructed a branch to change a secretary who has come under suspicion or has not safeguarded documents diligently enough.

Calling in copies of documents which have fallen into the hands of newspapermen and have been published, Broeder members of the Department of National Security and the Security Police can look for identification marks and identify the branch where the leak occurred. Sometimes head office stops leaks by changing the addressees. Circular 1/3/68: "In a previous circular it was mentioned that circulars would be sent to different members of your committee, and you were asked to supply safe addresses for all committee members. We intend to send the April circular to divisional chairmen. Your secretary must therefore advise us immediately if the address of your chairman has changed. If he will not be at home during the first week in April, let us know an address to use." The Broederbond will stop at nothing to trace leaks. The whole future of the organisation is tied up with its secrecy. If that is broken, it will lose its effectiveness: its members will be exposed to the harsh light of day. They know it, so they regard exposure as the biggest threat to their existence. On occasion they have called in members who are Department of National Security or Security Police agents to help stop leaks.

One trick is to make deliberate mistakes in a group of circulars sent only to certain branches. Should these appear in a newspaper the number of suspect branches is narrowed down. From there they can eliminate even further by calling back documents and looking for identification marks. In one circular (5/74/75) members are warned against using thin envelopes, the contents of which can be read without opening them. "We ourselves wrap documents in a blank sheet of paper if we use a lightweight envelope," the circular added.

"Do not assume naively that every Afrikaner in a leading position is a member – especially if they claim to have attended the inaugural meeting. Check by phoning the office (Circular 9/72/73).

"Telephone inquiries must be limited to the absolute minimum. The caller must identify himself with his membership number and date of birth. Only our own telephone number must be used for this, and not that of FAK."

The October 1977 circular said: "Your attention is drawn to the fact that Professor Dawid de Villiers of Stellenbosch (also known as Heilige Dawid) is not a member. It appears he is accepted as one, and has already been given information about our organisation and the Ruiterwag."

Most secret of all are *Bondsraad* meetings. The meeting place is usually kept a secret until the last possible moment. The lengths to which they go is clearly illustrated in another circular. Notice that the date of the meeting is not given in this circular, but was disclosed in a previous one. If this circular falls into the hands of non-members they would not know it was a Broederbond document, or where and when the meeting was to take place.

STRICTLY CONFIDENTIAL

September 15, 1964

To all branch secretaries

Dear Friend,

The date of the annual meeting was given in paragraph 10 of Circular 5/64/65 of August 3 1964. You are requested to inform your delegate immediately to report between 6.45 and 7.00 on the morning of the first day, that is the Tuesday at the entrance to Kempton Park station.

There he will meet a Mr Lombard who will be wearing a white flower in his buttonhole.

If your delegate arrives late because of unforeseen circumstances, he must phone the Johannesburg telephone number given in the extraordinary circular of June 17. He must use a *public phone* and ask to speak to Jan, giving his membership number and date of birth. Arrangements will be made to take him to the meeting place.

The usual letter of identification from his branch must be given to him. The letter must be shown to Mr Lombard when the delegate is asked for it. It must, however, be handed over only when the delegate reaches the meeting place.

Nobody will be allowed to attend without a letter of identification.

Warn your delegate to be careful where and with whom he discusses his visit. He must be especially careful at the place where he stays. As few people as possible must know of his visit.

The delegate must please bring a coat in case it gets cold or starts to rain.

Yours faithfully,
Chief Secretary.

Delegates to regional or annual meetings are strongly discouraged from staying in hotels, or even with friends or relatives who are non-members, because it would increase the security risk. The office has a list of members prepared to accommodate Broeders during meetings. Broeders are told not to discuss the meeting with anyone when they apply for leave from work and tell their families they are going away. The venues of annual meetings have, on occasion, been changed to ensure strict security.

Broeders are encouraged to offer lifts to fellow members to reduce the number of cars parked outside the meeting place. They are not to park all their cars in one place, but scatter them around the suburb to avoid attracting attention (Circular 9/72/73). Meeting places are guarded by members. No delegate can get into a meeting without a letter of identification signed by his branch chairman and secretary. The guards also patrol the grounds to prevent eavesdropping.

Branches with lax security measures get a reprimand from head office: "It still appears that there is insufficient control at meetings, especially at meetings of two branches or more. Recently a nonmember walked into a meeting while it was in progress, because there was no guard at the door. Branches must keep the tightest control at the entrance to a meeting. It is essential that an identity document such as an identity card, book of life or passport be produced with the usual letter of identification to gain entry to a meeting."

The Executive Council recently forbade the employment of black or coloured staff at gatherings, especially at *braais*. "Sometimes they are within hearing distance of the meeting place," a circular warned.[2] It ordered members to report breaches of this rule "so that action can be considered."

The size of the meeting may also constitute a security risk. "Where more than 350 members are expected, the Executive Council's prior permission must be obtained. The measures taken to ensure the meeting's secrecy and safety must be reported to the Executive" (Circular 5/75/76).

Members are warned against introducing their wives to other members. They are encouraged to hold branch meetings in houses where the wife, children and other relatives are away for the evening. They must serve refreshments themselves and not use servants and other non-members for that purpose. Circular 2/3/66: "As requested by a number of branches, we point out once again that the introduction of wives to friends (members) at branch meetings and gatherings is not in accordance with our strict requirements of secrecy and creates embarrassment for many friends (members)."

Members are discouraged from eating together in a public place after a meeting "because it can place our secrecy in jeopardy" (Circular 10/70/71). Branches are told to keep only brief minutes of meetings and to use membership numbers instead of names (Circular 4/63/64).

Some documents are regarded as so important that ordinary members are not allowed to keep them. The chairman's report of the 1972 annual meeting is one of them, "to be discussed at meetings from time to time. Otherwise it must not leave the possession of the secretary. All documents taken from the secretary by members must be carefully recorded to ensure that they are returned in time. The Executive Council urgently requests branches to see that documents concerning the annual meetings (or any other confidential documents of our organisation) do not fall into the wrong hands."

In Circular 6/71/72 members on their way to the annual meeting are warned not to assume that fellow-travellers are also delegates. "Be prepared to give an acceptable reason in case you are questioned about your trip. Although an air trip is very convenient, a sudden increase in air bookings might lead to questions. If you can travel in some other way, by all means do so."

Until 1964 gatherings of Broederbond members on holiday were acceptable to the Executive, but the serious leaks in the early 1960s changed its attitude. Circular 2/9/64: "The Executive Council has decided that holiday gatherings must be stopped. This decision has been taken on the insistence of friends (members) all over the country. It has been pointed out that these gatherings unjustifiably jeopardised our confidentiality."

Broeders are, of course, forbidden membership of other secret or semi-secret organisations. They are also barred from "international" organisations like Lions International, Rotary, Round Table and Jaycees. The ban does of course not apply to Rapportryers, Junior Rapportryers, Vryburgers and Ruiterwag (Circular 2/10/70).

Even members' dress has been discussed as a potential security risk. Broeders are required to attend meetings in dark suits, but some of them pointed out that this might arouse suspicion, for instance at a farm on a Saturday afternoon. The Executive solemnly considered this and announced at the annual meeting in 1970: "In certain areas in the country where safari suits are normally worn, it attacts a lot of attention if members go to meetings in dark suits. The dignity of the occasion must, however, always be recognised. A safari suit with long trousers will, in certain circumstances, be acceptable. Shorts, colourful sportswear, multi-coloured shirts, etc, are not acceptable."

Broederbond officials employed at head office face "a difficulty in explaining where they work, without jeopardising the secrecy of the organisation." For this reason they are normally associated with the public, cultural arm of the Bond, the FAK, which has offices in the same building.

Dr Piet Koornhof's position was thus explained in Circular 1/8/62: "The Executive Council has pleasure in announcing that friend Dr Piet Koornhof, previously deputy secretary of the National Party in the Transvaal, has been appointed chief secretary of our organisation. To the outside he will be known as Director of Cultural Guidance of the FAK ... The Executive has been fortunate in making an arrangement with the FAK whereby his appointment is associated with a public position. Although friends (members) can reach him by phoning our normal number or that of the FAK, they are requested to dial 344064 instead. This number does not appear in the telephone directory."

The double game the Broederbond plays with the FAK is clearly illustrated by the scores of warnings in circulars that members must not phone the FAK concerning Bond matters because some FAK officials are not Broeders. This strange attitude towards an organisation which the Broederbond founded as its own public "cultural arm", and housed in the same building, reflects their concern with secrecy. Over the years the Broederbond has actually warned members against FAK officials, though they are ostensibly working for the same "Afrikaner cause." FAK officials learning of this must have been astounded by the lack of "brotherly love." Some of the officials mentioned in warnings because they were not members were Mr J G du Plessis, F J Pretorius, H S van der Walt, J Taljaard, C Young, O S Smit, W McDonald and L Lemmer.

All in all the Broederbond organisation is a masterpiece of secretiveness. The Executive Council and head office are continuously aware of documents held by branches because they must report them monthly after their meetings. Branches must also report to head office every month on who attended the meetings. Not only does this strengthen the organisation by virtually compelling members to attend meetings, it also serves a security purpose. The organisation quickly spots people losing interest or becoming "cool" towards the Bond. These people are an obvious security risk. Branches are told to find out the reason for an individual's loss of interest. If it cannot be traced to something acceptable such as illness in the family or a problem at work, the member is taken to task. If he still fails to respond, all documents are taken from him, he is required to promise not to break the oath of secrecy, and he is expelled.

There are also strict instructions against making disclosures to prospective members before they have been accepted. The fact that a candidate's name has been circulated does not mean that he will become a member, and Broeders are warned not to speak to him about it in any circumstances. The present Broederbond chairman, Professor Gerrit Viljoen, has condemned the "recklessness" of Broeders who congratulated him in "mixed" company after his election in 1974. In Circular 1/11/74 Professor Viljoen deplores this "loose-lipped attitude" and calls on all branches to pay renewed attention to it.

Even funerals of Broeders or their wives have security implications for the Bond. In 1964 (Circular 3/11/64) the wife of the chairman of a Witwatersrand branch died. Members of the branch wanted to sprinkle soil ceremoniously on her coffin. The initial reaction from the Executive was positive, especially as it would eliminate blacks from "this intimate function." However, other members were quick to point out the security risk of members thus identifying themselves as Broeders. A month later, in December 1964, the Executive warned against this practice and in the circular of 1/5/69 they condemned it for security reasons.

One of the biggest security problems the Broederbond has faced since its membership increased dramatically in the 1960s concerned the venue for annual general meetings and those of the *Bondsraad.* As each branch is entitled to send a delegate, they would total more than 700. The dilemma is described in an extraordinary circular of June 12 1973. "As you know, the annual meeting of 1972 decided on a meeting every two years to which branches could each send one delegate. On this occasion the Executive Council is elected. We already have 711 branches increasing by at least 25 annually. This implies that we could expect more than 700 delegates at the next annual meeting.

"In the past few years we have been able to meet in suitable barns on selected farms. On the only occasion we have deviated from this since 1963 – in 1970 – we experienced many problems. It was then found that a public hall should not be used for an annual meeting because it is not as secure as a farm. (The Press discovered the venue.) The Executive does not know of a member's farm where more than 700 people could meet. (The place where we met in 1972 is no longer available.) There are other places at our disposal, but they cannot accomodate enough people.

"Furthermore, it must be recognised that when we have a major annual meeting our members cannot be confident of anonymity in hotels. For secrecy's sake delegates must stay with members, as has happened in the past few years. This means that annual meetings can take place only in the Pretoria-Witwatersrand-Vereeniging area, or in Cape Town and the surrounding area, where there are enough members to provide accomodation.

"After careful consideration of all these matters, the Executive Council has reached the conclusion that we must establish our own meeting place. We have started, therefore, to acquire a venue in the Pretoria-Witwatersrand-Vereeniging area. When necessary, and if a suitable venue becomes available in the Cape Town area, the Executive will consider it.

"The Executive is aware that in time the venue or venues may become known as our property and has decided, therefore, that they must be used intensively by such organisations as the Voortrekkers, church youth organisations, ASB, Junior Rapportryers, *Nasionale Jeugraad,* FAK and *Volkspelebeweging,* for youth meetings, youth leader courses etc. When a venue is used intensively for other purposes, our own meetings will draw less attention and it will be providing a service to the community.

"The necessary security arrangements will be made. Apart from a barn or hall seating 1 000 to 2 000 people, additional facilities must be supplied such as accomodation for about 60 people, a kitchen, toilets, tables and chairs, a caretaker's house and camping area. A committee including an architect and a consulting engineer has already been formed to advise the Executive. We expect to provide a meeting place which will do our organisation proud without wasting money on luxuries."

The chairman concludes by saying that the project or projects will be financed by the Christiaan de Wet Fund, and makes an appeal for contributions. The Broederbond meeting place near Hartebeespoort Dam was completed in about two years, almost exactly as planned. Full details are given in a special circular which says the farm will be managed by the Jeugraad of the FAK.

"The Hartbees-Jeugterrein of about 100 hectares is west of Hartebeespoort Dam in a natural, wooded area. It is 2km from the Skeerpoort Post Office next to the tarred road to Brits, and about 75km from Johannesburg Railway Station on the exit route from Hans Strijdom Drive through Randburg. From Church Square in Pretoria it is 50km if you take Church Street West exit. Do not turn off before you reach the T-junction at Skeerpoort. The meeting place is half a kilometre from the T-junction on the right.

"Apart from a big hall and kitchen there are two ablution blocks, one with separate bath and showers for men and women. There are three huts housing 15 people each and three huts which could take six people each. (Therefore 63 men and 63 women: total 126.) There is also a two-roomed leader's hut with its own bathroom and three beds in each room. There is kitchen equipment the use of which must be arranged in advance. Address inquiries to the Camp Manager, Box 6772, (Tel. 724-3054) Johannesburg 2000, or Box 99 (Tel. 29) Skeerpoort 0232."

In a later circular (3/5/76) notice is given that Broeder H S Hattingh, the manager/caretaker of the farm, has a new number during office hours: 31-3775 or 31-4326. The telephone number on the farm remains Skeerpoort 29.

The circular says the gates of the Broederbond meeting place will be kept locked at all times, and that prior arrangements to enter should be made with the manager. The farm is not available for "ordinary holidays" and Broeders attending meetings there are instructed not to make work for the blacks employed to clean the ablution blocks each morning. Occupants of the huts are responsible for cleaning them.

Broeders are encouraged to travel in groups to the meeting place, because large numbers of cars could attract attention and constitute a security risk. After the meeting, the traffic leaving the farm is staggered for the same reason.

The Broederbond's secrecy is perhaps the major issue criticised by Afrikaners who have not been invited to join. The organisation has been attacked for secrecy at church synod meetings. It defended its "confidentiality" at a Southern Transvaal *Nederduitse Gereformeerde* synod in April 1963. "The Bond's membership and activities are regarded as confidential. In documents and statements by the Bond on this issue, the confidentiality is justified as follows:

"(a) The Church, the Government, companies and other organisations rely on confidentiality and secrecy in pursuing their aims. Secrecy is embraced for practical reasons and not as a matter of principle – it is not intrinsically either good or bad. (b) It is, in the first place, the function of the State to take action if the secrecy observed by any organisation leads to subversion and damages other organisations or individuals. (c) The Bond is a democratic organisation and all its activities are reported to representatives from all branches at regular annual congresses. Any untoward activities will be revealed here and can be challenged. The Church similarly trusts certain members, who are also national leaders, to act as responsible Christians. (d) Although individuals may admit membership when a situation absolutely demands it – when they have permission from the Executive – membership is regarded as confidential because only persons whose strength of character, leadership and faith, and who are prepared to make sacrifices without expecting financial or other gain, are invited to join the Bond. This being the case, the release of the names of members could provoke resentment among other Afrikaners who are not members."

The Broederbond rationalises, of course, that it must be secret to be able to serve Afrikanerdom: "A stigma attaches to members whose identities are revealed. This makes it impossible for them to function properly" (Circular 3/9/68).

The fact that every action of the Bond is cloaked in secrecy enables it to scheme safely behind closed doors without fearing that non-members will discover how it influences policy and pushes its members into influential positions. The obsessive secrecy is illustrated by the instruction that Bond affairs must not be discussed between husband and wife or father and son – even if the son belongs to the Ruiterwag, the junior Broederbond. The organisations have the same fundamental aims, but where a father belongs to the Broederbond and his son to the Ruiterwag they must not discuss this.[3] "Open discussion of the two organisations' activities (between father and son) is strongly condemned and must not be allowed in any circumstances. It is a violation of confidentiality which the Executive Council will view in a serious light."

This kind of discipline has helped to make the Broederbond the most powerful underground organisation in the Western world. Members in powerful positions can deal with its enemies anonymously in scores of ways. Their secrecy is, indeed, their strength.

1. Formerly the Bureau For State Security.
2. Circular of May 3 1976.
3. August 1 1977.

23 *Discipline and Watchdog Committees*

Major factors in the effectiveness and success of the Broederbond are the strict discipline and code of conduct imposed on its members. The Executive Council exercises its authority with the bossy efficiency of a school principal and, through its terrier-like "head prefect" the chief secretary keeps the organisation running smoothly. The monthly circular letters are full of goadings and proddings to keep this discipline at peak performance. This is a typical example:

"The Executive Council is determined to do all in its power to sharpen up the internal discipline of our organisation and has therefore decided to introduce the following arrangements, among others. When branches do not respond to requests and papers *(skrywes)*, the circular letter and other documents can be withheld, the expansion of membership suspended by cancelling the annual quota of new members and deferring nominations, and in certain cases the branch chairman and/or secretary can be summoned to meet the Executive Council's committee for branch and membership matters. In exceptional cases it can even be decided to abolish a branch.

"It happens, unfortunately, that branches sometimes neglect to respond to inquiries from the Executive Council, with a consequent hold-up in the handling of nominations and other matters. The Executive Council would appreciate it if branch executives would pay particular attention to this" (Circular 5/76/77 of July 1 1976).

A constant source of displeasure to the Executive Council is the tardy payment of financial dues, and branches are forever being rapped for not being up to date. The maintenance of strict secrecy and the proper guardianship of the organisation's confidential documents are also regularly emphasised in the monthly letters. Regular attendance at meetings is another matter of constant concern to the Executive Council. Even if there are good reasons, branch executives are instructed to "approach friends whose attendance has been below 60 per cent and to see what arrangements can be made to improve their attendance" (Circular 4/73/74 of May 29 1973). These are the bread-and-butter rules and regulations of the organisation. Persistent contravention can eventually result in the offender's expulsion.

Other reasons for this drastic step are detailed in the monthy circular 6/76/77 of August 3 1976.

"It is not customary to reveal the reasons for termination of membership but in response to inquiries the Executive Council discloses the following general reasons. They should not be linked to specific cases, and it should be remembered that some Broeders had their membership terminated at their own request in view of the reasons stated.

1. Divorce in circumstances inconsistent with continued membership.
2. Refusal to quit the Herstigte Nasionale Party, or joining that party.
3. Conviction on a serious criminal charge.
4. Laziness, failure to carry out instructions and poor cooperation.
5. Loss of interest.
6. Alcohol abuse.
7. Regular participation in Sunday sport.
8. Transfer from a sister church to a sect."

From a study of Broederbond documents it appears that the most common reason for termination of membership is divorce. The stern Calvinistic ethic of the organisation regards divorce as a breach of a sacred union and generally an uncompromising stand is taken against it, although recently there appear to be signs of a slight softening in this attitude.

There are firm instructions to branches on handling a divorce. "Branches and friends are reminded that every instance in which a member is involved in a divorce must be reported to the Executive Council by the branch executive. The branch executive must also do everything in its power to stand by the friend in the difficult circumstances to an extent consistent with our members' way.

"The friend must confidentially inform the branch executive about the matter, and cease attending meetings until it has been reported to the Executive Council and a decision on the matter has been reached. If he does not do this voluntarily, the branch executive must ask him not to attend meetings.

"The branch executive must, as far as possible, obtain full details of the circumstances leading up to the event and present them to the Executive Council. While the Executive Council wishes to point out once again that divorce is regarded in a serious light, the branch executive is free to recommend that a Broeder involved should retain his membership and specify reasons for such recommendation.

"After considering the circumstances leading to the divorce, the friend involved must also ask himself whether his circumstances are consistent with continued membership of our organisation" (Circular 11/6/77 of February 2 1977).

Whenever memberships are terminated, whatever the reason, the names of the former Broeders are circulated in the monthly letters in the following form.

TERMINATION OF MEMBERSHIP

The following people are no longer members of our organisation and Broederbond matters may therefore not be discussed with them.

A P Meiring, furniture manufacturer/farmer, Hendrina, 3404.
C R Serfontein, farmer, Edenville, 6021
(Circular 7/77/78 of September 1 1977.)

Considering the organisation has about 12 000 members, the number of terminations is comparatively small. In 1976/77 there were 34 (Circular 3/77/78 of May 2 1977). The 1970/71 figure was 10 and 28 Broeders left in 1971/72 (Secretarial report of the Executive Council).

The Broederbond's code of conduct demands of its members an exacting degree of diligence, dedication and sacrifice. They are expected to work virtually day and night for the objectives of the organisation. "It is also necessary to emphasise that each individual member is actually a work-unit for the organisation. In the first place (and this priority is mentioned deliberately, because for many nation-savers their actual work is a side issue) it is every member's task not only to deliver fine achievement in his daily work, his profession, his work circle, but also to strive in his daily tasks not only to promote himself but also the Afrikaner cause, and to honour and enrich the Afrikaner nation. We save and serve our nation, in the first instance, not after 5pm but through the quality and intensity and application of our service and work activities during working hours.

"But over and above that, it is expected that the work-unit that every member represents will also give service in organisations outside of his normal work connections and professional life. After work he dare not pull on his slippers every day and go and sit on the sidelines and critically appraise party, church, sport and cultural activities; he must judiciously and to the utmost of his ability contribute to our ideals through outside organisations" (Circular 7/73/74 of October 1 1973).

This strong sense of discipline and motivation, instilled into every member of the organisation – and, by their influence, into Afrikanerdom as a whole – is a fundamental factor in the Broederbond's remarkable record of success.

One of the Broederbond's most powerful instruments for the pursuit of its ideals is the system of watchdog committees which operate quietly, efficiently and in total secrecy. There are watchdog committees for almost every aspect of national policy. The members are prominent Broeders who supervise the implementation of Broeder policies, see that Broeders get effective control of key areas, check that they perform their duties properly, and advise Cabinet Ministers on policy matters.

The Broederbond calls these committees "task forces", and their existence has been one of the best kept Broeder secrets. A full list of the members of the various committees was circulated only once to branches, in 1968. Continuity of service is of the utmost importance, so many members have been serving on them for years and know their subject inside out. The watchdog committees are appointed by the Executive Council and because the names are no longer circulated, ordinary Broeders do not know them. Even more in the dark, of course, are non-Broeders who are being watched without knowing it. They include secretaries of departments and the staffs of provincial administrations, control boards and public bodies; their performances in the implementation of policy are carefully scrutinised by the watchdogs of the Broederbond's "police force".

Any slackness or deviation from policy can be spotted almost instantly, enabling the Executive Council to take corrective action by leaning on the appropriate authority. Individuals who become obstructive can be replaced by more enthusiastic members. In this way the watchdog committees play a powerful role in seeing that the Broederbond influence in South Africa is administered with meticulous effect. The watchdog committees comprise the intellectual cream of the Broederbond, and their work is financed by the central Broederbond fund. Their expenses of about R12 000 include trips, meetings and accommodation.

These committees also act as think-tanks for the Broederbond. They deliberate on policies and study every facet before making recommendations to the Executive Council. Once accepted there, the recommendations will almost certainly become Government policy. According to Circular 2/5/77 the master plan for whites was drawn up by one of these committees. Another committee was busy studying ways and means of increasing the effectiveness of the civil service, the political future of the coloured people, blacks and Indians. Yet others were studying aspects of universities for blacks, Afrikaans universities, educational matters, foreign relations, security, youth affairs, political "resistance literature", and sport (3/2/75).

The list circulated in 1963 indicates the calibre of those who serve on the watchdog committees. They are all prominent in their fields and, according to the Broederbond, represent "the best brainpower in South Africa, if not in the whole world." The committees are never disbanded or reshuffled. Changes occur only when people die, retire from public life or enter entirely new fields.

The list is published in full below, giving the positions the members then held.

Watchdog committee for non-White affairs

Professor J P van S Bruwer, former Commissioner-General in South West Africa, was the chairman until his death. Professor Bruwer was also the convener of the Bantu Group.

Mr M C Botha, at the time a Deputy Minister, was also a watchdog in the Bantu group. He quit when he became Minister of Bantu Administration and Development and Bantu Education.

Others who have served include the late Dr W W Eiselen, who was Commissioner-General and former Secretary of Bantu Administration.

J P Dodds – a former senior official of the Department of Bantu Administration.

Professor E F Potgieter – then rector of Turfloop.

I P van Onselen – senior official of the Bantu Affairs Department.

Dr H J van Zyl – former Secretary of Bantu Education.

Ds C W H Boshoff – son-in-law of Dr Verwoerd and a Professor of Theology.

Dr P G J Koornhof – former Broederbond secretary and now Minister of Sport and Recreation.

Prof G van N Viljoen, Rector of the Rand Afrikaans University and Broederbond chairman.

M T de Waal.

F S Steyn, former MP, later an ambassador, today a judge. He is no longer a member of the task force.

J H T Mills, former Secretary of the Transkei Civil Service.

S F Kingsley, former Director of Bantu Affairs, Pretoria municipality.

Dr P J Riekert, The Prime Minister's former economic adviser.

Prof P F D Weiss, former Director of Africa Institute, who later joined the HNP. He, of course, is out.

Associate members: J H van Dyk, Dept of Bantu Administration and Development; Prof H du Plessis; Prof P J Coetze (formerly Anthropology Department dean and a member of the HNP); W J Grobelaar; P W Botha (at the time Deputy Minister of Coloured Affairs and now Minister of Defence and now Prime Minister); J L Boshoff, (former Rector of Turfloop); Dr A A Odendaal; Dr F C Albertyn.

Coloured group

Convener: F D Conradie, former MEC for the Cape and a member of the Broederbond Executive, now MP.

Mr Kobus Louw, former Secretary for Coloured Affairs, and vice-chairman, SA Rugby Board.

A C van Wyk.

Indian group

Convener; Prof S P Olivier, Rector, Indian University College.

Rev R J J van Vuuren.

Technical and natural science matters

Chairman: Dr E J Marais, Rector of University of Port Elizabeth.

Dr H O Mönnig, member of Prime Minister's Scientific Council.

Dr A J A Roux, head of Atomic Board.
Dr S M Naude, Scientific Adviser to the Prime Minister.
Professor L J le Roux.
Associate members: Dr C M Kruger, former manager, Iscor; Dr B C Jansen, head of Onderstepoort; Dr A W Lategan, Dr S J du Toit, Dr O R van Eeden, Prof Dr P W Groenewoud, Prof H L de Waal (former chairman of SA Akademie vir Wetenskap en Kuns), Dr D M de Waal, Prof P S Zeeman, Prof R Truter, Prof J M le Roux, Dr L A Prinsloo, Prof C A du Toit, Prof A P Malan, Dr J M de Wet, Dr S J du Plessis, Prof P J G de Vos, Dr C C Kritzinger and G H Loubser (General Manager of SA Railways).

Youth affairs

Chairman: Ds J S Gericke, former Moderator of the NG Kerk.
Ds C L van den Berg, youth minister for Ned Hervormde Kerk.
Dr S C W Duvenage, professor at Potchefstroom University. Prof J E Pieterse.
Dr M Swart, former head of Rapportryers.
J F P Badenhorst, head of Voortrekker youth movement.
W S J Grobler, then FAK secretary. Former MP.
H J Moolman.
O de P Kuun (secretary), then a senior Broederbond official.
Dr J C Otto, former MP and headmaster.
R W J Opperman, head of Olympics Committee and senior Perskor official.
Dr A P Treurnicht, former Broederbond chief and now a Deputy Minister.
Ds J E Potgieter, then NG Kerk student minister.
Dr D J Coetzee.

Agricultural

Chairman: S P Botha, Minister of Water Affairs and of Forestry.
A J du Toit, G J Joubert, J E de V Loubser, W A A Hepburn, P W van Rooyen, H E Martins, then an MP and Deputy Minister of Transport.
P S Toerien, C C Claassens.
Dr J C Neethling, senior official of Department of Agriculture.
Dr R D Henning, senior official of Water Affairs Department.

Associate Members: J M C Smit, Dr B C Jansen, Dr C M van Wyk, S J Brandt, Dr J G van der Wath, De la H de Villiers, S Reineke, D Grewar, N J Deacon, A M Lubbe, Adv P R de Villiers, L C R Bürhmann, S P Malan, P J H Maree, G Radloff, W v d Merwe, Prof S A Hulme, J P Hamman, C D C Human, S J J van Rensburg, P J Kruger.

Africa

Chairman: Prof P F D Weiss.

W C du Plessis, a former Administrator of South West Africa.

Dr T E W Schumann.

Prof Dr A J H van der Walt.

Prof J H Coetzee, University of Potchefstroom.

P J Cillie, former editor, *Die Burger.*

B J van der Walt, then MP and former Administrator of South West Africa.

Dr C P C de Wet, D B R Badenhorst, M A du Plessis.

Planning

Chairman: Dr P S Rautenbach – who today is head of the Public Service Commission.

Dr H O Mönnig.

Dr E J Marais.

Dr P J Riekert.

J F W Haak, then Minister of Economic Affairs.

Dr P M Robbertse, head of Council of Social Sciences.

Prof S Pauw, former Rector of Unisa.

Prof L J le Roux

Prof S A Hulme

P Z J van Vuuren, then an MEC, now MP

W W S Haveman, Administrator of Natal.

Dr F J Potgieter

M A du Plessis

J J Marais

P J V E Pretorius

Dr H Steyn

A J du Toit

J H Niemand, former Secretary of Community Development Department.

Press matters

P A Weber, former managing director Nasionale Pers.

P J Cillie, former editor, *Die Burger,* now Professor of Journalism, Stellenbosch.

M V Jooste, managing director, Perskor.

H P Marnitz, former editor, *Die Vaderland.*

J J van Rooyen, former editor, *Die Transvaler.*

C D Fuchs, formerly SABC.

J H Steyl, Transvaal secretary, National Party.

Steve de Villiers, SABC.

Associate members: H H Dreyer (Nasionale Pers); D J van Zyl (Nasionale Pers); T J A Gerdener (former Minister of the Interior and Administrator of Natal, since suspended from Broederbond).

Economic

Chairman: Dr A J Visser – former Senator.

J F W Haak, then Cabinet Minister.

Dr M S Louw.

Prof C G W Schumann.

Prof W J Pretorius.

C H J van Aswegen.

C J F Human.

H de G Laurie.

Dr P E Rousseau – former head of South Africa Foundation.

Dr J G van der Merwe.

Dr F P Jacobz.

Dr M D Marais.

J A Hurter – head of Volkskas.

T F Muller.

W Pauw.

P K Hoogendyk.

D v d M Benade.

R P Botha.

Associate members: Dr T W de Jongh, Governor, Reserve Bank; Dr A D Wassenaar, S J Naude, Dr H L F Snyman, P J F Scholtz, P J C van Zyl, G J J Visser, G D Wessels, J N Swanepoel, D M Hoogenhout, F J Marais, Dr E L Grove, A J Marais, J P van Heerden, L G van Tonder, E Cuyler, a former Senator, G J van Zyl, P G Carstens, J J Venter, J G H Loubser, B P Marais, Prof H J Samuels, former head of the Armaments Board.

Education

Chairman: Prof H J J Bingle, former Rector of Potchefstroom University.

Prof S Pauw, former Rector, Unisa.

Dr G J Jordaan, then chairman, National Education Advisory Council.

Dr P M Robbertse, head of Council for Social Research.

A J Koen, then Director of Education in Transvaal.

J H Stander, then Director of Education in Natal and an Executive Council member.

S Theron.

E E van Kerken, then Director of Education, Free State.

A G S Meiring, then Director of Education, Cape.

M C Erasmus, then Secretary for Education.

Ds P M Smith, senior leader of Hervormde Kerk.

Associate members: Dr W K H du Plessis; Prof G J J Smit; A J van Rooyen; Dr P A Conradie; S C M Naude.

Religious deferability

Chairman: Ds P M Smith.

Ds J du P Malan, NGK Minister.

Prof B J Engelbrecht, NHK.

Prof S P van der Walt, Gereformeerde Kerk.

Prof T N Hanekom, Stellenbosch University.

Ds S J Gericke, NGK Moderator – member of the Executive Council.

Prof F J M Potgieter, Stellenbosch University.

Ds D P M Beukes, NGk – member of the Executive Council.

Prof S du Toit – Gereformeerde Kerk.

Prof E P Groenewald, Pretoria.

Dr A P Treurnicht.

Prof H du Plessis.

Prof F J van Zyl – Hervormde Kerk.

Prof P S Dreyer – Hervormde Kerk.

Africa and world committee

Chairman: Dr P J Meyer.

Dr P E Rousseau.

S P Botha.

J A Marais, former MP.
J A Hurter.
M A du Plessis.
Gen H van den Bergh, former security chief, and head of BOSS (then Colonel).
Dr P Koornhof.
Dr E J Marais.

Relations with English

Chairman: Prof S Pauw.
Dr P J Meyer.
Prof H J Bingle.
F D Conradie.
S A Hofmeyr.
Dr G F C Troskie – headed committee dealing with the "Jewish problem".

Sport committee

This committee was headed for a long time by Prof A N Pelzer. Others on it were Mr Johan Claassen, former Springbok rugby captain, Mr Kobus Louw and Mr R J Opperman.

The Immigration Committee was headed by Dr Piet Koornhof.

A task force to combat communism, liberalism and other enemies such as Freemasonry was headed by Prof F J van Zyl.[1]

1 Report which was reproduced in the *Sunday Times*.

24 *Contact between Members and Subsequent Influence on Policy etc.*

As in all other aspects of its organisation, the Broederbond has a model procedure for contact between members. This contact is deliberate, planned and sustained, and enhances the Bond's tremendous influence. It ensures maximum influence on policy matters because members know exactly whom to approach on any aspect of local, provincial or state policy. It also enables Broeders to identify each other when they come to make appointments to key posts, when contracts are awarded or business propositions crop up.

The branch operates as a small unit, meeting at least once a month. Discipline is strict and members are compelled to attend. There they form friendships, and they protect each other's interests in business. Branch delegates attend the annual meeting putting them in touch with nearly 1 000 Broeders from all over the country. Regional meetings ensure that Broeders in each area meet regularly and get to know each other well. Broeders are linked too by the monthly newsletter reporting on candidates proposed, blackballed or accepted. At all times a Broeder knows about new members entering the organisation.

Among the most effective ways the Broederbond has devised to put members in touch with each other are the compulsory meetings for groups with a common interest or career. For example, Broeders who are teachers in Pretoria are required to meet at least twice a year. The same goes for doctors, lawyers, policemen and every other interest group. It is at meetings of this kind that tactics, programmes of action, take-over of a key position and similar projects can be discussed. Broeders in the same profession meet each other face to face, and it is only to be expected that this should have an effect on filling vacancies and achieving promotions.

The Broederbond vigorously disputes claims that it pushes members into top positions. It cites its rule stating that members must not abuse their positions. This sounds right and proper, but the position in reality is totally different: Broeders do hold top positions in almost every sphere of South African life. How this came about and is being perpetuated is a matter of implementing the basic Broederbond philosophy that it is an organisation of "genuine Afrikaners" serving Afrikanerdom at all times.

The key lies in this: to serve Afrikanerdom as they see it, they must do everything in their power to ensure that genuine Afrikaners have control of key positions. To them, obviously, "genuine Afrikaners" mean Broeders. Why else were they handpicked by extremely strict criteria to join this exclusive organisation of Super-Afrikaners? If you are a Broeder, your opportunities to serve Afrikanerdom in your occupation and elsewhere are ensured as you are pushed higher and higher up the ladder. This curious attitude to the aims of the Bond achieves two objectives: the Broeders can claim to serve Afrikanerdom and not their selfish interests, while the Broederbond's influence increases daily with more and more Broeders taking over key positions.

Analysis of one aspect on its own will prove that the Broederbond does not serve Afrikanerdom as a whole, and in fact that it is impossible for an organisation to achieve that broad ambition. A study of the Broederbond reveals clear evidence of Afrikaner snobbery among members, no matter how much they protest their real aim is to uplift the poor Afrikaner worker. The fact of the matter is that very, very few Afrikaner workers belong to the organisation. There are fewer than 10 miners for instance. Although the Bond manipulated miners as a contribution to the 1948 election victory (see Chapter 5) it seems they do not feel at home in its ranks. For this reason there has been a campaign to recruit more mining members in recent years. It has failed dismally. There was even an attempt to establish under Broederbond control a secret organisation for workers. Although they financed it heavily, that failed too.

The reason is simple: the Broederbond has become the home of the rich and powerful Super-Afrikaners. They have been so successful in advancing their own careers and finances, by being Broeders, that the gap between them and the Afrikaner worker has become wider and wider. The true Afrikaner worker will simply not be comfortable in that company.

Although the Broeders are very guarded in the secret documents, having learnt what harm a leak can do, it is easy to see how they can improve their own positions.

The clearest evidence is that Broeders do hold almost all the top public positions. To ascribe this to pure coincidence would be extremely naive. There is a definite link between the Broederbond's Executive Council and the Cabinet.

Co-operation between the Government and the Broederbond is extremely close. Professor A N Pelzer outlined it in his historical review of the Broederbond at the 50th anniversary in 1968. "The understanding (between the Government and the Bond) has always been of the best. This fortunate state of affairs can be attributed to the fact that the political leaders were normally members of the Afrikaner Broederbond and the problems were discussed in a spirit of Brotherhood."

There are several indications that members can call on Brothers in top positions to use their influence. Circular 6/10/66 discusses members who write directly to Cabinet Ministers, secretaries of departments and other "friends in responsible circles" as they are called in the circular, chiefly about policy matters and staff vacancies, but seemingly about anything else for that matter. "Notwithstanding repeated requests, some branches and members still write about our affairs to friends in responsible circles, like directors of education and departmental secretaries, at their official addresses. This has resulted in the contents becoming known to their private secretaries or other staff to the great embarrassment of the member. It is no use marking letters "confidential" because this is not noticed in an office handling so many letters. In every case these members' home addresses should be used.

"For obvious reasons we cannot give these home addresses in circulars. They can, however, be obtained from our office. You can also send letters to us for onward transmission. Please bring this matter to the attention of all your members."

In his 1968 annual report the chairman, Dr Piet Meyer, made it clear that members of Parliament or MPCs who are Broeders should be asked for help. "Branches are increasingly approaching the Executive Council or the office to resolve local problems. In most cases branches have neglected to raise these matters through normal channels, Broeders who are their MPCs or MPs or officials on local authorities."

Evidence of direct links between the Prime Minister, his Cabinet and the Broederbond Executive is conclusive. Not only did Mr Vorster, when he was South Africa's Premier, attend Broederbond meetings, he held one in his official residence, Libertas. Cabinet Ministers attend Broederbond Executive Council meetings when policies affecting their departments are discussed. "Regular in-depth discussions about policy matters are held with Broeders in responsible circles (Cabinet) who are invited to attend Executive Council meetings."[1]

And further: "Many queries from branches to the Executive Council are referred to friends in responsible circles (Cabinet) and their replies are then relayed back to the branches." The compulsory meetings of interest and professional groups constitute a most important opportunity for Broeders to plan strategy and get together to fill vacancies. The purpose is stated quite bluntly in the secret documents: "These meetings are used to promote Afrikanerdom inside a vocational or interest group.[2] Central committees must take the initiative in getting together members of professional groups to discuss, separately from branch meetings, the promotion of the Afrikaner's interest in their town or city." The Executive Council or the professional or interest group can instruct members "to extend the influence of our organisation and serve the Afrikaner's interests more effectively."

The same circular says several meetings were held between Cabinet Ministers and the Bond whose views were considered sympathetically "on every occasion." More liaison is considered essential; the Broeders in the Cabinet should be asked "as a matter of urgency" to attend meetings and gatherings of the Broederbond.

It is the stated aim of the Broederbond to control every facet of South African life. Through their contacts the Broederbonders know in advance about the establishment and siting of new universities, hospitals, harbours, oil-from-coal plants and other important projects. In earlier years the secret Broederbond circulars contained advertisements for staff vacancies and the names of relevant officials. After this was leaked the practice was officially stopped, but by word of mouth at Broeder meetings and elsewhere it may be presumed to continue.

"Doctor for Merweville. Hopetown: doctor and attorney. Contact Broeder J A Wiid, P O Witput (1966). Holiday resort manager for Hartenbosch. Salary 7 200 x 450 – R9 900. Apply to Executive Director, ATKV, P O Box 4585, Johannesburg. Do not mention this organisation or our newsletter (1/10/77). A by-election for the Free State vacancy on the Medical Council will be held shortly. All doctors can take part. The name of Dr Izak J Venter of Bloemfontein has been mentioned as meriting support. Secretaries must inform doctor Broeders not present at the meeting" (1/9/77).

The secret October 1969 newsletter also revealed Broeder tactics influencing appointments in the public service. It warned Broeders in the civil service to be on their guard against public servants and magistrates "whose attitude is not right" and might have made "wrong recommendations" resulting in the appointment of "hostile persons". It exhorted them to "neutralise the negative influence" of officials who opposed public servants' membership of organisations such as Rapportryers. "Friends draw attention to the fact that it is expected of civil servants such as magistrates to make recommendations for certain appointments. Where the attitude of the officials is not right, wrong recommendations are often made and hostile persons are appointed. We should be on our guard against this. Such officials can also dissuade subordinates from joining Rapportryers and other Afrikaans organisations. Where such cases occur, appropriate action should be taken to neutralise the negative influence." The special relationship with the former Prime Minister is once again revealed in Circular 9/69/70. "The Executive Council regrets that serious embarrassment has been caused in this manner to our Prime Minister, especially in view of the fact that he is doing more than could be expected normally of a friend (member) in his position by attending meetings of our organisation and even holding a meeting at his home." The extension of the Broederbond's influence, and its deliberate policy of pursuing this at all times, was emphasised by the Reverend J H Jooste in September 1972. He was then chairman of the HNP and said General H J van den Bergh, as head of the Security Police, had handed in a list of policemen to be accepted as Broederbond members.

One of the most significant secret documents is the one calling on Broeders to use their influence to get the right people on the Bantu Administration Boards which regulate the lives of blacks in urban areas. "Because the composition of these boards is of such great importance in promoting the policy of separate development, friends (members) who are involved in these organisations (town councils, chambers of commerce and industry, agricultural organisations) *must use their influence to ensure that* well-disposed persons are nominated for the boards" (January 12 1973).

The Broederbond system of forming caucuses is often discussed in the secret documents. The Broeders push their members into top positions in organisations, and almost invariably they confer in secret before general meetings to decide how to steer the organisation and vote in their preferred office-bearers. In any organisation this tactic can be most effective as long as it does not conflict with the spirit of the organisation – which is most unlikely to happen because the Broeders tend to be articulate, intelligent, and superb organisers.

The practice was strongly condemned by Professor A van Selms, former professor of Semitic Languages at the University of Pretoria. In his pamphlet *Church and Secret Organisations,* with special reference to the Freemasons and the Broederbond, he pointed to the danger for the church arising from members of secret bodies being committed to prior decisions to fill posts with their own people and nominate speakers who would take a preordained line. Professor van Selms added: "There is no point in arguing or discussing matters with them at the meeting. They cannot talk and act in accordance with their own insight and conscience. They are bound before they come to the meeting."

An example of this pre-planning appears in a circular announcing: "An official meeting of the directors and members of the country's 22 Bantu Administration Boards will be held in Pretoria from October 21-24 1974. Broeders who are chairmen of boards are requested to make discreet contact with friend H P P Mulder[3] of the West Rand Administration Board. A letter of identification must be carried."

The caucus technique is again exemplified in connection with farming. "Some branches point out that some friends (members), and Afrikaners in general, fail to play active roles as office-bearers in agricultural co-operatives and on their boards of directors. Friends (members) are invited to use their influence to ensure that well-disposed and capable Afrikaners are elected to these boards. There is great anxiety among friends (members) in organised agriculture over the lack of concern and active participation of well-disposed people in the various agricultural organisations. These friends (members) point out that control of the managements and executive committees of organised agriculture was captured with great effort and sacrifice years ago, and it is disturbing to hear lately of subtle infiltration by hostile elements. It must be remembered that the rank and file choose the congress delegates and decide who will hold the reins at the top. Committees of branches in agricultural areas are cordially but urgently requested to investigate and ensure that matters are put right in good time through plain speaking. Chairmen should take the lead in this" (22/11/76).

The comprehensiveness of the Bond's interests is indicated by a selection of recommended contacts. "Divisional Council Congress, August 10 1971, East London. Contact B van Deventer of Riversdale (3/71/72). Further police training for Broeders at the S A Police College. Contact Dominee J G Odendaal (1/71/72). Public Service Association, October 20-21 1975, Port Elizabeth. Contact personally the secretary, Broeder R H Landman (7/75/76). Friends visiting Oshakati can contact Broeder J M de Wet, Commissioner-General and member of the Bond's Executive Council, or Broeder Kolonel W Schoon of the Security Police (1/6/77).

"Divisional Congress, August 16 1977, Burgersentrum, George. Friends (Broeders) are invited to a meeting on the evening of August 16. Please bring a letter of introduction to identify yourself (2/5/77). Divisional Council Congress, August 1963, East London (2/63/64).

"Medical Congress, July 1963, Johannesburg (2/63/64). Agricultural Union (3/63/64). Public Service Association (3/63/64). National Woolgrowers' Congress (3/63/64). Members attending the congresses can get names of contacts from the office. Give your membership number when inquiring by post. Branches in congress venues must send us a list of contacts as soon as possible. Contact must be made discreetly and letters of introduction are absolutely essential (3/63/64).

"Cape Municipal Congress, April 20-24, Port Elizabeth (1/64/65). Divisional Council Congress, Cape Town (4/71/71). Friends can contact friend R Barry of Calitzdorp or B van Deventer of Riversdale. A meeting of friends (members) will probably take place on the evening of August 12. Friends R v R Barry of Calitzdorp, A T de Bod of Oudtshoorn, B P Badenhorst of Springbok and B van Deventer of Riversdale will be the contacts.

"Craven Schools Rugby Week. Friends can contact P Krynauw of Transvaal (2/5/77). During Parliamentary sessions branches are urged to check that members of Parliament attend meetings, and report their attendance record. The link man, for years, until he becomes a Commissioner General, was Dr R McLachlan, MP for Westdene. South African Teachers' Union: contact Broeder B Naude, 9 Tuintseron Street, Paarl (Tel 2327). Annual meeting of the SA Society of Technical and Commercial Teachers from August 30-September 1, Johannesburg. Contact Broeder M J Smit van Rensburg. A letter of introduction must be shown to attend a meeting of Broeders (2/6/75). Congress of SA Society for the Advancement of Education, January 17-18 1974, Cape Town. Contact Dr J de le R Cilliers, the secretary treasurer.

"Broeders visiting Salisbury can contact Broeder T C de Klerk, director of the Genootskap van Regte Afrikaners. The offices of the GRA are at Gedenkgebou, Jameson Avenue, Salisbury, telephone 25484. Mr de Klerk's home phone is 55274."

Other documents are full of similar lists of contacts. For the purposes of this book, however, it is obviously impossible to include them all.

Particularly interesting is the special circular of March 1972 concerning the Cape Municipal elections. It is several pages long and devoted entirely to revealing just how the National Party is to capture most of the municipalities in the Cape Province. "1972 is municipal election year in the Cape. Determined planned action is urgently necessary to ensure control. This will demand of us interest, active participation, and the right talent! If we cannot rule at the basic level, where the country's policy is ultimately implemented, we will not be able to rule on the higher level.

"If the control of a town or city is in the hands of a well-disposed committee which administers effectively, it is obvious that a sound foundation is laid for favourable elections on higher government levels. It is equally important that central control over the Cape Municipal Association and the United Municipal Council will be in the right hands.

"A factor which escapes the attention of too many whites, especially Afrikaners, is the fact that the eventual success or failure of the policy of separate development and the preservation of Nationalist control will depend on the extent to which coloured people accept the policy and are prepared to help implement it. Apathy can be interpreted by coloured people as policy antipathy."

The document quotes a study by the National Party executive in the Cape as showing 31 municipalities and 23 divisional councils still under the control of the United Party.[4] "It must be borne in mind too that many councils considered to be Nationalist are poorly motivated and cannot be relied on to implement Government policy consistently and loyally. The position regarding controlling bodies is even more serious. The Executive Committee of the Municipal Association of South Africa is controlled by people who are not well-disposed to our political philosophy." Then there is a clear reference to Jewish participation, although the group is not named. "It is noticeable that certain other minority groups, generally very rich and of high intelligence, are very active in protecting their interests on the municipal level.

"Through vigorous participation they ensure that their interests and aspirations are well represented. They fill the vacuum left by us, and thus get much more than their fair share of influence over community matters – and also, as a bonus, the honour of wearing the chain of office fairly regularly."

All members are called to action, as are the Broederbond's financial institutions, organised agriculture, and commerce and industry where members are in control. These bodies are urged to make capable men available to fight the election, and to help them financially. A plan of action is suggested. (a) All "well-disposed" people must join the ratepayers' organisations in their areas. "The aim must be to get control of these bodies as soon as possible. This is of cardinal importance, because they usually nominate the official candidates." (b) Participation in the activities of the ratepayers' organisation must be strongly recommended. "Choose a few inspired leaders and let them stimulate the others. (c) "Registration of voters for the next election must immediately be planned in detail." A clever way is suggested to get a majority – ignore your opponents and register only your supporters. (d) Municipal council boundaries are decided on the new voters rolls. "In this connection we can play an influential part and have a golden opportunity for early and appropriate action, ensuring a delimitation that will favour the right candidates as much as possible. Especially important is the right distribution of well-disposed voters." (e) As much money as possible must be collected – lack of money must not prevent a favourable election result. (f) Suitable candidates must be found without delay, so that they have time to streamline their campaigns.

As shown by this relatively brief series of extracts from the secret Broederbond documents, the organisation's striving for influential positions on every decision-making body in South Africa is tireless and their methods extremely thorough. Their success in this respect is, therefore, hardly surprising.

1. Broederbond document, *Our Organisation*, circulated June 1974.

2. Ibid.
3. Manie Mulder, brother of the Minister of Plural Relations, Dr. Connie Mulder.
4. Then the official Opposition in Parliament, the United Party has since disbanded.

25 *Economic and Other Institutions formed by the Broederbond*

The Broederbond's aims crystallised over a number of years. It became clear to them that total control of South Africa could only be achieved if the Broederbond was successful in seven fields: strengthening its influence generally, so that the "cream" of Afrikanerdom would eventually become members; by getting control of the Afrikaner's cultural life; by dominating the Afrikaner's religious life; by controlling the public service and the teaching profession; by political control of South Africa, through the Afrikaner; by taking control of the Afrikaner worker; the economic upliftment of the Afrikaner.

Strengthening the Broederbond's influence was an ongoing process from the beginning. A delicate balance had to be maintained, recruiting more members without lowering standards. Because members took an oath not to reveal anything about the Broederbond, it became a safe haven in which members, by supporting each other, were pushed into top positions, sometimes not even knowing who did the pushing. If a non-member achieves a top position and is eligible in terms of their rules, they will try and draw him into their ranks. This will ensure that Broeders lower down can expect "protection".

The Broederbond has always realised that it would never be in a position to work in the open, because this would destroy the organisation. On the other hand, there was a strong need for public bodies, controlled by it, which would implement its aims. In some cases, Broeders took over control of existing bodies through effective organisation. In others, where there was a need for an organisation, they simply formed one, controlling it through their own people from the beginning and financing it, if this was necessary.

This was the case with the *Federasie van Afrikaanse Kultuurverenigings.* In 1928 the Broederbond consisted of only 12 branches and 263 members. The organisation was far too small to control Afrikaans culture, even if it was prepared to work in the open. There were scores of small cultural bodies all over the country which had to be brought under one umbrella for effective control. And this is exactly what the Broederbond did. In one fell swoop, it brought all those bodies under its wing, ensuring control in perpetuity.

It was the Broederbond secretary, Ivan Lombard, who took the lead in inviting all recognised Afrikaans cultural bodies to serve on an organising committee, which would arrange a national congress. The congress took place on December 18 and 19 1929 in Bloemfontein. The FAK was established with the aim of promoting Afrikaans and protecting the Afrikaner's own national culture.

As Professor Pelzer stated at the 50th anniversary: "The FAK was the creation of the Afrikaner Broederbond and the intimate relationship between the two organisations has progressed in an undiminished way since." There are more than 2 000 Afrikaans cultural organisations affiliated to the FAK. Its offices are in the Broederbond building, Die Eike. The Broederbond has sponsored an FAK magazine, *Handhaaf,* in which Broederbond policies are aired from time to time. Staff is sometimes exchanged between the two organisations. To give Dr Piet Koornhof a cover while he was secretary of the Broederbond, he was publicly known as cultural adviser to the FAK.

The top Broeders always know what is happening in the FAK because they sit on the highest bodies of the organisation. As has already been noted, however, the reverse is not true and Broeders are sometimes warned in circulars not to discuss Broeder affairs with some top FAK officials in Die Eike, because they are not all members. Many thousands of Afrikaners actively engaged in cultural affairs all over the country do not appear to be good enough to join the ranks of the Super-Afrikaners.

The Broederbond, directly or indirectly, through leading members, was also responsible for the establishment of cultural organisations for the hundreds of thousands of postal workers, railway workers, policemen etc. By controlling these bodies, and having the ultimate safeguard (firm control of the federal body, the FAK) the Broederbond had brought off a spectacular coup barely six years after it had got off the ground. It would be almost impossible to do anything about this situation now or in future years. The fate of all Afrikaans cultural organisations is firmly linked to the Broederbond.

For the youth, the Voortrekker movement was formed in opposition to the Boy Scouts and Girl Guides. The Broederbond desired a purely Afrikaans organisation. When asked what to do about the Voortrekkers, General J B M Hertzog, the former Prime Minister who attacked the Broederbond in public, said Afrikaans parents should leave their children in the organisation, but take the movement out of Broeder hands. This has proved impossible. The organisation is rife with Broeders, mostly teachers who are officers in the Voortrekkers. In some years the movement has even been helped financially by the Broederbond. The leader of the Voortrekkers is Mr J F Badenhorst, a top Broeder.

The Rapportryers, formed as an Afrikaans counter to Lions, Rotary etc, was also formed by the Broederbond, as was the Ruiterwag, the Bond's secret youth movement. These organisations make an ideal training ground for future Broeders. Young Afrikaners are involved in organisations where they can be carefully scruitinized for some years to see if they may qualify for the Broederbond's high standard of admission.

Another secret organisation, the *Afrikaner-Orde,* was disbanded on instruction of the former Prime Minister, Mr Vorster. The *Afrikaner-Orde* was formed in the forties by Dr Albert Hertzog and his supporters. They wanted to take control of the Pretoria City Council and formed a secret organisation in Pretoria to achieve this aim (see Chapter 11). It was never seen as opposition to the Broederbond, of which Dr Hertzog was an executive member for many years. The *Afrikaner-Orde* succeeded in getting a majority on the city council, and later had about 2 000 members. When Mr Vorster saw the split between himself and Dr Hertzog approaching he persuaded the Broederbond to agree that the *Afrikaner-Orde* should disband, before it became a dangerous weapon in the hands of the ultra rightwing Herstigte Nasionale Party. A compromise was reached: the *Orde* would disband and the names of its members would be submitted for Broederbond membership in the usual way. Mr Vorster's gamble worked, for out of the 2 000 members, less than 200 were accepted by the Broederbond.

What the *Afrikaner-Orde* experience did show was how relatively easily a secret organisation could take control – through routine elections – of a city. That is, of course, a microcosm of what the Broederbond itself has done in South Africa as a whole.

Another cultural organisation formed by the Broederbond, is the *Maatskappy vir Europese Immigrasie,* whose aim it is to Afrikanerise immigrants from Europe (see Chapter 8).

The *Afrikaanse Studentebond* to which most students at Afrikaans universities and teacher training colleges belong, was formed by leading Broeders, among them Dr Nico Diederichs and Dr Piet Meyer. They broke the hold of the National Union of South African Students (NUSAS) on Afrikaans campuses and replaced it with this purely Afrikaans organisation. The *Afrikaanse Studentebond's* organiser has offices in the Broederbond's headquarters at Die Eike, and the organisation is heavily under Broederbond influence.

Another organisation formed by the Broederbond was the South African Bureau for Racial Affairs (SABRA). It serves as a think-tank on racial matters, but strictly within the framework of the Government's policy of separate development. It organises youth camps for young high school leaders, where they are lectured on various aspects of Government policy. Through the discussions, they are able to keep a finger on the pulse of the thinking of Afrikaner teenagers. SABRA also organises symposia on Government policies; its staff give lectures at meetings and prepare publications for general consumption. Municipalities and other institutions become members and finance the organisation, although the Broederbond is always prepared to make up the shortfall in funds. The present chairman is a leading Broeder, Professor C H W Boshoff, son-in-law of the late Dr Verwoerd. The director, Dr C J Jooste, is also an active Broeder.

With its unique network of organisations, the Broederbond is in an excellent position to influence the Afrikaner youth and to select the best among them for future membership. From primary school level, it can keep watch on them, study their behaviour, their weaknesses and strengths. Primary school children get drawn into the Voortrekkers, who meet regularly every week and at weekend camps. The leaders among Standard V pupils are also picked for "survival camps". High school children may also belong to the Voortrekkers and leaders are picked for survival camps, leadership camps, and SABRA youth camps. University students can become Voortrekker officers, attend youth camps as teachers and belong to the *Afrikaanse Studentebond.* Post-university or young working Afrikaners can belong to one of the FAK's many affiliates or join the Rapportryers. The elite among them will be asked to join the secret Ruiterwag, the Broederbond's youth wing. This is an ideal training ground from which the Broeders can pick and choose members for the Bond. Through this careful observation, almost from the first day an Afrikaans child enters school, the Broederbond is assured of the best selection. It is almost impossible for them to overlook the budding young Super-Afrikaners after so many years of careful scrutiny.

The Broederbond has been directly responsible for the establishment of three institutions of higher learning in recent years: the *Goudstadse Onderwyskollege,* the first Afrikaans teacher training college in Johannesburg, the Rand Afrikaans University, likewise the first in Johannesburg, and the bilingual University of Port Elizabeth.

Port Elizabeth fell into the natural sphere of influence of Rhodes University at Grahamstown. It was therefore to be expected that Rhodes should look to Port Elizabeth as an area in which a satellite campus could develop and a branch was consequently established there. The instruction was obviously in English.

The Broederbond decided matters would be otherwise. They lighted on a clever ploy: a purely Afrikaans university was not feasible, because Port Elizabeth was not an "Afrikaner" city, and to replace the Rhodes branch by an Afrikaans university would have drawn too much criticism. What could be better than a *bilingual* university under Broederbond control?

In the same year that Rhodes established its Port Elizabeth branch (1961), leading Broeders in the Eastern Province held a secret meeting on a Steytlerville farm.[1] It was decided that Rhodes be closed down in Port Elizabeth and the Government be asked, for tactical reasons, to establish a bilingual university there instead.

The blow to Rhodes became public after Port Elizabeth's mayor, Mr Monty van der Vyver, had visited the Minister of Education, Senator Jan de Klerk, in Cape Town. Mr van der Vyver triumphantly announced in February that the Government had agreed to the establishment of a new university. Only later did Senator de Klerk's secretary write officially to Rhodes University to say the Cabinet had decided in principle to establish a dual-medium college in 1965.

The rector of the University of Port Elizabeth is Professor E Marais, who is on the Broederbond's Executive Council, and several leading Broeders serve on the university's council. The composition of the council does not reflect a 50-50 partnership between Afrikaans and English as was originally suggested. Even before the establishment of UPE, the Broederbond started secretly recruiting Afrikaans students for the new bilingual university.

"With a view to the establishment of a university in Port Elizabeth ... that especially friends (members) in the area use their influence so that as many Afrikaans students as possible enrol there. Friends (members) over the whole country can, of course, help in this" (secret Circular 2/6/64).

For many years, the anti-Government influence of the liberal University of the Witwatersrand had been a thorn in the flesh of the Broederbond. Furthermore, the massive Witwatersrand complex was without an Afrikaans university. As early as 1953, some leading Broeders had started striving for the establishment of an Afrikaans university. In the forefront was Dr Piet Meyer who felt far too many young Afrikaners were forced to attend the University of the Witwatersrand and that its influence should be countered.

In November 1963 a meeting was called to discuss a new Afrikaans university. It was attended by representatives of big Afrikaner businesses, local and provincial governments, education, religion and culture in Southern Transvaal. The meeting decided to proceed with the plans proposed, and once again had the support of the Minister of Education, Senator Jan de Klerk, himself a Broeder. Dr I J van der Walt said at the meeting: "It must have a Christian national basis to counteract the liberal character of the existing university on the Rand."[2]

Twelve of the fourteen members of the committee to approach the Government on the formation were Broeders. The committee consisted of the executive of the *Goudstadse Onderwyskollege* and representatives of the East and West Rand and the Vereeniging-Vanderbijlpark areas. The members of the executive were: the chairman, Dr Piet Meyer, also chairman of the joint committee, the SABC and the Broederbond; Mr J P van der Spuy, then MP, until 1961 Broederbond chief secretary and later Minister of Education; Ds J G Griessel of Linden, one of the Broederbond spokesmen at the NGK synod in April 1963; Mr Eben Cuyler, prominent Broeder, later a Senator; Mr A W Muller, principal of the college and Mr A Z Human, vice-principal, both Broederbond members; Mr J C van Tonder, a headmaster and also a Broederbonder. Four Broeders from other areas were elected: Dr P Koornhof, then Broederbond secretary; Ds C H W Boshoff, son-in-law of the late Dr Verwoerd; Dr J J van der Walt and Dr A J Visser, an Afrikaans businessman, later MP and Senator.

The result was the Rand Afrikaans University, the most modern university in South Africa, firmly under Broederbond control. Although the university has only 4 000 students, it was designed to cater for 50 000. Its ultra-modern library has computer links with renowned universities in the rest of the world and can trace even the most rare book in seconds. The chancellor of the university was the late Dr Nico Diederichs, former State President and chairman of the Broederbond. The chairman of Council, Dr Piet Meyer, is also chairman of the SABC and a former Broederbond chairman. The rector, Professor Gerrit Viljoen, is the present Broederbond chairman. The university this year awarded honorary doctorates to two leading Broeders, Mr Sybrand van Niekerk, Administrator of the Transvaal, and Mr J G H Loubser, head of the South African Railways.

The council of RAU is well stocked with Broeders and the staff list reads like a Broederbond "Who's Who".

The Auckland Park-Melville-Westdene complex in Johannesburg is now dominated by Broederbond-controlled institutions. Within a five-mile radius from the Broederbond headquarters, Die Eike, can be found: SABC, *Goudstadse Onderwyskollege,* Perskor, Rand Afrikaans University, J G Strijdom Hospital and *Vorentoe Hoërskool.*

In the sphere of trade unions, the Broederbond played a role in gaining control through the *Nasionale Raad van Trustees.* In taking over the Mineworkers' Union it managed to swing six constituencies on the Witwatersrand in 1948, thereby giving the National Party a majority (see Chapter 5).

One of the first problems facing the Broederbond in its early years was the fact that by 1938 there were 300 000 Afrikaners who could be termed "poor whites". After the emotional oxwagon trek, the Broederbond instructed the FAK to arrange the *Ekonomiese Volkskongres* (Economic National Congress). This took place in Bloemfontein from October 3–5 1939, and the young Dr H F Verwoerd, later Prime Minister, drew national attention for the first time through his participation.

According to a Broederbond document circulated in April 1969, the congress was later seen as "one of the most important milestones in the development of the history of the Afrikaner nation." It added: "Its greatest value was that it deflected the Afrikaner's eyes from his poverty and made him conscious of his great potential on the economic front."

It was at this congress that the Afrikaner discovered the key to success for his own economic upliftment: pool Afrikaner money, establish Afrikaner concerns, support Afrikaner concerns. They were told that if every Afrikaans family contributed only 25 cents, mighty financial power could be unleashed. With this aim in mind the *Reddingsdaadbond* was formed.

The April 1969 Broederbond circular states: "The strength of the *Reddingsdaadbond* was that it went to the nation with a new message and vision. It brought a message of strength to a nation which had almost become disheartened in its struggle against poverty. To a nation which regarded a position of economic subservience as almost natural, it presented the ideal of an Afrikanerdom which would not only be employee, but also employer, not only a foreigner in the economic life of his fatherland, but also the proud owner of material power, which rightfully belonged to him. Today, we can look back thankfully to the work of the *Reddingsdaadbond*. The work it did is indestructible and the tracks indelible."

The moving force behind the *Reddingsdaadbond* from which scores of Afrikaans businesses sprang, was Dr Nicholaas Diederichs, former chairman of the Broederbond, Minister of Finance and State President.

Nicholaas Diederichs was born at Ladybrand on November 17 1903. He went to school at Boshof and to the University College of the Orange Free State where he graduated MA. He studied in Europe at the Universities of Cologne, Berlin and Leyden and graduated D.Litt et Phil with distinction. On his return early in 1929, Dr Diederichs was appointed lecturer and in 1934, professor of political science and philosophy at the University College of the Orange Free State. In 1938, he returned to Europe for further study and returned to the University in 1939. He relinquished his professorship in 1940 when he was asked to become director of the *Reddingsdaadbond*.

In the first eleven years of its existence, the *Reddingsdaadbond* mobilised more than R30-million for Afrikaans business enterprises. Its operation was terminated in 1946. The number of Afrikaans businesses grew from 3 710 in 1939 to 13 047 in 1949. The turnover increased from £61-million to £322-million in a year. The *Reddingsdaadbond* was also instrumental in the establishment of the co-operative movement on the platteland and started two commercial high schools, later taken over by the State.

One of the Afrikaans business grants started by the Broeder-

The late Dr Nico Diederichs. Ex-State President and Broederbond chairman.

bond was *Volkskas. Volkskas (Koöperatief) Beperk* was formed by 55 Broeders, under chairmanship of the Broederbond chairman, Professor J C van Rooy, on April 3 1934. From its humble beginnings in a private home in Pretoria, it has grown into one of the top three banks in South Africa today. Its taxed pofit in 1977/78 was R16 828 000 and total group assets R2 923 000. All the Board members are Broeders: Dr J A Hurter (chairman), Dr A J du Toit, Dr J S Gericke, M V Jooste, A J Marais, Dr M D Marais, Dr T F Muller, Dr S J Naude (recently retired), Mr D C H Uys, Mr D P van Huysteen (managing director), Mr H O de Villiers, Dr Hilgaard Muller, Dr W C du Plessis (retired).

Federale Volksbeleggings, another Afrikaner giant in today's business world, was started by the Broederbond as a direct result of the *Ekonomiese Volkskongres.*

"The aim of the organisation was to pool a part of Afrikaner capital in one company, and to make it available for the establishment or takeover of commercial and industrial concerns."[3]

Its taxed profits in 1976 were R8,6-million, and its assets R500-million, and the top management are all Broeders: Dr P E Rousseau (chairman), Mr C J F Human (managing director). Directors are: Dr W B Coetzer, Dr W J de Villiers, S A Hofmeyr, Dr S J Naude, P J F Scholz and Dr A D Wassenaar.

Out of *Federale Volksbeleggings* emerged *Federale Mynbou,* which started with only R120 000 share capital. Mr Wennie du Plessis described in his book,[4] how he was instrumental in *Federale Mynbou's* establishment. After he had resigned from the civil service, rather than resign from the Broederbond, a choice given to him by Smuts, the Broederbond helped him financially. Broeders like Danie Malan, Professor S P E Boshoff and Willem van Heerden, editor of *Die Vaderland,* all offered him positions, but instead he and his brother bought a small coal mine. They were given financial assistance by *Federale Volksbeleggings,* which then established *Federale Mynbou.*

Another Broeder, Willem Heckroodt, deputy general manager of the Railways, made trucks available to transport coal to Lourenco Marques (Maputo). From there it was shipped to Ireland, their first consignment netting them £30 000. The great breakthrough for *Mynbou* came in 1957, however, when an Escom contract put them in a position to increase production by 300 per cent.[5]

Its biggest coup was in January 1965, when *Federale Mynbou* gained effective control of General Mining, one of the large gold mining companies. In 1974, it obtained 29,9 percent in Union Corporation, another gold mining group, and in 1976, its effective control in General Mining increased from 44 per cent to 62,7 per cent. Union Corporation became an affiliate of General Mining.

The annual turnover is R2 000-million, and the total assets R2 400-million. General Mining alone made an after-tax profit of R86,3-million in 1977/78. The Board of Directors also accommodates many Broederbond members, with Dr W B Coetzer as chairman.

Even Dr Anton Rupert's mighty Rembrandt Tobacco empire, now spread all over the world, had humble beginnings under Broederbond auspices. Older members still remember how Voorbrand Tobacco Corporation – Rembrandt's predecessor – distributed its products at Broederbond meetings.

"We were asked to smoke and cough for *volk* and *vaderland*," one of them told us with a chuckle.

In recent years, Dr Rupert wanted to resign from the Broederbond. He thought the Bond's narrow Afrikaans image would damage his image as an outgoing international businessman. Other Broeders speculated that he wanted to live in Switzerland, which was more centrally situated for effective control of his empire. However, Dr Piet Meyer, Broeder chairman at the time, went to see him and persuaded him to stay in the organisation.

The mergers between the two large Broederbond-controlled building societies, *Saambou* and *Nasionaal* into *Saambou-Nasionaal,* created another giant. Its assets are R629 161 000.

The managing director is a Broeder, Mr A J Marais. The new general manager, Mr C du P Kuun, was formerly on the staff of the Broederbond. Other Broeders on the Board of Directors are: Dr J A Hurter (chairman), Dr M A Marais, Dr P J Meyer, Dr Hilgaard Muller, Mr G J van Zyl, and Dr A J du Toit.

It is impossible, in a book which covers an extremely wide field, to describe the Broederbond's influence on Afrikaans business in full. It is almost a subject for a book on its own. Even the massive Sanlam group, although established before the Broederbond was well off the ground, did not escape its influence. It benefited immensely from the economic awakening and "support your own" spirit unleashed in Afrikanerdom by the Broederbond and as the Bond grew, its members slowly but surely took over top positions in Sanlam. The chairman, Dr A D Wassenaar, the retired managing director, Mr Pepler Scholtz, and the new managing director, Dr Wim de Villiers, are all members.

From Sanlam, Santam and *Federale Volksbeleggings,* grew a host of affiliates, with branches in virtually every aspect of business life.

It is one of the many wonders of the Afrikaner Broederbond that it could have achieved so much on the economic front in only a few decades. On that strength alone, it has proved to be an organisation unique in today's world, with superb secret organisation, strict discipline and a determination seldom seen in any other organisation in history.

1. *Sunday Times,* June 16 1963.
2. *Sunday Times,* November 10 1963.
3. Professor A N Pelzer, *Historical Review of the Afrikaner Broederbond,* 1968.
4. *Die Goue Draad – Op die Trekpad van 'n Nasie,* Afrikaanse Pers, 1970.
5. Chairman's review, June 1978.

26 *The Ruiterwag*

One of the Broederbond's prime objectives from its inception has been to capture the minds of young Afrikaners and harness them to the organisation's Christian National cause. This explains its obsession with holding key positions in education throughout South Africa. It was inevitable, then, that the Broederbond would establish a junior organisation. What is extraordinary is that the Broederbond's overwhelming compulsion to maintain secrecy extends to its own creations. The Broederbond's junior organisation does not know, and is not allowed to know, that it is totally controlled by "Big Brother".

The junior body, the Ruiterwag, was founded in Bloemfontein on September 4 1956 under the direction of Professor H B Thom, Rector of the University of Stellenbosch and then chairman of the Broederbond, Dr P J Meyer, head of the South African Broadcasting Corporation and a member of the Broederbond Executive (and later to become the longest serving chairman of the organisation to date), and three other members of the Executive Council: Professor S Pauw, Dr S J Naude and the late Professor J Keyter. On August 17 1957 the second Watchpost, as a Ruiterwag branch is called, was established in Johannesburg. By the end of 1974 there were more than 200 Watchposts across the face of South Africa.

Basically, the aims and objectives of the Ruiterwag are exactly the same as those of the Broederbond itself. Membership follows the same exclusive pattern of the parent body and is also by invitation only. Provided they can meet all the exclusive Afrikaner requirements laid down by the Broederbond, males who have left school and are between 18 and 28 years old can become members of the Ruiterwag.

The swearing-in ceremony of the Ruiterwag[1] bears a striking resemblance to that of the parent body. After the customary prayers and scripture readings, the initiation master reads the full name of the aspirant and says: "You appear here because you have indi-

Prof H B Thom. Ex-Broederbond chairman, now a university principal.

cated a desire to join the ranks of the Ruiterwag. Before you are told what is intended and what demands will be made of you as a Ruiter, you must in true good faith and sincerely undertake:

"Firstly, to maintain the strictest secrecy about all matters concerning the Ruiterwag that may come to your knowledge;

"Secondly, never to join or be associated with any other secret movement without the permission of the *Hoofwag* (Chief Guard);

"Thirdly, to submit yourself to instant expulsion if the executive decides you have failed in this binding undertaking in any way."

The ceremony continues on these lines.

INITIATION MASTER: If after what you have heard you have

doubt in your mind, you now have the chance to go in peace. No one will hold it against you. *(A few moments of silence.)*
INITIATION MASTER: By not leaving us, you have indicated that you remain firm in your intentions. It can now be revealed to you that the Ruiterwag was born out of the urge to help promote the freedom and self-determination of the Afrikaner nation in all spheres of life.

Because the youth of a nation is the fountainhead of its vitality and development, the Ruiterwag wishes to weld together with firm bonds of mutual trust and love of nation a hard core of picked young men prepared unconditionally to pledge their service to the people and to the honour of God.

You, accordingly, do not come here to seek recognition of actions or achievements in the past, but to offer yourself in unselfish service to the nation and to become a Ruiter on the Road of South Africa. There will be no exit from this road for you. The song of the progress of the Ruiterwag will always echo in your ears and out of the people's past will come the call: Be prepared, be faithful. For this you must know, that he only can become a Ruiter who measures up to these demands:
ASSISTANT INITIATION MASTERS *stand behind the aspirant and intone:*
SPEAKER A: To subscribe to the Protestant faith and honour it;
SPEAKER B: To accept his own nationhood and to maintain it as a responsibility imposed by God;
SPEAKER A: Firm in principle and strong in character;
SPEAKER B: Comradeship, a spirit of sacrifice, fidelity and self-discipline;
SPEAKER A: To be able to give responsible leadership, and also to be able to subject himself to well-considered leadership.
INITIATION MASTER: Are you prepared to carry out these principles and faithfully to base all your actions on them? *(Gives the candidate's full name).* What is your answer?
ASPIRANT: Yes.
INITIATION MASTER: Because very rigorous demands are made of members of the Ruiterwag, it is necessary that you should carefully consider what is expected of a Ruiter.
SPEAKER A: The Ruiterwag wants you to remain always honest and true to the highest Afrikaner traditions;
SPEAKER B: The Ruiterwag wants you to strive always for unity among all right-thinking Afrikaners;

SPEAKER A: The Ruiterwag wants you to be faithful in the smallest things, and in your labours to seek only your due;
SPEAKER B: The Ruiterwag expects you faithfully to attend every meeting of your Wagpos *(Watchpost or branch)* and to co-operate actively with other Ruiters in a spirit of genuine unity and comradeship;
SPEAKER A: The Ruiterwag expects that you will submit yourself to such censure and discipline as the executive may have to apply under the standing orders.
INITIATION MASTER: You now know the significance of the choice which you must make, and you have another chance to consider these high demands. If you cannot face this call and this task, then you had better depart in peace. *(A few moments of silence.)*
INITIATION MASTER: Now that you have had plenty of time to consider your decision, you are asked to give the following undertakings:
To serve God and your people faithfully to the death without expecting honour or reward;
To maintain the utmost secrecy about all Ruiter matters;
Never to join or to co-operate with other secret organisations without the permission of the Hoofwag;
Always to carry out the instructions of those set above you and to work honestly, faithfully, and in good heart with all other Ruiters;
To regard all your promises as binding unto death, no matter what punishment is meted out to you and even if you are deprived of membership.

Do you solemnly and unconditionally promise this in the full realisation of the seriousness of your promises? *(Gives the candidate's full name.)* What is your answer?
ASPIRANT: Yes
INITIATION MASTER *(intones):*
The struggle that our fathers began,
Will rage till we have died or won,
That is the oath of Young South Africa.[2]

A Ruiter's membership lapses when he turns 33. Obviously, the Ruiterwag provides fertile recruiting grounds for the Broederbond, but membership of the junior organisation does not guarantee admission to its elite ranks. Former Ruiters have to go through the same recruitment process as any other candidate before they can join the Super-Afrikaners.

The Ruiterwag's organisational structure is a carbon-copy of the Broederbond's. Branches are called Watchposts, there is the equivalent of an Executive Council, and there is a congress every two years known as the Watch Council *(Wagraad)* to elect a president and a president's council. There is a minimum of two Broeders on the president's council.

At each Watchpost there is a Chief Guard and it is mainly through him that the Broederbond exercises control.

A document entitled *The Ruiterwag* was circulated to Broeders in November 1974. "The power to nominate Chief Guards," it said, "rests exclusively with the Executive Council (Ruiters believe that nominations come from the Council of Chief Guards). The Chief Guard, who must always be a member of the Broederbond, must take a vital interest in youth and have special knowledge of youth or have close association with youth, must be equipped to assume leadership, and must also be prepared to devote time and energy to the interests of the Ruiterwag ...

"The Chief Guard must be older than the Ruiters, but young enough in spirit to involve himself in the interests, concerns and aspirations of the youth. The Chief Guard must regard his office as a position of exceptional trust, associated with the highest responsibility, and in his duties he must at all times remain conscious of the Broederbond's aims for the Ruiterwag. At the same time he must beware of imposing his own outlook, desires, ambitions and personality. He must, on the contrary, strive to encourage the Ruiters' own initiative, decisiveness and leadership."

The document goes on to describe how Watchposts are in practice established by Broederbond branches who report to the Executive Council that the necessary potential exists in their areas. The Executive Council appoints Chief Guards and Assistant Guards *(Hulpwagte)* from Broeders nominated by the branches.

To co-ordinate the grand design for the Ruiterwag, the appointed Broeders assemble in the Council of Chief Guards. This body meets separately when a Watch Council meeting takes place every other year. It acts on behalf of the (Broederbond's) Executive Council, "although the Executive Council actually has final say in all matters that involve the Ruiterwag."

The Council of Chief Guards elects an executive of three members who can co-opt other members if necessary. If the president of the Ruiterwag is a Broeder, as is usually the case, he also has a seat on the executive. One of the recent Ruiterwag presidents was a prominent Broeder, Mr Dawie de Villiers, National Party

MP for Johannesburg West and a popular former Springbok rugby captain. It is the task of the executive of the Chief Guards to advise the Broederbond Executive Council on all matters relating to the Ruiterwag.

The Broederbond document continues with its explanation of how it maintains control over the Ruiterwag. "The Chief Guard acts as a link between the Broederbond and the Ruiterwag, without this ever being made known to the Ruiterwag. It is thus necessary that the Chief Guard serves on the executive of his (Broederbond) branch, where there is only one branch and one Watchpost in a town or area. Where there is one Watchpost in an area with more than one (Broederbond) branch, the Chief Guard serves on the executive of the (Broederbond) Central Committee.

"The Chief Guards must ensure that the greatest measure of cooperation is achieved between the Broederbond and the Ruiterwag, without the Ruiters realising they may be included in a larger plan of action. The extent of liaison between the Broederbond and the Ruiterwag was discussed comprehensively at the 1973 (Ruiterwag) Watch Council. The then president presented this declaration, which was drawn up in consultation with the (Broederbond) Executive Council.

'"I am often asked if there is any official liaison between these organisations. In this connection, I can give this answer frankly and with the knowledge and approval of the Broederbond leadership. Although these two organisations in many respects have common concerns, the Ruiterwag exists independently and separately from the Broederbond.

'"There is contact and liaison at the highest level between the two organisations: between the President's Council, through the president, and the Broederbond leadership. At all other levels, the two organisations maintain complete confidentiality towards each other. For the sake of complete clarity, I want to repeat: the two organisations exist independently. There is, therefore, in no respect an overlap of membership from one to the other.

"'The Broederbond is, just like the Ruiterwag, completely autonomous in the admission of its members, and applies its own criteria for recruitment. To sum up, we can put it like this: we are independent spiritual partners. Let us each in his own area and in his own way, with sacrifice and application, serve that goal which is greater than people or organisations.

"'In the light of these comments, a question arises about the

Ruiterwag's influence on external activities. Just because the President's Council liaises with the Broederbond at high level, it must not be inferred that this represents any channel of authority to the outside whereby the Ruiterwag can exercise any influence ... I would like to repeat: the President's Council, by the very nature of the Ruiterwag as a secret organisation, has no external authority. The power of the Ruiterwag arises, as far as I am concerned, from the activities of its members. The Ruiterwag is just as strong, vigorous and influential as its members.

"'Nevertheless we can, with a view to further discussion, make these points in connection with liaison. (1) It is possible for the President's Council to direct requests or make recommendations on behalf of the (Ruiterwag) to the Broederbond. As an independent organisation the Broederbond is, however, in no way bound to take action on this... This channel of action is not the most effective for the Ruiterwag.

"'(2) Consideration can be given to empowering the President's Council, where it is in the interests of the Ruiterwag, to liaise with former members in key positions. (3) The President's Council can be given authority, in highly exceptional cases ... to negotiate with any person whose integrity is above suspicion.'"

The deceptions in this denial are breathtaking. The claim that the two organisations are independent of each other is incorrect. From the inception of a Ruiterwag Watchpost, the Broederbond is in control. The very document which contains this passage disclaiming any significant interaction, details the machinery that exists to enable the Broederbond to pull all the strings in the Ruiterwag.

To claim there is no overlap in membership is also incorrect. In fact, the very president who was making the declaration was a member of the Broederbond, Dawie de Villiers. All the Chief Guards of the Ruiterwag have to be Broeders, and at least two members of the Ruiterwag President's Council ... and, according to the Broederbond document, "usually the majority" are members of the Broederbond.

The Ruiterwag also has to report to the Broederbond Executive Council. One such report was submitted on May 25 1967. It was a family affair, symbolising the close links between the two organisations. The report is signed by the Chief Secretary of the Ruiterwag, I A Meyer. His father was none other than Dr Piet Meyer, at that time Chairman of the Broederbond Executive Council receiving the report. Young Meyer's report inter alia thanks the Broederbond Executive for its continuing financial help. "From the financial statement it is clear that the salaries and travel costs of the officials, as well as the office rent and the travel allowances made available to the Watchposts, are not paid for by the Ruiterwag. Accept for this our special thanks."

At that stage the average age of the Ruiterwag's 1 300 members was 27,9 years. Teachers made up the bulk of the members. There were 240 of them, followed by 172 clerks in the public or private sectors, 141 students, 76 farmers, 73 professors and lecturers, 58 ministers of religion, 43 secretaries and accountants, 37 lawyers, 133 engineers, 27 salesmen and 21 agriculturalists. There were 18 Ruiters in the South African Defence Force, 16 in the South African Broadcasting Corporation, 10 working in municipalities, 10 policemen, five in the prisons service, five journalists, and two members of Parliament. Like its parent body, the Ruiterwag also has front organisations: the Junior Rapportryers, "whose secretariat is managed by us," the report says.

Apart from these manifestations of interlocking activity between the two organisations, the Broederbond is also actively involved in recruiting for the Ruiterwag. The Broederbond document *The Ruiterwag* instructs Broeders to keep an eye out for promising young men and pass names on to the Broederbond secretariat for transmission to the Ruiterwag's secretariat.

There is, however, a measure of confidentiality between the two organisations at grassroots level. The Broederbond document on the Ruiterwag says: "As the confidential nature of the membership and activities of the Ruiterwag is strongly impressed upon Ruiters, it is not right and would seriously jolt their faith if members of the Broederbond ... in some thoughtless way let it be known that they were aware of young men's Ruitership. To eliminate this risk it is essential that the names of Ruiters are not revealed to (Broederbond) branches."

To further protect the Broederbond-Ruiterwag relationship, there are strict guidelines for fathers who become aware that their sons are Ruiters. Open discussions of the two organisations' activities are strictly forbidden. They would constitute a breach of confidentiality that would be "regarded by the Executive Council in a most serious light," adds the document.

If a branch inadvertently starts recruiting a Ruiter when it already has one Broeder with dual membership, the Chief Guard in his double-agent role must instruct the branch to halt the recruitment process. This practice of dual membership again exposes the flaw in the Broederbond's declaration about the Ruiterwag. In fact, the document goes on to say that while dual memberships ought to be limited they are sometimes necessary.

Certainly a Ruiter who becomes a Broeder must not resign his junior membership too suddenly, "as this raises too many questions among his Ruiter colleagues and also unnecessary doubts about his integrity."[4]

The move across from membership of the Ruiterwag to membership of the Broederbond is done with typical caution and stealth. When a Ruiter reaches 33 he must resign. As this age approaches, years earlier in some cases, the path to the Broederbond is prepared. Discreetly the Chief Guard who serves on the branch Executive of the Broederbond can start directing their attention towards a promising prospect. But only when the branch has made a formal proposal can the Chief Guard reveal that the prospective member is a Ruiter. This is attractive to the branch, because he does not count in their regular annual quota of two new members.

1. Vatcher, W H, *White Laager*, pp 285-287.
2. Jong Suid-Afrika (Young South Africa) was the original name of the Broederbond.
3. Broederbond document, *The Ruiterwag*.
4. Ibid.

27 *Conclusion*

On October 3 1978, early in the morning, the quiet main road between Hartebeespoort Dam and Brits, north of Johannesburg, began to carry an unusually heavy amount of traffic. Cars bearing registration numbers from all parts of South Africa streamed along the road. In each car, dressed in dark suits, were two, three, sometimes four or five men. Some wore hats, some were bareheaded. The cars were mostly expensive models. Mercedes Benz and BMW were particularly favoured makes. As the time moved on toward 8.00 a.m., the unseasonal traffic began to reach a peak. Local inhabitants, taking their children to school, or heading off towards their rural occupations, stared in amazement at the unaccustomed sight.

The stream of cars moved from all directions to a focal point, where they swung off the tarred road, passed between two stout gates set into a heavy-security fence, and were swallowed up in the dense bush on the other side. An onlooker, peering intently beyond the gates, might have perceived through the dust of the assembling cars, a checkpoint manned by two men. Each car stopped at the checkpoint, while its occupants allowed some sort of document to be scrutinised, before receiving the satisfied nod of one of the guards to send it on its way once more. The onlooker would see no more as the cars disappeared one by one over the brow of a hill a short way beyond the entrance.

By 8.30, the stream had dried to a trickle as a few late-comers dribbled into the gates. Before 9.00 a.m., the most regular user of the rural road would have not the slightest inkling that nearly 1 000 sombrely dressed men were gathered unseen in their midst.

Meanwhile, a little later in the same day, across at the Union Buildings in Pretoria 50 km away, a new South African Prime Minister presided over his first Cabinet meeting. There, too, cars arrived and disgorged their occupants who, clutching their briefcases, mounted the wide concrete steps and disappeared through the portals of power.

The two apparently unconnected events had important common factors. The new Prime Minister, Mr P W Botha, presiding over his Cabinet colleagues, is a member of the organisation that had mysteriously gathered 50 km away, as are most of the men who sat around the table with him that morning. The organisation is, of course, the Broederbond.

Both meetings, in different ways, were manifestations of Afrikaner power. With only one exception, the Cabinet consists of Afrikaners wielding power granted them by the white South African electorate. With no exceptions, the Broederbond meeting was a gathering of Afrikaners. The power of the two organisations assembling that morning is mutually dependent. Mr Botha must be acutely aware that, even if he chooses to maintain a more distant relationship with the Broederbond than have his predecessors, he cannot afford to alienate himself from it. To do so would be to antagonise an organisation of influential individuals that could easily concert a nationwide backlash of well-placed Afrikaners, whose Broeder loyalties and discipline would transcend any loyalty to one renegade. Likewise, the Broederbond is aware that, for the continued achievement of its aims, a sympathetic Prime Minister and Cabinet is important. If the Broeder-Cabinet relationship continues on traditional lines, the two will slot comfortably side-by-side into an intimate liaison, exerting an horizontal influence on each other, each mutually aware of the strength and importance of the other and respectfully aware of their shared constraints.

By the end of that day, however, one of the partners in that relationship had been jarred by an intrusion into its carefully protected secrecy. The sombrely-dressed Broeders arriving at the organisation's bushveld shrine, a 100 hectare meeting place, dominated by a huge hall built like a modern Dutch Reformed Church, were shocked to be confronted at the gates by two parked cars containing a team of *Sunday Times* journalists, gathered there as a result of information in the authors' possession. As each car entered the gates, its registration number was recorded. In turn, the newspapermen's car registration numbers were taken. They were also placed under surveillance by uniformed army personnel manning a military radio from a civilian mini-bus. One of the *Sunday Times* cars was followed most of the way back to Johannesburg.

Later in the day, the authors and a photographer flew over the secret venue in a helicopter. On their first circuit of the meeting place, a handful of Broeders emerged from the church-like hall

The Broederbond's top-secret, purpose-built conference centre photographed from a Johannesburg Sunday Times *helicopter during the 1978* Bondsraad.

and peered upwards. When the helicopter came round again, they had returned to their meeting.

The unwelcome attention evoked an unusual response. That night the Broederbond issued a statement to the Press,[1] announcing that it had met. The theme of the meeting had been *The Battle Preparedness of the Afrikaner.* Papers were delivered on the following subjects:

The total onslaught against South Africa in the international field;
The struggle for the spirit of the Afrikaner;
Activation of the youth;
The quality of the Afrikaner's cultural contribution in this battle.

Among other things, it was decided to publish a scientific-historical study of the first 50 years of the Broederbond (1918–1968). The study had been written by Professor A N Pelzer of the University of Pretoria.

To the general Press, unaware that the *Sunday Times* had been monitoring the meeting, it was an unexpected windfall to receive a statement from the Broederbond. One newspaper had posters up all over Johannesburg, proclaiming that the Broeders had come into the open. They did not realise then that they were playing a role in a clever tactical move by the Broederbond to take the wind out of the sails of the Sunday exposé they knew was coming. The following afternoon, *The Star* carried a report saying the "highly secretive Afrikaner Broederbond has taken the first step to bring its activities more into the open." It quoted the Broederbond chairman, Professor Gerrit Viljoen, as saying it would be a "reasonable assumption" that the organisation was moving more into the open. But he immediately cast shadows of doubt on that assumption when he said although there were various reasons for this new openness he did not wish to discuss them.

The announcement that the organisation would publish its own book was another tactical move – to counter *this* book, the pending publication of which had been reported in two Afrikaans newspapers at that time. The tactic adopted showed an unusual, but not entirely new, approach by the organisation to breaches of its secrecy. But Professor Viljoen's refusal to discuss the very factors which led to this supposed candour reveals the extent of the reformation. All the Broederbond really announced in that statement was what it knew three million *Sunday Times* readers were going to be told five days later. It is the authors' opinion that when the heat of this exposé, and the publicity that will accompany it has cooled, the Broederbond will pursue its path of secrecy as energetically as before. That is certainly the pattern of the past.

It has been its custom to respond to exposure to scrutiny by ignoring it completely in the correct belief that, eventually, the publicity, operating by its design into a vacuum, will fizzle out. Past practice has been to quietly ride out the storm, while it effects an internal repair job. This has entailed setting itself new targets, like an immediate increase in membership to prove to its members that Afrikaners were not antagonistic to the organisation, and would jump at the opportunity of accepting an invitation to join.

This was aimed at morale boosting inside the organisation and will probably be done again. Organisationally, new improved methods of secrecy were invariably introduced, such as delivery of correspondence by hand for some time after the exposures. Activities were accelerated to keep members' attention fully occupied. Thus, after the 1963 exposés, the Executive set a target of R1-million for the Christiaan de Wet Fund by 1968. This was achieved and served the useful purpose of diverting attention from public criticism of the organisation's workings.

"Treason" committed by members in giving away secrets, is felt deeply in the Broederbond. One gets the impression that, after the initial outburst of anger, an atmosphere of almost religious mourning descends on the members. It is like a death in the family. One of the Broeders – one of the hand-picked Super-Afrikaners – has betrayed them. The unthinkable has happened, in spite of all the stringent secrecy measures and oaths before each other and God. Far from trying to understand why a Broeder would do such an "ungodly" thing, they dismiss him as a "traitor", to be banished to an Afrikaner Limbo. To them, the organisation cannot be wrong, because it is a gift from God. It is during this time that the organisation's inner strength and the belief in its calling, carried the members through the crisis.

At the first subsequent *Bondsraad* meeting, delegates from all over the country might take part in a symbolic exercise to reaffirm their loyalty to each other in the face of the "treason." Around a campfire under the starlit bushveld sky, they might revive an old Afrikaner tradition by piling rocks one on top of the other into a rugged cairn. In this emotion-laden gesture, Broeders have, in the past, cemented a new bond of determination and spiritual strength. After singing the *Bondslied* and the National Anthem, they go their separate ways, renewed, leaving behind their primitive, crude monument.

Another tactic the organisation has employed to patch up cracks in its defences, is to make members swear a new oath of allegiance, reconfirming their absolute loyalty to the principles of the organisation. They have done this twice in the past, and on both occasions only relatively few members declined, thus cutting themselves adrift from the Broederbond ranks. The oath thus serves a dual purpose: it strengthens the resolve of the members who elect to take it and, at the same time, calls those who may have been harbouring doubts for years, but who never had an opportunity to retire gracefully.

Whatever the tactics used on each respective occasion of crisis, the one immutable factor has remained the organisation's will to sustain itself in secrecy. Many Afrikaners will concede that against the historical background outlined in this book there probably was a need for an organisation like the Broederbond in the twenties. But today, they argue, the Afrikaner has political control, he can protect his language and is making vast economic progress. There is no doubt that the vast majority of Afrikaners would like the Broederbond to become an open cultural organisation. In a scientific study of attitudes of whites in the upper-income bracket, only 26 per cent of National Party supporters rated the Broederbond as "advantageous" to society, 15 per cent regarded it as "detrimental", 19 per cent noted a "mixed" reaction and 37 per cent declined to answer the question.[2]

The question whether the Broederbond should drop its secrecy has been mentioned from time to time in the organisation, but never very seriously. The former chairman, Dr Piet Meyer, once speculated on the possibility that the Broederbond could "take the Afrikaner into its confidence" to tell them what it has achieved – and to ask them for help to raise the Christiaan de Wet Fund to R10-million. Nothing has ever come of this. One of the founders, Mr Henning Klopper, expressed the horror of the Broederbond leaders even at the thought of opening the organisation.

At the 1968 *Bondsraad* meeting, he said: "Earlier today, there was reference to the question asked by many: has the Broederbond not reached its aim with the attainment of the Republic? Has the time not, perhaps, arrived, that we can disband or retire, to let things develop naturally? If that is so, Broeders, we must ask ourselves: Who will give us the Government of the country? Who will give us the future Prime Ministers? Who must form them? Where must they come from? Where will we find them . . . Dare somebody still ask the question: has the Afrikaner-Broederbond not served its purpose? He dare not ask such a question! No Broeder dare ask such a question! Remove the Afrikaner-Broeder from the life of Afrikanerdom, and what remains . . And who is the Republic? It is the Afrikaner-Broederbond's Broeders."

In 1972 calls were made by the Afrikaans newspapers, *Die Vaderland* and *Rapport,* for the Broederbond to drop its secrecy. Both calls were very tentative, published once, and never pursued with any vigour. In the same year, the veteran political commentator, Schalk Pienaar's membership was revealed. Mr Pienaar wrote that this had caused him acute embarrassment. He posed the question whether the Broederbond, because of an over-emphasis on secrecy, is not itself to blame for the fact that so much scandal is circulated about it.

"The point is that in the general Afrikaner life, there is a weighty question mark hanging over the Bond. The right or wrong of the question mark can be discussed, but the fact of the question mark cannot be reasoned away." Pienaar said the belief existed that members of the Bond possessed powers and privileges in which Afrikaners of equally high rank did not share. Together with this belief was the idea that the Bond was in a position to dictate Government policy and action in the life of the Afrikaner.[3]

But the Broederbond never took serious note over the concern about its secrecy – because secrecy is its greatest weapon, as it admits itself. As recently as 1976, Professor Gerrit Viljoen said in his chairman's address: "We can state unambiguously that South Africa and the Afrikaner never needed the Afrikaner Broederbond more than today."

It is clear, therefore, that it is wishful thinking to expect the Broederbond to change its role and drop its secrecy. It has been effective because it operated in secrecy, and its members were protected by it. Very little of what they had done, as described in this book could have been achieved if their members had operated openly. The Broederbond's stock reply is: What about the Freemasons, or the Sons of England? This book concerns the Broederbond, and is based on factual material. Perhaps such factual material about the Freemasons and the Sons of England could form the basis of studies by other writers in future.

Two myths about the Broederbond have now been exposed. Firstly, the claim that it is a purely cultural organisation. Why the obsession with secrecy if it is an innocent cultural organisation, and why can every Afrikaner who means well with his language and culture not become a member? One is amazed, in fact, in studying the documents on how little time the Broeders spend on purely cultural affairs. Almost none of today's important Afrikaans authors – the bearers of the language and culture – belong to the organisation. It was for the express purpose of looking after the Afrikaner's cultural interests that the FAK was formed by the Broederbond. This left them free to give attention to almost every other aspect of South African life, and to put the Broederbond stamp firmly on the Republic they created.

Secondly, that the Broederbond is not involved in politics. The influence of the Broederbond and its interference in politics is proved beyond doubt in this book. The evidence was supplied by the Broederbond itself – in its own secret documents. There is also a naive belief in some circles that the Broederbond has lost its influence. We could find no evidence of this. On the contrary, the Broederbond appears as strong and influential as ever. A new Nationalist Prime Minister and State President have just been elected. No Nationalist can become Prime Minister if he is not a Broeder – neither can he rule the country effectively without the organisation's support.

There is no doubt that the Broederbond could, theoretically at least, be an influential *verligte* force, working for change in the country. It has the brainpower in its ranks and through its think-tanks and unique organisation in the remotest corners of the country, the way to influence public opinion. The present chairman, Professor Viljoen, is also more pragmatic than his predecessors. The problem lies in the history and make-up of the Broederbond. Since its formation, the Broederbond developed an obsession with Afrikanerdom, that it must be protected, promoted and that it must rule. Shortly after that, a new obsession – separation of the races – came to the fore. On these two pillars, the Bond moulded itself and recruited members around it. The importance of education and religion in moulding the minds of the people necessitated heavy recruitment in these areas. The result is that the preponderance of members come from the most conservative elements of Afrikaner society – teachers, ministers of religion, and farmers.

They cannot, and have no wish to, make any significant changes. Every prerequisite for "change" in Broederbond documents is that it must take place within the framework of separate development. There is not a single exception to be found anywhere. The *verligtes,* like Professor Viljoen and others, are captives of a situation. The whole organisation and its membership was built on *verkrampte* pillars, and there is very little room in which to manoeuvre. This book is full of evidence of just how *verkramp* the Broederbond is, and the time test for Professor Viljoen's *verligtheid* would be for him to state in public with just how many of these Broederbond pronouncements he disagrees.

A reader of the *Rand Daily Mail* wrote:

"*Surprise Verligte*

I find it surprising that Professor Gerrit Viljoen, Rector of Rand Afrikaans University, is cast in a *verligte* mould by the RDM.[4] Here is a man with a Broederbond background owing his position to Broederbond backing and dedicated to maintaining permanent division in the ranks of South Africans through separate institutions from cradle to grave.

"This man regards it as a great mistake to impose on blacks a policy worked out by whites alone, yet goes on to assure us there can be no power sharing and that Afrikaners will insist on separate schools (for themselves) and separate residential areas (for all whites).

"His million-dollar question: 'How do Afrikaners maintain

their identity if they lose power?' has an obvious answer – by making themselves loved instead of disliked by others, and by accepting others as equal South Africans. Both of these concepts, however, are foreign to the Broederbond."

The future of South Africa is inevitably tied up between Afrikaner nationalism and black nationalism. In Afrikaner nationalism, the Broederbond plays the dominant role – a role Inkatha is progressively filling in black nationalism. Inkatha was formed in 1928, ten years after the Broederbond; both claim they are cultural organisations. While Inkatha was dormant for years, and was only revived in recent times by Chief Gatsha Buthelezi, the Broederbond worked day and night to take control of the country. The difference now is that Inkatha has to work in the open and will probably be banned if it becomes a secret organisation. Like the Broederbond, Inkatha is heavily involved in politics and in the end the crucial question for South Africa may well be whether these two organisations can reach political accommodation which would satisfy both sides. It seems an unlikely prospect.

In fact, any kind of political accommodation seems an unlikely prospect while the Broederbond continues to play such an influential role in the affairs of South Africa. Nationalist politicians are fond of repeating, correctly, from public platforms that South Africa is a plural society, a society of various cultures and races. They earnestly tell their public audiences, correctly, that any solution to South Africa's complex problems must take account of this political reality. Yet how much confidence can one place in the sincerity of their proclaimed desire to find an equitable accommodation for all the elements of the population, when one knows that they are secretly pledged to serve the exclusive interests of Afrikanerdom? How much faith can there be in their public utterances of conciliation, when one knows, or suspects, that in secret conclave the real commitment remains Afrikaner domination? It seems inevitable that while the Broederbond lurks beneath the political surface in South Africa, any moves towards dialogue will be fraught with suspicion and mistrust.

Doubts are placed on much-vaunted exercises like the recent meetings between Professor Viljoen and Dr Nthato Motlana, the prominent Sowetan political figure. Rightly or wrongly, there will be unavoidable doubts about the real significance of such talks. On the one hand, the man with whom they are dealing is recognised as a leading Afrikaner academic, described as a *verligte*. On the other hand, they know they are dealing with a man who heads a secret organisation, which firmly subscribes to, and was at least partly responsible for, the policy of apartheid which they equally firmly reject. Rightly or wrongly, doubts can hardly be expected to be dispelled when, shortly after such talks at the Rand Afrikaans University, Dr Motlana was banned from addressing a meeting at the University of the Witwatersrand. Can any move by the Government be taken at face value, or should it be judged in terms of the National Party's overwhelming membership of a secret organisation striving for Afrikaner interests?

When the Afrikaans Church pronounces on matters of national importance, is it influenced by the Broederbond, to which most of its leaders belong? When appointments or promotions are made, are they straightforward rewards of competence and diligence, or is some secret nepotism at work? However unkind, unwarranted, or misguided such questions may in fact be, they will continue to exist as long as any secret presence is known to be flourishing beneath the troubled surface of South African society. The authors agree with the observation of Dr Brian du Toit, who in a sociological study dealing with the role of secret societies in various parts of the world, came to the following conclusion:

"A closed, or semi-closed organisation, originates in order to fulfil a need in the society. When, however, the crisis is past, this organisation must dissolve; otherwise, it grows like a cancer in the society and causes internal dissension and feelings of suspicion, injustice and hostility among those who are frustrated."[5]

If the hope of a lasting peaceful political solution for South Africa is to have any prospect of achievement, many grotesque distortions, historical, sociological, economic and political, will have to be overcome. It is a formidable task for a country whose reserves of human goodwill are already stretched. When to those distortions are added the dimensions of mistrust and suspicion, the hope enters the realm of wishful optimism – at best, an unreliable agent for success.

1. SAPA, October 3 1978.
2. Van der Merwe, H W, Ashley, M J, Carton, N C J, Huber, B J, *White South African Elites*, p 146.
3. *Rapport*, September 24 1972.
4. *Inside Mail*, August 1 1978.
5. *Beperkte Lidmaatskap*, p 2.

"The Afrikaners ... did have a tough time, they did have a struggle, they did make a remarkable comeback, they are indisputably on top – but somehow they have got to get over their feelings of vindictive triumph about it and stop being as arrogant and brutal as they can be in their worst moments. In their best moments there are no nicer ... people. But they have got to relax. Nobody can make them do it, it will have to come from within. It may pay the Broederbond to issue a directive, because it is time for them to begin to show a little maturity... That, too, is one of the few genuine ways to create national unity. They can't get it with the basic attitude too many of them still cling to."

Allen Drury, *A Very Strange Society*

Selected Bibliography

1. Brotz, H, *The Politics of South Africa: Democracy and Racial Diversity,* Oxford University Press, 1977.
2. Cronje, G A, *'n Tuiste vir die Nageslag,* Publicite Handelsreklamediens, 1945.
3. De Klerk, W A, *The Puritans in Africa,* Pelican Books, 1976.
4. Du Plessis, W C, *Die Goue Draad – Op die Trekpad van 'n Nasie,* Afrikaanse Pers Boekhandelaars, 1970.
5. Du Toit, Brian, *Beperkte Lidmaatskap,* 1955.
6. Friedman, Bernard, *Smuts: A Reappraisal,* Hugh Keartland, 1975.
7. Hancock, W K, *Smuts, The Fields of Force,* Cambridge, 1962.
8. Huddlestone, Trevor, *Naught for Your Comfort,* Hardingham and Donaldson, Johannesburg for Collins, London, 1956.
9. Kestell, D E and Van Velden, J D, *The Peace Negotiations between Boer and Briton in South Africa,* R Clay, London, 1912.
10. Krüger, D W, *The Making of a Nation,* Macmillan, 1971.
11. Kruger, R, *Goodbye Dolly Gray,* Pan Books, 1977.
12. Malan, M P A, *Die Nasionale Party van Suid-Afrika. Sy Stryd en sy Prestasies,* Elsiesrivier, 1964.
13. Malherbe, E G, *Education in South Africa,* Vol 2, Juta, 1977.
14. *Military Intelligence Report on the Afrikaner Broederbond,* 1944.
15. Naude, Louis, *Dr Albert Hertzog, Die Nasionale Party en die Mynwerkers,* Nasionale Raad vir Trustees, 1969.
16. O'Meara, Dan, *The Afrikaner Broederbond 1927-1948: Class Vanguards of Afrikaner Nationalism,* Journal of Southern African Studies, Vol 3, 1977.
17. Pelzer, A N (ed), *Verwoerd Aan Die Woord 1948-1962,* 1963.
18. *Report of the D H Botha Commission of Inquiry into Secret Organisations,* 1964.
19. Serfontein, J H P, *Die Verkrampte Aanslag,* Human & Rousseau, 1970.
20. *South Africa in Travail,* South African Institute of Race Relations, 1978.
21. *Standard Encyclopaedia of Southern Africa,* Vol 3, Nasionale Opvoedkundige Uitgewery, Cape Town, Nasionale Boekhandel, London, 1970.
22. Swart, C F, *Politieke Profiele ten opsigte van Kontemporêre Aangeleenthede van die Blanke Grootstedelike Bevolking van die Witwatersrand,* Rand Afrikaans University, 1977.
23. *The Speeches of General the Rt. Hon. J C Smuts,* Truth Legion, 1941.
24. Troup, F, *South Africa: An Historical Introduction,* Penguin Books, 1975.
25. Van den Heever, C M, *Generaal J B M Hertzog,* Afrikaanse Pers Boekhandelaars, 1944.
26. Van der Merwe, H W, Ashley, M J, Charton, N C J, Huber, B J, *White South African Elites,* Juta, 1974.

27. Van der Poel, J, *Selections from the Smuts Papers,* Vol VII, Cambridge University Press, 1973.
28. Van Jaarsveld, F A, *Van Riebeeck tot Verwoerd 1652-1966 Inleiding tot die Geskiedenis van die Republiek van Suid-Afrika,* Voortrekkerpers, 1971.
29. Van Rooyen, J J, *Die Nasionale Party – Sy Opkoms en Oorwinning – Kaapland se Aandeel,* Elsiesrivier, 1956.
30. Van Selms, A, *Church and Secret Organisations,* pamphlet.
31. Vatcher, H W, *White Laager, The Rise of Afrikaner Nationalism,* Pall Mall, London, 1965.
32. Watts, H L, *A Social and Demographic Portrait of English-Speaking White South Africans,* 1974.
33. Welsh, David and van der Merwe, H W (eds), *Student Perspectives in South Africa,* Cape Town, 1972.
34. *What the Soldier Thinks,* Union Defence Force, 1944.

SELECTED INDEX

APPENDIX

Broederbond Membership List

The following list of members of the Broederbond is, by far, the most complete ever published. Over the years, not more than 400 names have been published in newspapers – this list contains about 7 500 names. This represents about 60% of the organisation's membership. The names not available were those who joined before 1962/1963, except in cases where they were nominated for the Executive, or were mentioned for some reason or other in the documents. It was impossible for the authors to trace the progress or movements of the 7 500 members. The key to reading the list is, therefore, contained in the date at which a person became a member – a teacher who joined in 1962 might by now be a professor at a university. Readers who want to trace the membership of an individual must, therefore, know his initials and something of his background.

The list contains, from the left, the name, initials, age, address, occupation, year in which he joined and where he lived previously.

The member's age, occupation and address apply to the year in which he joined.

Although everything possible has been done to ensure the accuracy of the list, it is possible that some of the names circulated by the Broederbond did not become members. Others could have been expelled, or resigned without it being reflected.

The fact of the matter is, however, that these names appear in Broederbond documents as members of the organisation at some stage or another.

Broederbond Membership List

A

Abrie P.L., 31, Sanlam Nylstroom, Streeksbestuurder 1975, Groblersdal
Ackerman J.J., 41, Krabfontein Hanover, Boer, 1975, Pretoria
Ackerman J.M., 34, N G Gemeente Pk Vanzylsrus, Predikant, 1967, Bredasdorp
Ackerman P.C., 30, P/A Chrysler Motorkorp Pretoria, Bestuurder Markbeplanning, 1976
Ackerman T L, 40, Pres Steynstraat 1 Bethulie/Volkskas, Bestuurder, 1971, Pretoria
Ackermann D J, 32, Volkskas Sannieshof, Rekenmeester, 1968, Petrusville
Ackermann N C, 32, P/A N G Kerk Skuilkrans Pretoria, Predikant, 1973, Fochville
Adendorff K, 42, Universiteit van Pretoria, Professor, 1974, Johannesburg
Agenbach H P M, 48, Avontuur A PK Wallekraal, Boer, 1967, Garies
Agenbach H P M, 39, Hoërskool Vredendal, Onderwyser, 1967, Lutzville
Agenbacht J F, 50, S A Polisie Calvinia, Dist Kommandant, 1965, Garies
Agenbag J F, 39, Dept Onderwys Kuns & Wet Pretoria, Studiebeampte 1967
Agenbag P J, 39, P/A Skool vir dowe Bantoe-Kinders Witsieshoek, Onderhoof, 1977 Knysna & Worcester
Aggenbach G A, 32, Môrelig Bredasdorp, Boer, 1966, Garies
Ahlers G H, 42, Dirleton Waterpoort, Boer, 1976, Belfast Dist
Ahlers H J, 37, Hoërskool Lyttleton, Onderhoof, 1964, Pretoria
Albers J B, 33, Broedershoek Melmoth, Boer, 1965
Alberts B C, 26, Yskor Pretoria, Ingenieur, 1967,Thabazimbi
Alberts H W, 32, P/A Munisipaliteit Potchefstroom/Indiër & Kleurlingsake, Bestuurder, 1975, Witbank
Alberts H W N, 39, Perseel 149 Derdepoort/Onderwyskollege Pretoria, Snr Lektor, 1970, Calitzdorp
Alberts J L M, 33, Primêre Skool Windhoek, Onderwyser, 1964,Gobabis
Albertse G J J, 38, P/A Landbo Tegn Dienste Lutzville, Navor Beampte, 1976, Stellenbosch
Albertse G P S, 30, Waverleyweg 24A Bloemfontein, Prokureur, 1965
Albertyn C, 41, Doornstraat 21, Arborpark, N G Predikant, 1972, Despatch
Albertyn C F (Lid Nr 1759), Porterville, Redakteur/Boer
Albertyn F C (Dr), Lid U R Nie-Blanke Kommissie 1973
Albertyn J T, 46, Lourensrivierweg 67 Strand, L V, 1977
Alheit W, 44, N G Kerk Worcester-Vallei, Predikant, 1967, Carnarvon
Allers M J R, 43, P/A Volkskas Venterstad, Bestuurder, 1977, Alberton
Allison G L, 38, Alemeinweg 13 Port Shepstone, Konstruksie Kontrakteur, 1974, Boksburg
Anderson A, 31, P/A Bank v d OVS Bloemfontein, Bemarkingsbestuurder, 1973, Ladybrand
Anderson H J R, 48, Dept Verdediging Pretoria, Majoor, 1966, Bloemfontein
Anderson L A P, 38, P/A W N N R Pretoria, Navorser, 1968
Anderson N C, 34, P/A Agricura Bpk Silverston, Tegniese Beampte, 1964, Barberton
Ankiewicz L, 32, Barnardskop PK Villiers, Boer, 1974
Annandale H J L, 31, Pospersoneel Mtubatuba, Klerk, 1967, Dundee
Appel M J F, 34, Santam Graaff-Reinet, Bestuurder, 1966, Pretoria
Appelgryn A C, 45, Rusoord PK Pom Pom Vryburg, Boer/Slagter, 1967
Arangies J, 38, P/A U O V S Bloemfontein, Snr Lektor, 1975, Potchefstroom
Archer A, 27, Môrelighostel Moorreesburg, Onderwyser, 1966, Stellenbosch
Archer A H, 40, Settlement Trompsburg, Boer, 1969
Archer J, 40, V D Merwestraat 24 Kiblerpark Johannesburg, Skoolhoof, 1977
Archer W E C, 38, Badsfontein Trompsburg, Boer, 1964
Arendt F W, 35erhoof, 1968, Witbank
Aucamp M W W, 33, Jukskeilaan 34 Farrarmere Benoni, Tandtegnikus, 1971, Delmas Johannesburg

Aucamp P, 32, P/A P U vir C H O Potchefstroom, Bibliotekaris, 1969, Durban
Aucamp P, 35, Brink Roos & du Toit Bellville, Ouditeur, 1970
Aucamp P J, 31, Doncasterweg 3 Nigel, Onderwyser, 1968, Potchefstroom
Aucamp R S, 30, Geref Pastorie Middelburg K P, Predikant, 1977
Aucamp W, 38, P/A Landdroskantoor Hennenman, Landdros, 1975, Pretoria
Aucamp W A S, 42, P/A Sanlam Bloemfontein, Wyksbestuurder, 1964, Colesberg
Augustyn P J, 32, S A Polisie — Versekeringsfonds Pretoria, Asst Sekretaris, 1964, Williston
Auret A de T, 26, Lucasvleivlakte Pofadder, Boer, 1975
Auret F de T, 44, Posbus 7 Pofadder, Sakeman/Boer, 1966, Die Strand
Auret J G, 47, Kromstraat 8 Alexanderbaai/Staats Alluviale Delwery, Installsie Voorman, 1975, Garies
Auret J P, 31, Cam Kiddiestraat 5 Kimberley, Onderwyser, 1971, Garies
venant P J, 27, Seunshostel Mosselbaai, Onderwyser, 1966, Paarl
Ayres J, 48, O'Haraweg 13 Turffontein/Grosvenor Motors, Adm Bestuurder, 1976, Johannesburg

B

Baard A P, 32, Mediese Forum Port Elizabeth, Geneesheer, 1967, Stellenbosch
Baard C, 34, P/A Witwatersrandse Kollege vir Gevorderde Tegniese Onderwys, Dosent, 1975, Vanderbijlpark
Baard J A, Kaapstad, Het Bondsraad in 1966 bygewoon,
Babst C F, 33, Goedehooplaan 7 Robertson, Onderwyser, 1974
Badenhorst A A, 34, Hoërskool Louis Trichardt, Onderwyser, 1965, Nylstroom
Badenhort A R, 25, Grensstraat 50 Parys,Onderwyser, 1972, Holshaus
Badenhorst B J G W, 32, Saambou-Nasionale Bouvereniging, Potchefstroom Beleggings-bestuurder,
1974, Bloemfontein
Badenhorst C H, 33, Waaikraal Belfast, Boer, 1975
Badenhorst C H J, 43, P/A Noord-Kaapse B A R ABB, 1975, Postmasburg
Badenhorst D B R, Lid van Uitvoerende Raad se Afrika Kommissie 1973
Badenhorst D H, 46, P/A S A S & H Upington, Stasiemeester, 1969, Graskop
Badenhorst F H B, 47, P/A Dept van Landbou Tegn Dienste Potchefstroom, Tegnikus, 1965 Stellenbosch
Badenhorst F J, 33, Oranjestraat 7, Oberholzer, Onderwyser, 1975, Heidelberg Tvl
Badenhorst F J, 42, Mahemsvlei Klerksdorp, Boer, 1969
Badenhorst H J, 34, De Wetstraat 27 Alberante-Uitbreiding Alberton, Geneesheer 1977, Bellville
Badenhorst H J, 38, V D Lindestraat Annlin Pretoria, Besturende Direkteur, 1977
Badenhorst J A C, 28, Newmansfordlaad 2 Queenspark Bulawayo, N G Predikant, 1974, Witbank
Badenhorst J B, 37, P/A Hoërskool Vredenburg, Onderwyser, 1967, Albertinia
Badenhorst J F P, (Lid Nr 1949) Skoolhoof — Boksburg-Noord — Voorgestel U R 1968/ Hoof van Voortrekkers
Badenhorst J H, 46, Tochgekregen Dewetsdorp, Boer, 1974
Badenhorst J J, 46, Dept Arbeid Pietermaritzburg, Asst Inspekteur, 1966, Bloemfontein
Badenhorst J P, 37, P/A Usko Aluminiumkorporasie Richardsbaai, Voorman/Passer, 1976, Vanderbijlpark
Badenhorst L J, 31, P/A Noordwes Koöp Lichtenburg, Inspekteur, 1965, Delareyville
Badenhorst L P, 37, Zondachsfontein Ogies, Boer, 1977
Badenhorst Piet, Wolmaransstad, Skoolinspekteur, 1966
Badenhorst P C, 29, Pan PK Komatipoort, Boer, 1974, Pretoria
Badenhorst P J W, 31, P/A S A Weermag Welsynsdiens/S A Vloot, Welsynsoffisier, 1974 Pretoria
Badenhorst P P, 37, P/A Afdelingsraad Springbok, Sekretaris, 1967, Humansdorp
Badenhorst Z B, 45, N G Kerk Chrismar Bellville, Predikant, 1967, Kimberley
Baker I D, 29 H/V Vrystaat- & Krugerstraat Standerton, Vise-Hoof, 1977 Heidelberg
Bakker P C, 36, P/A Hoër Tegn & Handelskool Vereeniging, Onderwyser, 1974, Bothaville
Bakkes J M, 32, Greystraat Tarkastad, Onderwyser, 1971, Kroonstad
Barker E R, 42, Blenheimweg 51 Pinetown/P/A Brownskool Pinetown, Adjunk-Hoof, 1976, Standerton

Barkhuizen A J, 44, P/A Nedersetting Charlesville, Boer/Superintendent, 1974, Jagersfontein
Barkhuizen P, 30, Loubad Distr Waterberg, Asst Sekretaris NTK, 1977
Barkhuizen P R, 26, Darlingstraat 29 Murraysburg, Landdros (Waarnemende), 1977, Swellendam
Barnard A T, P/A Santam Kaapstad, Beleggingsekretaris, 1964, Pretoria
Barnard B J H, 37, Hoewe 7 Pumulani Landbou;Hoewes Pretoria, Navorser/Onderstepoort, 1973, Delmas
Barnard C J, 37, N H Weeshuis Krugersdorp, Huisvader, 1966, Vanderbijlpark
Barnard C N, 33, Maraisstraat 71 Kroonstad/S A U K, Ingenieur, 1976, Johannesburg
Barnard D A, 31, Prov Koshuis Joubertstraat 8 Witrivier, Onderwyser, 1971, Delmas
Barnard F, 30, Lancestraat 11 Baysville Oos-Londen, Bourekenaar, 1976, Bloemfontein
Barnard G R , 41, P/A Hoërskool Villiers, Skoolhoof, 1977, Pretoria
Barnard H D, 38, N G Pastorie Vredendal, Predikant, 1970, Swellendam
Barnard H J, 37, S A Polisie Pretoria, Kaptein, 1968, Kaapstad
Barnard H M J, 30, Kameeldrif PK Corona (Brits), Boer, 1976
Barnard J L, 37, Prinshof Skool Pretoria, Vise-Hoof, 1977, Belfast
Barnard J P, 41, Alfredstraat 77 Stutterheim, N G Predikant, 1973, Babanango
Barnard L G, 49, Goudveldse Hoërskool Roodepoort, Onderwyser, 1965
Barnard M C, 32, Omega Umtali, Boer, 1966
Barnard M C, 34, P/A Borman Snyman & Barnard Potgietersrus, Prokureur, 1968
Barnard M C, 34, P/A Opleidingkollege Wellington, Dosent, 1974, Warrenton
Barnard M J, 31, P/A N P van Natal Durban, Hoofsekretaris 1968, Pietermaritzburg
Barnard P J, 30, Sesdelaan 4A Mellville/Hoërskool Vorentoe Johannesburg, Onderwyser, 1970, Pretoria
Barnard P J, 33, Universiteit Pretoria, Student, 1969, Swellendam
Barnard P R, 34, Liebenbergstraat Upington, Geneesheer, 1970
Barnard S G, 33, Badenhorststraat 105, Fairland Johannesburg, Vise-Hoof, 1976, Florida
Barnard S S, 47, P U vir C H O Potchefstroom, Professor, 1975,Fochville
Barnard W, 47, P/A Nywerheidsafd Sentraal Wes-Koöp Kroonstad, Hoofbestuurder, 1968, Otavi S W A
Barnard W A, 37, Turnerstraat 3 Delahaye Bellville/Sanlam, Bestuurder Personeel, 1977
Barnard W H M, 43, Posbus 155 Upington, Boer/Vervoerkontr, 1967, Oudtshoorn
Barnardo D J, 45, Sendingpastorie Koppies, Sendeling, 1964, Villiers
Barnardo J, U P E Kampus Somerstrand Port Elizabeth — (Skakel by U P E 4.2.76)
Barnardt T H, 35, Huis Jordaan Lingenstraat Kaapstad, Onderwyser, 1970, Uniondale
Barry R v R, Calitzdorp Gereelde skakel by afdelingsraadkongresse
Barry R v R, 30, P/A Roelou Barry Motors Robertson, Sakeman, 1967
Bartleman T W, 33, Goedemoed Marquard, Boer, 1967, Virginia
Barton A P, 39, Jessiestraat 19 Chrismar Bellville, Klerk, 1966, Kaapstad
Basson A J, 38, P/A N G Gemeente Pietersburg-Noord, Predikant, 1974, Jan Kempdorp
Basson A J (Lid Nr 4075) Piketberg — Boer — (Voorgestel U R 1968)
Basson A L, 33, Munisipaliteit Stellenbosch, Asst Stadstesourier, 1964, Standerton
Basson C J J, 33, Hoërskool Langenhoven Pretoria, Onderwyser, 1965
Basson D S, 35, Universiteit Stellenbosch, Dosent, 1976, Oudtshoorn
Basson G C, 40, Laerskool Grootfontein, Onderwyser, 1965, Omaruru
Basson G C, 39, Boekenhoutstraat 25 Birchleigh, Snr Uitgewer Perskor, 1971, Pretoria
Basson H P, 27, Bromptonweg 18, Bloemfontein/N G Gemeente De Bloem, Predikant, 1971, Stellenbosch
Basson J A, 42, Durbanstraat 61, Worcester/S A S & H, Werksvoorman, 1976, Uitenhage
Basson J A, 32, Ramonalaan 144, Erasmusrand/P/A Von Wielligh & Verba Pretoria, Ingenieur, 1976,
Basson J H, 37, P/A S A Polisie Brandfort, Luitenant, 1975, Pretoria
Basson J T (Basie), 39, Longlaan 439 Ferndale Randburg, Eiendomsagent, 1975, Bloemfontein
Basson M, 30, P/A Dept Landbou Tegn Dienste Middelburg Tvl, Voorligtingsbeampte, 1964,
Pretoria
Basson M H M, 30, Baviaanskloof PK Eendekuil, Boer, 1969
Basson M M, 32, H T S N Diederichs Krugersdorp, Onderwyser, 1968, Randfontein

Basson N J S, 31, Onderwyskollege Pretoria, Dosent, 1967
Basson N J S, 41, Holgatfontein Nigel, Boer, 1970, Devon
Basson P A, 29, Rheboksdam Malmesbury, Boer, 1968
Basson S P, 29, Langzeekoegat Devon, Boer, 1964
Basson S W, 49, P/A Montagu;Eksekuteurskamer Barrydale, Takbestuurder, 1967, Montagu
Basson W D, 37, P/A Laerskool Eendracht, Skoolhoof, 1969, Evander
Basson W H, 46, Bosjeskop Nelspruit, Boer, 1975, Ventersdorp
Becker J M, 33, Ericastraat 4 Parow-Noord — (Finansies) (Med Nav) Asst Sekretaris, 1977
Becker R C, 44, P/A Weakley & Becker Otjiwarongo, Rekenmeester, 1969, Outjo
Bedford J A, 25, Privaatsak 814 Witsieshoek, Asst Rekenmeester 1971, Pretoria
Bedford J A, Departement van Bantoe-administrasie & ontwikkeling, Rundu, 1977
Beetge A P S, 35, Van Zylstraat 16 Rustenburg, N G Predikant, 1971, Viljoenskroon
Beetge G P, 36, Potgieterstraat 11A Eastleigh (Edenvale), Wes-Randse B A Raad, 1977, Halfweghuis
Beezhold P E, 32, P/A S A Weermag Pretoria, Kolonel (ING), 1975
Behr P J, 42, D F Malanrylaan Sandspruit PK Honeydew, Diamantslyper, 1972, Randburg
Bekker A, 32, Lugmagbasis Bloemspruit, Majoor, 1974, Ysterplaat
Bekker C J, 24, P/A Hoërskool van Kerken Bloemfontein, Onderwyser, 1965
Bekker E H, 40, Harmony Goudmyn Virginia, Hoofgeoloog, 1974, Roodepoort
Bekker G, 48, Rosslands Colesberg, Boer, 1970, Rietbron
Bekker H O, 28, N G Pastorie Pietermaritzburg, Predikant, 1970, Johannesburg
Bekker I L, 29, Geref Kerk Sinoia Rhodesië, Predikant, 1977, Potchefstroom
Bekker J A, 35, Uitval oor Kuruman, Boer, 1973
Bekker J B, 35, P/A Bekker Rollermeule Bethal, Sakeman, 1965
Bekker J H, 33, Kabolk Upington, Boer/Onderwyser, 1972, Kimberley
Bekker J H, 34, Doringbos Rietbron, Boer, 1977
Bekker L P, 41, P/A N G Pastorie Clanwilliam, Predikant, 1974, Stellenbosch
Bekker M J, Calitzdorp, Senator (Lid nr. 2012)
Bekker M J, 35, P/A Volkskas Petrus Steyn, Rekenmeester, 1974, Harrismith
Bekker P M, 60, P/A Onderstepoort Pretoria, Skeikundige, 1968
Bekker P M, 29, P/A Universiteit Pretoria, Snr Lektor/Advokaat, 1974
Bell G M, 30, Kendal 28 Eversdal Durbanville, Geneesheer, 1977
Bell J U, 28, Kightleystraat 28 Brandfort, Onderwyser, 1967, Bothaville
Bell J W, 38, Esperanto Ceres, Boer, 1965, Senekal
Benade A J S, 36, Quentinweg 13, Robertsham Johannesburg, Fisioloog, 1975, Braamfontein
Benade D v d M, Lid U R Ekonomiese Kommissie 1973
Benade J G, 34, P/A Witwatersrandse Tegn Kollege Johannesburg, Snr Lektor, 1968, Petrus Steyn
Benade J G, (Lid Nr 10657), Putneyweg 19 Rossmore Johannesburg, Snr Lektor
Benade J G, 46, S A S Tugappelraad,Boksburg Voorgestel vir die U.R., Voorsitter, 1976, Tsumeb
Benade J M, (Lid Nr 1732), Rustenburg-Noord, Predikant, 1965
Benade P T, 39, Signallaan 5 P/A Hoërskool Vryburger (Elandsfontein), Adjunk-Hoof, 1975, Alberton
Benade S J, 38, P/A Munisipaliteit Vanderbijlpark, Stadstesourier, 1967, Boksburg
Benade Z L, 44, P/A Hoër Tegn Skool Tom Naude Pietersburg, Waarn Hoof, 1970, Johannesburg
Benecke F C, 33, Yorkstraat 26 Nigel, Onderwyser, 1977, Tzaneen
Beneke C F, 34, Tradouw P K Afrikaskop, Boer, 1968, Kestell
Beneke M J, 36, Sitrus Köop Malelane, Bestuurder, 1964, Patentie
Beneke S J, 38, P/A Tegn Afd Hoofposkantoor Mtubatuba, P & T Tegn, 1974, Ladysmith Natal
Benninghoff W, 38, Lyrastraat 34, Waterkloofrif Pretoria, Tandarts, 1977, Bothaville
Benson M C, 43, P/A Tuckners Vleishandelaars Linden Johannesburg, Bestuurder, 1967
Bergh A V, 28, P/A Sek Skool M T Steyn Philippolis, Onderhoof, 1974, Bloemfontein
Bergh M M, Posbus 7 Bothaville, 1962
Bergh O M P, 46, Landdroskantoor Calvinia, Landdros, 1965, Malmesbury
Bergh S J (Lid Nr 4856), Skoolhoof — Uitenhage —Voorgestel vir die UR in 1968

Bernard N J, 37, PK Balfour Kaap, Boer/Slagter, 1968, Tarkastad
Bernard P B, 29, Boogstraat 2, Naudeville Welkom, Onderwyser, 1971, Bloemfontein
Bernado J, Universiteit van Port Elizabeth
Berry J S, 40, N G Pastorie Barkley-Oos, Predikant, 1967, Bultfontein
Besselaar J F, 34, Edinburg Witputstasie, Boer, 1965, Hopetown
Bester A, 35, P/A Volkskas BPK Lindley, Rekenmeester, 1974, Pretoria
Bester A J, 46, Onverwacht Molteno, Boer, 1973
Bester A J J, 36, Hoër Landbouskool Bekker Magaliesburg, Onderwyser, 1977, Vryburg
Bester A N E, 40, Varsfontein Graafwater, Boer, 1969
Bester A W, 35, Hoërskool Reivilo, Onderwyser, 1969, Paarl
Bester C, 38, N G Kerk Birchleigh, Predikant, 1977, Verwoerdburg
Bester D J, 33, Menellstraat 9 Sasolburg/Hoërskool, Onderwyser, 1971, Koppies
Bester D W S, 35, N G Pastorie Paul Roux, Predikant, 1967, Port Shepstone
Bester E C, 26, Hoërskool Glencoe, Onderwyser, 1965
Bester H, 36, Sanlam De Doorns, Wyksbestuurder, 1968, Worcester
Bester H J, 39, Volkskas, — Phalaborwa, Bestuurder, 1965, Louis Trichardt
Bester H P, 38, Eerstelaan Petrusville/Volkskas, Bestuurder, 1971, Bloemfontein
Bester H S G, 31, P/A Libanon-Goudmyn Venterspos, Mynkaptein, 1974, Meyerton
Bester J B, 43, P/A Dept Landbou Tegn Dienste Pretoria, Asst Hoof, Bemarkingsnavorsing, 1968, Port Elizabeth
Bester J B, 45, P/A Onderstepoort Pretoria, Snr Tegn Beampte, 1968
Bester J C, 32, St Petersweg 60 Southernwood Oos-Londen, Handelaar, 1969
Bester J J, 37, N G Pastorie Birchleigh, Predikant, 1966, Piketberg
Bester J P, 39, S A S & H Komga, Stasiemeester, 1965, Loerie
Bester L, 29, Parkridgesingel 8 Port Elizabeth, Geneesheer, 1977
Bester M de B, 41, Citruslaan 24 Fort Victoria/Morgenstersending, Onderwyssekretaris, 1970, Paarl
Bester M J A, 28, P/A S A Polisie Heilbron O V S,, Adj-Offisier, 1968, Odendaalsrus
Bester N, 44, Hoërskool Hofmeyr, Skoolhoof, 1973, Balfour K P
Bester P J R, 38, Colin Fraserstraat Philippolis, Gesondheidsinspekteur, 1967, Bloemfontein
Bester P M, 33, P/A Hoërskool Vanderbijlpark, Onderwyser, 1969, Heidelberg Tvl
Bester P S, 42, P/A N G Pastorie Williston, Predikant, 1969
Bester S M, 33, Blouwater Molteno, Boer, 1965
Besuidenhout J J D, 32, Robyn Pongola, Boer, 1971, Vryburg
Beukes C J, 36, P/A Hoërskool Fakkel Johannesburg, Onderwyser, 1973, Randfontein
Beukes C J, 44, Hoërskool Oudtshoorn, Onderhoof, 1969, Barkly-Oos
Beukes C J, 30, Piet Retiefstraat 88 Monumentdorp/S A L, Snr Klerk, 1976, Krugersdorp
Beukes D P M (Lid Nr 2735), Linden-Park 1965 — Predikant — Voorgestel U R 1968
Beukes G J, 31, P/A U O V S Bloemfontein, Snr Lektor, 1974
Beukes J C, 34, Posbus 48 Pofadder, Onderwyser, 1974, Luitzville
Beukes J S, 31, P/A Universiteit Pretoria, Lektor, 1967, Meyerton
Beukes J W, (Lid Nr 7723), Grabouw, 1963
Beukes M J du P., 29, Mollieweg 28 Delarey, N H Predikant, 1970, Sannieshof
Beukes P J, 29, Mispah Grabouw, Boer, 1973
Beukes P J C, 29, Wilgerboschdam Hofmeyr, Boer, 1965
Beukes S G, 40, Kruppstraat Windhoek, Skoolhoof, 1971
Beukes T E, 34, Rhodesiese Spoorweë Gwelo, Betaalmeester, 1967
Beyers A S (Lid Nr 3686), Lichtenburg — Voorgestel U R 1968, Boer
Beyers A S, 25, Blaauwbank Lichtenburg, Boer/L P R, 1971
Beyers J A (Lid Nr 7725), Venterspos, 1963
Beyers N, 30, P/A N G Pastorie Kempton Park, Predikant, 1969, Stellenbosch
Beylefeld M H, 37, Smalstraat 42 Vryheid, Onderwyser, 1977, Boshoff
Beylefeld P J, 33, Wichita Woonstel 104 Johnsonstraat Sunnyside/(Dept v/d Eerste Minister), Navorser, 1971, Bloemfontein
Beyleveld E, 34, Kerkstraat Wepener, Prokureur, 1967, Bloemfontein
Beyleveldt B J (Lid Nr 5749) Organiseerder Christiaan De Wet Fonds 1972
Bezuidenhout C D, 29, De Poortje Steytlerville, Boer, 1965
Bezuidenhout D, 34, P/A Hoërskool Wessel Maree Odendaalsrus, Onderhoof, 1968, Bloemfontein

Bezuidenhout G, 32, Hoogstraat 8 Middelburg Tvl, Prokureur 1971, Walvisbaai
Bezuidenhout G P, 41, Proteasteeg 460 Lynnwood, Mediese Student, 1970, Klerksdorp
Bezuidenhout G P, 38, P/A Winchessterridge Primary School Johannesburg, Skoolhoof, 1973, Pretoria
Bezuidenhout G S, 33, P/A Yskor Pretoria, Waarn Hoof Bemarking, 1973
Bezuidenhout G W L, 33, Newton Walker & Venter Potchefstroom, Rekenmeester, 1965, Klerksdorp
Bezuidenhout H J, 34, Meesterlaan Outjo, Onderwyser, 1972, Upington
Bezuidenhout J, 36, P/A Machangana — Regeringsdiens Soutpansberg, Direkteur van Landbou, 1973
Pretoria
Bezuidenhout J C, 43, PK Levubu oor Louis Trichardt, Boer, 1967, Krugersdorp
Bezuidenhout J G, Bondsraad 1971 — Kleurlingsake (Brakpan-Wes)
Bezuidenhout J S, 35, Krugerkoshuis Rustenburg, Onderwyser, 1968, Potchefstroom
Bezuidenhout J W S, 31, Hoofstraat Wellington/Hugenote Laerskool, Onderwyser, 1971 Kakamas
Bezuidenhout P F G (Fritz), 41, The Prairie Welkom, Boer, 1975
Bezuidenhout P H, 39, P/A Cwaka Landbou-Kollege, Empangeni, Hoof, 1974, Marble Hall
Bezuidenhout P J A, 43, Swartkop PK Brandfort, Boer, 1968.
Bezuidenhout P J A, 27 Martina Brandfort, Boer, 1977, Pretoria
Bezuidenhout P J J, 42, Skoolweg 58 Amanzimtoti/Hotelle & Vakansie-Oorde, Hoof, 1976 Empangeni
Bezuidenhout P L, 37 P/A Yskor Pretoria, Dataverwerkings, 1967
Bezuidenhout P R, 39, Vlaklaagte Christiana, Boer, 1964
Bingle H J J (Lid Nr 1663), P U vir C H O Potchefstroom — Rektor — Voorgestel U R 1968
Bingle P W, 27, Geref, Pastorie Carolina, Predikant, 1967, Potchefstroom
Bingle P W, 41, Hoërskool Hans Strijdom Naboomspruit, Onderwyser, 1964, Potchefstroom
Bischoff A A, 47, P/A P U vir C H O Potchefstroom, Snr Lektor, 1969, Swartruggens
Bisschoff C A, 44, P/A Rondalia Groep MPYE Pretoria, Besturende Direkteur, 1973
Bisschoff I J, 42, Hoërskool Vorentoe Johannesburg, Onderwyser, 1966
Blaauw M S, 27, Huis 175 Oshkati, Onderwyser, 1975, Keetmanshoop
Blaauw W J, 39, Offisierslaan 22 Militêre Basis Potchefstroom/S A Weermag, Kaptein, 1970, Bellville
Blanché J P I, 37, P/A Lewis Appliances Boksburg Hoof Navorsing & Ontw, 1975
Blignault N J, 43, Hoskingstraat 51 Brenthurst Brakpan, Onderwyser, 1977, Pietersburg
Blignault W D, 27, N G Pastorie Postmasburg, Predikant, 1977, Stellenbosch
Blignaut C J J, 38, Dept Indiërsake Pretoria, Snr Adm Beampte, 1967, Heidelberg Tvl
Blignaut J B, 45, P/A Laerskool Akasia Pretoria, Skoolhoof, 1966
Blignaut J B, 35, Kerkstraat Belfast, Apteker, 1964
Blignaut J G B, 31, P/A Die Residensie Otavi, Landdros, 1970, Tsumeb
Bloem G N, 26, Delportstraat 19 Elsburg, N H Predikant, 1970, Fochville
Bloem P A, 34, P/A Stadsraad Edenvale, Asst Stadstesourier, 1968, Kempton Park
Bloemhof W J, 35, P/A S A L M Ysterplaat, Majoor, 1975, Pretoria
Blofield C H P, 41, Luton Dendron, Boer, 1969, Pietersburg
Blomerus J H, 32, Aspelingstraat 52, George, Voorligtingsbeampte, 1976, Ermelo
Blomerus J M, 43, Akasialaan 12 Durbanville, Radioloog, 1974, De Doorns
Blomerus W J, 40, Twello Bosbou Korp (Edms) Bpk Barberton, Asst Rekenmeester, 1967, Sutherland
Blomerus Z M, 29, Rietgat Britstown, Boer, 1969
Bodenstein C J, 47, Serowelaan 10 Fynnlands Bluff/P/A Vakleerlingskool Durban, Dosent 1977, Germiston
Bodenstein J C, 37, P/A H T S John Vorster Pretoria, Onderwyser, 1968
Boersma A, 33, Bassonstraat 278, Erasmia Pretoria, Onderwyser, 1976, Middelburg Tvl
Boettger R J, 34, Sabie-Sand-Koöp Hazyview, Handelsbestuurder, 1970, Rustenburg
Boltman F H, 33, Kalkgat Calvinia, Boer, 1965
Bondesio M J, 30 Minnesotaweg 301 Fairy Glen Pretoria, Snr Lektor, 1977
Bondisio G F, 37, Brandkraal PK Winterton, Boer, 1974, Koster
Boneschans H (Lid Nr 3423), Ondervoorsitter Huurraad — Allenweg 26 Bedfordview
Booker T D, 36, P/A Sendingkerk Worcester, N G Predikant, 1975, Robertson
Boonzaaier H J A, 38, Sentrale Aksepbank Johannesburg, Sekretaris, 1973, Stellenbosch

Boonzaaier Niek, Wolmaransstad, Oud-Onderwyser, 1966
Boonzaier H D, 37, Georgestraat Ashton, Onderwyser, 1969, Bonnievale
Booyens B (Prof), Universiteit van Stellenbosch
Booyens C J, 33, P/A Hoër Landbouskool Merensky, Vise-Hoof, 1975, Sannieshof
Booyens G, 30, P/A Sanlam Potchefstroom, Wyksbestuurder, 1968, Ventersdorp
Booyens J J, 43, Doordriftsstraat 55 Ventersdorp, Onderwyser, 1969
Booyens T J, 45, P/A S A Polisie Pretoria, Offisier, 1975, Venterstad
Booyse J P, 31, Burgershall Witrivier, Boer, 1967, Belfast
Booysen B, 37, Kollegeweg 38 Graaff-Reinet, Snr Dosent, 1977, Uitenhage
Booysen C H Z, 34, Genl Dan Pienaarweg 90 Bloemfontein, Verhoudingsbeampte Munisipaliteit, 1977
Booysen J A L, 41, P/A Dept van Justisie Pretoria, Ondersekretaris, 1974
Booysen J H, 36, Volkskool Tweespruit, Skoolhoof, 1967, Bloemfontein
Booysen J J H, 29, Posbus 23 Shannon, Onderwyser, 1964, Welkom
Booysen J R, 36, Hoewe 159 Sonskyn/(OVS Tegniese Kollege), Instrukteur, 1976
Booysen J R, Plaasimplemente-tegnieke P/s X20542, Bloemfontein, 1977
Booysen P de K, 34, P/A Fonteine Apteek Verwoerdburg, Apteker, 1974, Pretoria
Booysen S L, 37, P/A Menlopark Hoërskool Pretoria, Vise-Hoof, 1974
Borchardt C F A, 34, Rulestraat 39, Kroonstad, Bestuurder Agrico, 1976, Bloemfontein
Borman J C H (Lid Nr 7679), Prokureur — Potgietersrust — 1962
Borman J G, 35, Oosthuizenstraat 15 Middelburg, Prokureur, 1973, Pretoria
Bornman C H, 38, Zenithstraat 30 Solheim Germiston/Volkskas, Asst Rekenmeester, 1970, Wesselsbron
Bornman H G, 36, Atheloon PK Verkeerdevlei, Boer, 1975
Bornman J J, 32, P/A Ficksburg Motor Garage Ficksburg, Verkoopsman, 1974
Borstlap G P, 36, Barry Richterstraat Bloemfontein/Weerkundige Buro — Dept Vervoer, Hooftegnikus, 1970, Kimberley
Bos N J, 37, P/A Lydenburg Hospitaal, Klerk, 1967, Maandagshoek
Bosch A S du P, 33, Volkskas Albertinia, Rekenmeester, 1966, Somerset-Oos
Bosch G S, 33, Kaaplandse Landbou-Unie Paarl, Asst Organiseerder, 1967, Beaufort-Wes
Bosch J C, 26, Veeplaas Enkeldoorn, Boer, 1975, Fort Victoria
Bosch J C D, 39, Suikerboskop Witbank, Boer, 1975
Bosch J D, 30, P/A Sasol Sasolburg, Bedryfsingenieur, 1966, Stellenbosch
Bosch J L, 33, Barry Hertzogrylaan 11 Florida, Geoloog N O K, 1973
Bosch O J H, 30, N G Pastorie PK Vansylsrus, N G Predikant, 1971, Stellenbosch
Bosch P F C (Pieter), 43, Fouriesrust Brandfort, Boer, 1975
Boshof L, 35, Richterstraat Pionierspark, Windhoek, Bestuurder National Chemical Products, 1973, S W A
Boshoff A, 29, N G Sendingpastorie Mayfair-Wes, Johannesburg, Sendeling, 1965, Schweizer-Reneke
Boshoff C H, Oud L P R vir Wolmaransstad 1966
Boshoff C W H, Professor — Hoof Dept Godsdiens & Sendingwetenskap, Universiteit van Pretoria (Dr Verwoerd se Skoonseun & Voorsitter v Sabra)
Boshoff D J H, 45, Kaalplaas Dist Delareyville, Boer, 1976, Blyvooruitsig
Boshoff F, Rusape Rhodesië (Woon 1966 se Bondsraad by)
Boshoff F J, 28, P/A N H Gemeente Umtali, Predikant, 1974, Pretoria
Boshoff F P, Skakelsekretaris van die A B 1971
Boshoff F P J, 36, B D F Konstruksie Mpy Tzaneen, Pad & Huisbouer 1973, Pretoria
Boshoff G S, 35, N G Pastorie Kirkwood, Predikant, 1966, Stellenbosch
Boshoff H C, 35, P/A Skool vir Serebraalverlamdes Port Elizabeth, Onderhoof, 1964, Kroonstad
Boshoff H C, 33, Haarburgersingel 3 Bloemfontein/Klerewinkel-Bestuurder, 1975
Boshoff H J, 34, Watson Shipping Jan Smutslughawe, Skeepsagent, 1963, Paarl
Boshoff H P, 32, Hoërskool Grenswag Kokstad, Onderwyser, 1973, Colesberg
Boshoff H P, 29, Deerpark Tzaneen, Onderwyser, 1974, Lydenburg
Boshoff H S, 41, Laerskool Montagu, Onderwyser, 1965, Oudthoorn
Boshoff J, 40, P/A Smuts & Koch Malmesbury, Kredietbestuurder, 1973, George
Boshoff J L (Prof), Turfloop, Rektor
Boshoff J R (Lid Nr 6563), Stadsklerk van Bloemfontein in 1973
Boshoff L F, 33, P/A Coca-Cola Brakpan, Bestuurder, 1964

Boshoff L P J, 40, West Koöp Mpy Bpk/Döngesstraat 26 Kroonstad, Onderdelebestuurder 1970
Boshoff L P J, 37, Emily Hobhouselaan 10 Pretoria, Argitek, 1974, Bloemfontein
Boshoff M C, 34, Toeslaan Upington, Boer, 1971
Boshoff W H, 30, Vorentoe PK Mooirivier, Boer, 1968
Boshoff W J, 27, Hoërskool Vanderbijlpark, Onderwyser, 1965
Boshoff W L, 33, P/A Hoërskool Piet Potgieter Potgietersrus, Onderwyser, 1968, Linden
Boshoff Z C P, 39, P/A N G Pastorie Olifantshoek, Predikant, 1975, Stellenbosch
Bosman A M, 32, Linduvaal 12 Lochvaal, Chiropraktisyn, 1976, Benoni
Bosman A S, 28, Eeufeesstraat 11 Pretoria-Noord, Bouaannemer, 1972, Koster
Bosman D J, 39, Dept van Mynwese Brakpan, Chemiese Ontleder, 1973
Bosman D L, 46, Genl Beyerstraat 91 Pretoria-Noord, Direkteur Bosnavorsing, 1976
Bosman H J, 29, Norwoodweg Port Shepstone, Onderwyser, 1971, Kaapstad
Bosman H L, 36, S A Weermag Durban, Majoor, 1977, Walvisbaai
Bosman H S B, 42, Hoërskool Lichtenburg, Onderwyser, 1966, Johannesburg
Bosman I J, 38, S A Polisie Katima Mulilo, Offisier (Veiligheid), 1976, Springs
Bosman J, 32, Federale Volksbeleggings Kaapstad, Sekretaris, 1966, Johannesburg
Bosman J, 28, Vergesig W/S 614 Vermeulenstraat 106 Pretoria, Ingenieur Afd Nas Paaie, 1976, Stellenbosch
Bosman J J, 45, Suidwes Koöp Makwassie, Takbestuurder, 1970, Wepener
Bosman J P, 42, Leafontein PK Boons, Boer, 1970
Bosman J P, 31, P/A Capro Edenvale, Reklamebeampte, 1969, Verwoerdburg
Bosman J S, 33, Eikelaan 16 Grabouw, Kontrakteur, 1977
Bosman P, 39, Die Vlakte Somerset-Wes, Boer, 1970
Bosman P E, 32, Dave Noursestraat 3 Unitaspark Vereeniging, Boer/Vervoerkontrakteur, 1971
Bosman P E K, 36, P/A Kommandokrygskool Kimberley, Kommandant, 1968, Pretoria
Bosman P J, 44, Trevelloe Estates PK Shangani Rhodesië, Boer, 1968, Sinoia
Bosman T J, 31, Eerstestraat Vegkopuitbr Heilbron/Sanlam-Verteenwoordiger, 1977
Bossert C F, 44 Hoër Landbouskool Bekker Magaliesburg, Onderwyser, 1967, Vryburg
Bosua T A, 38, Weerburo Pretoria, Hoofweerkundige, 1965
Botes A, 27, S A S & H Johannesburg, Asst Ingenieur, 1966, Germiston
Botes A C, 31, S A Polisie Dewetsdorp, Adj-Offisier, 1976, Bloemfontein
Botes H C, 35, Voortrekkerstraat Hoopstad, Sakeman/Boer, 1969
Botes J A, 25, Enodia Prov Koshuis Bethal, Onderwyser, 1967, Johannesburg
Botes J A W, 36, P/A Hoër Handelskool Mike Erasmus Potgietersrus, Onderhoof, 1970, Naboomspruit
Botes J J, 42, Voorspoedkoshuis Middelburg TVL Adj-Hoof Hoërskool, 1971, Bethal
Botes N S (Lid Nr 2667), Skoolhoof Pretoria — Voorgestel U R 1968
Botes P J, 34, Munisipaliteit Roodepoort, Elektroteg Ingenieur, 1965, Standerton
Botes P W, 32, Mooistraat 11 Bethal, Geneesheer, 1973, Pretoria
Botes W L F, 38, N G Pastorie Balfour, Predikant, 1964, Welkom
Botha A, 36, Greylingstraat Harrismith, Onderwyser, 1964, Johannesburg
Botha A, 32, Junior Hoërskool Andries Pretorius Durban, Onderwyser, 1974
Botha A C, 30, Strydomsrus Elliot, Boer, 1968
Botha A D, 46, P/A N H Pastorie Elsburg, Predikant, 1974, Koedoesrand
Botha A H, 29, N G Kerk Rietfontein-Suid Pretoria, Predikant, 1967
Botha A J, 42, Langkuil Warmbad, Boer, 1964, Bronkhorstspruit
Botha A J J, 41, Ottosdalse Laerskool, Vise-Hoof, 1973 Heidelberg
Botha A M S, 46, Skoolraad Piketberg, Sekretaris, 1969, George
Botha A P J, 32, Middelbare Skool Volmoed, Skoolhoof, 1967, Victoria-Wes
Botha B C (Lid Nr 7724), Brakpan-Wes, 1963
Botha B F, 28, Ardnel Somerset-Oos, Boer, 1965
Botha C D, 42, Brakpan Dist Wolmaransstad, Boer, 1975, Schweizer-Reneke
Botha C J, 30, Landdroskantoor Pearston, Landdros, 1968, Pretoria
Botha C J, 34, P/A Du Rand Louw & Botha Pietersburg, Rekenmeester, 1976, Roodepoort
Botha C M, 34, P/A Universiteit van Zoeloeland/Siyayistraat Mtumzini, Lektor, 1975, Port Elizabeth
Botha C S H, 34, Lisbonlaan 22, Robertsham Laerskool Theo Wassenaar, Adj-Hoof, 1975, Dundee

Botha D, 39, Farmers Folly 48 Lynnwood, Spesialis Internis, 1963, Pretoria
Botha D E, 36, P/A Hoërskool Hexvallei, Skoolhoof, 1974, Springbok
Botha D H, 36, P/A Tegn Kollege Pietermaritzburg, Onderwyser, 1966, Weza Natal
Botha D J, 29, Piet Retiefstraat 34, Ladybrand, Onderwyser, 1977, Bloemfontein
Botha D W, 30, Hartebeesfontein Tarkastad, Boer, 1965
Botha D W S, 33, Yskor Pretoria (Hoogoonde), Asst Superintendent, 1972, Springs
Botha E G (Lid Nr 7687), Wolseley, Boer, 1962
Botha F A, 36, Welvaart Outjo, Boer, 1976
Botha F J, 42, P/A Sanlam Johannesburg, Asst Bestuurder, 1974, Bellville K P
Botha F J, 44, J L Clark Katoenmaatskappy Jan Kempdorp, Asst Bestuurder, 1969, Kempton Park
Botha F J, 37, Vrederus Maclear, Boer, 1969
Botha F J, Posbus 4 Devon (Tree op as skakel by Radarstasie Devon vir Militêre Dienspligtiges, 1967
Botha F J P, 43, Geluk PK Gerdau, Boer/Verteenwoordiger - (Triomf), 1974
Botha F J P R, 34, P/A Uniestaalkorporasie Vereeniging, Hoof Instrumente, 1977
Botha F T, 41, Armadastraat 12 Rustivia Germiston, Onderwyser, 1969
Botha G, 44, Weltevrede Florida, Blomkweker, 1969, Pretoria
Botha G C, Praat oor Christelike sake by Bonsraad van 1969 (Swellendam)
Botha G D, 37, Waverleyweg 35A Bloemfontein, Ing Provinsiale Administrasie, 1974, Windhoek
Botha G G, 34, Sasolbemarkingsmaatskappy Florida, Besigheidsbestuurder, 1966, Bloemfontein
Botha G W V, 28, P/A Geref Kerk Rustenburg-Noord, Predikant, 1968, Potchefstroom
Botha Hannes (Prof), President S A Atletiek Vereniging
Botha H C, 27, Harmony Matatiele, Boer, 1970, Franklin
Botha H J, 31, S A Weermag Pretoria, Kaptein, 1966
Botha H J, 31, P/A Saambou De Aar, Takbestuurder, 1965, Johannesburg
Botha H K, 28, Landboukollege Glen Bloemfontein, Dosent, 1970
Botha H L, 40, S A S Polisie Burgersdorp, Speurder-Sersant, 1974
Botha H P, 37, Robert Koch-Gebou Pretoria, Geneesheer, 1964, Koffiefontein
Botha H P, 28, P/A Stadsraad van Kempton Park, Adj-Stadsingenieur, 1975, Pretoria
Botha H P, 40, S A W Bluff Durban, Vloot-Kommandeur, 1963, Pretoria
Botha I M, 32, Mariusstraat 4 Witfield, Onderwyser, 1975, Germiston
Botha J, 38, P/A Onderwyskollege Wellington, Dosent, 1975, Paarl
Botha J, 30, Donellstraat 3 Marquard, Onderwyser, 1973, Harrismith
Botha J, 41, Vastfontein Pk Pyramid, Boer, 1971, Pretoria
Botha J A, 34, Ansongebou Ansonstraat Robertsham/Laerskool Dalmondeor, Vise-Hoof, 1977, Heidelberg
Botha J A v Z, 42, P/A Yskor Pretoria, Ouditklerk, 1968
Botha J C, 32, P/A Volkskas Winburg, Rekenmeester, 1974, Kestell
Botha J C, 31, Waltonstraat 5, Ladysmith, Onderhoof, 1973, Pietermaritzburg
Botha J C, 39, Blaauwboschfontein Boshof, Boer, 1970
Botha J F, 43, Perseel 7Q1 Jan Kempdorp, Boer, 1965, Mafeking
Botha J F, 40 P/A N G Pastorie Potchefstroom, Predikant, 1969, Zambië
Botha J G H, 46, P/A Nywerheidshof Pretoria, Sekretaris, 1968
Botha J H, 31, Normandiehof 22 Adcockvale Port elizabeth, Onderwyser, 1970, Graaf-Reinet
Botha J J, 36, P/A S A Weermag Pretoria, Kommandant, 1976, Pretoria
Botha J L P, 35, P/A Dept v Bantoe-Admin Pretoria/Koöp van Bantoetuislande, Hoof Vakkundige, 1977
Botha J N, 38, P/A S A S Telekommunikasiediens Nelspruit, Asst Voorman, 1973, Pretoria
Botha J P, 34, P/A S A Polisie Witbank, Kaptein, 1974
Botha J P, 34, Wentzelkoshuis Wolmaransstad, Onderwyser, 1971, Potchefstroom
Botha J P, 44, P/A Unisa Pretoria, Snr Lektor, 1977, Rustenburg
Botha J P, 37, Drakensbergrylaan 67 Waterkloofpark Pretoria, Argitek, 1968
Botha J P L (Lid Nr 7694), Boshoff, Skoolraad-Sekretaris, 1962
Botha L C, 34, P/A Munisipaliteit Lydenburg, Asst Klerk van die Raad, 1976, De Aar
Botha L J, 38, Geluk Danielsrus, Boer, 1975, Bethlehem

Botha L J, 34, Westview Spesiale Middelbare Skool Port Elizabeth, Skoolhoof, 1974, Bergvliet Kaap
Botha L J, 26, Spesbona PK Danielsrus, Boer, 1967, Bethlehem
Botha L J, 30, P/A Hoër Seunskoshuis Ellisras, Onderwyser, 1969, Pretoria
Botha L R, 47, Hoër Landbouskool Morgenzon, Hoof, 1966, Pietersburg
Botha L R, 52, S A Polisie Benoni, Kaptein, 1964, Port Elizabeth
Botha M C, Bloemfontein-Noord — Praat oor Rooms Katolieke by Bondsraad van 1967
Botha M C, Oud-Hoofinspekteur v Onderwys OVS — Samel fondse in vir Oranje Volksfeeshuis in 1971
Botha M C, Oud-Minister
Botha M C, 36, P/A Hlobane Trading Co Vryheid, Bestuurder, 1963, Volksrus
Botha M F, 29, Leër-Gimnasium Heidelberg Tvl, Kaptein, 1972, Bloemfontein
Botha M F, 38, Afdelingsraad Hofmeyr, Sekretaris, 1964, Middelburg K P
Botha M G, 38, Die Burger Kaapstad, Joernalis, 1973
Botha M J, 35, Derdestraat 32 Jozini, Gesondheidsinspekteur, 1967, Pongola
Botha N F, 38, Klipdrif Ottosdal, Boer, 1970
Botha O C, 32, Rietkuil Ottosdal, Boer, 1974, Boksburg
Botha O P S, 33, Voorbedacht Matjiesrivier, Boer, 1965
Botha P A, 33, Donkinplein Caledon Geneesheer (By 1966 Bondsraad praat hy teen Bankrekenings by Buitelandse Instellings), 1964, Kaapstad
Botha P A, 37, Lime Acres Danielskuil, Kampong-Bestuurder, 1974, Kimberley
Botha P B, 27, Stasieweg Clocolan, Ingenieur L T D, 1971, Pretoria
Botha P B, 42, N G Kerk Theunissen, Predikant, 1967, Senekal
Botha P C, 44, P/A Onderwyskollege Pretoria, Registrateur, 1977, Heidelberg
Botha P D B, 31, Durbanweg Colesberg, Onderwyser, 1972, Warrenton
Botha P J, 34, P/A S A U K Johannesburg, Adm Assistent, 1968, Pretoria
Botha P J, 39, Dunnstraat Jagersfontein, Geneesheer, 1965, Gobabis
Botha P J, 27, Landdroskantoor Witbank, Asst Landdros, 1964, George
Botha P J, 43, P/A Laerskool Ogies, Skoolhoof, 1975, Pretoria
Botha P J, 37, P/A Volkskas Villiers, Bestuurder, 1974, Kroonstad
Botha P R, 49, Braklaagte Dordrecht, Boer, 1977
Botha P R, 31, Parkstraat Pretoria, Argitek, 1965, Ladysmith
Botha P W, Eerste Minister en Minister van Verdediging
Botha R A, 34, "The Falls" Barkly-Oos/S A S & H, Klerk, 1974,Bedford
Botha R C, 28, Gertrudestraat 23, Naudeville, Onderwyser, 1970, Bloemfontein
Botha R F, 36, Dept Buitelandse Sake Pretoria (Tans Minister van Buitelandse Sake), Regsadviseur, 1969
Botha R P (Lid van U R se Ekonomiese Kommittee — 1973)
Botha S J, 28, N H Pastorie Symhurst Germiston, Predikant, 1964, Westdene
Botha Schalk J, (Lid Nr 728) Direkteur van Maatskappye Pretoria (Hartebeesspruit)
Botha S P, 37, Afrikaanse Springstowwe Coligny, Verteenwoordiger, 1967, Lusaka
Botha S P (Fanie) (Lid Nr 4418), Louis Trichardt, Minister van Arbeid en Mynwese
Botha S W, 43, Palmietfontein Ventersdorp, Geneesheer, 1968, Vredefort
Botha T J, 40, P/A Lever Bros Boksburg, Bestuurder, 1963, Steynsburg
Botha T J, 29, N O K Johannesburg, Tekstielbeampte, 1965, Durban
Botha T J N, 1965 (6 April) word Hoofsekretaris van A B in plek van Piet Koornhof
Botha T J P, 40, P/A Hoërtegniese Skool Kroonstad, Adjunk-Hoof, 1976, Excelsior
Botha T P A, 33, P/A Koshuis Kamieskroon, Onderwyser, 1969, Parow
Botha T S, 31, Kanonfontein PK Boshof, Boer, 1967, Wesselsbron
Botha W C, 32, P/A Krygstuigproduksieraad Pretoria, Produksiesupt, 1967
Botha W F, 27, Sheeprun PK Men Amalfi, Boer, 1968, Cedarville
Botha W F, 28, Cove rock Greenfields Oos-Londen, Winkelier, 1977, Maclear
Botha W J, 29, Oog van Wonderfontein Bank, Onderwyser, 1968, Potchefstroom
Botha W J J, 39, Annaniël Marquard, Boer, 1976, Henneman
Botha W J v H, 34, Remskoenstraat 396, Die Wilgers Uitbr 9 Pretoria, Stadsbeplanner, 1976 Kaapstad
Botha W S, 48, Witfontein PK Rosslyn, Sakeman, 1976, Vryburg
Bothma B, 37, P/A Santam/Willemsestraat 2, Vanderbijlpark, Koste-Taksateur, 1976, Johannesburg

Bothma B C, 43, P/A Eastern Free State Tractors Ltd, Boer/Direkteur, 1977, Bethlehem
Bothma C A, 25, Poskantoor Laingsburg, Klerk, 1965, Merweville
Bothma G P, 38, Jim van Tonderskool Bethal, Skoolhoof, 1973, Vereeniging
Bothma H, 40, Eversdalweg Durbanville, Argitek, 1975, Bellville
Bothma H J W, 34, De La Reyweg 20 Lyttleton/SAL, Offisier, 1970, Kloofsig
Bothma I G, 31, P/A S A Vloot Simonstad, Luitenant-Kommandeur, 1974, Saldanha
Bothma J A, 33, Waaihoek Hekpoort, Onderwyser/Boer, 1976, Kempton Park
Bothma J H, 30, Hoërskool Burgersdorp, Onderwyser, 1967, Lansdowne
Bothma L, 47, Willowmorese Handelskoöp, Bestuurder, 1974, Riversdal
Botma A J, 36, P/A Suidwes Koöp Bpk Makwassie, Takbestuurder, 1967
Botma D E, 39, P/A Tiki Eiendomsagente Alberton, Eiendomsverkoopsman, 1975
Botma J, 24, Eureka Prins Alfred Hamlet Gydo, Boer, 1970
Botma M C, 35, Posbus 152 Walvisbaai, Boukontrakteur/Boer, 1965, Wolmaransstad
Bouwer A G H, 35, P/A Landdroskantoor Bloemhof, Landdros, 1968, Lichtenburg
Bouwer E J P, 30, Florencestraat 73 Bellville, Boukontrakteur, 1976
Bouwer E L, 31, Whiteheadweg 13 Penford Uitenhage, Geneesheer, 1967, Colesberg
Bouwer J, 35, S A Kinderhuis Ivanhoestraat Kaapstad, Vise-Hoof, 1977
Bouwer J J, 31, Rooilaagte Niekerkshoop, Boer, 1963
Bouwer P B B, 45 P/A Laerskool Parksig Vanderbijlpark, Skoolhoof, 1976
Bouwer S E, 47, Culverwellstraat 12 Viljoenskroon, Posmeester, 1977
Bouwer W E, 41, Hoërskool Hangklip Queenstown, Onderhoof, 1966, Potchefstroom
Bouwer W J, 34, Altebly Kirkwood, Boer/Verteenwoordiger Agricura, 1975
Boyazoglu J G, 39, P/A S A Ambassade Parys Frankryk, Landbouraad L T D, 1976, Pretoria
Bradley J E, 28, P/A Bantoesakekomm Nongoma, Vakk Beampte, 1970, Pongola
Brand C v H, 27, N G Pastorie Gordonsbaai, Predikant, 1966, Worcester
Brand D G, 38, De Villiersstraat 6 Worcester, Boukontrakteur, 1974, Worcester
Brand D J, 37, 15delaan 15 Bellville, Sekretaris, 1971
Brand D P, 44, Chavonnestraat 59, Welgemoed Bellville, Onderwyser, 1976, Mashaba (Rhodesië)
Brand E J J, 28, Huis Toekoms Nieuwoudtville, Onderwyser, 1977, Vredendal
Brand F J J, 36, Cameronweg 2 Highland Hills Pinetown, Onderwyser, 1975, Tsumeb
Brand F J J, 34, P/A Volkskas Bpk Robertson, Rekenmeester, 1966, Wellington
Brand G J, 33, P/A Landdroskantoor Porterville, Asst Landdros, 1974, Robertson
Brand H P, 47, P/A Constantiaskool PK Retreat, Onderwyser, 1976, Worcester
Brand J F E, 46, Windellstraat, 3 Plattekloof Parow/Dept Binnelandse Inkomste, Adm Beheerbeampte, 1976
Brand J J, 46, Hondevlei PK Groot Mist Springbok, Boer/Winkelier, 1969
Brand L v W, 34, Losperplaas Loeriesfontein, Boer, 1973
Brand P M A, 37, Posbus 48 Kirkwood/Laerskool, Skoolhoof, 1970, Alicedale
Brand W J A, 30, Gondolalaan 3 Robindale/(Rand Mines), Regsadviseur/Mynsekretaris, 1977, Bloemfontein
Brandt E, 26, Munisipaliteit Krugersdorp, Asst Lokasie Supt, 1965, Potchefstroom
Brandt F J B, 42, Laerskool Durbanville, Onderwyser, 1966, Morreesburg
Brandt H B, 36, P U vir C H O Potchefstroom, Snr Lektor, 1972, Bloemhof
Brandt L de J, 43, Cilliersstraat 20 Lindey/Volkskas, Bestuurder, 1976, Pretoria
Brandt R B, 28, S A Polisie Johannesburg, Luitenant, 1969, Stellenbosch
Brandt S J, Lid van die U R se Landbou Kommittee 1973
Brazelle J A, 32, Laerskool Hartswater/Janviljoenstraat, Skoolhoof, 1970, Lady Frere
Brazelle R R, 30, P/A Penegare Kollege Taung K P, Onderwyser, 1975, Pretoria
Bredell G S, 37, P/A Navorsingsinst vir Sitrus & Subtropiese Vrugte Nelspruit, Wetenskaplike, 1975, Pretoria
Bredenkamp D C B, 39, Wolknit Korp Bpk, Rustenburg, Besturende Direkteur, 1974, Pretoria
Bredenkamp P, 33, P/A Landbou-Hoërskool Brits, Onderwyser, 1965, Benoni
Breedt A, 29, P/A U P Pretoria, Lektor, 1969, Krugersdorp
Breedt J, 43, Northridgelaan 27 Sunnyridge Germiston, Sakeman, 1977, Roodepoort
Breedt D J, 33, Careystraat 4 Strubenvale Springs, Onderwyser, 1974, Rustenburg
Breedt J S, 40 Susannasdeel Ogies, Boer, 1971, Pretoria
Breitenbach T C, 30, Ross Gradwellstraat 2 Uitenhage, Onderwyser, 1975, Graaff-Reinet

Bressel L C, 32, P/A N G Kerk Venterspos, Predikant, 1973, Johannesburg
Brewis D J, 35, Skoolstraat Ariamsvlei/S A Polisie, Adj-Offisier, 1976, Mafeking
Breyer J P, 46, Hopefield PK Lehmansdrift, Boer, 1968, Queenstown
Breytenbach A P J, 38, P/A Laerskoolkoshuis, Onderwyser, 1973, Nelspruit
Breytenbach H S, 39, Regent Circus 3 Tamboerskloof Kaapstad, Mondchirurg, 1969, Pretoria
Breytanbach J J v Z, 35, Vilonelstraat Steynsrus/N F S, Bestuurder, 1971, Frankfort
Breytenbach T, 35, St Johnstraat 91, Kokstad/S A Polisie, Luitenant, 1970, Pietermaritzburg
Breytenbach W N, 37, Droogskoonmakers Bukesstraat 19 Kokstad, Sakeman, 1973, Pretoria
Breytenbach W P, 33, P/A C & I Accounting Salisbury, Rekenmeester, 1975, Darwindale
Briedenhann J A L, 43, Erfenis Verkeerdevlei, Boer, 1977, Bloemfontein
Briedenhann J C, 41, P/A Manhattan Diamond Cuttingworks Johannesburg, Diamantslyper, 1967
Briel D S, 36, Hartebeesfontein PK Brits, Boer/Tuinbeplanner, 1976, Skeerpoort
Briers C J, 52, P/A Tvlse Prov Adm Pretoria, Verkeershoof, 1968
Brill J R, 34, P/A Hoër Tegn Skool Benoni, Onderwyser, 1970, Brakpan
Brink A, 33, Hoërskool Petrus Steyn, Onderwyser, 1967, Boshoff
Brink A J, 45, P/A Stadsraad Brits, Stadsklerk, 1975, Pretoria
Brink C J D, 28, P/A Brink Apteek Evander, Apteker, 1965, Bethal
Brink C T, 43, P/A Emmarentia Geldenhuysskool Warmbad, Onderhoof, 1965, Potchefstroom
Brink D, 46, N G Pastorie Uitenhage, Predikant, 1966, Ysterplaat
Brink D J, 43, Tordan Tengwe Karoi, Boer, 1976, Salisbury
Brink D J J, 30, Lime Acres Danielskuil, Elektrotegn Ing Northern Lime, 1970, Braamfontein
Brink D S v d M, (Lid Nr 4798) Prokureur en L U K Rustenburg
Brink H, 38, Afrikaanse Pers Bpk Doornfontein, Rekenmeester, 1966, Sasolburg
Brink J G, 48 S A B S Pretoria, 1ste Vakkundige Beampte, 1968
Brink J H, 47, Yskor Pretoria, Klerk, 1968
Brink J M, 31, Readmanstraat 109 Wilkoppies/Reyneke Brink & Kie, Geoktrooieerde Rekenmeester, 1970, Pretoria
Brink L C, 35, P/A Bester Beleggings Pretoria, Fin Bestuurder, 1975, Kempton Park
Brink L J, 32, P/A Dept Gevangenis Pollsmoor, Kaptein, 1973, Ceres
Brink N J, 47, Myburgh PK Viljoenskroon, Boer, 1964
Brink S J, 39, S A S & H Werkwinkels Soutrivier, Asst Voorman, 1967, Bloemfontein
Brink T C S, 33, Mosesriviermond Marble Hall, Boer, 1977, Brits
Brink W C J, 36, Stilfontein Goudmyn, Geoloog, 1966, Potchefstroom
Brits B S, 43, P/A Hoërskool Aliwal-Noord, Vise-Hoof, 1975, Maclear
Brits C P, 31, Hendrikspan PK Morgenzon, Boer, 1973, Bethal
Brits J C, 29, Hoërskool Maclear, Onderwyser, 1966, Delmas
Brits J P, 25, Hoërskool Parys/Schanette Woonstelle Nr 9, Onderwyser, 1970, Bloemfontein
Brits L H, 44, P/A Airite (Edms) Bpk Robertsham Johannesburg, Tegn Direkteur, 1976, Pretoria
Brits M J B, 40, Soft Plaas Macheke, Boer, 1976, Marandellas
Brits P B, 41, Lekkerwater Marandellas, Boer, 1976
Brits R J F, 30, Ivan Smutslaan 23 Kenmore Krugersdorp, Onderwyser, 1977
Brits S G, 39, P/A Noordkaapland Suiwel Koöp Kimberley, Rekenmeester, 1968, Ladysmith
Brits W F, 44, Staatsdienskommissie Pretoria, Inspekteur, 1965, Smithfield
Brits Y, 41, Uniestraat 13 (a) Parys, Organiseerder FAK, 1971, Vereeniging
Britz A J H, 44, P/A Amalgamated Engineers Union Durban, Sekretaris, 1968
Britz A W, 45, P/A C N Venter & Kie Durban, Prokureur 1967, Pietermaritzburg
Britz C J, 30, Kildareweg 2 Empangeni/Hoërskool, Onderwyser, 1970, Pretoria
Britz C J vZ, 40, 13e Straat 3 Greymont/Hoërskool Vorentoe, Onderwyser, 1971, Waterval Boven
Britz F W A, 39, Trust Bank Kaapstad/(Pros & Stelsels), Hoofbestuurder, 1976, Bellville
Britz G, 40, Hugo Naudelaan 7 Langerug Worcester/S A S & H, Snr Klerk, 1973, Cradock
Britz G J, 28, Landbou-Kollege Weston Mooirivier, Onderwyser, 1973, Estcourt
Britz R M J, 33, N G Pastorie Lady Grey, Predikant, 1975, Jamestown

Britz T F, 37, Groenfontein Vierfontein, Boer, 1969, Ventersburg
Broekman S W B, 40, Die Meerstraat 90 Pietersburg/S A Polisie, Kaptein, 1971, Middelburg Tvl
Bronkhorst P C, 41, P/A Helammyn Swartruggens, Mynspeurder, 1973
Brönn W F, 34, Reitzstraat Robertson, Geneesheer, 1965
Broodryk C J, 33, P/A Goudstadse Onderwyskollege Johannesburg, Snr Dosent, 1967
Broodryk D J, 38, P/A Westelike Graan-Koöp Malmesbury, Fin Sekretaris, 1967, Germiston
Broodryk M 32, Bo-Burgstraat 1 Wellington, Dosent/Opleidingskollege, 1971, Oviston
Brown C H 39, H/V Trotter & Hedgestraat Knysna, Sakeman, 1969
Brown E, 34, Universiteit Kollege van Zoeloeland Empangeni, Snr Lektor, 1966, Durban
Brown E L, 40, P/A BVS Umtata, Amptenaar, 1975, Grahamstad
Bruce G, 37, Dublinweg 38 Evander, Asst Posmeester, 1973, Riebeeck-Wes
Bruinette K E, 31, Bruinette Kruger & Hugo, Randburg, Ingenieur, 1969, Pretoria
Brümmer F J, 33, Dundonstraat 2, Wolmaransstad, Onderwyser, 1969, Pretoria
Brummer H J, 29, Bellstraat 1, Bethlehem, Tandarts, 1967, Pretoria
Brummer J G, 49, Munisipaliteit Johannesburg, Gesondheidsinspekteur, 1966
Brüssow A V, 46, U O V S Bloemfontein, Professor, 1976
Bruwer A A B, 28, Hoër Landbouskool Jacobsdal, Onderwyser, 1965, Reitz
Bruwer B E C, 40, P/A S A S & H Johannesburg, Skeikundige, 1969
Bruwer H J, 34, Maldonweg 67 Lynwood Glen Pretoria/Van Zyl Scheepers & Bruwer, Ouditeur, 1971, Klerksdorp
Bruwer J H, 33, P/A O'Kiep Copper Co, Geoloog, 1973, Worcester
Bruwer J J, 36, Strubenpark 321 Lynwood Pretoria/Landbou Ing Dienste, Hoof, 1968
Bruwer J L O, 40, N G Pastorie Stella, Predikant, 1965, Bray
Bruwer J M, 39, Munisipaliteit Swartruggens, Gesondheidsinspekteur, 1964, Pietersburg
Bruwer J P v S (Lid Nr 5022), Port Elizabeth, Professor
Bruwer W J, 37, N G Pastorie Swartruggens, Predikant, 1970, Sinoia Rhodesië
Bruyns M M, 38, Munisipaliteit Oudtshoorn, Stadstesourier, 1966, Malmesbury
Büchner A E, 27, Piesangbeheerraad Pretoria, Statistikus, 1966, Sandvlakte
Büchner J L B, 41, Kleinhoek PK Paterson, Boer, 1971
Buckle J P, 37, P/A Goulding & Smith Germiston, Begrafnisondernemer, 1963, Warrenton
Buckley J L, 39, Hoër Tegniese Skool de Wet Nel Huisklomp Kroonstad, Onderwyser, 1977, Welkom
Bührmann J R (L C R SN), 34, De Emigratie Ermelo, Boer, 1970
Bührmann J R, 35, Weltevrede Ermelo, Boer, 1968
Bührmann L C R, Lid van die U R se Landbou Komittee 1973
Buitendag C G, 29, P/A N P du Plessis Apteek Wolmaransstad, Apteker, 1973, Potchefstroom
Buitendag F J H, 40, Dunwoodielaan 80 Waverley Pretoria, Herv Predikant, 1971, Duiwelskloof
Buitendag H P, 45, Brindleyweg 21, Mondeor Johannesburg, Diamantslyper, 1975, Johannesburg
Buitendag J G E, 32, Mediese Sentrum 204 Voortrekkerstraat/Everglade Gardens 312 Lakeweg Gemiston, Tandarts, 1970
Burden H W, 26 P/A Landbou Koöp Brandvlei, Boekhouer/Boer, 1977, Loeriesfontein,
Burger A H, 32, P/A Brink le Roux & Myburgh Kakamas, Rekenmeester, 1973
Burger A J, 43, Yorkstraat 8/Landdroskantoor Wellington, Landdros, 1975, Paul Pietersburg
Burger A P, 46, P/A S A Polisie Bloemfontein, Sersant, 1968, Pretoria
Burger A P, 32, P/A Brian Sandrock Pretoria, Argitek, 1966
Burger B, Cecil Rhodeslaan 10, Mafeking
Burger B, 37, P/A S A Lugmag Mafeking/S A L, Kaptein/Tegn Offisier, 1974, Pietersburg
Burger C J, 37, Aero-Marine Durban, Takbestuurder, 1966, Johannesburg
Burger C R, 37, Laerskool Soebatsfontein, Skoolhoof, 1968, Kamieskroon
Burger C W, 26, Kingwillrylaan Graaff-Reinet, N G Predikant, 1977, Stellenbosch
Burger D A, 29, P/A N G Pastorie Alexanderbaai, Predikant, 1976, Kuilsrivier
Burger E J C, 43, Volkskool Wilgehof, Hoof, 1966, Karibib
Burger H A J, 41, Hoërskool Aberdeen, Skoolhoof, 1964, Brandvlei
Burger H L, 36, N G Pastorie Kroonheuwel Kroonstad, Predikant, 1964, Kimberley
Burger I S W, 34, P/A S A U K Johannesburg, Nuuskommentator, 1973, Pretoria

Burger J, 33, Montgomerylaan 2 Witbank, Ouditeur, 1966, Kimberley
Burger J A, 37, Skouterrein Milnerpark, Afd Sekretaris WLG, 1977, Florida
Burger J A, 33 Longstraat 19 Kempton Park, Prokureur 1975, Potgietersrus
Burger J de V, 30, Dept Landbou Vredendal, Voorligtingsbeampte 1967, Malmesbury
Burger J G, (Lid Nr 7706), Vaalharts/Dordrecht, Onderwyser, 1962, Vaalharts
Burger J G, 31, Beckstraat 22 Hennenman, N G Predikant, 1976, Edenvale
Burger J J, 36, Hugostraat 8 Monumenthoogte Kimberley/U O V S, Skakel-en-Ontw Beampte, 1973, Bloemfontein
Burger J J, 46, Rietfontein PK Putfontein, Boer, 1970, Germiston
Burger J J B, 34, P/A Wedgehill oor Prieska, Boer, 1967
Burger J J D, 29, Townsendstraat 193 Goodwood, Onderwyser, 1977, Lambertsbaai
Burger J K, 38, P/A Volkskas Wolseley, Bestuurder, 1975, Paarl
Burger J M, 39, P/A Volkskas Florida, Bestuurder, 1973, Primrose
Burger J S, 38, P/A S A Lugmag Pretoria, Adj-Offisier, 1975
Burger K A, 29, Ladismithse Saaiboere Koöp, Sekretaris, 1973, Wellington
Burger P, 37, Varkenskraal De Rust, Boer, 1966
Burger P A, 34, P/A Dept van Mynwese Alexanderbaai, Personeelbeampte, 1967, Pretoria
Burger P A Z, 42, Bysteek oor Brandvlei, Boer, 1973
Burger P J, 43, P/A Karl Bremer Hospitaal Bellville, Patoloog, 1968, Garies
Burger P J, 39, Northern Canners Politsi, Bestuurder, 1964, Heidelberg
Burger R J L (Lid Nr 7695), Komati Sekretaris/Boekhouer, 1962
Burger T F, 32, P/A Mediese Fakulteit Stellenbosch, Geneesheer, 1974, Johannesburg
Burger W, 40, Brandwag Montagu, Boer, 1974
Burger W A, 44, S A Polisie Randburg, Adj-Offisier, 1965, Porterville
Burger W P, 32, PK Skansklip oor Brandvlei, Boer, 1972
Burger W T, 31, 2deLaan 28 Heidelberg Tvl/S A Weermag, Majoor, 1976, Saldanha
Burke G A, 38, Spes Primêre Skool Goodwood, Onderhoof, 1966, Grabouw
Burmeister H F, 48, P/A Hoërskool Jansenville, Skoolhoof, 1968, Ugie
Burmeister J F, Hudsonstraat 36 Newton Park Port Elizabeth, 1971
Butler P W, 26, A H S Lynwoodweg 1 Pretoria, Onderwyser, 1973
Buurema H, Wolmaransstad, Skoolhoof, 1966
Buys B R, 43, Sannasposweg 61 Bloemfontein/Dept Prov Paaie, Snr Adm Asst, 1971
Buys C J H, 47, P/A Dept van Landbou Tegn Dienste Johannesburg, Vleisgradeerder, 1968
Buys C S W, 33, P/A Munisipaliteit Ermelo, Arbeidsbeampte, 1970, Vryburg
Buys G H, 37, Geref Kerk Delmas, Predikant, 1968, Uitschot Wes-Tvl
Buys I Z, 38, Paardeplaats Hartbeesfontein, Boer, 1977
Buys J, 41, P/A Engelsmedium Laerskool Rynfield Benoni, Onderwyser, 1965
Buys J C, 39, Kerkstraat 164, Nylstroom, Stadsklerk, 1971, Schweizer-Reneke
Buys J J, 40, Volkskool Brandfort, Skoolhoof, 1966, Bloemfontein
Buys J J J, 35, P/A Van Niekerk & Buys Witbank, Landmeter, 1970, Aliwal-Noord
Buÿs J P, 34, Volkskas Phalaborwa, Rekenmeester, 1970, Bothaville
Buys L J, 40, Geref Pastorie Middelburg Tvl, Predikant, 1963, Barkly-Oos
Buys M E L, 39, P/A W P Vrugte-Navorsingstasie Somerset-Wes, Snr Vakkundige Beampte, 1963, Klerksdorp
Buys M S, 33, Jordanstraat 31 Windhoek/S W A Adm, Staatsamptenaar, 1975, Prieska
Buys P J, 28, P/A Geref Kerk Odendaalsrus, Predikant, 1975, Potchefstroom
Buys R R, 40, Koppies, 1965
Buys S, 28, Possak 501 Oshakati, Geneesheer, 1974, Pretoria
Buys S B, 41, Prov Koshuis Standerton/Hoërskool, Vise-Hoof, 1971, Breyten
Buys S B, 37, Döngesstraat 25 Kroonstad, Apteker (Hospitraal), 1977, Virginia
Buys S P B, 30, Geref Pastoria Barkly-Oos, Predikant, 1964, Westdene
Buys W J, 41, P/A Vleissentraal Klerksdorp, Hoofbemark Beampte, 1974, Ventersdorp

C

Calitz J, 35, Cape Hotels Port Elizabeth, Rekenmeester, 1964, Calitzdorp
Calitz L P, 31, Eerstelaan 18 Marlands Germiston, Onderwyser, 1972, Pretoria
Carelson H L, 30, P/A S A Spoorweë Pretoria, Passer, 1968, Durban
Carstens A J, 31, Unisa Pretoria, Adm Klerk, 1977, Benoni
Carstens A J, 40, Nuwehoop Köop-Wynkelder Rawsonville, Bestuurder, 1970, Worcester

Carstens C, 32, Huis Esterhuizen Stella, Skoolhoof, 1967, Keimoes
Carstens H S, 37, P/A Sanlam Durbanville, Asst Bestuurder, 1975, Brackenfell
Carstens J, 33, Bothastraat 18 Westonaria, Landdros, 1971, Voortrekkerhoogte
Carstens J E, 39, Rembrandt Paarl, Sekretaris, 1963, Wellington
Carstens P G, Lid van U R se Ekonomiese Kommittee in 1973
Carstens P P, 38, P/A Westelike Graanboer Korp Tulbagh, Bestuurder, 1968, Paarl
Cawood J, 38, Nell Mapiustraat 1 Stellenbosch/Universiteit van Stellenbosch, Snr Lektor (Opv), 1975, Hopefield
Celliers A B, 42, Uniewinkels Kaapstad, Bestuurder, 1966, Heilbron
Celliers A W, 36, N G Kerk Nigel, Predikant, 1967, Pretoria
Celliers J G, 31, Unionstraat 9 Dundee, Geregsbode, 1964, Durban
Celliers J Z, 32, Rodewal Ermelo, Boer, 1976
Celliers S, 46 S A S & H Standerton, Klerk, 1965
Celliers W C, 32, J G Strijdomdam Jozini, Geneesheer, 1973, Standerton
Chamberlain H J, 39, Devonweg 42 Bluff Durban, Elektroniese Tegn(W N N R), 1976, Kaapstad
Changuion L J S, 34, Universiteit van die Noorde PK Sovenga, Lektor, 1975, Pretoria
Christensen A S, 29 Le Rouxstraat 7 Robertson, Onderwyser, 1972, Die Strant
Church H R, 43, S A S & H Bloemfontein, Snr Klerk, 1970
Church S du T, 27, P/A N G Kerk Odendaalsrus, Predikant, 1968, Stellenbosch
Church S J, 46, Venter & du Preez Bothaville, Sakeman, 1964, Kroonstad
Cillie C D, 49, Oorsprongberg Bethlehem, Boer, 1964, Wellington
Cillié F J, 27, P/A N G Pastorie PK Paterson, N G Predikant, 1974, Paarl
Cillie G G, Stellenbosch — Die Pieke
Cillie J F, 38, Bakenberg Sendingstasie PK Suswe, Geneesheer, 1975, Pretoria
Cillie P J, 30, "WERK & Leef" Sunnyside Pretoria, Adj-Parlementêre, Klerk 1971, Kaapstad
Cillie P J, Professor (Joernalistiek) Stellenbosch Redakteur Die Burger tans Voorsitter Nasionale Pers
Cilliers A B, 38, P/A Athlone skool vir Blindes Bellville, Skoolhoof, 1968, Port Elizabeth
Cilliers A v Z, 42, Landdroskantoor Knysna, Landdros, 1967, Lyttleton
Cilliers B, 30, Clarkweg 22 Pietermaritzburg/Univ Natal, Lektor, 1971, Bloemfontein
Cilliers C H, Hoër Terrasweg 4 Menlo Park Pretoria — Skakel by Univ van Pretoria 4.2.1976
Cilliers D H (Lid Nr 732) Professor — Universiteit van Pretoria — Voorgestel vir die UR 1968
Cilliers J, 33, Kleinfontein Swellendam, Boer, 1965
Cilliers J A H, 34, Voorslag PK Warden, Boer, 1973, Theunissen
Cilliers J F, 29, Lake Banaghar Chrissiesmeer, Boer, 1971, Heilbron
Cilliers J L le R, Sekretaris/Tesourier by Kongres van S A
Vereniging vir Bevordering van die Opvoedkunde in Kaapstad
1974
Cilliers P H K, 34, P/A H F Verwoerdhospitaal/Beechstraat 177 Lynnwoodrif Pretoria, Chirurg/Lektor, 1975
Cilliers P J, 41, S A S & H Upington, Betaalmeester, 1966
Cilliers P J v d M, 29, P/A Hoërskool Pretoria-Wes, Onderwyser, 1968
Cilliers W C (Jnr), 27, Sieringbank PK Ascent, Boer, 1970, Vrede
Claase E, 40, Sasol Sasolburg, Chem Ingenieur, 1967, Viljoenskroon
Claasen J N, 39, Diasstraat Westonaria, Hysbakbestuurder, 1966, Carletonville
Claasen J Y, 45, Buro vir Staatsveiligheid Pretoria, Inligtingsbeampte, 1974, Durban
Claasens J G, 36, Orab Mariental, Boer, 1977, Kamanjab
Claassen D G, 33, 6de Laan Heidelberg Tvl, Hoof van Werke, 1975, George
Claassen Johan, Gewese Springbok Kaptein
Claassen J D, 45, N G Pastorie Sidwell Port Elizabeth, Predikant, 1965, Kirkwood
Claassen N, 30, P/A Onderstepoort Pretoria, Skeikundige, 1965, Nylstroom
Claassen P J, 29, Leeuklip Stoffberg, Onderwyser, 1974, Ohrigstad
Claassens C C, Lid van die U R se Landbou-Kommittee 1973
Claassens C J, 28, F C U Pofadder, Skaap & Woldeskundige 1971
Claassens D J, 30, Foylelaan 50 Crosby Johannesburg, Hervormde Predikant, 1972, Hartbeesfontein
Claassens F L, 27, Laerskool Mariental, Onderwyser, 1965, Worcester
Claassens G C D, 37, P/A Dept van Waterwese Patensie, Ingenieur, 1967, Worcester
Claassens H C, Estcourt — Praat oor Kommunisme By Bondsraad van 1969

Claassens H C, 33, Allendale Greytown, Boer, 1968, Nongoma
Claassens H L, Florida — Ondersteun Afrikaanse Sake-Ondernemings By Bondsraad van 1966
Claassens J J, 32, Hoërskool Sasolburg, Onderwyser, 1973, Mariental
Claassens W K, 40, Norriseep Onseepkans, Boer, 1970
Clark A, 32, S A Huis Trafalgarplein Londen (Gewese Privaatsekretaris van Dr Carel de Wet), Minerale Attaché, 1974, Kaapstad
Clark H W J, 39, Paulinestraat 46 Constantiakloof/Roodepoort Wes Laerskool, Vise-Hoof, 1976, Ontdekkers
Clase F E, 39, Oranjehof Koshuis Boshof, Onderwyser, 1969, Brandfort
Classen J J, 27, Noordstraat Koster, Onderwyser, 1965, Pretoria
Classen R W, 34, Argitek AFD S A U K Johannesburg, Projekleier, 1973
Cloete A, 42, Ravensteynweg 24 Kampsbaai, Fabrieksbestuurder, 1972, Bloemfontein
Cloete A J, 32, Rhebokskraal McGregor, Boer, 1966, Pretoria
Cloete B D, 38, Randstraat 73 Koster/Volkskas, Bestuurder, 1971, Pretoria
Cloete C de M, 34, Constantia Skool PK Retreat, Onderwyser, 1967, Rustenburg
Cloete C S E, 45, Spoorwegpolisie Bloemfontein, Luitenant, 1967, Pretoria
Cloete F S M, 29, Mutual Plein 10 Ermelo, Tandarts, 1969, Johannesburg
Cloete G, 35, P/A Volkskas Vanderbijlpark, Rekenmeester, 1973, Empangeni
Cloete J C, 41, Dept van Sport & Ontspanning Pretoria, Skakelbeampte, 1973
Cloete J C L, 34, "Bluegum" PK Bainsvlei, Boer, 1968, Windhoek
Cloete J J, 34, Uitkyk Sutherland, Boer, 1966
Cloete P C, 37, N G Pastorie Vrede-Wes, Predikant, 1966, Johannesburg
Cloete S A, 36, Olifantsvlei Eikenhof, Speurder, 1968, Sterkstroom
Cloete T T, 44, P/A Universiteit van Port Elizabeth, Professor, 1968, Potchefstroom
Coertze H J, 34, Tweepanne Distrik Wolmaransstad, Boer, 1968, Schweizer-Reneke
Coertze J A, 39, P/A Adamas Paper Mills Port Elizabeth, Bestuurshoof, 1977, Springs
Coertze J H, 41, S A S & H Johannesburg, Klerk, 1964
Coertze P J, Gewese Hoof van Antropologie Dept, Professor
Coertze R D (Lid Nr 7673) Pretoria, Lektor, 1962
Coertze T F, 48, Merrivale Pietermaritzburg, Hoof B S V, 1976, Durban
Coertzen C R, 43, Skoolterrein Hoërskool Die Bult George, Onderhoof, 1972, Kaapstad
Coertzen J F, 39, 12de Laan 1 Thabazimbi/Gesondheidskomittee, Sekretaris, 1970, Witrivier
Coetsee D A, 45, Pretoriaweg 171 Germiston, Onderwyser, 1969, Heilbron
Coetsee E, 31, P/A Sanlam Klerksdorp, Verteenwoordiger, 1968, Durban
Coetsee F P, 33, Hoërskool Christiana, Onderwyser, 1964, Potchefstroom
Coetsee J A, 34, President Ingenieurswerke, Besturende Direkteur, 1973, Sasolburg
Coetsee M J, 39, P/A Primêre skool/Pres Reitzstraat 1 Harrismith, Adj-Hoof, 1975, Ladybrand
Coetsee S, 32, P/A S A S & H Oos-Londen, Timmerman, 1963, Burgersdorp
Coetsee W D, 42, Ansonstraat 64 Robertsham, Rekenmeester, 1972, Bloemfontein
Coetser P P J, 42, Yskor Vanderbijlpark, Instrumentingenieur, 1968, Pretoria
Coetzee A C A, 33, Hoogestraat 181 Potgietersrus, Apteker, 1967, Potchefstroom
Coetzee A G (Lid Nr 7768), Knapdaar
Coetzee A J, 33, Geref Pastoria Colesberg, Predikant, 1966, Marnitz Tvl
Coetzee A J, 33, P/A Wolnit Bpk Randfontein, Adj-Hoofbestuurder, 1967, Rustenburg
Coetzee A J, 27, Klippan PK Rykaartspos, Boer, 1973, Ventersdorp
Coetzee A J A, 39, Bergstraat 25 Springbok, Mynkommissaris, 1975, Windhoek
Coetzee A L, 28, P/A Geref Kerk Uitschot Vermaas, Predikant, 1968, Potchefstroom
Coetzee A P, 31, Grensstraat 26 Parys, Tekenaar, 1969, Johannesburg
Coetzee A P, 36, P/A O'Kiep Kopermaatskappy Nababeep, Rekeninge Klerk, 1973, Alexanderbaai
Coetzee A P S, 33, P/A N G Kerk Vryheid-Suid, Predikant, 1970, Randgate
Coetzee C, 41, Hartebeesfontein PK Brits, Sakeman/Bio Chemikus, 1975, Witbank
Coetzee C F C, 28, Geref Pastoria Louis Trichardt, Predikant, 1973, Potchefstroom
Coetzee C F C, 39, S A Polisie Florida, Majoor, 1968, Johannesburg
Coetzee C G, 28, Landbou Tegn Dienste Potchefstroom, Navorser, 1966, Bloemfontein
Coetzee Chris J, Gewese Rektor Potchefstroom Universiteit, Professor
Coetzee C J S, 42, Hoërskool Coligny, Onderhoof, 1967, Ventersdorp

Coetzee C M, 33, Steyldrift Oudtshoorn, Boer, 1966
Coetzee C N, 33, Caledonstraat Ficksburg, Boer, 1968
Coetzee D, 39, Harleystraat Oostersee Parow/Santam, Takbestuurder, 1970, Oudtshoorn
Coetzee D J, 37, P/A Sanlam Springbok, Takbestuurder, 1975, Mariental
Coetzee D J, 40, Farqarweg 155 Ladysmith/S A Polisie, Kaptein, 1971, Dundee
Coetzee D J (Dr), Lid van U R se Jeugkomitee in 1973
Coetzee D P, 25, P/A Albert Koöp Venterstad, Bestuurder, 1967, Burgersdorp
Coetzee F A J, 30, P/A BBK Durban, Organiseerder, 1975
Coetzee F C T, 39, Amakayastraat 1 King Williamstown, Direkteur van Landbou, 1972, Middelburg KP
Coetzee F J, 41, P/A Sasol-Gasskema Sasolburg, Bestuurder, 1964, Pietersburg
Coetzee G H J, 43, Reitzstraat 48 Meyerton/Hoërskool D F Malan, Onderhoof, 1972, Florida
Coetzee G J, 38, P/A Nas Boekhandel Johannesburg, Bestuurder, 1965, Port Elizabeth
Coetzee G J, 30, P/A O'Kiep Koper Mpy Ingenieur, 1974, Stellenbosch
Coetzee G J J, 37, Du Toitstraat 62A Porterville/Volkskas, Bestuurder, 1972, Bellville
Coetzee G J S, 37, Onderwyskollege Potchefstroom, Snr Dosent, 1966, Pretoria
Coetzee H B, 32, P/A Tvlse Raad Ontw Buitestedelike Geb (Dept Hoofing), Klerk, 1975, Germiston
Coetzee H J, 37, P U vir CHO Potchefstroom, Rekenmeester, 1968
Coetzee I, 32, Doverweg 20 Wentworth Durban/S A Polisie, Kaptein, 1971, Vryheid
Coetzee I S, 43, Poskantoor Marble Hall, Posmeester, 1965, Petrusberg
Coetzee J, 35, Munisipaliteit Krugersdorp, Snr Kom Klerk, 1965, Boksburg
Coetzee J, 39, P/A S A Polisie Johannesburg, Adj-Offisier, 1975, Randfontein
Coetzee J A, 44, Drostdy Mosselbaai, Landdros, 1970, Pretoria
Coetzee J A, 44, Vermaas, Winkelier/Boer, 1973, Zeerust
Coetzee J C, 34, Bergsigkoshuis Greyton, Skoolhoof, 1966, Kaapstad
Coetzee J C, 32, P/A Landdroskantoor Venterstad, Landdros, 1966, Middelburg K P
Coetzee J C, 39, P/A Pestrol Johannesburg, Besturende Direkteur, 1968, Ottosdal
Coetzee J C, 31, Hongerkloof Steynsburg, Boer, 1967
Coetzee J C van Z (Lid Nr 7726), Alberton 1963
Coetzee J E, 30, Vaalbank Reddersburg, Boer, 1976, Edenburg
Coetzee J G, 41, Goudfontein PK Rooihoogte KP, Boer, 1967, Middelburg K P
Coetzee J G du P, 34, Offisierslaan 28 Potchefstroom/S A Weermag, Offisier, 1976, Pretoria
Coetzee J H, 27, De Aar, Onderwyser, 1967, Piketberg
Coetzee J H, 36, Geref Pastorie Edenvale, Predikant, 1963, Potchefstroom
Coetzee J H, 43, Bloemhof PK Kayaseput, Boer, 1968
Coetzee J H (Prof) (Lid Nr 2300) Dekaan van Kunsfakulteit P U vir CHO Potchefstroom — 1963 — Voorgestel U R 1968
Coetzee J H F, 34, P/A Hoërskool Staats President C R Swart Pretoria, Onderwyser, 1975, Middelburg
Coetzee J J, 43, 2de Laan 3 Springbok, Sakeman, 1976, Plettenbergbaai
Coetzee J J H, 29, P/A Sasol Sasolburg, Asst Opleidingsbeampte, 1966, Bloemfontein
Coetzee J L, 34, N G Kerk Johannesburg-Suid, Predikant, 1964, Pretoria
Coetzee J N, 45, P/A Personeelafdeling Hoofbestuurder S A S & H Johannesburg, Klerk, 1964
Coetzee J N, 30, P/A Laerskool Oranje Maitland, Onderhoof, 1967, Touwsrivier
Coetzee J N C J, 39, Kestellstraat 163 Potgietersrus, Onderwyser, 1972, Groblersdal
Coetzee J P, 45, Krygsproduksie Pretoria, Direkteur, 1964, Vereeniging
Coetzee J S, 34, Essenhoutstraat 19 Phalaborwa, Prokureur, 1966, Bethulie
Coetzee K H S, 36, Graafwater S A Polisie Lambertsbaai, Sersant, 1965, Nuwerus
Coetzee L, 29, P/A Onderstepoort Pretoria, Dosent, 1966, Pretoria
Coetzee L C, 35, Bernardistraat 6, Paarl/Saambou, Bestuurder, 1971, Pretoria
Coetzee N, 30, Louwsrus Jamestown, Boer, 1970
Coetzee N C, 43, P/A Yskor Pretoria/Med Fonds, Klerk, 1968
Coetzee N J A, 35, P/A Johann Rissikskool Johannesburg, Onderwyser, 1965, Piketberg
Coetzee N P, 32, Magaliesberg Graankoöperasie, Sekretaris, 1976, Stellenbosch
Coetzee P A A, 41, Perseel 57 Hardap Nedersetting Mariental, Boer, 1976, O'Kiep
Coetzee P C, 32, PK Mfolozi, Onderwyser, 1967, Pretoria
Coetzee P F, 33, 8eLaan 124 Roodepoort-Noord, Onderwyser, 1968, Eikenhof

Coetzee P H, 27, N G Kerk Graskop, Predikant, 1967, Pretoria
Coetzee P H, 36, P/A Dreyer Drukkers & Uitgewers Bloemfontein, Adm Beampte, 1972
Coetzee P J, 38, Brightonrylaan 11 Summerstrand Port Elizabeth, Kinderarts, 1966, Lichtenburg
Coetzee P J (Dr), Klerksdorp Redakteur van Kerkblad — 1963 (By Bondsraad 1969 gepraat oor Christelike sake)
Coetzee P J, 36, Athene Plaas Cashel, Boer, 1972, Vereeniging
Coetzee P J, 37, P/A Pretoriase Onderwyskollege, Dosent, 1974, Potgietersrus
Coetzee P J, 39, P/A Hoërskool Voortrekker Boksburg, Vise-Hoof, 1975 Magaliesburg
Coetzee P K, 40 Kandelaarsrivier Oudtshoorn, Boer, 1976
Coetzee S F, 28, Blaauwputs Goabeb Bethanie, Boer, 1976, Goabeb
Coetzee S F, 33, P/A Windhoek Hoërskool, Vise-Hoof, 1974, Keetmanshoop
Coetzee S J, 41, Holpan Dist Marico, Boer, 1971, Lichtenburg
Coetzee S J, 42, P/A Feedo Nywerhede Harrismith, Besturende Direkteur, 1974
Coetzee S J J, 41, Skoolstraat Bultfontein, Vise-Hoof, 1975, Bloemfontein
Coetzee S P B, 46, Schalk Coetzee Apteek Vereeniging, Apteker, 1970, Residensia
Coetzee W C, 41, RandCarbide Witbank, Skeikundige, 1964, Murraysburg
Coetzee W J (Lid Nr 7699), Welkom, Joernalis, 1962
Coetzee W J, Haarburgersingel 9 Bloemfontein (Vrystaatse Streekdirekteur vir Republiekfees 1971)
Coertze C R F, 35, P/A S A Weermag Pretoria, Sersant-Majoor, 1968
Coetzer F C, 31, P/A Merriespruit Primêre Skool, Vise-Hoof, 1975, Welkom
Coetzer F J, 36, P/A Universiteit Stellenbosch, Snr Lektor, 1974
Coetzer J C, 44, Sudburylaan 1236 Queenswood/Universiteit van Pretoria, Hoof Fisiese Beplanning, 1977
Coetzer J H, 36, S A S Polisie Johannesburg, Luitenant, 1967, Durban
Coetzer J J, 43, Western Holdingsmyn Welkom, Klerk, 1966, Groblersdal
Coetzer J P, 41, Laerskool Kalie de Haas Meyerville, Skoolhoof, 1965, Heidelberg
Coetzer J P J, 41, Dept Justisie Pretoria, Ondersekretaris, 1966, Port Elizabeth
Coetzer P A, 46, S A S & H Pretoria, Bonuswerkinspekteur, 1968
Coetzer P W J, 36, Kameeldrif Hoewe 96, Pretoria, Ingenieurs Opmeter, 1974
Coetzer W C, (Lid Nr 7769), Vryheid, 1963
Collins H A, 29, Dept Inligting King Williamstown, Streekverteenwoordiger, 1967 Stellenbosch
Collins J, 47, Hoër Handelskool Pietersburg, Waarn Hoof, 1970, Lagersdrif
Colyn C F, 29, Piet Retiefstraat 48 Tiervlei, Onderwyser, 1970
Colyn R H N, 31, P/A Gevangenisterrein Baviaanspoort, Kaptein, 1971, Vereeniging
Combrinck F P, 45, P/A Ontv van Inkomste Johannesburg, Snr Aanslaer, 1969, Bloemfontein
Combrinck H A, 32, Freemanville Klerksdorp, Onderwyser, 1966, Voortrekkerhoogte
Combrinck H C, 42, P/A Uniestaalkorp van S A Bpk,Vereeniging Ingenieur, 1974,
Combrinck L W, 31, Malanstraat 22 Worcester, Tandarts, 1964, Rustenburg
Combrink A V, 34, Combrink Apteek H/V Boven- & Kockstraat Rustenburg, Apteker, 1971, Potchefstroom
Combrink H J B (Dr), Andrelaan 7 Presidentrif/R A U, Snr Lektor, 1971, Pretoria
Combrink J C, 39, Dahliastraat Belfast, Vise-Hoof, 1974, Heidelberg Tvl
Combrink J H, 26, P/A Prok-Genl Pietermaritzburg, Staatsadvokaat, 1965, Kimberley
Combrink P, 42, N G Pastorie Upington, Predikant, 1964, Niekerkshoop
Combrink P M, 38, Vaalkop Koedoeskop, Boer, 1973, Warmbad
Conradie A B, 28, S A Polisie Kaapstad, Luitenant, 1965, Sutherland
Conradie A E B, 31, P/A Volkskas Bpk Thabazimbi, Rekenmeester, 1967, Sasolburg
Conradie A F, 33, Syferpan Coligny, Boer, 1975
Conradie C du P, 39, Western Reef Goudmyn Orkney, Personeelbestuurder, 1967, Fochville
Conradie D, 34, P/A Munisipaliteit Pietersburg, Adj-Stadstesourier, 1974, Rustenburg
Conradie D L, 41, Lot — H 104 Hluhluwe, Boer/Sakeman, 1977, Pretoria
Conradie E L, 43, Lanseracweg 11 Stellenbosch/Buro v Studente Voorligting, Hoof, 1975 Somerset-Wes
Conradie F D (Lid Nr 4765), Oranjezicht Kaapstad — L V (Voorheen L U K) — Voorgestel vir Uitvoerende Raad 1968

Conradie F J (F SN), 37, P/A Pastorie Vanwyksdorp Dist Ladismith K P, Predikant, 1970, De Doorns
Conradie H A, 31, Stofberg & Conradie Worcester, Prokureur, 1968, Bellville
Conradie H F, 37, P/A Nasionale Pers Bpk Kaapstad, Hoofrekenmeester, 1968
Conradie H J, 36, P/A Minister van Vervoer Pretoria, Klerk, 1965, Johannesburg
Conradie J B, 37, Schubertstraat 9 Potchefstroom, Argitek, 1972, Klerksdorp
Conradie J D L R, 40, Potgieterstraat 6 Brits, Geneesheer, 1970, Lichtenburg
Conradie J F T, 44, P/A Yskor Pretoria, Afdelingshoof, 1963
Conradie J G J, 34, P/A Traverso Durbanville, Rekenmeester, 1964, Parow
Conradie P, 32, P/A Hoërskool Wolmaransstad, Onderwyser, 1967, Lyttelton
Conradie P A (Dr), Opvoedkundige
Conradie P D G, 33, Offisierslaan 1 Militêre Basis Potchefstroom, N G Kapelaan, 1974, Stellenbosch
Conradie P J, 43, Universiteit van Stellenbosch, Snr Lektor, 1970, Pretoria
Conradie P J, 26, Leeufontein Murraysburg, Boer, 1976, Graaff-Reinet
Conradie P J (Lid Nr 2973), S A S & H Johannesburg — Voorgestel U R 1968, Afdelingsbestuurder
Conradie P J, 33, Annastraat 5 Lambton Nr 2, Germiston, Onderwyser, 1968, Potchefstroom
Conradie P J, 53, Doornhoek Schweizer-Reneke, Boer, 1965
Conradie P J T, 43, Saaiplaas PK Matjiesfontein, Boer, 1968, Laingsburg
Conradie P v G, 41 Werda Nuy/Worcester, Boer, 1966
Conradie R P, 44, Dorpsigstraat 23, Stellenbosch (Skakel by Universiteit Stellenbosch 1976), Adm Beampte, 1964, Bloemfontein
Conradie T A, 37, P/A Sasol Sasolburg, Bedryfsingenieur, 1964, Robertson
Conradie W S, 30, Wilanda Biesiesvlei, Boer, 1970
Conradie W S, 33, Posbus 4 Vermaas, Boer, 1971
Conradie W S, 32, Kaallaagte PK Biesjesvlei, Boer, 1969
Cooke B, 28, Tradouwshoek Barrydale, Boer, 1964
Cornelissen A, 31, P/A Provinsiale Biblioteek Bloemfontein, Organiseerder, 1969, Kaapstad
Cornelissen C P, 42, P/A Volkskas Markstraat Johannesburg, Onder-Rekenmeester, 1968 Prieska
Cornelius H J, 39, H T S Tom Naude Pietersburg, Onderwyser, 1968, Krugersdorp
Cornelius L F B, 33, Utrechtstraat 37 Vryheid, Onderwyser, 1976, Johannesburg
Cornelius M J, 39, Dorpstraat 1, Pietersburg, Onderwyser, 1968, Krugersdorp
Corver T G, 39, Alma Pk Warden, Boer/Sakeman, 1968
Cowley R, 44, P/A Hoërskool Pearson Port Elizabeth, Skoolhoof (Adj), 1974, Gansbaai
Crafford C P de W, 46, S A Polisie Pretoria, Majoor, 1966, Grootfontein
Crafford C P de W 30, 28ste Laan 810 Rietfontein/S A Polisie, Luitenant, 1976, Johannesburg
Crafford D, 33, Rivonisendingstasie Acornhoek, Sendeling, 1968, Vaalharts
Crafford D F, 38, P/A Nederlandse Bank Kaapstad, Klerk, 1963, Ladismith
Crafford D J, 26, Chinota Plaas Inyazura, Boer, 1970, Umtali
Crafford D J A G, 37, Afdelingsraad Mafeking, Asst Sekretaris, 1966, Riversdale
Crafford J A, 42, Crafford Du Toit & Vennote Pretoria, Rekenmeester, 1965
Crafford J E, 53, Chinota Plaas Inyasura, Boer, 1964, Fort victoria
Crafford J M, 40, Langeberg Köop Boksburg, Bestuurder, 1964, Franschoek
Crafford W A 29, Rooilaagte Plaas Inyazura, Boer, 1974
Craffort D L, 27, Militêre Basis Rundu/S A Weermag, Soldaat, 1977, Bethlehem
Crause C A, 39, Universiteitskollege Fort Hare, Professor, 1968, Pretoria
Crause H J P, 26, Jan van Riebeeckrylaan 33 Stilfontein, N G Predikant, 1976, Stellenbosch
Crause T D, 33, P/A Impala-Apteek Vereeniging, Apteker, 1968, Potchefstroom
Cronje A P J, 40, Volkskool Allanridge, Skoolhoof, 1970, Hennenman
Cronje B J, 42, N G Pastorie Brandfort, Predikant, 1965, Edinburg
Cronje C P R, 31, Nas Padveiligheid Pretoria, Welsynsbeampte, 1975
Cronje G, 46, Pilgrimsrust Dordrecht, Boer, 1976
Cornje G F P, 34, "Hou Aan" — Theunissen, Boer, 1966
Cronje H J, 37, Cyferfontein Edenburg, Boer, 1963
Cronje H J O, 37, Hopefield Viljoenskroon, Boer, 1977, Bloemfontein

Cronje J, Farrelweg 7, Greenside Johannesburg — (Skakel by R A U 4.2.76)
Cronje J, Voorsitter van Johannesburg Sentrale Komitee
Cronje J, 36, Suid-Natalse Hoër Handelskool Port Shepstone, Vise-Hoof, 1972, Pretoria
Cronje J C J, 39, Poskantoor Bethlehem, Klerk, 1964, Senekal
Cronjé J I, 29, Cable Hill 13 Simonstad/S A Vloot, Welsynsoffisier, 1972, Pretoria
Cronjé J J A, 39, Magazynstraat 44A Pietersburg, Onderwyser, 1976, Messina
Cronjé J M, 49, Julianastraat 2 Oberholzer, Sendeling, 1964, Madzimoyo
Cronje J P, 35, Posbus 82 Malelane, Boer, 1975, Witrivier
Cronje J P, 34, P/A Munisipaliteit Brandfort, Tesourier, 1975, Witbank
Cronje J P, 36, P/A Noord-Wes Koöp Lichtenburg, Hoof Bereken Afd, 1976, Pretoria
Cronje N L, 42, Joubertspark Dist Dewetsdorp, Boer, 1967, Bloemfontein
Cronje N R, 48, Lincolnshire Memel, Boer, 1966
Cronjé N S, 28, Harry Millerweg Estcourt, Onderwyser, 1972, Kaapstad
Cronje P C J S, 45, Minalaan 9 Adamayview/Vleissentraal, Koöp Amptenaar, 1970 Louis Trichardt
Cronje P J, 32, P/A S A Weermag Potchefstroom, Sportoffisier, 1975, Oudtshoorn
Cronje P J, 40 Keyterstraat 11 Oudtshoorn, Onderwyser, 1973, Knysna
Cronje P J, 42, S A S & H Johannesburg, Klerk, 1965, Kimberley
Crots F P, 36, Smitswinkel Marken, Boer, 1975, Pretoria
Crous G I, 24, Seunskoshuis Pk Williston, Onderwyser, 1967, Graaff-Reinet
Crous J J, 32 P/A Groothoek Hospitaal PK Koringpunt, Geneesheer, 1965, Heidelberg Tvl
Crouse Cas, Unisa Pretoria (Universiteitsraad), Statistikus, 1974
Crouse C F, 29, Unisa Pretoria, Snr Lektor, 1966, Krugersdorp
Crouse M, 39, Palmietrivier — Pk Jansenville, Boer, 1966
Crouse M J, 49, S A S & H Johannesburg, Snr Klerk, 1966, Cradock
Crowther N A S, 31, Avonmouthsingel 10 Somerstrand Port Elizabeth, Professor/UPE 1975, Pretoria
Crowther R F, 33, Andries Pretoriusstraat Reddersburg, Skoolhoof, 1973, Rouxville
Crowther R F, 31, Militêre Kamp Bethlehem, Kaptein, 1965, Kestell
Cruywagen A G, 43, P/A Stadsraad Germiston, Verkeershoof, 1974, Krugersdorp
Cruywagen J S, 42, Volkskas Umtata, Rekenmeester, 1977, Leeudoringstad
Cruywagen P H, 37, Gardenweg 10 Norwoord, Insp van Plofstowwe, 1965, Bellville
Cruywagen W A, Minister van Onderwys en Opleiding
Cuyler A du P, 32, Thringstraat 10, Kroonstad, Veearts, 1977, Potchefstroom
Cuyler E (Lid Nr 4580), Gewese Stadsraadslid vir Johannesburg & Senator

D

Dafel D J, 33, Die Residensie Louwsburg, Landdros, 1975, Port Shepstone
Dafel H J, 39, Vierdestraat 127 Naboomspruit, Apteker, 1972, Wolmaranstad
Dahms J S, 38, Umgenistraat Drieriviere Vereeniging, Chirurg, 1966, Bethal
Dames J C, 44, Alusaf Richardsbaai/Bantoe Administrasie, Personeelbeampte, 1973, Newcastle
Dannhauser A G, 39, Natalse Landbou Koöp Hluhluwe, Takbestuurder, 1966, Bergville
Dannhauser D J J, 34, N G Kerk, Sinoville Pretoria, Predikant,1973, Vereeniging
Dannhauser L P, 41, D F Malanlaan 199 Lyttelton/Lugmag, Kaptein, 1968, Elsburg
Da silva A A, 30, N H Kerk Pretoria-Wes, Predikant, 1973, Johannesburg
Davel D L, 38, Engelbrechtstraat Viljoenskroon, Skoolhoof, 1976, Sasolburg
Davel E J, 39, Groenvlei Carolina, Boer, 1972
Davel H J S, 41, Yskor Vanderbijlpark, Ingenieur, 1974, Krugersdorp
Davel J, 30, Kalkkrans Utrecht, Boer, 1969
Davel J G A, 30, Koppie Alleen Badplaas, Boer, 1976
Davel W J, 34, Frisgewaagd Utrecht, Boer, 1974
Davids A J, 35, Oosweg 6 Otjiwarongo, Prokureur, 1974, Outjo
Davids F J, 29 P/A Yasbeck & Kie Oos-Londen, Prokureur, 1965
Davis C P, 35, P/A H F Verwoerdhospitaal Pretoria, Kliniese Assistent 1974, Rustenburg
Deacon N J, Lid van Uitvoerend Raad se Landbou Komittee in 1973
De Beer A, 37, Avondale Manskoshuis Onderwyskollege Pretoria, Snr Dosent, 1970, Johannesburg
De Beer A B, 38, "Duminy" Witrivier, Boer/Sakeman, 1977, Ottosdal

De Beer A J, 35, P/A Florida Hoërskool Florida, Onderwyser, 1974, Johannesburg
De Beer A S, 34, Dept Kommunikasiekunde R A U Johannesburg, Lektor, 1977, Bloemfontein
De Beer B H, 37, Stoplekmotors Parys, Sakeman, 1973, Lichtenburg
De Beer C K, 34, Eddie se Beerstraat 15 Bloemfontein, Bestekopnemer, 1973
De Beer C S, 33, N G Pastorie Elsburg, Predikant, 1970, Stellenbosch
De Beer D L, 39, P/A Geref Kerk Potgietersrus, Predikant, 1975, Potchefstroom
De Beer D P, 35, President Versekeringsmpy Johannesburg, Versekeringsklerk, 1969, Nylstroom
De Beer D W, 33, P/A Gen Min and Finance Corp Randburg, Personeelbestuurder, 1975 Bellville
De Beer E J, 36, P/A Laerskool D F Malherbe Vanderbijlpark, Onderhoof, 1969, Pietersburg
De Beer F C, 33, Krugerstraat 19, Bronkhorstspruit, Prokureur, 1976, Potchefstroom
De Beer G, 33, Goudstad Onderwyskollege Johannesburg, Snr Lektor, 1966, Langlaagte
De Beer G A, 28, Underhof 18 Selectionpark, Onderwyser, 1968, Springs
De Beer F, 41, P/A Hoërskool Jan De Klerk Krugersdorp, Onderhoof, 1965, Boksburg
De Beer G J E, 30, P/A Radio Bantoe Johannesburg, Hoof Swahilidiens, 1973, Pretoria
De Beer I I, 39, Crowstraat 2 Horison Roodepoort, Diamantslyper, 1975, Johannesburg
De Beer J, 48, Switchstraat 56 Power Park Johannesburg, Voorman Elektrisiën, 1971, Burgersdorp
De Beer J, 46, Woodlandsrylaan 1152, Queenswood Pretoria, Adj-Staatsdrukker, 1968
De Beer J G W, 31, Shipleyweg 7, Ferryvale Nigel, Prokureur, 1976, Potchefstroom
De Beer J J I, 44, Eeufeesstraat 21 Pretoria-Noord, Onderwyser, 1968
De Beer J J J, 31, P/A Hoër Tegn Skool Pietersburg, Onderwyser, 1974, Pretoria
De Beer J L, 33, Witbank PK Davel, Boer, 1971, Pretoria
De Beer, J L P, 37, P/A Afdelingsraad Barkly-Oos, Sekretaris, 1969, Rossouw
De Beer J P, 46, P/A Hoërskool Ellisras, Skoolhoof, 1967, Pietersburg
De Beer J M, 40, P/A Sanlam Vereeniging, Taksekretaris, 1967, Bellville K P
De Beer M J, 36, Sanlam Vryburg, Verteenwoordiger, 1968, Johannesburg
De Beer N J, 38, P/A BAR Ooskaap/Wodehousestraat 99 Queenstown, Personeelbeampte, 1975, Sterkstroom
De Beer P, 41, P/A S A Weermag Pretoria, Brigadier, 1976
De Beer P, 29, Du Toitstraat 15 Kiblerspark, Onderwyser, 1971, Pretoria
De Beer P J, 35, P/A N H Kerk Johannesburg-Wes, Predikant, 1975, Eikenhof
De Beer R J, 34, Boersemastraat 29 Universitas Bloemfontein, N G Predikant, 1973, Benoni
De Beer S A, 31, Weseindestraat 8 Postmasburg, Hoofvoorligtingsbeampte, 1971, Pretoria
De Beer S J, 27, N G Pastorie Komatipoort, Predikant, 1968, Stellenbosch
De Beer S J, 33, Albertusstraat 24 Wilkeville, Onderwyser, 1966, Stilfontein
De Beer S J, 30, Cloverstraat 9 Dersleypark, Volksraadslid, 1974, Magaliesburg
De Beer S J, 38, Markplein Adelaide, Prokureur, 1964, Steynsburg
De Beer S J M, 30, Van Bruggenstraat 30 Witbank/Vakleerlingskool, Onderwyser, 1970, Pretoria
De Beer T L, 27, P/A Francis Dix Bird & Kie Johannesburg, Ouditklerk, 1963, Boshoff
De Beer V, 31, P/A S A Spoorweë Pretoria, Skeikundige, 1967, Môregloed
De Beer W C M, 31, P/A N Herv. Pastorie Koster, Predikant, 1969, Coligny
De Beer Z, 41, Voorwaarts Seunskoshuis Pietersburg, Onderwyser, 1968, Waterberg
De Beer Z A J (Lid Nr 7727) Mafeking, 1963
De Beer Z H, 41, Afr. Pers. Bpk Johannesburg, Advertensie Werwer, 1964, Potchefstroom
De Bod A T, Lid van Afdelingsraad Oudtshoorn
De Bod S C, 41, Drostdy Koppies, Landdros, 1975, Pongola
De Bruin A J, 35, Nictus Boukontrakteurs Windhoek, Ingenieur, 1974
De Bruin B D L, 33, Duncanstraat 4 Brenthurst Brakpan, Hoof-Yker, 1975
De Bruin J G, 29, K O P Paul Roux, Verteenwoordiger, 1964, Fouriesburg
De Bruin M, 39, Lathamstraat 49 Irenepark, Narkotiseur, 1971, Pretoria
De Bruin M H, 40, Keatslaan 25, Orkney, Vakleerlingopleiding-Instrukteur, 1973, Vryburg
De Bruin M M, 34, Van Riebeeckstraat 38, Carolina, Weg-Inspekteur, 1974, Potchefstroom
De Bruin T D, 25, Volkskas Messina, Rekenmeester, 1965, Hennenman
De Bruin T F, 35, Lushof PK Vanzylsrust, Boer, 1968
De Bruyn, A36, Kingshoofweg 428 Lynnwood Pretoria/De Bruyn Skoenwinkels, Direkteur, 1971

De Bruyn A J, 37, N G Kerk Mayfair-Wes Johannesburg, Predikant, 1968, Glaudina
De Bruyn B C, 35, Krygstuigraad Pretoria, Best (Radar & Rekenaars), 1977, Jan Kempdorp
De Bruyn E, 30, Munisipaliteit Elliot, Stadsklerk, 1965, Senekal
De Bruyn F R P, 36, Geref Kerk Carletonville, Predikant, 1967, Port Elizabeth
De Bruyn F R P, 27, P/A Munisipaliteit Welkom, Bibliotekaris, 1965, Pietersburg
De Bruyn F R P, 35, Geref Pastorie Freemanville Klerksdorp, Predikant, 1973, Zastron
De Bruyn G A F, 35, S A S Bank — Oos-Londen, Bestuurder, 1967
De Bruyn J H, 32, Landbou Tegniese Dienste Ladybrand/Joubertstraat 46 Ladybrand, Tegnikus, 1976, Bethlehem
De Bruyn J J, 36, P/A NOK Johannesburg, Asst-Bestuurder, 1975, Middelburg K P
De Bruyn J R, 38, Laerskool Kuilsrivier, Onderhoof, 1969, Port Elizabeth
De Bruyn P J, 37, Geelhoutweg 481 Randparkrif 1 Randburg, Asst Makelaar, 1977, Groblersdal
De Bruyn P J, 32, Geref Kerk Vereeniging — Oos, Predikant, 1967, Silverton
De Bruyn S M, 45, Staatsmynopmeter Roodepoort, Hoof, 1964, Randfontein
De Clercq J, 34, P/A Dept Bantoetale Universiteit Stellenbosch, Snr Lektor, 1969
De Dock D H, 31, Schoongezichtstraat 5 Stellenbosch, Snr Lektor, 1968, Pretoria
Deetlefs N J, 34, Eureka Rawsonville, Boer, 1974
Deetlefs P P, 28, Porterstraat 82 Rawsonville, Boer, 1965, Goudini
Deetlefs P P du T, 31, Simonsberglaan 2 Durbanville, Geneesheer, 1975, Bellville
Degenaar B P D, 39, Wilgervlei Delareyville, Boer/Sakeman, 1974
Degenaar P J, 28, Plot 105 Sandspruit PK Honeydew/Cottesloeskool, Vise-Hoof, 1971, Roodepoort
De Graaf H, 26, Wingateweg 69 Montclair Durban, Tandarts, 1964, Pretoria
De Haas P, 35, Tiekiedraai Mkuzi, Boer, 1968, Mkweleni
De Haas S H, 44, Fernwood Mtubatuba, Boer, 1966, Volksrust
De Jager A J, 40, Kafferstad Hendrina, Boer, 1966
De Jager A J, 44, P/A Spoorwegpolisie Kaapstad, Kaptein, 1977, Esselenpark
De Jager A J, 28, "Corndale" Aberdeen, Boer, 1970
De Jager C L (Lid Nr 4644), Pretoria (President Kruger), Professor
De Jager C J, 26, Ankerhof Evander, Prokureur, 1968, Springs
De Jager C P, 33 P/A Jos De Waal & Kie Vryburg, Rekenmeester, 1974
De Jager C P, 35, P/A Ontvanger van Inkomste Pretoria, Rekenmeester, 1974, Stellenbosch
De Jager F A, 38, Hoërskool Villiera Pretoria, Onderhoof, 1965
De Jager G F, 43, P/A S A S & H Pretoria, Klerk, 1965, Bloemfontein
De Jager H J, 48, Rheboksfontein, — Mosselbaai, Boer, 1966
De Jager J A, 35, P/A Hoër Handelskool Tygerberg Parow, Onderhoof, 1969, Ladysmith Natal
De Jager J C L, 41, Rooirandjies Thaba'Nchu, Boer, 1966
De Jager J D U, 40, Framestraat 8(a) Middelburg, Sakeman, 1971, Ermelo
De Jager J H, 41, Delamarestraat 18 Robertsham Johannesburg, Geneesheer, 1967, Boksburg
De Jager J H, 40, Schreiwers Claim Harrismith, Boer, 1969
De Jager J H S, 40, Hoërskool Voortrekker Bethlehem, Onderhoof, 1965, Vrede
De Jager J J, 50, Uitkoms Hopetown, Boer, 1963, Griekwastad
De Jager J J, 32, Walterlaan 32, Waverley Pretoria, Geref Predikant, 1972, Potchefstroom
De Jager J J v N, 40, Drylaan 10 Theunissen, Onderwyser, 1972, Petrus Steyn
De Jager J S, 34, Blomstraat 1 Parow-Noord, Vise-Hoof, 1976, Uitenhage
De Jager J T H, 55, N G Pastorie Marandellas, Predikant, 1967, Fouriesburg
De Jager J T H, Salisbury-Praat oor Afrikaner in Rhodesie by 1969 se Bondsraad
De Jager L P, 34, Elektriese Installasies Stadsraad Windhoek, Inspekteur, 1972, Pietermaritzburg
De Jager N J, 37, P/A Hoërskool Goudrif Germiston, Onderhoof, 1965, Potchefstroom
De Jager N P J, 31, Hoofstraat Kenhardt/S A Polisie, Sersant, 1971, Gariep
De Jager P J, 49, Kingsweg 59 Bedfordview, Hoofbestuurder Vetsak, 1971, Ermelo
De Jager P T, 33, PK Besters Ladysmith, Boer, 1974, Pietersburg
De Jager P W, 32, Voortrekkerstraat Reivilo/Hospitaalraad, Sekretaris, 1970
De Jager S, 39, P/A Dirkie Uysskool Johannesburg, Skoolhoof, 1963, Tzaneen

De Jager S H F, 33, Toy Oosthuizenstraat, Bethlehem/Munisipaliteit Klerk v/d Raad, 1977, Brits
De Jonge J C, 38, Kampstraat Hoopstad/Hoërskool, Skoolhoof, 1970, Vierfontein
De Jongh A J, 42, P/A N G Pastorie Glenwood Durban, Predikant, 1970, Schweizer-Reneke
De Jongh C, 39, P/A S A Lugmag Pretoria, Luitenant, 1968
De Jongh C L, 38, "Vaatjie" Philadelphia, Plaasbestuurder, 1969, Moorreesburg
De Jongh J P N, 46, Hoërskool — Uniondale, Hoof, 1966, Nieuwoudville
De Jongh J V, 38, Klipfontein PK Ratelfontein, Boer, 1963, Graafwater
De Jongh P E, 42, Volkskas Bpk Du Preezstraat Bredasdorp, Bestuurder, 1970, Ficksburg
De Jongh T W (Dr), President van die Reserwe Bank
De Jongh W H, 34, P/A Lutzville Wynkelder Lutzville, Bestuurder, 1975, Upington
Dekker A J, 39, Jansensingel Phalaborwa/Frans Du Toit Hoërskool, Skoolhoof, 1970, Nelspruit
Dekker D J M, 29, P/A N G Sendingpastorie Hluhluwe, Sendeling, 1969, Vryheid
Dekker F A J J, 43, Wesstraat 84 Vryheid, Veeartsenydienstegnoloog, 1973, Pretoria
Dekker G (Prof), Gewese Voorsitter van die Sensorraad 1963
Dekker L W, 29, P/A Samuels Viljoen & Dekker Bloemfontein, Rekenmeester, 1963
De Klerk A J, 39, P/A Wag-'n-Bietjie Handelaars Dordrecht, Sakeman, 1968, Port Elizabeth
De Klerk B D, 34, Stephanopark 14 Vanderbijlpark, Onderwyser, 1971, Morgenzon
De Klerk B D, Robertson (Afdelingsrade)
De Klerk B J, 31, Meulstraat, Potchefstroom, Gereformeerde Predikant, 1977, Gobabis
De Klerk C J, 38, Clifton Graaff-Reinet, Boer, 1965
De Klerk F W, 27, P/A Theo Rood Boshoff & De Klerk Vereeniging, Prokureur, 1964, Potchefstroom
De Klerk F W, Minister van Pos — & Telekommunikasiewese, Volkswelsyn & Pensioene
De Klerk H, 34, Federale Mynbou Johannesburg, Afdelingsbestuurder, 1966 Potchefstroom
De Klerk H J, 29, P/A Meyer Nel & Kie Bethlehem, Ouditeur, 1975, Bloemfontein
De Klerk I J, 37, Mondorp Bpk Johannesburg, Bemarkingbestuurder, 1974
De Klerk Jan (Lid Nr 2490), Senator
De Klerk J A, 35, Prov Seunskoshuis Hoërskool Klerksdorp, Snr Assistent, 1971, Potchefstroom
De Klerk J J, 34, P/A Hoërskool Vredefort, Skoolhoof, 1966, Jagersfontein
De Klerk J J, 42, P/A Geref Kerk Boksburg-Suid, Predikant, 1974, De Aar
De Klerk J N, 31, Residensieweg Outjo/Landbou Tegniese Dienste, Voorligter, 1974, Otavi
De Klerk J P A, 43, Opleidingsdepot S A Polisie Pretoria, Adj-Offisier, 1964, Krugersdorp
De Klerk N R, 33, Dankfontein Jamestown, Boer, 1970
De Klerk P S A, 49, Eeufeesweg 52 Bayswater/S A S &H Bloemfontein, Snr Klerk, 1975, Pietermaritzburg
De Klerk S J, 34, Ncandu Park Primêre Skool, Vise-Hoof, 1976, Utrecht
De Klerk T C, 32, Jacksonweg 11 Hatfield Salisbury/Rhodesiese Lugdiens, Diens-Amptenaar, 1970, Enkelddoorn
De Klerk T C, 41, P/A Volkskas Bpk Karasburg, Bestuurder, 1970, Windhoek
De Klerk T C, Genootskap van Rhodesiese Afrikaners, Direkteur Gedenkgebou, Jamesonlaan, Salisbury
De Klerk T G, 36, Krenzstraat Outjo, Onderwyser, 1972, Gobabis
De Klerk W A, 29, Dept Lande Vryburg, Inspekteur, 1963
De Kock A D, 33, P/A Afdelingsraad Stellenbosch, Padinspekteur, 1973, Caledon
De Kock A J, 38, Volkskas Ladysmith, Rekenmeester, 1965, Frankfort
De Kock A J L, 35, Skoolraad Fraserburg, Sekretaris, 1966, Paarl
De Kock C J J, 38, Welgemeen Hertzogville, Boer, 1967, Reitz
De Kock D J, 38, P/A Albert Ko-operasie Venterstad, Bestuurder, 1963, Burgersdorp
De Kock E L (Jnr), 44, Platrug Philadelphia, Boer, 1970
De Kock G, 29, H/v Greef- & Riebeeckstraat Reivilo, Rekenmeester, Volkskas 1977, Vanwykssvlei
De Kock G L, 29, Papiesvlakte PK Stella, Plaasbestuurder, 1970, Komga
De Kock G P L, 31, P/A Uniewinkels Vereeniging, Streeksbestuurder, 1975, Potchefstroom
De Kock G W, 45, P/A Primêre Skool Wonderboom-Suid, Skoolhoof, 1975, Pretoria
De Kock H C, 29, Kalbaskraal-Plaas Kalbaskraal, Boer, 1975

De Kock J A, 35, "Die Hoek" PK Cedarville, Boer, 1972
De Kock J H, 44, Barry Hertzoglaan 18 Greenside Johannesburg, Ginekoloog, 1968
De Kock J M, 33, Remhoogte Philadelphia K P, Boer, 1969
De Kock J N, 32, Marynastraat Hennenman, Tandarts, 1963, Pretoria
De Kock L V, 42, P/A Landdroskantoor Boksburg, Landdros, 1965, Springs
De Kock M, 46, Eekhoringlaan 45, Monumentpark Pretoria, Landdros, 1976, Bellville
De Kock M C, 33, Banhoekweg 13 Stellenberg/Sanlam, Snr Beampte, 1977, De Doorns
De Kock N A, 34, S A S & H Bloemfontein, Vakman, 1966, Reitz
De Kock P S, 36, Van Zyl Scheepers & Bruwer Pretoria, Openbare Rekenmeester & Ouditeur, 1974
De Kock S A, 32, Friedenheim Nelspruit, Boer, 1968, Inyazura, Rhodesië
De Kock S D, 32, P/A Munisipaliteit Randburg, Asst Stadsingenieur, 1965, Stellenbosch
De Kock W N, 40, Rustig Orchard (De Doorns), Boer, 1965, De Doorns
De Kok J A, 33, Schikfontein Heidelberg Tvl, Besturende Direkteur, 1971, Vanderbijlpark
De Koker W J H, 38, P/A Volkskas Meyerton, Bestuurder, 1967, Pretoria
De Koning L W, 41, P/A Munisipaliteit Brakpan, Markmeester, 1967, Krugersdorp
De Korte G J, 35, 22eLaan 692 Rietfontein/Universiteit Pretoria, Adm Beampte, 1975 Potchefstroom
De Korte H J C, 39, Oertelstraat Schweizer-Reneke, Geneesheer, 1967, Klerksdorp
De La Bat R S, 28, P/A K W V Paarl, Marknavorser, 1965, Worcester
De Lange A F, 36, P/A S A Spoorweë Pretoria, Passer, 1968, Oos-Londen,
De Lange B J, 37, Vlakplaas PK Ladysmith, Boer & Vee-Inspekteur, 1967
De Lange B J, 30, Hoërskool Kensington Johannesburg, Onderhoof, 1966, Bethal
De Lange C J, 44, Gemsbokstraat 3 Loevenstein, Oor-Neus-& Keelarts, 1974, Volksrust
De Lange D, 41, Delvillesingel 2, Dellville Germiston, Ingenieur, Evkom, 1970, Brakpan
De Lange G L, 29, P/A Kinderoord Ugie, Rekenmeester, 1971, Port Elizabeth
De Lange J F, 31, Amatolary 108 King Williamstown, Onderwyser, 1974, Uitenhage
De Lange J J, 29, Thornegrove Pearston, Boer, 1970
De Lange N, 40, P/A Hoërskool Jan De Klerk Krugersdorp, Onderwyser, 1969
De Lange P J, 36, P/A Munisipaliteit Malmesbury, Stadsklerk, 1976, Porterville
De Lange W J, 33, S A Vloot Durban, Luit-Kommandeur, 1973, Simonstad
De La Rey J H, 33, Onderwyskollege Heidelberg Tvl, Dosent, 1964, Pretoria
De Leeuw C P, 30, P/A Mostert & Erasmus Bloemfontein, Ingenieur, 1968
Delport D S, 37, Aroma Dealesville, Boer, 1973 Bothaville
Delport G P, 38, P/A Kantoor van die Afdelingsbestuurder S A S & H Johannesburg, Snr Klerk, 1968
Delport H P J, 39, Volkskas Bpk Witbank, Bestuurder, 1964, Carolina
Delport J H, 49, Perseel IE4 Tadcaster, Boer, 1967, Migdol
Delport J P, 42, Geenspoor PK Hertzogville, Boer, 1967, Hoopstad
Delport J T, 29, Universiteit Port Elizabeth, Prokureur, 1969, Kirkwood
Delport L P, 40, P/A Volkskas Silverton, Rekenmeester, 1974, Louis Trichardt
Delport M J de V, 33, Anniesvelden Ventersburg, Boer, 1977, Kaapstad
Delport M J de W, 33, Beckerstraat Ladismith K P, Voorligtingsbeampte, 1967, Caledon
Delport P, 38, P/A Munisipaliteit Pretoria, Hoof Eiendomme Afdeling, 1965, Rustenburg
Delport P J, 37, Ertjiesdam PK Caledon, Boer, 1969
Delport P J, 32, Vanzylstraat 31 Bloemfontein/P/A Oorlogsmuseum, Hoof Vakk Beampte, 1976, Tarkastad
Delport P W J, 37, S A Polisie Aucklandpark, Kaptein, 1967, Bloemfontein
Delport W H (Lid Nr 4572) — Port Elizabeth-Wes L V (Voormalige Springbok)
De Meyer O, 43, Greybestraat 79 Rynfield Benoni, Landdros, 1977, Pretoria
De Meyer W A, 43, 21eLaan 926 Rietfontein/Doeltreffendheid Poswese, Asst Direkteur, 1970, Pretoria
De Munnik E O, 38, P/A Verdedigingskollege Voortrekkerhoogte/S A Weermag, Kommandant, 1975, Bronkhorstspruit
De Necker J G H, 43, Waterval Rustenburg, Sielkundige T O D, 1975, Potchefstroom
De Nysschen J J, 40, Troystraat 169, Pretoria, Sekr/Org Landmeters & Stadsbeplanners, 1977, Coligny
De Smit J T, 37, P/A Santam Ceres, Takbestuurder, 1975, Pretoria
De Swardt A J E, 35, Simpsonstraat Oudtshoorn, Onderwyser, 1973, George
De Swardt A V, Wolmaransstad, Prokureur, 1966

De Swardt D M S, 32, N G Pastorie Cornelia, Predikant, 1967, Magogong
De Swardt G J, 30, P/A Hoërskoolkoshuis Vredendal, Onderwyser, 1965, George
De Swardt J B, 38, Lankgelê PK Windmeul/Sasko, Asst Hoofbestuurder, 1976, Bellville
De Swardt J E I, 32, Malanstraat Calvinia, Geneesheer, 1970
De Swardt J J, 36, Universiteit van Pretoria, Snr Lektor, 1964, Kroonstad
De Swardt S S (Oom Salie), Saasveld-Bousbou-kollege
Privaatsak X531 George, Inwonende Koshuisvader, 1977
De Ville R J, 31, P/A van Heerden Schoeman & De Ville Standerton, Prokureur, 1969, Pretoria
De Villiers, 41, Suikerbosrylaan 1 Vereeniging, Radioloog, 1977, Pretoria
De Villiers A B, 32, P U vir C H O Potchefstroom, Lektor(Geografie), 1977, Allanridge
De Villiers A G, 44, Welgevonden Makoppa, Boer, 1977
De Villiers A J, 48, Uitzicht Napier, Boer, 1967
De Villiers C B, 37, Wes-Tvlse Bantoe-Administrasie Raad/Arbeid & Behuising, Direkteur, 1977, Orkney
De Villiers C F (Dr), Universiteit van Pretoria
De Villiers C F, 31, Baie Bome Sunsetview Pretoria/Assosiasie Internasionaal, Direkteur 1975, Klerksdorp
De Villiers C G, 39, Smitstraat 135 Fairland/GOK, Snr Dosent, 1970, Heidelberg Tvl
De Villiers Dawie LV (Gewese Springbok Kaptein), Voorsitter van Ruiterwag 1972
De Villiers De La H
De Villiers D J, 34, Signalberg Grunau S W A, Boer, 1966
De Villiers D J, 27, N G Kerk Wellington, Predikant, 1968, Stellenbosch
De Villiers D P, Sasolburg (Het Bondsraad van 1966 Bygewoon)
De Villiers D P (Lid Nr 5348) — Voorgestel U R 1968, Advokaat
Oranjezicht, Kaapstad
De Villiers D R, (Lid Nr 7707), Kestell, Sendeling/Lektor, 1962
De Villiers E E, 44, Munisipaliteit Carletonville, Elektro Ingenieur, 1964, Witbank
De Villiers G G, 35, Heuwellaan Warmbad, Med Praktisyn, 1970
De Villiers H J, 34, Harringtonstraat 10 Brits, N G Predikant, 1971, Springs
De Villiers H M, 32 Weltevreden Suider-Paarl, Boer, 1968
De Villiers I A, 42, Oubees PK Soebatsfontein, Boer, 1970
De Villiers I A v N, 34, Goldberglaan 5 Bethlehem/Primêre Skool Jordania, Vise-Hoof, 1972, Ficksburg
De Villiers I J, 30, Beckerstraat 8 Southcrest Alberton/RAU, Lektor, 1974, Germiston
De Villiers I J S, 44, Lourentia Vrede, Boer, 1976
De Villiers I L, 42, N G Pastorie Otjiwarongo, Predikant, 1964, Pretoria
De Villiers I W B, 33, Kingshoofweg 454 Lynnwood, Advokaat, 1970, Bloemfontein
De Villiers J, 37, P/A J C Lourens & Seuns Pongola, Sakeman, 1968, Stellenbosch
De Villiers J, 25, La Rochelle Malelane, Boer, 1965
De Villiers Johan, Hennenman — Kla oor Sondagkoerante 1971
De Villiers J A, 32, Joubertstraat Caledon, Skrynwerker, 1967, Stanford
De Villiers J A, 37, Chrissieskool PK Chrissiesmeer, Onderwyser, 1963, Springs
De Villiers J B M, 46, P/A Ons eie Koöp Garies, Bestuurder, 1969
De Villiers J I, 35, P/A Sasol Sasolburg, Personeelhoof, 1966, Pretoria
De Villiers J H, 40, Die Vlakte Barrydale, Boer, 1964
De Villiers J J H, 39, Hillside Mamreweg Malmesbury, Boer, 1969, Durbanville
De Villiers J S, 34, "Shalimar" Hectorspruit, Boer, 1975, Malelane
De Villiers J W, 32, Jakkalskuil Petrusville, Boer, 1966
De Villiers M H A, 34, Lothair Skool Chrissiesmeer, Onderwyser/Boer, 1969, Ermelo
De Villiers M J, 30, P/A S A Polisie Balfour, Sersant, 1975, Brakpan
De Villiers M P R, De Doorns — 1966 Bondsraad Bygewoon
De Villiers P, 28, Goldberglaan 9 Bethlehem/Sekondêre Skool Voortrekker Bethlehem, Onderwyser, 1970, Vrede
De Villiers P, 36, Schoongezicht Suider-Paarl, Boer, 1968
De Villiers P C, 31, Touwstraat 23 Drie Riviere/Uskor Vereeniging, Ingenieur, 1970 Klerksdorp
De Villiers P J de B, 38, Malan en Vennote Upington, Prokureur, 1974, Johannesburg
De Villiers P J S, 30, Posbus 51 Bank, Onderwyser, 1966, Pretoria
De Villiers P P H, 33, P/A N G Kerk Danie Theron Eikenhof, Predikant, 1968, Walvisbaai

De Villiers P R, Advokaat — Lid van Uitvoerende Raad se Landbou Komitee 1973
De Villiers P J C, 42, Van der Merwestraat Barberton, Apteker, 1974, Pretoria
De Villiers R, 39, P/A C P De Leeuw De Villiers Basson & Rascher, Bourekenaar, 1976, Stellenbosch
De Villiers R M, (Lid Nr 855), Kempton Park, Predikant
De Villiers Steve, S A U K
De Villiers S A, 34, Aurora Vrede, Boer, 1968
De Villiers S J, 30, V O S Langebaanweg Saldanha/S A Lugmag, Majoor, 1971, Durban
De Villiers S M, 40, P/A SAUK Johannesburg/Bantoediens, Hoof, 1963, Pretoria
De Villiers W J, 33, Sanlam Paarl, Verteenwoordiger, 1967, Bellville
De Villiers W J, 39, P/A Volkskas Aliwal-Noord, Bestuurder, 1974, Harrismith
De Villiers W J, 51, General Mining Johannesburg, Besturende Direkteur, 1973, Welkom
De Vleeschauwer C A M, 46, Goudstad Onderwyskollege Johannesburg, Departementshoof 1966, Stellenbosch
De Vos D J J, 33, P/A Afrikaans Hoër Seunskool Pretoria, Onderwyser, 1975, Welkom
De Vos E, 43, P/A Holland Afrika Verkope Johannesburg, Besturende Direkteur, 1968
De Vos F C, 46, Driefontein Kinross, Boer, 1974
De Vos G de la B, 44, Huis Frank Joubert Prieska, Skoolhoof, 1975, Indwe
De Vos J S, 37, S A S & H Bloemfontein, Klerk, 1965
De Vos P J G (Prof), Lid van Uitvoerende Raad se Wetenskap Komitee 1973
De Vos P W, 47, Hell's Gate PK Buhrmansdrift, Onderwyser, 1969, Potchefstroom
De Vos P W, Posbus 222 Mafeking (Skakel vir seuns wat opleiding ontvang by Radaropsporingstasie Nr 3 te Klippan Mafeking)
De Vos W, 33, Geref Kerk Bloemfontein-Wes, Predikant, 1968, Bethlehem
De Vries A H, 39, Boland-Koöp Wynkelders, Bestuurder, 1970, Rawsonville
De Vries A J M, 26, Buro vir Ekonomiese Ondersoek Stellenbosch, Ekonomiese Navorser, 1967, Wellington
De Vries C G, 40, P/A Paarlse Opleidingskollege, Rektor, 1973, Franschhoek
De Vries G P C, 33, P/A Saambou Pretoria, Beleggingsbestuurder, 1968, Bloemfontein
De Vries M J, 33, Universiteit Stellenbosch, Professor, 1967
De Waal A N, 33, P/A Triomf Kunsmis Johannesburg, Kontrak-Besigheidsbestuurder, 1975, Alberton
De Waal D M (Dr), Lid van Uitvoerende Raad se Wetenskap Komitee 1973
De Waal H L (Dr), Gewese Voorsitter van die Akademie vir Wetenskap en Kuns
De Waal J A, 40 Sasolburg, Vakkundige Beampte, 1964, Parys
De Waal J C, 46, P/A Verbruikers Koöp Bpk Kaapstad, Sekretaris, 1968
De Waal J G, 35, Pretoriuslaan 1803/Die Lytteltonse Hoërskool, Onderwyser, 1971, Carletonville
De Waal J G K, 39, Uniewinkels Pretoria, Direkteur, 1966, Bellville
De Waal J J, 32, Motetema Bantoekollege Groblersdal, Onderhoof, 1972, Middelburg Tvl
De Waal M J, 36, Volkskas Paarl, Rekenmeester, 1966, Williston
De Waal M T, Gedien op Uitvoerende Raad se Nie-Blanke Sake Raad in 1973
De Waal P E, (Lid Nr 5109), Zeerust, Professor/Boer
De Waal S W P, 42, Gholfstraat 17 Christiana, Sakeman, 1970, Kakamas
De Waal T J, 26, Marshallweg 12 Athlone Park/S A Titan Products Chemikus, 1970, Stellenbosch
De Waal W P, 34, P/A Sasol Sasolburg, Ingenieur, 1967, Stellenbosch
De Wet Abel, Wolmaransstad — N P Komitee 1966
De Wet A D, Ottosdal (By Bondsraad van 1966 het hy gepraat oor Mieliesake)
De Wet A J O, 45, Kollegestraat Jansenville/Volkskas, Bestuurder, 1972, Bloemfontein
De Wet B G S, 38, P/A Kaapvaal Trust Randburg, Boedelberedderaar, 1977, Johannesburg
De Wet Carel (Dr)
De Wet C J, 40, De Villiersstraat Carnarvon/Volkskas, Bestuurder, 1972, Tzaneen
De Wet E R, 29, Dept van Mynwese Witbank, Inspekteur 1967, Middelburg Tvl
De Wet F P, 44, Mosenthalstraat Adendorp/Hoër Volkskool Graaff-Reinet, Onderwyser, 1970, Vryburg
De Wet H, 46, P/A Suid-Apteek Potchefstroom, Apteker, 1968
De Wet J C J, 44, Delbata Verkeerdevlei OVS, Boer, 1967, Bethlehem
De Wet J E, 37, Maxwellstraat 12 Risiville/Hoërskool Drie Riviere, Vise-Hoof, 1974, Nylstroom

De Wet J F, 27, De Wets Karavaankamp Margate, Karavaankamp-Bestuurder & Eienaar, 1971, Johannesburg
De Wet J I, 44, Farrelweg 13 Hazeldene Germiston, Boukontrakteur, 1973, Krugersdorp
De Wet J J, 32, Smitstraat 252 Fairland Randburg, Direkteur v Maatskappye, 1971, Linden Johannesburg
De Wet J J, 29, Nooitgedacht Smithfield, Boer, 1966
De Wet J J, 39, P U vir CHO Potchefstroom, Professor, 1973, Rustenburg
De Wet J M (Jannie), Outjo S W A Voormalige Kommisaris-Generaal
De Wet J M (Dr), Lid van Uitvoerende Raad se Wetenskap Komitee in 1973
De Wet J P, 30, PK Witputstasie Telpoort, Boer, 1964, Hopetown
De Wet J P, 35, Dagbreek Friersdale, Boer, 1971, Keimoes
De Wet J S, 35, Hoërskool Alberton, Onderhoof, 1977, Bronkhorstspruit
De Wet L J, 29, W G A, Cradock, Verteenwoordiger, 1964, Hopetown
De Wet L J C, 41, P/A Bantoesake-Adm Raad, Direkteur Finansies, 1974, Bloemfontein
De Wet P G J, 39, Navorsingsinstituut Nelspruit, Hoofplaasbestuurder, 1973, Burgershall
De Wet P J, 28, P/A P R de Wet & Van Der Merwe 2eStraat Koppies, Prokureursklerk, 1977, Newcastle
De Wet P J, 43, Departement Toksikologie Pretoria, Hooftegnikus, 1974, Fauresmith
De Wet P J K, 40, Motor Industriële Beleggings Bpk Kaapstad, Besturende Direkteur, 1966 Paarl
De Wet P le R, 35, Artois Wolseley, Boer, 1967, Rawsonville
De Wet P V, 46, Lulu Heilbron, Sakeman/Boer, 1974, Johannesburg
De Wet P W (Lid Nr 7728), Pietersburg, 1963
De Wet R, 42, P/A Universiteit Durban-Westville, Hoofbibliotekaris, 1975, Pretoria
De Wet R D J, 32, N G Pastorie Tuinplaas, Predikant, 1975, Stilfontein
De Wet S D, 40, Noord-Wes Koöp Migdol, Takbestuurder (Handel), 1974, Johannesburg
De Wet T J, 28, Disasingel 5 Blomtuin Bellville/Trust Bank, Dataverwerker, 1971 Vanderbijlpark
De Wet W, 46, Bellview Enkeldoorn, Boer, 1970, Bloemfontein
De Wet W, 32, Friedenstal Outjo, Boer, 1974
De Wet W de V, 34, Le Chasseur Robertson, Boer, 1964
De Wet W F, 30, La Mascotte Lady Grey, Boer/Verteenwoordiger, 1970, Smithfield
De Wit C P, 26, Bo-Scholtzkloof Prins Albert, Boer, 1973
De Wit D C, 31, Stellenhof 4 Kuilsrivier, Dosent Denneoord, 1974, Vanwyksdorp
De Wit D C de V, 39, Tweedestraat Koppies, Waarnemende Hoof 1974, Bloemfontein
De Wit D J, 38, Grootrivier Ladismith, Boer, 1964
De Wit J V (Lid Nr 7708), Pretoria, Hoof Speurder
De Wit P, 35, Uitkyk Heidelberg K P, Boer, 1971, Swellendam
De Wit W A, 34, Premier Metal Works Umtali, Bestuurder, 1967, Gatooma
De Witt H G, 44, S A Polisie Pretoria, Brigadier, 1974
De Witt J H J, 29, P/A N G Kerk Witbank, Predikant, 1968, Pretoria
De Witt J J, 44 P/A Landdroskantoor Vanwyksvlei, Landdros, 1968, Vryheid
De Witt J J, 34, P/A Vetreën Isando, Afdelingshoof, 1975, Boksburg
De Witt J T, 37, Opleidingskollege Oudtshoorn, Dosent, 1970, Malmesbury
De Witt P J, 45, Heynsvlakte Carnarvon, Boer, 1963
Dicke J T G, 30, Merensky Hoër Landbouskool Spitsrand Duiwelskloof, Boer/Onderwyser, 1970
Dickenson W S J, 37, Dalmada Kleinhoewes, Pietersburg, Onderwyser, 1971, Potgietersrus
Dippenaar D J, 30, Hoërskool Goedehoop Germiston, Onderwyser, 1963, Brakpan
Dippenaar E J J, 36, P/A N G Kerk Tiervlei, Predikant, 1968, Warmbad, SWA
Dippenaar J A S, 36, P/A Hoërskool E G Jansen Boksburg, Onderwyser, 1973, Brakpan
Dippenaar M C, 30, Nkhensani N G Sendingstasie Giyani, Predikant, 1974, Pretoria
Dippenaar R J, 31, P/A Raad op Atoomkrag Pretoria, Metallurg, 1977
Dodds J P, Voorheen Senior Amptenaar by Bantoe Administrasie
Donald P R, 39, Gen Hertzogweg 136 Drie Riviere Vereeniging, Rekenmeester Uniestaal, 1976, Sasolburg
Dorfling L, 42, Seven Oaks Vrede, Onderwyser, 1977, Frankfort
Dorfling L M, 46, Brakhill PK Kirkwood, Boer/L P R, 1967, Uitenhage
Doubell G C, 35, P/A Meyer Nel & Kie Senekal, Ouditeur, 1974, Bloemfontein

Doubell W J C, 33, Streatleylaan 11 Aucklandpark Johannesburg, Snr Adm R A U, 1977, Pretoria
Dowd J J, 36, S A Polisie Strand, Luitenant, 1977, Heidelberg
Doyer P J v D, 31, Heuningklip Badplaas, Boer, 1976, Carolina
Dreyer A C, 31, Tomstraat 59 Potchefstroom/P U vir C H O, Lektor, 1972, Bloemfontein
Dreyer A E L, 39, Chesterweg 662 Bryanston, Geneesheer, 1971, Pretoria
Dreyer A G, 29, Prinsloo & Dreyer Johannesburg, Tandarts, 1963, Durban & Pretoria
Dreyer C H, 40, Glen Alpinedam PK Tolwe, Boer, 1967
Dreyer H C, 36, Zooihuis Sannieshof, Boer, 1975
Dreyer H H, Nasionale Pers (1973)
Dreyer H J, 39, Anthonysingel 49 Empangeni/Universiteit van Zoeloeland, Professor, 1976, Pretoria
Dreyer J, 30, Versaillesstraat 12 Bloemfontein, Landbou Navorser, 1976
Dreyer J A, 42, P/A National Chamber of Milling Johannesburg, Sekretaris, 1970, Windhoek
Dreyer J A, 29, Skulpspruit PK Ascent, Boer, 1970
Dreyer J J, 39, S A S Polisie Johannesburg, Adj-Offisier, 1966, Pretoria
Dreyer J J, 45, Rietdraai PK Lichtenburg, Boer, 1966
Dreyer J N, 39, Wolwepan Vermaas, Boer, 1970, Sannieshof
Dreyer J P, 32, Omkyk Dist Lichtenburg, Boer, 1975, Biesiesvlei
Dreyer J S, 40, N G Kerk Hartenbos, Predikant, 1968, Postmasburg
Dreyer L A, 29, P/A Hoërskool Kempton Park, Onderwyser, 1965, Swartruggens
Dreyer N, 34, Parkrylaan 7 Arcadia, Onderwyser, 1964
Dreyer P J, 37, Florenceweg Bellville, Skoolhoof, 1965, Vredendal
Dreyer P J, 43, Landdroskantoor Tzaneen, Asst Landdros, 1964, Vereeniging
Dreyer P K, 44, P/A Hoër Tegniese Skool Tom Naude Pietersburg, Onderwyser, 1965, Rustenburg
Dreyer P S (Prof), Hervormde Kerk
Dreyer S A P, 40, Palmstraat Strand, Prokureur, 1977, Morreesburg
Dreyer S J, 36, P/A Meintjes Vermooten & Zondagh Pretoria, Hoofklerk, 1966
Dreyer T F, 43, S A Weermag Pretoria, N H Predikant, 1967, Brits
Dreyer T F, 31, Killaloe Pos Retief, Boer, 1966
Dreyer T F J, 33, Ned Herv Pastorie Oberholzer, Predikant, 1966, Warmbad Tvl
Dreyer T J F, 28, P/A N H Kerk Nooitgedacht, Predikant, 1975, Krugersdorp
Dreyer T P, 31, P/A Universiteit Stellenbosch, Snr Lektor, 1968, Worcester
Dreyer W P, 26, Prinsloo Dreyer & Dreyer Johannesburg, Tandarts, 1967
Driescher A 37, N G Kerk Edleen Kempton Park, Predikant, 1977, Durban
Drotskie J J, F A K Verteenwoordiger vir Witwatersrand & Suid-Oos Transvaal
Drotskie J J, 26, Die Vaderland Johannesburg, Joernalis, 1966, Stellenbosch
Dry G C, 29, Biesiesdal Steekdorings, Boer, 1968, Vryburg
Dry J G, 36, Dept Landbou Petrusburg, Voorligtingsbeampte, 1966, Brandfort
Dubbelman P, 45, Loonraad Pretoria, Ekonomiese Adviseur, 1977
Du Bois A J, 33, Geluksoord Koelenhof Bondsraad 1971 gehou op Geluksoord, Boer, 1965
Du Bois N W, 46, Hoërskool Hopefield, Skoolhoof, 1964, Kaapstad
Du Buisson D I, 36, Tafelberg Senekal, Boer, 1969
Du Buisson N J, 33, Fallopiusstraat Nr 8 Hospitaalpark/Primêre-Skool Wilgehof, Onderhoof, 1971, Bloemfontein
Du Buys A J, 32, Killicklaan 659 Mayville Pretoria/Volkskas, Klerk, 1976, Pietersburg
Duminy P A, 33, P/A Universiteit Kollege Fort Hare, Professor, 1965, Pretoria
Duminy T L, 38, Spiegelsrivier PK Heidelberg KP, Boer, 1967
Dupisani J, 38, Agstestraat 92 Walvisbaai/S A B S, Voedselinspekteur, 1975, Windhoek
Du Plessis A J, 43, Volkskas Frankfort, Bestuurder, 1966, Boksburg
Du Plessis A J, Bellville (Karl Bremer) Open 1969 Bondsraad met Skriflesing & Gebed
Du Plessis A J, 34, Geref Kerk Bellville, Predikant, 1967, Virginia
Du Plessis A P, 37, Universiteit Kollege van Zoeloeland Eshowe, Professor, 1965, Pretoria
Du Plessis A S, 35, P/A Yskor Vanderbijlpark, Klerk, 1965, Pretoria
Du Plessis A S, 35, P/A Van Wyk & Louw Raadg Ing, Siviele Tegnikus, 1975, Florida
Du Plessis A S, 30, P/A Wesco Randburg, Fin Bestuurder, 1975, Bellville
Du Plessis B C, 39, Volkskas Steynsrus, Bestuurder, 1965, Vryburg

Du Plessis B J, 31, Cheviotweg 14 Floridaheuwels/International Business Machines, Verkoopsverteenwoordiger, 1971, Johannesburg
Du Plessis C A, 31, Hoërskool Edenburg, Skoolhoof, 1964, Bothaville
Du Plessis C J, 44, Greenstraat Witfield, Onderwyser, 1966, Christiana
Du Plessis C J, 39, Ostendweg 10 Germiston/Distillers Corp Wadeville, Bestuurder, 1971, Elsburg
Du Plessis C N, 51, Oosthuizenfontein Philipstown, Boer, 1970
Du Plessis C R, 28, P/A Le Roux Matthews & Du Plessis Johannesburg, Prokureur, 1968
Du Plessis D, 30, African Homes Trust Durban, Inspekteur, 1964, Pretoria
Du Plessis D F H F, 44, Gerrit Maritzlaan 130 Dalview Brakpan, Sakeman, 1965, Wolmaransstad
Du Plessis D G C, 32, P/A Geref Kerk Orkney, Predikant, 1967, Johannesburg
Du Plessis D H C (Lid Nr 8), Direkteur van Maatskappye (Stigterslid van A B Voormalige Hoofbestuurder van S A S & H & Voorgestel vir die U R in 1968)
Du Plessis D J, 30, Uitkyk Wellington, Boer, 1977
Du Plessis D J, 28, Meulstraat 6 Potchefstroom/Interad Edms Bpk/SWK Besturende Direkteur 1977
Du Plessis D J, 29, P/A Laerskool Newlands, Onderwyser, 1976, Randburg
Du Plessis D J, 30, Mannstraat 89 Riviera Pretoria, Geneesheer, 1973
Du Plessis D P, 37, Kleinvlei PK Brandfort, Boer, 1965
Du Plessis D P, 43, Bosmanskop Hendrina, Boer, 1975, Bapsfontein
Du Plessis D T, 35, Gloudinaweg 237 Murrayfield Pretoria, Ekonoom, 1977, Klerksdorp
Du Plessis E, 35, Fouriestraat Vredefort, Geneesheer, 1963, Potchefstroom
Du Plessis F Jv Z, 31, Laerskool Mopane, Skoolhoof, 1977, Pietersburg
Du Plessis F R de V, 30, Boland Reivilo, Boer, 1967, Kuruman
Du Plessis G, 38, Gracelaan 56 Parkhill Germiston, Geref Predikant, 1970, Roodepoort
Du Plessis G F, 43, P/A Meyer Nel & Kie Johannesburg, Ouditeur, 1963, Hertzogville
Du Plessis G F, 28, Landbounavorsingsinst Döhne, Vakkund Beampte, 1965, Rustenburg
Du Plessis G F C, 35, P/A Yskor Vanderbijlpark, Asst Supt, 1965, Pretoria
Du Plessis G G, 37, P/A Dr Du Plessis & V/D Merwe Lancet Hall Johannesburg, Oogarts, 1967, Zeerust
Du Plessis G J, 43, P/A Onderwyskollege Potchefstroom, Dosent, 1977, Klerksdorp
Du Plessis G M, 34, P/A Stadsraad Tzaneen, Hoofgesondheidsinspekteur, 1974, Springs
Du Plessis G N, 34, Dept Van Gevangeniswese Pretoria, Luitenant, 1965, Clanwilliam
Du Plessis G P, 26, Noordstraat Barkly-Wes, Passer & Draaier, 1966, Paarl
Du Plessis H (Prof), Dien op Uitvoerende Raad se Nie-Blanke Komitee in 1973
Du Plessis H A, 41, Van Heerdenstraat 24 Kroonstad/S A Polisie, Majoor, 1972, Worcester
Du Plessis H B, 32, S A Polisie Uitenhage, Luitenant, 1977, Despatch
Du Plessis H E, 33, Westfalia Landgoed Duiwelskloof, Landbou-Ingenieur, 1973, Tzaneen
Du Plessis H G W, 31, Joseph Bosmanstraat 466 Silverton/Unisa, Lektor, 1976
Du Plessis H J, 39, Parkstraat Aranos, Sakeman, 1975, Oudtshoorn
Du Plessis H S, 30, P/A Onderwyskollege Potchefstroom, Snr Dosent, 1977, Witpoort
Du Plessis H T J, 45, P/A Albertono-Verwe (Edms) Bpk Alberton, Sekretaris, 1969, Bloemfontein
Du Plessis I D, 41, Willowweg 6 Northcliff/S A S & H Johannesburg, Snr Klerk, 1974
Du Plessis J, 49, P/A Afd Krygsproduksie Dept van Verdediging, Snr Admin Beampte, 1965, Capital Park
Du Plessis J, 35, 'Smidsrus' Distr Bloemfontein, Boer, 1965, Shannon
Du Plessis J, 41, Vergelegen Oudtshoorn, Boer, 1974
Du Plessis J, 33, Modderfontein Tarkastad, Boer, 1970
Du Plessis J, 37, Auto Motors Woonstel Molteno/Quix Products, Boer/Fabriekswerker, 1970
Du Plessis J A, 40, N G Pastorie Maclear, Predikant, 1977, Stellenbosch
Du Plessis J B, 25, Provinsiale Koshuis Trichardt, Onderwyser, 1968, Bethal
Du Plessis J B, 44, Leo Epsteinstraat 13 Northcliff Johannesburg, Landmeter/Evkom, 1976, Linden Johannesburg
Du Plessis J C, 39, Tweefontein Bronkhorstspruit, Boer, 1975, Vredefort
Du Plessis J C M D, 53, P/A Tvlse Prov Adm Pretoria, Rekenmeester, 1968
Du Plessis J D, 43, P/A Dept van Binnelandse Inkomste Bloemfontein, Admin Beampte, 1968

Du Plessis J E, 43, P/A Staatsdienskommissie Pretoria, Adj-Sekretaris, 1974
Du Plessis J G, 35, P/A F A K Johannesburg, Snr Admin Beampte, 1969, Durban
Du Plessis J G (Lid Nr 7680), Trichardt, Predikant, 1962
Du Plessis J H, 43, Voortrekkerstraat Hofmeyr', Onderwyser, 1968, Riebeeckkasteel
Du Plessis J H, 34, P/A Laerskool Gariep, Skoolhoof, 1968, Marchand
Du Plessis J H, 30, Tredouxstraat Beyerspark/PA Moodie & Moodie Boksburg, Prokureur, 1977, Potchefstroom
Du Plessis J H, 36, P/A Lean Cecil & Du Plessis Johannesburg, Rekenmeester, 1973, Primrose
Du Plessis J J, 33, P/A Kantoor van die Staatsprokureur Johannesburg, Snr Staatsprokureur, 1968, Kaapstad
Du Plessis J J, 39, Southeystraat 5 Adcockvale Port Elizabeth, Onderwyser, 1976, Uniondale
Du Plessis J L, 36, P/A Santam Bank Bellville, Bestuurder, 1968, Ceres
Du Plessis J M, Havemanstraat 6 Kroonstad, Onderwyser, 1971
Du Plessis J N S, 42, P/A Opleidingskollege Wellington, Dosent, 1974, Stellenbosch
Du Plessis J P, 31, Koninginstraat Ladismith K P, Landdros, 1972, Ceres
Du Plessis J P, 29, P/A Hoërskool Carletonville, Onderwyser, 1963, Fochville
Du Plessis J S, 31, P/A N G Kerk Robertson-Oos, Predikant, 1975, Grahamstad
Du Plessis J v V, 35, Geref Kerk Edenvale, Predikant, 1967, Beestekraal
Du Plessis J W, 38, Caltex Olie Maatskappy Bloemfontein, Verteenwoordiger, 1967
Du Plessis J Z, 42, Verwagting Cradock, Boer, 1975
Du Plessis L S, 33, Rietkol Delmas, Veearts/Boer, 1975, Estcourt
Du PLessis L v Z, 39, Mimosastraat Kirkwood, Volkskasbestuurder, 1970, Oos-Londen
Du Plessis M A (Lid Nr 7756), Pretoria, 1963
Du Plessis M A, Lid van Uitvoerende Raad se Afrika & Wêreld Komitee asook Beplannings Komitee van 1973
Du Plessis M C F, 41, P/A Landboukollege Glen, Dept Hoof, 1965, Standerton
Du Plessis M J, 37, S A Weermag Potchefstroom, Kolonel, 1970, Rustenburg/Bloemfontein
Du Plessis M J, 27, P/A Geref Kerk Roodepoort, Predikant, 1976, Potchefstroom
Du Plessis M J H, 33, P/A P U vir CHO Potchefstroom, Professor, 1973
Du Plessis Nick, Wolmaransstad (N P Komitee)
Du Plessis N F, 35, Sam Jossel & Kie Barry Hertzogrylaan 30 Florida Park, Aandelemakelaar, 1970
Du Plessis Org, Wolmaransstad N P Komitee, 1966
Du Plessis P, 33, Geref Kerk Delareyville, Predikant, 1967, Tzaneen
Du Plessis P, 45, "Sonderend" Erasmia Pretoria, Onderwyser, 1966, Linden
Du Plessis P, 40, Doornhoek Thabazimbi/Yskor, Passer, 1976, Pretoria
Du Plessis P A, 34, Mauchstraat 17 Rynfield Benoni, Produksie-Bestuurder, 1968
Du Plessis P A du P, 46, P/A Hartbeesport Landbou Navorsingstasie Brits, Bestuurder, 1969, Rustenburg
Du Plessis P C, 44, S A Lugdiens Johannesburg, Klerk, 1966, Mayfair
Du Plessis P G, 34, Kerkstraat Dealesville, Sakeman, 1970, Bloemfontein
Du Plessis P G W, 34, Van Riebeeckstraat Amsterdam, Vise-Hoof, 1971, Birchleigh
Du Plessis P G W, 36, P/A R A U Johannesburg, Professor, 1968, Port Elizabeth
Du Plessis P J, 29, P/A Munisipaliteit Villiers, Stadsklerk, 1968, Senekal
Du Plessis P J L, 33, Geref Kerk Kuruman, Predikant, 1974, Tsumeb
Du Plessis P J S, 33, P/A Cilliers Liebenberg & Du Plessis Bloemfontein, Bourekenaar, 1967, Hennenman
Du Plessis P J V, 42, La Cavestraat 4 Despatch/Goodyear Motorbandfabriek, Klerk, 1970
Du Plessis P L, 41, Bealsdale Komga, Boer, 1967, Lusaka
Du Plelssis P T C, 29, Klipspruit 132 — Lydenburg, Boer, 1966
Du Plessis S F, 30, P/A Landbou-Navorsingsinstituut Nelspruit, 1969, Bloemfontein
Du Plessis S F, 43, P/A Hoërskool Brits, Onderhoof, 1967
Du Plessis S J, 33, P/A Fedmis Harrismith, Verteenwoordiger, 1974, Viljoenskroon
Du Plessis S J (Dr), Lid van Uitvoerende Raad se Wetenskap Komitee 1973
Du Plessis S J P, 41, 26steLaan 319 Villieria Pretoria, Adj-Sekretaris/Tesourie, 1971
Du Plessis S W, 34, Huisviljoen Bredasdorp/Hoërskool, Onderwyser, 1971, Touwsrivier
Du Plessis T A, 34, P/A Fochvillese Laerskool Fochville, Vise-Hoof, 1973, Potchefstroom

Du Plessis T A, 41, Hoewe 69 Heatherdale Pretoria-Noord/Dept van Beplanning, Hoofdirekteur, 1971
Du Plessis T C, 42, Rusplaas Dist Gobabis, Boer, 1974, Leonardville
Du Plessis T C, 42, Kareelaan 11 Kathu/Yskor, Ingenieur, 1977, Pretoria
Du Plessis W A, 25, "Alfa" Barkly-Wes, Boer, 1966
Du Plessis W J, 45, P/A R A U Johannesburg, Registrateur, 1968, Lyttelton
Du Plessis W J, 34, Jupiterstraat 34 Waterkloofrif Pretoria, Prokureur, 1976
Du Plessis W J, 33, S A Polisie Durban, Luitenant, 1975, Durban
Du Plessis W J, 34, Stellastraat 5 Chrismar (Belville), Geneesheer, 1976, Pretoria
Du Plessis W K H (Dr), Opvoedkundige
Du Plessis W S, 32 P/A Hoërskool Lansdowne Kaap, Onderwyser, 1969, Beaufort-Wes
Du Plooy C E G, 52, S A S Polisie Burgersdorp, Speursersant, 1966, Pinelands
Du Plooy C W, 34, Bisschoffstraat 8 Nelspruit, N G Predikant, 1971, Witfield
Du Plooy F S, 40, Lisztstraat 49 Vanderbijlpark, Ingenieur, 1978, Derby
Du Plooy F S, 34, Verlies Lichtenburg, Boer, 1975
Du Plooy G, 33, Warmbadweg Thabazimbi/Landbou Tegniese Dienste, Voorligtingsbeampte, 1976, Warmbad
Du Plooy G D, 37, Sanlam Burgersdorp, Verteenwoordiger, 1968, Oos-Londen
Du Plooy J C, 35, Allenstraat 76 Kroonstad, Onderwyser, 1969, Zastron
Du Plooy J S, 42, Geref Pastorie Olifantshoek, Predikant, 1973, Molteno
Du Plooy J S, 30, P/A Geref Kerk Postmasburg, Predikant, 1968, Vanderbijlpark
Du Plooy M, 33, Cypress — Singel Welkom, Sakeman, 1970, Bloemfontein
Du Plooy R A, 42, P/A Hoërskool Koster, Onderwyser, 1977, Vanderbijlpark
Du Pré J J, 39, Broungerstraat 3 Molteno, Verteenwoordiger Bkb, 1977, Steynsburg
Du Preez A B, Professor — Kweekskool Pretoria — Voorgestel vir Uitvoerende Raad 1968
Du Preez A J J, 35, P/A Noordwes Koöp Lichtenburg, Snr Klerk, 1964
Du Preez A J J, 26, Bainestraat 9 Rynfield Benoni, Onderwyser, 1965
Du Preez C J H, 34, Redelinghuysstraat Barberton, Prokureur, 1968, Thabazimbi
Du Preez C M R, Hoër Landbouskool Tweespruit
Du Preez F A, 38, Brosterstraat 8 Bethlehem/Brand Wessels & Kie, Prokureur, 1970, Harrismith
Du Preez F H, 41, Hoërskool Edenvale, Onderwyser, 1964, Nylstroom
Du Preez G J, 39, Essenbosch Karreedouw, Onderwyser, 1970, Alexandria
Du Preez H B, 42, Afr Hoërskool Germiston, Adj-Hoof, 1969
Du Preez H C, 37, P/A Farmabond (Edms) Bpk Potgietersrus, Apteker, 1973, Pretoria
Du Preez H J, 36, Palmoord Prov Koshuis Bethal, Onderwyser, 1974, Potchefstroom
Du Preez H P, Waboomkraal Distrik George, 1963
Du Preez I G, 32, P/A Hoërskool Windhoek, Onderwyser, 1968, Pretoria
Du Preez J J, 32, P/A Stadsraad Vanderbijlpark/Dept Parke & Ontspanning, Hoof, 1974, Johannesburg
Du Preez J J, 39, Hoofweg 91 Strand, Inspekteur SP KL, 1970, Kimberley
Du Preez J J, 33, Aquilalaan 124 Waterkloofrif-Uitbr/Hoërskool Wonderboom Pretoria, Onderwyser, 1976
Du Preez J J, 38, Jean Rouxstraat 29 Neserhof Klerksdorp, Onderwyser, 1976, Steenbokpan
Du Preez J S, 32, Sarel Cilliesstraat 2 Westonaria, Asst. Klerk van die Raad, 1970, Devon
Du Preez J T, 29, Vlaklaagte Blackhill Transvaal, Boer, 1967
Du Preez L J, 34, PK Jagfontein Gatsrand, Boomkweker, 1967
Du Preez L W, 41, Queenstraat 13 Irene Verwoerdburg, Argitek, 1972, Lyttelton
Du Preez M B, 37, Wolhuterskop PK Reddingshoop/Magaliesburg Sitrus Koöp, Bestuurder, 1973, Rustenburg
Du Preez M J, 36, Departement van Poswese Pretoria, Tegnikus, 1965, Nylstroom
Du Preez M L, 35, Harperse Apteek Benoni, Aptekersklerk, 1970
Du Preez N J, 41, P/A Môrester Bandediens Pietersburg, Sakeman, 1968, Louis Trichardt
Du Preez N P, 30, P/A Datons-Vetsak Nigel, Hoof Chemiese Afd, 1976, Pretoria
Du Preez N T, 32, P/A Munisipaliteit Tzaneen, Adj Direkteur Adm, 1977, Pretoria
Du Preez P J, 38, P/A Stadsraad Pretoria, Markmeester, 1967, Bellville
Du Preez P J, 44, Sanlam Vereeniging, Takbestuurder, 1964, Bellville
Du Preez P J, 34, Stasiestraat Malelane, Snr Ouditeursklerk/Bestuurder, 1971, Nelspruit
Du Preez P J, Posbus 39 Breyten, 1963

Du Preez P L, 40, P/A Sanlam Johannesburg, Pensioenebestuurder, 1976, Springs
Du Preez R B, 33, Militêre Basis Rundu/S A Weermag, Offisier, 1977, Oudtshoorn
Du Preez S J, 38, N G Pastorie Koppies, Predikant, 1965, Brits
Du Preez S P J, 34, Boabablaan 3 Birchleigh Kempton Park, Geneesheer, 1976, Pretoria
Du Preez W M, 44, Gevangenisterrein 77 Pretoria, Kolonel, 1967, Groot Brakrivier
Du Preez W P, 27, Brandwag Molteno, Boer, 1969
Du Preez W P, 37, Komatiedraai Komatipoort, Landboubestuurder, 1977, Barbeton
Du Preez W P J, 36, Excelsiorkoshuis Swellendam/Hoërskool J G Meiring, Onderwyser, 1970, Kaapstad
Du Raan G, 46, Coopersdal Komatipoort, Boer, 1970, Standerton
Du Raan J H, 36, Paveystraat 17 Baileypark Potchefstroom, Sakeman, 1968
Du Rand A, 41, De Jager Venter & Du Rand Pietersburg, Rekenmeester, 1970, Wepener
Durand H J, 40, Twaalfdestraat 110 Parkmore Sandton/S A S & H, Asst Supt Beplanning, 1975, Kaapstad
Durand J C, 36, Wolraadstraat 5 Boksburg-Suid, Dept Hoof G O K, 1977, Piet Retief
Du Randt A H G, 32, Konstitusie Adelaide, Onderwyser, 1973
Durandt J A, 47, Spoorwegkollege Esselenpark, Predikant, 1965, Hanover
Durandt L C, 32, Posbus 146 Vrede, Prokureur, 1965, Bloemfontein
Du Row W A, 33, Kroonbult Clocolan, Boer, 1976
Durr J A, 27, Volharding PK Davel, Boer, 1966
Du Toit A, 36, N G Pastorie Duiwelskloof, Predikant, 1964, Durban
Du Toit A B, 36, William Alexanderstraat Christiana/Westra Meule, Bestuurder, 1970, Viljoenskroon
Du Toit A F, 35, Baskop Vredefort, Wetenskaplike Genetikus, 1971, Pretoria
Du Toit A G, 31, P/A W N N R Pretoria, Navorser, 1973
Du Toit A G, 37, P/A Tvlse Prov Adm Pretoria/Carinusstraat 180 Meyerspark, Snr Werkstudiebeampte, 1977
Du Toit A G, 29, P/A Bolandse Eksekuteurskamer Paarl, Personeelbestuurder, 1969, Upington
Du Toit A J, 35, Idolweg 40 Lynwood Glen Pretoria, Siv Ingenieur, 1973, Port Elizabeth
Du Toit A J, Lid van Uitvoerende Raad se Beplannings-en Landbou Komitees 1973
Du Toit A N, 47, P/A Rembrandt Mpy Durban, Adm Bestuurder, 1974, Pinetown
Du Toit A P T, 30, Majuba Manskoshuis Stellenbosch, Snr Lektor, 1977, Rawsonville
Du Toit A S, 32, Abiliastraat Kilnerpark Uitbr 1 Pretoria, Snr Dosent U P, 1971, Pretoria
Du Toit B A, 29, 'N G Kerk Germiston, Predikant, 1967, Stellenbosch
Du Toit B J, 33, P/A R A U Johannesburg, Eksamenbeampte, 1975 Durban
Du Toit B J, 40, Darnysbos Hopetown, Boer/Klerk, 1971
Du Toit C A (Prof), Lid van Uitvoerende Raad se Wetenskap Komitee 1973
Du Toit C G, 34, Krokodilkraal Dist Thabazimbi, Boer, 1975, Koedoeskop
Du Toit C J E, 34, Francis Drake Place 14 Constantiakloof Florida/Bank van Johannesburg, Regsadviseur, 1977, Bellville
Du Toit C J F, 28, Piet Retiefstraat Steytlerville, Onderwyser, 1967, Paarl
Du Toit D, 34, S A Polisie Golela, Luitenant, 1969, Leslie
Du Toit D G, 38, Majuba Malanstasie, Boer, 1964, Wellington
Du Toit D J, 34, Freeanweg 15 Rondebosch K P, Sakeman, 1974
Du Toit D J, 24, P/A Hoërskool Greytown, Onderwyser, 1969, Pietermaritzburg
Du Toit D J, 27, Quarta Woonstelle Bosmanstraat Stellenbosch, Onderwyser, 1972
Du Toit D J, 32, P/A Suikerbekkie-Glansvrugte-Fabriek Malmesbury, Bestuurder, 1974
Du Toit D J E, 42, Droëfontein Langebaanweg, Boer, 1967, Hopefield
Du Toit E F, 33, De Tyger Laerskool Parow/Haarlemsingel 31 Stellenberg, Onderwyser, 1976, Parow-Oos
Du Toit F J, 34, Opsaal Seunskoshuis Kroonstad, Onderwyser, 1968, Heilbron
Du Toit F J, 35, P/A N G Gemeente Valhalla-Suid, Predikant, 1976, Cradock
Du Toit F P, 30, P/A N G Gemeente Selectionpark Springs, Predikant, 1974, Cornelia
Du Toit F P, 28, Vaalrivierskool Standerton, Onderwyser, 1971, Witbank
Du Toit F P, 28, N G Pastorie Zebediela, Predikant, 1969, Stellenbosch
Du Toit G, 28, Pollackstraat Robertson, Prokureur, 1971, Grahamstad
Du Toit G A, 33, Skoollaan 50 Sunnyridge, Onderwyser, 1966, Ermelo
Du Toit G F, 33, P/A Amkor Vereeniging, Produksiebestuurder, 1975, Pretoria
Du Toit G G, 27, Posbus 57 Vanderbijlpark, Apteker, 1965, Johannesburg

Du Toit G G, Hentystraat 20 Vanderbijlpark, 1973
Du Toit G J, 38, Longfellowlaan 35 Orkney, Onderwyser, 1965, Potgietersrus
Du Toit G J, 30, Talana-Woonstelle No 3 Wrenschweg Parow/Trust Bank, Afdelingshoof, 1971, Nuwerus
Du Toit G M, 44, Witfontein Fraserburg, Boer, 1967, Nelspruit
Du Toit H, 46, P/A St Helena Goudmyn Welkom, Geneesheer, 1965, Warden
Du Toit H A J, 27, Vissersingel 3 Aliwal-Noord, Tandarts, 1972, Ceres
Du Toit H D A (Prof), Ormondeweg 30 Pretoria
Du Toit H L K, 41, Yorkstraat 55 George, Geneesheer, 1966, Worcester
Du Toit H M, 27, P/A S A Polisie Worcester, Luitenant, 1973, Wynberg
Du Toit H W, 33, Scottstraat 18 Bellville/Evkom, Snr Toetsingenieur, 1971, Otjiwarongo
Du Toit J, 44, Ameland Vivo, Boer, 1974, Pretoria
Du Toit J A, 38, P/A Bolandse Eksekuteurskamer Moorreesburg, Takbestuurder, 1969, Paarl
Du Toit J B, 33, P/A Hoër Tegn Skool Welkom, Adjunk-Hoof, 1975, Theunissen
Du Toit J B, 41, Leebstraat Murraysburg, Sakeman, 1968
Du Toit J C, 37, P/A N G Kerk Vredendal, Predikant, 1975, Nieuwoudtville
Du Toit J C, 39, Johannesburgweg 13 Kew/Edgars, Bestuurder, 1970, Florida
Du Toit J F, 42, Alewynspoort/Die Transvaler, Sportredakteur, 1970, Kliptown
Du Toit J F, 28, Biesiesvlei Belmont, Boer, 1976
Du Toit J F J, 52, Sanlam Worcester, Takbestuurder, 1966, Ermelo
Du Toit J G M, 37, P/A Volkskas Pretoria, Rekenmeester, 1973, Randburg
Du Toit J H, 35, Tasmania Griekwastad, Boer, 1976
Du Toit J H, 39, La Rochelle Over-Hex, Boer, 1965, Worcester
Du Toit J H H, 33, N G Gemeente Rayton, Predikant, 1974, Derdepoort
Du Toit J I, 43, P/A O T K Bethal, Hoof-Inspekteur, 1965, Ermelo
Du Toit J J, 42, Lanbou Tegn Dienste Pretoria, Navorser, 1965, Stellenbosch
Du Toit J J, 30, H F Verwoerd Hospitaal Pretoria, Geneesheer, 1975, Koedoeskop.
Du Toit J J, (Lid Nr 6262), Geneesheer — Port Elizabeth-Noord — Voorgestel vir die U R in 1968
Du Toit J J, 37, Ouplaas Prince Alfred Hamlet, Boer, 1977, Middelburg
Du Toit J J F, Kensington
Du Toit J M, 31, P/A Hoër Landbouskool Kroonstad, Onderwyser, 1969
Du Toit J P, 34, Remkuil Caledon, Boer, 1977
Du Toit J P, 27, Belhambra Woonstelle Humansdorp/Arkade Apteek, Apteker, 1975 Potchefstroom
Du Toit J P, 47, Eikeboom PK Hermon, Boer, 1969
Du Toit J P, 34, Remountstraat 11 Ladysmith, Landmeter, 1970, Pretoria
Du Toit J R v D, 36, Vlakplaas Koppies, Boer, 1972, Belfast
Du Toit J S, 48, Dept Verdediging Bloemfontein, Snr Klerk, 1965, Pretoria
Du Toit M, 37, P/A Goudwesskool Carletonville, Vise-Hoof, 1974, Westonaria
Du Toit M A, 36, P/A Vleisraad Kaapstad, Klerk, 1965, Seepunt
Du Toit M D, 41, Tweelingsfontein, Ventersdorp, Boer, 1965, Koppies
Du Toit M H J, 28, Hofmeyrstraat Montagu, Onderwyser, 1974, Riebeeckkasteel
Du Toit M J, 34, Stuartstraat 698 Deernes Pretoria, Snr Adm Beampte, 1976
Du Toit M S, 34, P/A S A Weermag Upington, Majoor, 1975, Monte Vista
Du Toit M v B, 28, Uiterste Hoek Clocolan, Boer, 1965, Ficksburg
Du Toit N, 35, P/A BAR Postmasburg, Gebiedsbestuurder, 1975, Sasolburg
Du Toit N J, 36, P/A S A Polisie Aucklandpark Johannesburg, Adj-Offisier, 1968
Du Toit N M J, 43, Weslaan 47 Florida, Opleiding Tegn Poswese, 1971, Port Elizabeth
Du Toit O J J, 37, P/A S A Weermag Pretoria, Kolonel, 1974
Du Toit P, 41, S A Polisie (Veiligheid) Burgersfort, Kaptein, 1974, Pretoria
Du Toit P E, 34, P/A Sendingkerk Laingsburg, Predikant, 1974, Malmesbury
Du Toit P E J, 42, P/A Diamantmyn Swartruggens, Hysbakbestuurder, 1963
Du Toit P G, 31, Coetzerstraat Reddersburg, Onderwyser, 1970, Loxton
Du Toit P J, 44, D M Tomlinson & Kie Swellendam, Rekenmeester, 1970, Ashton
Du Toit P J, 41, Middelplaas Cornelia, Boer, 1970, Piet Retief
Du Toit P J, 31, Esterhuyzenstraat 7 Carnarvon, Onderwyser, 1974, Victoria-Wes
Du Toit P J, 42, N G Pastorie Worcester, Predikant, 1967, Marikana
Du Toit P J S, 35, Leeufontein Potchefstroom, Onderwyser/Boer, 1969, Kroonstad

Du Toit P S (Spiere), 30, Kloovenburg Riebeeckkasteel, Boer, 1966, Petrusville
Du Toit R E, 38, Rusfontein Rawsonville, Boer, 1975
Du Toit R P, 37 Hoërskool Boshof, Onderhoof, 1973, Shannon
Du Toit S, P U vir CHO Potchefstroom, Registrateur, 1963
Du Toit S (Prof), Professor Semitiese Tale P U vir CHO Potchefstroom, 1963
Du Toit S J (Dr), Lid van die U R se Wetenskap Komitee in 1973
Du Toit S J, 34, Rudweg 10 Dunnottar/Stadsraad Nigel, Rekenmeester, 1976
Du Toit S P, 27, Anex Elandsfontein Griekwastad, Boer, 1967
Du Toit S W J, 28, Voortrekkerstraat Krugersdorp, Tandarts, 1965, Chrissiemeer
Du Toit T A, 39, Duncanstraat 4, Brenthurst Brakpan, Adjunk-Hoof,, 1977
Du Toit Z B, 34, P/A Universiteit van Stellenbosch, Lektor in Fisika, 1975, Rawsonville
Duvenage A P C, 30, Geref Pastorie Auckland Park Johannesburg, Predikant, 1965, Eikenhof
Duvenage A P C, 42, N G Sendingkerk Klerksdorp, Predikant, 1967, Thabazimbi
Duvenage A S, 36, Volkskas Volksrust, Bestuurder, 1965, Middelburg K P
Duvenage H J P, 48, Laerskool Burgershoop/Chancliff Krugersdorp, Skoolhoof, 1970, Vereeniging
Duvenage J G, 33, Goedverwachting Vereeniging, Boer, 1975, Pretoria
Duvenage J P, P U vir C H O Potchefstroom, Snr Lektor (Aardrykskunde), 1963
Duvenage P S, 30, Pres Hoërskool Ridgeway Johannesburg, Onderwyser, 1973, Boksburg
Duvenage S C W (Prof), P U vir CHO Potchefstroom/Hoffmanstraat 30 Potchefstroom — Lid van die U R se Jeugkomitee in 1973 — Skakel by Universiteit in 1976
Duvenhage G P J (Lid Nr 7709), Kuruman, Boer, 1962
Duvenhage J G, 32, Universiteit van Pretoria, Snr Lektor, 1967, Westonaria
Duvenhage J P M, 33, Hertzogville, Landdros, 1963
Duvenhage M d W, 28, Bothasmoed PK Vanzylsrus, Boer, 1969
Duvenhage W I, Kuruman- By Bondsraad van 1966 praat hy oor Die Rapportryers
Dwyer L H, 30, P/A Hoërskool Oliftanshoek, Onderwyser, 1975, Niekerkshoop
Dyson S B, 37, President Krugerstraat 165, Rynfield Benoni, Geneesheer, 1976, Pretoria

E

Earle P A, 43, Combustion Eng (Pty) Ltd Johannesburg, Besturende Direkteur, 1966, Stellenbosch
Ebersohn A J J, 35, Orpenstraat Smithfield/Hoërskool Genl Hertzog, Skoolhoof, 1977, Bloemfontein
Ebersohn G G (Lid Nr 7700), Pretoria, Ouditeur, 1962
Ebersohn J F P, 33, N G Bantoekerk Springs, Predikant, 1967, Stellenbosch
Ebersohn P C, 49, P/A Munisipaliteit Springs, Vervoerinspekteur, 1963
Ebersöhn W C, 32, Clodestraat Bettysbaai, Kurator van Botaniese Tuine, 1973, Oos-Londen
Ehlers C B, 33, P/A Hoër Tegn Skool Randfontein, Onderwyser, 1966
Ehlers C F, 41, Doreg Landbouhoewes No. 27 Pretoria, Prokureur, 1971
Ehlers C F B H, 35, P/A Munisipaliteit Sasolburg, Klerk van die Raad, 1969, Harrismith
Ehlers J, 45, S A Polisie Tzaneen, Adj-Offisier, 1976, Johannesburg
Ehlers J G, 38, P/A Ross & Jacobsz Pretoria, Prokureur, 1975, Brits
Ehlers J H, 38, P/A Goede Hoop Sitruskoöp Citrusdal, Sekretaris, 1967, Paarl
Ehlers J J H, 46, C J Langenhovenstraat 52 Parow;Noord/S A S & H, Skakelbeampte, 1977 Kaapstad
Ehlers R, 41, P/A Hoërskool Brandwag Uitenhage, Vise-Hoof, 1976, Stellenbosch
Ehlers T J, 30, Comosastraat 697 Dorandia Pretoria, Onderwyser, 1974
Eksteen A J, 39, P/A Hoër Volkskool Potchefstroom, Adj-Hoof, 1967, Kempton Park
Eksteen C J, 35, Landdroskantoor Krugersdorp, Snr Landdros, 1976, Sasolburg
Eksteen D F, 42, Eerstelaan 11 Linden/S A U K, Joernalis, 1976, Londen
Eksteen F J, 28, Krygstuigraad Pretoria, Projekingenieur, 1974, Lyttelton
Eksteen G D, 32, Droëvlei Klipheuwel, Boer, 1974, Malmesbury
Eksteen I, 36, Robyn Inyazura, Boer, 1966, Winburg
Eksteen L C, 47, Buffelsfontein PK Crecy (Naboomspruit), Boer, 1976, Kroonstad
Eksteen L L, 33, Melkbosfontein Piketberg, Boer, 1974
Eksteen T J C, 31, P/A Merino Stoettelers Vereniging Graaff-Reinet, Sekretaris, 1973, Ermelo

Eksteen Z J, Groblersdal (Rustende Lid Nr 2754)
Ellis A F, 35, P/A Dept van Waterwese Pretoria, Booringenieur, 1968
Ellis A J M, 35, P/A S A S & H Bloemfontein, Vakleerlinginstrukteur, 1974
Ellis A P, 41, Dept van Justisie Pretoria, Adm Beampte, 1964, Ladismith
Ellis M C, 42, 4deLaan 25 Heidelberg Tvl/Volkskas Bpk, Bestuurder, 1970, Kempton Park
Ellis P H, 41, P/A S A Polisie Benoni, Adj-Offisier, 1966, Brakpan
Eloff C L, 38, Universiteit van die Noorde Pietersburg, Professor, 1974, Bloemfontein
Eloff D J, 41, P U vir CHO Potchefstroom, Snr Lektor, 1968
Eloff F C (Prof), President van Noord-Tvlse Rugby-Unie
Eloff S J P E, 37, Jorissenstraat 49a Pietersburg, Sjirurg, 1967, Krugersdorp
Eloff T, 41, P/A Provinsiale Koshuis Northam, Skoolhoof, 1974, Keetmanshoop
Eloff T, 29, P U vir CHO Potchefstroom, Lektor, 1977 Rustenburg
Eloff W, 39, P/A Bantoe-Beleggingskorp Pretoria, Sekretaris, 1969, Johannesburg
Eloff W G, 34, Villageweg 423 Menlo Park Pretoria, Tandarts, 1966, Bloemfontein
Els A L, 50, Honingkop Heilbron, Boer, 1964
Els C J, 47, Cranston Cathcart, Boer, 1965
Els C J, 46, Uithoek Koppies, Boer, 1970, All Days
Els G v R, 42, Voss Laerskool/PK Mamogagaleskraal (Brits), Skoolhoof, 1966
Els J C, 30, Fronemanstraat 52 Marquard, Onderwyser, 1965, Brandfort
Els J C, 31, Volkskas Bpk Wesselsbron, Rekenmeester, 1964, Kempton Park
Els J H, 40, Oshakati Owambo, Snr Inligt. Beampte, 1973, Umtata
Els J M, 32, Universiteit Fort Hare, Snr Lektor, 1972, Johannesburg
Els N J, 39, S A Polisie Van Ryn Benoni, Kaptein, 1967, Nelspruit
Els N J, 41, S A S & H Port Elizabeth, Klerk, 1964, Fort Beaufort
Els P le R, 32, Empilisweni Sterkspruit, Geneesheer, 1975, Pretoria
Els R J, 40, P/A Hoërskool Ben Vorster Tzaneen, Onderwyser, 1967, Nylstroom
Els W C, 47, Nooitverwacht PK Vermaas, Boer, 1975, Odendaalsrus
Els W P, 38, P/A Munisipaliteit Standerton/Bantoesake, Asst Direkteur, 1973, Bethlehem
Engelbrecht A M, 34, Keetmanlaan Keetmanshoop, Opmeter/Tekenaar, 1970, Stellenbosch
Engelbrecht A S, 32, P/A Volkskas Pretoria, Ekonoom, 1965, Potgietersrus
Engelbrecht B J (Prof), N H Kerk
Engelbrecht C A, 38, P/A S A Polisie Middelburg K P, Luitenant, 1975, Noupoort
Engelbrecht C J, 29, Hoërskool Nico Malan Humansdorp, Onderwyser, 1964, Noupoort
Engelbrecht C V, 33, H/v Grensweg & Groeneweide Bellville, Prokureur, 1971, Burgersdorp
Engelbrecht D C, 39, P/A O'Kiep Koper Mpy Nababeep, Hoof Drukkery, 1974, Garies
Engelbrecht D E, 34, Albertonse Hoërskool, Onderhoof, 1973, Lydenburg
Engelbrecht F W T, 35, Prinsloostraat 18 Bronkhorstspruit/Hoërskool Erasmus, Vise-Hoof, 1971, Groblersdal
Engelbrecht G C, 43, P/A Bantoe-Onderwys Bloemfontein, Inspekteur, 1964, Fouriesburg
Engelbrecht G C, 32, Katjiepieringstraat 14 Cottesloe, Snr Dosent G O K, 1971, Meyerton
Engelbrecht G C, 36, Poortje PK Oranjeville, Onderwyser/Boer, 1974, Deneysville
Engelbrecht G J, 35, P/A Hoër Tegn Skool Middelburg, Onderwyser, 1973, Nylstroom
Engelbrecht G P, 31, Hoërskool President Vasco, Onderwyser, 1967, Kanoneiland
Engelbrecht G S, 38, De Kokstraat 3 Môrelig Bethlehem, Vise-Hoof, 1974, Zastron
Engelbrecht H J, 35, Swartfontein Vierfontein, Boer, 1971, Bronkhorstspruit
Engelbrecht H J, 38, S A Polisie Pretoria, Kaptein, 1965, Johannesburg
Engelbrecht I J, 38, Drs Engelbrecht & Fourie Randfontein, Geneesheer, 1968, Pretoria
Engelbrecht J, 40, P/A Sybokhaarraad Port Elizabeth/Aragonweg 28 Adcockvale, Bemarkingsbeampte, 1975, Pretoria
Engelbrecht J, 40, P/A Delmas Koöp, Sekretaris, 1974, Springbok
Engelbrecht J A, 39, P/A Afdelingsraad Steytlerville, Sekretaris, 1974, Uitenhage
Engelbrecht J A, 38, N G Pastorie Nuwerus, Predikant, 1974, Vryburg
Engelbrecht J F, 35, Monumentweg Omaruru/P/A Sentramark SWA (Edms) Bpk, Bestuurder, 1977, Pretoria
Engelbrecht J P, 46, P/A Meyer Nel & Kie, Bloemfontein, Ouditeur, 1969, Reitz
Engelbrecht J P, 45, Carinusstraat 208 Meyerspark Pretoria, Inspekteur van Onderwys, 1975, Umtata
Engelbrecht J P J, 35, Beaufortstraat 7 Goodwood/S A S & H, Asst Statistikus, 1977, Parow

Engelbrecht J S, 32, Loopstraat 4 Parys, Onderwyser, 1968, Heilbron
Engelbrecht J W, 33, Plot 317 Glen Austin, Sakeman, 1976
Engelbrecht M C, 41, Uitkoms — PK Ladybrand, Onderwyser, 1966 Bethlehem
Engelbrecht M G, 28 Janestraat Touwsrivier/S A S & H, Elektrotegn Ingenieur, 1973, Johannesburg
Engelbrecht N, 34, Privaatsak X1020, Nylstroom, Onderwyser, 1974, Benoni
Engelbrecht P H S, 32, P/A Spoorwegbegrafnisgenootskap Germiston, Asst-Sekretaris, 1977, Primrose
Engelbrecht P J B, 31, N G Kerk Luipaardsvlei, Predikant, 1968, Pretoria
Engelbrecht P T, 43, P/A E F S Tractors Bethlehem, Kredietbestuurder, 1975, Kroonstad
Engelbrecht R, 27, P/A S A Polisiekollege Pretroria, Adj-Offisier, 1975, Vredendal
Engelbrecht R, 35, Orpenstraat Smithfield, Geneesheer, 1967, Pretoria
Engelbrecht S A, 34, Talanalaan 285, Villieria Pta/Hoofstad Uitrusters, Besturende Direkteur 1976
Engelbrecht S W B, 33, P/A Unisa Buro vir Universiteits-Navorsing, Snr Navorser, 1977, Niekerkshoop
Engelbrecht W J, 33, Volkskas Thabazimbi, Bestuurder, 1966, Springs
Engels M N, 42, Tampansbrand Dist Kuruman, Boer, 1975, Keetmanshoop
Enslin J H, 38, Leonardville, Sekretaris Dorpsbestuur, 1971
Enslin J S, 40, Dept Doeane & Aksyns Port Elizabeth, Admin Beampte, 1964, Middelburg Kaap
Enslin P J J S, 27, Geref Pastorie Pongola, Predikant, 1965, Piet Retief
Enslin S J M, 49, P/A Venda-Regeringsdiens Sibasa, A B B, 1975, Pretoria
Enslin T H, 39, Brakvlei Heilbron, Boer, 1971
Erasmus A M, 38, Laerskool Aughrabïes, Skoolhoof, 1965, Vryburg
Erasmus B, 32, Virginia Senekal, Boer, 1973
Erasmus B P, 46, Libenri King William's Town, Sakeman/Boer, 1974
Erasmus D F, 35, Ned Herv Pastorie Kieserville — Open Bondsraad van 1966 & 1969 met Skriflesing & Gebed, 1965, Ventersdorp
Erasmus D J, 33, P/A S A S & H Nelspruit, Elektro Tegn Ing, 1975, Pretoria
Erasmus D J, 33, Witfontein PK Birchleigh, Boer, 1971
Erasmus D L, 37, P/A Voorbereidingskool Mafeking, Skoolhoof, 1974, George
Erasmus E H, 40, Bergzichtstraat Malmesbury, Geneesheer, 1966, Springbok
Erasmus F C, 34, V O S Langebaanweg K P, Vlieënier, 1971, Pretoria
Erasmus F D, 52, Beerpoort Steytlerville, Boer, 1967
Erasmus F N, 33, Jakarandastraat 27 Cradock, Veearts, 1977, Middelburg K P
Erasmus G C, 37, Solwaystraat 19 Bellville/Dept Kleurlingbetrekkinge, Adm Beampte, 1972, Worcester
Erasmus G F, 25, Greytownse Hoërskool, Onderwyser, 1977, Paulpietersburg
Erasmus G J (Lid Nr 6011), Predikant — Voorgestel vir die U R in 1968
Erasmus H J, 29, Mediese Sentrum Dundee, Geneesheer, 1968, Durban
Erasmus J A, 33, Dept Bosbou Eshowe, Klerk, 1963, Knysna
Erasmus J A, 44, Hoewe 167 Kameeldrift Pretoria, Geneesheer, 1973, Amalia
Erasmus J C, 27, P/A Geref Kerk Keetmanshoop, Predikant, 1974, Potchefstroom
Erasmus J C, 28, N G Pastorie Kestell, N G Predikant, 1970, Vryburg
Erasmus J de J, 29, Goedgedacht Bethal, Boer, 1975
Erasmus J E, 41, Kleingeluk Strandweg Stellenbosch, Snr Lektor, 1967, Steytlerville
Erasmus J G, 35, Mimosastraat 12 Birchleigh/Steyn & Meyer, Ouditeur, 1971, Potgietersrus
Erasmus J J, 38, Grosmannstraat Wesselbron, Sakeman, 1966
Erasmus J J A, 30, Kampstraat 14 Vryburg/Saambou-Nasionaal, Takbestuurder, 1975, Rustenburg
Erasmus J M, 35 Buffelsfontein Matlabas, Boer, 1969
Erasmus J M, 37, P/A Universiteit Pretoria, Staatsveearts & Dosent, 1968, Pietersburg
Erasmus J M, 32, Beckerstraat Ladismith, Skoolraadsekretaris, 1964, Kirkwood
Erasmus K G, 33, Moedverloren Leslie, Boer, 1977, Pretoria
Erasmus L A, 45, P/A S A Lugmag Pretoria, Kaptein, 1968
Erasmus L J, 40, P/A Veiligheidspolisie Krugersdorp, Luitenant-Kolonel, 1977, Pretoria
Erasmus L J B, 37, Vlakplaas Koppies, Boer, 1965, Heilbron
Erasmus L M, 34, N G Kerk De Bloem, Predikant, 1967, Soutpan O V S

Erasmus M C, Voormalige Sekretaris van Onderwys
Erasmus M G, 35, P/A Universiteit Zoeloeland Empangeni, Snr Lektor, (Privaatreg) 1974, Fort Hare
Erasmus P F, 30, Bekkersrust Bethal, Boer, 1974
Erasmus P J E, 32, De Witskraal P K Hammanskraal, Boer, 1975, Pretoria
Erasmus P J E, 29, Witfontein PK Kaalfontein, Boer, 1965
Erasmus R P, 40, Inmalkaar Thabazimbi, Boer, 1965, Odendaalsrus
Erasmus S J, 30, Rooiribbokstraat 74 Waterkloof-Uitbr Pretoria, Regsadviseur, 1973 Bloemfontein
Erasmus S J P, 38, Hoër Tegn Skool Ficksburg, Instrukteur, 1966, Ventersburg
Erasmus W J, 38, P/A Stadsraad Rustenburg, Stadsklerk, 1973, Lichtenburg
Erasmus W L, 37, Koedoe Apteek Vanderbijlpark, Apteker, 1967, Durban
Erlank A, 44, P/A Laerskool Ferndale Randburg, Onderwyser, 1968, Florida
Erlank B J, 34, P/A Boland Bank Victoria-Wes, Bestuurder, 1977, De Doorns
Erlank C, 33, P/A Kreosootwerke Kareedouw, Sekretaris, 1969, Louis Trichardt
Erlank E, 27, N G Pastorie Tweeling, Predikant, 1966, Harrismith
Erwee A J, 29, Fritsche H 26 Pionierspark Windhoek, Geneesheer, 1976, Pretoria
Erwee J H, 36, Phillip Wesselsbron, Boer, 1968, Brandfort
Espach J B, 33, Burgerlaan 115 Verwoerdburg, Asst Sekretaris A T K B, 1971, Witbank
Espost V A, 43, P/A Laerskool Epping, Skoolhoof, 1964, Touwsrivier
Esterhuizen H C, 44, Bultfontein Hutchinson, Boer, 1964
Esterhuizen H L, 29, P/A St Andrews College Grahamstad, Onderwyser, 1974, Bloemfontein
Esterhuizen J J B, 36, C C v Dykstraat 3 Krugersdorp, Landdros, 1976, Vredendal
Esterhuizen J M, 38, Diepdrif Graskop, Boer/Handelaar, 1969
Esterhuizen W C, 38, Pastoriestraat 13 Keetmanshoop, Boer/Sakeman, 1967
Esterhuyse A E, 32, Residensieweg Outjo, Onderwyser, 1972, Gobabis
Esterhuyse A J, 39, P/A Universiteit Stellenbosch, Voorligtingsbeampte, 1967, Paarl
Esterhuyse H de W, 43, Arbeidersfontein Williston, Boer, 1975
Esterhuyse H G, 28, Volstruisfontein Williston, Boer, 1972
Esterhuyse W P, 30, P/A Universiteitskollege vir Indiërs Durban, Snr Lektor, 1967, Stellenbosch
Eyssen J C B, 41, Afd Publikasies Dept v Inligting Pretoria, Onderhoof, 1964, Babanango

F

Faasen C A, 31, Hoërskool Robertson, Onderwyser, 1974, Jan Kempdorp
Faasen J, 38, Allemanskraal Aberdeen, Boer, 1965, Somerset-Oos
Faasen P D, P/A Vic Armstrong T S M/Californiastraat 93 Crosby Johannesburg, Drukperswerktuigkundige, 1975
Fabricius P H, 43, P/A S A Polisie Paarl, Kaptein, 1968, Riversdal
Farrel P J, 41, Mooimeisierust Afrikaskop, Boer, 1971, Bethlehem
Faul C M (Dr), Molenstraat 71 Potchefstroom — Skakel by Militêre Opleidingskamp op Potchefstroom, 1966
Faul M, 38, S A Weermag Pretoria, Majoor, 1969, Ottosdal
Faul M A, 33, U O V S Bloemfontein, Professor, 1965, Potchefstroom
Faure J M B, Kurator — Letterkundige Museum Bloemfontein — was lank Lid van die U R
Faure J M B (Lid Nr 1256) Bloemfontein (Adj-Direkteur van Onderwys), Voorgestel vir die U R in 1968
Faure P H, 34, Hendrik Boomstraat 11 Worcester, Geneesheer, 1975, Bloemfontein
Faurie W H (Lid Nr 2000), Komatipoort, Boer/L V
Fechter L F, 25, P/A Fechter & Fechter Knysna, Rekenmeester, 1964
Felstead P G H, 46, Serfonteinstraat 15 Libradene Boksburg/Laerskool Elsburg, Skoolhoof 1976, Primrose
Felstead P G H, 35, P/A Setotoloane-Hoërskool PK Lutasrus, Skoolhoof, 1965, Dendron
Fensham F C (Lid Nr 7026), Professor (Semitiese Tale) — Lid van die U R (Voorgestel vir die U R in 1968)
Ferreira B A, 33, Molenstraat 59 Potchefstroom/S A Weermag, Kommandant, 1971, Bloemfontein
Ferreira B P, 29, P/A Hoërskool Vryburger Primrose, Onderwyser, 1974, Potchefstroom

Ferreira C J, 37, P/A Van Zyl Wegner Maritz & Vennote Letsitele, Ouditeur, 1976, Nelspruit
Ferreira C J, 33, P/A Bergers-Motorhawe Koster, Bestelklerk, 1968, Lichtenburg
Ferreira D M, 41, Elinus Cradock, Boer, 1972
Ferreira E, 41, P/A S A Polisie Bultfontein, Adj-Offisier, 1968, Boshoff
Ferreira F H, 37, Brightonrylaan 3 Somerstrand Port Elizabeth/Fordmotor Mpy, Direkteur (Personeel), 1970
Ferreira G T, 47, S A S & H Johannesburg, Personeelsuperintendent, 1964, Langkloof K P
Ferreira J B G, 37, Hoërskool Colesberg, Hoof, 1966, Redelinghuys
Ferreira G T, 44, Privaatsak Snyberg Uniondale, Boer, 1976
Ferreira I J, 44, Gum Tree Grove Utrecht, Boer, 1974, Philippolis
Ferreira I P H (Dr) (Lid Nr 7710) Bloemfontein, 1962
Ferreira J M, 37, Breëstraat Joubertina, Onderwyser, 1967, Dordrecht
Ferreira J T (Lid Nr 7758), Port Elizabeth, 1963
Ferreira L, 42, McGaghey 17 Boksburg/P/A Stadsraad, Klerk van die Raad, 1971
Ferreira L H, 34, P/A Munisipaliteit Ficksburg, Stadstesourier, 1967, Kroonstad
Ferreira M, 40, Singel Thorn Enkeldoorn Rhodesië, Boer, 1969
Ferreira P M, 32, Ascot Clocolan, Boer, 1972
Ferreira O J O, 33, R G N Pretoria, Geskied Navorser, 1974, Thaba'Nchu
Ferreira S E S, 38, 4deStraat 128 Naboomspruit, Sakeman, 1977, Groblersdal
Ferreira V N (Nic), 42, 3eLaan 15 Heidelberg Tvl, Posmeester, 1974, Virginia
Fischer H J, 40, P/A S A Polisie Pretoria, Kaptein, 1974, Vryburg
Fischer K J, 43, Roodekrans Morgenzon, Boer, 1969
Fick J C, 29, P/A Randse Afrikaanse Universiteit Johannesburg, Dosent, 1975, Pretoria
Fick J I J, 34, P/A Naude & Naude Bloemfontein, Rekenmeester, 1969
Fick J J, 31, Valencia Bergville, Boer, 1966 Devon
Fick J J, 31 Welkom Reitz, Boer, 1964, Devon
Fick L H, 30, Vaalplaas Dist Caledon, Boer, 1970
Fick L H, 31, Koedoebult P/S 1037 Waterpoort, Boer, 1971, Vryburg
Fick L H, 36, Vlaklaagte PK Dealesville, Boer, 1964
Fick M P, 45 Hoërskool Christiana, Sekretaris, 1966
Fick S J, 30, P/A Munisipaliteit Kempton Park, Asst Hoofgesondheidsinspekteur, 1973, Kimberley
Filmalter L J, 37, P/A Yskor Pretoria, Skeikundige, 1964, Thabazimbi
Firmani O M, 32, Seunskoshuis Springbok, Onderwyser, 1968, Parow
Fitzgerald P, 36, Earlstraat 36, Newcastle, Geneesheer, 1967, Durban
Fivaz A M, 33, P/A Hoërskool Bultfontein, Onderwyser, 1965, Vereeniging
Fogwell P C, 31, Servaasstraat 18 Flamwood Klerksdorp, Onderwyser, 1971, Heidelberg Tvl
Fölscher J C E, By 1965 Bondsraad praat hy oor Moedertaal Onderwys, (Nelspruit)
Fouche A F, 38, Conradie & Miller Witbank, Bestuurder, 1964, Ermelo
Fouche D R, 33, Geref Kerk Groblersdal, Predikant, 1974, Potchefstroom
Fouche J, 40, P/A General Mining Johannesburg, Hoof-Geoloog, 1973, Barberton
Fouche J H, 39, Cedarstraat 94, Corriemoore, Geoktrooieerde Rekenmeester, 1972, Pretoria
Fouche J J (Lid Nr 1899) Gewese Staatspresident
Fouche J P, 29, P/A Hoërskool Napier, Onderwyser, 1976, Robertson
Fouche J P, 45, S A Polisie Pretoria, Lid van Veiligheidspolisie, 1974, Delmas
Fouche L, (Lid Nr 7790) Pretoria, 1962
Fouché L B, 31, Rooikoppies Lady Grey, Boer, 1973
Fouche P A, 38, Perseel 6L6 Magagong, Boer, 1967, Marioko
Fouché P M, 37, Elandskraalskool PK Mooinooi, Skoolhoof, 1967, Brits
Fourie A B, 39, P/A Dept Hoër Onderwys Pretoria, Snr Vakk Beampte, 1968
Fourie A B, 30, P/A Usko Vereeniging, Ouditeursklerk, 1969, Bethlehem
Fourie A J, 35, P/A Stadsraad Vanderbijlpark, O & M Direkteur, 1966, Pretoria
Fourie C A, 39, Volkskas Barkly-Oos, Bestuurder, 1968, Pretoria
Fourie C E, 39, P/A Hoërskool A J Koen Bloemhof, Onderwyser, 1977
Fourie C J, 44, Yskor Pretoria, Snr Klerk, 1974, Steynsrus
Fourie C M, 32, Clongowna PK Hennenman, Boer, 1969
Fourie D A, 38, Tvlse Onderwysdepartement Brakpan, Sielkundige, 1967, Pretoria
Fourie D J, 34, Appeldoorn Dordrecht, Boer, 1977

Fourie D J, (Lid Nr 7791, Pretoria, 1962)
Fourie D P, 35, Liddlesdale PK Holfontein, Boer, 1969
Fourie F I H, 35, P/A N G Kerk Griekwastad, Skriba, 1969, Douglas
Fourie G J, 42, VanderWaltstraat Noupoort, Onderwyser, 1964, Oudtshoorn
Fourie H, 37, S A Polisie Paul Roux, Sersant, 1966, Sannieshof
Fourie H, 29, Westridingweg Ferrivale Nigel, Geneesheer, 1974, Pretoria
Fourie H P, 38, P/A Unisa Pretoria, Snr Lektor, 1974
Fourie I S, 39, Nieuwerus Koelenhof/Rupert Internasionaal, Skeikundige, 1976, Paarl
Fourie J, 33, P/A Veiligheidspolisie Brakpan, Luitenant, 1975, Napier
Fourie J, 26, Voorwaarts-Koshuis Steynsrus, Onderwyser, 1968, Dordrecht
Fourie J, 33, S A Weermag Pretoria, Majoor, 1964, Bloemfontein
Fourie J, 38, Opleidingskollege Paarl, Dosent, 1964, Stanford
Fourie J, 38, Salisburystraat 69 Bellville/P/A Volkskas Bpk Bellville, Rekenmeester, 1977, Joubertina
Fourie J, Posbus 8 Tempe, Kommandant, 1967
Fourie J A, 33, Joe Petra Petrusville, Boer, 1972, Philipstown
Fourie J A C, 42, P/A Volkskool Senekal, Onderwyser, 1967, Heilbron
Fourie J C, 30, Hoërskool Koshuis Sannieshof, Onderwyser, 1972, Johannesburg
Fourie J C H, 28, P/A Hoërskool Christiana, Onderwyser, 1966, Reivilo
Fourie J F, 37, Langplaas Dist Barkly-Wes, Boer, 1977
Fourie J H, 32, P/A Fiskor Phalaborwa, Superintendent, 1975, Sasolburg
Fourie J H, 33, Junior Koshuis Excelsior, Onderwyser, 1967, Brandfort
Fourie J J, 40, Katima Mulilo/S A Weermag, Majoor, 1976, Erasmia
Fourie J J, 28, P/A N G Gemeente Bloemfontein, Predikant, 1974, Stellenbosch
Fourie J J, 38, P/A Landbank Pretoria, Hoof Stelselontw, 1973
Fourie J J (Lid Nr 4805), Professor — Bloemfontein — Voorgestel vir die U R in 1968
Fourie J J H, 44, P/A Hospitaalraad Senekal, Sekretaris, 1975, Winburg
Fourie J M, 40, Robinson Getroude Kwartiere Randfontein/Laerskool Rapportryer, Skoolhoof, 1970, Stilfontein
Fourie J M, 40, P/A N H Kerk Nylstroom, Predikant, 1968, Benoni
Fourie J M, 47, Rooipoort Philipstown, Boer, 1974
Fourie J P, 45, Tennyson 75 Lombardy-Oos Johannesburg, Motorhandelaar, 1970, Yeoville
Fourie J S, 33, Handelsingel 4 Despatch, Onderwyser, 1969, Kirkwood
Fourie J S, 29, Laerskool PK Vivo, Onderwyser, 1969, Pretoria
Fourie J S, 47, P/A Foskor Phalaborwa, Produksiebestuurder, 1975, O'Kiep
Fourie J S, 38, P/A Ferreira & Fourie Bethal, Prokureur, 1974, Lydenburg
Fourie L D, 40, Berg-en-Dal Ashton, Boer, 1973, Klerksdorp
Fourie L de J, 35, Brink Roos & Du Toit Johannesburg, Ouditeur, 1965, Bloemfontein
Fourie L J, 37, P/A Bobs Motors Bulawayo, Onderdelebestuurder, 1976, Durban
Fourie L J F, 27, Slangfontein Kransfontein, Boer, 1973, Kestell
Fourie L M, 32, Van Graanstraat Potchefstroom, Onderwyser, 1977, Gobabis
Fourie M T S, 38, N G Gemeente Braamfontein, Predikant, 1970, Melville
Fourie N, 43, P/A Cullinan Holdings Ltd/Millweg 24 Olifantsfontein, Produksiebestuurder 1975, Rustenburg
Fourie N, 39, P/A Sentrale Makelaars Kempton-Park, Versekeringsmakelaar, 1976, Johannesburg
Fourie N J, 38, "Wag-'n-Bietjieshoek" Vryheid, Boer, 1970
Fourie N J, 29, S A Polisie Kempton Park, Speursersant, 1964, Groblersdal
Fourie N P, 45, Transvaler Boekhandel Johannesburg, Bestuurder, 1964
Fourie O J, 50, Opleidingskollege Wellington, Dosent, 1965, Oudtshoorn
Fourie P A C, 47, P/A Dept Pos & Tel Pretoria, Adm Beampte, 1968
Fourie P C, 37, U O V S Bloemfontein, Professor, 1967, Pretoria
Fourie P J, 34, Broomweg 21 Casseldale Springs, Onderwyser, 1977
Fourie P J, 30, S A Polisie Goodwood, Kaptein, 1974, Calvinia
Fourie P J, 35, Visserstraat 4 Strubenvale Springs, Landdros, 1967, Heidelberg Tvl
Fourie P J, 39, P/A Raad op Atoomkrag (Isotoop Navorsing), Pretoria Wetenskaplike, 1975
Fourie P J, 38, S A Polisie Devon, Adj-Offisier, 1975, Brakpan
Fourie P J V, 30, Posbus 30 Randfontein, Tandarts, 1963, Pretoria
Fourie P R, 45, Meriba Bethlehem, Boer, 1969
Fourie P S, 25, P/A Riversdalse Koöp/Proteastraat 4 Albertinia, Graangradeerder, 1975

Fourie R G, 27, Hoërskool Hennenman, Onderwyser, 1964, Potchefstroom
Fourie S, 35, U O V S Bloemfontein, Snr Lektor, 1966, Beaufort-Wes
Fourie S O S, 30, Vergenoegd Schweizer-Reneke, Onderwyser, 1970
Fourie S P, 37, Soetdorings Vryburg, Boer, 1973
Fourie W A, 33, Kwaggalaagte Kinross, Boer, 1970, Brits
Fourie W A, 33, Breitingstraat 20 Windhoek, N G Predikant, 1977
Fourie W A H, 37, S A Polisie Johannesburg, Sersant, 1964, Napier
Fourie W A J, 47, Gevangenis Opleidingskollege Kroonstad, Bevelvoerder, 1964, Pretoria
Fourie W M, 32, P/A Wilfour Wonings Randburg, Boukontrakteur, 1968, Fouriesburg
Fourie W W, 28, Erskinestraat 123 Greytown, Prokureur, 1976, Muden
Franzsen P J J, 29, N G Sendingpastorie Riebeeck Kasteel, Sendeling, 1964, Knysna
Fraser H C, 35, Lewis Construction Bpk Johannesburg, Sekretaris/Rekenmeester, 1965
Friedrich M L, 46, P/A Dept Gemeenskapsbou Bloemfontein, Streekverteenwoordiger, 1976, Pretoria
Friis J J, 28, Skoolstraat Philippolis, Onderwyser, 1969, Bloemfontein
Friis T F, 30, Skool vir Dowe Bantoekinders Tshilidzini, Vise-Hoof, 1974, Thaba 'Nchu
Fritz A S, 36, Leicesterweg 4A, Grahamstad, Landdros, 1976, Kimberley
Froneman P A, 35, P/A Keevy Steyn & Vennote Johannesburg, Ingenieur, 1974, Venterstad
Frylinck P C H, 41, Stadsraad Roodepoort, Adm Assistent, 1966, Randfontein
Fuchs C D, Voorheen S A U K
Fuchs F G, 33, P/A Sanlam Nigel, Verteenwoordiger, 1975, Bethal
Fuchs W D, 31, Drakensberg-Boekhandel Durban, Bestuurder, 1967, King Williamstown
Furstenberg F J, 32, P/A Volkskas Trompsburg, Rekenmeester, 1969, Pretoria

G

Garbers F H C, 44, Die Landdros Kroonstad, Asst Landdros, 1966, Witbank
Garbers P G C, 32, Hoër Seunskool Stoffberg Brakpan, Onderwyser, 1966, Heidelberg
Gauché J G, 42, Luckhofstraat Springbok, Myn-Eienaar, 1965, Johannesburg
Gauché J H, 26, Flamingo Sisal Mkuze, Boer, 1974
Gaum F M, 27, N G Pastorie Kuruman, Predikant, 1967, Stellenbosch
Gavera J P, 34, P/A N G Pastorie De Rust, Predikant, 1976, Queenstown
Gebhardt J W L, 41, P/A N G Moedergemeente Wellington, N G Predikant, 1976, Bethlehem
Geers P J, 40, P/A Stadsraad Verwoerdburg, Stadsklerk, 1977, Edenvale
Geertsema G, 43, S A Wolraad Pretoria, Ekonoom, 1964
Geertsema G J, 29, Nataliestraat 59 Murrayfield Pretoria, Tandarts, 1973
Geertsema J C, 24, P/A Dept Wiskunde Universiteit Pretoria, Lektor, 1965, Swartruggens
Geldenhuis J A, 33, Dept van Verdediging Pretoria, Kommandant, 1966, Tempe
Geldenhuis P J, 43, Strydfontein 71 Pretoria-Noord/Yskor, Navorser, 1976, Phalaborwa
Geldenhuis P J, 38, De Friedlandstraat 11 Pretoria/SALM Kollege, Snr Direkteur Opl., 1976, Kaapstad
Geldenhuys A, 41, Uitkyk Protem, Boer, 1966, Rhodesië
Geldenbuys B H, 35, Derdestraat 63 Linden/S A Weermag, Loods, 1973, Potchefstroom
Geldenbuys B L, 29, Smutsstraat 75 Randgate, N G Predikant, 1971, Stellenbosch
Geldenbuys D J C, 33, P/A A T K B Pretoria, Sekretaris, 1967, Carolina
Geldenhuys D J du P, (Lid Nr 7711) Queenstown, Landdros, 1962
Geldenhuys D M, 39, P/A Nas Bouvereniging Cradock, Takbestuurder, 1968, Middelburg K P
Geldenbhuys F G, 44, Universiteit van Pretoria, Professor, 1967
Geldenhuys G J, 34, Ruimte Dirkie Uysstraat Malmesbury, Vise-Hoof, 1971, Worcester
Geldenhuys H A, 38, PK Rietkuil Oor Hendrina, Onderwyser, 1974, Vaalwater
Geldenhuys H J, 42, Dept van Handel Pretoria, Hoofvakkundige Beampte, 1975, Londen
Geldenhuys I G, 30, Sonneskyn Kroonstad, Boer, 1967
Geldenhuys J G, 34, V D Merwestraat 72 Warmbad/S A Polisie, Luitenant, 1970, Pietersburg
Geldenhuys J J, 39, P/A S A Weermag Windhoek, Bevelv Kommandement, 1975, Luanda Angola
Geldenhuys J M, 49, Kliplaagte Lichtenburg, Boer, 1964
Geldenhuys J N, 34, P/A Nasionale Koerante Port Elizabeth, Bestuurder, 1963, Kaapstad

Geldenhuys J N L, 37, Loevrestraat 34 Courtrai Suider-Paarl/S A Polisie, Kaptein, 1977, Kaapstad
Geldenhuys M L, 33, P/A Kouebokveldse Aartappelkoöperasie Gydo, Bedryfsbestuurder, 1972, Prins Alfred Hamlet
Geldenhuys P J, 45, Laerskool Philadelphia, Skoolhoof, 1977, Bellville
Geldenhuys S, 30, P/A Boland Bank Worcester, Bestuurder, 1975, Kaapstad
Geldenhuys S P, 32, P/A Hoërskool Mafeking, Onderwyser, 1973, Levubu
Geldenhuys W S, 34, Tivotoord 28 Howick/Ciba Geigy, Teg Beampte, 1977, Ysterplaat/Nelspruit
Gelderblom B C, 45, P/A K W V Paarl, Sekretariële Asst, 1977, Paarl
Gelderblom I J, 40, Katbergstraat 6 Noordheuwel Krugersdorp/Uniewinkels, Streeksbestuurder, 1971, Pretoria
Genade A B, 27, Vissery-Ontw Korp Knysna, Navorser, 1966, Parow
Genade G J, 29, S A S & H Kaapstad, Meulmaker, 1964, Parow
Genis E G J, 28, Laingshoogte PK Graafwater, Boer, 1971
Genis L M, 36, Huis 77 O'Kiep/O'Kiep Copper Co, Geoloog, 1972, Vredendal
Genis M C de G, 31, Lefanyane PK Gilead, Boer, 1966, Potgietersrus
Gerber A, 27, N G Pastorie Brandvlei, N G Predikant, 1972, Stellenbosch
Gerber F A, 35, Hoërskool Dr Malan Meyerton, Onderhoof, 1966, Rustenburg
Gerber F A, 35, P/A Laerskool Kanoneiland, Skoolhoof, 1977, George
Gerber H J, 31, P/A Poskantoorpersoneel George, Adm Assistent, 1975
Gerber H T, 37, S A Polisie Delmas, Bevelvoerder, 1975, Springs
Gerber H W, 38, Versfeldweg 124 Vrijzee/S A S & H, Asst-Ingenieur, 1975, Wolseley
Gerber H W, 45, Laerskool Prieska, Skoolhoof, 1973, O'Kiep
Gerber J, Wolmaransstad, Onderwyser, 1966
Gerber J J, 39, Springbokweg 8 Loevenstein, Vise-Hoof, 1974, Kuilsrivier
Gerber P (Lid Nr 7759), Molteno, 1963
Gerber S H, 34, P/A S A Polisie Vredehoek Kaapstad, Luitenant, 1969, Riviersonderend
Gerber S J, 37, P/A Norwood Coaker-Fabriek Ladybrand, Apteker, 1967, Bloemfontein
Gerber T J, 31, Kaallaagte Vermaas, Boer, 1973, Zeerust
Gericke H S, 41, S A Lugdiens Johannesburg, Beplannings-Assistent, 1967, Bethlehem
Gericke J G, 42, Boeresake Parow, Verkoopsbestuurder, 1969, Kaapstad
Gericke J H O, 38, Louis Raymondstraat 10 Unitaspark Vereeniging, Vise-Hoof Laerskool, 1977, Potchefstroom
Gericke J S (Dr), (Lid Nr 1999), Predikant — Stellenbosch — Voorgestel vir die U R in 1968
Germishuizen H F, 31, P/A Oos-Tvlse Bantoesake Adm Raad Witrivier, Klerk, 1974
Germishuizen J C, 32, P/A Everest De Kock & Vennote Scholtzstraat 82 Witfield, Elektrotegn Ing, 1970, Boksburg
Germishuizen J C, 39, Bantoesake Admin-Raad NOVS Bethlehem, Bestuurder Bantoedorp, 1977, Standerton
Germishuizen W P, 45, Elim Waterbron, Direkteur, 1971, Maclear
Germishuys L J A (Dr) (Lid Nr 7696) Heilbron, 1962
Gerryts B A, 40, P/A N G Pastorie Malvern Durban, Predikant, 1976, Pretoria
Gerryts E, 43, P/A Vernuwings Sanlam Bellville, Hoofklerk, 1963, Kuilsrivier
Gerryts E D, 30, Unisa Pretoria, Bibliotekaris, 1970
Gersbach H C, 38, Waterklip Vredenburg, Boer, 1966
Gertenbach F P du T, 32, N G Kerk Bulawayo, N G Predikant, 1973, Upington
Gertenbach J D, 34, Seunskoshuis Volksrust/Hoërskool, Onderwyser, 1970, Ermelo
Gertenbach M P, 28, P/A N G Pastorie Louwsburg, Predikant, 1974, Stellenbosch
Geustyn P J, 41, P/A Geustyn Forsyth & Joubert Pretoria, Ingenieur, 1967, Papendorp
Geyer A, 30, "Beau Geste" Politsi, Boer, 1970
Geyer H, 39, Weltevrede PK Bailey, Boer, 1967, Queenstown
Geyer H J, 29, N G Pastorie Dendron, Predikant, 1975, Klerksdorp
Geyer H J, 40, Dept van Landbou Umtata, Hoofvakkundige, 1967, Ermelo
Geyer J C H, Malmesbury, Skakel by Afdelingsraadkongres in Oos-Londen in 1968
Geyer J C, 29, Munisipaliteit van Randburg, Stadsklerk, 1973, Klerksdorp
Geyer J P, 31, P/A Volkskas Kusweg Strand, Asst Rekenmeester, 1976, Malmesbury
Geyer L M, 37, Gevangenisterrein 39 Pollsmoor, Kaptein, 1975, Kroonstad
Geyer P (Reitz), Praat oor Jeugweerbaarheid by Bondsraad van 1969
Geyser A P, 28, Landdroskantoor Fouriesburg, Landdros, 1968, Carolina

Geyser C A C, 31, Residentstraat 42B Bloemhof, Geneesheer, 1969, Pretoria
Geyser J, 47, P/A S A S & H Pietersburg, Snr Amptenaar, 1969
Geyser O, 34, Universiteit van Port Elizabeth, Snr Lektor, 1967, Durban
Geyser P A, 30, P/A Ned Herv Pastorie Delareyville, Predikant, 1974, Johannesburg
Geyser P R, 34, Voortrekkerweg 30 Mafeking, Tandarts, 1967, Pretoria
Gie F W, 39, P/A S A S & H Parow, Tekenaar, 1975, Germiston
Gildenhuys A, 41, P/A Van der Merwe & Gildenhuys Pretoria, Prokureur, 1977
Gildenhuys B J P, 46, Oosthuizenstraat 9 Middelburg Tvl, Boer, 1971, Naboomspruit
Gildenhuys H J, 31, Egertonweg 21 Ladysmith, Geneesheer, 1965, Lydenburg
Gildenhuys J D, 42, Sekondêre Skool Jim Fouche Bloemfontein, Skoolhoof, 1973, Winburg
Giliomee P J, 28, Koppie Alleen Perdekop, Boer, 1967
Gillaume G, 30, PK Limburg Potgietersrus, Boer, 1963, Rustenburg
Gilliland J, 37, P/A Yskor Pretoria, Meganiese Ingenieur, 1970
Gobrechts O O, 37, Templeton Hostel Bedford, Onderwyser, 1967, Ashton K P
Gobregts C, 31, Hoofstraat Bonnievale, Geneesheer, 1964, De Doorns
Gobregts J P, 32, Langenhovenstraat 9 Soneike Kuilsrivier, Snr Klerk Viskor, 1975, Kaapstad
Goosen A C, 29, P/A NG Pastorie Reddersburg, N G Predikant, 1976, Parow
Goosen C J, 37, P/A G O K Johannesburg, Dosent, 1974, Pretoria
Goosen F P, 36, P/A Poskantoor Molteno, Posmeester, 1968, Oudtshoorn
Goosen G P, 39, Die Drosdy Voortrekkerstraat Humansdorp, Landdros, 1971, Pretoria
Goosen H P, 36, Krabfontein Rouxville, Boer, 1966
Goosen O J A, 32, Churchstraat 38 George, Landmeter, 1973, Port Elizabeth
Goosen O J J, 44, Scaffelweg 5 Floridaheuwels/United Transport Holdings, Streeksuitv Beampte, 1976, Brixton
Goosen P A J, 28, Neusuckly Hertzogville, Boer, 1970
Goosen P D, 43, Harmonie Leydsdorp, Boer, 1973, Ermelo
Goosen P J, 32, Bloukop PK Mopane, Vakman/Boer, 1968, Messina
Goosen P S, 29, Kerkstraat 11 Rouxville, Landdros, 1977, Humansdorp
Goosen S M, 44, P/A Vaal Potteries Meyerton, Verkoopsbestuurder, 1968, Ellisras
Goossens A P G, 34, Du Plessisstraat 12 Baillie Park Potchefstroom, Snr Lektor (Farmasie), 1971
Gough J P, 28, S A Polisie Tugela Ferry Greytown, Adj-Offisier, 1965, Van Rhynsdorp
Gous A G S, 27, Noordstraat Barkly-Wes, Diamantkoper, 1965, De Aar
Gous H P F, 44, S W A Admin Windhoek, Staatsamptenaar, 1965
Gous H P H (Lid Nr 7730), Grootfontein, 1963
Gous J H, 34, N G Sendingkerk Kimberley, Predikant, 1968, Albertinia
Gous J J, 29, Tolo Niekerkshoop, Boer, 1966
Gous J P, 46, Neilersdrif Keimoes, Boer, 1965
Gous J P, 30, Albertstraat 2 Uitenhage, Geneesheer, 1975, Peddie
Gouws B J, 36, Volkskas Mafeking, Bestuurder, 1967, Cradock
Gouws D J, 36, Volkskas Piet Retief, Bestuurder, 1964, Pretoria
Gouws H J, 37, Vaalkop Dist Delareyville, Boer, 1973
Gouws H J S, 30, N G Pastorie Dullstroom, Predikant, 1970, Pretoria
Gouws J H, 40, P/A Franlem Ingenieurs Firma Welkom, Besturende Direkteur, 1974, Pretoria
Gouws J J, 52, S A Polisie Kaapstad, Kolonel, 1965, Boksburg
Gouws J S, 31, Devonlaan 3 Brakpan, Hoof Opleidingsbeampte, 1970
Gouws P A M, 43, Paul Krugerrylaan 10 Krugersdorp, Sakeman, 1967, Bloemfontein
Gouws R B J, 47, Tvlse Prov Adm Pretoria, Eerste Adm Beampte, 1965
Gouws S J L, 31, Dept Opvoed Universiteit Pretoria, Snr Lektor, 1967, (Tans Prof by RAU)
Gouws S W, 36, Rooivlakte Hankey Patensie, Boer, 1971, Port Elizabeth
Gräbe J, 30, N G Pastorie Fauresmith, Predikant, 1966, Groblersdal
Gräbe J G C, 43, Atterburyweg 407 Menlopark/P/A Dept van Beplanning Pretoria, Ondersekretaris Personeel, 1977, Rayton
Gräbe P H G, 46, Kerkstraat Vryheid Natal, Skoolhoof, 1967, Durban
Gräbe P J, 34, Lindfieldweg 61 Lynnwood Manor Pretoria, Professor/UP, 1976
Gräbe P J W, 37, Munisipaliteit Vryheid, Stadsklerk, 1965, Weenen
Gravett L, 31, Hospitaalweg 25 Middelburg Tvl, Onderwyser, 1969, Amersfoort
Gravett W H, 33, Sonopstraat Volksrust/Laerskool Pionier, Onderhoof, 1970, Nylstroom

Greeff A J, 30, Daffodilstraat 11 Arcon Park/Uniestaal Vereeniging, Personeelhoof, 1970, Meyerton
Greeff E H D, 36, Ouplaas Knysna, Sakeman, 1974, Magaliesburg
Greeff G P, 39, P/A Randburgse Hoërskool Randburg, Adj-Hoof, 1970, Warmbad
Greeff H, 44, P/A S A Spoorwegpolisie Sterkstroom, Speursersant, 1965, Indwe
Greeff H G, 31, S A S & H Paulpietersburg, Klerk, 1967, Ladysmith
Greeff O P W, 28, Beryllaan-Suid 1027 Lyttelton, Geneesheer, 1977, Pretoria
Greeff R, 47, P/A Buro vir Staatsveiligheid Kaapstad, Snr Adm Beampte, 1974, Parow-Suid
Greeff S M, L P R Oudtshoorn
Gresse D A, 37, 7deLaan 112 Fairland/Goudstad Onderwyskollege, Snr Lektor, 1970, Krugersdorp
Gresse J B, 42, P/A Gerrit Maritzlaan 43, Krugersdorp, Prokureur, 1975
Grewar D M, Posbus 32, Gumtree, 1963
Grewar D Mc K (Lid Nr 6700), Boer & L U K — Ficksburg — Lid van die U R se Landbou-Komitee in 1973 Voorgestel vir die U R in 1968
Greybe L, 37, P/A Laerskool Dirkie Uys Moorreesburg/Pleinstraat 6, Skoolhoof, 1977, Beaufort-Wes
Greyling A C, 35, Madelainestraat 22 Mangoldpark/Skoolkliniek, Hoof, 1974, Port Elizabeth
Greyling A J, 34, P/A Bantoe-Onderwys & U O V S, Snr Navorser, 1975, Taung
Greyling B C, 30, Greylingsrust Makwassie, Boer, 1967
Greyling C P, 45, P/A Landbou Tegn Dienste Bloemfontein, Hoofvakk Beampte, 1969, Stellenbosch
Greyling D J, 29, S A Weermag Pretoria, Kaptein, 1966, Brits
Greyling E (Dordrecht, Skakel met pers by 1969 se Bondsraad
Greyling F, 30, Louwstraat 8 Rouxville, Onderwyser, 1974, Ladybrand
Greyling F J D, 34, Fonteinstraat 5 Discovery, Onderwyser, 1975
Greyling F L, 42, Afr Pers Johannesburg, Verkoopsbestuurder, 1966, King Williamstown
Greyling H L, Voorsitter van Kleurling Ontwikkelings Korporasie
Greyling J A (Ds), 42, P/A Dept Bantoe-Onderwys Pretoria, Insp Godsdiensonderwys, 1963, Umtata
Greyling J A, 32, Posbus 238 Leslie, Geneesheer, 1967, Devon
Greyling J H, 32, Hoërskool Dr E G Jansen Boksburg, Onderwyser, 1966, Heidelberg Tvl
Greyling J J, 44, Negendestraat 18A Fochville, Asst Sekretaris, 1972, Brakpan
Greyling J J, 36, Ashlaan 7 Robin Acres/Standard General Versekerings Mpy, Asst Alg Bestuurder, 1970, Bellville K P
Greyling J T, 38, P/A S A U K Johannesburg, Hoof Nuusdiens, 1968
Greyling M D, 32, Schuman Woonstelle Nr 9 Jasmynlaan Bloemfontein Santam Bank, Sekretaris, 1975, Oudtshoorn
Greyling P J, 47, S A Polisie Krugersdorp, Kaptein, 1965, Smithfield
Greyling P J, 35, Breckettstraat 44 Vereeniging, Onderwyser, 1966, Makwassie
Greyling P J, 30, Ruigtevlei PK Matlabas, Boer, 1977, Hoopstad
Greyvenstein F W, 41, P/A Gevangenisterrein Goedemoed, Hoofbewaarder, 1975, Dordrecht
Greyvenstein G P, 30, Voortrekkerstraat Piketberg/Vlok & V D Spuy, Prokureur, 1970, Springbok
Greyvenstein G P, 30, De Villierstraat 52 Barkly-Oos, Werktuigkundige, 1971
Greyvenstein J, 34, Ulundilaan 528 Mountainview Pretoria, N G Predikant, 1970, Koedoeskop
Griesel J D (Lid Nr 7731), Schweizer-Reneke, 1963
Griesel J J, 30, Imhoff Auretstraat Paarl, Onderwyser, 1970, Ermelo
Griesel P A, 33, N G Pastorie Leeudoringstad, Predikant, 1966, Brakpan
Griessel G A J, 42, Karlstraat Schoemanville PK Hartebeespoort, Lektor Unisa, 1976, Brits
Griessel R D, 42, P/A Raad op Atoomkrag Pretoria, Elektrisiën, 1976
Griffiths J M, 44, Botha Landbouhoewes Randgate, Sakeman, 1971, Krugersdorp
Grimbeeck C L, 39, Carterstraat 52 Vanderbijlpark, Onderwyser, 1967, Middelburg Tvl
Grobbelaar B F, 41, P/A Volkskas BPK Memel, Bestuurder, 1970, Pretoria
Grobbelaar C S, 35, P/A Volkskas Bpk Pretoria, Klerk, 1974, Lindley
Grobbelaar F, 36, P/A Poskantoor Kestell, Posmeester, 1974, Cradock
Grobbelaar F R, 35, Tautestraat 6 Oudtshoorn, Geneesheer, 1974, Hanover
Grobbelaar G J, 40, Wes Einde Kimberley, Prinsipaal, 1963

Grobbelaar H R, 38, Weltevrede Petrusburg, Boer, 1968
Grobbelaar J A , 37, Seunskoshuis Die Fort Grootfontein, Onderwyser, 1973, Kuruman
Grobbelaar J C C, 32, Brenton PK Tosca, Boer, 1972, Vryburg
Grobbelaar J G, 31, P/A B S B Carnarvon, Verteenwoordiger, 1966, Cradock
Grobbelaar J J, 29, Woburnlaan Benoni, Geneesheer, 1964, Ficksburg
Grobbelaar J S W, 45, Noelstraat 8 Chrisville/S A Polisie, Sersant, 1970, Marquard
Grobbelaar L P, 41, Volkskas Vrede, Bestuurder, 1965, Pretoria
Grobbelaar M J, 41, Stadskouburg Johannesburg, Hoofbestuurder, 1969, Pretoria
Grobbelaar P de v (Umtali), Open 1965 se Bondsraad met Skriflesing & Gebed
Grobbelaar P J v d M, 41, Perseel IK6 Magogong, Boer, 1968, Salisbury
Grobbelaar P W, 30, Schilpadfontein Darling, Boer, 1974, Petrusburg
Grobbelaar W J, Lid van die U R s e Nie-Blanke-sake Komitee in 1973
Grobbelaar W P, 40, Nooitgedacht Navorsingstasie Ermelo, Verantwoordelike Beampte, 1967, Kroonstad
Grobler C G, 33, Rotherystraat Nelspruit/V Zyl Wegner Maritz & Vennote, Ouditeur, 1977, Pretoria
Grobler C J, 42, Gretna Settlers, Boer, 1975
Grobler C J F, 35, P/A Drs Retief Grobler & Vennote Sasolburg, Geneesheer, 1970, Nelspruit
Grobler D G, 29, P/A Kommissaris — Gen Umtata, Inligtingsbeampte, 1964, Windhoek
Grobler G H, 32, Dinamietfabriek Somerset-Wes, Skeikundige, 1964, Oos-Londen
Grobler G J, 38, Smithfield Ermelo, Boer, 1973
Grobler H M, 46, Bantoeskool vir Dowes Thaba 'Nchu, Skoolhoof, 1966, Pretoria
Grobler H P, 29, P/A S A Veiligheidspolisie Johannesburg, Luitenant, 1969, Mayfair Johannesburg
Grobler J, 32, Steynsvlei Krugersdorp, Tandarts, 1977
Grobler J F, 29, Naboomstraat 42, Wilropark, Onderwyser, 1976, Roodepoort
Grobler J H, 37, P/A Afd Bodemkunde Landboukollege Potchefstroom, Hoof, 1963, Middelburg K P
Grobler J H, 32, Smithfield Ermelo, Boer, 1966
Grobler J H, 31, Charles Hofmeyer Koshuis Standerton, Onderwyser, 1968, Marico
Grobler J H, 40. Sitrusnavorsingsinst Nelspruit, Hoof, 1966, Pretoria
Grobler J H, Tungstenstraat 59, Proklamasieheuwel, Pretoria, 1973
Grobler J H F, 51, S A S (Bedryf) Johannesburg, Hoofsuperintendent, 1967, Pretoria
Grobler J J, 33, P U vir C H O Potchefstroom, Professor (Wiskunde), 1977, Carletonville
Grobler J J, 39, Granadaweg 23 Evander, Onderhoof, 1970, Bethal
Grobler J M, 34, Californiastraat 83 Crosby Johannesburg/Trustbank, Adm Bestuurder, 1970, Durban
Grobler J P, 32, P/A N G Kerk Johannesburg, Pastorale Sielkundige, 1969, Grasmere
Grobler M J, 33, Klipeiland Bronkhorstspruit, Onderwyser, 1970
Grobler M J, 24, Kalkfontein Grecy, Boer, 1970
Grobler M M, 35, Loopstraat 1 Brandfort, Vise-Hoof, 1977, Welkom
Grobler N J, 29, Kortstraat Swartruggens, Geneesheer, 1969, Kempton Park
Grobler N J, 36, Geref Pastorie Nelspruit, Predikant, 1964, Waterberg
Grobler N M J, 42, Blesbokspruit PK Piet Retief, Plaasbestuurder, 1971, Golela
Grobler P, 31, Rubenstraat 66 Mindalore Krugersdorp, Onderwyser, 1977
Grobler P B, 28, N G Pastorie Marble Hall, Predikant, 1974, Stellenbosch
Grobler P D F, 39, Melsheuwel Grootvlei, Boer, 1975
Grobler P H, 31, Rouxstraat Rouxville, Onderwyser, 1971, Maclear
Grobler P H, 37, P/A Lagrange Böhmer & Du Plessis/9e Straat 12 Menlopark Pretoria, Geboue Inspekteur, 1976
Grobler P J, 33, Bothastraat 22 Warmbad, N G Predikant, 1971, Brits
Grobler P S, 32, P/A Yskor Pretoria, Klerk, 1968
Grobler S J, 43, P/A F A Jonker & Vennote Lichtenburg, Ouditeur, 1974, Pretoria
Grobler S P N, 33, P/A Standard Telephones & Cables Boksburg, Onderbestuurder Data-Verwerking, 1974, Durban
Grobler T J, 30, St Iveswoonstelle 15 Hullstraat Florida/New Graphis Edms Bpk, Direkteur, 1970, Newlands
Grobler W S J, Voormalige L V en FAK-sekretaris
Groenewald A J, 51, Aktekantoor Pretoria, Hoofakteondersoeker, 1965, Bosbokrand

Groenewald B, Posbus 368 Adverteer vir Musiekonderwysers 1963, Posbus 368 Schweizer-Reneke
Groenewald B J, 40, P/A S A Spoorweë Pretoria, Asst Prod Ingenieur, 1968, Wolseley
Groenewald B J J, 25, P/A S A Polisie Hobhouse, Adj-Offisier, 1975, Bethlehem
Groenewald E P (Prof) (Lid Nr 2118), Dekaan Teologiese Fakulteit Universiteit van Pretoria
Groenewald F P, 38, Koelmanweg 76 Alphenpark Pretoria, Hoofnavorsings Beampte R G N, 1976, Bloemfontein
Groenewald H B, 42, Nelsonweg 16 Pinetown Natal/Sanlam, Wyksbestuurder, 1970, Butterworth
Groenewald H J P, 43, Welverdiend PK Brandfort, Boer, 1966
Groenewald J C, 32, Windsorlaan 19 Pietermaritzburg, N G Predikant, 1976, Stellenbosch
Groenewald J P, 34, Edgarstraat 23 Jansenpark Boksburg, Onderwyser, 1976
Groenewald M D, 24, Bothashof Salisbury, Onderwyser, 1968
Groenewald M J, 25, P/A Landdroskantoor Paul Roux, Landdros, 1968, Uitenhage
Groenewald P G, 36, Goedemoed Brandvlei Worcester, Boer, 1967
Groenewald P H, 33, P/A S A Lugmag Pietersburg, Majoor, 1969, Pretoria
Groenewald P J, 35, N G Gemeente Sonlandpark, Predikant, 1977, Vereeniging
Groenewald P W (Dr), Lid van die U R se Wetenskap Komitee 1973
Groenewald W L, 44, Kafueweg 14 Emmarentia Johannesburg, Narkotiseur, 1974, Mondeor Johannesburg
Groesbeek A J J, 41, Witkop Nigel, Boer, 1967
Gronum W v H, 32 P/A S A S & H Johannesburg, Chemikus, 1969, Potchefstroom
Grosskopf J G, 43, S A Buro v Standaarde Pretoria, Hoofwetenskaplike, 1970, Kroonstad
Grotius F, 31, P/A Transvaalse Suikerkoöp Komati, Arbeidsbeampte, 1975, Vanderbijlpark
Grove E L (Dr), Lid van die U R se Ekonomiese Komitee in 1973
Grove G R J, 37, Goedehoop Trichardt, Boer, 1965
Grove I J, 45, P/A Onderwyskollege Pretoria, Lektor, 1968
Grove P J, 39, P/A S A Polisie Du Plooysburg, Sersant, 1973, Douglas
Grové W, 32, P/A Veiligheidspolisie Middelburg, Kaptein, 1975, Victoria-Wes
Grove W M, 41, Old Missionweg 103 Wentworth Durban, N G Predikant, 1970, Newcastle
Gunning T, 31, Japie Krige 57 Unitaspark Vereeniging, Siviele Ingenieur, 1971, Vanderbijlpark
Gunter C F, 39, Laerskool Silverton, Onderhoof, 1970, Vereeniging
Gunter S J, 30, Van Reenenstraat 12 Robertson, Apteker, 1974
Guthrie C J, 46, Bedford-Oord 7 Cowies Hill, Apteker, 1974, Estcourt
Guy W J, 35, P/A Lawsons-Volvo Elsburg, Bemarkingsbestuurder, 1975, Klerksdorp

H

Haak J F W, Voormalige Minister
Haak P A (Jnr), 40, P/A Haak's-Motorhawe Pretoria, Sakeman, 1968
Haarhoff L, 43, Rubinstraat 7 Parys, N G Predikant, 1977, Marendellas
Haasbroek C F S, 36, S A Polisie Potchefstroom, Speursersant, 1964, Kuruman
Haasbroek G D, 44, P/A Laerskool Parow-Noord, Onderhoof, 1969, Bellville
Haasbroek G D, 29, P/A Hoërskool Koshuis Piet Retief, Onderwyser, 1976, Potchefstroom
Haasbroek I J, 45, N G Kerk Pietermaritzburg, Predikant, 1967, Bergville
Haasbroek J B, 35, Inhoek Leeudoringstad, Boer, 1968
Haasbroek J B, 30, N G Pastorie Elsburg, Predikant, 1966, Pretoria
Haasbroek J D K, 33, Genoa Vryburg, Boer, 1977
Haasbroek L C S, 35, N G Pastorie Vredefort, Predikant, 1964, Viljoenskroon
Habig W G, 31, N G Pastorie Tsumeb, Predikant, 1966, Vanderbijlpark
Haefele W J, 33, Wildebeesfontein Oranjeville, Onderwyser, 1965, Welkom
Hager J v S L, 40, Seodin Kuruman, Sakeman, 1973
Hahn W F, 31, P/A Landdroskantoor Springfontein, Landdros, 1974, Barkly-Wes
Hall G L, 34, S A Yster Staal & Verwante Nywerhede Vereeniging, Organiseerder, 1967, Springs
Hambly A T , 32, Edgeworthlaan 1 Darrenwood/Vereeniging Cons Mills, Sekretaris, 1970, Johannesburg
Hamersma H, 35, Klooflaan 4 Waterkloof Pretoria, Oor- Neus- & Keelaarts, 1964, Rustenburg

Hamersma P J, P U vir C H O Potchefstroom, Professor, (Fisiologie), 1963
Hamersma T K, 34, St Martin Noorder-Paarl, Boer, 1969, Wellington
Hamilton J H, 35, Skoolkliniek Bellville Handelstraat 93 Arauna Brackenfell, Hoof van Kliniek, 1970, Worcester
Hamman D S, 32, Militêre Basis Grahamstad, Majoor, 1971, Pretoria
Hamman E M (Prof), Universiteit van Pretoria, Rektor
Hamman J J L, 40, P/A S A U K Johannesburg, Rubriekbestuurder, 1969, Bloemfontein
Hamman J P, Lid van die U R se Landbou-Komitee in 1973
Hamman P F, 40, P/A Dept Waterwese Windhoek, Hoofskeikundige, 1973, Williston
Hamman W B, 43, S A S & H Heidelberg Tvl, Klerk, 1964, Lichtenburg
Hamman W P, 40, Gen Mining & Finansköop/Randburg, Personeelbestuurder, 1977, Phalaborwa
Hammann H J R, 37, P/A Hoërskool Bellville, Onderhoof, 1973
Hancke H P, 29, Palmietfontein Bethal, Boer, 1975
Hancke J G, 46, P/A Prov Adm Bellville, Werkswinkelhoof, 1969, Worcester
Hanekom A P, 37, PK Groblershoop, Sakeman , 1977
Hanekom C, 29, Universiteit Kollege van die Noorde, Snr Lektor, 1963, Bloemfontein
Hanekom D A, 37, P/A Dept van Kleurlingsake Kaapstad, Afdelingshoof, 1967, Paarl
Hanekom D J, 34, Hoër Tegniese Skool Tom Naude Pietersburg, Onderhoof, 1967, Kroonstad
Hanekom F, 44, S A S & H Treineafdeling Johannesburg, Klerk, 1967, Stellenbosch
Hanekom H A C, 41, Windelshoek PK Eendekuil, Boer, 1967, Piketberg
Hanekom J H L, 41, Boland Ogies, Geneesheer, 1973, Worcester
Hanekom J W J, 40, v d Merwestraat De Aar, N G Predikant, 1977, Stellenbosch
Hanekom P J, 45, De Villiersstraat 12 Worcester, Onderwyser, 1974, Calvinia
Hanekom P M, 32, S A Weermag Pretoria, Kommandant, 1970, Oudtshoorn
Hanekom T N (Prof), Stellenbosch
Hansen R, 33, S A Polisie Somerset-Oos, Adj-Offisier, 1965, Middelburg Kaap
Harley C B, 38, P/A Hoërskool Vereeniging, Vise-Hoof, 1975, Balfour
Harley S, 40, Orientstraat Arcadia Pretoria, Insp van Onderwys, 1975, Potchefstroom
Harmse C J B, 29, S A Polisie Potgietersrus, Adj-Offisier, 1964
Harmse G D, 34, Laerskool Danville Pretoria, Onderhoof, 1964, Vanderbijlpark
Harmse J H, 28, P/A Genl De La Reyskool Roodepoort, Waarnemende Vise-Hoof, 1974, Pretoria
Harmse J W J, 47, P/A S A Polisie Kuruman, Luit-Kolonel, 1975, Durban
Harris B C, 33, P/A Hoërskool Monument, Krugersdorp, Onderhoof, 1973, Balfour
Harris M P, 30, P/A Geref Kerk Schweizer-Reneke, Predikant, 1974, Port Elizabeth
Hart T M, 33, Pretoriase Tegn Kollege Pretoria, Dosent, 1968
Hartman J A, 27, Almera Villiers, Boer, 1969
Hartman J B, 34, Universiteit van Pretoria, Snr Lektor, 1974
Hartman J P, 32, P/A Hoërskool Nababeep, Onderwyser, 1977, Kaapstad
Hartman M H, 26, PK Sunland, Boer, 1965
Hartman S L, 37, Levubu, Boer, 1965, Krugersdorp
Hartman W R, Inspekteur v Onderwys — voorheen Hoër Handelskool Brakpan — (Skakel by Kongres
van Vereniging vir Tegniese & Beroepsonderwys in Oos-Londen van 3 tot 6 Okt 1966) (Skakel by Prinsipale Konferensie van die Dept Nasionale Opvoeding 4.2.1976)
Hartzenberg C H (Lid Nr 6221), Lid van die Staatdienskommissie Voorgestel vir die U R in 1968
Hartzenberg F, 28, Kleinuitschot Sannieshof, Boer, 1964
Hartzer P D, 36, P/A Addington Hospitaal Durban, Fisikus, 1965, Pretoria
Harvey F N, 35, P/A Noordweg Koöp Migdol/Graandepot, Bestuurder, 1971
Harvie G, 29, Laerskool Groblershoop, Onderwyser, 1977, Upington
Hassler D A (Lid Nr 7736), Sutherland, 1963
Hattingh A, 30, Beresfordweg Oos-Londen, Onderwyser, 1964, Queenstown
Hattingh B, 43, Van der Stellaan 15 Bethal, Streekbestuurder/Vetsak, 1977, Pretoria
Hattingh C, 30, Bakovenfontein Beaufort-Wes, Boer, 1968
Hattingh C A, 30, Vindragersfontein Merweville, Boer, 1967
Hattingh C J, N G Pastorie Môrelig Bethlehem, Predikant

Hattingh C P, 37, P/A Munisipaliteit Krugersdorp, Bestuurder Drankafdeling, 1963, Alberton
Hattingh C P, Tvlse Helpmekaar Studiefonds 1969 (O/B 14/8/69)
Hattingh D, 32, P/A Hoërskool Hopefield, Onderwyser, 1972, Stellenbosch
Hattingh D J, Heidelberg Tvl — by Bondsraad van 1965 praat hy oor "Sieklike" Eenheidsgedagte
Hattingh G A, 33, Geref Pastorie Pietersburg, Predikant, 1969, Pretoria
Hattingh G C, 35, P/A N G Gemeente Edenvale, Predikant, 1976, Jan Kempdorp
Hattingh G E, 48, Rietfontein Dist Cullinan, Boer, 1967, Lyttelton
Hattingh H S, Reisende Amptenaar van A B 1970
Hattingh I, 39, S A S & H Kaapstad, Personeelklerk, 1966, Riversdale
Hattingh I, 31, Cyfergat PK Villiers, Boer, 1967
Hattingh J H, Posbus 14111 Lyttelton Verwoerdburg — (Direkteur van Maatskappy vir Europese Immigrasie vanaf 1968) (Praat oor Kultuur Bondsraad 1965)
Hattingh J H P, 32, O V S Munisipale Pensioenfonds Kroonstad, Sekretaris, 1966, Edenville
Hattingh J J, 27, N G Kerk Nahoon Oos-Londen, Predikant, 1968, Stellenbosch
Hattingh J J H, 35, P/A Stone & Seuns Vasco, Kosteberekenaar, 1969, Beaufort-Wes
Hattingh J L, 34, Liebenhof Seunskoshuis Bethal, Onderwyser, 1974, Wolmaranstad
Hattingh J P, 32, P/A Hoërskool Klerksdorp, Onderwyser, 1973, Rustenburg
Hattingh J P, 31, Vaalbank Frankfort, Boer, 1977
Hattingh J W, 37, P/A Hoër Handelskool, Onderhoof, 1967, Zeerust
Hattingh M C, 33, Albertonse Hoërskool Alberton, Onderhoof, 1968
Hattingh M J, 47, Allenweg 43 Selectionpark Springs, Waarnemende Skoolhoof, 1963, Bedfordview
Hattingh M J, 32, Koshuis Hoërskool Grens Oos-Londen, Onderwyser, 1973
Hattingh P, 40, Uitvlug PK Dullstroom, Boer, 1969
Hattingh P A, 31, Innes Chambers Johannesburg/Lyntonlaan 5 Darrenwood, Advokaat, 1970, Florida
Hattingh P W, 37, Koeëlfontein Merweville, Boer, 1966
Haupt I, 47, P/A Dept Poswese Kaapstad, Telekommunikasie-Ingenieur, 1974, Kimberley
Hauptfleisch C J V, 37, P/A Komani Hospitaal Queenstown, Sekretaris, 1965, Bloemfontein
Hauptfleisch G J, 36, P/A R A U Johannesburg, Professor, 1969, Pretoria
Havemann J C T, 35, Universiteit van Port Elizabeth, Jnr Lektor, 1974, Pretoria
Havemann W W B (Lid Nr 4405) Administrateur Natal
Havenga G S, 38, P/A Volkskas Bpk Brandfort, Bestuurder, 1969, Pretoria
Havenga J F, 41, Gevangeniswese Kroonstad, Opperbewaarder, 1964, Griekwastad
Havenga J J, 44, S A S & H Johannesburg, Asst Bemarkingsbestuurder, 1970, Kimberley
Havenga J J D, 27, Donald Murraylaan 33 Bloemfontein, Ouditeur, 1977, Middelburg K P
Havenga J L D, Posbus 8701 Johannesburg, Helpmekaarstudie-fonds 1962
Havinga A, 46, P/A Daton's Kempton Park, Administratiewe Bestuurder, 1975, Vereeniging
Havinga C, 42, Elandsfontein Brits, Onderwyser, 1964, Swartruggens
Havinga H, 38, Volkskas Riviersonderend, Bestuurder, 1969, Kaapstad
Haxton J, 47, Viljoenstraat 4 Viljoenskroon/Hoërskool Salomon Senekal, Adj-Hoof, 1971, Pietermaritzburg
Hay D, 32, Sebastianhof Noordeinde Port Elizabeth, Onderwyser, 1973
Hay E, 39, N G Kerk Jeugbearbeiding Kaapland, Predikant, 1974, King Williamstown
Hay L, 35, Delphiniumrylaan 34 Westering Port Elizabeth, Onderwyser, 1977
Hayward S A S (Lid Nr 5710), L V vir Graaff-Reinet — Lid van die U R — Adjunk-Minister van Landbou
Hechter L G, 48, Renosterhoek Hartbeesfontein, Boer, 1973, Klerksdorp
Hechter L P J, 50, S A Lugmag Pretoria, Kommandant, 1964
Heckroodt W H L, 44, Padfieldweg 78 Pinetown/Indiërsake, Vakinspekteur, 1975, King Williamstown
Heese C A D, 37, P/A Dept van B A en Ontwikkeling, Supt Rehabilitasie, 1975, Edenvale
Heese D C, Posbus 222, Kaapstad, 1962
Heer J C, 35, P/A Drs Hefer & Tyers Kaapstad, Tandarts, 1970, Pretoria
Hefer W J, 40, Hoërskool Ben Viljoen Groblersdal, Skoolhoof, 1967, Potgietersrus
Heigers I L, 33, N G Pastorie Kroonstad-Suid, Predikant, 1970, Vrede
Heigers J L, 33, Dinglerstraat 20 Rynfield Benoni, Onderwyser, 1975, Brakpan

Heine W J, 26, Heuweltop Eshowe, Boer, 1969
Helberg A H, 29 P/A Albertonse Hoërskool, Onderwyser, 1964, Vaalwater
Helberg A N, 30, P/A Geref Pastorie Zeerust, Predikant, 1965, Ellisras
Helberg P J, 36, P/A P U vir C H O Potchefstroom, Lektor, 1967, Pretoria
Hendricks N J, 33, Riekertsvraag PK Crecy, Boer, 1970
Hendriks C H, 36, Davidsonstraat Vaalwater/P/A N T K, Takbestuurder, 1976, Edenburg
Hendrikse J A, 34, P/A Hoërskool Reivilo, Onderwyser, 1977, Loeriesfontein
Hendriksz P J, 31, Voortrekkerstraat 1 Edenburg, Tegnikus Poskantoor, 1976, Philippolis
Hendriksz P J, 33, Bethesda Marquard, Boer, 1975
Hendriksz P J R, 50, Bethesda Marquard, Boer, 1964
Henning C R, 30, Yskor Pretoria, Navorser, 1965, Potchefstroom
Henning D S, 39, Kommandoskool Brakpan, Onderhoof, 1965, Huntly
Henning J J, 35, P U vir C H O Potchefstroom, Snr Lektor, 1967, Kroonstad
Henning J W R, 30, P/A Prov Adm Bloemfontein, Padingenieur, 1969, Bethlehem
Henning O A, 31, P/A Hoërskool Rouxville, Skoolhoof, 1970, Zastron
Henning P D (Dr), Senior Amptenaar Watersake 1973
Hennop O J, 34, Gouda Marken, Boer, 1975, Klerksdorp
Henstock J G J, 37, Hoërskool Knysna, Onderwyser, 1963, Joubertina
Hepburn W A A, Lid van die Uitvoerende Raad se Landbou-Komitee in 1973
Herbst A J O, Ondersekretaris van A B in 1971 & Sekretaris van Jeugsake in 1976 & 1977
Herbst Dries (Lid Nr 7633)
Herbst D A S, 29, Die Transvaler Johannesburg, Asst Nuusredakteur, 1967, Potchefstroom
Herbst H J, 46, Verkyk Volksrust, Boer, 1967, Vrede
Herbst J G, 30, Berglaan 557 Pretoria-Noord, Onderwyser, 1975
Herbst W M, 33, Rabestraat Potgietersrus (Fin Bestuurder Slattery), 1974, Pretoria
Herholdt A N J, 34, Universiteit v d Noorde Sovenga, Dosent, 1973, Kaapstad
Herman L T I, 37, P/A N G Pastorie Fichardtpark Bloemfontein, Predikant, 1974, Paarl
Herman M, 33, Tweerivier PK Beestekraal, Boer, 1977
Herman S, 30, Pres Brand Volkskool Bloemfontein, Onderhoof, 1977, Ficksburg
Hermann M N, 38, P/A Nas Suiwel Koöp Heilbron, Afdelingbestuurder, 1975, Pretoria
Heslinga P F, 33, Jamorna PK Tzaneen, Boer, 1974, Pretoria
Hetzel F W M, 49, Vergenoeg Christiana, Boer, 1970, Hertzogville
Heunis A J, 43, Koöp Sitruspakhuis Rustenburg, Bestuurder, 1965, Alexandria
Heunis J C, 37, P/A Heunis & Heunis George (Tans Minister van Ekonomiese Sake), Prokureur & L P R, 1965
Heunis O B, 43, Tarnlaan 27 Goldwater/Laerskool Excelsior P E, Vise-Hoof, 1971, Ceres
Heydenrych H J, 38, Unielaan 12 Stellenbosch, Snr Lektor, 1974, Vaalharts
Heyl A M, 35, Golflaan 8 Randpark Randburg, Tandarts, 1976, Pretoria
Heyl P J (Lid Nr 703), Skoolhoof — Ermelo — Voorgestel vir die UR in 1968
Heymann R A, 38, Lanquedoc Petrus Steyn, Boer, 1967, Oos-Londen
Heyns C F, 35, N G Kerk Harmonie (Virginia), Predikant, 1974, Klawer
Heyns G F, 33, Thealsingel 4 Bloemfontein/Hoërskool Sentraal, Adj-Hoof, 1970, Jagersfontein
Heyns H S, 45, Oakdene Fort Beaufort, Boer, 1967, Langlaagte
Heyns J A, Stellenbosch — Praat oor Christelike Sake by 1969 Bondsraad
Heyns J D, 36, Brugwater PK Thabazimbi, Boer, 1964, Middelburg, Tvl
Heyns J M, Aftonwoldweg 3 Ashton Manor Kempton Park
Heyns J M, 31, P/A Pro Rege Pers Bpk Potchefstroom, Sekretaris, 1965, Bethlehem
Heyns M, 34, Grootpan PK Paul Roux, Boer, 1967
Heyns M, 39, Groenpan Senekal, Boer, 1965
Heyns M G, 27, Brill-Huis Grey Kollege, Onderwyser, 1968, Marquard
Heyns M L, 30, Dept Landbou Tegn Dienste Fraserburg, Voorligtingsbeampte, 1964, Koffiefontein
Heyns M R, 30, De Villiersstraat 11 Bellville, N G Predikant, 1970, Bothaville
Heysteck A S, 28, P/A Geref Kerk Walvisbaai, Geref Predikant, 1973, Potchefstroom
Heystek A M, 32, Sybrand V Niekerkstraat 8 Meyerton, Programmeerder/SAUK, 1972, Vereeniging
Heystek A M, 41 P/A Fabricated Steel Manufacturing Co Germiston, Tekenaar, 1967, Primrose
Heystek A S L, 35, Uniestaal Korp Vereeniging, Inst Werktuigkundige, 1964, Germiston

Heystek G M, 40, Toekoms Harrismith, Boer, 1972, Lichtenburg
Heystek H, 43, P/A Sasol Sasolburg, Bestuursrekenmeester, 1968, Pretoria
Heystek J F, 36, P/A B B K Pietersburg, Asst Bestuurder Sisal Fabriek, 1977, Pretoria
Heystek M C, 37, Lawsonlaan 117 Waverley/Hoërskool Pres C R Swart Pretoria, Onderwyser, 1970, Waterberg
Heystek N P, 34, P/A Geref Kerk Bellville-Oos, Predikant, 1974, Worcester
Hickman J A P, 38, Bosmanstraat Paarl/Boland Bank Bpk, Fin Bestuurder, 1972, Philipstown
Hiemstra R C, (Lid Nr 4152), Lid van die U R 1964/1965, Adj-Kommisaris-Genl, Pretoria
Higgo G, 38, N G Pastorie Worcester, Predikant, 1966, Kroonstad
Hillebrand J J, 43, Fairview Brandfort, Boer, 1974
Hillebrand S J, 31, "Vrede" Bultfontein, Boer, 1965
Hindley W R, 44, P/A Klerksdorpse Hoërskool, Adj-Hoof, 1973, Potgietersrus
Hoek Beyers, Sekretaris van Sport
Hoffman A M, 46, Scheepersstraat 21 Bethal, Prokureur, 1967, Stellenbosch
Hoffman D W, 29, Welgeleë Warmbad, Boer, 1972, Inyazura Rhodesië
Hoffman S S B, 47, Laerskool Vaalwater, Hoof, 1964, Krugersdorp
Hoffmann J E, 37, P/A Hoërskool Reivilo, Vise-Hoof, 1975, Dendron
Hofmeyer B J, 31, Janette Vryburg, Boer, 1977, Klerksdorp
Hofmeyer H S, 32, Navorsingsinst Vee-en Suiwelkunde Pretoria, Snr Vakkundige, 1969
Hofmeyr J H (Lid Nr 6068) Chirurg — Oos-Londen-Voorgestel vir die U R in 1968
Hofmeyr J H, 30, Tritoniastraat Riversdal, Prokureur, 1975
Hofmeyr J H, 32, Hoërskool Genl Hertzog Witbank, Onderwyser, Germiston, 1967
Hofmeyr S, "Verhoudinge met Engelse" 1973
Hollenbach H H, 34, "Poortjie" PK Villiers, Onderwyser, 1970, Randburg
Hollenbach J H, 37, Van Zylstraat Schweizer-Reneke, Tandarts, 1967, Port Natal
Holmberg D J R, 30, Greystraat Dordrecht, Geneesheer, 1965, Virginia
Holtshauzen L J, 36, Heroldsbaai George/S A Weermag, Majoor, 1976, Bloemfontein
Homan C J, 47, Kenmare Krugersdorp, Onderwyser, 1968, Rustenburg
Honiball J R, 41, Dorisstraat 1 Homestead/S A S & H (Germiston), Persoonlike Sekr Hoofbestuurder, 1972, Randfontein
Hoogenboezem J, 37, Vlieland PK Vivo, Boer, 1974, Pietermaritzburg
Hoogenboezem J, 45, Tamboekiesfontein Heidelberg, Boer, 1976, Johannesburg
Hoogendyk C F, 28, Weslaan 312 Ferndale, Rekenmeester, 1974, Linden
Hoogendyk P K
Hoogenhout D M, Lid van die U R se Ekonomiese Komitee 1973
Hoon J C, 40, Volkskas Uniondale, Bestuurder, 1969, Bethlehem
Hoon J H, 30, P/A N P Kantoor Kimberley, Organiseerder, 1967, Mosselbaai
Horak R B, 42, Irving Steynstraat 25 Casseldale Springs, Vert/Total, 1977, Steynsburg
Horn G F, 41, N G Pastorie Greenhills Randfontein, Predikant, 1969, Marico
Horn G P J, 39, Northstraat 94 Wynberg Johannesburg, Vervoerkontrakteur, 1975
Horn V P B (Lid Nr 7770), Florida 1963
Horn W J G, 34, P/A Nasionale Bouvereniging Port Elizabeth, Onderbestuurder, 1968
Hough A H L, 39, Landdroskantoor Groblershoop, Landdros, 1976, Trompsburg
Hough A J, 33, Perseel 27 D 7 Bull-Hill Warrenton, Boer, 1977
Hough A R, 40, P/A Total Mpy Johannesburg, Bemarkingsbestuurder, 1965, Kaapstad
Hough C C, 31, Perseel 27E9 Bull-Hill Warrenton, Boer, 1973, Hartsvallei
Hough D J, 26, Hough & Lategan Pietersburg, Prokureur, 1964, Johannesburg
Hough J A, 43, P/A N G Kerk Randburg, Predikant, 1967, Danielskuil
Hough M J, 41, Hoër Tegn Skool Pietersburg, Onderwyser, 1964, Christiana
Hough O S, 31, P/A Laerskool Barberton, Skoolhoof, 1973, Seymour
Hough W J, 47, Droogefontein Teviot Kaap, Boer, 1965
Howard A J, 42, P/A Hoërskool Senekal, Onderwyser, 1967
Howard J J N, 51, Dept Binnelandse Sake Pretoria, Adj-Sekretaris, 1965, Rouxville
Hudson J W, 39, P/A Kapteineseunsskool Nongoma, Skoolhoof, 1969, Middelburg Tvl
Hugo C G, 34, P/A Volkskas Bloemfontein, Rekenmeester, 1973, Piketberg
Hugo E A K, 37, Universiteit Pretoria, Snr Lektor, 1974, George
Hugo F, 39, P/A Bruinette Kruger Stoffberg & Hugo Pretoria, Ingenieur, 1975, Brakpan
Hugo F D, 34, Keurboschweg De Doorns, Geneesheer, 1966, Graaff-Reinet
Hugo G, 39, Julius Jeppestraat 107 Waterkloof Pretoria, Prokureur, 1971, Stellenbosch

Hugo G J, 32, P/A N G Moedergemeente Vanderbijlpark, Predikant, 1976, Bloemfontein
Hugo G J, 35, P/A Volkskas Messina, Bestuurder, 1966, Pietermaritzburg
Hugo G R, 43, Aan De Doorns, Boer, 1964
Hugo J G, 30, Bronkhorststraat Phalaborwa/Foskor, Waarn Stelselontleder, 1971, Benoni
Hugo J H, 41, Goldberglaan 43 Bethlehem, Onderwyser, 1977, Pretoria
Hugo J J, 45, "Oskoppie" Petrusburg, Boer, 1970
Hugo J M, 30, Kerkstraat Frankfort, Geneesheer, 1967, Koppies
Hugo J P, 47, Tafelkop Davel, Boer, 1964, Paarl
Hugo J P J, 41, Volkskas Bpk Zeerust, Bestuurder, 1964, Lindley
Hugo J S, 42, Land & Landboubank van S A Pretoria, Asst-Hoof (Korttermynvoorskotte), 1975, Kroonstad
Hugo M, 37, Bonnievale Victoria-Wes, Boer, 1970
Hugo N, 37, P/A Raad op Atoomkrag, Hoof Esksp Beampte Lewenswetenskap, 1974, Pretoria
Hugo P F, 42, Kleinstraat Touwsrivier, Boer, 1970
Hugo P H J, 33, Carvalhostr 46 Meyerton/Maize Products, Wyksbestuurder, 1970, Germiston
Hugo P J P, 35, P/A N G Pastorie Swellendam, Predikant, 1967, Port Elizabeth
Hugo R C, 40, Rhenosterhoek Groot Marico, Boer, 1977
Huisamen A H J, 28, P/A Dept Justisie Kempton Park, Staatsaanklaer, 1964, Welkom
Huisamen S W L, 45, P/A S A Polisie Johannesburg, Luitenant, 1965, Calvinia
Hulme S A (Lid Nr 5382), Landbou Tegniese Dienste Pietermaritzburg Voorgestel vir die U R in 1968, Professor & Hoof Streeksbeampte
Human B, 41, P/A Human Motors Bloemfontein, Sakeman, 1965, Longlands
Human C D C, Lid van die U R se Landbou-Komitee in 1973
Human C J F, Lid van die U R se Ekonomiese Komitee in 1973
Human G J J, 39, Rozenstraat Utrecht, Skoolhoof, 1975, Rustenburg
Human H J, 29, P/A SAUK Johannesburg, Org Afr TV Programme, 1973, Pretoria
Human H J, 30, P/A Union Carriage & Wagon Co Nigel, Hoofklerk, 1968, Pretoria
Human H J, 31, P/A Hoërskool Parys, Onderwyser, 1968
Human J, 28, Blesbokstraat 14 Bethal, Prokureur, 1975, Pretoria
Human J H, 41, S A Lugdiens Johannesburg, Snr Klerk, 1965, Germiston
Human J J, 39, N G Pastorie Windhoek-Oos, Predikant, 1967, Lyttelton
Human J J, 43, Skoolplaas Warrenton, Boer, 1965
Human J J, 34, "Klipgat" Victoria-Wes, Boer, 1974
Human J N, 39, "Vrede" PK Lindeshof, Boer, 1964, Caledon
Human J U, 34, P/A Transvaalse Landbou-Unie Pretoria, Asst Sekretaris, 1974, Coligny
Human J W D, 44, Vista Paterson K P, Boer, 1970
Human M P, 32, Soutpanslaan 78 Quellerina, Aandelemakelaar, 1974, Florida
Human O, 45, P/A Die Vaderland se Kinderstrand Glenmore, Bestuurder, 1969, Johannesburg
Human P J, 52, P/S Pearsons-Hunt Olifantshoek, Boer, 1970, Beaufort-Wes
Human P J, 28, N G Pastorie Mispa, Predikant, 1965, Verkeerdevlei
Human P J, Warrenton — Praat oor Sestiger boeke by 1967 se Bondsraad
Human S v S B, 36, N G Gemeente Gaskop, Predikant, 1976, Bonaeropark
Human W A, 30, Weltevrede PK Scheepersnek, Boer, 1965, Vryheid
Hurter D, 32, P/A Tsumeb Corporation Tsumeb, Ingenieur, 1967, Bethal
Hurter D A, 30, Goedgedacht PK Syferbult, Boer, 1968, Pretoria
Hurter J A (Lid Nr 3298), Besturende Direkteur Volkskas Pretoria — Voorgestel vir die U R in 1968
Hurter J H, 31, Hoërskool Otto du Plessis Port Elizabeth, Onderwyser, 1977, Ermelo
Hurter J J, 32, P/A Van Zyl Le Roux en Hurter Pretoria, Prokureur, 1974, Klerksdorp
Hurter M J, 48, P/A BVS Pretoria, Ouditeur, 1975
Huysamen A P R, 38, P/A Baardsmotorhawe Hopefield, Rekenmeester, 1965, Worcester
Huysamen F F, 40, Du Toitstraat 70 De Aar, Skoolraadsekretaris, 1970, Vryburg
Huysamen J J, 31, Damplaas Louis Trichardt, Handsetter Kirstendrukpers, 1972, Kakamas Johannesburg
Huysamen P J, 46, S A S & H Behuisingsraad, Florida, Sekretaris, 1964, Kakamas
Huyser J, Leërgimnasium Heidelberg Tvl, Kommandant, 1968

Huyser P B, 31, S A Lugmag Pretoria, Majoor, 1969, Potchefstroom
Huyzer J F, 30, S A Weermag Pretoria, Majoor, 1966, Potchefstroom

I

Immelman C O, 34, Gelnwoodweg Lynnwood Glen/Menlopark Hoër, Vise-Hoof, 1976, Pretoria
Immelman G J, 38, Larkspurlaan Virgina, Prokureur, 1968, Hennenman
Ipland J, 36, Moedverloren PK Leslie, Boer, 1964, Paarl

J

Jackson J T, 38, Assegaaiboschfontein Riversdal, Boer, 1975
Jacobs A A, 35, Hoër Volkskool Potchefstroom, Onderwyser, 1969
Jacobs A S, 40 Dept van Beplanning Pretoria, Adj-Ekonomiese Adv, 1968, Graskop
Jacobs A S, 41, S A S Polisie/Jenningsweg 6 Amalinda, Oos-Londen, Kaptein, 1970, Ventersdorp
Jacobs B, 36, Hamawasha Tzaneen, Boer, 1965
Jacobs C D, 31, Saambou Rissikstraat Johannesburg, Bestuurder, 1967, Bloemfontein
Jacobs C R, 31, N G Gemeente Springs-Oos, Predikant, 1973, Karoi
Jacobs D H, 38, Landsboroughstraat 21 Robertsham, Voorman, 1975, Johannesburg
Jacobs D J, 37, Universiteit van Fort Hare Alice, Asst Reg Finans, 1977, Witrivier
Jacobs D J J, 34 Chipsteadlaan 69 Marlborough Park Durban, Onderwyser, 1968, Bloemhof
Jacobs D J L, 35, Laerskool Glaudina Schweizer-Reneke, Hoof, 1963, Benoni
Jacobs D J N, 42, Berylstraat 42, Carletonville, Posmeester, 1973, Pretoria
Jacobs D J S, 33, Elandsdrift Marble Hall, Boer, 1973, Rustenburg
Jacobs D M, 38, N G Pastorie Augrabies, Predikant, 1969, Bellville
Jacobs D P, 41, Boerenstraat 242 Vryheid, Onderwyser, 1973
Jacobs D S, 31 Caledonweg 82 Nigel, Onderwyser, 1970, Heidelberg Tvl
Jacobs D S, 39, Volkskas Greytown, Bestuurder, 1973, Kaapstad
Jacobs E S, 30, Vogelstruisfontein Kroonstad, Onderwyser, 1967, Springfontein
Jacobs E S, 39, Reivilo Suiwel Koöp Reivilo, Sekretaris, 1973
Jacobs F J, 25, Koshuis Jagersfontein, Onderwyser, 1968, Bloemfontein
Jacobs H W J, 46, Departement Binnelandse Inkomste Pretoria, Eerste Administratiewe Beampte, 1967
Jacobs I J C, 48, Middeldeel Edenburg, Boer, 1967
Jacobs J C, 37, Yskor Pretoria, Hoof Prysevaluering, 1976
Jacobs J H, 35, Universiteit van Port Elizabeth, Adjunk-Registrateur, 1974 Pretoria
Jacobs J H, 39, Koedoesnek Postmasburg, Boer, 1969
Jacobs J H H, 33, N H Pastorie Bloemhof, Predikant, 1975, Grootfontein SWA
Jacobs J J, 41, Hoër Tegniese Skool Witbank, Onderwyser, 1970, Bronkhorstspruit
Jacobs J J de V, 24, Laerskool Grabouw, Onderwyser, 1965, Riebeeck-Wes
Jacobs J L, 42, Kaalspruit Stella, Boer, 1976, Amalia
Jacobs J P, 41, Hoewe 211 Rodenbeck Bloemfontein, Skoolhoof, 1970, Marquard
Jacobs L M, 31, F A K Johannesburg, Rekenmeester, 1973, Roodepoort
Jacobs M J, 43, Hutchinsonstraat 9 Bloemhof, Sakeman, 1968, Germiston
Jacobs P P, 35, Universiteit Port Elizabeth, Senior Lektor, 1973, Pretoria
Jacobs P T, 37, N H Pastorie Welkom, Predikant, 1965, Pretoria
Jacobs S G, 39, N G Pastorie Monte Vista Kaap, Predikant, 1974, Piketberg
Jacobs W D, 36, Westelike Koöp Kroonstad, Rekenmeester, 1968, Vanderbijlpark
Jacobs W J S, 34, Goudstad Onderwyskollege Johannesburg, Dosent, 1973, Florida
Jacobsen E S, 33, Pretoria Tegniese Kollege, Lektor, 1972 Witbank
Jacobsz F P (Lid Nr 7055), Uniestaal Korporasie Vereeniging, Hoofbestuurder (Voorgestel vir die U R in 1968)
Jacobsz J F, 34, Nasionale Party Phalaborwa, Organiseerder, 1966, Rustenburg
Jacobsz L A, 30, Cardiffweg 60 Clubview-Oos Verwoerdburg, Onderwyser, 1971, Leslie
James G L, 30, Landdroskantoor Odendaalsrus, Assistent Landdros, 1968, Stanger
Jamneck J J, 38, Federated Employers Johannesburg, Eisebestuurder, 1970
Jamneck L, 49, Pasteurboulevard Nr 5 Vanderbijlpark, Pleisteraar, 1963, Dewetsdorp
Janeke C M, 39, Nelliestraat 109 Krugersdorp, Onderwyser, 1966, Vereeniging

Jansen A, 32, Koekepanstraat Jan Kempdorp, Onderwyser, 1972, Philipstown
Jansen B C (Dr), Lid van die U R se Landboukomitee in 1973
Jansen B C (Dr), (Lid Nr 6979) Onderstepoort Pretoria, Hoof (Voorgestel vir die U R in 1968 & Lid van die U R se Landbou Komitee in 1973)
Jansen E A, 35, Jannie Rouxtehuis Barkly-Wes, Huisvader, 1975, Dewetsdorp
Jansen F S J, 32, De Klerkstraat 58 Potgietersrus, Onderwyser, 1977, Amsterdam Tvl
Jansen J A, 44, Uitkoms Koöp Hobhouse, Hoofbestuurder, 1975, Reitz
Jansen J C, 41, S A Polisie Durban, Kapelaan, 1966, Utrecht
Jansen J H, 40, Christiaan Beyersstraat 46 Westonaria, Magasynmeester (Kloof Goudmyn) 1977, Alldays
Jansen J P 44, Universiteit Stellenbosch, Professor, 1968, Queenstown
Jansen W B, 37, "Robyn" Pongola, Boer & Oud-Predikant, 1965, Paul Pietersburg
Jeppe W J O, 33, Libertaslaan 3 Karindal/Universiteit Stellenbosch, Senior Lektor, 1970, Worcester
Jerling J C, 34, Olga Kirschstraat 11 Ridgewag Johannesburg, Admin Bestuurder (Saambounasionaal) 1971, Upington
Johnston C J, 34, Welgelegen Haarlem, Boer, 1974
Jonck D, 39, Volkskas Pretoria, Boedelklerk, 1965, George
Jonck L M, 43, Duvenage Keyser & Jonck Oudtshoorn, Prokureur, 1975, Bloemfontein
Jones M du P, 38, Oberjones P/S C873 Oor Vryburg, Boer/Bou-Aannemer, 1976, Lichtenburg
Jonker D B, 34, Huis Loots Uniondale, Onderwyser, 1977, Strydenburg
Jonker G C, 30, S A Polisie Malvern Johannesburg, Sersant, 1965, Koster
Jonker G C (Lid Nr 9050), Churchillaan 18 Primrose Germiston, Stoorklerk
Jonker G J J, 33, N G Kerk Fynnland Durban, Predikant, 1975, Empangeni
Jonker J P L, 42, Die Pastorie Bothaville-Noord, N G Predikant, 1971, Stellenbosch
Jonker L N, 34, Weltevrede Bonnievale, Boer, 1974
Jonker P, 44, Marine Products Laaiplek (Vredenburg), Fabrieksbest/Ingenieur, 1967, Lambertsbaai
Jooste A, 39, Canon Rodgersweg Estcourt, Prokureur, 1976, Christiana
Jooste B B, 47, Bairdstraat 6-8 Uitenhage, Geneesheer, 1965, Colesberg
Jooste C J (Lid Nr 7712), Hartbeesfontein, Boer, 1962
Jooste C J, 43, Departement V Beplanning Pretoria, Demograaf, 1966, Durban
Jooste C J, 40, Bergwater Prins Albert, Boer, 1968, Bellville
Jooste C J (dr), Direkteur van SABRA, 1967
Jooste E, 32, Die Strand Hoërskool Strand, Onderwyser, 1976, Agter-Paarl
Jooste F E, 39, De Beerstraat 782 Wonderboom-Suid, Onderwyser, 1968
Jooste F J, 36, Munisipaliteit Karibib, Stadsklerk, 1975, Windhoek
Jooste J A, 34, Geref Pastorie Burgersdorp, Predikant, 1964, Windhoek
Jooste J A, 29, Sarel Cillierslaan Warden, Geneesheer, 1964, Vereeniging
Jooste J A, 27, Santos Woonstel 3 Wembleyrylaan Oos-Londen, Adj-Offisier (Veiligheidspolisie), 1973, S W A
Jooste J A, 38, Acquillalaan 89 Waterkloofrif Nr 2 Pretoria Senior Rekenmeester Ko-operasie pers van S A Silverton, 1977, Burgerspark
Jooste J A, 41, Possak 947 Upington, Boer/Sakeman, 1969
Jooste J G, 37, P/A W G A Edenburg OVS, Verteenwoordiger, 1968, Brandfort
Jooste J H (Lid Nr 5221), Direkteur C K A Pretoria — Voorgestel vir die U R 1968
Jooste J J, 45, P/A Hoërskool Ladysmith, Onderhoof, 1974, Balfour
Jooste J P, 39, Lorindalaan 155 Murrayfield Pretoria, Adj-Dir Biometrie LTD, 1976
Jooste J S, 31, Dinastraat 26 Meiringspark, Onderwyser, 1977, Lichtenburg
Jooste Koos L P R, Op N P Komitee Wolmaransstad in 1966
Jooste L K, 42, P/A Croesus Gold Mining Co Langlaagte, Bestuurder, 1965, Primrose
Jooste M V, 54, P/A Afrikaanse Pers (1962) Bpk, Johannesburg, Besturende Direkteur, 1963, Bloemfontein
Jooste P, Hoër Landbouskool Tweespruit, 1971
Jooste P L, 28, Mondeor Boulevard 12 Johannesburg, Navorser (Kamer v Mynwese), 1977, Stellenbosch
Jooste P P, 32, N H Kerk Standerton, Predikant, 1975, Meyerton
Jooste P W, 43, Hoërskool Nigel, Onderwyser, 1964, Brits
Jooste P W, 45, Onderwyskollege Potchefstroom, Senior Dosent, 1967, Rustenburg

Jooste S J J, 40, Swartfontein Vierfontein, Boer, 1971, Viljoenskroon
Jooste W A, 45, Herefordstraat Groblersdal, Predikant, 1976, Perdekop
Jooste W J, 39, P U vir CHO Potchefstroom, Plantsiektekundige, 1973
Jordaan A (Dr), 38, W N N R Pretoria, Skeikundige, 1975
Jordaan A J J, 40, Coronationmyn Vryheid, Hoofmagasynmeester, 1965, Middelburg
Jordaan A L, 32, Dan Louvre Strandfonteinweg Wetton Kaap, Boer/L P R, 1977
Jordaan C F P, 38, Roodepoort 18 Pietersburg, Boekhouer/Stoetboer, 1976
Jordaan C G, 26, Childrensweg 70 Bergvliet, Onderwyser, 1968, Worcester
Jordaan C L, 30, N G Gemeente Potchefstroom-Suid, Predikant, 1973, Pretoria
Jordaan D A H, 37, Stilfontein Goudmyn, Hoof-Ondersoekbeampte, 1974, Bloemfontein
Jordaan D H, 28, Reitzstraat Warmbad, Sakeman, 1969
Jordaan F, 35, Departement Landbou-Tegniese-Dienste Adelaide, Voorligtingsbeampte, 1972, Queenstown
Jordaan F R, 37, Posbus 46 Klerksdorp, Internis, 1965, Bothaville
Jordaan G B, 39, Hoër Tegniese Skool Springs, Onderwyser, 1967, Rustenburg
Jordaan G J (Dr), (Lid Nr 2631), Nasionale Onderwys Adviesraad Pretoria, Voorsitter, 1973
Jordaan H C W, 27, Panorama-Apteek Sabie, Apteker, 1966, Walvisbaai
Jordaan J B, 33, Idastraat 18 Oberholzer, Tandarts, 1965, Krugersdorp
Jordaan J C, 31, Hoërskoolkoshuis Sannieshof, Onderwyser, 1973, Germiston
Jordaan J D, 43, P A T Nylstroom, Assistent Padinspekteur, 1974, Potgietersrus
Jordaan J H L, 44, S A Polisie/Glanvillelaan 13 Crosby Johannesburg, Kaptein Veiligheidstak), 1972
Jordaan J J, 52, TWB Motors Warmbad Tvl, Direkteur v Maatskappye, 1967, Springs
Jordaan J L, 33, Keyterstraat 34, Oudtshoorn, Offisier (S A Weermag), 1977, Johannesburg
Jordaan P, 38, Kroonstad West Boere Koöp Welkom, Bestuurder, 1966, Ventersburg
Jordaan P, 33, N G Pastorie George, Predikant, 1973, Pretoria
Jordaan P C, 33, Raad van Kuratore van Minerale Baddens, Rekenmeester, 1969, Hartenbos
Jordaan R P (Lid Nr 7760), Alice, 1963
Jordaan S F, 30, Van Heerdenstraat Kibler Park, Amptenaar (Buro S V), 1973, Rosettenville
Jordaan S P, 34, De Beerstraat 441 Wonderboom-Suid Pretoria, Onderwyser (Hoërskool Wonderboom), 1971
Jordaan S T, 36, Sanlam Port Elizabeth, Taksekretaris, 1964, Cradock
Jordaan W G, 38, S A S & H Kinross, Hoofklerk, 1975, Maclear
Jordaan W G, 45, Hoërskool Edenvale, Adjunk-Hoof, 1975, Johannesburg
Jordaan W F, 31, Voortrekkerstraat Prieska, N G Predikant, 1974, Williston
Jordaan W M, 33, Trengrovelaan 9 Uniepark Stellenbosch, Rekenmeester (Volkskas), 1971, Villiersdorp
Jordt H C, 38, Rustenburg Platinamyn, Instrukteur, 1975, Marikana
Jorison P, 36, Rietfontein PK Kameeldrif, Skoolsielkundige, 1972, Pretoria
Joubert A, 40, Austinstraat 26 Klerksdorp, Oogarts, 1965, Pretoria
Joubert A B, 44, P/A Nasionale Paaie Garies, Snr Klerk, 1968, Kamieskroon
Joubert A J, 32, P/A Santam Springs, Hoofinspekteur, 1969, Bethal
Joubert A J M, 30, P/A S A Weermag Heidelberg, Majoor, 1974, Potchefstroom
Joubert B J le R, Haweweg Westcliff Hermanus, 1963
Joubert C J, Brookstraat 30 Brooklyn Pretoria/Komitee van Ondersoek na Kultuurverspreiding, Sekretaris, 1971
Joubert D J, 47, Theronstraat De Bruinpark/Volkskas, Bestuurder, 1971, Reitz
Joubert E (Dr), 36, Kerkstraat 40 Windhoek, Navorser/Natuurbewaring, 1975, Pretoria
Joubert F J, 29, Cedarweg 20 Thornton/Poskantoorklerk, 1976, Maitland
Joubert F J, 30, Draaihoogte PK Suider-Paarl, Boer, 1967
Joubert F J, 50, Arixomaweg 6 Thornton, Sanlamverteenwoordiger, 1968, Maitland
Joubert F J, 41, P/A Natalse Parkeraad St Lucia, Navorsingsbeampte, 1973, Tanzanië
Joubert F P, 43, PK Lagersdrif, Skoolhoof, 1965, Heidelberg
Joubert G J, 30, Pastorie Kenhardt, N G Predikant, 1977, Paarl
Joubert G J, 27, 19eLaan 923 Wonderboom-Suid Pretoria/Hoërskool, Onderwyser, 1970
Joubert G J, Lid van die U R se Landbou-Komitee in 1973
Joubert G J (Lid Nr 5084), S A Polisie Pretoria, Brigadier
Joubert G J V, 36, Hoogestraat 131 Potgietersrus, N G Predikant, 1971, Amsterdam
Joubert H J S, Boksburg, Praat oor Staatskole by 1969 se Bondsraad

Joubert H J S, 43, Munisipaliteit Boksburg, Stadstesourier, 1965, Ermelo
Joubert I J, 39, Munisipaliteit Brandfort, Stadsklerk, 1964, Bultfontein
Joubert J, 37, P/A Landbou Tegn Dienste Parys, Voorligtingsbeamapte, 1968, Ficksburg
Joubert J, 34, Hoewe Enkeldebos Pretoria, Onderwyser, 1975, Johannesburg
Joubert J A, 29, F R Cronje & Van Loggerenberg Winburg, Prokureur, 1965, Bloemfontein
Joubert J A, 30, Lentelus Barrydale, Boer, 1972
Joubert J A, 31, Swartbergstraat Laingsburg, Geneesheer, 1973, Stellenbosch
Joubert J A, 38, P/A Volkskas Bpk Winburg, Rekenmeester, 1970, Pretoria
Joubert J B, 30, Meisieskoshuis Springbok, Onderwyser, 1975, Upington
Joubert J C, 42, Eldoret Ing Werke, Besturende Direkteur, 1967, Kenia
Joubert J C J, 45, S A S & H Johannesburg, Elekt Tegn Ing, 1965
Joubert J D de B, 40, P/A Geustyn Forsyth & Joubert Pretoria, Ingenieur, 1965, Bloemfontein
Joubert J de V, 37, Pietersburgstraat 107 Pietersburg, Streekverteenwoordiger, 1973, Pretoria
Joubert J H, 38, P/A Triomf Kunsmis (Grootdraai), Verteenwoordiger/Boer, 1976, Pretoria
Joubert J J (Lid Nr 7677), Senekal, Onderwyser, 1962
Joubert J J, 32, The Prairie Marseilles Ladybrand, Boer, 1965
Joubert J J, 44, Potgieterweg 120 Verwoerdburg, Inspekteur van Onderwys 1971, Sasolburg
Joubert J J de V, 30, Tandheelkundige Afd Nevilleweg 14 Voortrekkerhoogte, Onderbevelvoerder, 1970, Pretoria
Joubert J P, 25, Somerset-Oos PK Steynsrus, Boer, 1964
Joubert J P (Jnr), 25, Makawaansbank Steynsrus, Boer, 1969
Joubert J S, 42, P/A S A P Balfour & Joubertstraat Balfour, Adj-Offisier, 1970, Greylingstad
Joubert J W J (Lid Nr 7674), Phalaborwa, Boer, 1962
Joubert L C, 33, P/A Laerskool Delville Germiston, Onderhoof, 1966, Pretoria
Joubert L J, 35, Hoërskool Goudveld Welkom, Onderhoof, 1964, Carolina
Joubert M H, 40, Sanlam Bellville, Asst Sekretaris, 1965
Joubert N J D, 42, Haasfontein PK Wolwefontein, Boer, 1975, Natal
Joubert P J J, 43, Gemsbokplek 1 Sunnyridge Germiston/S A Polisie, Adj-Offisier, 1975, Elsburg
Joubert P J W (Lid Nr 7735), Germiston, 1963
Joubert S J, 34, Edwardslaan 160 Westonaria, Onderwyser, 1976, Leeudoringstad
Joubert S W, 37, P/A K W V Paarl, Sekretaris, 1975, Alberton
Joubert W N, 41, P/A Volkskas Otjiwarongo, Bestuurder, 1967, Pretoria
Joubert Z F, 26, Stilfontein PK Chipinga, Boer, 1966
Jubelius C, 51, Grootfontein Jansenville, Boer, 1967
Jubelius J J, 33, Grootfontein Jansenville, Boer, 1975, Kroonstad
Jurgens F X, 31, Dellstraat 24 Parowvallei, Onderwyser, 1975, SWA
Jurgens M v R, 40, Perseel 161 Benoni Kleinplasies, Boukontrakteur, 1968, Benoni
Jurgensen E, 32, Elim Koshuis Dealesville, Onderwyser, 1973, Ladybrand
Jute M J S, 43, Viljoenstraat 22 Carolina, Volkskasbestuurder, 1970, Pretoria
Jute R A, 33, P/A Laerskool Môrewag Port Elizabeth, Vise-Hoof, 1973, Garies

K

Kahl O G, 39, P U vir C H O Potchefstroom, Snr Lektor, 1970, Pretoria
Kampfer J F, 36, Listerstraat 23 Windhoek, Onderwyser, 1966, Springbok
Kampfer J G D, 44, Rusten Olifantshoek, Boer, 1973, Deben
Kannemeyer J W F G, 46, Otjakatjongu Omaruru, Boer, 1975
Kapp D S, 42, Bothastraat Lady Grey, Boukontrakteur, 1974, Cala
Kapp J J, 31, P/A S A Polisie Durban, Luitenant, 1975, Vanderbijlpark
Kapp P H, 31, Alanrylaan 36 Mangoldpark, Lektor, 1971, Port Elizabeth
Kapp P H (Dr), Wealesingel 15 Northcliff Uitbr 22 Johannesburg, (Skakel by RAU), 1976
Kapp P W, 33, Amaryllisstraat 12 Uitenhage/P/A Gubb & Inggs) Personeelbestuurder, 1977, Port Elizabeth
Kasselman J P H, 39, Vogelstruispan Wesselsbron, Boer, 1973
Kayser F, 28, N G Pastorie Jamestown, Predikant, 1967, Barkly-Oos
Keevy C M, 31, Carringtonweg 28 Kimberley, Geneesheer, 1966, Douglas
Keevy J M (Gen) (Lid Nr 8125) S A Polisie Pretoria, Kommissaris, 1964, Cradock

Keller M, 44, Volkskas Napier, Bestuurder, 1968, Wellington
Kellerman A S, Wellington Praat oor Jeugsake by 1969 Bondsraad
Kellerman G P, 33, P/A Sendingpastorie Noupoort, Sendeling, 1965, Verkeerdevlei
Kellerman J, 39, P/A Gesamentlike Pensioenfonds (Parow), Sekretaris, 1974, Porterville
Kellerman J J, 33, Verbruikers Köop Moorreesburg, Sekretaris, 1965, Kaapstad
Kellerman J S, 31, N G Kerk George, Predikant, 1968, Stellenbosch
Kellermann W H, 39, Shannonpad 12 Kenmare Krugersdorp, Voedsel Tegnoloog, 1974, Stellenbosch
Kemp A, 34, Blouleliesbos PK Pineview, Alg Handelaar, 1969
Kemp J J, 36, S A Polisie Johannesburg, Luitenant, 1965, Pietermaritzburg
Kemp K G, 32, Onderwyskollege Pretoria, Dosent, 1964
Kemp M J, 38, P/A Alan Hudson & Kie Nelspruit, Verkoopsbestuurder, 1974, Witbank
Kemp P J, 34, Oshoek PK Mont Pelaan (Memel), Boer, 1965
Kemp P S, 37, P/A Kemp Motors (Edms) Bpk Kareedouw, Sakeman, 1968
Kemp S G, 39, Soetdorings Molenstraat Potchefstroom/Onderwyskollege, Dosent, 1973, Roodepoort
Kemp S le R, 31, De Hoop Uniondale, Boer, 1975, Springbok
Kempff D, Potchefstroom, Sluit 1965 Bondsraad af met skriflesing & gebed
Kesting P D, 34, Kesting Brand & Vennote Pretoria, 1967
Keulder A J, 46, Christelike Uitgewers Mpy, Willoughbystraat 65 Kenmare, 1970, Pretoria
Keulder H F, 28, P/A Provimi Vervoermaatskappy Durbanville, Verteenwoordiger, 1974, Port Elizabeth
Keulder J, 33, Bezuidenhout Uitrusters Johannesburg, Direkteur, 1967
Keulder P C, 34, P/A U O V S Bloemfontein, Snr Lektor, 1976, Johannesburg
Keuler A G, 38, Volkskas, Hennenman, Bestuurder, 1966, Johannesburg
Keun A J, 26, P/A Hoërskool Louis Trichardt, Onderwyser, 1975, Pretoria
Keyser J H, 49, Landdroskantoor Mafeking, Landdros, 1965, Vredenburg
Keyter H C A, 31, Mooimeisieshoek, Excelsior, Boer, 1967, Clocolan
Keyter J J, 39, Hans Strydomlaan Lyttleton, N G Predikant, 1971, Vryburg
Keyter W J, 33, Jonaskraal Napier, Boer, 1972
Keyzer A Z, 30, N G Pastorie PK Lykso, Predikant, 1975, Pretoria
Kielblock A M, 34, Esperancestraat 42 Parow-Oos, Eienaar Motorhawe, 1973
Kilian A P, 30, N G Pastorie Burgersdorp, Predikant, 1975, Stellenbosch
Kilian A P, 47, Leeufontein coligny, Boer, 1971, Harrismith
Kilian D H, 48, P/A Rembrandt Tabakkoöp Stellenbosch, Personeelbestuurder, 1967 Weenen
Kilian F H, 40, Voorspoed Skool Magogong, Skoolhoof, 1976, Oos-Londen
Kilian G C, 33, Ayliffstraat Dordrecht/Hoërskool, Onderwyser, 1976, Murraysburg
Kilian H J, 40, Gruntergully 11 Meerensee Richardsbaai/Alusaf, Produksievoorman, 1976, Amanzimtoti
Kilian H J, 36, Landdroskantoor Graskop, Landdros, 1967, Bethlehem
Kilian J D, 39, Quothquan Distr Barberton, Boer, 1969
Kilian J J, 32, P/A Hoërskool Bothaville, Onderwyser, 1974, Bloemfontein
Kilian N M, 34, Rietgat Coligny, Boer, 1968
Kilian P J du P, 30, P/A Rembrandt Paarl, Asst Fabriekbestuurder, 1968
Kingsley S F, Vise-Voorsitter van Noord — Tvlse Rugby Unie/Voormalige Stadsklerk van Pretoria
Kirchner M H, 31, P/A Yskor Thabazimbi, Asst Res Ingenieur, 1967, Sishen Kaap
Kirstein F E, 38, Klippoortjie-Steenkoolmyn Ogies, Mynbestuurder, 1964, Johannesburg
Kirsten J S, 42, P/A Laerskool David Brink Rustenburg, Onderhoof, 1969, Brits
Kirsten T M, Middelburg Tvl (Woon Bondsraad van die 1966 by)
Kitching S C, 37, P/A Sasol Sasolburg, Prod Voorman, 1967, Upington
Kitshoff J S, 34, P/A N O K Johannesburg, Asst Sekretaris, 1966, Pretoria
Klaasen J H, 30, Vaal Reefs Orkney, Mynamptenaar, 1969, Bothaville
Klazinga W, 41 P/A Douglas Koöp Douglas, Aankopebestuurder, 1969, Lichtenburg
Kleinhaus, J F, 55, P/A S A Polisie Johannesburg, Brigadier, 1975, Mayfair-Wes
Kleinhaus T, 38, Landdroskantoor Hendrina, Asst Landdros, 1965, Steytlerville
Klem A D, 27, Namakwalaan 10 Alexanderbaai, Onderwyser, 1966, Tulbagh
Kleu S J, 32, Parkside Ladismith K P, Onderwyser, 1977, Willowmore
Kleyn W H, 40, N G Gemeente Olifantshoek, Predikant, 1973, Ermelo

Kleynhans E P J, 47, P/A Volkskool Viljoensdrif, Skoolhoof, 1968, Vereeniging
Kleynhans F A, 38, Afrikaanse Hoërskool Durban-Noord, Onderhoof, 1973, Potchefstroom
Kleynhans H G de K, 33, P/A Sanlam Bloemfontein, Verteenwoordiger, 1974
Kleynhans H J, 33, Burgerrechtstraat 838 Bloemhof, Onderwyser, 1973, Potchefstroom
Kleynhans H J, 43, Altena Winburg, Boer, 1975, Kroonstad
Kleynhans H J, 38, P/A S A Buro v Standaarde Pretoria, Adm Beampte, 1969, Bethal
Kleynhans H J, 31, P/A Koöperasie Ladybrand, Klerk, 1966, Excelsior
Kleynhans J J, 33, "The Retreat" Excelsior, Boer, 1975, Welkom
Kleynhans J J, 33, Steynstraat 118 Pietersburg, Onderwyser, 1974, Bethal
Kleynhans J J A, 40, Joubertstraat Ladybrand, Prokureur, 1973, Rouxville
Kleynhans J W, 33, Kaapweg 430 Port Elizabeth, 1977
Kleynhans J W, L P R Algoa
Kleynhans N J, 35, Standard Telephones Boksburg, Personeelbestuurder, 1973, Johannesburg
Kleynhans P H, 44, P/A S A S & H Port Elizabeth, Klerk, 1977
Klinck B, 33, Lenastraat 12 Naudeville, Onderwyser, 1973, Johannesburg
Klopper A H, 30, P/A Geref Kerk Volksrust, Predikant, 1973, Potchefstroom
Klopper C C E, 49, Yskor Vanderbijlpark, Snr Ing Asst, 1967, Pretoria
Klopper D C, 40, P/A Hoër Tegn Skool Brakpan, Skoolhoof, 1974, Potchefstroom/Pretoria
Klopper I S, Praat oor Infiltrasie in Internasionale Organisasies by Bondsraad van 1966
Klopper J F, 35, Spreeukloof Kookhuis, Boer, 1971
Klopper J H, 41, Vlakplaas Utrecht, Boer, 1964
Klopper M J, 36, P/A Vaaldriehoekse Tegn Kollege Vanderbijlpark, Snr Lektor, 1969, Kroonstad
Kloppers B, 28, Provinsiale Koshuis Hendrina, Onderwyser, 1967, Roodepoort
Kloppers G J, 40, P/A Dept Pos & Tel Pretoria, Adm Beampte, 1968
Kloppers G R, 36, Erasmusstraat Ladybrand, Amptenaar B V S, 1975, Pretoria
Kloppers H J, 33, Scottstraat 5 Messina, Rekenmeester/Ouditeur, 1971, Louis Trichardt
Kloppers J J, 41, Bertramstraat 10 Rynfield Benoni, Onderhoof, 1964, Rustenburg
Kloppers J J K, 32, Kmdt Senekalstraat 76 Dan Pienaar Bloemfontein, Professor/UOVS, 1970, Randfontein
Kloppers L B, 31, Weavindlaan 340 Eldoraigne/Yskor Pretoria, Snr Amptenaar, 1970, Pretoria-Wes
Kloppers M H O, 33, N G Pastorie Belfast, Predikant, 1966, Alkmaar
Kloppers P A, 34, Jan S de Villiers & Seun Kaapstad, Prokureur, 1970, Vredefort
Kniep L L, 39, Rothstraat 25 Ventersdorp, Prokureur, 1967, Bloemfontein
Knobel F M, 39, 6eStraat 61 Parkhurst, Johannesburg, Sakeman, 1973, Pretoria
Knobel H A, 36, Versien Bethlehem, Boer, 1974
Knoesen C, 31, Randse Rafinadery 20 Germiston, Asseseues, 1967
Knoetze A, 40, Poskantoor Oos-Londen, Superintendent, 1970, Bellville
Knoetze C, 30, Jomano-Hof Adcockvale Port Elizabeth, Onderwyser, 1964, Jansenville
Knoetze C H, Vaaldriehoekse Bantoesake Administrasieraad, Hoofdirekteur
Knoetze D, 34, Arthurstraat 58, Sydenham Port Elizabeth, Onderhoof, 1967, Oudtshoorn
Knoetze F W, 36, Roy Campbellsingel 49 Parow-Noord, Oordragsekretaris-Bonuskor, 1971, Porterville Kaap
Koch A C F, 45, Van Der Stelstraat 26 Bellville, Onderwyser, 1967, Observatory
Koch A C F, 42, N G Pastorie Mount Pleasant, Predikant, 1974, Stellenbosch
Koch C D, 40 P/A Hoër Jogenskool Paarl, Onderwyser, 1969, Calvinia
Koch G G V, 36, P/A K W B Harrismith, Streeksbestuurder, 1967, Moorreesburg
Koch J, 36, Kenilworth Memel, Boer, 1969
Koch P P, 40, P/A Laerskool Bergland Nelspruit (Pearl of the Mountain Nelspruit), Vise-Hoof, 1977, Windhoek
Kock A H, 28, P/A Onderwyskollege Durban, Lektor, 1969
Kock H L, 39 P/A Tegniese Kollege Stellenbosch, Snr Dosent, 1975, Paarl
Koegelenberg J H, 30, Voortrekkerstraat 4 Touwsrivier/S A Polisie, Adj-Offisier, 1975, Swellendam
Koekemoer D J, 32, Saturnstraat 26 Fisher's Hill, Onderwyser, 1969, Louis Trichardt
Koekemoer F P, 27, Johannes Calvyn-Koshuis Excelsior, Onderwyser, 1974, Hopetown
Koekemoer G P, 38, Langseekoegat Nigel, Boer, 1974

Koekemoer H J, 36, Meisieskoshuis Schweizer-Reneke, Onderwyser, 1973, Zeerust
Koekemoer J A, 35, P/A Hoërskool Vryburg, Onderwyser, 1975, Kenhardt
Koekemoer J C, 42, P/A N G Pastorie Marchand, Predikant, 1974, Robertson
Koekemoer J H, 32, N H Pastorie Kempton Park, Predikant, 1967, Bethal
Koekemoer J J, 41, "Grootpan" Lichtenburg, Boer, 1968, Nigel
Koekemoer J M, 32, V D Merwelaan 120 Meyerspark Pretoria/Dept Bantoe Admin & Ontw, Adm-Beheerbeampte, 1971
Koekemoer J P, 37, Sneeulaan 5 Quellerina Roodepoort/Trust Bank, Inspekteur, 1973, Potchefstroom
Koekemoer P G, 27, Hoërskool Goedehoop Germiston, Onderwyser, 1967
Koekemoer P J, 31, Magnoliaweg 9 Primroseheuwel/S A S & H, Tekenaar, 1975, Randburg
Koen A J (Lid Nr 2162), Direkteur van Onderwys Pretoria
Koen E J, 34, Klipplaatdrift Dist Ventersdorp, Boer, 1970, Rhodesië
Koen F R, 38, Olifantsfonteinskool, Onderhoof, 1967, Wakkerstroom
Koen J A A, 41, Hilldrop Newcastle, Boukontrakteur, 1974
Koen J G, 41, P/A Universiteit van Pretoria, Snr Lektor, 1967
Koen J J, 36, Volkskas Hoopstad, Bestuurder, 1965, Oudtshoorn
Koen M J, 28, Junior Koshuis Somerset-Oos, Onderwyser, 1973, Port Elizabeth
Kok G J, 43, Rondekop Patensie, Boer, 1977
Kok H G, 45, Rondekop Patensie, Boer, 1967
Kok J C, 32 P/A R A U Johannesburg, Snr Lektor, 1973, Port Elizabeth
Kok J H C, 45 P/A Susan Strykdomskool Nylstroom, Hoof, 1964, Louis Trichardt
Kok L A, 31, P/A R M B Alloys Middelburg Tvl, Produksiebestuurder, 1967, Germiston
Kok N J, 29, P/A Kaapse Tegn Kollege, Kaapstad, Lektor, 1973, Stellenbosch
Kolesky J, 34, Roosmarynstraat 6 Welkom, Onderwyser, 1977
Kolver A T, 33, Bokpost Philippolis, Boer, 1976
Kolver W R, 44, P/A M K T V Rustenburg, Hoofsekretaris, 1969
Köning F G W, 33, PK Louwsburg, Skoolhoof Laerskool, 1971, Port Shepstone
Koornhof P G J (Lid Nr 6844), Minister van Nasionale Opvoeding & Sport & Ontspanning/ Voormalige Sekretaris van die A B, Voorgestel vir die U R in 1968
Korf A W, 37, P/A African Explosives & Chemical Industries Ltd Kempton Park, Rekenmeester, 1974, Pretoria
Korf B J, 40, Laubscherstraat 6 Graaff-Reinet, Snr Prov Skatter, 1975, Queenstown
Korff J, 41, Die Residensie Melmoth, Bantoesakekommissaris, 1970, Sibasa
Koster G C, 43, Pilkington Tiles Meyerton, Skeikundige, 1969, Potchefstroom
Koster J H B, 33, Cornelia PK Warden, Boer, 1969, Potchefstroom
Kotze A B, 41, P/A Tegn Kollege Kroonstad, Onderhoof, 1965, Bloemfontein
Kotze A B, 38, P/A Volkskas Petrusville, Bestuurder, 1968, Kimberley
Kotzé A P J, 40, V Falkenhausenstraat 4 Windhoek, Snr Landdros, 1976, Usakos
Kotze C D K, 43, Venter-Montesfieldstraat Reddersburg, Boer, 1967, Burgersdorp
Kotze D J, 45, Koransrug Moorreesburg, Boer, 1974
Kotze D J, 36, Dept van Geskiedenis Unieversiteit Stellenbosch, Professor, 1967, Aurora
Kotzé D M, 46, Blanchelaan 9 Darrenwood Randburg, Elektrotegniese Ingenieur, 1971, Germiston
Kotzé E C B, 28, N H Pastorie Venterspos, Predikant, 1964, Johannesburg
Kotze F C (Lid Nr 7766), Vaalhartz, 1963
Kotze F J, 32, Hoërskool Randfontein, Onderwyser, 1965, Krugersdorp
Kotze G, 41, Walvisbaai, Tandarts, 1970, Pretoria
Kotze G D, 37, Madeliefiestraat 9 Welkom, Onderwyser, 1977, Virginia
Kotze G D, 41, Perseel 6A6 Jan Kempdorp, Boer, 1963, Amalia
Kotzé G D, 39, Sanlam Burgersdorp, Wyksbestuurder, 1967, Pretoria
Kotzé G J, Grootvlei Kamieskroon, Boer, 1965
Kotze G J, 35, Môreson Malmesbury, Onderwyser/Boer, 1964, Swartland
Kotze G J, 35, S A Noodhulpliga Parow, Skakelbeampte, 1965, Ottosdal
Kotzé G J M, 32, Presidentstraat 16 Bellville, Afd Pens Santam, 1973, Tiervlei
Kotzé H A, 47, S A Weermag Pretoria, Kolonel, 1967
Kotze H C, 31, P/A B S B Bredasdorp, Woldeskundige, 1967, Middelburg, K P,
Kotze H W, 40, P/A S A Polisie Worcester, Kaptein, 1969, Somerset-Wes
Kotze J, 43, P/A Santam Springs, Takbestuurder, 1968, Pretoria
Kotzé J A V, 39 Planchette Senekal, Boer, 1970, Zastron

Kotze J E, 43, Sandra Dist Marandellas, Boer, 1970, Umtali
Kotze J H, 37, PK The Heights Van Zylsrus, Boer, 1974, Koegas
Kotzé J H, 31, P/A Transvaler Johannesburg, Nuusredakteur, 1964
Kotze J J, 38, "Cibini" Hluhluwe, Boer, 1966, Kaapstad
Kotze J J, 36, Swartjiesbaai PK Velddrift, Boer, 1970, Hopefield
Kotzé J J N, 33, P/A Agricura Nelspruit, Verkoopsverteenwoordiger, 1973, Moorreesburg
Kotze J M, 41, Bergstraat 28 Paarl/Boland Bank Bpk, Bestuurder, 1976, Upington
Kotzé J M A, 46, P/A Universiteit van Port Elizabeth, Professor, 1974, Pretoria
Kotzé J N E, 38, S A Vloot Fynnland Durban, Offisier, 1964, Pretoria
Kotze J P, 37, Willemsrivier Nieuwoudtville, Boer, 1965
Kotze K, 31, Uitsig Aliwal-Noord, Boer, 1970
Kotze L C v d M, 33, Ernststraat 12 Jansenpark Boksburg, Landdros, 1975, Berville Natal
Kotze L E, 29, P/A Munisipaliteit Barberton, Klerk, 1965, Dordrecht
Kotze M C, 40, P/A Volkskas Aberdeen, Bestuurder, 1968, Delareyville
Kotze N J de R, 53, Malanstraat 13 Worcester, Prokureur, 1972, Bethlehem
Kotze P E, 37, Vosloostraat 6 Windsor Glen/N O K, Hoof Afd Ekonomie, 1977, Stellenbosch
Kotze P J, 30, Dameskoshuis Bethulie, Onderwyser, 1969
Kotzé P P A, 40, N G Pastorie Vincent Oos-Londen, Predikant, 1967, Phalaborwa
Kotzé S F, 33, Bothashof P/S 3900 Salisbury, Onderwyser, 1971, Springs
Kotze T N, 27, Willemsrivier Niewoudtville, Boer, 1965
Kotze W de V (Lid Nr 7701), Bloemfontein, Bestuurder, 1962
Kotzé W J, 35, P/A Dept Bantoe-Onderwys Pretoria, Ondewrwysbeplanner, 1967, Potgietersrus
Kotzé W J, 44, Nooitgedacht Jagersfontein, Boer, 1966
Kotzé W J, 43, Kasteelstraat 7 Windhoek/Stadsraad, Stadsekretaris, 1976, Odendaalsrus
Kotzee A L, 44, Tvlse Onderwys Dept Pretoria, Prof Assistent, 1964, Potchefstroom
Kotzer N J, 35, Gruisfontein PK Crecy, Boer, 1964, Vaalwater
Kramer C A, 35, Fronemanstraat Marquard/Volkskas, Rekenmeester, 1971, Ladybrand
Krantz D R, 30, Chipsteadlaan 77 Fynnland Durban, Onderwyser, 1974, Pretoria
Krause F J L (Fritz), 45, Hancockstraat 4 Klerksdorp, Onderwyser, 1975, Potchefstroom
Krause J C, 33, P/A NAS Suiwelkoöp Heilbron, Fabrieksbestuurder, 1977, Pretoria
Krause J J, 37, Bergstraat Paarl/Saambou Nasionaal, Bestuurder, 1974, Pretoria
Kretschmer E S, 38, Van Oordtstraat 1 Sasolburg/Dept Per/Sasol II, Bestuurder, 1977, Stellenbosch
Kriek A C, 39, Goudstad Onderwyskollege Johannesburg, Dosent, 1966, Villiers
Kriek H, 35, P/A Shiya Onderwyskollege Witsieshoek, Onderwyser, 1975, Pretoria
Kriek H J, 29, Wiggotstraat 4 Oudtshoorn/Santam Bank, Hoofklerk, 1975, George
Kriek J C, 34, Volksskool Heidelberg, Onderwyser, 1970
Kriek J G, 31, Markstraat 13 Odendaalsrus, Sakeman, 1977, Bloemfontein
Kriek J G, 30, Munisipaliteit Rosendal, Stadsklerk, 1965
Kriek L A, 33, N G Pastorie Rensburgdorp, Predikant, 1963, Vanderbijlpark
Kriek P du P, 30, Breëstraat Kuruman, Apteker, 1964, Schweizer-reneke
Kriek W J H, 47, S W A Adm Windhoek, Opmetingsbeampte, 1967, Newecastle
Kriel A L, 34, Rembrandtlaan 8 De La Haye/Sanlam, Uitv Beampte, 1971, Pretoria
Kriel C J, Durbanville — (Praat oor Kleurlinge by Bondsraad van 1971)
Kriel D J, 32, P/A N G Pastorie Arlington, Predikant, 1976, Marquard
Kriel D J, 37, Ottostraat 19 Bailliepark Potchefstroom, Dosent P O K, 1971, Pretoria
Kriel F, 39, P/A Hoërskool Hopetown, Onderwyser, 1974, Hopefield
Kriel F A J, Standerton — Praat oor Liberalistiese Aanslag op Jeug by Bondsraad van 1969
Kriel G G, 30, Waterkantstraat 14 Odendaalsrus, Onderwyser, 1975, Kroonstad
Kriel G H, 35, Griel Modderpoort, Boer, 1963, Ladybrand
Kriel G J, 31, P/A K W V Paarl, Wingerdboukundige, 1975, Stellenbosch
Kriel G J, 44, Sultana-Oord oor Upington, Boer, 1976
Kriel G P, 37, P/A S A S & H Durban, Klerk, 1969, Bloemfontein
Kriel H J, 29, M E Rothmanstraat 47 Parow, Prokureur, 1970, Wellington
Kriel H S, 40, Simpsonsingel 11 Dundee, Bantoesakekommissaris, 1972, Tzaneen
Kriel J D, 29, 25steLaan 803 Rietfontein Pretoria/Universiteit van Pretoria, Lektor, 1977
Kriel J D (Dr), Universiteit van Pretoria
Kriel L B, 35, Martinsonstraat 5 Stellenbosch/Oude Meester, Bemark Bestuurder, 1977, Linden

Kriel P, 34, P/A Munisipaliteit Salisbury, Welsynsbeampte, 1970, Pretoria
Kriel P B de W, 44, P/A S Stone & Seuns (Edms) Bpk Goodwood, Sekretaris, 1976, Milnerton
Kriel W J, 36, Olifantsweg 3 Petersfield Uitbr/Wits Kollege vir G T O), Lektor, 1977 Port Elizabeth
Krige H L, 35, R A U Johannesburg, Professor, 1968, Pietersburg
Krige J D, 37, Koningshoofweg 398 Lynnwood/P/A Geustyn Forsyth & Joubert), Ingenieur, 1976, Heidelberg Tvl
Krige J H R, 45, Hoërskool Voortrekker Bethlehem, Onderwyser, 1966, Reitz
Krige J J, 36, Noordstraat 79 Oudtshoorn Onderwyser, 1975, Aberdeen
Krige W A, 37, P/A S A Lugmag Pretoria, Majoor, 1974, Parow
Krige W A, Kleinmond, Predikant, 1963
Kritzinger C C (Dr), Lid van die U R se Wetenskap Komitee 1973
Kritzinger F M, 31, Lourenstraat 14 Nelspruit, Onderwyser, 1970, Pretoria
Kritzinger J D, 43, Transvaalse Suikerkoöp Malelane, Hoofbestuurder, 1967, Durban
Kritzinger J H, 32, Smaldeel Edenville, Boer, 1973
Kritzinger J J, 27, Volkskool Hennenman, Onderwyser, 1967, Bloemfontein
Kritzinger J J, 31, Suurfontein PK Doornpoort, Onderwyser, 1975, Oos-Rand
Kritzinger J T, 36, Ilfordweg 10 Bulawayo/Rhodesië Railways, Personeelbeampte, 1973
Kritzinger L, 42, Markstraat Vryheid, Onderhoof, 1968, Ladysmsith Ntl
Kritzinger L J, 31, Turnbullstraat 21 Empangeni, Veearts, 1968, Pretoria
Kritzinger N M, 46, PK Louterwater Langkloof, Boer, 1966, Tweerivieren
Kritzinger T I, 28, P/A N G Sending Misgund-Oos, Sendeling, 1969, Joubertina
Kritzinger W G, 32, Oranjestraat 92 Doringkloof Verwoerdburg/S A Weermag, Offisier, 1975, Ladysmith Ntl
Kruegel D F N, (Lid Nr 7686) De Aar, Boer, 1962
Krugel W F, 44, Nuwehoopstraat 30 Maroolana Pretoria, Streeklanddros, 1975, Windhoek
Kruger A D, 35, P/A Avbob Pretoria, Handelsinspekteur, 1975, Roodepoort
Kruger A H, 43, P/A Volkskas Willomore, Bestuurder, 1967, Sannieshof
Kruger A J P, 43, Hoërskool Fakkel Johannesburg, Onderhoof, 1964, Krugersdorp
Kruger A S, 28, Badsfontein Venterstad, Boer, 1964
Kruger A S, 40, Hebron Smithfield, Boer/Veespekulant, 1968
Kruger B, 36, P/A Nel & Stevens Prokureurs/Cathcartstraat 275 GFreytown, Prokureur, 1975, Bloemfontein
Kruger B J, 36, Kinross/Posbus 52 Evander, Sakeman, 1976, Heidelberg
Kruger C D, 33, Schoonbeeksfontein Bethulie, Boer, 1967, Venterstad
Kruger C H J, 36, Tierweg 20 Monumentpark Pretoria, Bestuurder Rekenaars-Afd (Prov Adm), 1975
Kruger C J H, 38, Durbanse Onderwyskollege Vyfde Laan 32 Malvern Natal, Snr Lektor, 1970, Ermelo
Kruger C M (Dr), Voormalige Bestuurder van Ysksor
Kruger C P, 29, Lindcoit Dordrecht, Boer, 1970
Kruger D J, 43, Pospersoneel Ventersdorp, Posmeester, 1975, Bloemfontein
Kruger D J, 43, P/A W L Ochse Krugersdorp, Takbestuurder, 1967, Johannesburg
Kruger D J, 49, P/A Metalurgiese Afd Yskor Pretoria, Hoof, 1969
Kruger D W (Prof), P U vir CHO Potchefstroom, Professor (Geskiedenis), 1963
Kruger E L, 47, Albert Koöperasie Burgersdorp, Bestuurder, 1967, Aliwal-Noord
Kruger G A, 32, Elsie Maria Koshuis Potgietersrus, Snr Assistent, 1971
Kruger G D J (Ds), Markstraat 56 Grahamstad — Skakeling — Militêre Lotelinge Kantoor van die Kapelaan, S A 1-6 Militêre Basis Grahamstad, 1971
Kruger G H J, 42, Winkelstraat 3 Kuruman/GEFCO, Mynsekretaris, 1976, Johannesburg
Kruger G H J, 29, Kalkoenkrans Steynsburg, Boer, 1970
Kruger G L, 39, P/A Geref Kerk Rustenburg, Predikant, 1975, Benoni
Kruger G L, 45, Paarlstraat Standerton, Onderwyser, 1968
Kruger G P, 33, P/A Ou Mutual Benoni, Seksiehoof, 1964, Pretoria
Kruger G S, 40, P/A Veiligheidspolisie Pretoria, Kaptein, 1968
Kruger H B, 37, Van der Hoffweg 22 Potchefstroom, Snr Lektor, 1972, Bellville
Kruger W J, 40, P/A RAU Johannesburg, Adj Registr Fin, 1973, Bloemfontein
Kruger H P, 34, P/A Poskantoor Heilbron, Asst Posmeester, 1965, Vrede

Kruger H S J, 32, P/A De Klerk & Kruger Pretoria, Prokureur, 1975, Hatfield Pretoria
Kruger H W, 39, C G Marais & Kie Boshof, Prokureur, 1964, Bloemfontein
Kruger J A (Lid Nr 1865), S A S & H (Florida)-Voorgestel vir die U R in 1968, Hoofbestuurder
Kruger J C, 41, Munisipaliteit Springs, Asst Markmeester, 1966, Brakpan
Kruger J C, 43, Skietkolk Carnarvon, Boer, 1966
Kruger J D, 39, Sanlamgebou Krugersdorp, Rekenmeester, 1966, Florida
Kruger J F R, 34, Ansonstraat 78 Robertsham, Kaptein, 1973, Volksrust
Kruger J G, 32, Seaviewweg 49 Sea View Durban, Onderwyser, 1974
Kruger J G A, 35, Talanaweg 16 Noordeinde/Magnetiese Observatorium, Hooftegnikus, 1970, Sasolburg
Kruger J L, 39, P/A E J Kruger & Kie Johannesburg, Direkteur, 1967, Pretoria
Kruger J L, 39, P/A Gesondheidskomitee Devon, Sekretaris/Boer, 1967
Kruger J L, 33, P/A Lebowa-Regeringsdiens Fort Klipdam, Sekretaris Staatsdienskommissie, 1974, Pretoria
Kruger J M, 33, Van Bruggenstraat 20 Sasolburg/Sasol, Snr Rekenk Beampte, 1973, Pretoria
Kruger J M N, 36, Kiaatstraat 31 Kempton Park/Laerskool Impala, Adj-Hoof, 1970, Elsburg
Kruger J P J, 36, Lushof Lichtenburg, Boer, 1973, Biesiesvlei
Kruger J S, 38, Bantoebeleggingskorp Durban, Adm Bestuurder, 1973, Mafeking
Kruger J S J, 39, P/A Wolmarans & Kruger Port Elizabeth, Rekenmeester, 1965
Kruger J T (Adv), 44, Koningin Wilhelminalaan 7 Muckleneuk Pretoria, Minister van Justisie Polisie & Gevangenisse
Kruger L J, 33, E J Kruger & Kie Johannesburg, Sakeman, 1964, Mellville Johannesburg
Kruger M, 28, Meiringstraat Edenburg, Geneesheer, 1971, Ontdekkers
Kruger M, 37, P/A Noordkaapse BAR Vryburg, Direkteur, 1975, Lichtenburg
Kruger M A, 38, Geref Pastorie Swartruggens, Predikant, 1968, Aranos
Kruger M J, Posbus 7714 Johannesburg — Ondersekretaris van A B 1971 & Admin Sekretaris van A B, 1977
Kruger M S, 34, Soldierstraat 40 Ladysmsith, Onderwyser, 1976, Heidelberg
Kruger P, 38, Laerskool-Koshuis Lothair, Skoolhoof, 1975, Lydenburg
Kruger P, 40, Sanlam Aliwal-Noord, Wyksbestuurder, 1967, Elliot
Kruger P A, 35, Majuba-Manskoshuis G O K Cottesloe Johannesburg, Dept-Hoof, 1970, Rustenburg
Kruger P E J, 29, P/A S A Polisie Springs, Adj-Offisier, 1974, Nigel
Kruger P E J, 34, P/A Hoër Tegn Skool N Diederichs Krugersdorp, Onderwyser, 1968, Swartruggens
Kruger P J, Bloemfontein-Noord — Praat oor Landbou Sake by Bondsraad 1966 — Lid van U R se Landbou Komitee 1973
Kruger P J, 38, P/A Onderwysburo Dept Onderwys Pretoria, Assistenthoof, 1977, Bergsig
Kruger P J, 36, P/A Wolnavorsingsinstituut Port Elizabeth, Tekstielnavorser, 1969, Bloemfontein
Kruger P J H, 30, Volkskool Sand du Plessis Bloemfontein, Onderwyser, 1965
Kruger P J J, 33, Weshofkoshuis Christiana, Onderwyser, 1972, Kempton Park
Kruger P L, Tweedelaan 8 Thabazimbi, Skakel vir militêre dienspligtiges, 1971
Kruger P P, 38, O'Kulisstraat 30 Vanderbijlpark, Chirurg, 1975, Bloemfontein
Kruger P P, 35, P/A Geref Kerk Baysville Oos-Londen, Predikant, 1976, Reddersburg
Kruger P W, 45, S A Polisie Vereeniging, Majoor, 1964, Johannesburg
Kruger P W B, 32, Borderweg 314 Menlopark, Ingenieur, 1971, Pretoria
Kruger R A, 34, Ellisras Hoërskool, Onderwyser, 1966, Krugersdorp
Kruger S J, 43, Perseel J40 Slagboom, Boer, 1975, Marble Hall
Kruger S J, 34, P/A Sanlam Germiston, Wyksbestuurder, 1974, Kempton Park
Kruger S J P, 47, Vermootenstraat 92 Bethal/O T K, Handelslbestuurder, 1970, Standerton
Kruger T F, 38, Staatsvoorskotte Pretoria, Rekenmeester, 1967, Somerset-Oos
Kruger T G, 31, P/A T G Kruger Eiendomme Potchefstroom, Sakeman, 1977
Kruger T H F, 35, P/A Boland Bank Bpk Strand, Rekenmeester, 1974, Oudtshoorn
Kruger T J, 34, P/A New Graphis Industries Maraisburg, Direkteur, 1976, Potchefstroom
Kruger T J, 28, Keuningstraat 202 Meyerspark Pretoria, Advokaat, 1977, Potchefstroom
Krugfer T L P, 29, Singlehurstweg 46 Casseldale Springs, Onderwyser, 1971, Sundra
Kruger W A, F A K Verteenwoordiger vir Noord en Noordoos — Tvl
Kruger W A J, 47, P/A Kalie De Haas Laerskool, Skoolhoof, 1968, Nylstroom

Kruger W de K, Hoërskool Gimnasium Potchefstroom, 1963
Kruger W P, 44, P/A Yskor Pretoria, Snr Asst, 1968
Krynauw P, 35, Deodarweg 15 Primrose-Oos/Hoërskool Vryburger, Onderwyser, 1970, Alberton
Kühn A W J, 32, Fonteinstraat 13 Lindley, Vise-Hoof (Primêr), 1972, Kroonstad
Kühn C J J, 34, Victoriastraat Uniondale, Onderwyser, 1970, Lobatsi
Kuhn J M G, 32, Queensweg 95 King Williamstown, Hoof B S V, 1977, Pretoria
Kühn P G, 44, Landdroskantoor Harrismith, Landdros, 1967, Durban
Kühn W J, 43, P/A S A Weermag Pretoria, Kommandant, 1976, Pietersburg
Kuperus W L, 43, Knightstraat 4 Petersfield Springs, Geref Predikant, 1976, Siloam
Kuyler H, 38, Pastorie Bowdstraat Knysna, N G Predikant, 1972, Nababeep
Kuschke E R H, 39, P/A Grootte Schuur Hospitaal Kaapstad, Spesialis, 1968, Vredenburg
Kuun O de P, Amptenaar van die A B
Kuun P J C, 36, Eureka Hostel Willston Windhoek/St Augustinian Hoof Bantoe Opleidingskollelge, 1973, Nelspruit
Kuyler J, 27, P/A N G Pastorie Warrenton, Predikant, 1969, Stellenbosch
Kuyper E, 31, Kirkmanstraat PK Vaalwater, Onderwyser, 1971, Ellisras

L

Laas C J, 35, Tegniese Dienskorps Pretoria, Kaptein, 1965, Witbank
Laäs H J, 43, P/A S A S & H Kaapstad, Klerk, 1967
Labuschagne A J J, 43, Philadelphia Sendingstasie PK Dennilton Tvl, Predikant N G, 1970, Pretoria
Labuschagne C E G, 38, P/A Yskor Pretoria, Hoof Opl & Ontwikkeling, 1974, Vanderbijlpark
Labuschagne C J, 31, P/A Volkskas Jan Kempdorp, Rekenmeester, 1969, Oos-Londen
Labuschagne F J, 36, Geref Pastorie — Gobabis, Predikant, 1966, Potchefstroom
Labuschagne F L, 32, "Fanie" Gravelotte, Boer, 1971, Tzaneen
Labuschagne G J J, 35, P/A Ned Herv Pastorie Pietersburg, Predikant, 1969, Salisbury
Labuschagne J A, 39, Perseel 16 Pongola, Boer, 1964, Piet Retief
Labuschagne J C, 31, Chayneweg 11 Darrenwood, Advokaat, 1973, Potchefstroom
Labuschagne J E, 33, P/A Atlas Fabriek Kempton Park, Supt Finansies, 1968, Kensington
Labuschagne J F, 33, Kareestraat 8 Nelspruit, Sielkundige/Voorligter, 1976, Ermelo
Labuschagne J H, 31, P/A Monument Versekeringsmaatskappy Barbeton, Verteenwoordiger, 1970, Roodepoort
Labuschange J H, 42, Nolastraat 139 Buccleuch Sandton, Snr Klerk Verkeersafd S A L Johannesburg, 1973
Labuschagne J H, 35, Hoërskool Middelburg, Onderwyser, 1965, Lindley
Labuschagne J J, 35, P/A Munisipaliteit Sasolburg, Adj-Stadstesourier, 1975, Bloemfontein
Labuschagne J M, 41, N H Gemeente Louis Trichardt, Predikant, 1967, Pietersburg
Labuschagne J S, 43, Merwena Hostel Heidelberg K P, Skoolhoof, 1973, Parow
Labuschagne M A, 47, P/A Munisipaliteit Vereeniging, Dorpsbestuurder, 1969, Sharpeville
Labuschagne M C, 45, Posbus 7 Groot Marico, Onderwyser, 1967
Labuschagne M J, 29, Van Veldenstraat Brits, Onderwyser, 1966 Ventersdorp
Labuschagne N J S, 32, Vyfdestraat 20 Fochville, Tandarts, 1977, Westonaria
Labuschagne N W, 28, P/A Ludi Uitrusters Bpk Brakpan, Bestuurder, 1969, Boksburg
Labuschagne P G, 32, Kareepan Bloemhof, Boer, 1966
Labuschagne P W, 30, P/A van Riebeeck-Melkery Bellville, Motorwerktuigkundige, 1973
Labuschagne S P R, 44, Benjaminstraat 17 Robertsham/Langlaagte Tegn Skool, Onderwyser, 1977, Harrismith
Lagerwey T, 35, P/A Foskor Phalaborwa, Asst Meulsuperintendent, 1968, Stilfontein
La Grange A C d W, 28, Huis Koornhof Laingsburg, Onderwyser, 1969, Riviersonderend
La Grange D C, 35, P/A Hall-Thermotank Parow, Ingenieur, 1973, Table View
La Grange G J B, 40, Volkskas Lindley, Bestuurder, 1966, Dewetsdorp
La Grange O D, 39, Elgarstraat 3 Vanderbijlpark, Ass sup. Yskor, 1977, Pretoria
La Grange P A, 48, Personeelafd Dept Verdediging Pretoria, Offisier, 1965
La Grange P D F, 43, S A S Vaalwater, Stasiemeester, 1965, Olifantsfontein
Laing J J A, 25, Middelbare Skool Brackenfell, Onderwyser, 1967, Stellenbosch

Lambinon H J, 32, P/A Sasol Sasolburg, Snr Navorser, 1973, Pretoria
Lambrecht B J, 34, P/A Seunskoshuis Vanrhynsdorp, Onderwyser, 1969, Fraserburg
Lambrecht W H, 38, Emanuel Hartbeesfontein, Onderhoof, 1968, Pretoria
Lambrecht W J, 26, Charlestraat 26 Somerset-Oos, Geneesheer, 1968, Stellenbosch
Lambrechts D G, 33, Gloria Hendrina, Boer, 1973
Lambrechts P H S, Toekoms Pk Petrusburg, 1963
Lamprecht (Ds), S A Atletiek Vereeniging
Lamprecht C E, 43, Nicolsonstraat 222 Brooklyn Pretoria, Snr Skakelbeampte/Musikus, 1971, Johannesburg
Lamprecht C E, 34, Volkskas Aberdeen, Rekenmeester, 1969, Johannesburg
Lamprecht C W, 39, P/A Dep "Conex" Gwelo, Grondbew Beampte, 1968, Enkeldoorn
Lamprecht De V B, 34, Von Bondestraat 8 Universitas/U O V S, Snr Lektor, 1977, Stellenbosch
Lamprecht D M, 46, P/A Oakdale Hoër Landbouskool, Onderwyser, 1965, Postmasburg
Lamprecht H L J, 41, P/A Volkskas Vrede, Bestuurder, 1963, Pretoria
Lamprecht K K, 41, P/A N G Pastorie Verkeerdevlei, Predikant, 1977, Stellenbosch
Lamprecht P L M, 37, P/A Munisipaliteit Potgietersrus, Verkeershoof, 1977, Nelspruit
Landman C R, 27, Alexandria, Boer, 1963
Landman J C, 40, P/A Kinderoord Ugie, Rekenmeester, 1965, Bothashof
Landman J O, 39, Vaalbank Newcastle, Boer, 1970, Utrecht
Landman K P, 28, Hartbeesfontein PK Amersfoort, Boer, 1964
Landman M C, 42, Vermootenstraat 5 Bethal, Asst Sekretaris OTK, 1976, Standerton
Landman P J, 39, Denneysenstraat Molteno, Volkskasbestuurder, 1971, Bloemfontein
Landman R H, Sekretaris — Vereniging van Staatsamptenare
Landman S J, 26, P/A O T K Nigel, Takbestuurder, 1968, Middelburg Tvl
Landsberg E H K, 33, Du Pisanie-Koshuis Vereeniging, Onderwyser, 1970, Johannesburg
Lange F J, Praat oor Ondersteuning van Eie Sakeondernemings by Bondsraad van 1966 — Zeerust
Lange J, 30, P/A Liebenhof Koshuis Bethal, Onderwyser, 1963, Zeerust
Langenhoven J D, 34, Klipheuwel Buffeljagsrivier, Boer, 1965, Swellendam
Langeveldt S W, 32, Disalaan 20 Kleinmond, Skoolhoof, 1976, O'Kiep
Langley P J, 33, Matjesgoedkuil PK Devon, Boer, 1970, Vereeniging
Langley T (Lid Nr 7755) — L V Pretoria (Klapperkop) Woon 1965 se Bondsraad by
Lass H R, 41, Maylaan 15 Arconpark Vereeniging, Onderwyser/Hoërskool, 1970, Wolmaranstad
Lategan A J, 32, P/A Prokureur-Genl Kaapstad, Prof Assistent, 1965, Lutzville
Lategan A W (Dr), Lid van die U R se Wetenskap-Komitee-1973
Lategan B C, 32, Unielaan 15 Uniepark/Teologiese Skool N G Sendingkerk, Professor, 1965, George
Lategan B D, 27, Brakfontein Aberdeen, Boer, 1965
Lategan B G, 49 Wilgelaan 2 Nucam Oor Ermelo, Supt Evkom, 1975, Worcester
Lategan D, 34, Moseliestraat Pretoria-Noord/P/A Dept van Openbare Werke, Tegnikus, 1975, Dewetsdorp
Lategan E H W, 45, P/A Opleidingskollege Paarl, Dosent, 1974, Stellenbosch
Lategan H J, 43, N G Pastorie Nieuwoudtville, Predikant, 1970, Ottosdal
Lategan J H, 44, Diepkloof Magoebaskloof, Onderwyser, 1977, Steenbokpan
Lategan J J, 44, Cogliarie Zastron/Landbou Tegniese Dienste, Boer/Veldbeampte, 1977, Boksburg
Lategan D F, 34, Huis Archer Voortrekkerstraat Oudtshoorn, Onderwyser/Hoërskool, 1970
Lategan P H, 35, Grimbeekstraat Beaufort-Wes, Onderwyser, 1968, Grootfontein, S W A
Lategan W, 44, Hoër Tegn. Skool Oudtshoorn, Onderwyser, 1970
Laubscher C J, 37, Heuningkop Edenburg, Boer, 1973, Bethulie
Laubscher D E M, 37, Witdam Petrusburg, Boer, 1977, Bloemfontein
Laubscher E J, 37, S A B S Pretoria, Entomoloog, 1966, Wolmaransstad
Laubscher G J, 39, Hoërskool Ben Viljoen Groblersdal, Onderhoof, 1966, Potchefstroom
Laubscher H P, 43, S A S & H Heilbron, Klerk, 1966, Vredendal
Laubscher H W, 33, P/A Sanlam Heidelberg Tvl, Wyksbestuurder, 1967, Paarl
Laubscher J A B, Kolonel — S A Polisiehoofkwartier/Kontak vir Boeke na Grens (1973)
Laubscher N G, 28, P/A Geref Pastorie Nigel, Predikant, 1969, Potchefstroom
Laubscher R J, 42, Welgelegen Bainsvlei, Boer, 1973, Kroonstad

Laubscher S J, 37, Landbank Middelburg Tvl, Klerk, 1966, Heidelberg
Laufs D, 26, Geref Pastorie Bethulie, Predikant, 1974, Potchefstroom
Laurens R C, 30, P/A van Wyk De Vries Malan & Steyn Johannesburg, Prokureur, 1964
Laurie H de g, Adj-Besturende Direkteur Perskor
Lazarus E, 44, 7 DeLaan 77 Bellville, Onderwyser, 1967, Bredasdorp
Le Clus P, 35, P/A S A Lugmag Pretoria, Kommandant, 1974, Pretoria
Leeson T P, 37, P/A Electro Pneumatiese Installasies Kempton Park, Direkteur, 1969, Modderfontein
Leeuwner K A, 35, P/A De Klerk & Van Gend Kaapstad, Prokureur, 1974, Philipsotwn
Le Grange F A, 34, P/A Uniewinkels Bloemfontein, Streekbestuurder, 1973, Bethlehem
Le Grange J A, 42, P/A S A Polisie Komatipoort, Adj-Offisier, 1964, Pretoria
Le Grange J H B, 47, S A Polisie Stutterheim, Adj-Offisier, 1964, Hanover
Le Grange J M, 39, Volkskas BPK Barrydale, Bestuurder, 1970, Kaapstad
Le Grange J P, 45, P/A Yskor Pretoria, Snr Gesondheidsinspekteur, 1974, Oos-Londen
Lemmer H R, 42, Perseel J18 Marble Hall, Boer, 1973, Middelburg
Lemmer J C, 30, Palmstraat 7 Northmead-Uitbr No. 4 Benoni/T O Vereeniging, Adj-Sekretaris, 1970, Pretoria
Lemmer J J, 47, S A S & H Kazerne, Klerk, 1965, Zeerust
Le Riche E J L, 37, N G Pastorie Komatipoort, Predikant, 1966, Pretoria
Le Roux A du T, 34, Frank Townsendstraat Witrivier, Geneesheer, 1971, Pretoria
Le Roux A F, 35, Kruisstraat Potchefstroom, Onderwyser, 1966, Vryburg
Le Roux A J, 40, S A S & H Kaapstad, Landmeter, 1967, Johannesburg
Le Roux B, 34, Hans Strydomlaan 278 Lyttelton, Geneesheer, 1966, Pretoria
Le Roux C J P, 51, Hartbeesfontein skool, Skoolhoof, 1963, Bloemhof
Le Roux C R de W, 39, P/A Vereniging van Staatsamptenare Pretoria, Sekretaris, 1964, Windhoek
Le Roux D B, 41, S A Weermag Pretoria, Majoor, 1966, Bloemfontein
Le Roux D F, 36, Van Der Waltstraat Venterstad, Vise-Hoof, 1971, Franschhoek
Le Roux D F B, 39, P/A S A Spoorweë Vryheid, Ingenieursasst, 1974, Parow
Le Roux D J, 35, La Boroux Malanstasie, Boer, 1964, Wellington
Le Roux E, 36, P/A Volkskas Virginia, Rekenmeester, 1968, Windhoek
Le Roux E, 34, Dianaweg 402 Lynnwood Pretoria, Prokureur, 1965, Stellenbosch
Le Roux F, 45, Hoërskool Ventersdorp, Onderhoof, 1966, Potchefstroom
Le Roux F H, 32, P/A Landbou Tegn Dienste Nelspruit, Skeikundige, 1965, Pretoria
Le Roux F J D, 37, Slent Huguenot K P, Boer, 1967, Paarl
Le Roux F N F, 38, P/A IBM Suid Afrika (Edms) Bpk Johannesburg, Bestuurder/Inligtingstelsel, 1974, Kaapstad
Le Roux F P J, 29, Posbus 642 Welkom, Geneesheer, 1965, Edenville
Le Roux G C, 39, Doornkraal de Rust, Boer, 1976
Le Roux G D, 44, Kerkplein Prieska, Boer/Verteenwoordiger Sanlam, 1970
Le Roux G P V, 32, N G Gemeente Universitas Bloemfontein, Predikant, 1973, Port Elizabeth
Le Roux H, 38, Moultonlaan 63 Waverley, Abb Staatsdienskommissie, 1976, Pretoria
Le Roux H F, 38, P/A Die Volksblad Bloemfontein, Sportverslaggewer, 1973, Frankfort
Le Roux H J, 34, Maraisstraat Tulbach, Onderwyser, 1972, Oudtshoorn
Le Roux H J, 38, Coetzeestraat Belfast, Onderwyser, 1970, Wolmaransstad
Le Roux J, 33, Conistonsteeg 11 Malvern Johannesburg, Onderwyser, 1970, Pretoria
Le Roux Jannie, President Transvaalse Rugby Unie
Le Roux J E (Lid Nr 7689), Volksrust, Onderwyser, 1962
Le Roux J F, 44, Zwol Boshof, Boer, 1966, Vaalharts
Le Roux J F, 45, Van Veldenstraat 29 Brits, Apteker, 1969, Potchefstroom
Le Roux J F, 26, P/A N G Pastorie Soutpan, N G Predikant, 1974, Stellenbosch
Le Roux J F M, 34, P/A Stadsraad Westonaria, Supt (Elekt), 1976
Le Roux J G, 27, Vendome Huguenot, Boer, 1974
Le Roux J H, 29, Damfontein Smithfield, Boer, 1971
Le Roux J H, 34, S A Polisie — Badfontein, Sersant, 1965, Carolina
Le Roux J J, 42, Pennysingel 10A Kroonstad/Stanley Motors, Werksvoorman, 1970, Johannesburg
Le Roux J J, 29, Langenhoven Marble Hall, Boer, 1971, Caledon
Le Roux J M (Prof), Lid van die U R se Wetenskap Komitee 1973
Le Roux J N M, 34, Bakenskraal Oudtshoorn, Boer, 1970

Le Roux J P, 28, Edwardstraat 17 King Williamstown, Onderwyser, 1970, Knysna
Le Roux J P, 28, P/A Mayvilleskool Pretoria, Onderwyser, 1970
Le Roux L J (Prof), Lid van die U R se Wetenskap Komitee 1973
Le Roux M J, 33, J G Strÿdom Huis No. 2 6deStraat Jozini, Hoofingenieur, 1972, Somerset-Oos
Le Roux M J, 34, P/A Hoërskool Lyttelton, Onderwyser, 1965, Potgietersrus
Le Roux M P S, 46, P/A Afdelingsraad Kaapstad, Gesondh Opv Tegnikus, 1974, Wynberg
Le Roux P, 33, Kilmarnock Kransfontein, Boer, 1975, Middelburg KP
Le Roux P, 36, Yskor Pretoria, Meganiese Ingenieur, 1967, Gobabis
Le Roux P A, 37, P/A Nas Party OVS Welkom, Organiseerder, 1965, Williston
Le Roux P A F, 39, Levubu, Boer, 1971
Le Roux P G, 40, Kloppenspruit Smithfield, Boer, 1977
Le Roux P J, 43, Burgersdorp, Apteker, 1964, Williston K P
Le Roux P J, 38, Drostdy Laingsburg, Landdros, 1963, Grahamstad
Le Roux P J H, 27, Maranda Villiersdorp, Veearts/Boer, 1970
Le Roux P O, 50, Fouriestraat 9 Wellington/Hugenote Kollege, Dosent, 1970, Kaapstad
Le Roux R S, 44, 2eLaan Uitsig Wellington, Stadsklerk, 1971, Bredasdorp
Le Roux S C J, 43, Rouzelle PK Breërivier, Boer, 1965, Worcester
Le Roux S F du T, 39, Edenvale Headlands, Boer, 1970, Hobhouse
Le Roux S J, 37, Huis 77 PK Ulco, Skoolhoof, 1970, Vaalharts
Lessing C J H, 28, P/A Univ Biblioteek Potchefstgroom, Asst-Bibliotekaris, 1965
Lessing D G S, 29, Groenkloof Noupoort, Boer, 1968
Lessing I J (Ds), Potchefstroom, 1963
Lessing I J, 30, Spekboomstraat 34 Kempton Park, Bemarkingsbeampte O K, 1971, Potchefstroom
Lessing J, 31, P/A Afdelingsraad Humansdorp, Sekretaris, 1968, Willowmore
Lessing J C, 33, P/A Yskor Pretoria, Skeikundige, 1966, Potchefstroom
Lessing J P, 36, Hersovstraat 24 Sasolburg, Adj-Hoof Laerskool, 1970, Virginia
Lessing J P, 34, Oppermanstraat 2 Vaalpark Sasolburg, N G Predikant, 1977, Malelane
Lewies W A, 32, Durban Ellisras, Boer, 1975, Pretoria
Liebenberg A J, 35, P/A S A Weermag Heidelberg, Kommandant, 1974, Pretoria
Liebenberg C J, 41, Pumilanga — Fort Rixon, Boer, 1966
Liebenberg C J (Lid Nr 7737), Pretoria, 1963
Liebenberg C J, 42, O T K Amersfoort, Takbestuurder, 1966, Bethal
Liebenberg C J, 39, Stasiestraat Vredenburg, Geneesheer, 1966, Pretoria
Liebenberg C R, 35, P/A Hoërskool Carolina, Onderwyser, 1967, Nylstroom
Liebenberg D A, 27, Philipstraat 14 Ceres, Onderwyser, 1967, Upington
Liebenberg D J (Lid Nr 7681) Vredenburg, Fabrieksbestuurder, 1962
Liebenberg D J, 39, Tsumeb-Korporasie, Sweiservoorman, 1976, Johannesburg
Liebenberg D P, 38, Pienaarstraat 10 Brits, Raadg Ingenieur, 1973
Liebenberg F J, 41, P/A Staatsdrukker Pretoria, Hoof (Ink Afdeling), 1964, Carolina
Liebenberg G Z, 33, P/A Brink Roos & du Toit Paarl, Ouditeur, 1970, Vereeniging
Liebenberg H C, 41, Galeweg 6 Parktown Johannesburg, Uroloog, 1970, Stellenbosch
Liebenberg H D, 32, Plaas Villa Rose Usakos, Boer, 1977, Grootfontein
Liebenberg H L, 27, Mandalay Plaas Dist Gwelo, Boer, 1971, Salisbury
Liebenberg J A, 34, P/A Roodepoortse Munisipaliteit, Bibliotekaris, 1973, Sasolburg
Liebenberg J A C, 35, P/A S A Polisie-Kollege Pretoria, Sersant, 1967, Upington
Liebenberg J D v d M, 47, Kloofmyn PK Libanon, Hoofmynopmeter, 1966, Krugersdorp
Liebenberg J G, 34, P/A Volkskas Silverton, Klerk, 1973, Carolina
Liebenberg M P, 37, Hoërskool Richmond, Onderwyser, 1967, Mosselbaai
Liebebberg N M, 36, Kleinbroekskool Bothaville, Onderwyser, 1976, Welkom
Liebenberg P J, 34, Nywerheidsaksepbank Johannesburg, Bestuurder, 1967, Johannesburg
Liebenberg P W, 34, P/A P U vir CHO — Sentrum vir Interne Politiek/Sitastraat 14 Potchefstroom, Navorser, 1975, Port Elizabeth
Liebenberg S W, 35, P/A Raad op Atoomkrag Pretoria, Ingenieur, 1972, Stellenbosch
Liebenberg T A, 36, P/A Geref Kerk Virginia, Predikant, 1968, Ladybrand
Ligthelm C J, 37, P/A Alberton Verwe (Edms) Bpk, Skeikundige, 1967, Middelburg Tvl
Ligthelm J G, 44, O T K Graanafd Stofberg, Bestuurder, 1966, Blinkwater
Ligthelm N W, 45, Laerskool Totius Vanderbijlpark, Onderhoof, 1965, Vereeniging

Ligthelm S P, 44, P U vir CHO Potchefstroom, Professor, 1966, Alberton
Limbach K J, 35, Glencoe PK Hoedspruit, Boer, 1970, Messina
Linde D L S, 42, Wesselstraat Excelsior, Onderwyser, 1965, Verkeerdevlei
Linde F J, 38, N G Pastorie PK Soutpan, N G Predikant, 1971, Windhoek
Linde H J, 27, N G Pastorie Riversdal, Predikant, 1968, Stellenbosch
Linde J J, 45, Graspan Verkeerdevlei, Boer, 1965, Steynspruit
Linde P E S, 35, Kruitfontein Potchefstroom, Boer, 1967
Linde P J W, P/A Geref Kerk Schweizer-Reneke, Predikant, 1968, Paarl
Lindeque B G, 33, P/A Bantoe-Adm en Ont Pretoria, Pers Klerk, 1974, Pietermaritzburg
Lindeque G F, 32, Gillardrylaan 4 Cresta Randburg, Asst Direkteur Seifsa, 1974, Kaapstad
Lindeque J G, 32, P/A N G Pastorie Proklamasieheuwel, Predikant, 1969, Hartbeesfontein
Lindeque J G, N G Pastorie Katima Mulilo, Predikant, Skakel vir militêre dienspligtiges, 1977
Lindeque P J, 31, Voortrekkerstraat Balfour, Geneesheer, 1968, Clocolan
Lindeque R C, 27, N G Pastorie Alberton-Suid, Predikant, 1968, Klerksdorp
Lindeque W, 25, Eensaam Deneysville, Boer, 1970
Lion-Cachet J (Dr), 46, Murraystraat 367 Pretoria, Chirurg, 1965, Germiston
Lizamore B F, 48, Schoonoord Sekhukhune, Snr Bantoekommissaris, 1967, Pretoria
Lloyd C T, 36, Garmouthlaan 154 Bluff Durban, Onderwyser, 1977
Lloyd J, 45, P/A Poskantoor Potgietersrus, Superintendent, 1965, Robertson
Loader L J R, 27, P/A Volkskas Memel, Rekenmeester, 1974, Pretoria
Lochner G P, 39, Klein Langverwacht Kuilsrivier, Boer, 1970, Moorreesburg
Lochner G P, 33, Boustraat 5 Moret Randburg, Onderwyser, 1969, Johannesburg
Lochner J de V, 34, Mediese Navorsingsraad/Nederburgstraat Welgemoed Bellville, Vise-President, 1972, Stellenbosch
Lochner L J P W, 34, Hoër Seunskool-Koshuis Worcester, Onderhoof, 1965, Wolseley
Lochner T C, 30, Bayviewterras 7 Kaapstad P/A C L Lochner Argitekte Sanlamgebou, Argitek, 1976, Pretoria
Logan J C, 32, P/A Bantoe-Hoërskool Setotlewane, Onderhoof, 1967
Lohann C A, 39, Postmastraat Potchefstroom, Dosent/Onderwyskollege, 1970
Lombaard A C, 32, Fontein Adelaide, Boer, 1977, Adelaide
Lombaard D, 32, P/A Sennet en Wessels Pretoria, Ingenieur, 1973, Otjiwarongo
Lombaard E R, 38, Yskor Pretoria, Personeelklerk, 1964, Hobhouse
Lombaard J A C, 44, P/A Ladybrand-Koöp Excelsior, Bestuurder, 1969
Lombaard J C, 31, P/A Universiteit van Port Elizabeth, Lektor, 1974, Bloemfontein
Lombard J G E, 43, P/A Landdroskantoor Breyten, Landdros, 1969, Warmbad
Lombaard L C, P/A Karoo Vleisboerkoöp, Onderbestuurder, 1973, Upington
Lombaard L C, 37, Sanlam Kimberley, Taksekretaris, 1966, Port elizabeth
Lombaard M P, 36, Wildebeesthoek 309 J R Dist Pretoria, Snr/ABB Staatsdienskommissie, 1977, Benoni
Lombaard W A, 41, P/A Dept van Verdediging Pretoria, Majoor, 1963, Watervalboven
Lombard A C, 36, Posbus 44 Adelaide, Boer, 1963
Lombard B, 43, P/A Bantoe Admin Raad Noord-Kaap, Hoofrekenmeester, 1977, Strand
Lombard C A J, 39, P/A Volkskas Vredefort, Bestuurder, 1972, Boksburg
Lombard C J, 36, Vredestraat 9 Wolseley, Bestuurder Volkskas, 1972, Stellenbosch
Lombard D P, 38, Lulustraat 59 Mardelana, Staatsamptenaar B V S V, 1973
Lombard G, 30, P/A Randburgse Stadsraad, Snr Rekenmeester, 1975, Pretoria
Lombard H, 43, Rekenpligtige Dept S S A S Johannesburg, Klerk, 1963, Bloemfontein
Lombard H A, 39, N G Kerk Rondebosch, Predikant, 1972, Pretoria
Lombard H J, 31, P/A N G Kerk Roodepoort, Predikant, 1974, Potgietersrus
Lombard H L, Fouriestraat Boshof — Het vir Dokter Geadverteer — 1963
Lombard J (Lid Nr 7738), Springbok, 1963
Lombard J A, 51, P/A Universiteit Pretoria, Professor/Ekonomie, 1977
Lombard J J, 34, Deputasiestraat 158 Vryheid, Onderwyser, 1966, Utrecht
Lombard J Z P, 46, Smutsstraat Leeudoringstad, Sakeman, 1966, Pretoria
Lombard M S, 25, Boplaas Eikenhof, Boer/Saalperdteler, 1971
Lombard N D, 42, P/A Sanlam Vryheid, Wyksbestuurder, 1968, Estcourt Natal
Lombard P C, 33, G E Myn Gravelotte, Bestuurder, 1966, Johannesburg
Lombard P J, Donnerandweg 26 Dalsig Stellenbosch — Skakel by Universiteit, 1976
Lombard P L, 35, P/A Ernest Oppenheimer-Hospitaal Welkom, Statistikus, 1969, Piet Retief
Lombard P M, 49, Truter & Lombard Kaapstad, Prokureur, 1966, Tulbagh

Lombard S, 31, Ahrbeckstraat Prieska, Sakeman, 1968
Lombard T, 31, P/A Afdelingsraad Worcester, Banatoebeheerbeampte, 1966, Kimberley
Lombard T E, 26, N G Kerk Malmesbury, Predikant, 1968, Stellenbosch
Lombard W J H, 37, Houtvolop Schweizer-Renecke, Boer, 1977
Loock E L, 26, Lustfontein Willowmore, Boer, 1977
Loots B, 41, Die Drostdy Mosselbaai, Landdros, 1976, Sabie
Loots B P, Praa t oor Voortrekkers by 1965 Bondsraad
Loots F J N, 44, P/A Spoorwegpolisioe Bloemfontein, Kaptein, 1974, Kimberley
Loots F N J (Rustende Lid Nr 9051), 48, Pioneer Crusher Johannesburg/Reynoldstraat 30 Reynoldsview Kensington, Dept Hoof, 1965, Herbert K P
Loots F W, 47, S A Weermag Windhoek, Kommandant, 1965, Pretoria
Loots G J, 34, P/A Meisieskoshuis Schweizer-Reneke, Onderwyser, 1969
Loots H J, 39, P/A B B K Pretoria, Streekbestuurder, 1975, Waterberg
Loots J A J, 29, N G Gemeente Elsburg, Predikant, 1977, Kamanjab
Loots J H, 35, H/V V D Graaf-en Imhoffstraat Welgemoed, Wyksbestuurder, Sanlam, 1970, Wolseley
Loots J J, 49, Swenskuil Prieska, Boer/L V, 1964
Loots J M (Lid Nr 7763), Barkly-Wes, 1963
Loots P A, 41, P/A N G Kerk Parow-Sentraal, Predikant, 1974, Middelburg
Loots W J, 33, P/A S A Polisie (Veiligheidsafd), Kaptein, 1973, Prieska
Loots Z B, 29, Hoopstraat Jacobsdal, Onderwyser, 1966, Bethlehem
Loots Z M, 46, P/A Merino-Koöp Beaufort-Wes, Takbestuurder, 1967, Britstown
Loretz H J E, 44, Laerskool Nylstroom, Onderhoof, 1977, Pietersburg
Lotriet A H, 38, Bergkareelaan 375 Lynnwood Pretoria, Ingenieur (Raadg), 1976, Johannesburg
Lotriet C A, 33, Landdroskantoor Durban, Landdros, 1967, Pinetown
Lötter B S, 35, Crawfordsingel 74 Strubenvale Springs, Tand-Tegnikus, 1976, Pretoria
Lötter D C, 37, P/A Letaba Langoed Letaba, Bestuurder, 1964, Zebediela
Lötter D J B, 50, P/A Van Bazaar Pearston, Klerk, 1968
Lötter J D, 36, Tweeriviere PK Fullarton, Boer, 1969
Lötter L D, 42, W G A Port Elizabeth, Wolsorteerder, 1968, Jansenville
Lotter P H F, 44, P/A Moderne Skoonmakers Ermelo, Direkteur, 1968
Lötter P J M, 32, Koperlaan 30 Virginia, Onderwyser, 1973, Bloemfontein
Lotter W G, 33, Louw Geldenhuysskool Linden, Onderwyser, 1967, George
Lotz F J, 43, Odendaalstraat Meyerspark/W N N R Pretoria, Fisikus (Bounavorsing), 1970 Pretoria
Lötz J J, 37, P/A N G Pastorie Paterson, Predikant, 1966, Pearston
Lötz J v Z, 46, Tvlse Onderwysdept Pretoria, Snr Asst Navorsingsburo, 1967, Lydenburg
Lotz J W (Lid Nr 7683), Wakkerstroom, Boer, 1962
Lotz T J, 30, Mauritiusstraat 37 Meiringspark, Apteker, 1969, Potchefstroom
Loubser A C (Lid Nr 7713), Verkeerdevlei, Predikant, 1962
Loubser C H, 48, Dennesigstraat 4 Stellenbosch, Landmeter, 1967
Loubser F J, 47, P/A Ontv van Inkomste Bloemfontein, Inspekteur, 1964, Calvinia
Loubser J de V, Lid van U R se Landbou-Komitee in 1973
Loubser J G H, Algemene Bestuurder — S A S & H — Lid van U R se Wetenskap-Komitee in 1973
Loubser J S, 38, Van Riebeeck Mediese Gebou Schoemanstraat Pretoria, Chirurg, 1970
Loubser J W S, 35, Boterberg Philadelphia, Boer, 1970
Loubser M D, 35, Boesmanskop Loeriesfontein, Boer, 1977
Loubser M G, 41, P/A Brink Roos & Du Toit Bellville, Professor, 1967, Stellenbosch
Loubser M v d S, 45, Blaaubergplaas Melkbosstrand, Boer, 1971, Philadelphia
Lourens C J, 33, Philadelphia Hospitaal Dennilton/Dept Gesondheid, Adm Beampte, 1970, Rustenburg
Lourens D C, 40, Lateganstraat 53 Outjo, Sakeman, 1973, Keimoes
Lourens E M, 40, Bantoesake PK Witsieshoek, Kommisaris, 1967, Rustenburg
Lourens G H C, 40, P/A Laerskool Turffontein Johannesburg, Onderhoof, 1968, Frankfort
Lourens H C de W, 35, N G Gemeente Danie Theron Eikenhof, Predikant, 1977, Lobatsi
Lourens J J, 38, Magaliestr 34 Koster/Koster Koöp, Asst Hoofbestuurder, 1977, Rustenburg
Lourens J J B, 32, Bristol Cornelia, Boer, 1975

Lourens J P, 44, P/A Joy-Manufacturing Cosalto Johannesburg, Inspeksievoorman, 1969, Koppies
Lourens J P (Lid Nr 7774), Edingurglaan Clubview Oos Verwoerdburg — Werk by Atoomkragraad 1963
Lourens P C, 30, Rietkuil PK Villiers, Boer, 1974
Lourens W J, 33, Van Riebeeckstraat Montagu, Onderwyser, 1967, Albertina
Louw A A, 36, Dalmada 20 Pietersburg, Rekenmeester/Ouditeur, 1971, Pretoria
Louw A F M, 44, Fisantekraal Durbanville, Boer, 1976
Louw A H P, Laerskool Ceres, Onderhoof, 1965, Redelinghuys
Louw A J, 33, P/A Tegn Kollege Langlaagte, Onderwyser, 1965, Bronkhorstspruit
Louw A J, 46, Buro vir Statistiek Pretoria, Onder-Direkteur, 1966
Louw A J, 33, P/A Nas Party van S W A, L W ǗHoofsekretaris, 1975, Usakos
Louw A J P, Woon 1966 Bondsraad by (Bellville-Wes)
Louw A P, 42, N G Pastorie Môrelig Bethlehem, Predikant, 1966, Primrose
Louw A P v N, 47, Skool vir Serebraal Kreupeles Pretoria, Onderhoof, 1967, Pietersburg
Louw A W, 40, Parkstraat Karasburg, Boer/Klerk by Afd Paaie, 1971, Germiston
Louw C C de W, 39, P/A Henochsberg Germiston, Dept Bestuurder, 1974, Primrose
Louw C F, 30, P/A Rovicon Edms Bpk Bellville, Sakeman, 1973
Louw C I M, 50, Oranje PK Hendrina, Boer, 1964
Louw C J, 44, V D Merweweg De Deur, Slagter, 1975, Vereeniging
Louw C S, 27, P/A Marine Products Kaapstad, Ouditeur, 1967, Bellville
Louw D, 45, Dept Volkswelsyn Pretoria, Adm Beheerbeampte, 1966, Oos-Londen
Louw D F J (Lid Nr 7702), Fraserburg, Boer, 1962
Louw D F J, 45, Agterste van Zylsplaas Williston, Boer, 1969
Louw E, 33, P/A Koeberg-Trust Durbanville, Prokureur, 1965, Bellville
Louw E, 42, Dirkie Uysstraat 43, Harrismith, Onderwyser, 1970, Reddersburg
Louw G H, 38, Paarl Trust Bpk Paarl, Sekretaris, 1963
Louw G J J, 38, Residensie Jacobsdal, Landdros, 1968, Mooirivier
Louw G N, 31, Landboukollege Grootfontein, Navorser, 1965, Nieuwoudtville
Louw H, 40, Kransbos PK Knysna, Skoolhoof, 1977
Louw H A, 35, Dept Landbou Univ Stellenbosch, Professor, 1965, Paarl
Louw H A V, 34, P/A Mondorp Johannesburg, Rekenmeester, 1974, Pretoria
Louw I J, 40, P/A Boksburg-Benoni Hospitaal, Superintendent, 1965, Bethal
Louw I S, 44, P/A N G Sendingpastorie Hanover, Sendeling, 1965, De Doorns
Louw J, 45, S A Polisie Johannesburg, Adj-Offisier, 1964, Vredendal
Louw J A, 34, Kroonstad, Stadsingenieur, 1963
Louw J A G, 40, Losberg Carnarvon, Boer, 1973
Louw J B Z, 30, Transvalialaan 14 Uniepark/Universiteit van Stellenbosch, Snr Adm Beampte, 1971, Paarl
Louw J D, 45, Pres Steyn Goudmyn Welkom, Ambulansbeampte, 1967, Libanon
Louw J E, 33, Verdedigingshoofkwartier Potgieterstraat (Kontak vir Boeke na Grnes in
Please omit above line
Louw J E, 33, Verdedigingshoofkwartier Potgieterstraat Pretoria (Kontak vir Boeke na Grens in 1973), Kolonel, 1969, Bellville
Louw J G, 29, Samuels Viljoen & Dekker Bloemfontein, Ouditeur, 1967, Johannesburg
Louw J G, 40, Middeldeurvlei Pofadder, Boer, 1967, Carnarvon
Louw J H, 39, N G Pastorie Bethulie, Predikant, 1967, Luckhoff
Louw J L, 36, P/A Klein Karoo-Landboukoöp Oudtshoorn, Asst Bestuurder, 1967, Potgietersrus
Louw J P (Jr), 29, Hartebeeskloof Porterville, Boer, 1967
Louw J P, 43, Yskor Pretoria, Asst Bibliotekaris, 1964
Louw J P, Berryllaan Lyttelton 3 Verwoerdburg/Yskor, Amptenaar
Louw J v H, 28, Santam Port Elizabeth, Trustbestuurder, 1965, Porterville
Louw J W, 43, Dept Finansies Pretoria; Afdelingshoof, 1964, Windhoek
Louw J W, 38, Roulou Firgrove Stellenbosch, Boer, 1967
Louw Kobus, Vise-Voorsitter van S A Rugby Raad Voormalige Sekretaris van Kleurlingsake
Louw M S (Dr), Lid van die U R se Ekonomiese Komitee 1973
Louw N E, 28, Die Pastorie Gansbaai, N G Predikant, 1970, Stellenbosch
Louw N W, 31, Ebenhaezer Porterville, Boer, 1970
Louw P L R, 41, Forestweg 20 Oranjezicht, Joernalis, 1972, Kaapstad

Louw S C P, 47, Hoërskool Charlie Hofmeyr Ceres, Skoolhoof, 1974, Fraserburg
Louw W F, 34, N G Sendingpastorie Sibasa, Sendeling, 1965, Pretoria
Louw W F, 37, "Wildekeur" Oor Upington, Boer, 1973
Louw W J H, 38, Philadelphia Hospitaal Dennil,ton, Geneesheer, 1974, Utrecht
Louw W P (Lid Nr 7714), Bloemfontein, Kommandant, 1962
Louwrens F G, 38, Dassiefontein Keetmanshoop, Boer, 1974
Louwrens K J, 27, Laspoort Reddersburg, Boer, 1971, Smithfield
Low B, 41, Sanlam Krugersdorp, Wyksbestuurder, 1967, Johannesburg
Loxton A J (Lid Nr 7739), King Williamstown, 1963
Lubbe A M, 29, Posbus 535 Vanderbijlpark, Veearts, 1964, Pretoria
Lubbe A M, Lid van die U R se Landbou Komitee in 1973
Lubbe A N P, 33, Dept van Bantoe-Onderwys Pretoria, Snr Vakkundige Beampte, 1967, Graaff-Reinet
Lubbe B G, 34, Jongilizwe Tsolo Transkei, Onderhoof, 1969, Middelburg Tvl
Lubbe F C, 38, Alba Umfolozi/Eshowe, Boer, 1964, Fauresmith
Lubbe F v Z, Afrikaanse Taal & Kultuur Vereniging — Skakel by kongres op Hartenbos, 1976
Lubbe G J (Lid Nr 4230) Hartswater — Prokureur & LPR/Voorgestel vir die U R in 1968
Lubbe H, 39, Dept van Lande Pretoria, Adm Beampte, 1967, Pietersburg
Lubbe H J H, 42, Truter Kakamas, Boer, 1975
Lubbe H J P, 35, P/A S A U K Johannesburg, Org Suid-Sotho-Diens, 1967, Kempton Park
Lubbe J, 33, Lewerkiestraat 21, Cotswold Port Elizabeth, Onderwyser, 1977, Kimberley
Lubbe J C, 38, Volkskas Aberdeen, Bestuurder, 1966, Schweizer-Reneke
Lubbe J F F, 37, Hoërskool Kalahari Kuruman, Onderwyser, 1967, Danielskuil
Lubbe J H, 39, Mount Charles Groblershoop, Boer, 1975, Niekerkshoop
Lubbe J J, 36, P/A Hoërskool Durbanville, Vise-Hoof, 1977, Maitland
Lubbe J J F, 36, Spitskopstraat 17 Windhoek/Ont van Inkomste, Admin Beampte, 1977, Vereeniging
Lubbe J L, 44, P/A Stewarts & Lloyds Vereeniging, Hoof Verkoper, 1974, Oranjeville
Lubbe K P v W, 47, Dept Binnelandse Inkomste Virginia, Ontv van Inkomste, 1964, Petrusburg
Lubbe P S, 34, Militêre Basis Bethlehem, Soldaat, 1975, Potchefstroom
Lubbe W J, 31, Edenrus 401 Hamiltonstraat Arcadia Pretoria, N G Predikant, 1972, Stellenbosch
Lucas P A J, 40, P/A M J Joubert & Kie Tulbagh, Sakeman, 1974, Paarl
Luck H W, 40, Glypan PK Aranos, Boer, 1966, Gobabis
Luckhoff J R Pretoria (Woon 1966 se Bondsraad by)
Ludeke W, 40, Edenvale Lothair, Boer, 1973, Krugersdorp
Ludick J P, 34, P/A S A U K Pretoria, Streekbestuurder, 1968, Johannesburg
Ludik S J, 32, Dunbarstraat 38 Parowvallei, N G Predikant, 1977, Orania-Dist Hopetown
Luitingh L I, 34, Van Riebeeklaan Edenvale/Kensingtonse Hoërskool, Onderwyser, 1970, Heidelberg Tvl
Lutsch W J F S, 46, P/A Bonuskor Johannesburg, Groepsingenieur, 1966, Stellenbosch
Luttig G, 31, P/A Boland Bank Paarl, Asst Sekretaris, 1973
Lutz B F, 41, Charlie Ochsestraat 10 Cradock, Bou-Aannemer, 1970, Williston
Lutz J J, 34, Fed Volksbeleggings Kaapstad, Asst Bestuurder, 1966, Johannesburg
Luwes N J, 34, P/A Die Afrikaanse Handelsinstituut Johannesburg, Sakebestuurder Volkshandel, 1975

M

Maarschalk S T, 42, Keetstraat 1 Humansdorp, Landmeter, 1966, Willowmore
Maartens J H, 39, PK Biesiesvlei, Sakeman, 1967, Mahemsvlei
Maartens J J, 37, Klipkuil Reddersburg, Boer, 1965
Maartens J M, 29, Susanna Bethlehem, Boer, 1967
Maas L K, 26, Hoërskool Trompsburg, Onderwyser, 1967, Bultfontein
Maas O, 30, P/A Hoërskool Sutherland, Onderwyser, 1970, Brandvlei
Maas N J I V, 40, Jopie Fouriestraat 23 Tiervlei, Onderwyser, 1967, Somerset-Wes
Maass P J, 33, 2deLaan 56 Westdene Johannesburg/S A Polisie, Speurder Adj-Off., 1972
Mahne T C, 27, Leeupoort PK Fochville, Onderwyser, 1974, Carletonville
Malan A F, 41, Fairbairnstraat 4 Sasolburg, Rekenmeester Volkskas, 1975, Heidelberg, Tvl

Malan A J, 40, Strydomstraat 66 Heidelberg Tvl, Apteker, 1964
Malan A P (Prof), Lid van U R se Wetenskap Komitee 1973
Malan A S, 27, P/A Unie Staalkorporasie Vereeniging Admin Assistent, 1965, Pretoria
Malan C A P, 29, Leeukop Deneysville, Boer, 1970
Malan C W, 41 P/A Bantoeskool vir Dowes & Blindes Babanango, Hoof, 1966, Bosele
Malan D G, 37, P/A Karbochem Sasolburg, Bestuurder (Tegnies), 1973, Bloemfontein
Malan D J, 36, N G Pastorie Hartsvallei, Predikant, 1966, Otjiwarongo
Malan D J, Aasvoëlskop
Malan D J, 35, Benstraat 84 Erasmia Pretoria Hoërskool Elandspoort, Vise-Hoof, 1970, Groblersdal
Malan D J, 40, Dept van Gevangeniswese PK Goedemoed, Kaptein, 1970, Leeukop Gevangenis
Malan D J J, 34, Merrimanstraat 3 Welkom, Onderhoof, 1971, Kroonstad
Malan D S, 41, P/A Bakke & Kie/Petrastraat 3 Denneburg, Opl-en Pers Bestuurder, 1975, Strand
Malan E, 41, P/A Universiteit Westville, Snr Lektor, 1977, Bloemfontein
Malan E S, 36, Huis J J Muller Clanwilliam, Onderwyser, 1963, Calvinia
Malan F A, 38, Gordonstraat Mafeking, Apteker, 1971, Brits
Malan G F (Abe), 30, Damfontein Vereeniging, Boer, 1966, Stellenbosch
Malan G J, 42, Louis Bothalaan 30 Louis Trichardt/Soutpnasbergse Laerskool, Onderwyser, 1970, Delmas
Malan H D J P, 31, Presidentstraat 63 Potchefstroom, Stadsingenieur, 1970, Verwoerdburg
Malan H P, 45, P/A Sasol Sasolburg, Hoofklerk, 1967, Rhodesië
Malan H T, 30, PK Melmoth, Poskantoorklerk, 1963, Ladybrand
Malan J (Prof), Universiteit van S A
Malan J A, 32, P/A Laerskool Milnerton, Onderhoof, 1967, Tiervlei
Malan J de L, 42, Dept Publieke Werke Pretoria, Bourekenaar, 1964, Pretoria
Malan J de V R, 29, Hartbeesboek PK Rosslyn Pretoria, Kweker/Boer, 1968
Malan J du P, Brits — (Krokodilrivier) Woon 1966 Bondsraad by
Malan J du T, 27, P/A N G Pastorie Vanwyksvlei, Predikant, 1975, Stellenbosch
Malan J E, 34, P/A Dept Bantoe Adm & Ontw Qumbu, Snr Landbou Beampte, 1967, Mt Fletcher
Malan J F, 44, Libanon Klein Drakenstein, Boer, 1977, Paarl
Malan J H, 32, Albrechtstraat 122 Bloemfontein, Sekretaris VCHO, 1970
Malan J v L, 43, Glencrescent Oranjezicht, Oogarts, 1964, Vredenburg K P
Malan M A, 36, P/A S A Weermag Windhoek, Kolonel, 1967, Pretoria
Malan M M, 27, Hoërskool Menlopark Pretoria, Onderwyser, 1969, Brakpan
Malan P A, 32, Mispellaan Proteapark Rustenburg, Boukontrakteur, 1974, Johannesburg
Malan P C, 33, Rustfontein Bethal, Boer, 1966
Malan P G, 40, P/A Ing Afd Poskantoor Vereeniging, Snr Tegnikus, 1974, Bloemfontein
Malan P J, 37, Malanshoek Keimoes, Boer, 1970
Malan P J, 26, Derdelaan-Wes Clocolan, Geneesheer, 1963, Wellington
Malan P J W, 44, Schuttespos Parys, Boer, 1970
Malan S du P, N G Kerk, Predikant
Malan S F, 45, Atlas Vliegtuigkorp Kempton Park, Direkteur, 1966, Stellenbosch
Malan S F, 30, Allesverloren Riebeek-Wes, Boer, 1969
Malan S F, 33, Hornkranz Windhoek, Boer, 1971, Riebeeckkasteel
Malan S J, 33, P/A Hoërskool Riebeeck Randfontein, Onderwyser, 1976, Potchefstroom
Malan S P, 36, Beatonstraat Ladybrand, Asst Rekenmeester, 1975, Pretoria
Malan S P, Lid van die U R se Landbou Komitee in 1973
Malan S P, 37, Stadsraad Benoni, Onder Stadsklerk, 1967, Alberton
Malan S W, 28, Paardefontein Adelaide, Boer, 1964
Malan W C, 27, Parksteeg 9 Blairgowrie Randburg, Prokureur, 1972, Johannesburg
Malherbe C J, 31, Snel Droogskoonmakers Pretoria-Tuine, Sakeman, 1967
Malherbe D H P, 43, Harry smithstraat 19 Sasolburg, Messelaar, 1971, Ermelo
Malherbe D J, 42, Kweekkraal Riversdal, Boer, 1974
Malherbe F J, 43, Volkskas Swellendam, Bestuurder, 1964, Paarl
Malherbe G J, 35, Hartebeeskraal Paarl, Boer, 1966
Malherbe G J, 46, Hoërskool Tuine Pretoria, Onderhoof, 1967, Brits
Malherbe S G, 33, Porterstraat Rawsonville, Sendeling, 1964, Paarl

Malherbe S P v B, 30, La Dauphine Franschhoek, Boer, 1965
Malherbe U P, 33, P/A N G Kerk Fort Victoria, Predikant, 1976, Kuruman
Malherbe W J, 47, Stockwell Ashton, Boer, 1967
Malherbe W P M, 39, Yskor Pretoria, Geneesheer, 1964, Bloemfontein
Maloney J D, 36, N H Gemeente Oberholzer, N H Predikant, 1977, Pretoria
Mammes H E, 39, Dawellstraat 9 Wilkoppies Klerksdorp, Sakeman, 1965
Mammes P A, 39, P/A Vleissentraal Krugersdorp, Voorl Amptenaar, 1967, Klerksdorp
Marais A J, Steynsrus — Spreek kommer uit oor Versekeringswese op Platteland by 1966 se
Bondsraad. Lid van die U R se Ekonomiese Komitee in 1973
Marias A J, 44, Mullerstraat Bellville/Marais Pienaar & Vennote, Prokureur, 1970, Laingsburg
Marais A L, 31, W G A Steytlerville, Verteenwoordiger, 1964, Merweville
Marais A W C, 34, Tabakwoonbuurt Patensie, Onderwyser, 1968, Reivilo
Marias B, 33, Francina Geneva Stasie, Boer, 1965
Marais B P, Lid van die U R se Ekonomiese Komitee 1973
Marais C F, 32, Vale end Tarkastad, Boer, 1966
Marais C F, 36, N G Gemeente Horison, Predikant, 1965, Fraserburg
Marais C L, 38, Earlstraat 31, Newcastle, Onderwyser, 1966
Marais D, Predikant — Brewerweg 39 Somerstrand Port Elizabeth — Skakel by Univ van Port
Elizabeth 4.2.76
Marais D D, 37, Laerskool Dagbreek Windhoek, Skoolhoof, 1964, Paarl
Marais D F, 38, Laerskool Monument Krugersdorp, Adj-Hoof, 1973, Pretoria
Marais D J, 35, P/A Munisipaliteit Nigel, Klerk, 1963
Marais D P, 45, D F Malanstraat Parow-Noord, Skoolhof, 1975, Somerset-Oos
Marais D P, 38, Lemoenput Salt Lake (Douglas), Boer, 1973, De Aar
Marais E J (Lid Nr 4955), Rektor — Univ van Port Elizabeth — Voorgestel vir die U R 1968
Marais F A J, 35, Hoërskool Gerrit Maritz Pretoria-Noord, Onderwyser, 1964
Marais F J, Lid van die U R se Ekonomiese Komitee 1973
Marais G, 41, Besigheidskool Unisa Pretoria, Direkteur, 1973, Wolseley
Marais G C J, 40, S A S & H Kimberley, Snr Klerk Pers Ingen, 1973
Marais G E, 41, Poskantoor Potchefstroom, Superintendent, 1972, Bethal
Marais G H, 41, P/A S W A — Adm Windhoek, Adm Beheerbeampte, 1969, Pretoria
Marias H B, 41, P/A Marais & du Preez Pretoria, Ouditeur, 1967
Marais H I J, 40, Nkhensani N G Sendingstasie Gryani, Sekretaris, 1974, Vanderbijlpark
Marais I J, Onderwyskollege Durban, Lektor, 1965, Newcastle
Marais I P, 36, P/A Sasolburg, Gebied-Supt, 1970, Chloorkop
Marais J, 40 P/A Hoërskool Etosha Tsumeb, Vise-Hoof, 1975, Windhoek
Marais J, 30, P/A Geref Kerk Belfast, Predikant, 1975, Potchefstroom
Marais J B, 41, Regopkloof Adelaide, Boer, 1967
Marais J C, 32, Volkskas Bpk Brandfort, Rekenmeester, 1964, Humansdorp
Marais J du P, 40, P/A Dept van Arbeid Pretoria, Adm Beampte, 1968
Marais J F, 40, P/A Volkskas Strand, Rekenmeester, 1963, Pietermaritzburg
Marais J F K, 27, P/A Agrikollege Middelburg K P, Dosent, 1969, Stellenbosch
Marais J G, 44, P/A Benoni Steelite Windows, Besturende Direkteur, 1965, Johannesburg
Marais J I F, 46, Staatsdienskommissie Pretoria, Beroepsvoorligter, 1965
Marais J I F, 43, Kareefontein Wepener, Boer, 1969
Marais J J, 30, P/A Roberts Konstruksie/Van der Merwerylaan 131 Meyerspark Pretoria, Tegn Bestuurder, 1975, Alberton
Marais J J, 32, Krygskool Danie Theron Kimberley, Kapelaan, 1969, Bloemfontein
Marais J J, 30, Hoewe 117 Shannon, Werwingsbeampte, 1966
Marais J J, Lid van die U R se Beplanningskomitee in 1973
Marais J J F, 49, Groblersretriet PK Broedersput, Boer, 1966, Delareyville
Marias J L, 35, Timstraat 41 Morganridge Boksburg, Skoolsielkundige, 1977, Kempton Park
Marias J P, 37, Munisipaliteit Benoni, Skeikundige, 1966, Kimberley
Marais J S, 36, N G Pastorie Kimberley-Wes, Predikant, 1965, Williston
Marais L J, 38, P/A Hoërvolkskool Heidelberg Tvl, Onderwyser, 1969, Thabazimbi
Marais M D (Dr), Ekonoom
Marais M J, 46, P/A Onderwyskollege Pretoria, Dept Hoof Afrikaans, 1976, Potchefstroom

Marais N B, 43, Clifton Fort Beaufort, Boer, 1963, Bedford
Marais N E, 32, P/A Laer Volkskool Graaff-Reinet, Onderhoof, 1977, Somerset-Wes
Marais N v d M, Pietermaritzburg — Praat oor Vortrekkergedenkkerk by Bondsraad 1966
Marais P B M, 33, P/A Santam Kaapstad, Beleggingsekretaris, 1964, Ceres
Marais P C, 39, Kommandeurstraat 13 Welgemoed Bellville, Org T V Prog, 1977, Johannesburg
Marais P G, 30, P/A Haak Marais & Pienaar Bellville, Prokureur, 1963, Robertson
Marais P G B, 30, P/A Munisipaliteit Springs, Registrasiebeampte, 1966, Vrede
Marais P S, 42, P/A Otk Bethal, Sekretaris, 1976, Vrede (OVS)
Marais P S, 38, P/A Die Volksblad Bloemfontein, Redakteur-Buiteland, 1975, Bloemfontein
Marais P W, 31, P/A Human Motors Kimberley, Rekenmeester, 1967, Bethlehem
Marais S J, 45, Kerkstraat Colesberg, Geneesheer, 1965, Carnarvon
Marais T J T, 34, P/A Transvaalse Indiër Kollege Roodepoort, Lektor, 1974, Ontdekkerspark
Marais W, 37, Sunrise Dordrecht, Boer, 1975, Tarkastad
Marais W A L, 28, Vrede Petrus Steyn, Boer, 1971
Marais W C, 44, P/A Kempstad Beleggings Kempton Park, Direkteur van Mpye, 1970
Marais W D, 32, Welgemoed 11 Pinelands, Geneesheer, 1966, Kaapstad
Marais W J v d M, 40, Dept van Behuising Pretoria, Ingenieur, 1964, Ceres
Marais W T, 35, Omnia Boeredienste Pretoria, Direkteur, 1964, Pretoria
Maré G S, 40, P/A Tegn Opleiding S A Weermag (Verwoerdburg), Vise-Hoof, 1975, Brits
Maré J A G (Lid Nr 5340), Univ Kollege van Zoeloeland — Voorgestel vir die U R in 1968
Mare J C S, 43, T P A (Paaie-Afd) Lydenburg, Admin-Beampte, 1970, Ermelo
Mare J P, 40, Alaskaweg 3 Selcourt, Onderwyser, 1964, Ermelo
Marè P H C, 40, P/A Sanlam Krugersdorp, Wyksbestuurder, 1969, Magaliesburg
Maré P L, 44, Millerstraat Nelspruit, Prokureur, 1976, Witbank
Mare R, 35, Geref Kerk Empangeni, Predikant, 1977, Potchefstroom
Maree a, 25, Boerehael Ass Maatskappy Ficksburg, 1964, Brandfort
Maree A J B, Bestuurskomitee Middelburg Tvl, 1963
Maree A O S, 37, P/A Fauna Motorvervoermaatskappy Johannesburg, Bestuurder, 1970
Maree C G, Protealaan Kleinmond, Skakel vir vakansiesaamtrek, 1964
Maree C M, 30, Smitrus Tweeling, Boer, 1977
Maree D B, 30, Verblyden Bultfontein, Boer, 1964
Maree D J, 33, Seunskoshuis Senekal, Onderwyser, 1975, Winburg
Maree G de K, Voormalige L V
Maree G du P, 32, P/A Noristan Bpk Pretoria, Rekenmeester, 1974, Klerksdorp
Maree H O, 28, Onderwyskollege Pretoria, Dosent, 1967, Potchefstroom
Maree J, 38, De Hoop De Rust, Boer, 1971
Maree J F, 40, Voortrekkerweg Groblersdal/Landbou Tegniese Dienste, Snr Navor Beampte, 1977, Warmbad
Maree J G, Praat teen Nusas op 1965 Bondsraad
Maree J J, 31, Simonstraat 97 Bethal/S A Polisie, Sersant, 1977, Durban
Maree J P, 33, Strombergplaas Muldersdrift, Hoenderboer, 1970, Marquard
Maree L M, Ondersteun Afr Besighede-Bondsraad 1966
Maree M D, 34, P/A Volklskool Hoogland Bethlehem, Adjunkhoof, 1973, Virginia
Maree P H, 26, P/A N G Kerk Koshuis Verkeerdevlei, Onderwyser, 1965, Virginia
Maree P J H, Lid van die U R se Landbou Komitee in 1973
Maree R P, 33, P/A N G Pastorie Grabouw, Predikant, 1974, Botrivier
Maree W A , Praat oor Kleurlinge by 1971 se Bondsraad
Maree W L, 41, P/A N G Kerk Persburo Pretoria, Direkteur, 1968
Maritz A W A, 31, Steenbokhoorn PK Glen Lyon (Niekerkshoop), Boer, 1973, Postmasburg
Maritz A W A M, 41, Coné Postmasburg, Boer, 1969
Maritz C J, 32, P U vir C H O Potchefstroom/Solomonstraat 5, Lektor, 1971, Pretoria
Maritz G M, 47, Cullinanse Laerskool, Onderhoof, 1966, Bronkhorstspruit
Maritz G M S, 31, Roodekrans Ohrigstad, Boer, 1968
Maritz G N, 33, Hoërskool Colesberg, Onderwyser, 1967, Reivilo
Maritz G S, 39, Onderplaas Fraserburg, Boer, 1976
Maritz J G, 35, Blomkool Brandvlei K P, Boer, 1973
Maritz J H, 33, Hartbeeshof Kenhardt, Onderwyser, 1969, Kaapstad

Maritz J H, 38, Hudab Karasburg, Boer, 1975
Maritz L F H, 49, Blouklip PK Papkuil, Boer, 1965, Griekwastad
Maritz L S, 29, P/A S A Spoorweë Bloemfontein, Klerk, 1967
Maritz P, 26, Montweg 7 Grahamstad/Universiteit Rhodes, Dosent, 1970, Bloemfontein
Maritz P N, 39, P/A Senekal Landbou Koöp Mpy, Hoofbestuurder, 1974, Ficksburg
Maritz W J, 35, P/A Geref Pastorie Floridaheuwels, Predikant, 1969, Parys
Maritz W J B, 31, Groblerstraat 34 Springfontein/Suid-Vrystaat Vleiskoöp, Bestuurder, 1970, Vryburg
Marnitz H J, 36, Rioweg 6 Blairgowrie/SAUK, Omroeper, 1976, Randburg
Marnitz H P (Lid Nr 5164), Direkteur van Diamantsaak — Voorgestel vir die U R in 1968
Marnitz H P, voormalige Redakteur van die Vaderland
Marren A J W, 34, P/A Handelsmerkafdeling Rembrandt, Hoof, 1969, Johannesburg
Mars P W, 46, Jasmynstraat 4 Floridapark, Velspealis, 1976, Ontdekkers
Martins Herman
Martins P v d M, 31, Kritzingerstraat 223 Salieshoek, Onderwyser, 1971, Volksrust
Martins Theo f, Boer en L U K Volksrust — Voorgestel vir die U R in 1968
Martinson J H, 38, N G Pastorie Booysen, Predikant, 1966, Nylstroom
Marx C S, 35, Hoërskool Postmasburg, Skoolhoof, 1965, Noupoort
Marx G J B, 28, Louwstraat 29 Rouxville, Onderwyser, 1967, Brandfort
Marx P D, 36, P/A Alusaf Richardsbaai, Produksie Asst, 1975, Virginia
Marx P J, 30, Brakpan Wolmaransstad, Boer, 1977
Matthee C F, 32, N G Pastorie Stutterheim, Predikant, 1968, Weza Port Shepstone
Matthee C J, 38, Nuwejaarskraal Rietbron, Boer, 1964, Kaapstad
Matthee D J, 38, P/A Munisipaliteit Kempton Park, Snr Adm Asst, 1968, Edenvale
Matthee J A, 37, Dorpsigstraat 19 Stellenbosch, Professor, 1974, Bonnievale
Matthee J J, 44, Pellstraat 41 Beaconbaai Oos-Londen/S A S & H, Werksman, 1976, Port Elizabeth
Matthee L A, 37, Volkskas Queenstown, Bestuurder, 1965, Brits
Matthee P J, 48, Hoërskool Fochville, Prokureur, 1976, Pietermaritzburg
Matthiae U F A, 41, Sonskyn PK Orchard, Boer, 1977, Touwsrivier
Mauley J P, 41, Huis Nr 10 Koegasbrug, Onderwyser/Boer, 1977, Hofmeyr
Meier J H H, 33, P/A Eendrachtse Laerskool, Skoolhoof, 1972, Johannesburg
Meintjes J H, 51, 20steLaan 897 Rietfontein Pretoria, Onderhoof, 1968
Meintjies A S, 42, P/A General Mining & Federale Mynbou Krugersdorp, Sekretaris, 1975, Stilfontein
Meintjies D du B, 30, Chelsearylaan 3 Durban-Noord, Apteker, 1965, Vryheid
Meintjies E C, 31, Militêre Basis Kmdmt op/Port Elizabeth, Kaptein S A Weermag, 1976, Oudtshoorn
Meintjies G P, 41, P/A Laerskool Grootvlei, Skoolhoof, 1969, Welverdiend
Meintjies J P, 37, Karelstraat 5 Del Judor Witbank, Onderwyser, 1974, Bronkhorstspruit
Meiring A E, 32, Vredestraat 16 Malmesbury, Onderwyser, 1975, Parow
Meiring A G S, Voormalige Direkteur van Onderwys Kaap
Meiring D H, 27, PK Fort Hare, Snr Lektor, 1965, Bloemfontein
Meiring F J, 46, Magaliesbergse Tabakplanters Koöp Brits, Sekretaris, 1965
Meiring G C, 32, Skoolkoshuis Philipstown, Skoolhoof, 1975, Mosselbaai
Meiring H R, 39, Honingkloof Kestell, Boer, 1975, Bloemfontein
Meiring J G v G, 32, S A Reserwebank Pretoria, Tweede Asst, 1965, Stellenbosch
Meiring J J, 36, Ferreistraat Piet Retief, Steenmaker, 1965, Wakkerstroom
Meiring J W H, 28, K W V Suider-Paarl, Asst Sekretaris, 1965, Stellenbosch
Meiring P J, 46, C6 Oudestad Groblersdal, Boer, 1973, Brits
Meiring P L, 32, P/A Volkskas Bpk Steynsburg, Rekenmeester, 1969, Potchefstroom
Meisenholl F S, 35, N O K Johannesburg, Navorser, 1964, Reitz
Mentz J H W, 38, Onverwacht Louwsberg, Boer/Sakeman, 1965, Utrecht
Mentz N J, 41, Tvlse Onderwys Buro Pretoria, Vakkundige, 1965, Volksrust
Mentz P K, N G Pastorie, Kerkstraat 60 Middelburg Kaap, Predikant, 1962
Mey M T, 29, P/A Krygstuigraad Pretoria, Sen Vakk Beampte (Pers), 1975, Silverton
Meyer A C, 30, Elandsparkskool Boksburg, Onderhoof, 1964, Dullstroom
Meyer A J J, P/A Sanlam Bellville, Snr Beampte (Stelsels), 1976, S W A
Meyer A M, 22, Louis Trichardtstraat Somerset-Oos, Asst Landdros, 1965, Uitenhage
Meyer A S, (Lid Nr 3090), Malmesbury/West Graanboere, Bestuurder

Meyer B, 39, N G Pastorie Beaufort-Wes, Predikant, 1975, Omaruru
Meyer B C, 44, Uitkyk PK Leeuklip, Boer, 1967, Middelburg Tvl
Meyer C M W, 40, P/A S A Polisie Theunissen, Konstabel, 1966
Meyer f, 37, Horison Dameskoshuis G O K Johannesburg, Dosent, 1977, Witbank
Meyer G M, 27, Meyerton Outjo, Boer, 1966
Meyer H C, 34, Poplarstraat 93 Drie Riviere/P/A Laerskool Historia Vanderbijlpark, Vise-Hoof, 1975, Vereeniging
Meyer H R, 25, Damfontein Laingsburg, Boer, 1970
Meyer I (Izak) (Lid Nr 8410), Seun van Piet Meyer
Meyer I A, Ondersekretaris 1965
Meyer I A, 26, Hoërskool Helpmekaar Johannesburg, Onderwyser, 1964
Meyer I A, 30, P/A Unie Staalkorporasie Vereeniging, Asst Bedryfsing, 1965, Nylstroom
Meyer J, 36, P/A Palabora Mining co Phalaborwa, Sekuriteitsbeampte, 1977, Venterspos
Meyer J A, 29, Villa Campanulla No 7 Stellenbosch, Onderwyser, 1973, Tulbagh
Meyer J B W, 38, Kantoor van die Eerste Minister Pretoria, Privaatsekretaris, 1967
Meyer J C, 36, P/A Dept Nie-Blankesake Munisipaliteit Nigel, Werkevoorman, 1968, Middelburg Tvl
Meyer J de J, 42, Krugerstraat 17 Mount Pleasant Port Elizabeth, Onderwyser, 1970, Albertina
Meyer J E, 34, P/A Sanlam Graaff-Reinet, Wyksbestuurder, 1967, Potchefstroom
Meyer J G, 48, Palmietkuil Devon, Boer, 1974
Meyer J H, 40, P/A Laerskool Tjaart V/D Walt Port Elizabeth, Onderhoof, 1968, George
Meyer J H, 37, Pastoriestraat Alexandria, Geneesheer, 1964, Port Elizabeth
Meyer J J S, 46, Samancor Bestuursdienste Potgietersrus, Mynsekretaris, 1975, Johannesburg
Meyer J P C, 43, Eben Swemmerskool Pretoria, Vise-Hoof, 1964, Heidelberg
Meyer J S, 46, P/A Onderwyskollege Bloemfontein, Dosent, 1968, Pretoria
Meyer J W, 41, Von Abostraat Bothaville, Geneesheer, 1972
Meyer L J, 28, Van der Horst Koshuis Wolmaransstad, Onderwyser, 1964, Bronkhorstspruit
Meyer L W, 27, N G Pastorie Bergville, N G Predikant, 1971, Harrismith
Meyer M, 42, Susanna Reitz, Onderwyser/Boer, 1966, Petrus Steyn
Meyer M G J, 32, P/A Laerskool Thornton, Onderhoof, 1967, Paarl
Meyer M J, 40, P/A Veiligheidspolisie Pretoria, Majoor, 1969, Kaapstad
Meyer P F, 32, P/A Hoërskool Hans Strydom Naboomspruit, Onderwyser, 1963, Melkrivier
Meyer P J (Lid Nr 787), Voorsitter S A U K Johannesburg
Meyer P J, 40, Barkerstraat 28B Kokstad/S A Polisie, Luitenant, 1970, Welkom
Meyer P J S, 43, "Vaalbank" Winterton, Boer, 1967, Ladysmith
Meyer R F v d W, 30, Doringrug Humansdorp, Boer, 1964
Meyer S F, 35, P/A Volkskas Bpk Prieska, Rekenmeester, 1968, Patensie
Meyer T (Lid Nr 1348), Bothaville Voorgestel vir die U R in 1968, Boer/Geneesheer, 1968
Meyer T F, 37, Elandsvlei Bothaville, Boer, 1976, Schweizer-Reneke
Meyer T W S, Johannesburg — Praat oor Rolprente by 1965, Bondsraad
Meyer W, 49, Dis-Al Gobabis, Boer, 1966
Meyer W C, 33, P/A S A Weermag Bloemfontein, Majoor, 1968, Rouxville
Mills B, 46, P/A Dept van Vervoer Pretoria, Ondersekretaris, 1968, Dullstroom
Mills J H T (Lid Nr 4065), Sekretaris van Finansies Umtata Transkei — Voorgestel vir die U R in 1968
Minnaar A G, 39, P/A Hoërskool Fauresmith, Onderwyser, 1975, Edenburg
Minnaar A P, 32, Shipleyweg 5 Nigel, Onderwyser, 1970, Delmas
Minnaar J R, 35, Panorama Kiepersol, Boer, 1971
Minnaar P, 38, P/A RAU Johannesburg, Bibilotekaris, 1976, Durban
Minnaar P A, Posbus 9801 Johannesburg — Amptenaar van die A B 4.2.76
Minnaar W N, 37, Mediese Sentrum 410 Krugersdorp, Geneesheer, 1967, Pretoria
Minnie A P, 47, S A Polisie Groblersdal, Offisier, 1976, Potchefstroom
Mischke E v H E, S A U K Johannesburg, Kosteberekenaar, 1965, Hobhouse
Mitchell J F, 37, Riekertstraat 8 Ontdekkerspark/K O P, Handelbestuurder, 1971, Rustenburg
Mocke C H, 32, Afdelingsraad Kenhardt, Sekretaris, 1964, Citrusdal
Mocke H A, 35, P/A Efataskool vir Blindes Umtata, Hoof, 1969, Rustenburg
Moll J C, 28, U O V S Bloemfontein, Dosent, 1965

Moller C A, 34, P/A L M Nywerhede Bothaville, Bestuurder, 1967, Clocolan
Moller C J, 38, Deputasiestraat 98 Vryheid, Onderwyser, 1973
Möller F J, 42, Soutpansdrift PK Brits, Onderwyser, 1975, Carolina
Moller G S J, (Lid Nr 4083), Stellenbosch Voorgestel vir die U R in 1968, Predikant
Moller H F, 36, Kerkstraat 130 Strand, Rekenmeester, 1964, Welkom
Möller H F S, 36 Waverley Wolseley, Boer/Handellar, 1963
Moller J, 40, Landboudienste Bpk Dewetsdorp, Sakeman, 1964, Ermelo
Möller J L, 30, Telewarrenstraat 20 New Redruth Alberton, Veearts, 1973
Moller J P, 39, P/A B S B Trompsburg, Verteenwoordiger, 1969, Ceres
Möller J P M, 33, Cambellweg 46 Valhalla/S A Weermag, Offisier, 1971, Oudtshoorn
Möller J V, 46, Blakely P/S Kuruman, Boer, 1969
Moller P C, 32, Kerkstraat Prins Albert, Onderwyser, 1974, Jankempdorp
Moller P D S, 45, Platvlei Lichtenburg, Boer, 1966
Möller P du T, 36, Patryskloof PK de Wet Worcester, Boer, 1976, Worcester
Moller W, 31, P/A Volkskool Goedemoed oor Aliwal-Noord, Skoolhoof, 1968, Bloemfontein
Moller W C A, 34, P/A Hoërskool A J Koen Bloemhof, Onderhoof, 1967, Potchefstroom
Moller W C A, 32, 30steLaan 780 Villieria Pretoria, Med Student, 1977, Alberton
Monnig H O (Dr), Lid van die U R se Tegniese & Natuurwetenskap in 1973
Monnig H O, 43, Richmondlaan 38 Aucklandpark Johannesburg, Professor, 1971, Pretoria
Mooi E, 39, P/A Vereeniging Brick & Tile My, Werkebestuurder, 1963, Kaapstad
Moolman A T, 29, P/A S A S & H Johannesburg, Superintendent, 1967, Johannesburg
Moolman H C, 44, Brilsedam van Wyksvlei, Boer, 1965
Moolman H J, 41, S A S & H, 41, S A S & H Klerksdorp, Tegnikus, 1964, Bloemhof
Moolman H J (Lid Nr 6875), Elandsfontein Voorgestel vir die U R in 1968, Sakeman
Moolman H J, Lid van die U R se Jeugkomitee 1973
Moolman H J, 49, Constantia Viljoenskroon, Boer, 1965, Harrismith
Moolman J G, 34, N G Pastorie Queenstown, Predikant, 1968, Lusaka
Moolman J J, 40, PK Melmoth, Boer, 1972, Mkuze
Moolman J N, 28, S A Lugmag Kaapstad, Sersant, 1964, Prieska
Moolman J P F, 33, Universiteit van die Noorde Savenga, Dosent, 1973, Pretoria
Moolman J S, 36, Borderstraat 19 Kroonstad/Hoërskool, Onderwyser, 1972, Ladybrand
Moolman L, 37, N G Pastorie Vishoek, Predikant, 1964, Malmesbury
Moolman L A du T, 35, Standertonse Hoërskool Standerton-Wes, Skoolhof, 1977, Meyerton
Moolman W A, 57, Connanstraat Carnarvon, Rustende Boer, 1974, Mariental
Moore H J A, 42, Dept Onderwys Kuns & Wet Pretoria, Inspekteur Vakopleiding, 1966, Oudtshoorn
Morkel F W, 40, Breyerlaan 41 Waverley/S A B S Pretoria, Voorligter Nas Produktiwiteits Insti, 1977, Lichtenburg
Morkel H J T, 46, Muirweg 27 Rondebosch, Narkotiseur, 1973, Winburg
Morkel H M, 45, Smutsstraat Gobabis/S A Polisie, Majoor, 1973, Brakpan
Morkel J D, 44, P/A Middelbare Skool van Wyksvlei, Hoof, 1966
Morrison G d V (Lid Nr 4078), Cradock — Voorgestel vir die U R in 1968, L V
Mostert A J, 31, Kakamas, Onderwyser, 1965, Garies
Mostert C W, 39, P/A Theron v/d Poel & Kie Kaapstad, Ouditeur, 1965
Mostert F J, 32, S A Polisie Windhoek, Kapelaan, 1967, Petrusville
Mostert G C J, 41, Garies, Boer/Weksvoorman, 1971
Mostert H J G, 33, Sullivan Engineer Johannesburg, Ketelmaker, 1967, Malmesbury
Mostert J, 29, Eastwoodstraat 222 Arcadia Pretoria, Beampte B V S, 1975, Bloemfontein
Mostert J A, 30, Uitsig Bultfontein, Boer, 1972
Mostert J C, 45, Rooivlei PK Grootmist, Boer, 1972, Port Nolloth
Mostert J P, 37, N G Sendingpastorie Empangeni, Predikant, 1967, Louwsberg
Mostert J S, 39, P/A Hoërskool Carolina, Onderhoof, 1964, Zeerust
Mostert L J, 35, P/A S A Polisie Keimoes, Adj-Offisier, 1974, Pretoria
Mostert S H G, 34, P/A Delmas Koöp Bpk, Bestuurder Nywerheid en Ontw, 1975, Bethlehem
Moulder J E, 48, Platklipfontein Dist Pietersburg, Boer/Onderwyser, 1974
Mouton a, 33, Bergstraat 3 Linden-Uitbr, Direkteur, 1971, Johannesburg
Mouton F D (Lid Nr 7704), Fraserburg, Boer, 1962
Mouton H J, 38, Kolkie Tweeling, Boer, 1970
Mouton J A, 39, Kerkstraat Aberdeen/Volkskas, Bestuurder, 1970, Malmesbury

Mouton J C, 34, Moffatstraat 57 Warmbad/Landbou Tegn Dienste, Tegn Beampte, 1970, Pienaarsrivier
Mouton J D, 45, Dept Waterwese Pretoria, Eerste Adm Beampte, 1965, Stellenbosch
Mouton J P, 35, P/A Dept Volkswelsyn en Pensioene Pretoria, Adm Asst, 1968
Mouton L E, 40, P/A Parow-Oos Motors, Motorhandelaar, 1974, Upington
Mouton M M, 30, Kriedouwkrans Citrusdal, Boer, 1976
Mouton N V, 31, P/A Oranjerivierwynkelders/Keimoes, Bestuurder/Wynmaker, 1977, Paarl
Mouton P L, 30, W L Ochse & Kie Johannesburg, Direkteur, 1966
Mouton T H J, 30, Tygerbergstraat 20 Vrijzee Goodwood, Onderhoof, 1976, Goodwood
Mouton W L (Prof), Rektor U O V S Bloemfontein
Mudge P S, 32, Bynadaar Otjiwarongo, Boer, 1964
Mulder A H, 32, P/A Geref Kerk Innesdal Pretoria, Predikant, 1973, Louis Trichardt
Mulder A H, 28, Geref Pastorie Mopanistraat Randfontein, Predikant, 1971, Frankfort
Mulder A H, 39, P/A Sanlam Port elizabeth, Verteenwoordiger/Boer, 1974
Mulder C F, 33, P/A Hoërskool Sannieshof, Vise-Hoof, 1973, Pietersburg
Mulder C P (Lid Nr 4750), Minister van Plurale Betrekkinge — Voorgestel vir die U R in 1968 (Randfontein)
Mulder F E, 40, Volkskas — Edenville, Bestuurder, 1966, Pretoria
Mulder H P P (Manie), Wes-Randse Bantoesake — Administrasieraad
Mulder J C, 44, Hoër Seunskool Helpmekaar Johannesburg, Onderhoof, 1966, Brits
Mulder M S, 32, Cloetestraat 84 Ermelo, Onderwyser, 1965, Pretoria
Mulder M W, 43, Voortrekker Winkels Bethal, Asst Bestuurder, 1970, Ogies
Mulder P F S, 29, P/A Prov Vissery Inst Lydenburg, Hoof, 1974, Potchefstroom
Muller A L, 35, P/A Sanlam Bellville, Uitv Beampte, 1967, Johannesburg
Muller A M, 35, Klipbank Brandfort, Boer, 1967
Muller c, 31, Piet Retiefstraat 39 Standerton, Apteker, 1975, Warden
Muller C J, 37, P/A Direktoraat van Burgerlike Beskerming Pretoria, Adm Beampte, 1969, Kempton Park
Muller C M, 57, P/A Dept Handel en Nywerheid Pretoria, Staatsamaptenaar, 1968
Muller C P, 33, Chattan Humansdorp, Boer, 1969, Salisbury
Muller D v d B, 41, P/A S A Polisie Vereeniging, Kaptein, 1967, Durban
Muller E C C, 41, Dewetstraat 69 Horison/G O K, Dosent, 1970, Potchefstroom
Muller E R, 40, Vygielaan Flamieda Klerksdorp, Vise-Hoof, 1974, Ottosdal
Muller G L (Jr), 36, Lovedale Lindley, Boer, 1964
Muller Hilgard (Lid Nr 3380), Voormalige Minister van Buitelandse Sake
Muller H C, 41, Theron v/d Poel & Kie Kaapstad, Ouditeur, 1964, Riviersonderend
Muller H W, 29, P/A Nas Bouvereniging Bloemfontein, Onderbestuurder, 1968, Port Elizabeth
Muller H W S, 40, Volkskas Marquard, Bestuurder, 1967, Pretoria
Muller J A, 43, P/A Die Gevangenis Christiana, Opperbewaarder, 1968, Kroonstad
Muller J A, 33, Uitkyk Bultfontein, Boer, 1974
Muller J A, 41, Skadudal Herbertsdale, Boer, 1974
Müller J C, 29, Reginaldweg 29 Primroseheuwel, N G Predikant, 1977, Nigel
Muller J J F, 46, P/A Hoër Tegn skool Benoni, Onderwyser, 1969, Saldanha
Muller J J P, 32, N H Pastorie Bronkhorstspruit, Predikant, 1973, Pretoria
Muller J J v d L (Lid Nr 7690), Duiwelskloof S A Polisie, Sersant, 1962
Muller J L, 34, P/A Stadsraad Orkney, Klerk van die raad, 1976, Kempton Park
Muller J P, 32, Hoër Tegniese Skool Ficksburg, Onderwyser, 1973
Muller J R, 26, P/A Laerskool H F Verwoerd Kimberley, Onderwyser, 1968, Wolseley
Muller M J, 27, De cypher Carnarvon, Boer, 1977
Muller N C, 29, Cradockstraat 104, Graaff-Reinet, Prokureur, 1966, Kaapstad
Muller P, 35, P/A Landdroskantoor Fouriesburg, Landdros, 1974, Alexandria
Muller P H, Stellenbosch
Muller P J, 39, S A Vloot Simonstad, Luit-Kommandeur, 1963, Saldanha
Muller P J, 47, Laerskool Hangklip Queenstown, Hoof, 1965, Cathcart
Muller R T, 31, P/A Union Corporation Evander, Personeelbeampte, 1969, Springs
Muller S L, Minister van Vervoer
Muller T F (Lid Nr 3511), Yskor Johannesburg — Voorgestel vir die U R in 1968
Munnik A G, 32, P/A N G Pastorie Môregloed Pretoria, Predikant, 1964

Munnik J P, Praat oor Hartenbos Museum by 1966 se Bondsraad
Murray J K, 29, Landbou Tegniese Dienste Stellenbosch, PR Ing Ingenieursdns, 1973
Murray S, 40, V/D Vyverstraat Meiringspark Klerksdorp/Hoërskool Schoonspruit, Onderhoof, 1971, Florida
Mussman L E L, 30, Idastraat 11 Oberholzer, Onderwyser, 1964, Pretoria
Myburg A, 30, P/A Geref Pastorie Swartruggens, Predikant, 1967, Matlabas
Myburg G J C, 34, Uitvalse Barkly-Oos, Boer, 1969
Myburgh A, 39, P/A S A Spoorweë Pietersburg, Snr Klerk, 1975
Myburgh A A, 37, Hoërskool Genl Martiz Pietermaritzburg, Prinsipaal, 1972, Drierivier
Myburgh A J, 36, R O N H Pretoria, Asst Direkteur, 1964
Myburgh A P, 51, Nederlandse Bankgebou Pretoria, Advokaat, 1965
Myburgh A P R, 32, Parkweg 84 Oudtshoorn/Saadskoonmaakafdeling, Afdelingshoof, 1973
Myburgh B J, 34, Volkskas Bpk Vredefort, Bestuurder, 1965, Pretoria
Myburgh C C, 43, N G Kerk Sonhoogte, Predikant, 1975, Langlaagte
Myburgh C J (Lid Nr 7771), Springs, 1963
Myburgh E J, 38, Suidstraat 6 Swartruggens, Skoolhoof, 1973, Tuinplaats
Myburgh G, 27, P/A Hoërskool Kempton Park, Onderwyser, 1963, Lichtenburg
Myburgh H G, 34, Geduld Petrus Steyn, Boer, 1975, Johannesburg
Myburgh J H, 33, Suid-Westelike Koöp Mosselbaai, Hoofklerk, 1968, Steytlerville
Myburgh J J, 39, P/A Libanon Goudmyn Westonaria, Tekenaar, 1965, Bank
Myburgh J J, 29, Kingsheath Petrusburg, Boer, 1975
Myburgh J S, 36, P/A Vogelstruisbult-Myn Springs, Elektrisiën, 1964
Myburgh W H, 34, P/A Hoërskool Outjo, Onderhoof, 1966, Windhoek
Myburgh W P, 39, P/A Munisipaliteit Springs, Elek Inst Inspekteur, 1968
McDonald A T, 33, P/A N H Gemeente Bethal, Predikant, 1968, Dendron
McDonald D, 31, P/A Koedoe-Apteek Vanderbijlpark, Apteker, 1968, Pretoria
McFarlae L R, 27, Paul Roos Gimnasium Stellenbosch, Onderwyser, 1967, George
McFarlane L S, Praat oor Voortrekkers by 1966 se Bondsraad
McLachlan R (Dr), Kommisaris — Genl vir Lebowa was gereelde skakel by Parlement, L V Westdene
McLaren P J (Lid Nr 7703), Bloemfontein, Skoolhoof, 1962

N

Nagel A J, 42, P/A N G Kerk Aroab, Predikant, 1974, Stellenbosch
Nagel J J A, 43, Hoërskool Kalahari Kuruman, Onderwyser, 1976, Springbok
Nagel R, Ouditeur van A B
Naude A J, 38, Bloemhof Richmond K P, Boer, 1965
Naudé A P, 30, Posmeesterhuis Hoofstraat Utrecht, Posmeester, 1972, Harrismith
Naude A S, Lichtenburg — By 1969 se Bondsraad vra hy wat is beleid oor samewerking met Volksvreemde Organisasies
Naude B, Timberonstraat 9, Paarl (Skakel by SAOU-kongres, 1975)
Naude B C, 38, P/A Sasbank Roodepoort, Takbestuurder, 1968, Germiston
Naude B C S J, 32, P/A Opleidingskollege Paarl, Dosent, 1970, Stellenbosch
Naudé C, 41, P/A Prov Koshuis Groot Marico, Onderwyser, 1975, Middelburg Tvl
Naude C F, 37, McCabespruit Clocolan, Boer, 1977
Naude C J, 24, S A Polisie Cornelia, Sersant, 1972, Frankfort
Naude C P, 38, N G Pastorie Tzaneen, Predikant, 1969, Welkom
Naude F P, 48, Haaskraal Richmond, Boer, 1977
Naude H H, 31, P/A J J Serfontein-Hoërskool Queenstown, Onderwyser, 1964
Naude J, Posbus 9801 Johannesburg, 1967
Naude J I v Z, 36, Niekerksfontein Richmond K P, Boer, 1975
Naude M J, 45, N H Gemeente Robertsham, Predikant, 1968, Pretoria
Naude P J, 39, P/A N F S Tractors Wesselsbron, Bestuurder, 1967, Maseru
Naude R T, 34, Wellingtonstraat 20 Irene, Landboukundige, 1967, Krugersdorp
Naude S C M, Opvoedkundige
Naude S J (Lid Nr 788), Saakgelastigde van N G Kerk — Lid van die U R 1964 & 1965 — Lid van die U R se Ekonomiese Komitee 1973 (Bloemfontein)

Naudé S J, 25, Kollegelaan 1 Bloemfontein, Prokureur, 1963
Naude S M (Dr) (Lid Nr 2033), W N N R Pretoria Wetenskaplikle Advisuer vir Eerste Minister, President
Naude W I J, 47, P/A Yskor Pretoria, Sweiser, 1968
Naude W L E, 41, Reitzstraat 29 Vrede, Apteker, 1967, Heilbron
Neethling D A, 34, Swerwerskraal PK Limburg, Boer/Veearts, 1972, Potgietersrus
Neethling f, 37, Mountainviewsingel 15 Durbell Durbanville, Sakeman, 1977, Parow-Noord
Neethling J A, 30, Rondefontein Smithfield, Boer, 1975
Neethling J C (Dr), Dept van Landbou, Snr Amptenaar, 1973
Neethling J M, 30, Swerwerskraal PK Limburg, Boer, 1966, Potgietersrus
Neethling M de V, 30, Herschellstraat 109 Strand, Ingenieur, 1968, Klipdale
Neethling S W, 41, Dept Landbou Pretoria/P/A Minister v Landbou, Privaat Sekretaris, 1974
Nel A, 39, P/A Dept Aardrykskunde Univ van Stellenbosch, Professor, 1963, Worcester
Nel B M, 37, Dahlialaan 110 Doringkloof Verwoerdburg, Navorsingsbeampte Sabra, 1977, Swaziland
Nel C, 27, Sendingpastorie Philipstown, Sendeling, 1965, Keimoes
Nel C H, 35, Leniana PK Messina, Onderwyser, 1972
Nel C J, 32, P/A U O V S Bloemfontein, Snr Lektor, 1968, Hertzogville
Nel C J, 39, P/A Senekal Landbou Koöp, Hoofbestuurder, 1976, Pretoria
Nel C P, 45, P/A Meyer Nel & Kie Bellville, Prokureur, 1963, Wellington
Nel D P, 37, Hagilla Vierfontein, Boer, 1967
Nel D H, 43, Leeukuil 56 Sannieshof, Boer, 1966, Rietspruit
Nel D S, 28, P/A Hoërskool Vanderbijlpark, Onderwyser, 1967
Nel E P, 31, Rondawel Brandfort, Boer, 1970
Nel F, 30, Drakensberg Boekh (Edms) Bpk/Sakabulalaan 1 Yellowwood Park Durban, Bestuurder, 1977, Matatiele
Nel F D, 44, Duinekraal Grootfontein, Boer, 1977, Calvinia
Nel F v V, 37,Willow Terrace 12 Benoni/Van Aswegen Brs, Direkteur, 1976, Pretoria
Nel G, 37, S A Polisie Roodepoort, Speurder, 1965, Krugersdorp
Nel G H, 34, Lutherstraat 22 Windhoek/S A Polisie, Werwingsoffisier, 1977, Mafeking
Nel G S, 30, Kinderoord mir Smit Ugie, Onderwyser/Huisvader, 1972, Dordrecht
Nel H du P, 41, P/A Mieliebeheerraad Pretoria, Adm Beampte, 1964, Ficksburg
Nel H J, 41, P/A Maricodraaiskool PK Derdepoort, Skoolhoof, 1969, Pretoria
Nel H J, 44, Kujam Pofadder, Boer, 1971
Nel H W, 30, Maskewstraat 45 Rowhill Springs, Geneesheer, 1971, Pretoria
Nel J, 38, P/A Nas Suiwelkoöperasie Wesselsbron, Bestuurder, 1976, Heilbron
Nel J A, 36, Tambotiestraat 4 Newcastle, Supt Poskantoor, 1974, Estcourt
Nel J A, 31, Sonop PK Hertzog, Boer, 1969
Nel J A C, 29, Fanthorpeweg 213 Mondeor/Winchester Ridge Skool, Adjunk-Hoof, 1976, Johannesburg
Nel J C, 36, Boshoffstraat 48 Linton Grange, Skoolhoof, 1967, Vryburg
Nel J F, 37, Seunskoshuis Parys, Onderwyser, 1975, De Aar
Nel J G, 29, George Stegmann-Hospitaal Saulspoort, Sekretaris, 1964, Lichtenburg
Nel J H, 35, D F Malanrylaan 201 Northcliffe Johannesburg, Sakeman/Uitv Beampte (Overvaal Melkvervoer), 1977
Nel J H, 33, Randfontein Estates Goudmyn, Skofbaas, 1965
Nel J H, 28, P/A Landbou Koöp Vanrhynsdorp, Rekenmeester, 1967, Worcester
Nel J J, 40, P/A Volkskas Bpk Edenville, Bestuurder, 1970, Brits
Nel J J, 38, P/A Poskantoor Trompsburg, Posmeester, 1976, Alexanderbaai
Nel J J, 45, Agstestraat 88 Walvisbaai, Majoor/Distrikskommandant, 1971, Windhoek
Nel J L, 30, S A Polisie Barkly-Oos, Adj-Offisier, 1976
Nel J R, 30, Meisieskoshuis Leliehof, Onderwyser, 1977, Tweeling
Nel J S, 36, P/A Die Boere Koöp Versekeringsmaatskappy Paarl, Bestuurder, 1967, Malmesbury
Nel J v d L, 47, P/A Hoër Handelskool Uitenhage, Skoolhoof, 1970, Reivilo
Nel J W, 33, Gimnasium Hoërskool Potchefstroom, Onderwyser, 1969, Bloemfontein
Nel L A, 29, Doornsloot Vaalwater, Boer, 1974, Melkrivier
Nel L A, 40, N H Pastorie Volksrust, N H Predikant, 1972, Ellisras
Nel L C, 38, Saambou Pretoria, Ontwikkelingsbestuurder, 1965, Johannesburg

Nel M J, 46, Dept van Gevangenis Pretoria, Brigadier, 1964, Pietersburg
Nel M J, 42, P/A Poskantoor Port Elizabeth, Hoof Supt, 1977, Pretoria
Nel M S, 32, Bereaweg 4 Ladysmith, Tandarts, 1966, Pretoria
Nel M S, 44, Hopewell Lady Grey, Boer, 1966
Nel N, 41, Perseel 67 Pongola, Suikerboer, 1971
Nel N E, 32, P/A Univ van Zoeloeland, Snr Lektor, 1975, Stellenbosch
Nel N J, 34, S A U K Durban, Nuusredakteur, 1965, Pietermaritzburg
Nel P A, 33, Brandwagstraat 140 Silverton, Professor Unisa, 1972, Bloemfontein
Nel P A E, 33, S A Karakoelkoöp Upington, Handelsbestuurder, 1977, Ceres
Nel P C, 36, Meisieskoshuis Swakopmund, Onderwyser, 1969, Usakos
Nel P F, 46, P/A S A S & H Durban, Ouditeur, 1969, Oos-Londen
Nel P G, 37, Hoërskool Wonderboom-Suid, Onderhoof, 1965, Johannesburg
Nel P H E, 29, Hoërskool Koster, Onderwyser, 1971, Schweizer-Reneke
Nel P J, 41, Dept Inligting Pretoria, Inligtingsbeampte, 1964, smithfield
Nel P J, 44, Nuwestraat Pofadder, Boer/Sakeman, 1975
Nel P J C, 30, Sandrivierweg 82 Virginia, Geneesheer, 1967, Winburg
Nel R F, 27, "Avondale" Matatiele, Boer, 1977, Warmbad Tvl
Nel S J, 37, Boomplaas Lydenburg, Boer/Sakeman, 1974, Pretoria
Nel T C, 37, Hoër Tegniese Skool Pietermaritzburg, Hoof, 1964, Potchefstroom
Nel W A, 34, P/A Pietersburg Prov Hospitaal, Geneesheer, 1975, Pretoria
Nel W A S, 40, Tshilidzini Sendinghospitaal PK Shayandima, Hospitaalsekretaris, 1970, Pietersburg
Nel W J, 39, P/A Penge Asbestos (Edms) Bpk Pk Penge, Skofbaas, 1970, Senekal
Nel W S, 47, P/A S A Polisie Lady Grey, Sersant, 1974, Aliwal-Noord
Nell H J, 39, P/A Hoërskool Lindley, Skoolhoof, 1976, Koffiefontein
Nell J, 40, Varsitystraat 7 Tamboerskloof/Sanlam, Verteenwoordiger, 1970, Jansenville
Nell L J J, 34, P/A N H Pastorie Groblersdal, Predikant, 1975, Empangeni
Nell N J P, 40, P/A Stadsraad Kempton Park, Snr Adm Asst, 1973, Pretoria
Nelson H D, 33, Molenstraat 69 Potchefstroom, Dosent, 1971, Kimberley
Nelson J D, 39, Jansenstraat 15 Worcester, N G Predikant, 1976, Upington
Neser C, Wolmaransstad — op N P Komitee 1966
Neuhoff A F, 35, Louw Wepener 43 Vanderbijlpark, Skoolhoof/Ankerskool, 1972, Vereeniging
Nezar C W H, 38, Doornfontein PK Ottosdal, Boer, 1965
Niehaus A S, 46, Gummed Tapes Johannesburg, Verkoopsbestuurder, 1969, Kaapstad
Niehaus H W, 48, Munisipaliteit Citrusdal, Stadsklerk, 1976, George
Niehaus J H, 34, Elandstraat 29, Louis Trichardt, Oogkundige, 1977, Ladysmith
Niehaus P E, 39, P/A Ninham Shand & Vennote Kaapstad, Ingenieur, 1974, Strand
Nieman J J, 38, P/A Sasol Sasolburg, Asst Voorman, 1974, Hennenman
Nieman P J, 33, P/A N G Sendingpastorie Senekal, Sendeling, 1969, Upington
Nieman W A, 37, Volkskas Bpk Warden, Bestuurder, 1964, Boksburg
Niemand C W P, 44, Keithlaan 6 Pinepark Johannesburg, Boukontrakteur, 1969
Niemand J H, Sekretaris — Dept Gemeenskapsbou — Lid van die U R se Beplannings Komitee 1973
Niemand J J, 39, S A S & H Pietermaritzburg, Ketelmaker, 1966, Oos-Londen
Niemandt A D, 46, Wonderfontein Oberholzer, Boer, 1967, Zeerust
Niemandt A D, 40, Tsessebeweg 8 Nimrodpark/Springfield Body Builders, Bestuurder, 1970, Kempton Park
Niemann J J, 35, P/A S A S & H Bloemfontein, Klerk, 1964, Boshof
Nienaber A G, 36, P/A Munisipaliteit Hennenman, Asst Stadstesourier, 1967, Bethlehem
Nienaber J, 43, P/A Dept van Bantoe-Onderwys Vryheid, Inspekteur, 1969, Rouxville
Nienaber J J (Hanko), 31, P/A N O K Johannesburg, Hoofampt Bemarking, 1973
Nienaber P J, 32, Vredesverdrag Hennenman, Boer, 1974, Johannesburg
Nienaber P J (Prof)
Nienaber S P, 30, P/A S A Polisie Mbazwane, Adj-Offisier, 1968, Pietermaritzburg
Nieuwoudt A E C, 40, Hoofstraat Keimoes, Geregsbode/Boer, 1965
Nieuwoudt A J A, 39, Volkskas Bpk Benoni/Pretoriaweg 114 Rynfield, Rekenmeester, 1970, Wesselsbron
Nieuwoudt C F, 38, Universiteit Pretoria (Voorsitter van Noord-Tvlse Atletiekvereniging) Snr Lektor, 1965

Nieuwoudt D J, 37, Dept Mynwese Alexanderbaai, Werktuigkundige, 1965, Van Van Rhynsdorp
Nieuwoudt E, 41, P/A X O K Oos-Londen, Sekretaris, 1974, Umtata
Nieuwoudt E A, 31, Norbreck-Gebou 306 Tramwaystraat Kenilworth, Prokureursklerk, 1972, Johannesburg
Nieuwoudt E H W, 35, P/A S A Weermag Pretoria, Kommandant, 1975, Upington
Nieuwoudt G, 33, 12eLaan 17 Dagamapark Simonstad, Luit-Komdr, 1967, Saldanha
Niewoudt G G, 47, Staatsdelwery Alexanderbaai, Magasynmeester, 1964, Clanwilliam
Nieuwoudt G S, 41 P/A Bantoebewysburo Pretoria, Vingerafdrukdeskundige 1968
Nieuwoudt J, 36, Pigeonrylaan 3 Yellowwood Durban/PHK, Klerk Personeelafd, 1971, Pietermaritzburg
Nieuwoudt J A F, 31, Derryweg 4 Rondebosch, Teologiese Student, 1974, Wellington
Nieuwoudt J J, 46, Vlootkollege Gordonsbaai, Kaptein, 1974, Vishoek
Nieuwoudt J J, 48, Poplarlaan 18 Thornton/Prof Hosp Dienste Kaapstad, Ingenieur, 1970, Klawer
Nieuwoudt K J, 28, P/A S A Reserwebank Pretoria, Noteklerk, 1973, Pretoria
Nieuwoudt M M, 41, P/A N G Kerkkantoor Windhoek, Saakgelastigde, 1968, Ofjiwarongo
Nieuwoudt R W J, 37, Pres Steynstraat 27 Upington, Rekenmeester, F C U, 1973, Karasburg
Nigrini L M 28, Hoërskool Hopetown, Onderwyser, 1967, Vaalharts
Noeth J G, 41, Merino PK Vanzylsrus, Boer, 1969
Nöffke C F, 39, Die Transvaler Johannesburg, Redakteur, 1969, Londen
Nolte C B, 32, P/A Dept van Kultuursake Kimberley, Skakelbeampte, 1969, De Aar
Nolte G E, 37, Kleinfontein PK Groot Marico, Onderwyser, 1972, Heidelberg Tvl
Nolte J H, 40, De Rust PK Windmeul, Boer, 1969, Paarl
Nolte J v d L, 37, Kingfisherlaan 99 Elspark, Elsburg, Adjunk-Hoof, 1976, Alberton
Northnagel J A, 41, Elandsfontein Grasmere, Diamantslyper, 1968
Nortier D J, 36, Goedhartsingel 8 Bloemfontein, Prokureur, 1975, Worcester
Nortier W du T, 40, Vredelaan Ladismith K P, Skoolhoof, 1977, Herbertsdale
Nortje A C L, 37, Volkskool Rheederpark Welkom, Skoolhoof, 1968, Somerset-Oos
Nortje E P, 39, S A Polisie Stellenbosch, Speurdersersant, 1966, Oudtshoorn
Nortje D H, 33, Swartstraat 13 Nylstroom, Onderhoof, 1973, Potgietersrus
Nortjé J D, 34, Van Zylstraat 72 Brandfort, Skoolhoof, 1971, Bloemfontein
Nortje J H, 39, Vaalwater Fraserburg, Boer, 1964
Nortje N Z, 39, Danie Theronstraat 182 Pretoria-Noord, Skakelbeampte U P, 1976
Nortjé R, 32, Greylingstraat Harrismith, Apteker, 1963, Bethulie
Nortje S J, 38, P/A V Rensburg Boukontrakteurs/Camelfordweg 18 New Redruth Alberton, Boekhouer/Bestuurder, 1977, Johannesburg
Nortjé W, 38, P/A Volkskas Odendaalsrus, Bestuurder, 1963, Brits
Norval C D, 32, Stillerus Adelaide, Boer, 1964
Northnagel A E, 28, P/A Adj-Minister van Bantoesake & Ontwikkeling Pretoria, Privaatsekretaris, 1967
Nothnagel A J, 40, Horakstraat 27 Denneburg Paarl/Laerskool Drakenstein, Skoolhoof, 1976, Somerset-Wes
Nothnagel D C, 41, P/A S A Polisie Keimoes, Adj-Offisier, 1968, Ariamsvlei S W A
Notley P, 31, P/A Noordskool Sasolburg, Onderhoof, 1969, Heilbron

O

Obbes T J, 32, Barnardostraat 8 Kimberley, Prokureur, 1973, Johannesburg
Oberholster A G, 38, Coghillweg 78 Lynnwood Glen, Navorser-R G N, 1976, Bloemfontein
Oberholster A J, 30, De Villiersspruit PK Hamab, Boer, 1967, Karasburg
Oberholster E L P, 28, Kuruman, N G Predikant, 1966, Stellenbosch
Oberholster J J (Lid Nr 4444), Professor — U O V S Bloemfontein — Voorgestel vir die U R in 1968
Oberholzer D S, 27, Voortrekkerstraat Nieuwoudtville, Sakeman, 1968, Calvinia
Oberholzer G J, 36, Gordonweg 81 Northcliff Johannesburg, Adjunk-Hoof, 1976
Oberholzer J C, 33, P/A Hoërskool Outjo, Onderhoof, 1969, Gobabis
Oberholzer J F, 32, PK Marken Oor Potgietersrus, Geneesheer, 1963, Groot Marico
Oberholzer J H, 46, Hoofstraat Tsumeb, Sakeman, 1966, Kanoneiland
Oberholzer J P (Lid Nr 7402), Voorgestel vir die U R in 1968, Predikant, Pretoria

Oberholzer S O, 45, Drakensburg Ko-op Bpk Bethlehem, Kredietbestuurder, 1969, Warden
Ochse W L, 46, P/A Laerskool Glencoe, Onderhoof, 1969, Empangeni
Odendaal A A (Lid Nr 4098), Kestell Voorgestel vir die U R 1968 — Lid van die U R se Nie-Blanke Komitee 1973, Sendeling/Rektor
Odendaal A C, 31, P/A Munisipaliteit Kroonstad, Interne Ouditeur, 1968, Lindley
Odendaal A D, 39, P/A S A S Bedryfsafd Johannesburg, Klerk, 1974, Durban
Odendaal C H, 34, Laerskool Mountain View Pretoria, Onderhoof, 1966
Odendaal D C, 39, Cassilis PK Thomasrivier, Boer, 1964, Cathcart
Odendaal F H, 44, P/A Landboufakulteit Universiteit van Natal Pietermaritzburg, Rekenmeester, 1967, Bloemfontein
Odendaal F J, 44, P/A Rondalia Pretoria, Direkteur Toerisme, 1975, Pretoria
Odendaal G J B, 30, Mareestraat 16 Vrede, Tandarts, 1965, Pretoria
Odendaal J E, 33, Eskol Harrismith, Boer, 1975
Odendaal J G (Lid Nr 7740), Roodepoort, 1963
Odendaal J G, S A Polisiekollege Pretoria, Predikant, 1971
Odendaal L P, 41, Pres Steynstraat Memel, Skoolhoof, 1972, Vredefort
Odendaal P J, 41, Colinweg 17 Eldoraigne/Volkskas Elektr Data-Werking, Onderbestuurder, 1975, Pretoria
Odendaal P J, 45, Pikkewynlaan 35 Monumentpark Pretoria, Asst Direkteur Beplanning, 1976
Oelofse A N, 27, Nuwestraat 4 Dordrecht, Prokureur, 1964
Oelofse J C, 35, P/A Smit Peens & Oelofse Pretoria, Prokureur, 1965, Dordrecht
Oelofse L A, 26, Krigestraat Laingsburg, Geneesheer, 1969, Bellville
Oelofse L J, 46, Buffelskloof Sterkstroom (Oud-Lid), Boer, 1963, Hofmeyr
Oelofse N J, 40, Plaas Hoases Otjiwarongo, Boer, 1967, Outjo
Oelofse W R, 33, Seunskoshuis Claredonlaan Witbank, Onderwyser, 1971, Pretoria
Oelofsen R P, 30 P/A Sanlam Joubertina, Verteenwoordiger, 1968, Humansdorp
Oelofsen W, 34, 7deLaan Walmer Port Elizabeth/Universiteit Port Elizabeth, Professor, 1970, Pretoria
Oeschger P H, 33, Moleseylaan 24 Aucklandpark Johannesburg, Adj-Hoofbibliotekaris R A U, 1972
Oliver J J, 43, S A Polisie Honeydew, Adj-Offisier, 1974
Oliver J M, 41, P/A Volkskas Ficksburg, Bestuurder, 1968, Virginia
Olivier A J, 38, P/A Klein Karoo Landbou Koöp Oudtshoorn, Asst Hoofbestuurder/Sekretaris, 1968, Upington
Olivier A J, 43, Mynrust Dewetsdorp, Boer, 1973, Dewetsdorp
Olivier A S, 39, Prov Koshuis Hendrina, Skoolhoof, 1966, Klerksdorp
Olivier B J, 32, Drilrivier Clanwilliam, Boer, 1974
Olivier E, 32, Klopperstraat 159 Rustenburg, N G Predikant, 1972, Primrose
Olivier F B, 42, Dept Bantoe-Onderwys Tzaneen, Inspekteur, 1964, Pietersburg
Olivier F J, 38, P/A Afrikaanse Springstowwe en Chem Nywerhede Somerset-Wes, Superintendent, 1968, Stellenbosch
Olivier G C, 38, Wilcocksweg 29 Noordhoek Bloemfontein, N G Predikant, 1976, Bainsvlei
Olivier G C, 46, Universiteit Fort Hare PK Fort Hare, Professor, 1973, Pretoria
Olivier G C J J, 30, Hoewe 101 Shannon, Tel Tegn/P & T, 1977
Olivier G J C, 34, Elgarstraat 43, Vanderbijlpark, Sakeman, 1976, Nelspruit
Olivier I du P, 34, Berlin PK Petrus Steyn, Onderwyser, 1975, Bloemfontein
Olivier J, 33, P/A Opleidingskollege Oudtshoorn, Dosent, 1973, Parow
Olivier J H, 29, G O Kollege Eaglestraat Cottesloe Johannesburg, Snr Dosent, 1965, Pretoria
Olivier J H, 44, S A S & H Durban, Snr Klerk, 1977
Olivier J J, 34, Western Holdings Welkom, Monsternemer, 1964, Villiers
Olivier J J C, 29, P/A S A U K Bloemfontein, Omroeper, 1977
Olivier J L, 40, Olivier Burger & Du Toit/Ruggstraat 4 Kimberley, Geneesheer, 1973, Alicedale
Olivier J P J, 33, P/A Radio Bantoe Johannesburg, Nuusredakteur, 1966, Ladybrand
Olivier M J, 33, P/A Afrika — Instituut Pretoria, Navorsingsbeampte, 1964, Oudtshoorn
Olivier M J, 40, "Die Punt" Tweeriviere Langkloof, Boer, 1974
Olivier M J P, 44, P/A N G Pastorie Potchefstroom-Suid, Predikant, 1965, Delmas
Olivier N E, 46, P/A Dept van Arbeid Pretoria, Adm Beampte, 1968

Olivier P J S, 27, Gansvlei Koffiefontein, Boer, 1965
Olivier R, 37, Montery-Woonstelle Witbank, Geneesheer, 1966, Pretoria
Olivier S P, Rektor — Indiër Kollege Durban — Voorgestel vir die U R in 1968
Olivier T, 39, Goedgeloof Tweerivieren, Boer, 1972, Langkloof
Olivier W A S, 35, Uitkyk 612 L S Pietersburg, Boer, 1975
Olivier W G, 39, P/A Munisipaliteit Leeudoringstad, Stadsklerk/Tesourier, 1967, Klerksdorp
Olivier W J, 39, Kantoor van die Eerste Minister, Privaatsekretaris, 1967, Ladybrand
Olls W J, 40, Skoolplein Tulbagh, Skoolhoof, 1965, Humansdorp
Oosthuizen A J G, Voormalige Moderator van die N H Kerk, Predikant
Oosthuizen B J M, 40, S A Polisie Klerksdorp, Luitenant, 1967, Pretoria
Oosthuizen C J, 39, P/A Santam Kaapstad, Onderskrywingsbestuurder, 1971, Springs
Oosthuizen C J, 45, P/A Landdroskantoor Parys, Landdros, 1974, Bethal
Oosthuizen D J, 39, Clivedon Close 2 Salisbury/Sanlam, Bestuurder, 1970, Pietersburg
Oosthuizen F J, 37, Hoërskool Wessel Maree Odendaalsrus, Onderhoof, 1971, Viljoenskroon
Oosthuizen G C, 31, Die Landbank Lichtenburg, Snr Klerk, 1964, Hartbeesfontein
Oosthuizen G F, 38, Hoërskool Steynsburg, Skoolhoof, 1964, Dordrecht
Oosthuizen G H, 32, P/A Laerskool Voorwaarts Mamagalieskraal, Skoolhoof, 1970, Vereeniging
Oosthuizen G L (Dr), 31, Keulderweg Boksburg, 1963
Oosthuizen G L, 39, P/A Unisa Pretoria, Dosent, 1975
Oosthuizen G V E, 36, Amanxala Komatipoort, Winkelier/Boer, 1967, Pretoria
Oosthuizen H J, 34, Uniestaalkorp Vereeniging, Marknavorser, 1964, Frankfort
Oosthuizen J C, 32, Dudley Smithstraat 2 Boksburg, Geneesheer, 1972, Boksburg
Oosthuizen J F, 51, Bospan PK Carletonville, Boer, 1965, Albertinia
Oosthuizen J H, 45, Rietgat Koppies, Boer, 1977, Viljoenskroon
Oosthuizen J H, 42, P/A U O V S Bloemfontein, Snr Lektor, 1975, Heilbron
Oosthuizen J H J, 30, N G Pastorie Reddersburg, N G Predikant, 1970, Lady Grey
Oosthuizen J S, 37, Voortrekkerstraat Calitzdorp, Boer, 1966
Oosthuizen L, 34, P/A Dee Bee Afd Winkel Harrismith, Bestuurder, 1975, Ladysmith Natal
Oosthuizen L, 34, Gamka-Oos, Calitzdorp, Boer, 1970
Oosthuizen L D, 28, Clivedonhof 8 Diep Rivier Kaapstad, Ontw/Tekenaar, 1974
Oosthuizen L M, 38, Kirkwood, 1963
Oosthuizen M C C, 33, P/A Stadsraad Piet Retief, Stadsklerk, 1973, Umtata
Oosthuizen N J, 48, Gouritzmond PK Avondrust oor Albertinia, Alg Handelaar, 1963
Oosthuizen N J, 34, Raubenheimerstraat 125 Heilbron, Onderwyser, 1971
Oosthuizen N J, 42, Skoolstraat Swellendam, Onderwyser, 1968, Kraaifontein
Oosthuizen N L, 38, Marestraat Viljoenskroon, Apteker, 1973
Oosthuizen O, 43, P/A S A S & H Pietersburg, Distriksing, 1969, Johannesburg
Oosthuizen P, 36, Regsfakulteit Universiteit van Pretoria, Professor, 1973
Oosthuizen P C, 35, Hamiltonstraat 41 Harrismith, Onderwyser, 1972, Villiers
Oosthuizen P du T, 35, PK Sibasa, Landboukundige, 1974, Pietersburg
Oosthuizen P E, 28, N G Pastorie Aranos, Predikant, 1977, Pretoria
Oosthuizen P J, 32, PK Rietkuil/P/A Evkom, Snr Leierhand Instrumentasie, 1977, Sasol
Oosthuizen P P, 40, Proteapark Wolseley/S A Polisie, Adj-Offisier, 1971, Kaapstad
Oosthuizen R, 36, McKensiestraat 1 Vryburg, N G Predikant, 1972, Bultfontein
Oosthuizen R K, 36, Noudonzies Aughrabies, Boer, 1964
Oosthuizen S J D, 47, Seringboom Tsumeb, Boer/Sakeman, 1969, Outjo
Oosthuizen W C, 42, N G Kerk Skoonspruit, Predikant, 1967, Petrus Steyn
Oosthuizen W J, 40, Rooiheuwel Albertinia, Boer, 1964
Oosthuizen W J, 33, Charl Cillierstraat 82A Standerton, Geneesheer, 1973, Pretoria
Oosthuizen W J, 43, P/A Volkskas Cradock, Rekenmeester, 1969, Virginia
Oosthuizen W M, 38, S A Polisie Ladysmith, Speur Sersant, 1965, Tweespruit
Oosthuysen J H, 31, P/A Wes-Tvl Bantoe Admin Raad Potchefstroom, Direkteur Tegn Dienste, 1975, Pretoria
Oosthuysen W T, 36, Bothastraat Lady Grey, Skoolhoof, 1966, Ugie
Openshaw L J, 39, Laerskool Rynfield Benoni, Onderhoof, 1967
Opperman A J P, 40, Crosleyweg 7 Oos-Londen, Onderwyser, 1965, Cala
Opperman A W S, 33, Christina Ficksburg, Boer, 1976, Jankempdorp

Opperman B J, 38, Ernststraat 24 Jansenpark Boksburg, Onderwyser, 1970
Opperman C M, 35, Hakou Gobabis, Boer, 1974
Opperman C P J, 35, Universal Motors Otjiwarongo, Rekenmeester, 1965, Usakos
Opperman D H, 38, Delmas Steenkoolmyn, Hospitaal Supt, 1975, Kroonstad
Opperman D J, 40, Sabiweg 11 Selcourt Springs, Asst Elektr Ing, 1972, Edenvale
Opperman D P J, 33, P/A U O V S Bloemfontein, Lektor, 1974, Windhoek
Opperman G C, 33, Lyonsrust Ficksburg, Boer, 1976, Hartswater
Opperman J, 31, Moabsvelden Delmas, Boer, 1967
Opperman J A J, 35, Keeromstraat 18 Krugersdorp/Uniewinkels, Bestuurder, 1972
Opperman J H, 32, P/A Stadsraad Kempton Park, Bestuurder Nie-Blanke-Sake, 1973, Potchefstroom
Opperman Rudolf (Sport)
Opperman R W J, 31, De Hoop Smithfield, Boer, 1967, Potgietersrus
Opperman W M, 38, Volkskas Edenburg, Bestuurder, 1964, Pretoria
Orffer C J, 45, P/A Dept van Onderwys Kuns & Wetenskap Pretoria, Beheerbeampte, 1964
Orffer J H, 37, Lemietrivier Wellington, Boer, 1974
Orffer P L, 37, Reinderslaan 629 Pretoria-Noord/Volkskas, Rekenmeester, 1976, Vredendal
Oschman A G, 39, P/A Laerskool Newlands Johannesburg, Skoolhoof, 1969, Kaapstad
Otten P, 46, Bremnerstraat 4 Potchefstroom, Sakeman, 1970
Otto D J, 40, Volkskas Alberton, Bestuurder, 1965, Middelburg K P
Otto F P, 39, Laerskoolkoshuis Barberton, Onderhoof, 1973, Kaapmuiden
Otto G J, 42, P/A Spoorweë Bethlehem, Masjinis, 1969, Springs
Otto H J, 33, Murrelsingel 7 Framesby of P/A Hoërskool Cillié Port Elizabeth, Onderwyser, 1975, Kimberley
Otto J, 44, Allanstraat 59 Kroonstad, Onderwyser, 1974
Otto J C (Dr), Voormalige L V & Skoolhoof
Otto J F, 32, Gev Rehabilitasiesentrum Kroonstad, Adj Bevelv Offisier, 1967, Springs
Otto J P W (Lid Nr 12533), Adjunk-Hoofsekretaris van die A B met ingang 1 Feb 1976
Otto J S, Johannesburg — By Bondsraad van 29 & 30 Sept 1964 (Tweefontein) wys hy ,, Op die Ongekontroleerde aanwas van die Nie-Blanke bevolking en die implikasies daarvan"
Otto W H, 31, Wilkensstraat 105 Meiringspark, Onderwyser, 1975, Potchefstroom
Otto W M, 39, P/A Western Deep Level Goudmyn Carletonville, Seksiebestuurder, 1975, Randfontein

P

Paasch J H, 41, Karenweg 50 Illiondale Edenvale/A C & E I Modderfontein, Skeikundige, 1970, Roodepoort
Palm A P, 39, De Hoop de Doorns, Boer, 1964
Pansegrouw I, 30, Nonna PK de Wet, Onderwyser, 1965, Bellville
Papendorf E L, 46, Taeuber & Corrsen Durbanville, Bestuurder, 1966, Springs
Papendorf O L, 46, Piet Retiefstraat 31 Krugersdorp, Konsult Ingenieur, 1964
Papenfus B C du P, 36, Nooitgedacht Ohrigstad, Boer, 1973, Zambië
Papenfus P C, 45, Noordwes Motors Lichtenburg, Bestuurder, 1969, Coligny
Parsons E J H, 33, "Die Drostdy" Mcrgenzon, Landdros, 1964, Johannesburg
Pas Ques L J, Hoof — Hoërskool Eric Louw Messina — Skakeling Militêre Lotelinge O/B 2.10.67
Pauw D A, 30, P/A R A U Johannesburg, Snr Lektor, 1974, Pretoria
Pauw J G, 43, Sanlam Stellenbosch, Wyksbestuurder, 1969, Montagu
Pauw S (Lid Nr 1448), Lid van die U R se Ekonomiese Komitee 1973
Pauw W, Lid van die U R se Ekonomiese Komitee in 1973
Peach P P, 41, Prinshofskool Pretoria, Hoof, 1971, Umtata
Peacock R, 32, Ons koop Meisieskoshuis Pietersburg, Vise Hoof/Hoërskool, 1971, Lydenburg
Pellissier J v R, 27, Oranjeweg 2 Alexanderbaai, Geneesheer, 1973, Pretoria
Pelser A, 29, Servaasstraat 24 Flamwood/P/A Saambou Apteek Klerksdorp, Apteker, 1977
Pelser F J, 38, Voortrekkerstraat 58 Delareyville, Stadsklerk, 1973, Vryburg
Pelser G M M, 28, N H Pastorie Pretoria-Wes, Predikant, 1965, Groblersdal
Pelser J C, 42, Du Preez-Laager PK Eerste Myn Virginia, Boer, 1967, Lydenburg

Pelser N J, 43, P/A Saphar Laboratoriums Roodepoort, Afd-Hoof, 1975, Melville
Pelser P A, 38, Seunskoshuis Krugersdorp, Onderwyser, 1964
Pelser P C, 27, Genl Fickstraat Rosendal, Onderwyser, 1969, Marquard
Pelser P J, 34, Geref Pastorie Heidelberg, Predikant, 1964, Louis Trichardt
Pelser S C, 44, Nooitverwacht PK Bulgerivier, Boer, 1970, Welkom
Pelser W P J, 36, Rouxlaan 11 Frankfort/Snyman & Steyn Heilbron, Ouditeur, 1977, Sasolburg
Pelzer A N P, 30, Munisipaliteit Potchefstroom, Asst Direkteur, 1969, Germiston
Pelzer A N P (Lid Nr 3381), Professor — Eridanusstraat 46 Waterkloofrif Pretoria — Skakel by Univ Pretoria 4.2.76
Pentz N W, 44, N G Kerk Danskraal Monument Gemeente Ladismith Predikant, 1974, S W A
Pepler D R, 32, N G Kerk Nooitgedacht Port Elizabeth, Predikant, 1968, Robertson
Peters J, 38, Ranleighsingel 35 Durban-Noord, Geneesheer, 1976, Tsilidzini
Petersen V H, 26, P/A Rossouw Strydom en de Beer (Argitekte) Benoni, Tekenaar, 1973
Pfaff P H, 33, Pretoriusstraat 99 Heidelberg, Prokureur, 1974, Pretoria
Piek J G C, 30, S A S Polisie Johannesburg, Adj-Offisier, 1977, Elandsfontein
Piek S J, 30, P/A Marais & du Preez Pretoria, Rekenmeester, 1973, Reivilo
Piek W G, 38, Mooigelegen PK Roedtan, Boer, 1967, Pretoria
Pienaar A E, 42, Sanlam Chrissiesmeer, Boer & Verteenw, 1964, Pretoria
Pienaar A E, 35, Munisipaliteit Vanderbijlpark, Hoof Toetsafdeling Elektrotegn, 1974, Bultfontein
Pienaar A J, 34, Haldonweg 158 Bloemfontein, Adjunk-Hoof, 1971, Boshof
Pienaar A J, 42, Hoewe 55 Shannon, Akte-Inspekteur, 1963, Despatch
Pienaar A J, 39, Geluksfontein Vaalwater, Boer, 1974, Wynberg
Pienaar C G, 25, P/A SAUK Port Elizabeth, Omroeper, 1976, Johannesburg
Pienaar D C (Lid Nr 7741), Oudtshoorn, 1963
Pienaar D J, 41, PK Chipinga, Boer/Spoorwegamptenaar, 1967, Rusape
Pienaar D J, 37, P/A Hoër Jongenskool Paarl, Adjunk-Hoof, 1974, Vanderbijlpark
Pienaar E A C, 39, P/A S A Weermag Pretoria, Kommandant, 1968, Pretoria
Pienaar E W, 34, P/A Fisons Malmesbury, Vakkundige Beampte, 1967, Stellenbosch
Pienaar F, 37, P/A Sanlam Vryheid, Wyksbestuurder, 1965, Paardekop
Pienaar G, 31, Uitkyk Ficksburg, Boer, 1970
Pienaar G E, 42, S A S & H Pietermaritzburg, Klerk, 1964, George
Pienaar G G, 26, P/A M P L Underhay Tulbagh, Boer, 1964, Pretoria
Pienaar H J, 54, P/A Dept Pos & Tel Pretoria, Ondersekretaris, 1968
Pienaar H J, 43, P/A S A Polisie Oos-Londen, Kaptein, 1974, Benoni
Pienaar H J, 40, Beginsel Ventersburg, Winkelier/Boer, 1971, Welkom
Pienaar H P, 25, "Gooi Die Hoed" Winburg, Boer, 1970
Pienaar J A, 45, Jakkalsfontein De Aar, Boer, 1966, Sutherland
Pienaar J A, 36, Witklip Delmas, Admin Bestuurder, 1977, Bloemfontein
Pienaar J G, 41, P/A Veeartsenykund Fakulteit Onderstepoort, Asst Direkteur, 1977, Ngomo
Pienaar J J, 32, P/A Universiteit S A Pretoria, Lektor Unisa, 1966, Kimberley
Pienaar J J, 37, Kerkstraat 34 Lichtenburg/N W Koöp, Hoofaankoper, 1970, Klerksdorp
Pienaar J P, 25, Patmos Arlington, Boer, 1970, Lindley
Pienaar J P, 33, Deelfontein Winburg, Boer, 1973, Virginia
Pienaar J P, 31, P/A S A S & H Pretoria, Ingenieur, 1977
Pienaar J S J, 33, Leliespan Distr Lichtenburg, Boer, 1974
Pienaar K J, 36, P/A Grey Kollege Bloemfontein, Onderwyser, 1967
Pienaar L A (Lid Nr 5919), ambassadeur — Parys — Voorgestel vir die U R 1968
Pienaar L D (Lid Nr 7762), King Williamstown, 1963
Pienaar L D, 34, N G Kerk Belfast, Predikant, 1968, Brakpan
Pienaar L J, 37, Tiddysingel 8 Baysville Oos-Londen, Onderwyser, 1965, Mosselbaai
Pienaar S, 37, Hoërskool John Vorster Nigel, Onderwyser, 1973, Alberton
Pienaar S C, 24, Bergsig Koshuis Elliot, Onderwyser, 1969, Heidelberg Kaap
Pienaar S W, 45, P/A Transkeise Dept van Landbou Umtata, Sekretaris, 1965, Vryheid
Pienaar W D J, 40, P/A Durbanse Onderwyskollege/Hamiltonweg 23 Ashley Pinetown, Departementshoof, 1976, Vryheid
Pienaar W G, 30, 2deLaan 71 Edenvale, Onderwyser, 1968, Boksburg

Pienaar W J, 39, P/A Dept Landbou-Tegn Dienste Stellenbosch, Navorsingsbeampte, 1967
Pieters B J, 34, P/A Yskor Vanderbijlpark, Water-Tegnikus, 1968
Pieters H B, 42, N G Sendingpastorie Barkly-Wes, Predikant, 1977, Reitz
Pieters H J, 29, P/A Laerskool Boons, Hoof, 1973, Makwassie
Pieters H N, 25, Hoërskool Bekker Magaliesburg, Onderwyser, 1965
Pieters J A, 38, P/A Munisipaliteit Germiston, Rekenmeester, 1967, Krugersdorp
Pieters J H, 35, Afrikanerstraat 122 Vryheid/S A Polisie, Kaptein, 1972, Durban
Pieters M H, 31, N G Pastorie Krugersdorp-Suid, Predikant, 1964, Heilbron
Pieters W A, 40, Kromdraai Lindley, Graangradeerder/Boer, 1970
Pieters W D, 47, Venanatum Grootfontein, Boer, 1974, Outjo
Pieters W J, 37, Volkskas Zastron, Bestuurder, 1964, Lindley
Pieterse A J H, 31, P/A Universiteit van Pretoria, Snr Lektor, 1976, Klerksdorp
Pieterse D C, 31, Klipplaatdrift Amersfoort, Boer, 1970
Pieterse D J, 32, Mandarinweg 14 Primrose, Onderwyser, 1971, Germiston
Pieterse D P, 32, Brightonrylaan 11 Somerstrand Port Elizabeth/Ford Motor Mpy (SA), Bestuurder Arbeidsverh, 1976, Stellenbosch
Pieterse F P, 40, Alecweg 25 Sunnyrock Germiston/Asokor, Hoof Bestuurder, 1976, Kaapstad
Pieterse G J, Uitenhage — By 1966 se Bondsraad sê hy die Afrikaner moet meer militant wees om eie sake te steun
Pieterse H J, 30, N G Gemeente Wonderboomspoort, Predikant, 1967, Shabani
Pieterse J C, Pretoria — By 1966 se Bondsraad vra hy waarom Afrikaanse versekeringsmaatskappye werk gee aan nie-Afrikaanse argitekte
Pieterse J E (Prof), Universiteit Pretoria — 'n Stigterslid van Ruiterwag
Pieterse J J G, 36, P/A Monument-Versekering Johannesburg, Adm Bestuurder, 1969, Olifantshoek
Pieterse J L, 43, Nie-Blanke Sake Munisipaliteit Rustenburg, Direkteur, 1965, Pretoria
Pieterse J le R, 33, Groningen Smithfield, Boer, 1973
Pieterse J S J, 48, P/A Bantoe Adm en Ontwikkeling Sibasa, Bantoesake-Komissaris, 1968, Pretoria
Pieterse J V, 28, Hestersrus Odendaalsrus, Boer, 1976, Kroonstad
Pieterse J W, 45, Montana Vryburg, Boer, 1970
Pieterse P J, 38, Salisburyweg 89 Westville Natal, Radioterapeut, 1968, Johannesburg
Pieterse P J S, 34, Dept Landbou Tegn Dienste Potchefstroom, Navorsingsbeampte, 1965
Pieterse P W, 30, Madernastraat 16 Vanderbijlpark, Onderwyser, 1968, Phalaborwa
Pieterse S C, 41, P/A Volkskas Bpk Sutherland, Bestuurder, 1973, Kuilsrivier
Pieterse T J, 37, Maxwellstraat 14 Risiville Vereeniging, Onderwyser, 1976, Vereeniging
Pieterse W J, 35, P/A Landdroskantoor Vierfontein, Landdros, 1976, Johannesburg
Pietersen J C (Lid Nr 5667), Predikant — Kroonstad — Voorgestel vir die U R in 1968
Pietersen J D C, 30, Huis Venter Barkly-Wes, Onderwyser, 1973, Welkom
Pietersen J P, 30, Jakarandastraat 16 Swellendam, Voorligtingsbeampte, 1971, Villiersdorp
Pijpers H, 37, Ladysmithse Koöp Handelshuis Ladysmith, Bestuurder, 1965, Harrismith
Pistorius G J, 29, Rugbystraat 17 Victoria-Wes, Geneesheer, 1965, George
Pistorius H G, 36, P/A De Souza-Koshuis Lydenburg, Onderwyser, 1965, Heidelberg, Tvl
Poggenpoel D J, 33, P/A Vleissentraal Fraserburg, Boer/Skakelbeampte, 1963, Carnarvon
Poggenpoel J D, 34, P/A Middelkaroo Verbruikerskoöp Kenhardt, Onderbestuurder, 1963, Carnarvon
Poggenpoel S J, 48, P/A K W V Montagu, Hoofklerk, 1968, Carnarvon
Pohl E W, 49, Beckerstraat Olifantsfontein, Klerk, 1966, Bronkhorstspruit
Pohl R E, 35, Hoërskool Ben Viljoen Groblersdal, Onderwyser, 1977, Middelburg
Pont J W, 40, Frederickrylaan 503 Northcliff Johannesburg, Ortopeed, 1967, Rustenburg
Poolman J, 43, P/A R A U Johannesburg, Professor, 1973, Pretoria
Portwig E H, 35, Seymourstraat 19 Grahamstad, Onderwyser, 1973, Stellenbosch
Postma D, 34, P/A Geref Pastorie Bethlehem, Predikant, 1969, Dordrecht
Postma D J, 28, Eureka Dist Kimberley, Boer, 1975, Oos-Londen
Postma M, De Aar — Open 1968 Bondsraad met Skriflesing & Gebed
Postma M, 34, V/D Hoffweg 78 Potchefstroom, Onderwyser, 1977, Gobabis
Postma W, 35, Hawthornstraat 81 Kokstad, Tegn SAUK, 1974, Meyerton
Potgieter A, 29, S A Weermag Potchefstroom, Kaptein, 1967, Strand

Potgieter A H J, 35, Hoërskool Bonnievale, Onderwyser, 1966, Pretoria
Potgieter B J D, 51, P/A Eierraad Pretoria, Klerk, 1968
Potgieter C L, 35, Panoramalaan 76 Stellenberg/Sanlam Sanlamhof, Asst Bestuurder, 1975, Bellville
Potgieter C R, 48, Voortrekkerweg Humansdorp, Geneesheer, 1976, Pretoria
Potgieter D, 40, Yskor Pretoria, Asst Verkoops-Bestuurder, 1964, Bethlehem
Potgieter D S M (Lid Nr 7691), Elandsfontein, Vise-Hoof, 1962
Potgieter D S M, Woon 1966 Bondsraad by
Potgieter E F (Prof), Voormalige Rektor Turfloop
Potgieter F E, 37, Platkop Villiers, Boer, 1967
Potgieter F J, 34, Straussennestraat Keetmanshoop, Boer, 1966, Stellenbosch
Potgieter F J, 37, P/A Tegn Kollege Olifantsfontein, Instrukteur, 1968
Potgieter F J M (Lid Nr 2757), Professor — Stellenbosch — Lid van die U R se Beplanningskomitee 1973
Potgieter Gert, Springbok — Atleet/Tans verbonde aan Triomf Kunsmis
Potgieter H E, 33, Groutoord 19 Bellair Durban/G C Shave & Co, Hoofskeikundige, 1970
Potgieter H F R, 33, P/A Laerskool Jonkersberg, Skoolhoof, 1969, Despatch
Potgieter H G J, 43, Boriusstraat 20 Potchefstroom/P U vir CHO, Professor, 1976, Sasolburg
Potgieter H H J, 48, Laerskool Kirkwood, Onderwyser, 1964, Heidelberg
Potgieter H J, 30, Quarrystraat Steynsburg, Geneesheer, 1975, Uitenhage
Potgieter H L, 33, Mederastraat 76 Umtata, Sakeman, 1977, Mowbray
Potgieter H L, 35, Buffelskloof Calitzdorp, Boer, 1977
Potgieter H L, 38, Homes Trust Lewensversekering Kempton Park, Takbestuurder, 1975, Kaapstad
Potgieter H P, 32, V D Waltstraat 36 Venterstad, Afdelingsraad-Sekretaris, 1974, Vanrhynsdorp
Potgieter I F, 49, Dept Ontwikkeling Univ Stellenbosch, Eerste Adm Beampte, 1968, Johannesburg
Potgieter J C, 39, Erneststraat 21 Springs Uitbr, Organiseerder N P, 1970, Springs
Potgieter J D, 34, P/A Artillerieskool Potchefstroom, Kolonel, 1969, Pretoria
Potgieter J E (Ds), Stigterslid van Ruiterwag
Potgieter J F, 33, N G Pastorie Wonderboomplotte, Predikant, 1964, Pretoria
Potgieter J F, 41, Glengarrysingel 34 Humewood Uitbr Port Elizabeth, Direkteur/Beplannings Navorsing U P E, 1971, Pretoria
Potgieter J F W, 33, Cameronstraat 5 Petersfield, Onderwyser, 1967, Ogies
Potgieter J G, 47, Bloedrivier Utrecht, Boer, 1967
Potgieter J H, Dewetsdorp, Boer, 1961
Potgieter J H, 38, Wag-'n-Bietjie 1046 Grootfontein, Boer, 1967, Outjo
Potgieter J H, 31, Dorchester Alexandria, Boer, 1973
Potgieter J H, 30, P/A Rondalia Pretoria, Verteenwoordiger, 1968
Potgieter J J, 29, Seekoegat Komatipoort, Boer, 1967, Brits
Potgieter J M, 33, Sanlamgebou 106 Kroonstad, Advokaat, 1968, Bloemfontein
Potgieter J P, 33, Buitekantstraat 7 Middelburg Tvl, Onderwyser, 1968, Carletonville
Potgieter J W, 46, Laerskool Eric Louw Beaufort-Wes, Skoolhoof, 1967, Jan Kempdorp
Potgieter L G, 31, P/A Laerskool Andalusia Vaalharts, Onderwyser, 1967, Beaufort-Wes
Potgieter L J, 39, Dan Pienaarlaan 30 Florida-Noord, Besturende Direkteur van Adverkor, 1972, Johannesburg
Potgieter L J, 35, O T K Ogies, Skakelbeampte, 1972, Bronkhorstspruit
Potgieter L M, 34, Yskor Vanderbijlpark, Snr Prod Asst, 1964, Rustenburg
Potgieter M, 35, Volkskas Germiston, Asst Rekenmeester, 1975, Fochville
Potgieter M G, 36, P/A Lamberts Bay Holdings Lambertsbaai, Fabrieksbestuurder, 1977, Stompneusbaai
Potgieter M G, 34, Skoolhostel Bonnievale, Onderwyser, 1968, Port Elizabeth
Potgieter M J, 34, P/A Hoërskool Ogies, Onderwyser, 1975, Witrivier
Potgieter M J L, 43, Paardepoort Utrecht, Boer, 1969
Potgieter N J, 31, P/A S A Vloot Simonstad, Offisier, 1975, Saldanha
Potgieter P C, 28, N G Pastorie Vredenburg, Predikant, 1969, Stellenbosch
Potgieter P D, 33, Theunsweg 232 Murrayfield Pretoria/Uraanverrykingskorporasie Valindaba, Ingenieur, 1976, Bothaville

Potgieter P J J S, 33, P/A P U vir CHO Potchefstroom, Lektor, 1975, Otjiwarongo
Potgieter P R, 31, Demilander Petrus Steyn, Boer, 1967
Potgieter P T, 38, Vierde Privaatlaan 288 Villieria Pretoria, Onderwyser, 1966
Potgieter S L, 34, P/A Hoër Landbouskool Kroonstad, Onderwyser, 1975, Pietersburg
Potgieter S P, 48, P/A Mare & Potgieter Nelspruit, Prokureur, 1966, Ermelo
Potgieter S T, 39, P/A Landbou Tegn Dienste Pretoria, Pluimvee-Deskundige, 1966, Heidelberg, Tvl
Potgieter S T, 35, Hoërskool Etosha Tsumeb, Onderhoof, 1966, Gibeon
Potgieter T C, 31, Ouwerf PK Congoskraal, Boer, 1970, Alexandria
Potgieter T D, 45, Hoërskool Monument Krugersdorp, Onderhoof, 1969, Rustenburg
Potgieter T I, 43, Prov Admin Bloemfontein, Hoofverkeersbeampte, 1966, Kroonstad
Potgieter W A, 38, P/A G O K Johannesburg, Snr Dosent, 1974, Randburg
Potgieter W J, 45, Hoërskool Brits, Onderwyser, 1969
Pottas C D, 34, Kesselstraat 90 Fairland, Lektor/R A U, 1973, Pretoria
Powell G H, 35, Glen Avonweg Kempton Park/S A L, Lugvaarttegnikus, 1975, Johannesburg
Preller F T, 28, Bankstraat 117 Nigel, Onderwyser, 1967, Pretoria
Pretorius A J, 34, P/A Volkskas Barberton, Bestuurder, 1965, Pretoria
Pretorius A L (Lid Nr 7743) Pretoria, 1963
Pretorius A L, 32, Hoërskool Ogies, Onderwyser, 1968, Middelburg Tvl
Pretorius A P, 40, Cleveland Nottinghamweg Pietermaritzburg, Boer, 1974, Plooysburg
Pretorius C v N, 41, P/A N G Pastorie Meyerton, Predikant, 1969, Rothdene
Pretorius D H S, 34, S A Vloot Simonstad, Geneesheer, 1966, Pretoria
Pretorius D J, 44, P/A Hoërskool Schweizer-Reneke, Onderhoof, 1968, Wolmaransstad
Pretorius D J, 29, Dirkie Uysstraat 6 Franschhoek, Onderwyser, 1971, Queenstown
Pretorius D S B, 34, P/A Tegn & Ind Beleggings Stellenbosch, Personeelopl Beampte, 1975 Johannesburg
Pretorius F H, 42, S A Polisie Windhoek, Kaptein, 1963, Tsumeb S W A
Pretorius F J, 28, P/A Dept Landbou Tegn Dienste Pongola, Voorligtingsbeampte, 1967, Pietermaritzburg
Pretorius F J, 33, P/A Sanlam Middelburg Tvl, Takbestuurder, 1975, Alberton
Pretorius G C de B, 37, P/A G O K Johannesburg, Dosent, 1965
Pretorius G J, 45, Alaska Sinoia, Boer, 1976, Boshoff Zambië
Pretorius G P, 42, P/A S A Polisie Stella, Sersant, 1972, Derby
Pretorius G P, 44, S A S Polisie Johannesburg, Kaptein, 1965, Kimberley
Pretorius G R, 38, S A S & H Johannesburg, Klerk, 1967, Mafeking
Pretorius H, 30, S A S & H Barkly-Oos, Vervoerkontrakteur, 1977, Bloemfontein
Pretorius H A J, 33, Schoongesicht Hoekspruit Bantoe Hoërskool, Onderhoof, 1974, Hazyview Oos-Tvl
Pretorius H E, 34, Huis Erundu Otjiwarongo, Onderwyser, 1965, Usakos
Pretorius H J, 34, P/A Nie-Blankesake Munisipaliteit Potchefstroom, Brouerybestuurder, 1967, Nelspruit
Pretorius H J, 29, Pres Paul Krugerlaan 278 Bloemfontein, Onderwyser, 1973, Welkom
Pretorius H N, 37, P/A P U vir CHO Potchefstroom, Professor, 1975, Vereeniging
Pretorius H P, 27, Western Reefmyn Orkney, Skofbaas, 1966, Carletonville
Pretorius I A, 33, Battersea Park Dundee, Boer/Komdt S A W, 1977, Ventersburg
Pretorius I C, 34, Westphalstraat 37 Bloemfontein/Bank v/d OVS, Sekretaris, 1972, Clocolan
Pretorius J A, 36, Grusstraat 43 Waterkloofrif Pretoria, Tandarts, 1974
Pretorius J C, 39, P/A Naude & Naude Bloemfontein, Prokureur, 1968, Pretoria
Pretorius J C, 31, Sek Skool Sand du Plessis Bloemfontein, Onderhoof, 1977
Pretorius J C R, 50, Pretoriusmyn PK Baltimore, Boer, 1975, Waterberg
Pretorius J F, 37, Vredehoek Barkly-Oos, Boer, 1967
Pretorius J G, 33, Constantia Shannon, Onderwyser, 1967, Kafferrivierstasie
Pretorius J H J G, 41, Platfontein Barkly-Oos, Boer, 1966
Pretorius J H D, 32, Shepstonestraat 10 Brenthurst, Geneesheer, 1975, Pretoria
Pretorius J J B, 35, Lafniestraat Hendrina, Geneesheer, 1973, Heidelberg Tvl
Pretorius J L M, 35, P/A Universiteit Pretoria, Lektor, 1977
Pretorius J M, 39, P/A Federale Volksbeleggings Bloemfontein, Bestuurder, 1976, Johannesburg

Pretorius J N, 33, Springboklaan Middelburg Tvl, Landdros, 1977, Pretoria
Pretorius J v H, 41, P/A Vikor Vanderbijlpark, Ingenieur, 1967, Johannesburg
Pretorius L M, 45, Flowerstraat 174, Capitalpark Pretoria, Boekbinderinstr, 1968
Pretorius M, 34, P/A Pretorius Steyn & Lategan Pretoria, Argitek, 1967
Pretorius M de W, 32, P/A Spoorweghoofkantoor Johannesburg, Klerk, 1963, Potchefstroom
Pretorius M F, 28, P/A Premo-Dryco Staal (Muldersdrif), Direkteur, 1974, Krugersdorp
Pretorius M H O, 31, Jacobsdal, Geneesheer, 1965, Kirkwood
Pretorius M J, 37, Burgerstraat 4 de Rust, Onderwyser, 1975, Stella
Pretorius M W, 33, Ned Herv Kerk Voortrekkerhoogte, Predikant, 1973
Pretorius N J, 45, Nas Party van Tvl Johannesburg, Hoof-Organiseerder, 1965, Pretoria
Pretorius P, 46, P/A Boedel en Trustafd Volkskas, Bestuurder, 1976, Pretoria
Pretorius P A, 40, P/A Newton & Taylor Johannesburg, Graveerder, 1968
Pretorius P C, 37, P/A Bruinette Kruger Stofberg & Hugo Johannesburg, Ingenieur, 1975 Pretoria
Pretorius P H, 35, P/A Hoërskool Die Burger Maraisburg, Onderwyser, 1966, Johannesburg
Pretorius P J, 41, Mediese Fakulteit Pretoria, Professor, 1966, Steynsburg
Pretorius P J, 39, P/A Pos & Telekommunikasiewese Pretoria, Admin Beampte, 1975, Bloemfontein
Pretorius P J, 31, Kameeldrif Distrik Pretoria, Verteenwoordiger Sanlam, 1976
Pretorius P J V E, Lid van die U R se Beplanningskomitee 1973
Pretorius R de V, 41, Nuwe Uitbr Willowmore, Onderwyser, 1966, Darling
Pretorius S J, 36, S A Weermag Bloemfontein, Kommdt Sportoffisier, 1973, Boshof
Pretorius S P, 38, De Villierslaan 12 Kenridge Durban, Uitvoerende Beampte Sanlam, 1971, Mkhoma Malawi
Pretorius W C, 34, Bothastraat 4 Vrede/S A Polisie, Adj Offisier, 1971, Aberfeldy
Pretorius W G, 42, P/A S A S Werkwinkel Bloemfontein/Bendrylaan Campbellton Bloemfontein, Asst Voorman/Vak Opl, 1975
Pretorius W H, 33, P/A Yskor Pretoria, Klerk, 1968
Pretorius W J, 34, Roosstraat 255 Meyerspark Pretoria/S A S & H, Tekenaar, 1971, Pietermaritzburg
Pretorius W J, 33, Huis Derksen Kroonstad, Onderwyser, 1971, Villiers
Pretorius W J (Prof) (Lid Nr 5946) — Direkteur van Maatskappye — Voorgestel vir die U R 1968 — Lid van die U R se Ekonomiese Komitee 1973
Pretorius W J B, 45, Dept Onderwys Kuns & Wet Pretoria, Eerste Adm Beampte, 1965, Potchefstroom
Pretorius W J H, 34, P/A Unisa Pretoria, Snr Lektor, 1973
Pretorius W P J, (Lid Nr 7744), Barkly-Oos, 1963
Prince D S, 44, P/A Tegn Kollege Johannesburg, Onderhoof, 1966
Prins F E, 40, P/A S A S & H Worcester, Ingenieur, 1973, Mafeking
Prins F J, 32, Vryhof PK Mareetsane, Boer, 1971
Prins H A T, 41, S A S Polisie Fynnland Durban, Speurluitenant, 1965, Johannesburg
Prins H H J, 39, P/A Laerskool van Reede Oudtshoorn, Skoolhoof, 1968, Parow
Prins M J, 31, Jack Hindonstraat 29 Pretoria-Noord, Onderwyser, 1971
Prins T J, 53, Vadersgawe Ceres, Boer, 1967
Prinsloo A L, S A S & H Lichtenburg Sentraal
Prinsloo B D C, 29, Geref Pastorie Elliot, Predikant, 1964, Potchefstroom
Prinsloo C, Prys die Ruiterwag op Bondsraad van 1965
Prinsloo C L, 34, Olympia Okahandja, Plaasbestuurder, 1977
Prinsloo D S, 25, P/A Dept Staatsleer R A U Johannesburg, Lektor, 1974, Pretoria
Prinsloo F J, 33, P/A Laerskool Potgietersrus, Onderhoof, 1967
Prinsloo G D P, 43, H/v 8estraat & Van Riebeecklaan Delmas, Geneesheer, 1977, Dist Witbank
Prinsloo G F, 32, Totiusstraat 10 Marlands Germiston, Adj-Hoof Laerskool, 1970 Vereeniging
Prinsloo H F, 35, Honingkrans Smithfield, Boer, 1963
Prinsloo H F, 40, Kruidfontein Koster, Boer, 1973
Prinsloo H J, 33, P/A Hoër Handelskool Brakpan, Onderwyser, 1974

Prinsloo H P, 31, P/A Radiobantoe Johannesburg, Taalorganiseerder, 1967, Potchefstroom
Prinsloo I J, 39, De Boerstraat 7 Nylstroom, Prokureursklerk, 1973, Alberton
Prinsloo I J, 31, P/A Laerskool Selection Park, Onderhoof, 1977, Nigel
Prinsloo J, 36, P/A Meyer Nel & Kie Bloemfontein, Ouditeur, 1966, Potchefstroom
Prinsloo J A, 35, Occupation Imvani Queenstown, Boer, 1966
Prinsloo J J, 39, P/A Kunsrubber Mpy (Edms) Bpk Sasolburg, Hoofingenieur, 1967, Germiston
Prinsloo J J, Port Elizabeth-Noord
Prinsloo J J, 44, P/A Swartkops-Seesout Port Elizabeth, Bestuurder, 1967, Gravelotte
Prinsloo J L, 41, P/A Laerskool Akasia Pretoria, Onderwyser, 1968
Prinsloo J P N, 45, N G Pastorie Westonaria, Predikant, 1964, Bethal
Prinsloo J v N J, 37, Markslaan 3 Boksburg, Geneesheer, 1976, Brakpan
Prinsloo K P, 30, Lindfieldweg 71, Lynnwood Pretoria, Hoofnavorsingsbeampte, 1973 Pretoria
Prinsloo L A (Prof), Lid van die U R se Wetenskapkomitee 1973
Prinsloo M J, 33, Gerrit Maritzlaan Brakpan, Onderwyser, 1969, Rand Collieries Brakpan
Prinsloo M W, 33, P/A Stadsraad Brakpan, Asst Direkteur, 1967, Bronkhorstspruit
Prinsloo P F, 42, P/A Wagner Wagner Prinsloo & Van Wyk, Geneesheer, 1974, Belfast
Prinsloo P H, 35, S A Polisie Sundra, Sersant, 1965, Springs
Prinsloo P M, 35, Hofmeyerstraat 9 Westonaria, Tandarts, 1967, Pietersburg
Prinsloo W, 43, Westraat 10 Middelburg Tvl, Prokureur, 1974, Barberton
Prinsloo W P, 30, Buitestedelike Ontwikkelingsraad Pretoria, Klerk, 1974, Pretoria
Prinsloo W R, 26, Rondebult Boksburg, Boer, 1970
Prosch G C, 44, P/A Nas Bouvereniging Pretoria, Bestuurderassistent, 1968
Puren M F, 38, Gonakraal Somerset-Oos, Boer, 1970, Cradock
Putter A P, 31, S A Vloot Simonstad, Lt Kdr, 1967, Saldanha
Putter D J, 35, P/A Dept van Bantoe-Adm Pretoria, Inspekteur, 1969, Peddie
Putter N J, 45, Kerkstraat 15 Kempton Park, Snr Klerk/SAL, 1970, Germiston
Putter S J M, 37, Knopfontein PK Alma, Boer, 1976
Putter W J, 32, P U vir CHO Potchefstroom, Snr Dosent, 1968, Nylstroom

Q

Quass F P, 28, Lothburyweg 3 Aucklandpark/Hofmeyr v/d Merwe & Botha Johannesburg, Prokureur, 1977, Middelburg

R

Raath J P, 36, S A S & H (Personeelafd) Verwoerdburg, Klerk, 1974, Bloemfontein
Raath R B, 26, Brakwater Britstown, Boer, 1973
Raath R J, 54, Ingersolweg 67 Lynnwood Glen, Hoofrekenmeester, 1976, Pretoria
Raath R J, 30, P/A Ellaton Mining Supply Co, Direkteur, 1973, Ottosdal
Raath R J, 56, N G Pastorie Bronberg Pretoria, Predikant, 1964, Nylstroom
Raath W, 45, V Andelstraat 9 Dan Pienaar Bloemfontein, Sek Rek Sendingpers, 1977, Port Elizabeth
Raats J J, 32, Tweedelaan 2 Kleinmond, Skoolhoof Laerskool, 1971, Robertson
Rabe J P P, 47, Salamanderweg Saldanha, Sakeman, 1965, Hopefield
Rademeyer J R, 33, Jakkalskuil Petrusville, Boer, 1974, Riversdal
Rademeyer P de V, 28, P/A General Mining Johannesburg, Geoktr Rekenmeester, 1975, Ermelo
Radley W S (Lid Nr 962), Malelane, Boer/Winkelier
Omit above line please sorry
Radley W S (Lid Nr 962), Malelane Voorgestel vir die U R in 1968, Boer/Winkelier
Radloff F G T, 31, P/A McRobert de Villiers & Hitge, Prokureur, 1974, Pretoria
Radloff G, Lidv an die U R se Landbou-Komitee in 1973
Radloff J G, 27, Vlugopleidingskool PK Langebaanweg, Kaptein, 1973, Pretoria
Radyn C H, 31, Sivestraat 26 Kuilsrivier, Streeksekretaris Sanlam, 1975, Bellville
Rall C C, 49, Van Eckshof Douglas, Boer, 1965, Parys
Rall E, 40, Roosbank Heilbron, Boer, 1971, Johannesburg

Raal F R, 29, Somerville Leonardville, Boer, 1977, Aranos
Rall W H B, 29, Wesselstraat Bethlehem, Onderwyser, 1963, Harrismith
Range N J, 31, Die Hoërskool Douglas, Onderwyser, 1972, Uitenhage
Ras J M N, 46, Mobil Olie Maatskappy Jan Smuts Lughawe, Klerk, 1967, Standerton
Ras W J, 38, P/A Stadsraad Pretoria, Ondersupt Mamelodi, 1968
Rathbone I E, 35, Uitsig Steytlerville, Boer, 1966
Raubenheimer A J, Minister van Bosbou
Raubenheimer G J, 33, P/A Raubies Meubelhandelaar Meyerton, Bestuurder, 1976, De Deur
Raubenheimer J, 30, P/A Malan en Raubenheimer Vereeniging, Prokureur, 1963
Raubenheimer J G, 30, P/A Villiersdorpse Vrugte Koöp Bpk, Sekretaris/Rekenmeester, 1964, Humansdorp
Raubenheimer J J M, 38, Dept van Indiëronderwys "Môrewag" N G Kerk Jeugsentrum Nuttall Tuine Durban, Vakinspekteur, 1970, Rustenburg
Raubenheimer J J M, 34, N G Gemeente Bloemvallei, Predikant, 1967, Volmoed
Raubenheimer L J, 38, P/A Jan Krielskool Kuilsrivier, Skoolhoof, 1975, Worcester
Raubenheimer P L, 28, S A U K Johannesburg, Adm Asst, 1974, Wellington
Rauch J H (Lid Nr 1777), Pretoria, Brigadier (Afgetree)
Rautenbach G E, 34, N G Pastorie Arconpark Vereeniging, Predikant, 1967, Nelspruit
Rautenbach G F, 33, P/A Köhlerse Garage Witbank, Sekretaris/Rekenmeester, 1973, Witbank
Rautenbach G S, 26, Hoërskool Winburg, Onderwyser, 1964, Excelsior
Rautenbach K D, 37, 10destraat Boksburg, Kontroleur van Voorrade Stadsraad, 1971
Rautenbach P F, 33, Hoërskool Gimnasium Welkom, Onderhoof, 1967, Senekal
Rautenbach P S, Direkteur RONH en Voorsitter Permanente Komitee vir Nywerheids-Vestiging, Pretoria
Rautenbach R C, 43, Rooikoppies Standerton, Boer, 1967, Amersfoort
Rautenbach S J, 34, Roodepoortstraat Warmbad, Onderwyser, 1974, Pretoria
Rautenbach W d v W, 35, N G Pastorie Rustenburg-Wes, Predikant, 1965, Klaver
Redelinghuys E W, 40, Universiteit van Zoeloeland Empangeni, Registrateur, 1971, Alice
Redelinghuys H J, 35, P/A Dept Bantoe-Onderwys Pretoria, Onderwyser, 1968
Redelinghuys J A J, 42, Perdefontein Dist Pretoria/Universiteit Pretoria, Dosent, 1972, Villieria
Redelinghuys J P, 35, Mosterstraat Pionierspark/P/A Augistinium Bantoeskool Windhoek, Vise-Hoof, 1976, Karibib
Reinach H A, 29, Voortrekkerstraat Ceres, Tandarts, 1966, Pretoria
Reinecke C H S, 35, Primëreskool Fonteine, Adj-Hoof, 1976, Zastron
Reinecke C J, 50, P/A Durban Deep Myn 137 Roodepoort, Mynkaptein, 1965, Mayfair
Reinecke C J, 31, P U vir CHO Potchefstroom, Snr Lektor, 1973, Potgietersrus
Reinecke G H, 29, N G Pastorie Kempton Park-Noord, Predikant, 1966, Pretoria
Reinecke J J, 42, P/A Hoër Tegn Skool Middelburg Tvl, Onderwyser, 1966, Standerton
Reinecke J P, 34, P/A Munisipaliteit Empangeni, Adj-Stadstesourier, 1975, Graskop
Reineke S, Lid van die U R se Landbou-Komitee in 1973
Reitman D (Dr), 34, 24stestraat 60 Menlopark Pretoria, Kernfisikus, 1968, Bloemfontein
Reitmann E, 38, P/A S A U K Johannesburg, Sr Ingenieur, 1968
Rens J P, 34, Die Hoop Kruisrivier Uitenhage, Boer, 1968
Retief A E, 32, Kenridgelaan 36 Durbanville, Genetikus, 1974, Bellville
Retief B R, 33, P/A Kavalier Films Johannesburg, Skakelbeampte, 1970, Kaapstad
Retief D J, 40, Clydestraat 2 Murrayfield Pretoria, Uitgewer/Sakeman, 1976, Rustenburg
Retief F P, 33, Karl Bremer-Hospitaal Bellville, Internis, 1967
Retief F P, Skakel Sekretaris van die A B 1971/1977 — Streekrade, Sprekers, Afstigings Buite & Rustende Lede, navrae oor Lede, Statistiek, Vraelyste, Pos
Retief G M, 54, P/A Stadsraad Pretoria, Asst Bestuurder Nie-Blankesake, 1968
Retief J, 33, P/A Poskantoor Wendywood Johannesburg, Ingenieur Ukor, 1975, Randburg
Retief J J, 24, Groenkloof Graaff-Reinet, Boer, 1973
Retief J L, 29, Driehoeksfontein Murraysburg, Boer, 1975, Middelburg K P
Retief P J, 33, Koninginsingel 426 Lynnwood Pretoria, Spesialis, 1966, Alberton
Reynecke C C, 37, P/A Beplanningsadviesraad van die Eerste Minister Pretoria, Sekretaris 1969, Lichtenburg
Reynecke F J, 35, P/A S A Polisie Aliwal-Noord, Luitenant, 1964, Vryheid

Reyneke A F, 32, P/A Sentraal — Wes Koöp, Bestuurder, 1970, Bloemfontein
Reyneke A J, 30, Eureka Plaas Chipinga, Boer, 1973
Reyneke A M, 44, P/A Poskantoor Ermelo, Hoofingenieur, 1975, Pretoria
Reyneke D A, 28, Turnerweg 7 Ladysmith, Ouditeur, 1971, Vereeniging
Reyneke H J C, 34, Kightleystraat 32 Brandfort, Onderwyser, 1975, Winburg
Reyneke J C, 35, P/A S A Vloot Saldanha, Lt Kdr, 1973, Simondstad
Reyneke J H T, 36, Willsonstraat 267, Fairland Johannesburg, Internis, 1971, Bellville
Reyneke J P A, 44, P/A Baanbrekerskool Boksburg, Onderwyser, 1964
Reyneke M J, 36, Zuidesande Olifantshoek, Boer, 1970, Postmasburg
Reyneke S M, 33, Stiglingstraat Floridaheuwels, T V Regsseur, 1977, Port Elizabeth
Reynders L S v d V, 45, Ouditeurgeneraal Pretoria, Adm Beampte, 1966
Reynolds J H C, 42, Perseel N 8 Pongola, Boer, 1973, Ermelo
Rex E, 31, P/A N G Gemeente Primroseheuwel, N G Predikant, 1974, Vereeniging
Rheeder C G, 39, Hoërskool Calvinia, Onderwyser, 1973, Doringbaai (Weskus)
Rheeder J, 37, P/A Hugenote-Kollege Wellington, Registrateur, 1977, Bloemfontein
Rheeder L P, 36, Volkskas Fraserburg, Bestuurder, 1970, Vryburg
Rheeders H J H, 34, Hoërskool Randfontein, Onderwyser, 1968, Sasolburg
Richard B T, 39, P/A N G Kerk Naboomspruit, Predikant, 1973, Pretoria
Richards J, 41, Messina Transvaal Ont. Mpy, Passer/Draaier, 1973, Rhodesië
Richards W J, 44, U O V S Bloemfontein, Professor, 1966, Pretoria
Richter B W B, 28, Mieliespruit Bloemfontein, Boer, 1969
Richter C G F, 42, Leeukop Bloemfontein, Boer, 1964
Richter C J, 32, Mimosalaan Kuruman, Mynbestuurder, 1967, Carletonville
Richter G J, 35, S A Polisie Komatipoort, Sersant, 1963, Vaalharts
Richter H A, 31, P/A Union Corp Goudmyn Bracken Trichardt, Passer, 1965, Trichardt
Richter J, 35, Tvlse Prov Administrasie Johannesburg, Amptenaar, 1969, Rustenburg
Richter J G M, 44, PK Derdepoort oor Rustenburg, Geneesheer, 1967, Pretoria
Richter J H G, 45, Clarendonstraat 47 Mafeking, Direkteur Nutrak Spares (Edms) Bpk, 1971, Potchefstroom
Richter M, 35, P/A General Mining Johannesburg, Ouditeur, 1973, Potgietersrus
Richter R, 40, Bankdrift Koster, Boer, 1970, Swartruggens
Rieckert H J, 40, Spoorweghuis 278 Usakos/S A S & H, Masjinis, 1971, Luderitz
Riekert C J H, 42, Elandsfontein Mooinooi, Boer, 1967, Pretoria
Riekert H F P, 33, P/A Dept Verdediging Windhoek, Kaptein, 1964, Pretoria
Riekert H I, 33, Doringboomstraat Kempton Park/Bad, Snr Vakk Beampte, 1973, Nelspruit
Riekert J A, 33, P/A Anglo/Alpha Dudfield Lichtenburg, Produksie Bestuurder, 1975, Hennenman
Riekert P J, Lid van U R se Nie-Blanke Komitee 1973
Ries G A F, 42, P/A Die Burger Kaapstad, Politieke Beriggewer, 1974, Pretoria
Ries H E, 39, P/A Bluff Meat Supply Durban, Blokman, 1975, Bergville
Ritson W E, 40, Willem Coetzerweg 5 De Bruinpark/Usutu Koolmyne (Ermelo), Mynkaptein, 1976, Breyten
Robberts C S, 41, Emmasdalskool Heidelberg Tvl, Onderhoof, 1975, Pretoria
Robbertse G F (Lid Nr 2837), Ventersdorp, Hoofonderwyser
Robbertse J A, 42, Sefanjekraal — PK Rhenosterdoorns, Boer, 1966
Robbertse J D, 28, Hindenburg PK Fort Louis, Boer, 1967, Vryheid
Robbertse N, 33, P/A Altberg Sement Prod Hlobane, Sakeman, 1969, Vryheid
Robbertse N J, 28, Dept Landbou Tegn Dienste Brits, Voorligtingsbeampte, 1964, Vryheid
Robbertse P M, (Lid Nr 6546), Direkteur — Nasionale Buro vir Opvoedkundige & Maatskaplike Navorsing Pretoria
Robbertse W P (Prof), Dept van Wetenskap P U vir CHO Potchefstroom, Dekaan, 1963
Robbertse H C G, 30, P/A N G Kerk Doornkloof Verwoerdburg, N G Predikant, 1976, Vanderbijlpark
Roberts J G A, 34, P/A Clocolan Koöp, Verkoopsman, 1975, Reddersburg
Robertson C B, 41, Uitkyk PK Sinksabrug, Boer, 1967, George
Robins F W , 35, Munisipaliteit Johannesburg, Lokasie Supt, 1969
Robinson P J, 36, Eerstelaan 91 Newtonpark Port Elizabeth, N G Predikant, 1971, Vanderbijlpark
Robinson S, By Bondsraad 1965 Spreek hy hom uit teen die Jaag na 'n Hoë Lewensstandaard

Rode H, 31, Woodlandsrylaan 1199 Pretoria, Geneesheer, 1973
Röder E E, 40, P/A Spar Foodliner Sasolburg, Sakeman, 1976, Pretoria
Roeloffse J A, 40, P/A Volkskas Zastron, Bestuurder, 1975, Pretoria
Roelofse C B, 40, N G Pastorie Milnerton, Predikant, 1966, Groot Brakrivier
Roelofse C J, 34, Bellstraat Fort Beaufort, Landdros, 1976, Vredendal
Roelofse E P, 36, Roelcar (Eien) Bpk Strand, Besturende Direkteur, 1964, George
Roelofse J J, 33, P/A Hoërskool Hottentotsholland Strand, Onderwyser, 1970, Caledon
Roelofse W, 39, PK Anerley Natal, Sakeman, 1970, Ventersburg
Roelvert D M, 35, P/A Afd Nie-Blankesake Stadsraad Johannesburg, Dorpsbeplanner, 1969, Mayfair-Wes
Roesch N C, 37, Fernandi Meisieskoshuis Bethal, Onderhoof, 1972, Vanderbijlpark
Roets A L, 36, Miltonlaan 83 Orkney, Onderwyser, 1974, Olifantshoek
Roets C J, 27, N G Pastorie Lichtenburg-Oos, Predikant, 1969, Warren
Roets F C, 44, Suidrand Hospitaal Rosettenville, Sekretaris, 1965, Rustenburg
Roets F W M, 38, Hoërskool-Pietersburg, Onderwyser, 1966, Naboomspruit
Roets J B S, 38, Dept van Justisie Pretoria, Staatsprokureur, 1968, Pretoria
Roets J B S, 38, Watersonstraat 52 Sasolburg, Onderwyser, 1973, Kempton Park
Roets J C M, 40, Landdroswoning Cullinan, Snr Landdros, 1975, Florida
Roets M J, 31, P/A Distillers Korp Stellenbosch, Reklamebeampte, 1965, Durban
Roets P G W, 39, Blinkwater Sentrum Thabazimbi, Boer, 1971
Roggeband W J, 38, P/A Gebrs Roggeband Elfdestraat 8 Delarey Maraisburg, Besturende Direkteur, 1967, Linden
Rhode A W, 37, P/A van wyk & Louw Pretoria, Ingenieur, 1974, Senekal
Roode C D, 33, Kmdt Senekalstraat 19 Dan Pienaar Bloemfontein Skakel by U O V S 4.2.76, Professor, 1970, Pietersburg
Roode J E, 30, P/A Maizekor Silverton, Sakeman, 1977, Lichtenburg
Roode P N F, 35, P/A All-O-Matic Transmissions/Rosestraat 73 Florida, Rekenmeester, 1975, Heidelberg Tvl
Roodt E J, 34, Roodt Apteek Parys, Apteker, 1967
Roodt H J, 32, S A Polisie Port Elizabeth, Speursersant, 1966
Roodt I J, 41, Blaauwbank Lichtenburg, Boer, 1968
Roodt L, 39, Posbus 185 Welkom, Argitek, 1965, Johannesburg
Roos D J, 45, Meerhof Hartebeespoort, Skoolhoof, 1972, Pretoria
Roos J G W, 36, Wegestraat 031 Mindalore Witpoortjie, N G Predikant, 1971, Krugersdorp
Roos J H (Lid Nr 3831), Bellville-Wes (Voorgestel vir die U R in 1968), Predikant
Roos J J, 41, Rooikoppies 44 Brits, Boer, 1964
Roos J R, 31, Collettstraat 5 Adcockvale/Tegn Kollege P E, Rektor, 1970, Vereeniging
Roos S M, 48, Doreg 3 Rosslyn Pretoria, Beeldhouer, 1974, Groblersdal
Roos S P, 53, Skurweberg Dist Pretoria, Skoolhoof, 1968
Roos T J (Lid Nr 7772), Somerset-Wes, 1963
Roos W, 37, Blyvooruitzicht Laerskool, Onderhoof, 1963
Roos W J, 34, P/A R A U Johannesburg, Uinv Ingenieur, 1973, Pretoria
Rörich R B, 45, P/A Dept Justisie Grahamstad, Staatsadvokaat, 1974, Stellenbosch
Ross A T, 45, Outeniqua Hostel George, Onderwyser, 1967, Olifantshoek
Ross J J (Lid Nr 3018), Afgetrede Rektor Fort Hare — Voorgestel vir die U R in 1968
Ross W, 46, Magaliesbergse Doring Koöp Brits, Handelsbestuurder, 1964, Marikana
Rosslee D D, 40, P/A Julies Haarkappersalon Heidelberg Tvl, Dameshaarkapper, 1969, Pretoria
Rossouw A A, 40, Munisipaliteit Bellville, Berekeningsklerk, 1970, Parow
Rossouw B, 34, P/A Dept van Bantoesake Mooketsi, Adm Klerk, 1968, Springs
Rossouw B J M, 34, P/A Santam/Corristonweg 16 Rondebosch, Streekbestuurder, 1975, Bellville
Rossouw D G, 42, Erweestraat 34 Wesselsbron, Prokureur, 1976, Odendaalsrus
rossouw D J, 26, Sekondêre Skool Vanwyksvlei, Onderwyser, 1964, Prins Albert
Rossouw G, 49, P/A Amkor Johannesburg, Asst Sekretaris, 1967, Meyerton
Rossouw G U, 36, Faganstraat 4 Marlands Germiston, Vise-Hoof, 1975, Nelspruit
Rossouw H A, 32, P/A Hoërskool Bonnievale, Onderwyser, 1977, Stellenbosch
Rossouw H W, 32, P/A Universiteit Stellenbosch, Snr Lektor, 1966
Rossouw J D, 27, Badenhorststraat 4 Albertinia, Onderwyser, 1968, Van Wykslei
Rossouw J H, 30, P/A Dept Landbou Tegn Dienste Pretoria, Skeikundige, 1968

Rossouw J L A, 40, P/A Afrikaansmedium Noordskool Pietersburg, Adj-Hoof, 1969, Nylstroom
Rossouw J P H (Lid Nr 7745), Springbok, 1963
Rossouw M J (Lid Nr 7675), Klerksdorp, Onderwyser, 1962
Rossouw M J K, 30, P/A Dorpsraad Duiwelskloof, Gesondheids-Inspekteur, 1976, Pretoria
Rossouw P A, 44, Vaalbank Coligny, Boer/Verteenwoordiger, 1976
Rossouw P A G, 32, Afdelingsraad Piketberg, Gesond Inspekteur, 1965
Rossouw P D, 28, P/A Pieter Rossouw & Vennote Pretoria, Argitek, 1965, Uitenhage
Rossouw P L, 36, Milldenestraat 10 Tiervlei, Geneesheer, 1967, George
Rossouw S N, 47, Shaft Sinkers Johannesburg, Kontrakingenieur, 1974, Stilfontein
Rossouw T J, 38, P/A Welvaart Koöp PK Trawal, Bestuurder, 1969, Kaapstad
Rossouw W F, 37, P/A Parlement Kaapstad, Asst Hoofrekenmeester, 1977, Vishoek
Rothmann A, 30, N G Kerk Niekershoop, Predikant, 1967, Johannesburg
Rothwell T W, 29, Palmweg 50 Durban, Tandarts, 1963
Rosseau B G, 34, P/A Oosend Sitrus Pakhuis Witrivier, Bestuurder, 1965, Kakamas
Rosseau J W, 35, Die Eike Caxtonweg Meadowridge Kaapstad, Veearts, 1970, Wynberg
Rousseau P, 43, Perseel 177 Derdepoort, Argitek, 1970, Carletonville
Rousseau P E (Lid Nr 2712), Sasol Johannesburg, Besturende Direkteur
Rousseau P J, 29, Leedssingel 17 Pinetown, Prokureur, 1975, Graaff-Reinet
Roux A A, 40, Môresonlaan 4 Durbanville, Geneesheer, 1968, Bellville
Roux A A, 27, Die Erf PK Vyeboom, Boer, 1967, Villiersdorp
Roux A J A (Dr), Hoof van Atoomkragraad
Roux A P, 33, P/A Sentrale Vliegskool Dunnottar, Majoor, 1965, Pretoria
Roux A P, 34, Sentraal Wes Koöp Klerksdorp, Sekretaris, 1964, Strand
Roux D F, 32, Elandsrivier Villiersdorp, Boer, 1971
Roux D G, 30, 7 S A I Bourke's Luck Graskop, Kaptein, 1975, Ladysmith Natal
Roux D J, 31, P/A Orkneyse Laerskool Orkney, Onderwyser, 1963, Pretoria
Roux F du T, 31, Noblesfontein Victoria-Wes, Boer, 1971, Pretoria
Roux G H, By Bondsraad van 1965 praat hy oor die Kloof tussen die Godsdiens en die Wetenskap
Roux G J, 29, Goede Hoop Franschhoek, Boer, 1964
Roux H, 35, P/A S A Weermag Valhalla, Offisier, 1975, Muizenberg
Roux J A V A, 44, P/A Staatsdienskomissie Pretoria, Adm Beheerbeampte, 1965, Malmesbury
Roux J F, 37, P/A Munisipaliteit Klerksdorp, Bou-Inspekteur, 1974, Hartenbos
Roux J H J, 39, Plot 29 Vastfontein Pretoria, Onderwyser, 1972
Roux J P (Dr), 34, P/A Asst Komm van Gevangenisse (Verwoerdburg), Brigadier, 1975, Pretoria
Roux J P, 38, Maroelastraat 21 Birchleigh, Ingenieur, 1975, Pretoria
Roux J P, 31, Universiteit Kollege Wes-Kaapland/Bellville, Lektor, 1967, Pretoria
Roux J P, 44, S A S Johannesburg, Elektro Ingenieur, 1964, Pretoria
Roux J V (Lid Nr 7746), Waterpoort, 1963
Roux J W, 34, P/A C M R Kimberley, Sekretaris, 1967, Riversdal
Roux L A D, 43, P/A N G Kerk Stilfontein, Predikant, 1968, Reddersburg O V S
Roux M J, 33, P/A Distillers Stellenbosch, Adm Bestuurder, 1966, Paarl
Roux P D A, 37, P/A Hoërskool Vereeniging, Onderwyser, 1964, Vaalwater
Roux P E J, 42, Kerkstraat 8 Vryburg, Skrynwerker, 1977
Roux S T, 34, Monteithoord 7 Durban-Noord, Patoloog, 1974, Carolina
Roux G W A, 27, Eselskloof Britstown, Boer, 1970
Rust H E, 31, Kerkstraat 84 Wellington, Geneesheer, 1963
Rust N J A, 30, P/A Universiteit Stellenbosch, Lektor, 1975, Malmesbury
Rykaart H J, 37, Palmietfontein Ventersdorp, Boer, 1965
Ryke P A J, 40, P U vir CHO Potchefstroom, Professor, 1967, Grabouw

S

Saaiman J C, 36, Schamrockstraatr 3 Ferndale — Uitbr Nr 3, Asst-Sekretaris, 1971,, Pretoria
Saaiman P J, 36, Volkskas Krugersdorp, Rekenmeester, 1965, Potchefstroom
Saayman B, 33, Huis Koornhof Laingsburg, Onderwyser, 1975, Bellville

Saayman N J L, 43, P/A Volkskas BPK Clocolan, Bestuurder, 1975, Bellville
Saayman T I, 29, 7deLaan 3 Lugmagbasis Ysterplaat/S A Weermag, Navigator, 1976, Pretoria
Sadie J C, 39, Primêre Skool Utrecht, Onderwyser, 1965, Stellenbosch
Sadie J J J, 43, Hilton PK Macheke S R, Boer, 1966, Malmesbury
Sadie M, 38, Lucretia Winburg, Boer, 1966, Welkom
Samuels H J (Prof)
Sans P J, 39, PK Marchand, Onderwyser, 1963
Saunderson J W, 32, Pringlestraat 5 Vanderbijlpark, Dosent/G O K, 1977, Alberton/Johannesburg
Schaaf G W, 31, Avontuur Grootfontein, Klerk, 1968
Schabort P J, 34, Umgwezistraat 9 Emmarentia Johannesburg, Advokaat, 1970, Alberton
Schaffner V, 38, Luytstraat Frankfort, Apteker, 1967, Heidelberg Tvl
Schalkwyk A P, 45, Middelwater De Wildt, Motorhawe-Eienaar, 1977, Verwoerdburg
Scheepers C F, 32, P/A Ekonomiese Raadgewer V D E M (Verwoerdburg), Adjunk-Direkteur, 1976, Bellville
Scheepers C H H, 36, Herbert Bakerstraat 41 Groenkloof Pretoria, Openbare Rekenmeester & Ouditeur, 1972
Scheepers D J J, 37, N G Pastorie Wesselsbron, Predikant, 1965, Vryburg
Scheepers E, 32, Primêre Skool de Hoop, Onderhoof, 1976, Graaff-Reinet
Scheepers F A, 46, P/A Westransvaalse Bantoe-Adm Raad Potchefstroom, Direkteur, 1974, Ermelo
Scheepers G A, 46, Spoorwegkollege Esselenpark, Instrukteur, 1967, Davel
Scheepers G C, 34, Haarhofstraat 21 Groblersdal, Apteker, 1975, Sabie
Scheepers G J A, 40, S A S & H Vryheid, Werktuigkundige, 1977, Ladysmith
Scheepers G M J, 35, Jansenstraat 8 Ladysmsith, Fabriekseienaar/Ing, 1973, Pretoria
Scheepers H E, 45, Stilton PK Senlac Bray, Boer, 1975, Odendaalsrus
Scheepers H P, Ottosdal — By 1969 Bondsraad praat hy oor Godsdiensonderrig
Scheepers J A, 42, PK Hartland oor Paulpietersburg, Winkelier/Boer, 1974
Scheepers J F J, 34, P/A Van Zyl Scott Naude & Buys Pretoria, Ouditeur, 1974, Pretoria
Scheepers J H, 42, P/A Universiteit Kollege v d Noorde Pietersburg, 1969, Witsieshoek
Scheepers J H, 44, Sigoreibeheerraad Alexandria, Afdelingshoof, 1967
Scheepers J J, 32, Omdraai Bethlehem, Boer, 1964
Scheepers J J, 40, Van Veldenstraat Brits (N G Sending), Predikant, 1971, Carolina
Scheepers J K, 48, Ficks Alexandria, Boer, 1973, Pretoria
Scheepers J S K, 40, Genl Kockstraat 132 Welgelegen Pietersburg/Boland Bank, Takbestuurder, 1975, Pretoria
Scheepers L, 36, P/A Triomf Kunsmis/Kleinstraat 94 Ermelo, Landboukundige, 1977, Fort Beaufort
Scheepers S P P, 38, Ziervogelstraat Cradock, Tandarts, 1965, Winburg
Scheepers S W J, 35, Sewefontein Bethlehem, Boer, 1971
Scheepers T, 41, Laerskool Swartruggens, Skoolhoof, 1964, Lydenburg
Scheffer, Wolmaransstad, N P Komitee, 1966
Scheffer J H, 47, Andersonstraat 402 Menlopark Pretoria, Sakeman, 1968
Scheffer J H, 35, P/A Yskor Pretoria, Skakelbeampte, 1973, Johannesburg
Scheltema J C, 33, P/A Dept Landbou Barkly-Oos, Vakkundige Beampte, 1975, Aberdeen
Scherrer A J, 29, Kemptonweg Kempton Park, N G Predikant, 1971, Port Elizabeth
Schickerling J K, 39, Bosbult Delareyville, Boer, 1964
Schickerling W G, 46, Dept van Binnelandse Inkomste Pretoria, Ondersekretaris, 1965
Schieke K, 52, De Wetstraat 101 Krugersdorp, Skoolhoof, 1964, Morgenzon
Schlunz G I, 49, Bergzichtstraat Malmesbury, Elektrisiën, 1967, Kaapstad
Schlebusch P L, Minister van Binnelandse Sake
Schmidt A C J E, 36, Wykom Louwsburg Natal, Boer, 1968, Vryheid
Schmidt R, 31, P/A N G Sendingpastorie Molteno, Sendeling, 1965, Kimberley
Schmidt W W, 29, Kirkstraat Maclear, Sakeman, 1967, Pietersburg
Schneider D F, 34, P/A Universiteit van Stellenbosch, Snr Lektor, 1969, Paarl
Schneider D J, 34, Uitzicht Wellington, Veearts, 1964, Paarl
Schnetler J F, 30, Idastraat 9 Oberholzer, Veearts, 1967, Krugersdorp
Schoch A E, 42, Banhoekweg 191 Stellenbosch/Universiteit van Stellenbosch, Snr Lektor, 1977, Grootfontein

Schoeman A D, 40 P/A Yskor Pretoria, Asst Aankoper, 1963, Graaff-Reinet
Schoeman A M, 28, Vierdestraat 21 Fochville, Onderwyser, 1968
Schoeman Ben (Lid Nr 3613) Voormalige Minister van Vervoer — Voorsitter van Perskor
Schoeman C, 49, P/A S A Polisie Dordrecht, Sersant, 1968, Sterkstroom
Schoeman C F, 44, Esselenstraat 69 Potchefstroom, Professor, 1966
Schoeman C F S, 31, Leydstraat 25 Morehill Benoni, Tandarts, 1974, Pretoria
Schoeman C J, 46, S A S & H Koffiefontein, Stasiemeester, 1966, Oranjerivierstasie
Schoeman D H, 36, Ethelweg 8 Brandwacht Worcester, Onderwyser, 1974, Beaufort-Wes
Schoeman D W, 29, Moordenaarspoort Dordrecht, Boer, 1966
Schoeman G D, 44, Munisipaliteit Pretoria, Rekenmeester, 1966
Schoeman G S (Lid Nr 7715), Bloemfontein, Lektor, 1962
Schoeman H, Minister van Landbou
Schoeman H M, 34, P/A Cicira Opleidingskool Umtata, Skoolhoof, 1965, Pretoria
Schoeman H W, 45, P/A Stadsraad Pretoria, Adj-Klerk van die Raad, 1967, Worcester
Schoeman J, 32, P/A Joe Schoeman & Kie Springfontein, Prokureur, 1973, Pretoria
Schoeman J, 42, Lomangundiweg 47 Avondale Salisbury, Sakeman, 1966, Brokenhill
Schoeman J G, 34, S A Lugdiens Johannesburg, Loods, 1965, Kaapstad
Schoeman J H, 40 P/A Stewarts & Lloyds Vereeniging, Beplanner, 1974
Schoeman J H, 29, Marshallstraat 37b Pietersburg0P/A Pietersburgse Hoërskool, Onderwyser, 1974, Pretoria
Schoeman J J, 38, Kingsleystraat 9 Vanderbijlpark, Stadsgeneesheer, 1966, Fouriesberg
Schoeman J L, 30 P/A Huis Veldman Ermelo, Onderwyser, 1969, Vereeniging
Schoeman M G, 34, Brandbach Cullinan, Boer, 1975, Potchefstroom
Schoeman N M, 35, Transvalie Morgenzon Tvl, Boer, 1968, Hendrina
Schoeman P C, 37, S A Polisie Groblersdal, Adj-Offisier, 1963, Potgietersrus
Schoeman P G, P U vir CHO Potchefstroom, Asst Registrateur, 1963
Schoeman P J A, 30, Bronkhorstfontein Volksrust, Boer, 1967, Dordrecht
Schoeman P P, 34, P/A Hoërskool Sasolburg, Vise-Hoof, 1974, Vereeniging
Schoeman P S J A, 38, P/A Laerskool Graskop, Skoolhoof, 1964, Kennedy's Vale
Schoeman S E, 32, P/A Hoërskool Vaalharts, Onderwyser, 1975, Sterkstroom
Schoeman S J, 30, N G Pastorie Ladybrand-Noord, Predikant, 1970, Stellenbosch
Schoeman S J, 31, P/A S A Orrelbouers Pretoria, Bestuurder, 1963, Lydenburg
Schoeman S J, 38, Dept Wysbegeerte Universiteit Pretoria, Lektor, 1964, Brits
Schoeman T F, 39, P/A S A Weermag Pretoria, Kaptein, 1974, Pretoria-Noord
Schoeman W G, 36, P/A Zinkor Nigel, Voorman Passer, 1975
Schoeman W J, 38, Werke-Ontwerp en Tekenkant Yskor Newcastle, superintendent, 1973, Vanderbijlpark
Schoevers J E, 34, Stoeifontein Victoria-Wes, Boer, 1964
Scholtemeijer G J H, 29, P/A Sentraal-Wes Koöp Potchefstroom, Bemarkingbestuurder, 1973
Scholtz A P, 37, Mielieraad Pretoria, Asst Bestuurder, 1967
Scholtz C v Z, 30, Middelpost Kimberley, Boer, 1975, Ventersdorp
Scholtz D A, 30, Maripi Bantoe Opleidingskool/P/S Acornhoek, Onderwyser, 1967, Lydenburg
Scholtz D H, 34, P/A D J de Villiers Scholtz & v d Walt Johannesburg, Prokureur, 1974
Scholtz D J, 29, Huistenbosch Papkuil, Boer, 1975, Danielskuil
Scholtz D J, 27, Langenhovenweg Hopetown, Onderwyser, 1977, Paarl
Scholtz H C C, 40, Kremetart Nr 34 Gazankulu, Landdros, 1976, Ladysmsith Natal
Scholtz H J S, 40, Doornfontein, Ottosdal, Onderwyser, 1964, Danielskuil
Scholtz I P, 46, Laerskool Kroonrand Johannesburg, Skoolhoof, 1970, Kempton Park
Scholtz J A C, 49, N G Pastorie Nietverdiend, Predikant, 1964, Kuruman
Scholtz J A J, 38, Migdolskool Schweizer-Reneke, Vise-Hoof, 1974, Schweizer-Reneke
Scholtz J C, 31, N G Pastorie Amalia, Predikant, 1973, Stellenbosch
Scholtz J W K, 25, P/A Skoolraad Kokstad, Sekretaris, 1965, King Williamstown
Scholtz P A, 30 Jacobstraat 613 Gezine/S A Polisie Dept, Luitenant, 1976, Pretoria
Scholtz P F J, Lid van die U R se Ekonomiese — Komitee 1973
Scholtz P F R, 55, Rondebultskool Rondebult, Skoolhoof, 1973, Germiston
Scholtz P L, 41, P/A Onderwyskollege Graaff-Reinet, Dosent, 1963, Vanrhynsdorp
Scholtz P L, 36, N G Kerk Montagu, Predikant, 1967, Koës S W A
Scholtz P L, 48, Dept Arbeid Pretoria, Eerste Adm Beampte, 1964, Calvinia

Scholtz W C, 38, Snymanlaan 6 Brits, Geneesheer, 1975, Louis Trichardt
Scholtz W du T, 44, PK Jacobsdal, Boer, 1963
Schoombee J C L, Praat oor Onderwys by 1966 Bondsraad
Schoombie J M, 40, S A Polisie Ottosdal, Adj-Offisier, 1966, Vryburg
Schoombie H S, 30, P/A Dept Hoër Onderwys Pretoria, Personeelklerk, 1968
Schoombie J A, 36, P/A Tedelex Johannesburg, Kredietbestuurder, 1976, Pretoria
Schoombie J C, 31, N G Pastorie Uitenhage-Noord, Predikant, 1965, King Williamstown
Schoon W F, Veiligheidspolisie P/S 506 Oshakati, Luit Kolonel
Schoon W F, 40, Veiligheidspolisie/Buckinghamlaan 23 Pietermaritzburg, Majoor, 1971, Durban
Schoonbee G S, 43, Kalkfontein Groblersdal, Boer, 1973, Bronkhorstspruit
Schoonbee J A, 29, P/A Laerskool Piet Hugo Pietersburg, Onderwyser, 1974, Louis Trichardt
Schoonees P C, 37, P/A Afdelingsraad Worcester, Siviele Ingenieur, 1965, Stellenbosch
Schoonraad J, 40, Lornaweg 21 Kimberley/S A S Bank, Takbestuurder, 1971, Bloemfontein
Schoonraad P F J, 38, P/A Ysksor Pretoria, Klerk, 1968
Schoonwinkel J H, 34, Rissikstraat 15 Dagbreek/East Rand Engineering, Bestuurder, 1971, Bothaville
Schrader H D, 26, Huis 22 Oshakati, Geneesheer, 1975, Bellville
Schreiber F A, 38, P/A S A S Kantoor van die Hoofbestuurder, Johannesburg, Seniorklerk, 1967, Durban
Schreuder H A, 29, Humpatastraat Gobabis S W A, Geneesheer, 1971, Oshakati
Schreuder H A, 48, P/A Paryse Hoërskool, Vise-Hoof, 1974, Pretoria
Schreüder H F R, 44, Van Enkhuysenstraat Vredenburg, Hoofskakelbeampte, 1975, Pretoria
Schreuder H O, 44, P/A Munisipaliteit Wolmaransstad, Stadsklerk, 1968, Usakos S W A
Schreüder P M, 33, P/A Hoërskool Calitzdorp, Skoolhoof, 1967, Redelinghuys K P
Schreuder P v L, 31, Skuitjiesklip Vredenburg, Boer, 1964, Koringberg
Schroeder H F, 40, Laerskool Hendrik Vanderbijl Vanderbijlpark, Hoof, 1965, Marico
Schulenburg r, Op N P Komitee Wolmaransstad, 1966
Schultz D M, 36, Unisa Pretoria, Lektor, 1969, Johannesburg
Schultz J C, 31, P/A Hoërskool Alberton/Du Plessisweg 1 Florentia Alberton, Vise-Hoof, 1976, Pretoria
Schultz M J, 46, Endwell Aliwal-Noord, Boer/Klerk, 1974
Schulze G E Y, 32, Strydomstraat 28 Bailliepark Potchefstroom, Geneesheer, 1975
Schumann C G W (Prof), Lid van die U R se ekonomiese Komitee 1973
Schumann T E W (Lid Nr 1133), Ondervoorsitter Atoomkragraad Pretoria, — Voorgestel vir die U R in 1968
Schumann W A , 34, P/A Raad op Atoomkrag Pretoria, Navorsingsing, 1969, Stellenbosch
Schurink R W, 42, Zwagershoek Lydenburg, Boer, 1963
Schutte A P, 38, Universiteit van S A Preotira, Produksie Bestuurder, 1965, Schweizer-Reneke
Schutte B C (Prof), Onderwysfakulteit P U vir CHO Potchefstroom, Dekaan, 1963
Schutte C E G, 45, Cobhamweg 1163 Queenswood Pretoria, Skeikundige, 1968
Schutte C J H, 34, Proteaweg 69 Middelburg Tvl/S A Polisie, 1971, Pretoria
Schutte C J H, 27, Krompoort Venterstad, Boer, 1968
Schutte F R P, 30, Witbank Apteek, Apteker, 1964, Johannesburg
Schutte F R P, 32, Carterstraat 50 Vanderbijlpark, Onderwyser, 1971, Klerksdorp
Schutte G P, 38, P/A Unie Spoorweg Begrafnisonderneming Germiston, Klerk, 1964
Schutte I C, 38, P/A Sentra Oes Koöp Bpk Ficksburg, Adm Bestuurder, 1974, Bethlehem
Schutte J H, 44, P/A Gereformeerde Kerk Piet Retief, Predikant, 1975, Potchefstroom
Schutte J H P, 29, P/A Van wyk de Vries Malan & Steyn Fairlands, Prokureur, 1975
Schutte J H T, 45, S A U K Johannesburg, Hoof Programontw, 1965, Senekal
Schutte J W, 31, Matjespoort Willowmore, Boer, 1969
Schutte P C, 26, Kliniekskool Loopspruit, Onderwyser, 1968, Sannieshof
Schutte P J, 34, Barriestraat Vanderbijlpark, Geneesheer, 1967, Kroonstad
Schutte P J, 45, Klippan Sannieshof, Boer, 1964
Schutte S H, 34, S A Polisie Odendaalsrus, Luitenant, 1964
Schutte W J, 39, Morgenzon Dist Louis Trichardt, Boer, 1974

Schwartz H J, 28, Nas Visserye (Edms) Bpk Kaapstad, Bestuurder, 1970
Scott B J, 39, Swanepoellaan 3 Aldara Park/Brink Roos & Du Toit Randburg, Ouditeur, 1977, Pretoria
Scott L B, 31, P/A Hoërskool Genl Hertzog Witbank, Onderwyser, 1970, Groblersdal
Scribante O E, 45, Belvedere Schweizer-Reneke, Onderwyser, 1970
Seegers L S, 35, S A U K Johannesburg, Supt Suid-Sotho Diens, 1974, Krugersdorp
Senekal H E J (Lid Nr 3519), Pretoria, Hoofonderwyser
Senekal J B, 42, P/A Laerskool Jan Cilliers, Johannesburg, Skoolhoof, 1975, Randburg
Senekal J H, 36, Universiteitkollege van Zoeland, Professor, 1966, Johannesburg
Senekal M L, 40, Sewefontein Bryanston, Boer, 1969
Senekal P P, 34, Perseel 217 Kameeldrift/New World Apteek Pretoria, Apteker, 1970, Pretoria
Serfontein D D, 44, Danfordstraat 27 Bethal/Volkskas, Bestuurder, 1976, Hartswater
Serfontein D D, 33, Maroelastraat 16 Randparkrif 3 Randburg/Wonder-Tuinbou-Produkte, Bestuurder, 1975, Nelspruit
Serfontein F J, 30, De Wetlaan 5 Mosel Uitenhage, N G Predikant, 1977, Stellenbosch
Serfontein J A, 35, Spioenkop Springfontein, Boer/Ouditeur, 1970, Boshof
Serfontein J H, 42, P/A Volkskas BPK Marble Hall, Bestuurder, 1974, Fochville
Serfontein J H P, 31, P/A N G Pastorie Germiston, Predikant, 1977, Pretoria
Serfontein M, 41, Volkskas-Durban, Rekenmeester, 1966
Serfontein P R, 46, P/A Naude & Naude Bloemfontein, Prokureur, 1969
Sersfontein J D, 44, Durbanstraat 33 Fort Beaufort/Bantoe Hoërskool Healdtown K P, Onderhoof, 1971, Bloemfontein
Sevenster J J, 42, N G Pastorie Koffiefontein, N G Predikant, 1971, Stellenbosch
Sherman T W W, 42, Bonuskor Kaapstad, Sekretaris, 1964, Kimberley
Sidler L F H, 49, P/A Dept Gemeenskapsbou Pretoria, Klerk, 1966, Kimberley
Sieberhagen C F, 31, P/A N G Kerk Pretoria-Wes, Predikant, 1968, Vaalharts
Sieberhagen N, Spreek Bondsraad toe oor Kleurlinge
Siebert M A, 39, N G Gemeente Amersfoort, Predikant, 1977, Germiston
Siebrits A M, 37, Gladiatorstraat 90 Kempton Park/S A L, Kaptein, 1971, Franschhoek
Siepker A J, 46, P/A Dept Landbou Tegniese Dienste Middelburg K P, Asst Direkteur, Karoostreek, 1976, Pretoria
Siertsema H H, 41, P/A Hospitaal Krugersdorp, Superintendent, 1963, Klerksdorp
Simpson J A, 32, N H Pastorie Durban, Predikant, 1975, Bulawayo
Sinclair C, 32, De Unie Carnarvon, Boer, 1970, Victoria-Wes
Sipsma J, 33, David Baxter 29 Pietermaritzburg, Onderwyser, 1974, Brits
Skein E v E, 31, Posbus 3 Humansdorp, Prokureur, 1966, Oos-Londen
Skein T, 27, Die Rand Jansenville, Onderwyser, 1969, Port Elizabeth
Slabber J D, 32, Dept Landbou Tegn Dienste Queenstown, Streeksbeampte, 1964, Aliwal-Noord
Slabber J H W, 29, Sandkloof Malmesbury, Boer, 1970
Slabber L J, 37, Braklaagte Dist Bloemfontein, Boer/Verkoopsasst, 1973, Kimberley
Slabber M M, 29, Middelpos Malmesbury, Boer, 1970
Slabber P J W, 37, Leliefontein Hopefield, Boer, 1975
Slabbert B J, 38, Oviumbo-Oos Okahandja, Boer, 1977
Slabbert D, 28, Excelsior PK Danielsrus, Boer, 1964, Bethlehem
Slabbert J, 35, P/A N G Pastorie Reddersburg, Predikant, 1967, Bloemfontein
Slabbert J A J, 29, P/A S A S & H Soutrivier, Ingenieur, 1976, Strand
Slabbert J D, 38, Dudgeonweg 3 Rondebosch, Skoolhoof, 1975, Porterville
Slabbert M, 43, Tshiya Regeringskool Witsieshoek, Onderwyser, 1973, Soutpan OVS
Slabbert P H, 35, Sendingpastorie Brits, Sendeling, 1966, Leopoldville
Slabbert S, 44, S A S & H Johannesburg, Klerk, 1967, Pretoria
Sleigh J W, 38, P/A S A Vloot Kaapstad, Kaptein, 1976, Vredenburg
Sloet H A (Lid Nr 7767), Johannesburg-Noord, 1963
Smal P J, 38, P/A U P E Port Elizabeth/Rinalaan 19 Framesby, Lektor Opvoedkunde, 1975, Willowmore
Smal P J N, 44, N G Pastorie Mariasburg, Predikant, 1964, Pretoria
Small J G C, 35, Seselaan 35 Walmer Port Elizabeth/U P E, Professor, 1971, Pretoria
Smidt H C, 33, P/A Saambou Kaapstad, Rekenmeester, 1968
Smidt S A P, 39, P/A Volkskas Laingsburg, Bestuurder, 1975, Pretoria

Smit A, 33, Bo-Downes Calvinia, Boer, 1973, Fraserburg
Smit A A (Lid Nr 7684), Pretoria, Tandarts, 1962
Smit A C J, 32, N G Pastorie Sonhoogte Germiston, Predikant, 1964, Vereeniging
Smit A K, 35, Bospoort PK Politsi, Boer, 1965, Pietersburg
Smit A L, 40, P/A Indiërkollege Durban, Professor, 1965, Villiersdorp
Smit A P, 26, Voorspoed-Koshuis Middelburg Tvl, Onderwyser, 1963, Bloemhof
Smit A P, Praat oor Christelike Sake by 1969 Bondsraad
Smsit B C V, 46, David Glennysingel 7 Empangeni, Ingenieur, 1975, Pretoria
Smsit B F, 34, Malutilaan 12 Doringkloof/Unisa Pretoria, Dosent, 1976, Bloemfontein
Smit B H, 30, N G Pastorie Prieska, N G Predikant, 1970, Pretoria
Smit C F, 30, Universiteit Pretoria, Snr Lektor, 1974
Smsit C J, 38, Scottstraat 3 Messina, Onderwyser, 1967, Pretoria
Smit C J, 30, P/A Geref Kerk Randfontein, Predikant, 1977, Schoemansville
Smit C J B, 31, Parkrylaan 9 Arcadia Pretoria, Oor-Neus-en Keelarts, 1975, Potgietersrus
Smit C N, 34, P/A Dept van Bantoe Adm & Ont Windhoek, Hoof Vakkund Beampte, 1967, Pretoria
Smit D J, 30, P/A M E Wessels & Kie Bothaville, Ouditeur, 1974, Bellville
Smit D J, 42, Afdelingsraad Kenhardt, Sekretaris, 1973, Upington
Smit D J E, 30, Langstraat 42 Moselbaai, Onderwyser, 1971, Prieska
Smit D J v L, 38, Kaap de Goede Hoop Spaarbank Kaapstad, Rekenmeester, 1968, Tiervlei
Smit E, 35, P U vir CHO Potchefstroom, Snr Lektor, 1969, Ladybrand
Smit e, 34, Hoërskool Voortrekker Kaapstad, Onderwyser, 1963, Kimberley
Smit E G, 53, P/A Dept Hoër Onderwys Pretoria, Eerste Adm Beampte, 1968, Pretoria
Smit E H, 33, Maranda PK Gravelotte, Boer, 1969, Pretoria
Smit F A, 38, Volkskas Prins Albert, Bestuurder, 1967, Bellville
Smit F J, 45, Kerkstraat 19D Lydenburg, Posmeester, 1976, Kempton Park
Smit F P J, 34, Korhansrug Darling, Boer, 1974
Smit F P Z, 34, Groblerstraat Pieterburg, Onderwyser, 1974, Pretoria
Smit G C M, 44, Laerskool Jan Van Riebeeck Springs, Adj-Hoof, 1968, Heidelberg Tvl
Smit G G, 37, Landdroskantoor Boksburg, Landdros, 1967, Queenstown
Smit G J, 40, Komissarisstraat 1 Fouriesburg, Skoolhoof/Hoërskool, 1971, Virginia
Smit G J J (Lid Nr 2644), Kaapstad
Smit H C, 42, P/A S A Polisie Pretoria, Kaptein, 1968
Smit H H, Minister van Kleurling Betrekkinge
Smit H V, 40, P/A Hoërskool Sentraal Bloemfontein, Vise-Hoof, 1975, Hennenman
Smit H Z, 32, P/A Yskor Newcastle, Personeelbeampte, 1974, Vanderbijlpark
Smit J A, 40, P/A Yskor-Utiliteitswinkels Sishen, Bestuurder, 1975, Uis S W A
Smit J D A, 32, P/A Hoërskool Hofmeyr, Skoolhoof, 1967, Philipstown
Smit J F, 34, Soutpan Albertinia, Boer/Klerk, 1967, Riversdal
Smit J G O, 44, P/A Volkskas Koppies, Bestuurder, 1977, Kimberley
Smit J H, 34, Chesnutsstraat 74, Drie Riviere Vereeniging, Prokureur, 1976, Bultfontein
Smit J H, 29, Sanlam Calvinia, Verteenwoordiger, 1966, Aberdeen
Smit J H, 46, P/A Dept van Justisie Sonderwater, Werkswinkelbevelvoerder, 1968, Leeukop Gevangenis
Smit J H N, 35, Burensingle 3 Durbanville, Skoolhoof, 1973, Alberton
Smit J J, 32, P/A Dept van Vervoer Pretoria, Asst Hoofingenieur, 1974, Zeerust
Smit J J, 35, P/A A T K B Pretoria, Klerk, 1968
Smit J J, 32, P/A Alusaf Richardsbaai, Asst Supt Reduksie, 1973, Pretoria
Smit J J, 39, Sekondêre Skool Usakos, Onderwyser, 1974, Touwsrivier
Smit J J, 48, P/A S A Polisie Pretoria, Kaptein, 1969
Smit J J N, 39, Ebenhaeserskool Krugersdorp-Wes, Hoof, 1966, Brits
Smit J M C, 30, Murraystraat 32 Brooklyn Pretoria, Advokaat, 1968, Cradock
Smit J M C, Algemene Bestuurder Landbank
Smit J P 31, Antoinettestraat 4 Floridapark, Hoofkwaliteitsbeampte, 1968, Proklamasieheuwel
Smit J S, 36, Elvina Bethlehem, Boer, 1972
Smit J W, 29, Prieska Vleiskoöperasie, Boer/Sakebestuurder, 1976, Marydale
Smit K H, 32, Landdroskantoor Marquard, Landdros, 1974, Mosselbaai
Smit M C, 42, P/A Staatsvoorskotte Pretoria, Klerk, 1968
Smit M J, 39, Tegn Kollege Rustenburg, Onderhoof, 1970, Alberton

Smit M J, Skakel vir Afgevaardigdes na Kongres van Vereniging vir Beroeps-en Tegniese Onderwys 2.2.77
Smit M K, 25, P/A Laerskool Mariepskop P/S Klaserie, Onderwyser, 1975, Haenertsburg
Smit N W H, By 1966 Bondsraad Pleit hy dat steun vir Afrikaanse Instellings op Skool Universiteite & Kolleges Aandag Geniet
Smit O J, 31, Volkskas Schweizer-Reneke, Rekenmeester, 1965, Pretoria
Smit P, 32, Afrika-Instituut Pretoria, Navorser, 1969, Williston
Smit P A, 41, Driehoek Tsumeb, Boer, 1966, Otavi
Smit P D (Jnr), 30, Doornriviersvlei Barrydale, Boer, 1975
Smit P de V, 34, Lenteson Newcastle, Geneesheer, 1972, Pretoria
Smit P M J, 34, Huislandman Malmesbury, Onderwyser, 1966, Cradock
Smit P S, 39, Huyerstraat 26 Delmas, Sakeman, 1973
Smit S J J, 29, P/A S A Polisie Durban, Luitenant, 1969, Standerton
Smit T C, 30, Dept Opvoedkunde Univ Stellenbosch, Snr Lektor, 1965, Pretoria
Smit T S, 29, Bainstraat Barrydale, N G Predikant, 1977, Stellenbosch
Smit W, 33, Huis 1459/58 Derdelaan Tsumeb/Hoërskool Etosha, Onderhoof, 1971, Windhoek
Smith A J S, 43, S A S & H Olifantsfontein, Snr Instr Handel, 1975, Windhoek
Smith C C, 29, Bothstraat Kestell, Geneesheer, 1967, Bloemfontein
Smith C de J, 39, P/A B V S Pretoria, Adj Afdelingshoof, 1975
Smith C F, 43, Silverpineweg 125 Malanshof/Hoërskool Randburg, Vise-Hoof, 1970
Smith C J, 44, P/A Grey-Kollege Bloemfontein, Skoolraad-Sekretaris, 1970, Harrismith
Smith C L, 32, Van Rooyenshek Wepener/S A Polisie, Luitenant, 1970, Pretoria
Smith C M, 28, Neliesmith-Sportwinkel Bloemfontein, Sakeman, 1964
Smith D J, 33, P/A N H Kerk Newcastle, Predikant, 1973, Ogies
Smith D P, 42, Uysstraat 3 De Aar, Loodgieter, 1976, Makwassie
Smith D W L, 29, Durban Deep 199 Roodepoort, Skofbaas, 1967
Smith E J, 41, Cypherkuil Philipstown, Boer, 1964, Rhodes
Smith E J J, 32, Posbus 86 Koës, Boer, 1975
Smith F C, 45, P/A Laingsburg Keep Laingsburg, Bestuurder, 1968, Williston
Smith F W, 35, Middelbare Skool Cedarville, Hoof, 1964, Patentie
Smith G J, 28, Earlstraat 2 Newcastle, Onderwyser, 1968, Welkom
Smith G J, 48, Zasmlaan Waterval Boven/S A S & H, Werksvoorman, 1970, Brakpan
Smith H D, 38, N G Kerk Odendaalsrus, Predikant, 1973, Bloemfontein
Smith H J, 29, Trentstraat 42 Murrayfield Pretoria, Kernfisikus/W N N R, 1971
Smith H J, 30, Mizpah Rouxville, Boer, 1964
Smith J, 38, Plettenbergstraat Welgemoed Bellville, Rekenmeester, 1977, Stellenbosch
Smith J A J, 33, Impala-Koshuis Thabazimba, Onderwyser, 1968, Nylstroom
Smith J B, 38, Deepdene Wepener, Boer, 1970, Pretoria
Smith J H, 39, P/A Republikeinse Publikasies Durban, Voorradebestuurder, 1974, Lesotho
Smith M C, 28, Frisgewaagd Utrecht, Boer, 1970, Pretoria
Smith M D, 36, P/A Krystuigraad Pretoria, Ingenieur, 1973
Smith N J, 31, N G Pastorie Tsilinzini, Predikant, 1964, OVS
Smith N J S, 24, P/A Trust Bank Bethal, Bankklerk, 1969
Smith O, 32, P/A Welkom Goudmyn, Asst Ventilasie Supt, 1975, Zastron
Smith P F, 30, P/A Sysu Vakansiebelange Bpk Verwoerdburg, Mpy Sekr/Sakeman, 1974, Sunnyside
Smith P J, 33, P/A Volkskas Jansenville, Rekenmeester, 1966, Carolina
Smith P M (Lid Nr 3219), N H Kerk Pretoria, Predikant
Smith S C, 35, P/A Volkskas Bpk Pretoria, Ekonoom, 1974, Johannesburg
Smith W, 34, Gousblomstraat 16 Benoni, Klerk Stadsraad, 1971
Smook T, 26, Hangklip Hostel Queenstown, Onderwyser, 1970, Kimberley
Smuts H P v d M, 42, Sunny Grass Winterton, Boer, 1973, Lydenburg
Smuts N L, 44, Wilbotsdal 44 Randfontein, Sakeman, 1969
Smsuts s du T, 40, N G Sendinggemeente Oberholzer, Predikant, 1974, Malawi
Snijders H J C (Lid Nr 1971), Johannesburg, Predikant
Snijders J F A, 43, P/A Nederlandse Bank Kaapstad, Onderrekenmeester, 1965, Worcester
Snyders H J C, 42, Klipfontein Leeudoringstad, Boer, 1973
Snyman A de V, 26, Hoërskool Hoogenhout Bethal, Onderwyser, 1968
Snyman A F, 40, Retieflaan 351 Lyttelton, Landdros, 1974

Snyman A J, 43, P/A Pietersburg Bottling Co Louis Trichardt, Bestuurder, 1968, Pietersburg
Snyman B J, 49, Landdroskantoor Lydenburg, Landdros, 1965, Pretoria
Snyman C, 34, P/S Spesiale Middelbare Skool Milnerton, Skoolhoof, 1976, Oos-Londen
Snyman C F W, 33, P/A N G Kerk Grootfontein, Predikant, 1968, Stellenbosch
Snyman D P, 31, Anglo Vaal Johannesburg, Elektro Tegn Ing. 1966, Randleases
Snyman F J, 47, P/A Afr Woordeboekkantoor Stellenbosch, Hoofredakteur, 1963, Rietbron
Snyman G C, 40, P/A Raad op Atoomkrag Pelindaba, Wet Navorser, 1977, Pretoria
Snyman G J, 41, N G Pastorie Elandia Klerksdorp, Predikant, 1963, Carolina
Snyman G J, 33, Volkskas Kempton Park, Rekenmeester, 1964, Barkly-Wes
Snyman G P C, 49, Liverpool Koedoeskop, Boer, 1966, Pretoria
Snyman H, 47, P/A Veiligheidspolisie Despatch, Kaptein, 1976, Pretoria
Snyman H G, 36, Navorsingsinstituut vir Tabak P/S Rustenburg, Grondkundigeseksiehoof, 1970, Potgietersrus
Snyman H J, 37, P/A S W A Landbou-Unie Windhoek, Sekretaris, 1975
Snyman H L F (Dr), Lid van die U R se Ekonomiese Komitee 1973
Snyman H W, (Lid Nr 5574), Pretoria, Internis
Snyman J J, 34, Ysterhartstraat 48 Birchleigh, Snr Tegnikus/SAL, 1972, Alberton
Snyman J J, 28, Saambougebou Pietersburg, Argitek, 1964, Pretoria
Snyman J L J, 39, Geref Kerk Bloemfontein-Noord, Predikant, 1967, Paarl
Snyman J P, 40, P/A Volkskas Delareyville, Bestuurder, 1974, Marble Hall
Snyman J W, 33, P/A Landbounavorsingstasie Dundee, Navorser, 1969, Estcourt
Snyman N J, 40, Luctorlaan 262 Meyerspark Pretoria, Lektor U P, 1975, Nylstroom
Snyman N S, 30, P/A S A Speurdiens Kaapstad, Kaptein, 1974
Snyman P A, 36, Perseel 25D3 PK Hartsvallei, Boer, 1963, Vryburg
Snyman P J, 37, P/A Hoërskool Vryburg, Onderwyser, 1968, Lichtenburg
Snyman P M, 31, Orbankoshuis Otjiwarongo, Onderwyser, 1974, Bloemfontein
Snyman R P G, 34, Golfstraat 1 Comet Boksburg, Onderwyser, 1965, Marico
Snyman t, 31, Herv Pastorie Marikana, N H Predikant, 1973, Roodepoort
Snyman W J (Prof), Teologiese Fakulteit P U vir CHO Potchefstroom, Dekaan, 1963
Snyman W J, 32, Saambougebou Pietersburg, Geneesheer, 1965
Snyman W S, 34, Kerkstraat Heilbron, Rekenmeester, 1965, Pretoria
Sonnikus A J H, 37, S A Polisie Pietermaritzburg, Adj-Offisier, 1964, Kokstad
Spamer D J, 30, Noordstraat 2 Ladismith K P, Onderwyser, 1974, Vanwyksdorp
Spamer D W, 38, P/A Universiteit Pretoria, Sekretaris Med Fak, 1976
Spamer F J, 34, Villet & Kie Bredasdorp, Ouditeur, 1964
Spammer S J, 32, S A S & H Vryheid, Personeelklerk, 1964, Kokstad
Spangenberg J P, 44, Carringtonweg 16 Kimberley/diamantveld, Skoolhoof, 1970, Reivilo
Spies A J, 41, Volkskas riviersonderend, Bestuurder, 1967, Port Elizabeth
Spies A J, 39, N G Gemeente Vanderbijlpark-Oos, Predikant, 1965, Ladysmith
Spies A J, 45, 12destraat 93 Menlopark/Vleissentraal Pretoria, Veekundige Adviseur, 1976, Nelspruit
Spies A P, 35, S A S & H Kleinstraat De Doorns, Stasie Voorman, 1966, Van wyksdorp
Spies A S, 53, Dept Binnelandse Sake Pretoria, Staatsamptenaar, 1967, Rouxville
Spies D J, 40, P/A Allied Bouvereniging Parow, Beleggings Adviseur, 1977, Goodwood
Spies H J, 34, Andragstraat 4 Welgemoed/Superama, Mpy Sekretaris, 1972, Malmesbury
Spies L P A, Praat oor Gesonde Ontspanning vir die Kind by Bondsraad 1965
Spies M P D, 42, Munisipaliteit Afd Bantoesake Welkom, Adj-Direkteur, 1967, Klerksdorp
Spies N T, 44, Grasvalley Potgietersrus, Mynbestuurder, 1966
Spoelstra B, 35, Universiteit van Zoeloeland Kwa Dlangezwa, Snr Lektor, 1973, Potchefstroom
Spoelstra T T, 30, Nederlandse Bankgebou Pretoria, Advokaat, 1965
Spruyt O W, 40, Charlestraat 526 Menlopark Pretoria, Argitek, 1974, Pietersburg
Stadler J H E, 44, Casperlaan 560 Eloffsdal/S A Polisie Pretoria, Adj-Offisier, 1970, Pietersburg
Stafford B, 33, Laerskool Aranos S W A, Skoolhoof, 1970, Vryburg
Stafleu A, 43, Lapworthweg 7 Gresswold Johannesburg, Rekenmeester, 1966, Pretoria
Stals C L, 39, S A Reserwebank Pretoria, Asst van die Presidente, 1974, Pretoria
Stals E L, 28, Universiteit Stellenbosch, Lektor, 1967
Stals J P, 32, Hoewe Nr 70 Houtkop Vereeniging, Apteker, 1971, Caledon
Stals W A, 36, P/A U P Pretoria, Lektor, 1969, Standerton

Stander A H, 35, Hoërskool Touwsrivier, Onderhoof, 1969, Queenstown
Stander A H J, 50, Hoër Tegn Skool de Wet Nel Kroonstad, Hoof, 1966, Oudtshoorn
Stander A M, 32, P/A Laerskool Verkenner Port Elizabeth, Onderwyser, 1974, Knysna
Stander C H, 35, Keurboomstraat 22 Milnerton Kaapstad/Kaapse Trousseau-Huis, Bestuurder, 1978, Reitz
Stander F W, 41, Nywerheidskool Ottery Kaap, Onderhoof, 1965, Retreat
Stander H F, 43, Bothastraat 8 Rheederspark Welkom, Mynkaptein, 1966, Springs
Stander J, 37, Heidestraat Caledon, Onderwyser, 1976, Uniondale
Stander J C W, 41, Onderwyskwartiere PK Ganspan, Onderhoof, 1968, Uniondale
Stander J H, Voormalige Direkteur van Onderwys Natal
Stander J H (Lid Nr 770), Durban, Pensioentrakker (Voorgestel vir die U R in 1968)
Stander K, 44, Hendrick & Stander Saambougebou Kaapstad, Argitek, 1965, George
Stapelberg H J, 28, Hoopstraat 6 Bonnievale, Onderwyser, 1972, Umtata
Stapelberg J J, 51, S A Weermag Bloemfontein, Kolonel, 1965, Oudtshoorn
Starke U R, 35, PK Malelane, Boer, 1965, Durbanville
Starker L B, 43, Drostdy Dordrecht, Landdros, 1975, Oos-Londen
Stassen C J, 36, Culemborgsingel 15 Stellenberg, Onderwyser, 1972, Upington
Stassen D J, 33, Afdelingbestuurder S A S Kaapstad, Klerk, 1966
Stassen P J, 33, Hoofstraat Moorreesburg, Skoolhoof, 1972, Vredenburg
Steel H R, 39, P/A Goudstadse Onderwyskollege Cottesloe J H B, Lektor, 1963, Potchefstroom
Steenberg F J, 44, S A S & H Johannesburg, Hoofklerk, 1966, Wolmaransstad
Steenekamp A J, 24, Dennelaan Bainsvlei, Onderwyser, 1966
Steenekamp B B, 37, P/A Dept Bantoe-Adm & Ontw Pretoria, Staatsamptenaar, 1968
Steenekamp D S, 46, Perseel 69 Kakamas, Boer, 1977, Aliwal-Noord
Steenekamp J C, 34, Doornbos Magaliesburg, Boer, 1965, Johannesburg
Steenekamp J H, 31, N H Pastorie Crosby Johannesburg, Predikant, 1964
Steenekamp J H, 33, Lindesfarne Barkly-Oos, Boer, 1975
Steenekamp J S, 43, 8stestraat 91 Menlopark Pretoria, Onderwyser, 1965
Steenkamp A J, 35, Windhoek PK Dullstroom, Boer, 1965
Steenkamp A J, 30, P/A Mobil Oliemaatskappy Jan Smutslughawe, Klerk, 1963, Potchefstroom
Steenkamp C H, 29, N G Pastorie Jansenville, Predikant, 1967, Port Elizabeth
Steenkamp C J, 43, St Helena Goudmyn Welkom, Takelaar, 1966, Viljoenskroon
Steenkamp D F, 36, N G Kerkoshuis De Wetsdorp, Onderwyser, 1965, Bloemfontein
Steenkamp G A, 37, Doornlaagte Steenbokpan, Boer, 1967
Steenkamp G D J, 48, P/A Volkskas Bpk Edenville, Bestuurder, 1974, Pretoria
Steenkamp G J, 32, P/A Trustbank Kaapstad, Beleggingsbestuurder, 1975, Stellenbosch
Steenkamp H P, 35, Popularweg 6 Dalpark Brakpan, Snr Onderwyser, 1972, Brakpan
Steenkamp H S, 39, Hertzogstraat Hartswater Kaap, Apteker, 1967, Groblersdal
Steenkamp J H, 38, Vryheid cons Louwsburg/Ontevrede 124, Skeikundige, 1970
Steenkamp J J, 42, Prositstraat Otjiwarongo, Onderwyser/Boer, 1977, Windhoek
Steenkamp L J S, 28, P/A N H Pastorie Ogies, Predikant, 1975, Ogies
Steenkamp L P, 39, P/A S A L Jansmuts, Klerk, 1977, Johannesburg
Steenkamp L P, 28, Langebergplaas Durbanville, Boer, 1969, Stellenbosch
Steenkamp M D J, 34, Unitedgebou Kimberley, Advokaat, 1966, Bloemfontein
Steenkamp P E, 33, B S B Swellendam, Skaap & Woldeskundige, 1964, Calvinia
Steenkamp P W, 42, Boesmanstad Aranos, Boer, 1974
Steenkamp T J, 38, Pyppan Steenbokpan, Boer, 1975
Steenkamp W F, 32, Geref Pastorie Lambton, Predikant, 1966, Potchefstroom
Steenkamp W F, Kempton Park
Stegmann J A, 31, H/V Merrimanstraat & Vincentstraat Wolseley, Onderwyser, 1977, Ceres
Steinberg W F, 32, Leonoraweg 58 Selcourt Springs, Adj-Stadstesourier, 1970, Heidelberg Tvl
Steinmann R D, 33, P/A SAUK Johannesburg, Adm Beampte, 1973, Pretoria
Stemmet F J, 39, P/A Hoërskool Fakkel Johannesburg, Onderwyser, 1968, Pretoria
Stemmet J G le R, 31, S A Polisie Sunnyridge Oos-Londen, Luitenant, 1967, Kaapstad
Stemmet J F, 32, Hoërskool Sand Du Plessis Bloemfontein, Adj-Hoof, 1969, Kroonstad
Stephens J R, F A K — Verteenwoordiger vir Natal & Oos-Kaapland

Stevens J B, 41, S A Polisie Pretoria, Majoor, 1968, Johannesburg
Steyl A, 35, P/A Industrial Chemical Products Boksburg, Asst V D Besturende Direkteur, 1969, Bloemfontein
Steyl G B, 34, Rouxlaan Frankfort, Voorl Beampte Landbou, 1974, Bloemfontein
Steyl J F B, 29, Mysterie PK Likatlong, Boer, 1969
Steyl J H, Senator & Tvlse Sekretaris van N P
Steyl J L, 40, Tevrede Pk Likatlong oor Bloemfontein, Boer/Eiendomsagent, 1975, Thaba 'Nchu
Steyl J M, 47, P/A Sekondêre Skool Harrismith, Skoolhoof, 1973, Lindley
Steyn A S S, 31, Broadacres Winterton, Boer, 1976, Pretoria
Steyn B J, 42, S A U K Johannesburg (N G Uni Dienste), Hoof, 1966, Pietermaritzburg
Steyn C, 31, Monluwoonstel Nr 3 Markstraat Carnarvon, Onderwyser, 1971
Steyn C E, 43, Correllilaan 814 Mayville/P/A Yskor Pretoria, Produktiwiteits-Intensieveringsbeampte, 1976, Pretoria
Steyn C W (Lid Nr 7698), Louriesfontein, Predikant, 1962
Steyn C W A, 35, P/A Cicira Opleidingskool Umtata, Skoolhoof, 1970, Hennenman
Steyn D, 39, Universiteit Pretoria, Snr Lektor, 1967
Steyn D C, 37, Baden Montagu, Boer, 1970
Steyn D G, 49, Hardapbesproeiingskema Distr Gibeon, Boer, 1969, Grootfontein
Steyn D W, 35, Pumalani Hoewe No 24 Pretoria, Onderwyser, 1972
Steyn D W, 42, Munisipaliteit Pretoria, Elektro Ing, 1965
Steyn E, 33, P/A Boland Bank Bellville, Snr Klerk, 1975, Swellendam
Steyn F D, 35, Brandkraal Winterton, Boer, 1976, Lichtenburg
Steyn F L C, 39, P/A Afdelingsraad Kenhardt, Boer/Rekenmeester, 1975
Steyn F S, Regter
Steyn F S, 42, P/A National Bolts & Rivets Boksburg, Gereedskapverharder, 1967
Steyn G C T, 32, Sophiastraat 70 Fairland Johannesburg, Asst Bestuurder Vleissentraal, 1971
Steyn G D, 31, Caro Nome 8 Geldenhuyslaan Bonaero Park Kempton Park, Geneesheer, 1972, Pretoria
Steyn G F, 41, Volkskas Bronkhorstspruit, Bestuurder, 1964, Winburg OVS
Steyn G H (Lid Nrt 7296), Navorser — Onderwysburo Pretoria — Voorgestel vir die U R in 1968
Steyn G M, 34, N G Gemeente Universiteit-Oord Pretoria, Predikant, 1966, Belfast
Steyn H, 28, N G Pastorie Marble Hall, Predikant, 1967
Steyn H (Dr), Lid van die U R se beplannings-Komitee in 1973
Steyn H, 40, P/A Dept van Openb Werke Pretoria, Staatsamptenaar, 1968
Steyn H A, 36, PK Kanoneiland Keimoes, Boer, 1966
Steyn H J, 36, P/A S A B S Pretoria, Wetenskaplike, 1968
Steyn H L, 34, P/A Hoërskool Goudini Rawsonville, Onderwyser, 1966, Steynsburg
Steyn H S, 30, P/A P U vir CHO Potchefstroom, Snr Navorser, 1977, Pretoria
Steyn J A, 27, S A Polisie Residensia, Adj-Offisier, 1967, Vereeniging
Steyn J C, 32, P/A Hugenote-Hoërskool Wellington, Onderwyser, 1974, Barrydale
Steyn J D J, 40, N G Pastorie Potchefstroom-Noord, Predikant, 1969, Wepener
Steyn J G D, 41, P/A Yskor Pretoria, Mineraloog, 1967
Steyn J F, 25, Hoërskool Swartruggens, Onderwyser, 1966
Steyn J H, 42, P/A Volkskas Richmond, Bestuurder, 1967, Albertinia
Steyn J M L, 33, P/A Stadsraad Nigel/Nie-Blanke-Sake, Asst Bestuurder, 1968, Delmas
Steyn J P S, 35, P/A Volkskas Pretoria, Onderhoofrekenmeester, 1967, Cradock
Steyn J W, 45, Concordia Knysna, Hoof Bosbouer, 1963
Steyn J W, 36, P/A N T K Potgietersrus, Afdelingshoof, 1974, Pretoria
Steyn K K, 28, Corlinhof 9 Sesdestraat Linden/Hoërskool Linden, Onderwyser, 1970, Tzaneen
Steyn M C, 29, N G Pastorie Sunland Kirkwood, Predikant, 1966, Swellendam
Steyn P, 42, Bostonstraat 20 Bellville/Caltex Olie (SA) (Edms) Bpk, Rekenmeester, 1977, Bloemfontein
Steyn P, 29, P/A Sanlam Bellville, Uitv Beampte, 1968, Pretoria
Steyn P G, 33, P/A Oude Meester Kelders Stellenbosch, Sekretaris, 1967, Grabouw
Steyn P J, 40, Charmainelaan 24 Presidentrif Randburg, Chirurg, 1976, Pretoria
Steyn P J, 37, Landdroskantoor Cathcart, Landdros, 1967, Umzinto Natal

Steyn P J, 33, Geref Pastorie Wolmaransstad, Predikant, 1966, Windhoek
Steyn P M, 31, P/A Bezuidenhout & Steyn Potchefstroom, Geokt Rekenmeester, 1973, Klerksdorp
Steyn P P, 31, Begoniastraat 17 Welkom, Onderwyser, 1976, Odendaalsrus
Steyn P R, 41, Hoërskool Ermelo, Onderwyser, 1966, Heidelberg Tvl
Steyn P S, 34, Gatestraat 5 Otjiwarongo, Onderwyser, 1976, Potchefstroom
Steyn P S, 36, P/A T P A Pretoria, Asst Hoofing Paaiedept, 1978, Potchefstroom
Steyn P T, 28, Rietgat Theunissen, Boer, 1975
Steyn S H, 42, P/A Witwatersrand Gold Mines Employees Prov Fund/Longfellowstraat 99 Ridgeway JHB, Sekretaris, 1977, Forest Hill JHB
Steyn S J, 37, P/A Total Oliemaatskappy Johannesburg, Verkoopsbestuurder, 1967, Delareyville
Steyn W H, 33, Hutchinsonweg 21 Nigel, Geneesheer, 1973, Pretoria
Steyn W I, 41, P/A Staatsdienskommissie Pretoria, Direkteur Opleiding, 1966, Venterstad
Steyn W J, 26, Tiendelaan 59 Edenvale, N H Predikant, 1971, Pretoria
Steyn W J A, 27, Wildebeesvlei Venterstad, Boer, 1968
Steynberg A J, 32, Groenhofstraat 11 Freewaypark Boksburg/Elsburg Hoër Tegn Skool, Adj-Hoof, 1977, Edenvale
Steynberg M T, 36, P/A Saambou-Nasionaal Nelspruit, Bestuurder, 1974, Potgietersrus
Steynberg W F, 37, Eland Apteek Drie Riviere Vereeniging, Apteker, 1968, Smithfield
Steynberg W F U, 47, Sybrandskraal PK Sybrandskraal, Boer, 1970, Premiermyn
Stimie G, 35, Welgemoedstraat 3 Elsburg, Toetsbeampte/Elektrisiteitsafd, 1971, Germiston
Stockenstrom F F, 34, Sanlam Wesselsbron, Verteenwoordiger, 1966, Hoopstad
Stofberg J M, 34, Hospitaalweg 73 Middelburg, Apteker, 1973, Potchefstroom
Stofberg N E F, 38, Marine Products Durbanville, Eiendomsbestuurder, 1966, Philadelphia
Stofberg P J P (Lid Nr 5199), Geneesheer — Groblersdal — Voorgestel vir die U R in 1968
Stofberg T C B, 44, P/A Hoërskool Linden Johannesburg, Adj-Hoof, 1969, Germiston
Stoffberg P A, 41, P/A Bruinette Kruger Stoffberg & Hugo Pretoria, Ingenieur, 1974
Stoker H G, P U vir CHO Potchefstroom, Professor, 1963
Stoker P H, 37, Dept Fisika P U vir CHO Potchefstroom, Professor, 1964
Stolz H N P, 40, P/A Lydenburg Voorspoed Koöp, Stoorman/Inspekteur, 1977, Bronkhorstspruit
Stone G J, 56, P/A Sanlam Springbok, Verteenwoordiger, 1968
Stone H F, 42, Premier Diamantmyn Cullinan, Mynopmeter, 1964, Balmoral
Stone J D, 40, Wagnerstraat 31 Sasolburg, Bestuurder Sigma-Myn, 1976, Westonaria
Stone J v W, 45, P/A Geelwinkel Springbok, Boer/Sakeman, 1966
Stopforth S H, 36, Laerskool Jan De Villiers, Ariamsvlei, Skoolhoof, 1975, Otjiwarongo
Strachan L J, 36, P/A Hoërskool Eldoraigne Verwoerdburg, Onderhoof, 1977, Meyerton
Straszacker R L, 53, P/A Evkom Johannesburg, Voorsitter, 1965, Stellenbosch
Strating A (Lid Nr 6937), Professor — Wonderboom — Voorgestel vir die U R in 1968
Strauss A J, 40, Landdroskantoor Fauresmith, Landdros, 1966, Theunissen
Strauss C A, 43, P/A Bar Pietersburg, Rekenmeestger, 1976, Pretoria
Strauss D F M, 28, P/A U O V S Bloemfontein, Snr Lektor, 1974
Strauss E D, 33, Dept Landbou Rusape, Uitbreidingsbeampte, 1974, Beaufort-Wes
Strauss H J, 37, Jagkolk Brandvlei K P, Boer, 1974
Strauss H J, 39, Driekloof Pos Bulgerrivier/S A Weermag, Kaptein/Boer, 1974, Ottosdal
Strauss H J (Lid Nr 2512), Professor — O U V S Bloemfontein — Voorgestel vir die U R in 1968
Strauss J J, 34, Anniesdale Wepener, Boer, 1971
Strauss L J, 33, Engelbrechtstraat 18 Oatlands Krugersdorp, Dosent, 1973
Strauss N J, 37, P/A Pres Steyn-Myn Welkom, Personeelbeampte, 1966, Theunissen
Strauss P D, 31, N G Pastorie Despatch Eendrag, Predikant, 1968, Stellenbosch
Strauss W A, 40 Garrickstraat 54 Kenmare Krugersdorp/S A S & H, Asst Bemarking-Bestuurder, 1976, Durban
Streicher D H, 40, P/A Leslie Apteek Leslie, Apteker, 1969
Streicher J J Lid Nr 5166) Boer — Albertina — Voorgestel vir die U R in 1968
Streicher S F, 40, Kwaggalaagte Kinros, Boer, 1973
Streicher W B V, 35, Voortrekkerstraat 2 Pietersburg, Sakeman, 1968, Pietersburg
Stronkhorst J H, 40, Oaklaan 267 Ferndale Randburg, Chirurg, 1975, Johannesburg

Strümpfer P S H F, 33, N G Pastorie Belfast, Predikant, 1967, Burgersfort
Strumpher J W, 30, Dirkie Uystraat 15 Christiana, N G Predikant, 1977, Stellenbosch
Struwig D J, 38, Gedenkstraat 36 Bethlehem/Saambounasionaal, Bestuurder, 1976, Kroonstad
Struwig D J, 42, Elma-Oord 80 Riebeekstad, Ingenieur, 1971, Komtikragstasie
Struwig J H G, 32, Hoërskool Watervalboven, Onderwyser, 1964, Morgenson
Struwig K D, 45, P/A N G Gemeente Meyerspark, Predikant, 1973, Lichtenburg
Struwig P W v R, 25, PK Adams Mission Oor Durban, Onderwyser, 1967, Heidelberg Tvl
Strydom A, 28, N G Pastorie Vredenburg, Predikant, 1964, Oudtshoorn
Strydom a (Duimpie), 42, Dunboynelaan 10 Crosby/Nie-Blanke-Sake, Doeltreffendheidsbeampte, 1971, Johannesburg
Strydom A C (Lid Nr 7717), Ogies, Stasievoorman, 1962
Strydom A E, 42, Bentleystraat 12 Robertsham Johannesburg, Onderwyser, 1965, Paarl
Strydom A E, 38, Opaalstraat 105 Waverley Pretoria, Navorser/Rgn, 1977, Johannesburg
Strydom A H, 29, P/A U O V S Bloemfontein, Lektor, 1969
Strydom C D J, 43, S A S & H Johannesburg, Personeelklerk, 1967, Oos-Londen
Strydom C J, 41, P/A Volkskas Empangeni, Bestuurder, 1968, Memel
Strydom C P J, 33, Primêre Skool Hluhluwe, Skoolhoof, 1975, Pietermaritzburg
Strydom D T H, 34, Sesdestraat 57 Linden Johannesburg, Argitek, 1971, Pretoria
Strydom E, 41, Skiereilandse Kollege vir GTO Parow, Vise-Rektor, 1975, Port Elizabeth
Strydom g, 33, Drs Keet de Wet Strydom & Van Os Trust Bank Sentrum Kaapstad, Tandarts, 1973, Pretoria
Strydom G J, 31, S A Polisie Springs, Adj-Offisier, 1970, Uniondale
Strydom G J, 36, N G Pastorie Neilersdrif Keimoes, Predikant, 1967, Barrydale
Strydom G L, 32, P/A P U vir CHO Potchefstroom, Lektor, 1975, Vryburg
Strydom G R J, 32, Witbank Devon, Boer, 1970, Balfour
Strydom G S R, Posbus 28 Burgersdorp — Adverteer vir Hoofklerk in Burgersdorp Koöperatiewe Handelsvereniging in 1963
Strydom G S S (Lid Nr 7718), Virginia, Bestuurder, 1962
Strydom H D, 49, P/A Spoorweghostel Nelspruit, Huisvader, 1975, Breyten
Strydom H F, 33, Landbou Tegn Dienste Vryheid, Hoofveearts, 1964, Dundee
Strydom H J, 41, P/A Hoërskool Ben viljoen Groblersdal, Onderwyser, 1969
Strydom H M, 25, Hoërskool Petrusville K P, Onderwyser, 1968, Stellenbosch
Strydom J, 42, Wilmotstraat 18 Noupoort, Slagter, 1970, De Aar
Strydom J, 28, P/A Human Motors Bloemfontein, Bestuurder, 1973
Strydom J F, 39, Doornhoek Bishopstowe Pietermaritzburg, Boer, 1977, Badplaas
Strydom J H, 36, P/A Sanlam Durban, Takbestuurder, 1973, Johannesburg
Strydom J H, 33, Fredericklaan 49 Fynnland Durban, Onderwyser, 1971, Ermelo
Strydom J J S, Greytown — Woon 1966 Bondsraad by
Strydom J S, 32, P/A Hoërskool Voortrekker Bethlehem, Onderwyser, 1974, Bloemfontein
Strydom K C, 30, Gannakloof PK Willowmore, Boer, 1975
Strydom L, 48, Rietkuil Senekal, Boer, 1967
Strydom L J, 32, S A Polisiekollege Pretoria, Luitenant, 1974, Virginia
Strydom M J, 29, Berlynstraat 5 Heidelberg Tvl, Geneesheer, 1965, Kaapstad
Strydom O A W, 43, P/A Raad op Atoomkrag (Ontdekkers Park), Wetenskaplike, 1977, Sasolburg
Strydom P J, 37, Dassieskrans Jansenville, Boer, 1974
Strydom R T, 33, P/A Alusaf Empangeni, Veiligheidsbeampte, 1973, Newcastle
Strydom s, 35, P/A Greykollege Laer Bloemfontein, Skoolhoof, 1973
Strydom s, 38, Universiteit van Pretoria, Senior Lektor, 1963, Ventersdorp
Strydom S J, 32, Wortelkuil Jansenville, Boer, 1970
Strydom S J, 36, Grensstraat 31 Tzaneen/S A Polisie, Kaptein, 1970, Pretoria
Strydom S J, 38, Hoërskool Orkney, Onderhoof, 1963, Koster
Strydom S S, 35, Bartlettweg 37 Pinetown Natal, Skakelbeampte, 1971, Germiston
Strydom S T J, 34, Hoopstraat Jacobsdal, Posmeester, 1970, Hertzogville
Strydom W A, 49, Kanoneiland Kakamas, Onderwyser, 1964, Queenstown
Strydom W F, 29, P/A Laerskool Rietbron, Skoolhoof, 1977, Bellville
Strydom W M, 35, N G Pastorie Kenhardt, Predikant, 1965, Pretoria
Strydom W M de P, 42, Bezuidenhoutstraat 13 Glenmarais, Sakeman, 1976, Pretoria
Strydom W M L, 32, Tiendelaan 84 Bellville, Onderwyser, 1966, Humansdorp

Stuart C H, Oxfordsteeg 8 Lynnwood Manor Pretoria — Skakel by Universiteit van Pretoria 4.2.76
Stulting C H, 35, Gainsboroughstraat 31 De la Haye/S A S & H, Ingenieur, 1971, Kaapstad
Stulting G J, 33, Jansonstraat 2 Framesby Port Elizabeth, Prokureur, 1970, Grahamstad
Stulting J D, 25, P/A S A S & H Johannesburg, Fisikus, 1967, Ladismsith Kaap
Sutherland F C, 32, P/A Hoërskool Martin Huizen Kakamas, Onderwyser, 1973, Oost-Keetmanshoop
Swanepoel A, 32, Panoramarylaan 91, Stellenberg, Aktuaris, 1975, Bellville
Swanepoel A A, 32, Klawerhoek Rouxville, Boer, 1966
Swanepoel A C, 36, Beaufort Vryheid, Boer, 1969
Swanepoel A M, 37, 7deLaan 24 Kieserville Lichtenburg, N H Predikant, 1972, Warmbad Tvl
Swanepoel D E , 34, Ilex 11 Kempton Park/Munisipaliteit, Asst Klerk van die Raad, 1970 Pietersburg
Swanepoel D S, 29, P/A Laerskool Luipaardsvlei, Onderwyser, 1975, Witpoortjie
Swanepoel E J, 42, A E & C I Modderfontein, Personeelbeampte, 1973, Germiston
Swanepoel F, 31, P/A N G Pastorie Salisbury, Predikant, 1970, Pretoria
Swanepoel g, 37, P/A Dept van Landbou Tegn Dienste Pretoria, Vakk Beampte, 1968
Swanepoel G B H J, 37, Whites Portland Cement Lichtenburg, Elektrisien, 1964
Swanepoel G H J, 36, Tulbachstraat 3 Alberante, Sakeman, 1971, Alberton
Swanepoel G J, 33, Hoërskool Hottentots Holland Somerset-Wes, Onderwyser, 1964, Jamestown
Swanepoel G J P, 33, Alidastraat 24 De Aar/P/A J N Marais & Kie (Ouditeurs), Ouditeursklerk, 1977, Riversdal
Swanepoel H L (Lid Nr 2328), Professor in Regte Potchefstroom — Voorgestel vir die U R in 1968
Swanepoel J A, 46, Greylingstraat Potchefstroom, Onderwyser, 1968, Volksrust
Swanepoel J A, 47, Doornbult Delareyville, Boer/Oudonderwyser, 1969, Leeudoringstad
Swanepoel J A E, 45, Sandrif Vaalwater, Boer, 1974, Ronkins Pass
Swanepoel J G, 33, N G Kerk Burgersfort, Predikant, 1977, Kimberley
Swanepoel J J, 35, Mariasstraat 11 Welkom, Org N P, 1968, Virginia
Swanepoel J J, 30, P/A Inst vir Eietydse Geskiedenis UOVS, Navorser, 1975, Bloemfontein
Swanepoel J J H, 39, Fraaiuitsig Rouxville, Boer, 1969
Swanepoel J N, Lid van die U R se Ekonomiese Komitee in 1973
Swanepoel J W, 38, P/A Hoërskool Balfour, Onderhoof, 1965, Potgietersrus
Swanepoel J W, 43, P/A Noordwes Koöp Lichtenburg, Rekenmeester, 1968
Swanepoel K D, 37, Hoërskool Wonderboom Pretoria, Onderwyser, 1965
Swanepoel L, 31, Militêre Opleidingskamp Ladysmith, Veldkornet, 1968, Ingogo
Swanepoel L P, 41, P/A Anglo American Korporasie Johannesburg, Ingenieur (Elektron IKA), 1976, Aucklandpark
Swanepoel N J, 30, Vrystraat Koöperasie Reitz, Sekretaris, 1969, Paarl
Swanepoel P C, 41, Firwoodlaan 35 Hazelwood Pretoria/Dept van Eerste Minister, Beampte, 1970, Windhoek
Swanepoel P J, 40, P/A Ouditeur & Kontroleurgen Pretoria, Asst Ouditeur, 1968
Swanepoel S J N, 46, Hoërskool Vryburger Primrose, Adj-Hoof, 1976, Vanderbijlpark
Swanepoel W J, Port Elizabeth-Noord — Praat oor Kleurlinge by 1971 Bondsraad
Swanevelder C J, 42, Soeteweide 9 Stellenbosch/Universiteit van Stellenbosch, Snr Lektor, 1970, Saldanha
Swart A, George
Swart C A C, 31, Rosendal Ellisras, Boer, 1975
Swart C F, 33, Dept Sisiologie Universiteit van Pretoria, Lektor, 1969, Nylstroom
Swart C F, 43, N G Gemeente Klipriviersberg, Predikant, 1973, Orkney
Swart D A H, 42, P/A Pospersoneel Heilbron, Posmeester, 1974, Beaufort-Wes
Swart F J, 35, Suidweg 72 Rewlatch Johannesburg, Radiotegnikus, 1970, Pretoria
Swart H J, 29, Boshoffstraat 25 Nylstroom/Bayer Agro-Chem, Bestuurder, 1973, Pretoria
Swart H J, 27, Witbank Devon, Boer, 1967, Nelspruit
Swart J C, 29, Militêre Basis Tempe/S A Weermag, Majoor, 1973, Pretoria
Swart J C, 36, Posstal Buffeljagsrivier, Boer, 1967, Swellendam
Swart J H, 45, Leeufontein Bodenstein, Boer/Onderwyser, 1974, Coligny
Swart J J, 32, N G Pastorie Ottosdal, Predikant, 1966, Alberton
Swart J J, 29, P/A Dept van Poswese Smithfield, Tegnikus, 1968, Bloemfontein

Swart J J, 45, P/A Van den Bergh & Jurgens Edms Bpk Durban, Bemarkingsdirekteur, Johannesburg
Swart J J, 38, Henrystraat Albertinia, Telefonis P & T, 1976, Barrydale
Swart J J, 43, P/A Volkskas Bpk Warrenton, Bestuurder, 1970, Pretoria
Swart J S, 31, Appelbos Swellendam, Boer, 1976
Swart L J, 32, Leeukop Delareyville, Boek/Boekhouer, 1966, Potchefstroom
Swart L P, N G Kerk, Predikant, Malvern
Swart M (Prof), Hoof van Rapportryers
Swart M J, 28, Koesanie Buffeljagsrivier, Boer, 1970, Swellendam
Swart M J, 39, Lucasoord 8 Fynnland Durban, Prokureur, 1976, Kroonstad
Swart M L, 34, P/A Spoorwegkollege Esselenpark, Hoofklerk, 1968, Johannesburg
Swart N J, 30, P U vir CHO Potchefstroom, Professor, 1972
Swart N J, 29, Welstand Dist Bethal, Boer, 1976, Ogies
Swart P H, 41, S A Landbou-Unie Pretoria, Adj-Direkteur, 1975
Swart P J, 36, Hoërskool Vryheid, Onderwyser, 1964
Swart P L, 32, Drakenslaan 43 Quellerina (Maraisburg) Lektor/RAU, 1975, Johannesburg
Swart P S, 34, Smitstraat Pionierpark/Dept van Natuurbewaring, Adj-Direkteur, 1970, Tsumeb
Swart S P C, 33, Universiteit van die Noorde/Voortrekkerstraat 6 Pietersburg, Snr Lektor, 1972, Bloemfontein
Swart T J P, 34, Nuweland Vrede, Boer, 1976, Kroonstad
Swart T R, 42, S A Polisie Brakpan, Luitenant, 1970, Bloemhof
Swart V P, 30, P/A Universiteit van Stellenbosch, Fisikus, 1975
Swarts C C, 38, P/A Hawker Siddeley Brush Fabriek Germiston, Werks-Direkteur, 1964, Petrus Steyn
Swarts C J, 47, Haartbeesfonteinweg 53 Stilfontein/S A Polisie, Kaptein, 1977, Reneke
Swarts H B, 32, P/A Rouxville Handelshuis Koöp Bpk, Bestuurder, 1976, Smithfield
Swarts L D, 31, Skoolstraat Elliot, Onderwyser, 1966, Aberdeen
Swartz J L, 32, P/A Molopo Apteek (Edms) Bpk/McKenziestraat 66 Vryburg, Apteker, 1970, Potchefstroom
Swartz N J, 31, S W Tvlse Koöp Leeudoringstad, Kredietbestuurder, 1967, Kempton Park
Swiegers G J, 40, Rooipan Griekwastad, Boer, 1965
Swiegers J M, 33, Quaggasfontein De Aar, Boer/Ouditeur, 1977, Britstown
Swiegers L E, 29, Birkettstraat 23 Dundee, Tandarts, 1963
Symington M M C, 42, Rileystraat 120 Parowvallei, Snr Landdros, 1975, Sutherland

T

Tait P J, 34, "Die Hoop" PK Verkeerdevlei, Boer, 1965, Tweespruit
Taljaard C J, 31, Middelburg Transvaal, Standsingenieur, 1963
Taljaard C M L, Kensington
Taljaard C M L, 28, P/A C M L Taljaard & Seun Johannesburg, Besturende Direkteur, 1963, Belgravia
Taljaard E J, 37, S A S Bank Kaapstad, Bestuurder, 1966
Taljaard G F, 27, Hoërskoolkoshuis Piet Retief, Onderwyser, 1966, Pretoria
Taljaard H, 39, Suidweg 5 Linden Uitbr Johannesburg, Argitek, 1965, Witbank
Taljaard H J, 43, Pafurilaan 235 Sinoville Pretoria/Binnelandse Veiligheid, Ondersekretaris 1977
Taljaard J, 39, P/A Jongilizwe Kollege Tsolo Transkei, Hoof, 1975, Cala
Taljaard J J v/d M, 36, Nairobi Reitz, Boer, 1969
Taute J H F, 41, P/A Laerskool Delmas, Skoolhoof, 1974, Krugersdorp
Taute W, 32, P/A Hoër Seunskool Helpmekaar Johannesburg, Onderwyser, 1974, Ellisras
Taylor A C, 37, Danie Theronstraat Beaufort-Wes, Skoolhoof/Hoërskool, 1971, Barrydale
Taylor J H (Joe), 32, P/A N O K Johannesburg/Klein Nywerhede, Sekretaris, 1973, Sasolburg
Teichler M G, 34, Seunskoshuis Hoërskool Nelspruit, Vise-Hoof, 1972, Ermelo
Terblanche A B, 51, S A Polisie Pretoria, Majoor, 1964, Welkom
Terblanche D J J, 33, Arbeidsgenot Stella, Boer, 1973, Mafeking
Terblanche E, 34, W P Tabak-Koöp Paarl, Bestuurder, 1966, Oudtshoorn
Terblanche F, 31, PK Bergplaats oor George, Handelaar/Slagter, 1967
Terblanche F, 34, Goedehoop Molteno, Boer, 1967, Bethanie S W A

Terblanche F J, 40, Athlonelaan 26 Dalview Brakpan/Stofberg Seunskool, Onderwyser, 1976
Terblanche G, 25, P/A Pastorie Dealesville, N G Predikant, 1975, Thaba 'Nchu Distrik
Terblanche G A, 32, Eufeesweg 49 Bloemfontein/U O V S, Asst Regis Finansies, 1977
Terblanche G W, 42, Huis Nico Malan Uniondale, Onderwyser/Boer, 1970, Fullarton
Terblanche H, 43, P/A Volkskas Vryburg, Rekenmeester, 1974, Vereeniging
Terblanche H I, 48, Hoërskool Zastron, Onderhoof, 1967, Hobhouse
Terblanche H L, 37, Angleweg 34 Gonubie Oos-Londen, Ing Telekom/S A S, 1977, Kimberley
Terblanche H M, 47, Ruthstraat Brooklyn Pretoria, Staatsamptenaar, 1964, Mosselbaai
Terblanche J D V, 35, Hoërskool Dr Malan Meyerton, Skoolhoof, 1967, Rustenburg
Terblanche J J, 41, P/A S A Polisie Johannesburg, Adj-Offisier, 1968, Alexanderbaai
Terblanche J P, 47, Albertstraat 14 Robertson, Onderwyser, 1964, Adelaide
Terblanche N M, 45, P/A Bosveldse Koöp Potgietersrus, Bestuurder, 1970, Heidelberg
Terblanche P J J, 31, Kafferboomlaan 4 Thabazimbi, Vakleerling-Instrukteur, 1969, Brits
Terblanche P N J, 39, Acasiastraat 11 Riversdal/LandbouTegniese Dienste, Voorligt Beampte, 1977, Bredasdorp
Terblanche S E, 35, Sekondêre Skool Vierfontein, Onderwyser, 1974, Bloemfontein
Terblanche S E, 34, Universiteit Port Elizabeth, Senior Lektor, 1975, Stellenbosch
Terblanche S S, 33, Firlaan 38 Primrose-Oos, N G Predikant, 1971, Pretoria
Terblans H, 34, P/A Venter Broers Garage (edms) Bpk Burgersdorp Adm Bestuurder, 1975, Bloemfontein
Terblans P J, 36, P/A Hoërskool Sentraal Bloemfontein, Onderwyser, 1973
Terreblanche G F, 44, Bank Trompsburg, Boer, 1970, Parys
Terreblanche H J, 32, P/A Bank van Johannesburg Kaapstad, Streekbestuurder, 1970, Bloemfontein
Terreblanche S J, 35, P/A Universiteit Stellenbosch, Professor, 1969, Edenvale
Theart J N J, 48, S A S & H Kaapstad, 1963, Johannesburg
Theron A J, 37, Gedeelte 54 Witfontein 301 JR (Pretoria), Eiendomsagent, 1975, Villiers
Theron A J, 34, Karakoel Koöp Upington, Hoofvakk Beampte, 1969
Theron C, 24, Hoërskoolkoshuis Sannieshof, Onderwyser, 1966, Heidelberg
Theron D C, 37, Hoërskool Belfast, Onderwyser, 1963, Machadodorp
Theron D J, 42, Bethel Plaas Fort Victoria, Boer, 1974, Kaapstad
Theron E, 32, Koshuis Reivilo, Onderwyser, 1970, Calvinia
Theron F, 37, Hoërskool Jan Mohr Windhoek, Adj-Skoolhoof, 1974, Otjiwarongo
Theron F C F, 37, Monicaweg 472 Lynnwood/Dept V D Eerste Minister, Snr Amptenaar, 1970, Johannesburg
Theron F J, 38, P/A General Mining Finanskorp Johannesburg, Fin Ondersoekbeampte, 1975, Pretoria
Theron G, 44, P/A Hoërskool Standerton, Onderhoof, 1965, Potchefstroom
Theron G H, 32, N G Pastorie Luckhoff, Predikant, 1972, Ficksburg
Theron G M, 31, P/A Nas Koerante Port Elizabeth, Rekenmeester, 1965, Bellville
Theron H, 35, P/A N G Pastorie Kampersrus (Blyderivier), Predikant, 1974, Onderstepoort
Theron H J, 25, Prinspan Boshof, Boer, 1968
Theron J (Lid Nr 7719), Rustenburg-Noord, Boekhouer, 1962
Theron J A L, 28, U O V S Bloemfontein, Lektor, 1966, Pietersburg
Theron J C, 36, Doornhoek Thabazimbi, Geneesheer, 1964, Vryburg
Theron J D, 30, Fitzroystraat 137 Goodwood, Onderwyser, 1975, Tulbach
Theron J D, 32, Heuwelstraat Knysna, Landdros, 1973, Wellington
Theron J F, 39, Erfdeel Tulbagh, Boer, 1973
Theron J F, 34, Dunnstraat 6 Floridapark/S A S & H, Skeikundige, 1972, Johannesburg
Theron J G, 36, Landbou Kdt & Grondbesit Swartruggens Streekbeampte, 1974, Calvinia
Theron J J, 40, Inst vir Voedingsnavorsing Pretoria, Direkteur, 1967, Heidelburg
Theron J J, 32, Kleinharts Ottosdal, Boer, 1965
Theron J P, 34, Coetzeelaan 14 Selectionpark Springs, Onderwyser, 1976, Bronkhorstspruit
Theron J P, 33, P/A Universiteit van S A Pretoria, Finasbeampte, 1974, Stellenbosch
Theron L J, 34, S A Polisie Port Elizabeth, Kapelaan, 1966, Beaufort-Wes
Theron L P, 30, Witkoppies Dist Pretoria, Veearts/Boer, 1974, Oudtshoorn
Theron O J, 38, Uitsig Beaufort-Wes/S A S & H, Klerk, 1970

Theron P, 26, Sentrale Hoërskool Bloemfontein, Onderwyser, 1968, Senekal
Theron P D, 43, Kwaggashoek Swartruggens, Boer, 1965, Thabazimbi
Theron P J, 29, P/A Steel & Barnett Johannesburg, Rekenmeester, 1975
Theron P J, 49, S A Polisie Pretoria, Luit-Kolonel, 1964, Roodepoort
Theron P L, 38, Welgemoed Koës, Boer, 1977
Theron P L, 43, Kleinfontein Tulbach, Boer, 1967
Theron P P, 53, P/A Dept van Volkswelsyn Pretoria, Staatsamptenaar, 1968
Theron P T, 27, Hoërskool J G Meiring Goodwood, Onderwyser, 1970, Strand
Theron P W, 35, P/A Die Volksblad Bloemfontein, Adj-Hoofsubredakteur, 1974
Theron S, Opvoedkundige
Theron T A, 45, P/A Hoër Tegn Skool Rustenburg, Onderhoof, 1967, Uitenhage
Theunissen J B, 29, Bloemstraat 60 Bloemhof, Onderwyser, 1964, Ermelo
Theunissen J M, 32, Adamweg 12 Bertonpark Germiston, Onderwyser, 1977, Brakpan
Theunissen J M, 34, Freeziastraat Caledon, Begrafnisondernemer, 1975
Theunissen J R, 44, "Toggekry" PK Radium, Boer, 1973, Louis Trichardt
Theunissen M P, 45, P/A Gen Chem Corp Durban, Bestuurder, 1965, Modderfontein
Thiart B F, 39, Dept Fisiologie Universiteit Stellenbosch, Lektor, 1969, Somerset-Wes
Thiart D J G, 41, P/A Dept Immigrasie Pretoria, Klerk, 1967, Kimberley
Thiart J J, 39, P/A Saambou Nasionale Bouvereniging Pretoria, Bestuurder Dataverwerker, 1973, Elsiesrivier
Thom G, 36, P/A Hoërskool Petrusville, Vise-Hoof, 1974, Pretoria
Thom H B (Lid Nr 1773), Voormalige Rektor Stellenbosch Universiteit & Voormalige Voorsiter van die A B
Thomas G, 35, Uitkoms Proefplaas Grootfontein/Landbou, Tegniese Dienste Snr Tegnikus, 1974, Windhoek
Thompson J A, 43, Lodge PK Tuinplaas Nylstroom, Boer/Winkelier, 1974, Brits
Thuynsma W F, 32, P/A Hoërskool Delmas, Onderwyser, 1974, Hartswater
Toerien D F, 37, Snipestraat 21 Honey Hills Florida, Ingenieur NOK, 1976, Sasolburg
Toerien G P, 33, P/A JHB Cons Investm/Mulderstraat 2 Ontdekkerspark, Asst Bestuurder Mineraalontwikkeling, 1975, Roodepoort
Toerien M J, 39, Stellenbosch Universiteit, Snr Lektor, 1966, Johannesburg
Toerien P E C, 30 P/A S A Weermag Port Elizabeth, Majoor, 1974, Pretoria
Toerien P S, Lid van die U R se Landbou-Komitee 1973
Tolken P J L, 41, Baileystraat Koffiefontein, Sakeman/Motorhawe, 1977, Kimberley
Tolmie D, 40, N G Kerk Oudtshoorn-Noord, Predikant, 1973, Stilbaai
Tredoux A F, 32, Wilmotstraat 10 Noupoort, Landdros, 1973, Swartruggens
Tredoux J C, 31, V D Merwestraat Beaufort-Wes, Onderwyser, 1976, Victoria-Wes
Treurnicht A F (Lid Nr 4240), Adjunk-Minister — Voorgestel vir die U R in 1968 & Voormalige Redakteur van Hoofstad
Treurnicht A S, 36, Kalkfontein Groblersdal, Boer, 1967, Gutu Rhodesië
Triegaardt L G, 48, Foskor Phalaborwa, Asst Rekenmeester, 1964, Vanderbijlpark
Tromp J A, 34, Doornkom Hartbeesfontein, Boer, 1977, Outjo
Tromp J A, 48, Okaimpuro Okahandja, Boer, 1975
Tromp P J de W, 45, P/A Nictusgroep Windhoek, Direkteur van Mpye, 1969
Tromp W S, 46, Ozombusomasse Okahandja, Boer, 1975
Troskie C G, 45, Huntstraat 4 Aliwal-Noord, Geneesheer, 1966, Pearston
Troskie C J, 35, Hoërskool Brandwag Benoni, Onderwyser, 1967, Groot Marico
Troskie G C, 29, Waaifontein Springfontein, Boer, 1967, Pearston
Troskie G F C, (Lid Nr 2895), Kroonstad — (Voorgestel vir die U R in 1968), Geneesheer
Trouw A, 56, P/A Raad op Atoomkrag Pretoria, Onder-Sekretaris, 1968
Troux M, 40, Prinsloostraat 343 Bronkhorstspruit, Apteker, 1967, Roodepoort
Trümpelmann G W, 26, Kantoorstraat 14a Lydenburg, Veearts, 1974
Truter A W, 42, Hofstraat 23 Tuine Kaapstad/Volkshospitaal, Bestuurder, 1971, Bellville
Truter A W, 37, Herschellstraat 45 Strand, Onderwyser, 1967, Bredasdorp
Truter de V J D, 50, Groote Kerkgebou Kaapstad, Prokureur, 1964
Truter D J, 35, Parkweg 120 Oudtshoorn/Kleurling Opleidingskollege, Vise-Rektor, 1976
Truter F H, 35, Drostdy Karibib S W A, Landdros, 1971, Tsumeb S W A
Truter H C, 26, Bainstraat 28a Wellington, Tandarts, 1967, Kaapstad
Truter H F G (Lid Nr 7775), Springbok, 1963
Truter J H, 31, P/A Van der Wall & Vennote Bloemfontein, Sekretaris, 1974

Truter J J W, 37, P/A Volkskas Bpk Strand, Rekenmeester, 1969, Kaapstad
Truter J L, 31, S A Polisie Rundu S W A, Luitenant, 1977, Pretoria
Truter J T, 44, Frederickrylaan 177 Northcliff Johannesburg, Patente-Agent, 1973, Cottesloe
Truter L K, 28, P/A Tygerbergse Hoër Handelskool, Onderwyser, 1974, Oudtshoorn
Truter M B, 31, P/A Theron & Van de Poel Kaapstad, Rekenmeester, 1969, Hopefield
Truter M H G, 36, P/A Landbou-Koöp Beaufort-Wes, Bestuurder, 1964, Paarl
Truter R (Prof), Lid van die U R se Wetenskap-Komitee 1973

U

Ueckermann E C, 35, P/A Messina Tvl Develop Co Messina, Passer, 1965
Ueckerman S J, 43, O T K Bethal, Kredietbestuurder, 1967
Uitenweerde J D C, 46, P/A Reed & Uitenweerde Piet Retief, Landmeter, 1965, Ermelo
Underhay J P, 29, Brandwachtstraat 31 Stellenbosch, Onderwyser, 1976, Tulbagh
Ungerer O D J, 39, Volkskas Barkly-Oos, Bestuurder, 1972, Pretoria
Ungerer S J, 25, Bettiesdeel (2a) Cornelia, Boer, 1965
Untiedt F J, 48, P/A Raad op Atoomkrag/Bettie Prinsloostraat 7 Annlin Pretoria, Personeelbeampte, 1975, Pretoria
Uys C, 34, Posbus 13 Carolina, Prokureur, 1964, Ermelo
Uys C E G, 35, Blesbokweg 179 Waterkloofrif Nr 2 Pretoria/Bantoe Diskoteke S A U K, Snr Asst Organiseerder, 1971
Uys C J, 33, S A Polisie Pretoria, Luitenant, 1977
Uys C P, 38, Richardlaan 61 Homestead Germiston, Onderhoof, 1969, Pretoria
Uys D C, 29, Komarsekraal Bredasdorp, Boer, 1966
Uys D C, 47, Kafferskraal Bethal, Boer, 1964
Uys D C H, Voormalige Minister van Landbou, Senator
Uys D C J, 38, Van Zylstraat 17 Schweizer-Reneke, Voorl Beampte, 1977, Welkom/Bloemfontein
Uys D F, 42, S A S & H Pietersburg, Klerk, 1964, Waterval Boven
Uys D J, 52, P/A Nas Party Bethlehem, Organiseerder, 1966, Hennenman
Uys D J, 30, Havemannstraat 58 Viljoenskroon, Onderwyser, 1973, Bethlehem
Uys E W, 35, P/A Christianase Laerskool, Skoolhoof, 1974, Primrose
Uys G F, 35, P/A Uniestaalkorp Vereeniging, Prod Toesighouer, 1973
Uys H C S, 35, Sanlam Bellville, Asst Sekretaris, 1965, Potgietersrus
Uys H J, 37, Belmont, Boer, 1963, Douglas
Uys H J, 30, Hoofstraat Clanwilliam, Geneesheer, 1966, Caledon
Uys H J, 34, Keurvlei Barrydale, Boer, 1969
Uys H J, 29, Kadie Heidelberg K P, Boer, 1976
Uys H P, 36, Eeufeesstraat 60 Pretoria-Noord, Onderwyser, 1966
Uys J C, 34, P/A Kommissaris-Generaal Mafeking, Adm Beampte, 1965, Vaalharts
Uys J C I, 45, P/A Dept Arbeid Pretoria, Abb, 1975, Standerton
Uys J F (H J Sn), 36, Kadie PK Heidelberg K P, Boer, 1968
Uys J H (Lid Nr 7682), Umtata, Skoolhoof, 1962
Uys J J, 46, Witkop PK Bredasdorp, Boer, 1968
Uys J W, 28, Merino Bredasdorp, Boer, 1969
Uys M J, 32, Restawhile Heidelberg K P, Boer, 1967, Queenstown
Uys P A J, 41, Harmonielaan 5 Bellville K P, Onderwyser, 1966, Carnarvon
Uys P J, 43, P/A Gumbo-Grafietmyn Messina, Mynbestuurder, 1977
Uys P v R, 41, Bosheuwel Heidelberg K P, Boer, 1968
Uys W F, 33, Caledonrylaan 4 Drieriviere Vereeniging, Tandarts, 1968, Pretoria
Uytenbogaardt B J, 31, P/A S A Polisie PK Assen, Adj-Offisier, 1969, Simonstad

V

Vahrmeyer J, 33, Weberstraat 124 Silverton, Plantkundige Ltd, 1977, Pretoria
Van Aarde A M, 31, Hoërskool Wonderboom Pretoria, Onderwyser, 1964, Lichtenburg
Van Aarde G P, 31, Paardeplaas Hartbeesfontein, Boer, 1968, Bospoort
Van Aarde J A (Appel), 34, Dept Sielkundige Dienste Onderwysdept Port Elizabeth, Hoof, 1963, Kimberley
Van Aarde J J, 41, Buffelsdoring Maricodraai (Northam), Boer, 1967, Marico

Van Aardt B, 31, P/A KWB Ermelo, Voorligtingsbeampte, 1965
Van Aardt C P, 34, Ridgewayse Laerskool Johannesburg, Onderhoof, 1969, Carolina
Van Aardt H J, 35, Saambou Durban, Bestuurder, 1966, Pretoria
Van Aardt J H B, 30, Marathonweg 88 Grosvenor Durban, Adj-Hoof, 1971, Durban
Van Aardt J M H, 46, P/A Unisa Pretoria, Sen Lektor, 1974
Van Aardt W, 33, Klaberplek 7, Risiville Vereeniging, Hoof Opl en Pers Ontwikkeling Uskor, 1976, Pretoria
Van Antwerpen J P, 35 S A P Komatipoort, Adj-Offisier, 1977, Middelburg Tvl
Van Arkel J T de J, 32, Nederburghstraat 53 Welgemoed Kaap, Hospitaal Leraar NGK, 1975, Pretoria
Van Aswegen A M, 37, "Perseverance" Noupoort, Boer, 1965
Van Aswegen C H J (Lid Nr 4223), Voorgestel vir die U R in 1968, Hoofbestuurder Santam Kaapstad
Van Aswegen J D, 37, P/A Natalse Landbou Koöp Vryheid, Bestuurder, 1975, Greytown
Van Aswegen J D, 36, Forest Town Skool vir Serebraalgestremde Kinders Johannesburg, Skoolhoof, 1975, Discovery
Van Aswegen J D, 33, Elandskraal PK Mooinooi, Veiligheidsbeampte, 1973, Vereeniging
Van Aswegen P F, 30, Dept Nie-Blanke Sake Munisipaliteit Heilbron, Bestuurder, 1965, Lindley
Van Aswegen S W, 30, P/A Munisipaliteit Standerton, Komiteeklerk, 1965, Edenville
Van Aswegen V, 37, Waters Edge Plotte 40 Oberholzer, Rekenmeester, 1976, Potchefstroom
Van Aswegen W H, 43, Staffordstraat 39 Westdene Johannesburg, N G Predikant, 1976, Blyvooruitzicht
Van Aswegen W P G, 41, P/A Hoër Tegn Skool Kimberley, Adjunkhoof, 1977, Bloemfontein
Van Baalen C J, 37, P/A Laerskool Denneoord Brakpan, Skoolhoof, 1975, Bethal
Van Beek D J M (Lid Nr 7765), Stellenbosch, 1963
Van Biljon I J, 42, Universiteit Stellenbosch, Professor, 1967, Graaff-Reinet
Van Biljon J A, 44, Fonteinstraat, Dewetsdorp, Motorhawe-Eienaar, 1975
Van Biljon P G, 37, Maggie Vierfontein, Boer, 1969, Viljoenskroon
Van Biljon P J, 36, Humansgeluk PK Ottosdal, Boer, 1965
Van Biljon W J (Lid Nr 7748), Johannesburg (Linden-Noord), 1963
Van Blerk W J, 33, P/A S A Spoorweë Bloemfontein, Klerk, 1969, Brandfort
Van Brakel J P, 44, v Graanstraat 20 Potchefstroom/P U vir CHO, Snr Lektor, 1976
Van Buuren H J, 34, P/A Hoërskool Riebeeck Randfontein, Vise-Hoof, 1973, Standerton
Van Coller C L W, 39, Carrollstraat Dewetsdorp, Predikant N G, 1970, P E Sonheuwels
Van Coller D H, 39, P/A Drs Blake Van Coller & Jankowitz Germiston, Geneesheer, 1968, Virginia
Van Coller F J, 41, Volkskas Steynsrus, Bestuurder, 1967, Zastron
Van Coller G C, 41, Kerkstraat 149, Vryheid, Klerk S A S & H, 1975
Van Coller G P (Lid Nr 7749), Johannesburg, 1963
Van Coller J G, 35, N G Kerk Rustenburg-Wes, Predikant, 1975, Paarl
Van Deemter C H S, 43, P/A Landbou Tegn Dienste Fauresmith, Voorligtingsbeampte, 1970, Humansdorp
V D Ahee F M, 35, Rietfontein Murraysburg, Boer, 1964
V D Bank J P, 32, Harmonie-Goudmyn Virginia, Ventilasiebeampte, 1966, Vaalharts
V D Bend C, 49, 14de Laan 974 Wonderboom-Suid Pretoria, Asst Hoof Stat, 1975, Pretoria
V D Berg A, 27, St Iveslaan 7 Cotswold Port Elizabeth, Onderwyser, 1963, Worcester
V D Berg A C, 27, Exeter Ladybrand, Boer, 1977
V D Berg A D P, 42, Macphailstraat 40 Springs, Geneesheer, 1972, Pretoria
V D Berg A J, 48, P/A N O K Johannesburg, Hoofbestuurder, 1970, Ermelo
V D Berg A M (Dr), Johannesburg, Fak Sekretaris
V D Berg A R, 36, P/A R G N Pretoria, Asst Dir v Inst Psigometriese Nav, 1975, Pretoria
V D Berg A S (Lid Nr 7705), Pretoria, Onderwyser, 1962
V D Berg B, 36, Albertynstraat 1 Uitenhage, Tandarts, 1966, Kirkwood
V D Berg B L, 40, Robinsonweg 135, Fort Victoria, Shell-Depotbestuurder, 1970, Umtali
V D Berg C L (Ds), Jeugpredikant N H Kerk — Lid van die U R se Jeugkomitee, 1973
V D Berg D A, 36, P/A Brand & V D Berg Lindley, Prokureur, 1965, Bloemfontein
V D Berg D J, 32, P/A Ferre Metale Alberton, Pers — En Adm Bestuurder, 1973, Vereeniging
V D Berg D P J, 46, Greystraat Dordrecht, Stasiemeester, 1974, Stellenbosch

V D Berg E H, 32, De La Reystraat Hobhouse, Onderwyser, 1975, Dealesville
V D Berg G D P, 38, P/A Consolglaswerke Pretoria-Wes, Verkoopsbestuurder, 1976
V D Berg G J, 43, Pres Brandweg 4 Parys, Skoolhoof/Primêre Skool, 1971, Vredefort
V D Berg G P, Voormalige L V — Wolmaransstad
V D Berg G P, 46, Pres Brand Goudmyn Welkom, Kampongbestuurder, 1967, Ladybrand
V D Berg G P, 33, Gedenkstraat 38, Bethlehem, Bem Beampte Vleissentraal, 1975, Senekal
V D Berg H B, 39, P/A Afdelingsbest S A S & H Bloemfontein, Klerk, 1967
V D Berg H J, 29, P/A N G Pastorie PK Skeerpoort, Predikant, 1967, Warmbad
V D Berg J A, 42, Volkskas Carletonville, Bestuurder, 1966, Johannesburg
V D Berg J A, 35, Peacestraat 17 Tzaneen, N G Predikant, 1974, Pretoria
V D Berg J C, 35, Kerkstraat Warden, Onderwyser, 1964, Hobhouse
V D Berg J H, 35, P/A P U vir CHO Potchefstroom, Dosent, 1973, Klerksdorp
V D Berg M, 44, P/A Interbank Diskontohuis Bpk Johannesburg, Besturende Direkteur, 1974, Pretoria
V D Berg M A, 41, Conradweg 9 Homelake/Wright Anderson Engineers Randfontein, Ingenieur, 1970, Brits
V D Berg P J, 44, Eierkring Kaapstad, Bestuurder, 1964, Mosselbaai
V D Berg P J, 37, Linksfieldweg 41 Edenvale, Geneesheer, 1974, Carletonville
V D Berg P J B, 36, Oshoorn Lindley, Boer, 1969
V D Berg T M M, 34, P/A S A Polisie Nylstroom, Sersant, 1975, Groblersdal
V D Berg W J, 34, Dept Bantoe Adm & Ontwikkeling Dundee, Kommissaris, 1964, Alberton
V D Bergh A G, 38, P/A K O P Kempton Park, Bedryfsbestuurder, 1974, Meyerton
V D Bergh G N, 43, P U vir CHO Potchefstroom, Professor, 1975, Pietersburg
V D Bergh H J (Lid Nr 6745), Eerste Minister se Veiligheidsraadgewer/Sekretaris van Sekuriteit/Voorheen Hoof van die Buro vir Staatsveiligheid
V D Bergh J L, 32, P/A Federale Mynbou Johannesburg, Bestuurder, Fin Adm, 1968, Linden
V D Bergh J P J, 29, P/A Venm Edms Bpk Welkom, Sekretaris, 1967, Vereeniging
V D Burgh C, 32, Saambou Pietersburg, Takbestuurder, 1964, Bloemfontein
V D Colf A P, 35, Makamerstraat 47, Gobabis, Onderwyser, 1975, Koës
V D Colff C J, 39, S A Polisie Potchefstroom, Speursersant, 1966, Potchefstroom
V D Heever A I, 36, West Ridingweg 2 Nigel, Direkteur Melkery, 1976
V D Heever C, 34, Cowlestraat 48 Springs, Ingenieur Grinaker, 1973
V D Heever C M, 26, P/A M J v d Heever (Edms) Bpk Koppies, Sakeman, 1969
V D Heever D, 38, P/A N G Kerk Grootfontein, Predikant, 1976, Klawer
V D Heever D J, 47, Sanlam Johannesburg, Verteenwoordiger, 1964
V D Heever J A, 36, N G Pastorie Clanwilliam, Predikant, 1969, Kamieskroon
V D Heever L, 34, Veiligheidspolisie Bellville, Kaptein S A P, 1974, Linden
V D Heever L J, 30, Elandweg 44 Kempton Park, Prokureur, 1970, Pretoria
V D Heever M J, 46, Noordstraat Koppies, Sakeman, 1967, Senekal
V D Heever P J, 27, P/A Hoëveldse Hoër Landbouskool Morgenzon, Onderwyser, 1970, Springs
V D Heever P P, 39, Kontorogab Springbok, Boer, 1969
V D Heever S, 39, Volkskas Smithfield, Bestuurder, 1964, Pretoria
V D Heever W C, 50, Areb Springbok, Boer, 1967
V D Linde B S, 39, Putneyweg 104 Brixton Johannesburg, Vervoerkontrakteur, 1974
V D Linde G P L, 1966 Bondsraad — Was Voorsitter van Bloemfonteinse Sentrale Komitee
V D Linde J A, 35, Tweelingskop Olifantshoek, Boer, 1967, Postmasburg
V D Linde J A, 26, Allena PK Koopmansfontein, Boer, 1968, Postmasburg
V D Linde J A, 34, V D Linde Motors Postmasburg, Motorhandelaar, 1964
V D Linde J A, 32, Duitseput Griekwastad, Boer, 1977
V D Linde J A, 34, Rusfontein Bloemfontein, Boer, 1965
V D Linde J C, 38, Rietkuil Lindley, Boer, 1975, Hoopstad
V D Linde L J, 46, Poswerkersunie Johannesburg, Sekretaris, 1966, Petrusburg
V D Linden F J, 41, Kaallaagte PK Biesiesvlei, Boer, 1963
V D Lith A A, 36, Nie-Blanke Sake Munisipaliteit Pietersburg, Direkteur, 1965, Pretoria
V D Lith A J S, 34, T180 Lugmasbasis Pietersburg, Kommandant S A L, 1971, Kaapstad
V D Merwe A B (Lid Nr 7720), Jacobsdal, Boer, 1962
V D Merwe A B, 49, Dept Sielkunde Univ Stellenbosch, Professor, 1965, Hanover
V D Merwe A B J, 46, Vogelstruisdrif Moorreesburg, Boer, 1974
V D Merwe A D J, 42, Goedgeloof Breërivier, Boer, 1974

V D Merwe A J, 41, Sagtevrugteraad Kaapstad, Vrugte-Inspekteur, 1966, Goodwood
V D Merwe A J, 32, Erinvaleweg 16, Freewaypark Boksburg, Visehoof, 1976, Welkom
V D Merwe B P M, 39, Rabiestraat 3 Lydenburg, Klerk van die Raad, 1971, Sabie
V D Merwe C, 33, S A S & H Breyten/v Riebeeckstraat 51 Breyten, Terreinmeester, 1970, Witbank
V D Merwe C A, 33, Elandstraat 211 Wierda Park Pretoria, Sen Navorser U P, 1977, Witbank
V D Merwe C F, 37, P/A Nas Raad vir Opv en SOS Navorsing Pretoria, Hoofnavorsingsbeampte, 1967
V D Merwe C G, 27, Hoërskool Mariental, Onderwyser, 1972, Potchefstroom
V D Merwe C I, 37, Malgasfontein Coligny, Boer, 1965
V D Merwe C J, 40 P/A Primêre skool Heilbron, Onderwyser, 1974, Ladybrand
V D Merwe C J, 45, Skoolraadskantoor Oos-Londen, Skoolraad, 1968, Bellville
V D Merwe C J, 30, "Dagbreek" PK Ofcolaco, Boer/Veearts, 1975, Tzaneen
V D Merwe C J, 42, Cove Singel 9 Ladysmith, Prokureur, 1976, Dundee
V D Merwe C J H, 32, Marestraat 16 Pietersburg, Ass Rekenmeester Landbank, 1970, Kroonstad
V D Merwe C J N, 32, De Grootboom P K Steelpoort, Boer, 1968, Ermelo
V D Merwe C M, 49 Hoërskool Steynsrus, Skoolhoof, 1964, Odendaalsrus
V D Merwe C N, 36, Eeufeesstraat 17 Lydenburg, Geref Predikant, 1977, Standerton
V D Merwe C N, 39, Leeufontein Klerksdorp, Onderwyser, 1969, Pretoria
V D Merwe C P (Lid Nr 4731), Hoof Opleidingskollege Wellington — Voorgestel vir die U R in 1968
V D Merwe C P, 37, Hoërskool Frankfort, Onderwyser, 1964, Tweeling
V D Merwe C V, (Lid Nr 4079), LV Bloemfontein — Voorgestel vir die U R in 1968
V D Merwe D A, 39, S A Polisie Greytown, Konstabel, 1965, Newcastle
V D Merwe D B, 41, N G Pastorie PK Misgund-Oos, Predikant, 1964, Edenvale
V D Merwe D F, 47, N G Kerk Oudtshoorn, Predikant, 1968, Beaufort-Wes
V D Merwe D J, 38, P/A Munisipaliteit Welkom Adj-Stadstesourier, 1967, Dealesville
V D Merwe D J, 43, Eikelaan Grabouw, Onderwyser, 1970, Porterville
V D Merwe D S, 28, Hoërskool Wonderboom Pretoria, Onderwyser, 1964, Brakpan
V D Merwe D W, 32, Vierdelaan 27 Heidelberg Tvl, Geneesheer, 1976, Beaufort-Wes
V D Merwe E, 32, P/A S A S & H Uitenhage, Ingenieur, 1975, Pretoria
V D Merwe E J, 34, S A Reserwebank Pretoria, Senior Navorser, 1974
V D Merwe F A R, 30, Tulipstraat 119 Lynnwood Pretoria, Rekenmeester/Rentmeester, 1977
V D Merwe F E, 31, N G Pastorie Dordrecht, Predikant, 1973, Lady Grey
V D Merwe F H H, 32, Strydom PK Kommandodrift, Boer, 1964, Bothaville
V D Merwe F J, 32, P/A Windmeul Kunsmisfabriek Robertson, Streeksbestuurder, 1968, Paarl
V D Merwe F J, 32, Spes Bona Vrede, Boer, 1975, Louis Trichardt
V D Merwe F J, 33, Univ Stellenbosch, Senior Lektor, 1966, Calvinia
V D Merwe F J, 37, Coronation Hospitaal Johannesburg, Ginekoloog, 1965, Bethlehem
V D Merwe F J, 38, P/A Vleissentraal Aberdeen, Verteenwoordiger/Boer, 1973, Murraysburg
V D Merwe F P, 34, Diazstraat 42 Strand, Ouditeur, 1966, Paarl
V D Merwe G C, 27, P/A Unisa Pretoria, Lektor, 1973
V D Merwe G J, 37, Sanlam Springs, Streeksbestuurder, 1975, Johannesburg
V D Merwe G J, 36, Môrester Koue Bokkeveld, Boer, 1974, Clanwilliam
V D Merwe G P, 30, The Mall Woonstel Phalaborwa/Coetzee en V D Merwe, Prokureur, 1970, Klerksdorp
V D Merwe G P B, 44, Posbus 166 Louis Trichardt, Sakeman, 1970, Naboomspruit
V D Merwe G S S P 45, P/A Durban-Roodepoort-Deep Myn, Instrukteur, 1963, Wolmaransstad
V D Merwe H D K, 33, Schoemanstraat 1059 Hatfield Pretoria L V, 1968
V D Merwe H I, 32, Lemon Grove 34 Bulawayo, Modelmaker, 1973
V D Merwe H P, 34, Morgenstond Bonnievale, Boer, 1966
V D Merwe H S, 45 P/A Sentraal-Wes Koöp Klerksdorp, Asst Graanbestuurder, 1969, Ventersdorp
V D Merwe I, 39, Aalwynstraat 11 Jim Fouche-Park Welkom, Takbestuurder/Allied Bouvereniging, 1971, Kroonstad

V D Merwe I, 33, Hoërskool Zwartberg Prins Albert, Onderwyser, 1975, Bonnievale
V D Merwe I J, 37, Aberdeenweg 85 Clubview/S A Weermag, Kommandant, 1974, Saldanha
8 D Merwe I J, 37, Kronendal Ermel, Slaghuiseienaar, 1972
V D Merwe I S, 45, Ammunisiedepot 93 Jankempdorp, Bevelvoerder, 1964, Piketberg
V D Merwe J, 46, Skoolkoshuis Northam, Onderwyser, 1972, Fochville
V D Merwe J C, 37, Sinodale Sending Komm, N G Kerk in S A, Sakebestuurder/Scriba, 1974, Kaapstad
V D Merwe J C, 35, Mooidraai Postmasburg, Boer, 1970, Germiston
V D Merwe J C S, 33, Potgieterstraat 26 Upington, Onderwyser, 1976
V D Merwe J D, 36, Nu Plus-Ultra Dist Pietersburg, Boer, 1977
V D Merwe J D B, 35, Carrolsfarm PK De Wet, Asst Stadsklerk, 1973, Stellenbosch
V D Merwe, J D G, 37, P/A Hugenote Kollege Wellington, Dosent, 1964, Pretoria
V D Merwe J D G, Wellington — Praat oor Kommunisme by Bondsraad 1969
V D Merwe J G (Dr), Lid van die U R se Ekonomiese Komitee 1973
V D Merwe J G, 39, Landdroskantoor Potgietersrus, Landdros, 1967, Bloemfontein
V D Merwe J H, 40, Proteaweg 16 Kempton Park, Ingenieur S A S & H, 1971, Mosselbaai
V D Merwe J H, 52, Ebenhaesar Ceres, Boer, 1966
V D Merwe J H, 42, Tierkloof Porterville, Boer, 1965
V D Merwe J H, 30, Nuwejaarskuil Beaufort-wes, Boer, 1965, Aberdeen
V D Merwe J H P, 32, Rooipoort Laerskool Potchefstroom, Onderwyser, 1966, Kempton Park
V D Merwe J J, 48, Windsor PK Ellisras, Boer, 1968, Waterberg
V D Merwe J L, 31, Rautenbach's Kroonstad, Boekhouer, 1969
V D Merwe J L, 44, P/A Sasol Sasolburg, Instandh Voorman, 1968, Durban
V D Merwe J M, 44, Dorspan Boshof, Boer, 1976
V D Merwe J M, 34, "Conigenda" Otjiwarongo, Boer, 1975
V D Merwe J M H, 41, P/A S A Polisie Ladysmith Natal, Majoor, 1968, Volksrust
V D Merwe J P (Lid Nr 7750), Springbok, 1963
V D Merwe J S (Prof), P U vir CHO Potchefstroom Professor Aardrykskunde, 1963
V D Merwe J S, 29, Diepdrift Graskop, Boer/Argitek, 1964, Kroonstad
V D Merwe J S D, 32, N G Gemeente Bethlehem-Noord, Predikant, 1973, Marquard
V D Merwe J V, 31, Plaatjiesdam, Postmasburg, Boer, 1974
V D Merwe J V, 31, P/A S A Polisie Ficksburg, Kaptein, 1968, Pretoria
V D Merwe K W P, 35, Hoërskool Uniondale, Onderhoof, 1966, Upington
V D Merwe L C, Voorsitter van Christiaan De Wet Fonds Hoof Personeelbeampte van Volkskas Pretoria
V D Merwe L J, 45, P/A Geref Kerk Ventersdorp, Predikant, 1974, Silverton
V D Merwe M A, 41, Marchand, Boer/Sakeman, 1965, Kakamas
V D Merwe M C, 31, P/A Munisipaliteit Vereeniging Asst Stadsingenieur, 1973, Durban
V D Merwe M J, 36, Donkinstraat 44 Graaff-Reinet, Senior Assistent, 1971, Jansenville
V D Merwe M J, 34, Kildare Terra Firma Bray, Boer, 1964, Carnarvon
V D Merwe M J N, 40, Munisipaliteit Ermelo, Elektrisien, 1967
V D Merwe N, 43, P/A S A B S Pretoria, Asst Direkteur, 1967
V D Merwe N J, 32, N G Pastorie Karas, Predikant, 1975, Warrenton
V D Merwe O R, 32, P/A Hoërskool Ben Viljoen Groblersdal, Onderwyser, 1975, Springbokvlakte
V D Merwe P A, 30, Troyestraat 274 Muckleneuk Pretoria, N G Predikant, 1971, Krugersdorp
V D Merwe P A, Bethlehem — Woon 1966 se Bondsraad by
V D Merwe P J, 41, Van Warmelostraat 56 Pietersbsurg, Klerk S A S, 1977, Soekmekaar
V D Merwe P J, 29, Ellisrasse Hoërskool, Onderwyser, 1967, Nylstroom
V D Merwe P J, 45, Verversingsafd S A S Johannesburg, Inspekteur, 1966
V D Merwe P J J, 49, P/A Geoue Afd Prov Adm Bloemfontein, Hoof, 1966, Ceres
V D Merwe P J J (Jnr) 25, Leeufontein Petrusville K P, Boer, 1968, De Aar
V D Merwe P P J, 35, Hybernweg 7 Port Elizabeth, Landdros, 1975, Pretoria
V D Merwe P S, Otjiwarongo, 1971
V D Merwe P U, 31, Witklip PK Makokskraal, Boer, 1970, Pretoria
V D Merwe R A, 37, Hoërskool Porterville, Skoolhoof, 1975, Jansenville
V D Merwe R A T, 34, P/A Sanlam Durban, Taksekretaris, 1968, Bellville

V D Merwe S D, 31, N G Pastorie Vanderbijlpark, Predikant, 1964, Jeppestown
V D Merwe S J, 41, Morsfontein Steynsburg, Boer/Boekhouer, 1967, Fauresmith
V D Merwe S J, 30, Die Eike Constable, Boer, 1968, Beaufort Wes
V D Merwe S J, 40, Doakstraat 23 Hazeldene Germiston, Raadg Ingenieur, 1969, Queenstown
V D Merwe S J du T, 41, Albert Biesiesvlei, Boer/Onderwyser, 1970, Pretoria
V D Merwe S S, 42, Ninowweg 3 Valhalla of P/A Dept Justisie, Adj-Sekretaris, 1975, Queenstown
V D Merwe S W (Lid Nr 6571) — Voorgestel vir die U R in 1968 — Minister van Gesondheid
V D Merwe S W, 38, Dasklip Porterville, Boer, 1963, Kuruman
V D Merwe S W, 43, Atoomkragraad Pretoria, Hoofskakelbeampte, 1966, Bloemfontein
V D Merwe S W B, 37, Hoër Landbouskool Augsburg, Vise-Hoof, 1971, Bellville
V D Merwe W, Lid van die U R se Landbou-Komitee 1973
V D Merwe W A, 36, P/A Rautenbachs & Kie Vereeniging, Bestuurder/Dir., 1965, Kroonstad
V D Merwe W A H (Lid Nr 7776), Aliwal Noord, 1963
V D Merwe W G, 39, P/A S A Vlootgimnasium Saldanha, Kommandeur, 1967, Gordonsbaai
V D Merwe W H, 42, Dept Bantoe Adm & Ontwikkeling Umtata, Hoofvakkundige, 1967, Harding, Natal
V D Merwe W J, 35, P/A Santam Bloemfontein, Sekretaris, 1965, Johannesburg
V D Merwe W J, 27, Geref Pastorie Mooinooi Rustenburg, Predikant, 1966, Vereeniging
V D Merwe W J, 46, Helpmekaar Ceres, Boer, 1968
V D Merwe W J, 37, S A Veiligheidspolisie Vereeniging adj-Offisier, 1969, Oranjefontein
V D Merwe W J, 46, P/A Volkskas Bpk Hertzogville, Bestuurder, 1974, Bloemfontein
V D Merwe W J J, 32, P/A Hoërskool Brits, Onderwyser, 1976, Potchefstroom
V D Merwe W J S, 37, Wesselskop Winburg, Boer, 1977
V D Merwe W K, 42, P/A NAS Party Johannesburg, Streeksorganiseerder, 1963, Potchefstroom
V D Merwe W O, 30, Plot 138 Nooitgedacht, Rekenmeester/W L Ochse, 1977, Linden Johannesburg
V D Merwe W P O, 36, Jnr Seunskoshuis Gobabis, Onderwyser, 1970, Walvisbaai
V D Mescht, G F, 45, P/A African Life Ass. My Port Elizabeth, Agent, 1965, Steytlersville
V D Nest T F, 32, Worralweg 8 Nahoon Oos-Londen, Onderwyser, 1973, Oos-Londen
V D Riet J L, 43, Hoërskool Kakamas, Onderhoof, 1967
V D Ryst J W, 36, Groenfontein Koster, Boer, 1976
V D Sandt J M, 42, Grootvlei No 36 PK Pyramied, Onderwyser, 1976, Pretoria
V D Spuy G R, 31, Arumweg 164 Table View, Onderhoof, 1976, Uitenhage
V D Spuy S de w, 45, Langerug Worcester, Geneesheer, 1965, Rondebosch
V D Stoep F, 34, Universiteit Pretoria, Professor, 1966
V D Vloed J, 34, N G Kerk Turffontein Johannesburg, Predikant, 1975, Pretoria
V D Vyver D H, 37, P/A Instituut vir Taalonderrig Universiteit Stellenbosch, Direkteur, 1977, Bloemfontein
V D Vyver G C P, Bloemfontein
V D Vyver G T (Lid Nr 3291), L P R (L U K) Adelaide
V D Vyver I W, 41, De Rust Aberdeen, Boer, 1972
V D Vyver J A, 39, Hoërskool Langenhoven Queens Crescent 444 Lynnwood Pretoria, Onderhoof, 1972
V D Vyver J L, 33, Volkskas Prins Albert, Rekenmeester, 1970, Louis Trichardt
V D Vyver J S F, 33, Steyn V/D Vyver & De Jager Willowmore, Prokureur, 1966, Laingsburg
V D Vyver J S F, By 1966 Bondsraad Spreek hy kommer uit dat baie Afrikaanse Prokureurs op die Platteland werk aan Nie-Afrikaanse Prok-Firmas in Stede Toevertrou
V D Vyver M J, 34, Hoërskool Welkom, Onderwyser, 1965, Bultfontein
V D Wall M, 30, N G Pastorie Lykso (Vryburg), Predikant, 1963, Bloemfontein
V D Walt A, 32, Geref Kerk Heilbron, Predikant, 1967, Schweizer Reneke
V D Walt A, 29, Tweespruit Reitz, Boer, 1967
V D Walt A J, 48, P/A South Bakels (Edms) Bpk Johannesburg, Sekretaris/Rekenmeester, 1967, Melville
V D Walt A J H (Prof Dr)
V D Walt A L, 28, Fieldstraat 48 Lilianton Boksburg, Onderwyser, 1970, Kempton Park
V D Walt A T, 35, P/A Univ van Wes-Kaapland, Sen Lektor, 1974, Bloemfontein

V D Walt A G P, 34, P/A Gereformeerde Kerk Orkney, Predikant, 1974, Volksrust
V D Walt B, 39, 3destraat 18 Heilbron, Sekretaris NAS Suiwelkoöp, 1977, Pretoria
V D Walt B (Lid Nr 7777), Kimberley, 1963
V D Walt B J, 47, P/A S A Spoorweë Johannesburg, Ind Beampte, 1963, Auckland Park
V D Walt B J, 35, Pieter Raathlaan 22 Germiston, Prokureur, 1974, Eikenhof
V D Walt B J, Voormalige L V Ambassadeur in Kanada — Administrateur S W A
V D Walt C F, 39, Markstraat Ventersdorp, Telefoon-Superintendent, Sannieshof
V D Walt C P, P U vir CHO Potchefstroom, Woon 1965 se Bondsraad by, Sen Lektor (Politiek), 1963
V D Walt D C P, 32, P/A Vleissentraal Pretoria, Personeelbeampte, 1974, Pretoria
V D Walt D G, 34, Renosterkloof Stella, Boer/Sakeman, 1969, Bethal
V D Walt D J, 34, Umgenistraat 86 Drie Riviere Vereeniging, Garage-Eienaar, 1973
V D Walt D J, 35, Rietfontein, Middelburg K P, Boer, 1970, Venterstad
V D Walt D J, 36, P/A Munisipaliteit Alberton, Stadsingenieur, 1965, Pretoria
V D Walt E J, 26, P/A N G Kerk Willowmore, Predikant, 1968, Stellenbosch
V D Walt G H, 42, Rolfes Ltd Elandsfontein, Rekenmeester, 1964, Johannesburg
V D Walt G J, 45, Munisipaliteit Aliwal Noord, Voorman, 1965, Bethlehem
V D Walt G M, 39, P/A Petra Meubels Pretoria, Direkteur, 1964, Uniondale
V D Walt H A, 30, Van Iddekingelaan 12, Fichardtpark, Hoof Rekenmeester N G K, 1975, Bloemfontein
V D Walt H J, 35, P/A Geref Pastorie Odendaalsrus, Predikant, 1967, Middelburg Kaap
V D Walt H J D, 28, P/A Erasmus Jooste & Kie Klerksdorp, Prokureur, 1964, Potchefstroom
V D Walt H J S, 47, P/A Skiereilandse Tegn Kollege Bellville, Hoof, 1969, Bloemfontein
V D Walt H P, 41, V/D Walt & Fourie Scholtzstraat 39 Unisersitas Bloemfontein, Argitek, 1972, Kroonstad
V D Walt H P, 52, Sidney Settlers, Boer, 1977, Delmas
V D Walt I S, 44, Nooitverwacht PK Vermaas, Boer, 1973, Uitschot
V D Walt J, 35, Danspan Potgietersrus, Boer/Sakeman, 1964
V D Walt J C, 38, Jonesstraat 94 Pietersburg, Prokureur/Naude Jansen & V D Walt, 1970, Pretoria
V D Walt J C, 32, P/A Geref Pastorie Wolmaransstad, Predikant, 1970, Molteno
V D Walt J C, 37, Elsiesdam Hopetown, Boer, 1976
V D Walt J D, 33, Stillehoop Steynsburg, Boer, 1965
V D Walt J H (Lid Nr 1896) Pensioentrekker — Voorgestel vir die U R in 1968
V D Walt J H, 33, Platdoorn Potgietersrus, Boer, 1973
V D Walt J H, 34, P/A Mooirivier Motors (Edms) Bpk Potchefstroom, Besturende Direkteur, 1967, Colesberg
V D Walt J H, 32, Geref Pastorie Barberton, Predikant, 1966, Randburg
V D Walt J H, 25, Kleinfontein Noupoort, Rekenmeester/Boer, 1971
V D Walt J H P, 34, Hoërskool Petrusburg, Onderwyser, 1963, Odendaalsrus
V D Walt J J, 43, Schilpadpan Alldays, Boer, 1977
V D Walt J J, Kimberley
V D Walt J J A, 35, Univ Stellenbosch, Sen Lektor, 1974, Pretoria
V D Walt J J A, 43, P/A P U vir CHO Potchefstroom, Professor, 1969
V D Walt J L, 42, P/A NAS Bouvereniging Johannesburg, Takbestuurder, 1965, Port Elizabeth
V D Walt J L C, 27, N G Kerk Eshowe, Predikant, 1968, Stellenbosch
V D Walt J P, 37, Carletonville Hoërskool, Onderwyser, 1964, Potchefstroom
V D Walt J P, 44, PU vir CHO Potchefstroom, Hoof Tegnikus Instrumentmakery, 1974
V D Walt J P L, 31, Geref Kerk Suidheuwels Bloemfontein, Predikant, 1976, Reitz
V D Walt L, Pretoria
V D Walt L, 32, S A U K Johannesburg, Ingenieur, 1966, Springs
V D Walt L J, 33, P/A Geref Kerk Sishen, Predikant, 1977, Barberton
V D Walt L S, 39, P/A SAPPI Springs, Skeikundige, 1965, Benoni
V D Walt L S, 40, P/A Volkskas Venterstad, Bestuurder, 1968, Reitz
V D Walt M F, 30, Maraisstraat 49 De Aar, Predikant Geref Kerk, 1976, Potchefstroom
V D Walt M J, 41, Burgerstraat 18 Pietersburg, Prokureur, 1973, Potchefstroom
V D Walt M P A (Lid Nr 7751), Christiana, 1963
V D Walt N, 35, Prov Administrasie Bellstraat 15 Universitas Bloemfontein, Ingenieur, 1973, Louis Trichardt

V D Walt N S O, 39, Brakspruit Leslie, Boer, 1971, Kinross
V D Walt N S T, 40, Genl Conroystraat 14 Bloemfontein, Argitek, 1963
V D Walt N T S, 37, P/A Volkskas Bpk Orkney, Rekenmeester, 1975, Randfontein
V D Walt P, 37, P/A Van Rooyen en Van Der Walt Pretoria, Bourekenaar, 1968, Venterstad
V D Walt P C, 45, P/A Sasol Sasolburg, Kontraktebestuurder, 1967, Johannesburg
V D Walt P J, 32, P/A Eksteen en V D Walt Tzaneen, Siviele Ingenieur, 1975, Levubu
V D Walt P J, 40, Volkskas Carolina, Bestuurder, 1966, Bethal
V D Walt P J, 42, Tokat Gobabis, Boer,1969, Middelburg Tvl
V D Walt P J, 32, Departement v Verdediging Walvisbaai, Majoor, 1969, Pretoria
V D Walt P J, 36, Versekeringskorporasie Rondalia, Admin Bestuurder, 1975, Nylstroom
V D Walt P J J, 32, Gereformeerde Kerk Lydenburg, Predikant, 1967, Pretoria
V D Walt P S V, 26, Rouxstraat Bethulie, Onderwyser, 1968
V D Walt P T, 35, Skukuza Krugerwildtuin, Hoofnavorsingsbeampte, 1977, Middelburg K P
V D Walt R A, 37, Britsstraat 60 Standerton/Oska Eng, Klerk, 1977, Warden
V D Walt S C, 44, Laerskool Steynsburg, Skoolhoof, 1965
V D Walt S C, 36, Condreystraat 10 Kroonstad, Onderwyser, 1976, Randfontein
V D Walt S J, 40, Rondebultweg 226 Libradene/Laerskool J M Louw Boksburg, Skoolhoof, 1971, Primrose
V D Walt S J, 46, Brick & Tile Vereeniging, Beplanningsklerk, 1967
V D Walt S P, PU vir CHO Potchefstroom, Professor (Teologie), 1963
V D Walt T, 32, Gereformeerde Pastorie Krugersdorp, Predikant, 1966, Holland
V D Walt T (Prof), Molenstraat 65 Potchefstroom/PU vir CHO, Rektor (Skakel by Universiteit 1976)
V D Walt T A, 40, Lytteltonse Ingenieurswerke, Produksie Superintendent, 1973, Pretoria
V D Walt T F, 45, Herbert Bakerstraat 37 Groenkloof/Departement Handel Pretoria, Adj-Sekretaris, 1977
V D Walt T J, 31, Nola Nywerhede Randfontein, Tegniese Bestuurder, 1969, Sasolburg
V D Walt T N, 33, Stadsraad Rustenburg, Bestuurder Pers & Organisatoriese Dienste, 1975, Randburg
V D Walt T S P, 33, Holtzhausenweg 22 Potchefstroom, Lektor/PU vir CHO, 1977, Rustenburg
V D Walt W, 29, Wildfontein Noupoort, Werktuigkundige/Boer, 1973
V D Wath J G (Dr)
V D Watt H J P, 36, Karreedam Marquard, Boer, 1965
V D Watt L, 26, Van Zylstraat Brandfort, Prokureur, 1965, Excelsior
V D Watt P B, 27, N G Pastorie Bloemhof, Predikant, 1966, Amalia
V D Westhuizen A, 32, Minerale Bad Tshipise, Superintendent, 1964, Brits
V D Westhuizen B B, 39, Simmerskool Germiston, Skoolhoof, 1966, Springs
V D Westhuizen B N, 38, N G Sendinggemeente Katima Mulilo, Predikant, 1976, Elliot
V D Westhuizen C B, 27, Hoewe 224 Chartwell Sandton, Onderwyser, 1976, Potchefstroom
V D Westhuizen C F J, 33, Pigeonstraat 21 Elspark/S A Weermag, Majoor, 1976
V D Westhuizen C H, 43, Tegniese Skool Randfontein, Onderwyser, 1973
V D Westhuizen C J, 38, Mopaniestraat 4 Homelake Randfontein, Geregsbode & Eiendomsagent, 1964
V D Westhuizen C J, 40, Steelweld (Edms) Bpk/Randburg, Tegn & Bemarkingsbestuurder, 1974, Barkly-Wes
V D Westhuizen C V, 35, Bonfoi PK Vlottenburg, Boer, 1973
V D Westhuizen D B, 51, Carnarvon, Veeboer, 1963
V D Westhuizen F J, 29, Jozini Staatswaterskema Zoeloeland, Skoolhoof, 1968, Durban
V D Westhuizen G J, 46, Onderwyskollege Pretoria, Lektor, 1968
V D Westhuizen G M, 38, P/A Ontvanger van Inkomste Pietersburg, Senior Beampte, 1965, Tweeling
V D Westhuizen G P, 37, Cedarlaan 12 Robertson, Onderwyser, 1967, Noupoort
V D Westhuizen G P, 38, Buffelshoek Nylstroom, Sakeman, 1967, Louis Trichardt
V D Westhuizen G v S, 33, Swartrivier Koelenhof, Boer, 1970, Stellenbosch
V D Westhuizen H G, 27, N H Pastorie Hartswater, Predikant, 1964, Pretoria
V D Westhuizen H L, 45, P/A Sanlam Mafeking, Verteenwoordiger, 1964, Bloemhof
V D Westhuizen H L, 32, Stinkwater Niekerkshoop, Boer, 1971
V D Westhuizen H P, 39, V D Hoffweg 40 Potchefstroom, Onderwyser, 1966, Pretoria
V D Westhuizen H P, 36, Konservatorium vir Musiek Stellenbosch, Dosent, 1967, Bellville

V D Westhuizen I J O, 52, PK Rooirivier Oor Uniondale, Boer, 1964
V D Westhuizen I P, 36, Landdroskantoor Kenhardt, Landdros, 1967, Upington
V D Westhuizen J, 34, N G Kerk Cradock, Predikant, 1967, Paterson
V D Westhuizen J C, 35, Millinweg Kimberley/Landbou-Unie-N-KP, Sekretaris (Org), 1975, Paarl
V D Westhuizen J C, 44, Grootvlei Kamieskroon, Boer, 1975
V D Westhuizen J H, 34, Okavangoweg Grootfontein, Adj-Skoolhoof, 1970, Manina
V D Westhuizen J J, 29, Buitestedelike Gesondheidsraad Pretoria, Regsassistent, 1965
V D Westhuizen J J P, 27, Universiteitskollege van Zoeloeland, Klerk, 1965, Pretoria
V D Westhuizen J L, 34, S A Polisie Alberton, Kaptein, 1968, Germiston
V D Westhuizen N, 48, Sterkfonteinhospitaal Krugersdorp, Superintendent, 1966, Potchefstroom
V D Westhuizen N J, 35, S A Weermag Pretoria, Kommandant, 1974
V D Westhuizen P, 39, Senior Seunskoshuis Swakopmund, Onderwyser, 1976, Windhoek
V D Westhuizen P J, 33, Hartebeespoortdam/Hoërskool Brits, Onderwyser, 1968, Johannesburg
V D Westhuizen P J, 38, Zwartkop PK Ariamsvlei, Boer, 1965
V D Westhuizen P J, 35, Derdestraat 45 Kieserville/Sanlam, Verteenwoordiger, 1970, Potchefstroom
V D Westhuizen P J, 34, Carinusstraat 246 Meyerspark/Volkskas, Asst-Hoofrekenmeester, 1970, Silverton
V D Westhuizen P J, 45, Afrikaans Hoër Durban, Skoolhoof, 1974, Pietermaritzburg
V D Westhuizen P J W S, 30, Geref Sendingpastorie Drimiopsis, Sendeling, 1970, Potchefstroom
V D Westhuizen P W, 30, S A Weermag Oudtshoorn, Majoor, 1967, Walvisbaai
V D Westhuizen S A, 27, Santam Calvinia, Sekretaris, 1966, Bellville
V D Westhuizen S J, 33, Tempe Bloemfontein/S A Weermag, Kapelaan, 1977, Vereeniging
V D Westhuizen S M J, 33, Union Carriage & Wagon Co Nigel, Kontraktebeampte, 1974, Springs
V D Westhuizen W J, 41, Bantoe-Opleidingskollege Sibasa, Hoof, 1976, Marble Hall
V D Westhuizen W K, Erasmusstraat 244A Meyerspark Pretoria, Streekdirekteur Tvl (Republiekfees 1971)
V D Westhuizen W P, 30, Bell & Van Rensburg Naboomspruit, Apteker, 1965, Pretoria
V D Westhuizen J J N, 39, Departement Landbou Pinetown, Hoofvoorligtingsbeampte, 1967, Port Shepstone
V D Westhuizen O S, 32, Colin Gertenbach & De Vries Saldanha, Ingenieur, 1974, Bellville
Van De Venter A A, F A K-Verteenwoordiger Vir Wes-Tvl Noord-Kaapland & S W A
Van de Venter A A, 33, F A K Johannesburg, Administratiewe Beampte, 1969, Potchefstroom
Van Deventer B, Riversdal (Tree op as Skakel by Afdelingsraadkongres in Kaapstad in 1966)
Van Deventer D J, 43, S A Polisie Heilbron, Adj-Offisier, 1973, Hertzogville
Van Deventer F J, 32, Gereformeerde Kerk Germiston, Predikant, 1973, Middelburg K P
Van Deventer H T, 30, N H Pastorie Krugersdorp-Wes, Predikant, 1974, Pretoria
Van Deventer J H, 31, Nasionale Koerante Bloemfontein, Nuusredakteur, 1973, Pretoria
Van Deventer J J, 37, Drie Riviere Laerskool Vereeniging, Skoolhoof, 1974, Elsburg
Van Deventer J J, 34, N G Gemeente Selcourt Springs, Predikant, 1966, Stellenbosch
Van Deventer S P, Stadswaardeerder van Bloemfontein terwyl in diens van Munisipaliteit in 1973 Stadsraad se Hoof Bou-Inspekteur
Van Dyk A C, 32, Hoërskool Edenvale, Onderhoof, 1976, Potchefstroom
Van Dyk C C, 28, Oosthuizen & Van Dyk Bellville, Tandarts, 1965, Malmesbury
Van Dyk C J, 33, Sluiterstraat 50A Ermelo, Prokureur, 1971, Wepener
Van Dyk F J, 32, Lantanalaan 2 Edleen Kempton Park, Onderwyser, 1977, Edenvale
Van Dyk F J, 50, Kafferskraal Marikana/Sanlam, Boer, 1974, Bothaville
Van Dyk G J, 50, A S D Kantoor Alexanderbaai, Assistent Bestuurder, 1966, Pretoria
Van Dyk G P (Lid Nr 1784) Bantoe-Onderwys Pretoria, Sekretaris
Van Dyk J C J, 34, Volkskas Glencoe, Rekenmeester, 1969, Durban
Van Dyk J H, Departement Bantoe-Administrasie, 1973
Van Dyk J H, 40, Reynoldstraat 16 Dundee, Hoofventilasiebeampte, 1972, Vryheid
Van Dyk J J, 32, Hompestraat 040 Mindalore Krugersdorp Munisipaliteitbeampte 1977

Van Dyk J J, 30, Hoërskool Rustenburg, Onderwyser, 1965, Pretoria
Van Dyk J S, 42, V D Merwestraat Erasmia Pretoria, N G Predikant, 1970, Benoni
Van Dyk P J C, 36, Hoërskool Nylstroom, Onderwyser, 1965, Waterberg
Van Dyk T A, 35, S A Weermag Pretoria, Kommandant, 1964, Ermelo
Van Dyk T J, 39, Blakewayweg 40 Umtata/Bantoe-Onderwys, Skoolhoof, 1975, Nqamakwe
Van Dyk T J, 45, S A Lugmag Pretoria, Kaptein, 1968
Van Dyk S W, 36, Sinoville Pretoria, Adjunkhoof, 1975
Van Dyk W D, 36, Rooivlei P K Grootmist Port Nolloth, Boer, 1969
Van Dyk W J, 33, Napier, Boer, 1963
Van Eck D R, 39, Lusthof Lichtenburg, Boer, 1974
Van Eck J, 33, Hoërskool Williston, Onderwyser, 1974, Bellville
Van Eck S F, 32, Ulswater 8 Pinelands/Van Zijl & Robinson Finansiële Direkteur, 1971, Bredasdorp
Van Eeden A, 38, Tautestraat Machadodorp, Apteker, 1974, Swartruggens
Van Eeden C C C, 32, Michaelstraat 36 Wilkoppies Klerksdorp, Onderwyser, 1970, Potchefstroom
Van Eeden D, 45, PU vir CHO Potchefstroom, Professor, 1973
Van Eeden D P W, 41, Romastraat 10 Robertsham Johannesburg Adj-Offisier (SAP), 1968, Florida
Van Eeden F J, 34, P/A Yskor Pretoria, Chemikus, 1975, Vanderbijlpark
Van Eeden G, 40, Van Eeden Motors Germiston, Werktuigkundige, 1969
Van Eeden G J, 28, Kruisrivier Riversdal, Boer, 1973
Van Eeden H J A, 34, Elveystraat 2 Vanderbijlpark/Hoërskool, Onderwyser, 1976, Sasolburg
Van Eeden J A (Lid Nr 7752), Potchefstroom-Wes, 1963
Van Eeden J A, 27, Susannahswoning PK Sheridan, Boer, 1967, Fouriesburg
Van Eeden J A, 39, Nie-Blanke Sake Munisipaliteit Pretoria, Superintendent, 1964
Van Eeden J B, 32, Kerklaan 362 Lynnwood Pretoria, Onderwyser, 1965, Lichtenburg
Van Eeden J H, 34, Denisestraat 11 Brakpan, Onderwyser, 1973
Van Eeden J J, 38, P/A Nasionale Party (Tvl) Johannesburg Asst-Sekretaris, 1968, Randfontein
Van Eeden J S, 41, Hoërskool Hangklip Queenstown, Onderhoof, 1967, Springbok
Van Eeden J T, 34, Palmietfontein Klerksdorp, Boer, 1970, Delareyville
Van Eeden O R (Dr), Lid van die Uitvoerende Raad se Wetenskap-Komitee in 1973
Van Eeden T F J, 29, Oshoek Delareyville, Boer, 1974
Van Emmenis R, 35, Blairgowrie Construction Randburg, Direkteur, 1970, Johannesburg
Van Eyssen P J, 42, 113deLaan 32 Bellville, Rekenmeester & Fabriekskosteklerk, 1971, Strand
Van Garderen D S, 33, P/A Yskor Ellisras, Meganiese Ingenieur, 1977, Thabazimbi
Van Graan C H, 29, Vierdestraat 69 Springs/NG Kerk Werdapark, Predikant, 1970, Bellville
Van Graan E V, 32, Bank V/D OVS Bloemfontein, Finans & Statistiese Assistent, 1969 Kimberley
Van Graan H L, 32, N G Kerk Capital Park-Oos Pretoria, Predikant, 1973, Durban
Van Graan J A, 29, Monicalaan Flamwood Klerksdorp/General Mining & Finance Korp Bpk, Hoof-Projekgeoloog, 1976, Potchefstroom
Van Graan P H, 35, Rietfonteinweg Primrose Germiston, Tandarts, 1968, Pretoria
Van Heerden A, 49, Hutchinsonweg 44 Scottsville Pietermaritzburg, Regter, 1967, Durban
Van Heerden A, 45, Landbou Tegniese Dienste Pretoria, Asst Direkteur (Veeartseny), 1974, Vryburg
Van Heerden A F, 39, Witrivier Munisipaliteit, Stadstesourier, 1973, Meyerton
Van Heerden A J, 47, N G Kerk Wonderboom Pretoria, Predikant, 1968, Durban
Van Heerden A J N, 31, N G Pastorie Matubatuba, Predikant, 1964
Van Heerden C S, 28, Eloffskraal Murraysburg, Boer, 1966
Van Heerden C V, 42, Derdelaan 7 Vaalreef, Asst Ondergrondbestuurder, 1967, Springs
Van Heerden C v L, 42, Volkskas Bethulie, Bestuurder, 1974, Pretoria
Van Heerden C W C, 49, Departement van Verdediging Pretoria, Parl Assistent, 1968
Van Heerden F A J, 33, Oranjestraat 1 Lakeview/S A S & H, Klerk (Rekenkundig), 1972, Bloemfontein
Van Heerden F J, 45, Garies, Posmeester, 1973, Indwe

Van Heerden H, 37, Plaas "Cub" Outjo, Boer, 1970
Van Heerden H, 34, Burgerstraat 14 Lydenburg, Tandarts, 1965
Van Heerden H F, 34, Smithfield Handelshuis Koöp Bpk, Bestuurder, 1975, Barkly-Oos
Van Heerden H J V, 36, Vaalbank PK Hlobane, Boer, 1975, Christiana
Van Heerden H M, 35, Hockeylaan 5 Northcliffe Johannesburg, Sakeman, 1970, Biesiesvlei
Van Heerden H S, 35, Landdroskantoor Bethal, Senior Landdros, 1974, Roodepoort
Van Heerden I J, 30, Bosmanskop Hendrina, Sakeman/Boer, 1974, Lentz
Van Heerden I J, 31, Naudesfontein Sterkstroom, Boer, 1968
Van Heerden J D G, 31, Cullinan Refractories Olifantsfontein Personeelbestuurder, 1969
Van Heerden J L, 41, Gracelaan 66 Murrayfield Pretoria, Apteker (Sentra Apteek), 1977, Hercules Pretoria
Van Heerden J P, Lid van die Uitvoerende Raad se Ekonomiese Komitee in 1973
Van Heerden J P vd W, 41, Erasmusstraat 242 Meyerspark Pretoria Admin Beampte U P, 1977, Pretoria
Van Heerden L D, 42, Onderstetuin Murraysburg Kaap, Boer, 1969
Van Heerden L F, 43, Hoërskool Vereeniging, Onderwyser, 1965, Lydenburg
Van Heerden L J, 38, P/A Bantoekommissaris Potgietersrus, Add Bantoesakekomm, 1968, Sibasa
Van Heerden L J R, 42, Collinsingel 6 Sasolburg/Carbochem, Rekenmeester, 1976, Johannesburg
Van Heerden P D R, 39, P/A Karl Bremerhospitaal Bellville, Internis, 1970, Rustenburg
Van Heerden P J (Lid Nr 8649), Lisbonlaan 47 Robertsham Uitbr 1, Onderwyser
Van Heerden P J, 25, Laerskool Malvern Johannesburg, Onderwyser, 1965
Van Heerden P J R, 37, Volkskas Morgenzon, Bestuurder, 1966, Pretoria
Van Heerden P W, 45, S A S & H Oos-Londen, Voorman Grofsmid, 1970, Durban
Van Heerden R B J, 40, Esperancestraat 40 Oosterse Parow, Majoor (S A S Polisie), 1971, Pretoria
Van Heerden t, 34, P/A Sothodiens S A U K Johannesburg, Hoof, 1966, Randfontein
Van Heerden W F, 32, Sanlamgebou Durban, Tandarts, 1969, Pretoria
Van Heerden W F P, 35, Sybrand v Niekerkkoshuis Vereeniging, Onderwyser, 1964
Van Heerden W J S, 38, Genl Pretorius-Gebou Pretoria, Raadpl Ingenieur, 1964, Heilbron
Van Heerden W S, 38, Langstraat 1 Mosselbaai, Stadsklerk, 1976, Springs
Van Helsdingen J M, 31, Huis Keet Lydenburg, Onderwyser, 1977, Pretoria
Van Huyssteen B J, 39, Rivierstraat 18 Laingsburg, Volkskasbestuurder, 1972, Kaapstad
Van Huyssteen C F, 32, Lismorestraat 12 Kenmare Krugersdorp, Onderwyser, 1967, Ermelo
Van Huyssteen C F, 38, Schnehagestraat 2 Winburg, Elektrisiën, 1974, Bothaville
Van Huyssteen J S, 42, Midde-Vrystaatse Suiwelkoöp Senekal Handelsbestuurder, 1965
Van Huyssteen R, 39, Derdelaan Parys, Onderwyser, 1975, Vredefort
Van Huyssteen R J, 41, Dorpsbestuur Richardsbaai, Stadstesourier, 1976 Pietersburg
Van Huyssteen S S, 27, Volkskas Pietermaritzburg, Assistent Rekenmeester 1966, Matatiele
Van Huysteen G C, 32, Vyfdestraat 10 Marlands Germiston, Admin Beampte B B K, 1977
Van Huysteen G F, 26, Rietkuil Komspruit, Boer, 1964, Lindley
Van Huysteen S, 34, Sanlam Port Elizabeth, Verteenwoordiger, 1963, Knysna
Van Jaarsveld A A, 31, Rietfontein PK Uchab, Boer, 1964, Dordrecht
Van Jaarsveld A B J, 25, Fisons Bpk Standerton, Adviseur, 1965, Ficksburg
Van Jaarsveld A S, 47, Munisipaliteit Brakpan, Klerk v d Raad, 1965, Roodepoort
Van Jaarsveld J G P, 30, Jagterslust Grootfontein, Boer, 1967, Adelaide
Van Jaarsveld J P, 43, Wesselstraat 13 Boshoff, Onderwyser, 1974, Theunissen
Van Jaarsveld R J, 40, S A S & H Sannaspos Bloemfontein, Stasiemeester, 1967, Kaalspruitstasie
Van Jaarsveld S R, 29, Panmar Huis 604 Bloemfontein, Argitek, 1966
Van Jaarsveld S R, 40, Karroo Vleisbeurs Bpk Germiston, Hoofbestuurder, 1965, Bethulie
Van Kerken E E, Voormalige Direkteur van Onderwys van O V S
Van Kradenburg L P, 29, Twaalfdestraat 221 Walvisbaai, Hoërskoolonderwyser, 1972, Stellenbosch
Van Lill H, 28, Pienaarstraat Despatch, N G Predikant, 1977, Stellenbosch
Van Lill H, 32, E Ross-Hospitaal Witsieshoek, Geneesheer, 1976, Madwaleni

Van Loggerenberg A S, 44, Tehuis J A Kruger Elandsfontein (S A S), Assistent Bestuurder, 1977, Klerksdorp
Van Loggerenberg E, 31, Elizabeth Eybersstraat 59 Randhart, Lektor (RAU), 1975, Port Elizabeth
Van Loggerenberg J F, 45, Munisipaliteit Randfontein, Stadsklerk, 1967, Welkom
Van Loggerenberg J H, Open Bondsraad van 1966 met Skriflesing & Gebed (Bloemfontein)
Van Loggerenberg J P B, 33, P/A S A Lugmag Pretoria, Kommandant, 1969, Ermelo
Van Loggerenberg P H (Lid Nr 7773), Winburg, 1963
Van Loggerenberg P J S, 43, Robinweg 38 Yellowwoodpark Durban, Geregsbode, 1975, Pretoria
Van Lutterveld J, 34, Posbus 82 Oberholzer, Melkboer, 1970
Van Metzinger S, 30, Hans Strijdomlaan 14 Robindale Randburg, Sakeman, 1977, Johannesburg
Van Niekerk A A, (Lid Nr 7753) Johannesburg, 1963
Van Niekerk A I, 36, Rugseer Kenhardt, Boer, 1975, Stellenbosch
Van Niekerk A J, (Lid Nr 4989), Grootfontein, Boer
Van Niekerk A P, 34, Possak 57 Aroab S W A, Boer, 1965, Warmfontein
Van Niekerk A P J, 39, Suid-Wes Tvlse Landboukoöp Leeudoringstad, Produktehoof, 1974, Pretoria
Van Niekerk A S, 33, Grootkop Badplaas, Boer, 1970, Carolina
Van Niekerk B, 43, Krymekaar Springbok, Boer, 1964, Gamoep
Van Niekerk C A, 32, Ratelfontein Calvinia, Boer, 1967
Van Niekerk C C P, 34, Sesdelaan 225 Capital Park/WNNR Pta, Senior Tegn Assistent, 1976, Pretoria
Van Niekerk C J, 28, Boschoek Distrik Vrede, Boer, 1965, Harrismith
Van Niekerk C J, 30, Shannonweg 6 Uitbr 1 Bonaero Park, Geneesheer, 1970, Keetmanshoop
Van Niekerk C J du P, 39, Rietfontein-Suid/N G Pastorie
Van Niekerk C J du P, 39, N G Pastorie Rietfontein-Suid Pretoria, Predikant, 1965, Hobhouse
Van Niekerk C M, 32, Maritzstraat 12 Nelspruit/S A Polisie, Kaptein, 1972, Groblersdal
Van Niekerk C M, 33, P/A Staatsprokureur Pretoria, Wetsassistent, 1967, Brakpan
Van Niekerk C W, 37, Izak Lombardkoshuis Delmas, Onderwyser, 1971, Pretoria
Van Niekerk D H, 31, Erasmus Jooste & Kie Klerksdorp, Prokureursklerk, 1964, Pretoria
Van Niekerk D H, 42, Departement v Landbou Gobabis, Senior Beampte, 1969, Windhoek
Van Niekerk D J, 42, Edwardstraat 25 Waterkloof Pretoria, Hoofsekretaris (S A Akademie), 1971, Kaapstad
Van Niekerk E A, 38, S A S Polisie Esselenpark Pretoria, Luitenant, 1968, Windhoek
Van Niekerk E A, 30, N G Pastorie Potgietersrus, Predikant, 1965, Pretoria
Van Niekerk F, 44, Crafford du Toit & Vennote Brits, Rekenmeester, 1963, Malmesbury
Van Niekerk F C, 28, Voortrekkerstraat Grabouw, Onderwyser, 1966, Piketberg
Van Niekerk F J, 38, Brandwag Versekering Johannesburg, Hoof-Inspekteur, 1967
Van Niekerk G A, 33, Modderfontein Rustendburg, Senior Assistent, 1971, Heidelberg Tvl
Van Niekerk G J, 34, Edgars Johannesburg, Werkbestuurder, 1968, Boksburg
Van Niekerk G J C, 35, S A Weermag Oshakati, Kommandant, 1975, Pretoria
Van Niekerk G L, 30, Fullardstraat 19 Kroonstad, Bestuurder/Saambounas, 1971, Bloemfontein
Van Niekerk G P, 31, Donkerkloof Jagersfontein, Boer, 1969, Fauresmith
Van Niekerk G S, 31, Dept Volkekunde Univ Stellenbosch Jan v Riebeeckstraat 10 Wellington, Student/Tegniese Beampte, 1973, Keetmanshoop
Van Niekerk H A du T, 38, N G Sendingpastorie Op-die-Berg Gydo, Sendeling, 1969, Hennenman
Van Niekerk H C, 33, Oakridgelaan 8 Hadisonpark Kimberley Dept Binnelandse Inkomste, Inkomste Inspekteur, 1974, Jacobsdal
Van Niekerk H G, 39, Departement Sielkunde Univ Stellenbosch, Lektor, 1964, Fort Beaufort
Van Niekerk H J, 42, Helpmekaar Dewetsdorp, Boer, 1964
Van Niekerk H J, 44, Legal & General Ass Mpy Durban, Senior Klerk, 1974, Johannesburg
Van Niekerk I J M, 36, S A Polisie Bellville, Luitenant, 1964, Springbok
Van Niekerk J, 30, P/A K W V Wellington, Landbou-Ekonoom, 1975, Bellville

Van Niekerk J A, 26, Hoërskool Carolina, Onderwyser, 1966, Potchefstroom
Van Niekerk J D, 39, A E G SA /Kentlaan 180 Ferndale, Ingenieur, 1970, Alberton
Van Niekerk J C H, 37, S A S & H Beaufort-Wes, Gesondheidsinspekteur, 1963, Worcester
Van Niekerk J J S, 44, N G Kerk Elandsfontein, Predikant, 1967, Fort Beaufort
Van Niekerk J M, 39, N G Pastorie Carnarvon, Predikant, 1967, Vanzylsrust
Van Niekerk J O, 35, Waaiwater Warden, Boer, 1970
Van Niekerk J S, 33, Molopo Apteek Vryburg, Apteker, 1964
Van Nieker J W, 27, Kerkstraat Douglas, Onderwyser/Boer, 1967, Paarl
Van Niekerk M J, 30, Excelsiorkoshuis Hoër Volkskool Heidelberg Tvl, Onderwyser, 1971
Van Niekerk P, 46, Krugerlaan 46 Discovery, N G Predikant, 1970, Ficksburg
Van Niekerk P A F, 46, "Eendoring" Springbok, Boer/Sakeman, 1969
Van Niekerk P A L, 35, Paul Krugerstraat Durbanville, Skoolsielkundige, 1974, Kaapstad
Van Niekerk P J, 35, Volkskas Christiana, Bestuurder, 1964, Pretoria
Van Niekerk P L, 26, D'Arcystraat Douglas/S A Polisie, Konstabel/Boer, 1970
Van Niekerk P W, 42, Landdroskantoor Hammanskraal, Landdros, 1976, Rundu S W A
Van Niekerk P W le R, 29, Bornkhorstraat 59 Groenkloof Pta, Prokureur (Tim du Toit & Kie), 1977, Brooklyn Pta
Van Niekerk S C J, 36, Rainierstraat Malmesbury, Geneesheer, 1964, Kaapstad
Van Niekerk S G, 28, Louterbronnen Gumtree, Boer, 1964, Ficksburg
Van Niekerk S G J, (Lid Nr 2296) Pretoria (Waterkloof), Administrateur van Tvl (Voorgestel)
Van Niekerk S G J, (Lid Nr 2296) Pretoria — Administrateur v Tvl — Voorgestel vir die U R in 1968
Van Niekerk S T, 25, Hoërskool Witrivier, Onderwyser, 1970, Potchefstroom
Van Niekerk S W, 34, Elandsdrift PK Mooinooi Brits, Landdros, 1973, Nelspruit
Van Niekerk W A, (Lid Nr 7678) Vanrynsdorp, Boer, 1962
Van Niekerk W A, 29, Provinsiale Administrasie Pretoria, Geneesheer, 1967
Van Niekerk W J, 32, Dept Landbou Ekonomie & Bemarking Kstd Administratiewe Beampte 1966, Langlaagte
Van Niekerk W J L, 32, Taitstraat Mariental/S A S & H, Klerk, 1975, Riversdal
Van Niekerk W M, 45, Munisipaliteit Walvisbaai, Direkteur v Bantoesake, 1967, Heilbron
Van Niekerk W P, 27, N G Kerk Dullstroom, Predikant, 1967, Pretoria
Van Nieuwenhuizen A, 43, P/A Yskor Pretoria, Ingenieur, 1974
Van Nieuwenhuizen H P J, 32, Foskor Phalaborwa, Passer, 1969, Lydenburg
Van Nikkelen Kuyper G J E, 36, Harringtonstraat 49 Brits/Evkom, Ingenieur (Elektriese), 1971, Pretoria
Van Onselen I P, Voormalige Beampte van Bantoe-Administrasie
Van Oordt A G, 38, La Rocherylaan 13 Humewood Port Elizabeth, Bestuurder (Santam), 1971, Pretoria
Van Oudtshoorn M C B v R, 35, Bremnerstraat 27 Bailiepark/PU vir CHO, Professor, 1970, Ermelo
Van Pittius D M Gey, 39, Laerskool Vaalwater, Onderhoof, 1967, Naboomspruit
Van Pletzen J H, 46, Laerskool Wildehondpan Migdol, Skoolhoof, 1975, Orkney
Van Pletzen N L, 36, Reitzpark Primêre Skool Welkom, Skoolhoof, 1976, Bloemfontein
Van Pletzen P N, 41, Laerskool Wesbank Oudtshoorn, Hoof, 1966, Port Elizabeth
Van Putten J W, 36, Rooibosteebeheerraad Clanwilliam, Vakkundige Beampte, 1968, Graafwater
Van Reenen C, 36, Departement Bantoe-Onderwys Thaba 'Nchu, Onderwyser, 1975, Pretoria
Van Reenen D G B, 38, Pretorium Trust Bpk Pretoria, Assistent Rekenmeester, 1973, Kakamas
Van Reenen G L, 30, Lucasstraat Harrismith, Prokureur, 1973
Van Renen J, 34, Laerskool Bellville, Onderhoof, 1969
Van Rensburg A J, 32, Lindense Hoërskool Johannesburg, Onderwyser, 1973
Van Rensburg A J, 53, Crestlands Balfour, Boer, 1969, Kenia
Van Rensburg B D J, 29, Fraai-Uitzicht Ficksburg, Boer, 1970
Van Rensburg B H Janse, 50, Durban Deep 31 Roodepoort, Ventilasiebeampte, 1967, Maraisburg
Van Rensburg B J J, 42, Stadsraad Pretoria, Ouditklerk, 1968
Van Rensburg B W J, 31, Gelykwater Babanango, Boer, 1963
Van Rensburg C J J, 37, Aurora Aberfeldy, Boer, 1963

Van Rensburg C J J, 33, N H Pastorie Vryheid, Predikant, 1976, Witbank
Van Rensbsurg C J J, 31, Utrechtstraat 60 Vryheid, N G K Sendeling, 1971, Utrecht
Van Rensburg C J J J, 39, Vaalharts Landboukoöp, Bestuurder, 1975, Hartswater
Van Rensburg D E J, 32, N G Pastorie Victoria-Wes, Predikant, 1966, Aurora
Van Rensburg D J, 29, Klein Sabie Sabie, Onderwyser, 1967, Potchefstroom
Van Rensburg D J J, 26, Dept Landbou Tegniese Dienste Pretoria Landbou-Ingenieur, 1974
Van Rensburg E G, 46, Groenrant Uniondale, Boer, 1975
Van Rensburg E J J, 30 Van Riebeecklaan 220 Verwoerdburg/Yskor Tegniese Ontleder/Program, 1977, Kroonstad
Van Rensburg E S J, 43, S A Polisie Paarl, Luitenant-Kolonel, 1970, George
Van Rensburg E T J, 32, Malutilaan 40 Quellerina Johannesburg, Bestuurder (Fin Afd F V B), 1971, Bellville
Van Rensburg F C J, 39, Schoemansdrif PK Reitzburg, Boer, 1965, Schoemansdrif
Van Rensburg F W v L J, 40, S A Polisie Pietermaritzburg, Adjunk Offisier, 1966, Durban
Van Rensburg G F, 35, Hoërlandbouskool Jacobsdal, Onderwyser, 1974, Pretoria
Van Rensburg G F J, 35, Hoërskool Petrusburg, Onderwyser, 1967, Brandfort
Van Rensburg G F J, 37, Amkor Vereeniging, Veearts, 1965, Pretoria
Van Rensburg G F J, 35, N G Pastorie Swellendam, Predikant, 1969, Stellenbosch
Van Rensburg G J J, 33, Plesier Biesiesvlei, Boer, 1975 ,
Van Rensburg G P, 40, Winnepegstraat 33 Raceview Alberton, Adj-Direkteur (Nie-Blanke Sake), 1971, Springs
Van Rensburg H C J, 33, Laerskool Winkelhaak Evander, Onderwyser, 1974, Witbank
Van Rensburg H D J, 35, Hoërskool Nelspruit, Onderwyser, 1975, Randfontein
Van Rensburg H G, 25, H G Hollaagte Mosselbaai, Boer, 1974
Van Rensburg H I J J, 34, Fullardstraat 12 Kroonstad, Onderwyser, 1969
Van Rensburg H J M J, 36, Penrith Babanango, Boer, 1963
Van Rensburg H M J, 35, Alwynfleur Riversdal, Prokureur, 1965
Van Rensburg H M J, 40, N G Sendingpastorie Wellington, Sendeling, 1964, Kaapstad
Van Rensburg J A J, 39, Wolhuterskop Hertzogville, Boer, 1968
Van Rensburg J F J, 37, Bucklands Douglas, Onderwyser, 1967, Belmont
Van Rensburg J F J, 42, Calysteeg 1207 Queenswood Pretoria, Waternavorser (W N N R), 1976, Kimberley
Van Rensburg J F J, 39, Dealeweg 90 Dan Pienaar Bloemfontein, Landmeter, 1969, Winburg
Van Rensburg J F N J, 38, Republiek Bloemfontein, Onderwyser, 1976
Van Rensburg J G J, 39, Vlakfontein Swartfolozi Vryheid, Boer, 1974
Van Rensburg J H, 35, Skoongesig Sannieshof, Boer, 1971
Van Rensburg J H, 36, Mooivlakte Bainsvlei O V S, Boer, 1974, Bloemfontein
Van Rensburg J H J, 36, Glasgow Bloemhof, Boer, 1974
Van Rensburg J J, 30, Drieankerhof 416 Sunnyside Pretoria, Takbestuurder (Sanlam), 1977, Johannesburg
Van Rensburg J J J, 38, Langsloot Kinross, Fabrieksbestuurder, 1974, Potchefstroom
Van Rensburg J J J, 31, Volkskas Durban, Assistent-Rekenmeester, 1968, Benoni
Van Rensburg J J J, 35, Saambou-Nasionaal Port Elizabeth, Admin-Bestuurder, 1976, Kuilsrivier
Van Rensburg J L J, 32, Rooikoppies 417 Distrik Brits, Boer, 1974
Van Rensburg J L J, 26, Hoërskool Dundee, Onderwyser, 1973, Johannesburg
Van Rensburg J M P J, 33, Sasol Sasolburg, Hoof (Personeel Dept), 1973, Bellville
Van Rensburg J T J, 43, Rooikoppies 417 Distrik Brits, Boer, 1972
Van Rensburg L P J, 37, Hoërskool Vanderbijlpark, Vise-Hoof, 1974, Potgietersrus
Van Rensburg M C G J (Lid Nr 7234), Bloemfontein, 1963
Van Rensburg N A J, 38, Rooth & Wessels Vanderbijlpark, Prokureur, 1975, Zastron
Van Rensburg N F J, 35, S A Weermag Oudtshoorn, Kaptein, 1969, Pretoria
Van Rensburg N J J, 34, S A Koop-Ampt-Vereniging Paarl, Rekenmeester, 1968, Dundee
Van Rensburg N J J, 38, Duncombeweg 319 Mondeor Johannesburg, Kunslektor, 1974, Potchefstroom
Van Rensburg N M J, 41, Klopperstraat 12 Thaba 'Nchu, Landdros (Bophuthatswana Regeringsdiens), 1975, Tzaneen

Van Rensburg P J, 28, Cottesloehof 4 Heraldstraat Johannesburg, Onderwyser, 1971, Potchefstroom
Van Rensburg P J J, 37, S A Polisie Sabie, Sersant, 1965, Lydenburg
Van Rensburg R C J, 32, Malelane Sitruskoöp Malelane, Vervoerbestuurder, 1970, Reitz
Van Rensburg R J J, 42, Koöp Handelshuis Bpk Nylstroom, Bestuurder, 1964, Reivilo
Van Rensburg S A J, 38, Koolvelde-Handelshuis Witbank, Bestuurder, 1966, Middelburg
Van Rensburg S F J, 39, Van Riebeeck Mediese-Gebou 622 Pretoria Oogarts, 1967, Philippolis
Van Rensburg S H J, 32, Parkstraat Frankfort, Geneesheer, 1972, Bethal
Van Rensburg S J, 36, Christiaanstraat 18 Annlin Pretoria, Wetenskaplike (Raad op Atoomkrag), 1970, Stellenbosch
Van Rensburg S J, 34, Hoofstraat Greylingstad, Laerskool Onderwyser, 1971, Meyerton
Van Rensburg S J J, (Lid Nr 7594) Vleissentraal Pretoria, Hoofbestuurder (Voorgestel vir die U R in 1968 & Lid van die U R se Landbou-Komitee in 1968)
Van Rensburg S W J, 35, Amkor Newcastle, Skeikundige, 1964, Potchefstroom
Van Rensburg T C J, 43, Volkskas Hoofkantoor Pretoria, Bestuurder (Elektroniese Dataverwerking), 1976, Vrede
Van Rensburg T G J, 47, Human Motors Bloemfontein, Sekretaris, 1969
Van Rensburg T I J, 42, Spekboom PK Paterson, Boer, 1977
Van Rensburg V E, 41, Landdroskantoor Stanger, Landdros, 1975, Bethal
Van Rensburg W C J, 34, Whitegatestraat Glencoe, Prokureur, 1967, Pietermaritzburg
Van Rensburg W H J, 41, Sestiendelaan 2 Mosselbaai, Tandarts, 1970, Pretoria
Van Rensburg W J, 32, N G Gemeente Rietfontein-Suid Pretoria, Predikant, 1977, Brakpan
Van Rensburg W J J, 44, Onderwyskollege Potchefstroom, Departementshoof, 1967, Pretoria
Van Rensburg W J J, 38, S A S & H Johannesburg, Hoofklerk, 1969, Germiston
Van Rensburg W L J, 36, Landbou Fakulteit U O V S, Bloemfontein, Senior Lektor, 1973, Stellenbosch
Van Rensbsurg W L D M J, 32, Albert Koöp Jamestown, Bestuurder, 1967, Venterstad
Van Rensburg W M J, 43, Ottaweg 24 Kampsbaai/Nasionale Koerante, Rekenmeester, 1971, Kaapstad
Van Rheede v Oudtshoorn W P, 41, Beaufortstraat 66 Grahamstad, Griffier, 1967, Windhoek
Van Rooy A, 30, "Belasting" Letsitele, Boer, 1965, Rustenburg
Van Rooy D J, Emeritus Professor in Wiskunde P U vir CHO, Potchefstroom
Van Rooy G M, 35, Dept Verdediging Pretoria, Kaptein, 1964, Potchefstroom
Van Rooy H C, P U vir CHO Potchefstroom, Professor, (Biblioteekkunde), 1963
Van Rooy H F de W, 45, Boland Krugersdorp, Boer, 1964, Aliwal Noord
Van Rooy L, 34, Sitrusbeurs Plaston, Koordineerder, 1967, Queenstown
Van Rooyen A A C, 43, Delhi PK Letsitele, Boer, Reitz
Van Rooyen A C, 37, P/A S A Polisiekollege Pretoria, Luitenant, 1968, Knysna
Van Rooyen A J, Opvoedkundige
Van Rooyen A J L, (Lid Nr 4114), Johannesburg Noord Voorgestel vir die U R in 1968, Ginekoloog
Van Rooyen B D, 39, Merino Slagtery Port Elizabeth, Bestuurder, 1977
Van Rooyen C P F, 44, Daniel Malanrylaan 17 Floridapark, Verkoopsbestuurder, 1975, Pietermaritzburg
Van Rooyen D R D, 33, Laerskool PK Teebus (Steynsburg), Skoolhoof, 1969, Cradock
Van Rooyen D W, 35, Militêre Basis Doornkop Johannesburg, Offisier, 1977, Vereeniging
Van Rooyen E A, 39, Bechuanastraat 10 Kuruman, Afdelingsraadsekretaris, 1970, Upington
Van Rooyen E J, 33, Hoërskool Sybrand v Niekerk Sabie, Onderhoof, 1969, Heidelberg Tvl
Van Rooyen E R, (Lid Nr 7676), Langkloof, Assistent Landdros
Van Rooyen F, 34, Meyer Nel & Kie Welkom, Ouditeur, 1969, Bloemfontein
Van Rooyen G, 38, Slabbert Verster & Malherbe Johannesburg, Bestuurder, 1969
Van Rooyen G F M, 33, Lombard & v Rooyen Excelsior, Prokureur, 1965, Senekal
Van Royen G I, 45, Afdeling Hospitaaldienste Pretoria, Inspekteur, 1968, Mosselbaai
Van Rooyen G P, (Lid Nr 265), Krugersdorp Afgetrede Inspekteur v Onderwys
Van Rooyen G R, 49, N G Pastorie Ladysmith, Predikant, 1963, Vryheid
Van Rooyen H C, 37, N G Pastorie Jacobs Natal, Predikant, 1966, Vierfontein

Van Rooyen I, 30, Hoërskool Edenvale, Onderwyser, 1967, Zeerust
Van Rooyen I F O, 32, Derdelaan 88 Edenvale, Onderwyser, 1970, Wolmaransstad
Van Rooyen I M, Vryheid-Oos — Hy sê Buitelandse Besoekers moet by Afrikaners Tuisgaan
(Bondsraad 1965)
Van Rooyen J J, Voormalige Redakteur van die Transvaler
Van Rooyen J J, 40, Dekselfontein Alexandria, Boer, 1967
Van Rooyen J K, 30, Walker-Woodstraat Barberton, Hoërskool Onderwyser, 1971, Potchefstroom
Van Rooyen J W J, 45, Bluffweg 839 Grosvenor Durban, Inspekteur v Skole, 1967, Dundee
Van Rooyen K F, 32, Landsberghoek Potgietersrus, Oogkundige/Boer/Apteker, 1974, Hendrina
Van Rooyen L, 32, Onrecht PK Swartfolozi, Boer/Sakeman, 1973
Van Rooyen L, 47, Boshoek Vryheid, Boer, 1964, Hlobane
Van Rooyen M, 32, Universiteit Pretoria, Dosent (Ing), 1964, Senekal
Van Rooyen M M, 47, Gedenk-Kinderhuis Ladybrand, Direkteur, 1967, Steynsburg
Van Rooyen M S, 33, N G Sendingpastorie Hendrina, Predikant, 1968, Manzini
Van Rooyen P C, 42, Staatsdienskommissie Pretoria, Admin Beheerbeampte, 1970
Van Rooyen P G, 48, Provinsiale Koshuis Laerskool Witrivier, Onderwyser, 1965, Ermelo
Van Rooyen P H, 45, Nola Nywerhede Randfontein, Reklamebeampte, 1967, Johannesburg
Van Rooyen P T, 40, S A S & H Potchefstroom, Masjinis, 1965
Van Rooyen P W, Lid van die U R se Landbou-Komitee in 1973
Van Rooyen R H, 40, Hoërskool Caledon, Skoolhoof, 1974, Wittedrif
Van Rooyen R P, 35, Hoërskool Brandwag Benoni, Onderwyser, 1974, Meyerton
Van Rooyen R T J, 39, Yskor Pretoria, Personeelbeampte, 1966, Makwassie
Van Rooyen S C, 34, Sasolnuus Sasolburg, Redakteur, 1969, Oudtshoorn
Van Rooyen W F, 34, Sanguineweg Montroux Johannesburg, Ortopediese Chirurg, 1969, Pretoria
Van Rouendal L, 35, Wouterweg 7 Retiefpark Lichtenburg, Argitek, 1977, Pretoria
Van Ryneveld W, 33, Finsburylaan 12 Aucklandpark, Senior Lektor (RAU), 1971, Pretoria
Van Ryssen J C J, 33, Barnardstraat 9 Potchefstroom, Senior Lektor (PU vir CHO), 1977, Johannesburg
Van Rijkswijk A A, 33, Harmsfontein Burgersdorp, Boer, 1976
Van Schalkwyk A P J, 46, S W A Administrasie Windhoek, Mynkommissaris, 1968, Pietersburg
Van Schalkwyk D J, 34, Laerskool Grunau, Skoolhoof, 1971, Otavi
Van Schalkwyk F A, 30, Natal Apteek Durban, Apteker, 1967, Glencoe
Van Schalkwyk F G, 36, Shippardstraat 40 Meyerton/Hoërskool, Vise-Hoof, 1972, Heidelberg, Tvl
Van Schalkwyk G D, 33, Hoërskool Tulbach, Onderwyser, 1976, Paarl
Van Schalkwyk G J, 31, Goederverwachting Fraserburg, Boer, 1974
Van Schalkwyk G S, 46, Dept van Binnelandse Sake Pretoria, Verkiesingsbeampte, 1968
Van Schalkwyk H C H, 27, Senior Meisies Hostel Swakopmund, Onderwyser, 1970, Windhoek
Van Schalkwyk H P, 45, Stadsraad van Tzaneen, Hoofrekenmeester, 1975
Van Schalkwyk J J, 35, Pospersoneel George, Superintendent (Alg), 1977, Worcester
Van Schalkwyk J O T, 39, Moultonlaan 44 Waverley Pretoria, Onderhoof (Hoërskool), 1970
Van Schalkwyk J P, 46, Môrester Trompsburg, Boer, 1967
Van Schalkwyk O J, 41, Holsdam Barkly-Wes, Boer, 1970, Kimberley
Van Schalkwyk P, 32, H/V Waaiboom & Libertasstraat Freewaypark Boksburg, Onderwyser, 1974
Van Schalkwyk P, 29, Geref Pastorie Reddersburg, Predikant, 1977, Potchefstroom
Van Schalkwyk P G, 46, Bantoe-Administrasieraad Nelspruit, Hoofdirekteur, 1974, Carletonville
Van Schalkwyk P J, 48, Leerlingvlieënierskool Dunnottar, Hoof, 1969, Lyttelton
Van Schalkwyk P L, 29, Hoërskool Thornton, Onderwysersielkundige, 1973
Van Schalkwyk T J, 31, S A Weermag Heidelberg Tvl, Majoor, 1974, Pretoria
Van Schalkwyk W, 35, Du Toitstraat 43 Georgina Roodepoort, Onderwyser, 1977

van Schalkwyk W F T, 33, Outeniquaweg 19 Noordheuwel Krugersdorp, Ouditeur, 1977, Pretoria
Van Schalkwyk W V L, 36, S A Polisie Benoni, Luitenant, 1965, Carnarvon
Van Schoor A M, 55, Die Vaderland Johannesburg, Redakteur, 1965
Van Schoor M, 32, M J van Schoor & Seun Philadelphia, Nyweraar, 1967
Van Solms H J W, 36, Akademiestraat 8 Komga, Onderwyser, 1971, Graaff-Reinet
Van Staden B F, 29, Loubserstraat Kenhardt/Boere Saamwerk, Verteenwoordiger, 1971, Upington
Van Staden B J, 41, N H Pastorie Klerksdorp-Oos, Predikant, 1969, Pretoria
Van Staden D A, 39, Vrydelaan 8 Cashan (Rustenburg), Geneesheer, 1975, Boksburg
Van Staden F J, 31, Skoolterrein Marikana, Waarn Skoolhoof, 1975, Pretoria
Van Staden J A, 38, Stadsraad Nigel, Asst Stadstesoureir, 1966, Boksburg
Van Staden J F, 40, Hoë Boime Brakkloof Swartruggens, Boer, 1977, Rustenburg
Van Staden J F, 38, Sanlam Meyerton, Takbestuurder, 1974, Vanderbijlpark
Van Staden J M C, 35, Sewendelaan 30A Mellville Johannesburg, Sen Asst (Hoërskool D F Malan), 1971
Van Staden M J, 36, Piet Uysstraat 101 Muckleneuk Pretoria, Dept-Hoof Onderwyskollege, 1977, Brits
Van Staden M J, 48, S A Polisie Riviersonderend, Sersant, 1965, Gansbaai
Van Staden P R, 35, Palmietvlei PK Verkeerdevlei Boer, 1969, Oudtshoorn
Van Staden S J, 32, Hentystraat 6 Vanderbijlpark, Onderwyser, 1972, Pretoria
Van Straaten J A C, 41, Nassaustraat Ugie, Sakeman, 1968, MaClear
Van Straaten N J, 40, Esbikya Matatiele, Boer, 1966
Van Straten P F, 29, Kendal Maclear, Boer, 1975
Van Tiddens A H, 37, Jordaanspoort Pofadder, Boer, 1968
Van Tiddens H, 40, Middellandse Hoër Handelskool Cradock, Skoolhoof, 1974, George
Van Tonder A, Ondersekretaris van die A B
Van Tonder A, 24, Grahamweg 15 Malvern-Oos Johannesburg, Organiseerder, A S B, 1971
Van Tonder A F, 32, Golflaan 122 Clubview-Wes Pretoria, Vennoot (Meintjies Vermooten & Vennote), 1976, Klerksdorp
Van Tonder A J, 38, Universiteit van Stellenbosch, Assistent Registrateur, 1974
Van Tonder A J J (Lid Nr 10247), Somersetstraat 104 Kensington Johannesburg, Predikant
Van Tonder A J J, 34, N G Pastorie Newcastle, Predikant, 1967, Empangeni
Van Tonder D A F, 27, Weltevrede-Wes Dewetsdorp, Boer, 1965
Van Tonder D J, 29, Hoërskool Frikkie Meyer Thabazimbi, Onderwyser, 1965, Nylstroom
Van Tonder D R, 38, PK Beauty (Mogol), Boer, 1968, Piet Plessis
Van Tonder F J, 46, Sanlam Carnarvon, Verteenwoordiger, 1975, Prieska
Van Tonder G, 37, Harmonie Dewetsdorp, Boer, 1968
Van Tonder G, 34, Middelplaas Sannaspos (Bloemfontein), Boer, 1973
Van Tonder G, 38, Kromdraai PK Sannaspos, Boer, 1967
Van Tonder G F, 31, De La Reystraat 66 Koster, Onderwyser, 1974, Barberton
Van Tonder G J, 30, Magnoliastraat 13 Dalpark Benoni, Onderwyser, 1973, Brakpan
Van Tonder H P, 34, Deanelaan 18 Bloemfontein, Patoloog, 1967, Pretoria
Van Tonder J, 30, P/A Stadsraad Ermelo, Klerk van die Raad, 1964, Welkom
Van Tonder J A, 30, Jan Van Riebeeckweg Oudtshoorn, Onderwyser, 1973, Pretoria
Van Tonder J A, 31, Pilansbergstraat 6 Noordheuwel Krugersdorp, Adjunk-Hoof (Laerskool), 1976, Westonaria
Van Tonder J A (Lid Nr 5429), Grahamweg 15 Malvern Oos Germiston, L V
Van Tonder J C, 31, Laerskool Piet Retief, Onderwyser, 1966, Pretoria
Van Tonder J H, 46, Proklamasieheuwel Pretoria, Bou-Aannemer, 1965, Pretoria
Van Tonder J J (Lid Nr 3118), Pretoriusstraat 946 Arcadia Pretoria, Stadsingeneur
Van Tonder J M, 42, P/A Midde OVS B A R Welkom, Asst Streekdirekteur, 1974, Hennenman
Van Tonder L G, Lid van die U R se Landbou-Komitee in 1973
Van Tonder P C, 40, Rotsvlei Marandellas, Boer, 1967, Chipinga
Van Tonder P J H, 42, Blinkwater Potgietersrus, Boer, 1967, Vrede
Van Velden D, 33, Evkom Kimberley, Elektrotegn Ingenieur, 1975, Colesberg
Van Velden P G, 35, J D Crawford & Seun Beaufort-Wes, Prokureur, 1972, Stellenbosch
Van Vollenhoven W, 41, Raad vir Buitestedelikegebied Pretoria, Rekenmeester, 1973, Kroonstad

Van Vrede J J H, 41, Die Noord-Transvaler Pietersburg, Redakteur, 1975, Pretoria
Van Vuren H J, 39, Uitzicht 586 Pretoria/Hoofstad, Verslaggewer, 1973
Van Vuren J N, 37, S A Polisie Villiers, Sersant, 1967, Frankfort
Van Vuuren B G J J, 41, Saambou-Nasionaal Alberton, Bestuurder, 1974, Kempton Park
Van Vuuren C J, 29, Geref Pastorie Marnitz, Predikant, 1966, Postmasburg
Van Vuuren C J J, 31, Laerskoolkoshuis Morgenzon, Onderwyser, 1977, Florida
Van Vuuren C M, Open 1969 Bondsraad met Skriflesing & Gebed
Van Vuuren D, 32, Caledonstraat 17 Marlands Germiston, Dosent (Goudstad Onderwyskollege), 1973, Pretoria
Van Vuuren D M J, 40, P/A Kinross Mines Ltd (Evander), Klerk, 1967, Brakpan
Van Vuuren D P D J, 31, Uitkoms Rietbron, Boer, 1966
Van Vuuren F J J, 43, Hospitaalstraat 304 Nababeep, Mediese Praktisyn, 1971, Indwe
Van Vuuren G C J, 37, P/A Krygkor Pretoria, Rekenmeester, 1973, Alberton
Van Vuuren H G, 29, S A Polisie Cradock, Adjunk-Offisier, 1963, Kirkwood
Van Vuuren H P, 35, P/A Fedmis Landboukundige Afd Paarl, Landboukundige, 1975, George
Van Vuuren H S J, 32, Hoërskool Goudveld Welkom, Onderwyser, 1967, Westonaria
Van Vuuren I L J, 42, Wallisstraat 4 Potchefstroom, Dosent P O K, 1967, Zeerust
Van Vuuren J, 39, Taaibos Manskoshuis Universiteit Pretoria, Voorligtingsbeampte, 1963, Heidelberg
Van Vuuren J A J, 32, Pagel Beckerstraat 9 Flamwood, Apteker (KDM Apteker Klerksdorp), 1974, Bloemfontein
Van Vuuren J F, 36, Vrystaat Koöp Reitz, Rekenmeester, 1969
Van Vuuren J G J, 35, Lyttelton Ingenieurswerke, Bestuurder, 1973, Pretoria
Van Vuuren J H, 37, Vaalkraal Dewetsdorp, Boer, 1965, Bloemfontein
Van Vuuren J J J v R, 47, Poskantoor Ladybrand, Posmeester, 1969, Koppies
Van Vuuren J J M J (Lid Nr 7754), Heilbron, 1963
Van Vuuren J L J, 34, Volkskas Edenburg, Bestuurder, 1966, Bloemfontein
Van Vuuren J N, 42, N G Kerk Lyttelton-Noord, Predikant, 1974, Vanderbijlpark
Van Vuuren J N J, 43, Shippardstraat 13 Meyerton, Prokureur, 1965, Oberholzer
Van Vuuren J P, 35, -Forestraat 15 New Redruth Alberton, Geneesheer, 1966, Pretoria
Van Vuuren J P J, 41, Van Jaarsveldstraat 7 Parkdene Boksburg, Prokureur, 1971, Malmesbury
Van Vuuren J S J, 35, Makoeispan Biesiesvlei, Onderwyser/Boer, 1976
Van Vuuren L J, 38, Vredespruit PK Rietbron, Boer, 1968, Beaufort-Wes
Van Vuuren L M J, 42, Bosplaas PK Tuinplaas, Boer, 1974
Van Vuuren L R J, 39, Hoër Tegniese Skool Wolmaransstad, Onderwyser, 1966, Middelburg Tvl
Van Vuuren M, Florida (Praat oor Kultuursake by 1965 se Bondsraad)
Van Vuuren M V, 36, Matlala Sendinghospitaal PK Tsimanyane Mediese Superintendent, 1976, Kroonstad
Van Vuuren N A J, 38, Volkskas Bloemfontein, Rekenmeester, 1965, Colesberg
Van Vuuren P A J, 40, Voëlfontein Pk Petrusville, Boer, 1965
Van Vuuren P J, 31, Optima Kunsmis Bpk Durbanville, Landboukundige, 1970, Bellville
Van Vuuren P J J, 31, Agricura Pretoria, Navorsingsbeampte, 1964, Rustenburg
Van Vuuren P L, 46, Volkskas Parys, Rekenmeester, 1967, Bloemfontein
Van Vuuren P L J, 44, Poskantoor Groblersdal, Superintendent, 1975, Rustenburg
Van Vuuren P T J, 42, "Fairfax" Bergville, Boer, 1970, Heidelberg Tvl
Van Vuuren P Z J, Voormalige L V vir Langlaagte
Van Vuuren R J J, 43, N G Pastorie Sterkstroom, Predikant (J P Seun), 1966, Rietbron
Van Vuuren R J J (Ds), (Lid Nr 4413), Trompsburg (Voorgestel vir die U R in 1968 & Lid van die U R se Indiërkomitee in 1973)
Van Vuuren R J J, 43, S A Weermag Pretoria, Kommandant, 1967, Lyttelton
Van Vuuren R P J, 43, 26steLaan 905 Rietfontein Pretoria, Luitenant-Kolonel (S A Polisie), 1972, Germiston
Van Vuuren R W J, 46, Jadelaan 31, Lyttelton Manor, Kolonel (S A Weermag), 1976, Lenz
Van Vuuren S I J, 49, N G Pastorie Duiwelskloof, Predikant, 1970, Potgietersurs
Van Vuuren S M, 33, N G Pastorie Suidrand Johannesburg, Predikant, 1965, Durban
Van Vuuren T J J J, 32, S A S & H Johannesburg, Klerk, 1964, Koster
Van Wijck S J, 43, P/A Rembrandt Paarl, Fabrieksbestuurder, 1965, Krugersdorp

Van Wyk A, 48, S A Polisie Pretoria, Luitenant-Kolonel, 1969, Heidelberg
Van Wyk A, 46, Munisipaliteit Kempton Park, Lisensie/Verkeersbeampte, 1968, Nelspruit
Van Wyk A A, 40, Grootvlei, Cornelia, Boer, 1972
Van Wyk A A H, 47, P/A Staatsdrukker Pretoria, Staatsdrukker, 1968
Van Wyk A C, (Lid Nr 3108) Bultfontein, (Lid van die U R se Kleurlinggroep in 1973 & Voorgestel vir die U R in 1968, Administrateur v O V S
Van wyk A E, 43, Wolwepooret PK Kamieskroon, Boer, 1970
Van Wyk A J, 38, Junior Hoërskool Rosendal, Skoolhoof, 1967, Bloemfontein
Van Wyk A J, 29, Weltevrede Ventersburg, Boer, 1968
Van Wyk A J, 32, Afrika Instituut Pretoria, Senior Navorser, 1965, Bloemfontein
Van Wyk A J, 31, Volkskas Sutherland, Rekenmeester, 1967, George
Van Wyk A J, 38, Hoewe Kameeldrif Distrik Pretoria, Ingenieur (W N N R), 1976, Alldays
Van Wyk A J F, 31, P/A USKO Vereeniging, Assistent Ingenieur, 1965
Van Wyk A J J, 29, Tweedelaan Wes Clocolan, Geneesheer, 1966, Hertzogville
Van Wyk A L, 35, Hoërskool Transkei Umtata, Onderhoof, 1974, Herbertsdale
Van Wyk A M, 28, St Annessingel 27 Pinetown Natal, N G Predikant, 1971, Pretoria
Van Wyk A P, 29, Davies Theunissen & Vennote Springs, Prokureur, 1973
Van Wyk A W, 33, Randse Afrikaanse Universiteit Johannesburg, Senior Lektor, 1973, Port Elizabeth
Van Wyk B, 45, Ellenvilla Skoolpad Brackenfell, Sakeman, 1974, Parow
Van Wyk B A, 35, Vleissentraal Potgietersrus, Vakkundige Beampte, 1970, Upington
Van Wyk B P, 34, S A Polisiekollege Polkol Pretoria, Sersant, 1974
Van Wyk B R, 46, Doornkraal PK Riversdal, Stasievoorman, 1967
Van Wyk C J, 36, Universiteit Stellenbosch, Professor, 1968
Van Wyk C J H, 46, Skoolraad Johannesburg, Klerk, 1969, Rustenburg
Van Wyk C M (Dr), Lid van die U R se Landboukomitee in 1973
Van Wyk C M, 43, Perseel H50 Marble Hall, Boer, 1974, Middelburg Tvl
Van Wyk D A, 38, Tiendeweg Tsumeb, Apteker, 1972, Keimoes
Van Wyk D F H, 35, Soutpan PK Papkuil, Boer, 1964
Van Wyk D J, 36, Barnardstraat 39, Ontdekkerspark, Ouditeur (B A O), 1976, Sasolburg
Van Wyk D J, 33, P U vir CHO Potchefstroom, Senior Lektor, 1976, Bloemfontein
Van Wyk D J C, 27, N H Gemeente Springs, Predikant, 1968, Pretoria
Van Wyk D J L, 28, Graspan PK Prieska, Boer, 1970
Van Wyk F C (Lid Nr 4201), Bradfordstraat 8 Bedfordview Bestuurder (Volkskas)
Van Wyk G, 35, Riggstraat 4 Jansenpark Boksburg, Landdros, 1975, Wolmaransstad
Van Wyk G C, 34, S A S & H Kimberley, Senior Beroepskundige, 1974, Pretoria
Van Wyk G E, 34, Floridaheuwels, Blomkweker, 1967, Johannesburg
Van Wyk G F, 35, Mooiplaas Ermelo, Boer, 1967, Carolina
Van Wyk G J, 37, S A Polisie Springbok, Speurdersersant, 1964, Kamieskroon
Van Wyk G M, 43, Langpan Aranos, Boer, 1969
Van Wyk H A, 39, N G Sendingpastorie Port Nolloth, Sendeling, 1965, Orumana
Van Wyk H D, 33, Zooihuis Biesiesvlei, Boer, 1976, Sannieshof
Van Wyk H v d M, 33, Von Eckenbrecherstraat Windhoek, Rekenmeester, 1971
Van Wyk J, 34, Van Heerdenstraat Hofmeyr/Hoërskool, Skoolhoof, 1970, Fort Beaufort
Van Wyk J, 34, Landbou Tegniese Dienste Pretoria, Hoof Pensioene, 1976, Middelburg Kaap
Van Wyk J, 44, P/A Staatsdienskommissie Pretoria, Ondersekretaris, 1977
Van Wyk J, 41, Munisipaliteit Noupoort, Werke-Voorman, 1966
Van wyk J A, 30, Perseel 143 Grootdrink, Boer, 1965
Van Wyk J A du P, 35, S A Polisie Johannesburg, Sersant, 1965, Pilansberg
Van Wyk J C D, 38, Volkskas Wolseley, Bestuurder, 1965, Malmesbury
Van Wyk J D, 33, Weslaan 267 Presidentsrif, Professor, 1973, Pretoria
Van Wyk J D, 29, Universiteit Stellenbosch, Lektor, 1973
Van Wyk J D, 37, N G Pastorie Volksrust-Suid, Predikant, 1965, Durban
Van Wyk J F, 26, N G Pastorie Cradock, Predikant, 1970, Stellenbosch
Van Wyk J H, 30, Onzerus Brandfort, Boer, 1969
Van Wyk J H, 29, Vyfdestraat 4 Linden Johannesburg, Marknavorser (Sappi), 1973
Van Wyk J J C, 40, Klein Coné Postmasburg, Boer, 1967
Van Wyk J J P, 33, PU vir CHO Potchefstroom, Senior Lektor, 1968
Van Wyk J K, 43, Kamieskroon, Sakeman, 1964

Van Wyk J M, 42, P/A Warmbad Versoolwerke, Direkteur, 1965, Pretoria
Van Wyk J P R, 40, P/A S A Wolkommissie Port Elizabeth, Sekretaris, 1965, Pretoria
Van Wyk J S, 29, Gordonstraat Koffiefontein, Landdros, 1974, Bethlehem
Van Wyk J W F, 28, Militêre Basis Grahamstad, Kaptein, 1975, Saldanha
Van Wyk K P, 47, Nie-Blanke Sake Mun. Pretoria, Asst Bestuurder, 1966
Van Wyk L A, 32, PU vir CHO Potchefstroom, Senior Lektor, 1975, Pretoria
Van Wyk L A S, 29, Geref Pastorie Naboomspruit, Predikant, 1965, Rustenburg
Van Wyk L J, 39, Hoërskool Calvinia, Onderwyser, 1964
Van Wyk L S, 38, Riverpark 4 Vereeniging, Onderwyser, 1974, Heidelberg Tvl
Van Wyk M C, 31, Hoërskool Parow, Onderwyser, 1963, Ladismith Kaap
Van Wyk M J, 32, Bergstraat 1 Harrismith, Geneesheer, 1969, Warden
Van Wyk M J, 28, Hoërskool Erasmus Bronkhorstspruit, Onderwyser, 1965, Leeudoringstad
Van Wyk M J de B, 44, Munisipaliteit Bloemfontein, Klerk, 1966
Van Wyk O J O, 39, Sanlam Witbank, Wyksbestuurder, 1964, Lydenburg
Van Wyk P A, Bondsrade Het op sy Plaas Vergader
Van Wyk P A C, 37, P/A S A Spoorweë Ermelo, Klerk, 1968, De Aar
Van Wyk P G, 44, P/A Libanon Goudmyn, Elektrisien, 1973, Krugersdorp
Van Wyk P J R, 36, P/A Volkskas Kirkwood, Bestuurder, 1965, Bloemfontein
Van Wyk P P, 46, Remhoogte Protem (Bredasdorp), Boer, 1967, Ladismith Kaap
Van Wyk R C J, 25, Von Brandisstraat 8A Piet Retief, Apteker, 1976, Potchefstroom
Van Wyk R R, 39, N G Pastorie Nuwedorp, Predikant, 1964, Witfield
Van Wyk S, 30, Koedoe Koshuis Thabazimbi, Onderwyser, 1973, Heidelberg Tvl
Van Wyk S J P, 46, Eerstestraat 9 Melville Johannesburg, Kaptein (Veiligheidspolisie), 1971, Potchefstroom
Van Wyk S P, Pretoria (Praat oor Kleurlinge by 1971 se Bondsraad)
Van Wyk S P, 38, Departement Landbou-Ekonomie & Bemarking Pretoria, Onderhoof, 1966, Vereeniging
Van Wyk T P, 35, P/A Malan & Klopper Masadagebou Pta, Bourekenaar, 1975
Van Wyk W, Wolmaransstad (Lid van Nasionale Party Komitee 1966)
Van Wyk W C, 31, Universiteit Pretoria, Senior Dosent, 1969, Alberton
Van Wyk W J P, 37, Volkskas De Aar, Bestuurder, 1965, Pretoria
Van Wyk W L, 38, Departement Mynwese Pietermaritzburg, Geoloog, 1963, Vryheid
Van Wyk W P, 37, P/A Sentramark Klerksdorp, Streekverkoopsbestuurder, 1973, Sasolburg
Van Wyk W P J, 34, P/A N G Kerk Florida, Predikant, 1977, Brakpan
Van Wyk W P J, 42, S A Polisie Halfweghuis Tvl, Majoor, 1971, Johannesburg
Van Wyk W P V, 35, Munisipaliteit Virginia, Asst-Stadstesourier, 1967, Welkom
Van Wyk De Vries W, 29, S A Ambassade Trafalgar Plein Londen, Lid van Buro vir Staatsveiligheid, 1974, Port Elizabeth
Van Zijl D J, 35, Streakstraat 6 Nelspruit, Bode van die Hof, 1971, Pretoria
Van Zijl E, 35, S W A Administrasie Windhoek, Advokaat & L U K, 1967
Van Zijl N R J, 41, N G Pastorie Vryburg, Predikant, 1966, Delportshoop
Van Zyl A H, 39, N G Pastorie Kameeldrif (Pretoria), Predikant, 1964
Van Zyl A J, 37, Krygstuigproduksieraad Pretoria, Senior Administratiewe Beampte, 1968
Van Zyl A J, 37, Uniestaalkorporasie Vereeniging, Ingenieur, 1969
Van Zyl A J, 27, Dorpsbestuur Klawer, Sekretaris, 1967, Pretoria
Van Zyl B P, 38, Nova Hopetown, Boer/Scriba, 1973, Sand-Vet Skema
Van Zyl C, 41, Hoërskool Sentraal Beaufort-Wes, Onderhoof, 1966, Colesberg
Van Zyl C B, 36, "Goabeb" Usakos, Boer, 1968, Gobabis
Van Zyl C G (Sakkie), 42, P/A U O V S Bloemfontein, Dosent, 1975
Van Zyl C H, 28, S A Weermag Oshakati, Majoor, 1976, Saldanha
Van Zyl C J J, 34, Hoërskool Alberton, Onderhoof, 1964, Pietersburg
Van Zyl C J J, Natalspruit (Praat oor Afrikaanse Volksfeeste wat afgestomp het — Bondsraad 1966
Van Zyl D C B, 30, Tiendestraat 28 Greymont Johannesburg, Sakeman, 1968, Pretoria
Van Zyl D J, Nasionale Pers, 1973
Van Zyl D N, 31, N G Kerk Bellville-Wes, Predikant, 1975, Beaufort-Wes
Van Zyl D P, 36, Coronation Vryheid, Skoolhoof, 1964, Ladysmith
Van Zyl D R, 36, Sandfontein Trompsburg, Boer, 1967, Reddersburg
Van Zyl E J, 34, Augsburg Clanwilliam, Onderwyser, 1976, George

Van Zyl F J, (Pretoria), Hy spreek kommer uit oor Round Taule & Rotariërs by Bondsraad van 1965
Van Zyl F J (Prof), Hervormde Kerk
Van Zyl F J, 34, Kenridgelaan 21 Durbanville, Sekretaris F V B, 1970
Van Zyl F L, 41, S W A Drukkery Bpk Windhoek, Joernalis, 1968, Kaapstad
Van Zyl F W, 43, Breipaal Perseel 24A2 Ganspan, Boer, 1970,Warrenton
Van Zyl G A E, 45, Oubenheim Vredendal, Boer, 1963, Vanrhynsdorp
Van Zyl G A J, 45, Vyfdestraat 25 Naboomspruit, N G Sendeling, 1970, Valvinia
Van Zyl G J, 34, Villa Roux Sunnyside Pretoria, Onderwyser, 1965, Ceres
Van Zyl G J, Lid van die U R se Ekonomiese Komitee in 1973
Van Zyl G P, 44 Volkskas Middelburg Tvl, Rekenmeester, 1976, Senekal
Van Zyl H C, 47, Padvervoerraad Oos-Londen, Sekretaris, 1964, Pretoria
Van Zyl H G, 35, Sarel Celliersstraat Jacobsdal Onderwyser (Hoërskool), 1970, Bloemfontein
Van Zyl H J (Dr), Voormalige Sekretaris van Bantoe-Onderwys
Van Zyl H J, 32, W G A Willowmore, Verteenwoordiger, 1967, Steytlerville
Van Zyl H J, 31, Sekondêre Skool Zastron, Onderwyser, 1974, Senekal
Van Zyl H J G, 42, Kapteinsdrif Bonnievale, Boer, 1971
Van Zyl H J P, 33, S A Polisie Johannesburg, Luitenant, 1963, Waterberg
Van Zyl H L, 44, Veiligheidspolisie Parow, Sersant, 1970, Kaapstad
Van Zyl H M, 36, Hoërskool Schweizer-Reneke, Onderwyser, 1965, Wolmaransstad
Van Zyl H M A, 39, Vondeling van Rhynsdorp, Boer, 1974, Vredendal
Van Zyl H M A, 43, Karroovlakte PK Trimoa oor Klawer, Boer, 1975
Van Zyl I D, 32, Dwarsfontein Derby, Boer, 1977
Van Zyl I D, 44, Vosstraat 13 Trompsburg, Bestuurder, 1973, Bloemfontein
Van Zyl J A, 31, Elsstraat Verkeerdevlei, Adj-Off S A Polisie, 1973, Bultfontein
Van Zyl J A, 25, U O V S Bloemfontein, Dosent, 1967, Senekal
Van Zyl J A, 41, Laerskool Swartruggens, Onderhoof, 1966, Marico
Van Zyl J C, 43, Wilhelm PK Roadside, Boer, 1968, Vrede
Van Zyl J C, 41, P/A Yskor Pretoria, Hoof Bemarkingsstrategie, 1975, Roodepoort
Van Zyl J C, 42, P/A Hoërskool J J du Prees Parow, Onderwyser, 1963, Port Elizabeth
Van Zyl J D, 37, P/A Kemponville Apteek Bellville, Apteker, 1965, Paarl
Van Zyl J D A, 38, Landdroskantoor Amersfoort, Landdros, 1968, Brits
Van Zyl J F, 49, P/A Spoorwegdienskommissie Pretoria, Asst Supt, 1974, Johannesburg
Van Zyl J G, 34, Louisstraat Parkdene Boksburg, Onderwyser, 1966, Langlaagte
Van Zyl J H, 38, Kockstraat 176 Rustenburg, Geneesheer, 1964, Vosburg Kaap
Van Zyl J J M, 28, Buitehof Robertson, Boer, 1974, Springbok
Van Zyl J L, 28, Hillstraat Ficksburg/Ficksburg Koöp, Landboukundige, 1971, Pretoria
Van Zyl J M, 39, Sesdelaan Lichtenburg, Skoolsielkundige, 1976, Bethal
Van Zyl J N C, 29, Hoërskool Usakos, Onderwyser, 1970, Okahandja
Van Zyl J S, 28, S A S & H Bloemfontein, Klerk, 1966
Van Zyl J W, 43, Departement v Justisie Christiana, Landdros, 1964, Potgietersrus
Van Zyl L G, 48, Landbou Tegniese Dienste Ermelo, Navorsingsbeampte, 1967, Pretoria
Van Zyl L S, 33, Gouws & Gouws Saadhandelaars Magaliesburg, Bestuurder, 1975, Rustenburg
Van Zyl M C, 47, Unisa Pretoria, Professor, 1977, Saldanha
Van Zyl M F, 38, S A U K Bloemfontein, Streeksingenieur, 1969, Johannesburg
Van Zyl M J, 42, S A Polisie Pretoria, Kaptein, 1966, George
Van Zyl M M B, 31, Mulderstraat Residensie, Landdros, 1972, Lichtenburg
Van Zyl M S, 27, N G Sendingkerk Komga, Predikant, 1968, Louterwater
Van Zyl N H, 34, Southern Life Kimberley, Verteenwoordiger, 1977, Bellville
Van Zyl N J, 42, S A Polisie Potchefstroom, Luitenant, 1963, Welkom
Van Zyl O A W, 31, Swanepoellaan 7 Aldarapark Randburg, Siviele Ingenieur, 1975, Pretoria
Van Zyl P A, 37, Sanlam Kaapstad, Wyksbestuurder, 1967, Sasolburg
Van Zyl P E, 35, N G Kerk Leeu Gamka, Predikant, 1967, Kuilsrivier
Van Zyl P H S, 36, Hoërskool Carletonville, Onderwyser/Boer, 1965, Florida
Van Zyl P J, 30, Hoërskool Keimoes, Onderwyser, 1968
Van Zyl P J, 34, Dept Opvoedkunde PU vir CHO Potchefstroom, Lektor, 1973, Alice Kaap
Van Zyl P J C, Lid van die U R se Ekonomiese Komitee in 1973
Van Zyl S F, 40, PK Garies, Boer/Sakeman, 1965

Van Zyl S J, 37, Laerskool Pongola, Skoolhoof, 1970, Blyvooruitzicht
Van Zyl W A, 37, S A Polisie Oudtshoorn, Luitenant, 1963, Goodwood
Van Zyl W A, 29, Witdam PK Dealesville, Boer, 1970
Van Zyl W F J, 38, Yskor Pretoria, Rekenpligtige Assistent, 1967, Somerset-Oos
Van Zyl W G M, 45, Sesdelaan 14 Melville Johannesburg, Streekslanddros, 1975, Calvinia
Van Zyl W J, 30, Hoërskool Mariental, Onderwyser, 1974, Warmbad S W A
Van Zyl W J v d M, 44, Paardekop Citrusdal, Boer, 1969
Van Zyl Z, 29, Pretoriusstraat 29, Sasolburg, Onderwyser, 1966, Pofadder
Vaughan D J, 39, Windplaas Distrik Rouxville, Boer/Ingenieur, 1965, Kaapstad
Veenstra J, 38, Landbou Tegniese Dienste Pretoria, Assistent Hoofingenieur, 1973
Velthuysen G, 34, N H Kerk Duncanville, Predikant, 1976, Eloffsdal
Veltman N J, 33, Piercestraat 98 Heilbron, Apteker, 1973, Lydenburg
Venter A A, 27, Erasmus Jooste & Kie Klerksdorp, Prokureur, 1964
Venter A du P, 34, Smaldeel Burgersdorp, Boer/Klerk, 1973
Venter A H, 39, A R Fleischach & Kie Potchefstroom, Prokureur, 1965, Pretoria
Venter A J, 25, Postmasburgse Koöp Doornput, Takbestuurder, 1963, Postmasburg
Venter A J, 49, Agstestraat 96 Walvisbaai, Vise-Hoof (Hoërskool), 1970, Germiston
Venter A J, 42, Departement Hoër Onderwys Pretoria, Senior Vakkundige Beampte, 1968
Venter A L, 37, Elfdelaan 4 Thabazimbi/Poskantoor, Hooftegnikus, 1971, Mafeking
Venter C, 41, P/A O T K Bethal, Sekretaris, 1967
Venter C, 36, Apexgebou 11 Springs, Prokureur, 1965
Venter C F, 39, Gerhardstraat Lyttelton, Geneesheer, 1967
Venter C J, 47, Volkskas Mayville Pretoria, Bestuurder, 1975, Johannesburg
Venter C J H, 27, Geref Kerk Tzaneen, Predikant, 1967, Odendaalsrus
Venter C P, 40, Brink Roos & Du Toit Johannesburg, Ouditeur, 1969, Bellville
Venter C P, 42, Jooste Reyneke & Venter Johannesburg, Narkotiseur, 1970, Kestell
Venter C P, 42, Jooste Reynecke & Venter Johannesburg Greenhillweg 10 Emmarentia Johannesburg, Narkotiseur, 1970, Kestell
Venter de la R, 30, Ventersfontein Hutchinson, Boer, 1976
Venter D J (Lid Nr 6281.), Churchillaan 16 Primrose, Luitenant S A Polisie (Vrygestelde Lid)
Venter D J, 34, Madeleyweg 50 Strubenvale Springs, Vise-Hoof, 1975, Kimberley
Venter D J, 39, Pastoriestraat Springbok, N G Predikant, 1970, Piketberg
Venter D M J, 34, Tweepanne PK Glaudina, Boer, 1967, Potchefstroom
Venter E A, 31, Deqarweg 9a Gevangenisterrein Pta, Majoor (Gevangenis), 1970, Kroonstad
Venter E A, 31, P/A Hoërskool Wilgerrivier Frankfort, Onderwyser, 1973, Paul Roux
Venter F P, 34, Elandsdrif PK Marble Hall, Boer, 1968, Pretoria
Venter G H, 41, P/A G H Venter & Kie Kimberley, Rekenmeester, 1967, Johannesburg
Venter G J C, 30, N G Pastorie Kerkernberg, Predikant, 1966, Lusaka
Venter G S, 39, Laerskool Stulting Humansdorp, Skoolhoof, 1970, Burgersdorp
Venter H, P U vir CHO Potchefstroom, Professor (Afrikaans-Nederlands), 1963
Venter H, 41, P/A N G Kerk Keetmanshoop, Predikant, 1968, Ashton K P
Venter H H, 35, Herby Taylorstraat 10 Unitaspark, Onderwyser, 1975, Carletonville
Venter H J (Lid Nr 6245), Bankbestuurder Vryburg — Voorgestel vir die U R in 1968
Venter H J, 31, Kralingen Ermelo, Boer, 1965, Thabazimbi
Venter I J, 35, Medfontein 413 Bloemfontein, Velspesialis, 1967, Pretoria
Venter Izak J (Dr), Dermatoloog van Bloemfontein Omsendbrief 1.9.77 word broers dokters n, Landdros, 1974, Johannesburg
Venter J A, 37, Pomona Landgoed PK Bredett, Onderwyser, 1966, Kempton Park
Venter J A, 44, Nywerheidsaksepbank Johannesburg, Besturende Direkteur, 1967, Paarl
Venter J B, 40, P/A Saambou-Nasionaal Kroonstad, Takbestuurder, 1974, Kimberley
Venter J C, 34, Harmonie Burgersdorp, Geneesheer, 1964, Reddersburg
Veneter J D, 28, Geref Kerk Venterstad, Predikant, 1975, Potchefstroom
Venter J D, 36, Nas Buro vir Opvoedkundige Navorsing Asst Direkteur, 1964, Witbank
Venter J D, 33, Perseel E26 Marble Hall, Boer, 1970, Groblersdal
Venter J G, 37, N G Kerk Onze Rust, Predikant, 1967, Indwe
Venter J H, 33, Ludorfstraat 64 Brits, Kernfisikus/Raad op Atoom, 1977
Venter J H, 24, N G Kerkkoshuis Tweeling, Onderwyser, 1964, Philippolis
Venter J H, 31, S A Weermag Tempe, N G Veldprediker, 1966, Dewetsdorp
Venter J I, 40, Gravelotte Skool, Onderhoof, 1964, Benoni

Veneter J J, 39, Louis Trichardt BLVO 227, Vanderbijlpark, Geref Predikant, 1977, Potchefstroom
Venter J J, 36, Millstraat Adelaide, Tegnikus/Ltd, 1977, Stutterheim
Venter J J, 38, S A L Angelierstraat 30 Northmead, Benoni, Boordingenieur, 1972, Kempton Park
Venter J J, Lid van die U R se Ekonomiese Komitee 1973
Venter J J, 43, S A Polisie Pretoria, Majoor, 1968
Venter J J, 32, Yatessingel 3 Kimberley/Sanlam, Verteenwoordiger, 1970
Venter J J L, 39, P/A Venter & Seuns Parys, Direkteur, Boshof
Venter J S M, 30, S A Polisie Koster, Adj-Offisier, 1964, Boons
Venter L, 30, Bantoe-Hervestigingsraad Johannesburg, Superintendent, 1967, Potchefstroom
Venter L J, 32, Agrikura Salisbury, Sekretaris, 1969, Pretoria
Venter M, 47, 29steLaan 899 Rietfontein Pretoria, Administratiewe Beampte, 1968
Venter M, 31, Rynfieldse Laerskool Benoni, Onderwyser, 1968, Kensington
Venter M, 35, H/V Hilltop & Mainstraat Bordeaux Randburg, Predikant, 1963, Postmasburg
Venter M H, 32, Tvl Eiendomsagentskap Johannesburg, Onderbestuurder, 1975, Honeydew
Venter M J S, 27, De Beerstraat Jagersfontein, Onderwyser, 1967, Potchefstroom
Venter P, 33, Kareepoort Philippolis, Boer, 1974
Venter P, 27, Munisipaliteit Johannesburg, Senior Vertaler, 1969, Bloemfontein
Venter P F, 39, Wangemanstraat 297 Groenkloof Pretoria, Ginekoloog, 1964, Potchefstroom
Venter P J, 48, Kremetart Giyani/Dept Justisie Gazankulu, Sekretaris, 1977, Zeerust
Venter P J, 32, Radio Bantoe Johannesburg, Organiseerder, 1966, Lichtenburg
Venter P J, 36, Stadsraad Vanderbijlpark, Sen Verkeersinspekteur, 1974
Venter P J, 32, Oom Jacobstraat 52 Meiringspark, Asst Kosterekenmeester se Kantoor (Senr Wes Koöp), 1971, Potchefstroom
Venter P M, 39, Hoër Tegniese Skool Middelburg Tvl, Onderwyser, 1964
Venter P P, 34, Mittelstraat 13 Swakopmund, Onderwyser, 1975, Keetmanshoop
Venter P R, 25, Krugerskraal Hofmeyr, Boer, 1969
Venter P T, 37, Pietersburgstraat 57 Ladanna Pietersburg, N G Predikant, 1976, Ohrigstad
Venter P W, Klerksdorp (Sluit 1965 Bondsraad af met Skriflesing & Gebed)
Venter R V, 35, Geref Kerk Elandspoort, Predikant, 1969, Nigel
Venter S J, 28, Sterkloop Dullstroom, Boer, 1973, Ventersdorp
Venter S J J, 33, Jakkalsfontein PK Danielskuil, Boer, 1964
Venter S J P K, 43, Rooslaan 6 Huttenhoogte Newcastle, Werkekontroleur Yskor, 1976,
Venter T J J, 35, S A S & H, Bloemfontein, Bonus werk Inspekteur, 1970, Pretoria
Venter W, 29, Geref Pastorie Swartruggens, Predikant, 1973, Germiston
Venter W A J, 36, Voortrekkerwinkels Koöp Bethal, Afdelingshoof, 1966
Venter W H, 47, Lorrainestraat 43 Bayswater, Onderwyser, 1977, Rodenbeck
Vercueil G F, 28, Louishof 3 Crescentweg Wynberg Kaap, Onderwyser/ Student, 1975, Malmesbury
Vercuiel H J F, 32, PK Dendron, Boer, 1965, Pietersburg
Verhoef L H, 31, Foskor PK Phalaborwa, Geoloog, 1963, Sasolburg
Verhoef L H W, 38, Kentweg 258 Meyerspark Pretoria, Hoof Hidroloog (Dept Waterwes), 1977
Verhoef P A, Stellenbosch (Sluit 1969 en Bondsraad af met Skriflesing & Gebed)
Verhoef W, 35, Maatskaplike Navorsingburo Pretoria, Assistent Direkteur, 1965, Langlaagte
Vermaak C S, 27, Merino PK Melmoth, Boer, 1975, Pretoria
Vermaak D (Prof), U O V S Bloemfontein (Bantoe-Onderwys)
Vermaak D, 34, Hoërskool Calitzdorp, Skoolhoof, 1964, De Aar
Vermaak H D S, 37, Volkskas Louis Trichardt, Bestuurder, 1963, Pretoria
Vermaak J C, 40, Swartlaagte Edenville, Boer/Landmeter, 1968, Zastron
Vermaak J N, Bellefiedlaan 214 Mondeor JHB/Jabulani Bantoe Skool 38, Hoof, 1971, Krugersdorp
Vermaak M J, 44, Gesondheidskomitee Roadtan, Boer/Sekretaris, 1975
Vermaak N J, 40, PK Kareedouw, Onderwyser, 1965, Redelinghuys
Vermaak S J, 36, Munisipaliteit Walvisbaai (Bantoesake), Adj-Direkteur, 1973, Windhoek

Vermaak W A, 33, Raubenheimerstraat 145 Heilbron, Versekeringsmakelaar, 1977, Oudtshoorn
Vermaas L C F, 43, O T K Bethal, Ouditeur, 1969, Charl Cilliers
Vermuelen A, 26, PK Diskobolos Kimberley, Onderwyser, 1963
Vermeulen A A M, 26, Dagbreekkoshuis Kokstad, Onderwyser, 1967, Vanwyksvlei
Vermeulen C J, 23, Swart Koppie Philipstown, Boer, 1975
Vermeulen G du P, 40, Deelfontein Luckhoff, Boer, 1971
Vermuelen I J, 49, Swartkoppies Philipstown, Boer, 1967
Vermeulen J U, 48, Vrede Philipstown, Boer, 1964
Vermeulen M V A Lid Nr 7672, Durban, Predikant, 1962
Vermeulen S D, 36, Martinspan Hopetown, Boer, 1964
Vermeulen W C, 36, P/A I B M Kaapstad, Verkoopsbestuurder, 1973, Randburg
Vermooten J J, Ere-Ouditeur van A B
Verreynne G J, 39, Federale Mynbou Kuruman, Geoloog, 1969, Dunnottar
Verryne A A, 34, Sanlam Gebou Kimberley, Argitek, 1968, Mayfair-Wes
Versteeg, C, 34, Versteeg Potplantkwekery Wilgespruit, Besturende Direkteur, 1975, Florida
Verster A A, 30, P/A Hoerskool Grabouw, Onderwyser, 1976, Ceres
Verster, A A, S A Polisie Alexanderbaai, Luitenant, 1967, Calinia
Verster E, 37, P/A Dept Landboutegn Dienste, Asst Direkteur, 1977, Jan Kempdorp
Verster J D, 45, Syferfontein Ventersdorp, Boer, 1970, Potchefstroom
Verster J P, 26, S A Ambassade Trafalgar Plein London, Buitelandse Diensbeampte, 1977, Potchefstroom
Verster J P, 47, Lugverdedigingshoofkwartier Lyttelton, Brigadier, 1967, London Engeland
Verster T L, 34, Unisa Pretoria, Dosent, 1970, Louis Trichardt
Verster W C, 37, Laerskool Vredenburg, Skoolhoof, 1975, Port Elizabeth
Verwey G L, 36, Hoër Handelskool Parow, Onderhoof, 1969, Krugersdorp
Verwey J H, 48, Dept Sport & Ontspanning Pretoria, Ondersekretaris, 1975, George
Verwey J P, 33, S A Polisie Murraysburg, Sersant, 1964, Willowmore
Verwey J S, 40, S A Polisie Stellenbosch, Kaptein, 1968, Wynberg Kaap
Verwey T J P, 32, Hoëveldse Bantoe-Admin Raad Witbank, Direkteur Fin, 1974, Virginia
Verwoerd C A, 29, Eugene Maraisstraat 33 Sasolburg, Mediese Praktisyn, 1972, Pretoria
Victor G D (Jnr), Alma Christiana, Boer, 1973
Victor J A, 27, N G Pastorie Port Nolloth, Predikant, 1969, Middelburg K P
Viktor Z H, 44, P/A Uniewinkels Bellville, Bestuurder, 1964, Lainsburg
Viljoen A, 42, Dept Landbou Tegn Dienste Stellenbosch, Vakkundige, 1967, Piketberg
Viljoen A, 36, P/A Staatsdienskommissie Pretoria, Ondersekretaris, 1975, Pretoria
Viljoen A A, 42, Massey-Fergusan/Ringweg 136 Drie Riviere Finans-Ontleder, 1970, Bellville
Viljoen A C, 46, N G Kerk Hartebeesspruit, Predikant, 1968, Potchefstroom
Viljoen A D, 55, Paul Roux Straat 70 Bloemfontein, Sakeman/Burgemeester, 1965, Worcester
Viljoen A J, 27, P U vir CHO, Lektor, 1966, Postmasburg
Viljoen A J, 32, P/A Nakanas Port Nolloth, Boer, 1966
Viljoen A J, 31, Combrinckstraat Worcester, Juwelier, 1968
Viljoen A P, 28, N G Pastorie Aliwal-Noord, Predikant, 1971, Stellenbosch
Viljoen B G, 30 Oosstraat 92 Vryheid, Onderwyser, 1968, Pinetown
Viljoen C E M, 35, Vyfdelaan 14 Heidelberg Tvl, Medikus, 1967, Pretoria
Viljoen C J, 37, N H Pastorie Pretoria-Tuine, Predikant, 1970, Virginia/Randport
Viljoen D A, 33, Munisipaliteit De Aar, Klerk, 1966
Viljoen D C, 43, S A Droëvrugteraad Dwarsstr Uitsig, Bestuurder, 1970, Pretoria
Viljoen D J, Stofbergstraat 4 Universitas Bloemfontein (Skakel by U O V S 4.2.76)
Viljoen D J, 32, Raad v Ontwikkeling v Natuurlike Hulpbronne Pretoria, Assistent Direkteur, 1966, Winburg
Viljoen D J, 31, Sanlam Sinoia (Salisbury), Verteenwoordiger, 1974, Lichtenburg
Viljoen D R, 42, Winterhoek-Wes Tulbach, Boer, 1966
Viljoen E J, 39, Klipfontein Colesberg, Boer, 1977
Viljoen F, (Lid Nr 365) Johannesburg, Oud-Skoolhoof
Viljoen F H, 39, Griffithstraat 16 Aliwal-Noord, Skoolhoof, 1976, Postmasburg
Viljoen F J, 46, S A Weermag Lenz, Offisier, 1975, Pretoria
Viljoen F J, 32, Ferreirastraat 100 Nelspruit, Geneesheer, 1965, Pretoria

Viljoen F P, 37, Dromorestraat Kenmare Krugersdorp, Bemarkingsbeampte, 1971, Johannesburg
Viljoen G V N Lid Nr 6197, R A U Johannesburg Voorsitter van die A B — Voorgestel vir die U R in 1968
Viljoen H A J, 31, P/A N G Gemeente Crosby-Wes, Predikant, 1974, Pretoria
Viljoen H C, 34, Hoflaan 6 Stellenbosch, Professor, 1971, Stellenbosch
Viljoen I M, 45, S A S Bloemfontein, Insp Bantoe-Arbeid, 1964, Kroonstad
Viljoen J, 34, Wilgehof Bethlehem, Boer, 1970
Viljoen J B, 35, Volkskas Koppies, Rekenmeester, 1966, Winburg
Viljoen J C, 37, Sierraweg 8 Selcourt/Premier Beskuitjies Besturende Direkteur, 1976, Florida
Viljoen J C T, 36, Middelplaas Caledon, Boer, 1965
Viljoen J E, 41, P/A Yskor Pretoria, Seksievoorman, 1967, Rustenburg
Viljoen J F, 36, N G Kerk Graaff-Reinet, Predikant, 1967, Somerset Wes
Viljoen J H, 37, Langstraat 22 Mariental, Geref Predikant, 1972, Messina
Viljoen J H, 37, Laerskool Graveloote, Onderhoof, 1969, Zeerust
Viljoen J H, 33, Sergeantstraat 21 Universitas, Bloemfontein, Sen Lektor U O V S, 1977, Potchefstroom
Viljoen J H, 32, 4de Straat 17 Middelburg Tvl, Onderwyser, 1968, Nelspruit
Viljoen J H, 41, Eldorado PK Indwe, Boer, 1974
Viljoen J H, 28, Langfordhill Richmond Kaap, Boer, 1970
Viljoen J J, 33, Middelplaas Caledon, Boer, 1967
Viljoen J M B, 34, Pastoriestraat Bultfontein, Geneesheer, 1965, Wesselsbron
Viljoen J N, 40, Oakstraat 72 Northmead Benoni, Admin Beamapte (Ontvanger v Inkomste), 1971, Carolina
Viljoen J P, 36, P P Rus-Motors Potgietersrus, Bestuurder, 1973, Koedoesrand
Viljoen J T B, 43, P/A Borckenhagen & Louw Pretoria, Bourekenaar, 1964, Witbank
Viljoen J W, 30, Berlynstraat 18 Heidelberg Tvl, Tandarts, 1964
Viljoen Marais (Lid Nr 3226), Voormalige Minister van Arbeid — President of the Senate
Viljoen M D, 29, Diamantdoorns Schweizer-Reneke, Boer, 1964
Viljoen M J, 40, S A Weermag Potchefstroom, Offisier, 1973, Windhoek
Viljoen P, 35, Die Ster Tulbach, Boer, 1969
Viljoen P C, 36, Aanhou-Wen Lichtenburg, Onderwyser, 1966, Schweizer-Reneke
Viljoen P E, 34, Jim Fouchélaan 66 Universitas Bloemfontein, Lektor U O V S, 1971, Jagersfonteininsiale Hospitaal Bethlehem, Superintendent, 1969, Ntsiridinisending-stasie
Visagie I G, 41, Volkskas Petrusburg, Bestuurder, 1974, Bloemfontein
Visagie J A, 48, 23ste Laan 460 Villieria Pretoria, Onderwyser, 1968, Calvinia
Visagie J A N, 25, B S B Williston, Veldbeampte, 1966, Calvinia
Visagie J D, 45, Vredestraat 27 Wolmaransstad, Onderhoof, 1969, Coligny
Visagie J H, 36, S A Polisie Esselenpark Pretoria, Adj-Offisier, 1964, Bloemfontein
Visagie J H L, 37, Sterkfontein PK Middelpos, Boer, 1969
Visagie M L, 42, Tygerbergse Hoër Handelskool Parow, Skoolhoof, 1964, Worcester
Visagie R G, 38, Heidelbergse Onderwyskollege, Dosent, 1965, Bethal
Visagie S J J, 35, Readweg 20 Ladysmith P/A Dept Bantoe Onderwys, Onderhoof, 1975, Louis Trichardt
Visagie S W J, 37, Pinestraat 6 Drie Riviere Vereeniging, Landdros, 1971, Pofadder
Visagie W S, 38, De Puts Middelpos, Boer, 1973
Visser, 29, Elandsfontein Clanwilliam, Boer, 1965
Visser A C, 38, Nelstraat 18 Wellington/Droëvrugte-Koöp, Voedseltegnoloog, 1976, Pretoria
Visser A C, 37, Posbus 409 Oranjemund, Onderwyser, 1977, Oudtshoorn
Visser A J, 29, Clancliff Krugersdorp, Geneesheer, 1973, Pretoria
Visser A J (Dr), Voormalige Senator
Visser A L, 44, Nellie Swartskool Pretoria, Onderwyser, 1975, Steynsburg
Visser B J, 33, Sanlam Kimberley, Wyksbestuurder, 1967, Hopetown
Visser C E, 38, Vissershoek PK Richmond Kaap, Boer, 1967
Visser C F, 45, SP Mid Skool Baysville Oos Londen, Skoolhoof, 1968, Port Elizabeth
Visser C H J, 40, Hoër Seunskool Hugenote Springs, Onderwyser, 1969, Nylstroom
Visser C J, 30, P/A S A Polisie Klerksdorp, Sersant, 1974, Schweizer-Reneke

Visser C J, 42, Dept Pos- & Telegraafwese Pretoria, Adm Beheerbeampte, 1967
Visser C J, 28, Munisipaliteit Standerton, Rekenmeester, 1967, Boshof
Visser D C, 34, Klopperbos Nuy, Boer, 1977, Worcester
Visser D J, 30, Hexrivier Citrusdal, Boer, 1967
Visser D T, 41, P/A Randbank BPK Johannesburg, Hoofrekenmeester, 1974
Visser F A H, 44, Dept Gevangeniswese Pretoria, Kolonel, 1966, Kaapstad
Visser F J, 35, Swartklip Distrik Rustenburg, Onderwyser, 1969, Vryheid
Visser F J C, 33, Handelhuis Smithfield, Onderbestuurder, 1966, Humansdorp
Visser G H J, 35, P/A Groep II Skool Ogies, Onderwyser, 1965, Wakkerstroom
Visser G J, 40, P/A Porterville se Landbou Köop, Takbestuurder, 1965, Klawer
Visser G J F Lid Nr 3571, Johannesburg Noord Voorgestel vir die U R in 1968, Sakeman
Visser G J J, Lid van die U R se Ekonomiese Komitee in 1973
Visser G N, 32, Kom-Nader Cathcartstraat George, Onderwyser, 1975, Prieska
Visser G P, 27, P/A Dept Landbou Tegn Dienste, Voorligtingsbeampte, 1978, Fauresmith
Visser G R, 44, Hoërskool Emily Hobhouse Wepener, Skoolhoof, 1975, Dealesville
Visser H J, 35, P/A Hoërskool Greytown, Onderwyser, 1965, Ventersdorp
Visser H J, 29, Visserhoek Richmond K P, Boer, 1968, Richmond K P
Visser H J, 34, Hans Strijdomlaan 289 Verwoerdburg, Senior Onderwyser, 1971, Ventersdorp
Visser H J G, 46, P/A Hoërskool Die Burger, Onderwyser, 1973, Windhoek
Visser H L, 46, Volkskas Ladysmith, Rekenmeester, 1976, Belfast
Visser I J, 35, Korenfontein PK Swartruggens, Onderwyser, 1965
Visser J, 47, Eksteenskuil — Nedersetting Keimoes, Superintendent, 1974
Visser, J, 32, Mareestraat 12 Odendaalsrus, Prokureur, 1975, Welkom
Visser J, 35, Geref Kerk Germiston, Predikant, 1966, Potchefstroom
Visser J C, 43, S A Polisie Hoofkantoor Pretoria, Werwingsoffisier, 1967, Piketberg
Visser J G, 38, Boskor PK Kleinbos Distrik Humansdorp, Produksiebestuurder, 1972, Barberton
Visser J H, 28, K W V Paarl, Regsadviseur, 1966, Kaapstad
Visser J J C, 47, N G Pastorie Boston Bellville, Predikant, 1967, Laingsburg
Visser L J, 33, Impala Koshuis Thabazimbi, Onderwyser, 1974, Delmas
Visser O W N, 38, Edwardslaan 118 Westonaria, Motorhawe-Eienaar, 1968, Carletonville
Visser P A C, 35, Voortrekkerstraat Redelinghuys, Onderwyser, 1972, Kaapstad
Visser P D, 39, Collinsingel 12 Sasolburg, Instandhoudings-Beplanningsingenieur, 1972, Parys
Visser P L, 27, Hoërskool Ventersdorp, Onderwyser, 1968, Brits
Visser S M, 33, S A Weermag Walvisbaai, N G Kapelaan, 1975, Ohopoho
Visser T J K, 29, Oos Burgerstraat Fauresmith, Onderwyser, 1974, Bloemfontein
Vivier C de W, 44, Groote Schuurhospitaal Kaapstad, Asst Superintendent, 1967, Uitenhage
Vivier P M, 41, Melivanda Woonstelle 303 Bourkestraat Sunnyside Pretoria/Volkskas, Assistent Sekretaris, 1970, Kaapstad
Viviers M N O, 34, Rooseveltstraat 11 Robindale Uitbreiding, Bestuurder (Wilfour Wonings), Pietersburg
Viviers P J, 38, Hoërskool Lydenburg, Onderhoof, 1974, Pietersburg
Viviers P L, 36, Vakopleidingskool Westlake Kaap, Senior Onderwyser, 1976, Worcester
Viviers P M, 29, La Rochelleweg La Rochelle, Onderhoof, 1974, Parow
Vlok B, 42, Kavalierfilms Randburg, Besturende Direkteur, 1973, Bloemfontein
Vlok G J, 33, Kotze & Vlok Balfour, Prokureur, 1966, Brits
Vlok N, 33, Mirianastraat 237 Sinoville Pretoria, Geregsbode, 1977, Valhalla
Vlok W J, Perskor Handelsdrukkery Johannesburg, Afdelingsvoorman, 1974
Vlotman G C, 39, De rust PK Brandfort, Boer, 1967
Vogel G M, 31, Radienhof Leemhuisstraat Klerksdorp, Onderwyser, 1970, Nelspruit
Vogel J J, 35, N G Pastorie Tadcaster, Predikant, 1976, Balfour
Voigt C J, 38, Munisipaliteit Roodepoort, O & M Beampte, 1969, Kempton Park
Voigt J G, 38, Dwarsdeur Vredendal, Boer, 1968
Volschenk A D, 31, Laerskool Saffier (Tiervlei), Vise-Hoof, 1973, Warrenton
Volschenk J A M, 35, Sekondêre Skool Tweeling, Onderwyser, 1971, Kroonstad
Volschenk J E, 32, Outenique Proefplaas George, Hoof, 1974, Hartenbos
Volschenk J J, 38, Militêre Basis Doornkloof, Majoor/S A Weermag, 1977, Pretoria

Volschenk P G, 25, PK Adams Mission, Onderwyser, 1976, Alberton
Volsteedt A K, Bloemfontein (Praat oor Onderwys by 1966 se Bondsraad)
Volsteedt J A, 27, Grey Kollege Bloemfontein, Onderwyser, 1975
Von Molendorff G A S, 46, Laerskool Parow-Sentraal Parow, Onderhoof, 1967, Worcester
Von Solms S J H, 45, Nederlandse Bank Thabazimbi, Bestuurder, 1968, Johannesburg
Von Wielligh C L, 27, Hoërskool Ermelo, Onderwyser, 1966
Von Wielligh J H, 29, Hoërskool Walvisbaai, Onderwyser, 1975, Stellenbosch
Von Wielligh L A J, 36, Maskam Landboukoöp van Rhynsdorp, Bestuurder, 1973, Loeriesfontein
Von Wielligh P J, 36, Pakhuisdam Paarl, Boer, 1974
Voogt A J, 36, Churchillweg 6 Port Shepstone, Landdros, 1976, Umzinto
Voordewind W J, 38, P U vir CHO Potchefstroom, Lektor, 1965, Vanderbijlpark
Vorster A J D, 38, Volkskas Bpk Caledon, Bestuurder, 1965, Vereeniging
Vorster A P, 42, Pospersoneel Kimberley, Hooftegnikus, 1967, Johannesburg
Vorster B J (Lid Nr 3737), Staatspresident
Vorster B J, 28, Grootpan PK Marken, Boer, 1969, Potgietersrus
Vorster C J, 33, Laerskool Arborpark, Onderwyser, 1974, Pietermaritzburg
Vorster D J, 29, Cathcartstraat Somerset Oos, Onderwyser, 1977, Cradock
Vorster F H, 34, Leedsweg 56 Umtata, Onderwyser, 1965, Potchefstroom
Vorster G H L, 39, Tygerbergse Tegn Instituut Parow, Lektor, 1973, Bellville
Vorster G J, 34, Waaihoek Warrenton, Boer/Sakeman, 1973
Vorster H A, 36, S A U K (Radio Bantu)/Amatolary 111 King Williamstown, Ingenieur, 1975, Pretoria
Vorster H P, 49, Grootpan PK Marken, Boer, 1966, Potgietersrus
Vorster H T J, 44, Dordrechtstraat 29 Crosby, Klerk (SAUK), 1972, Potchefstroom
Vorster I, 32, De Klerk Vermaak & Vennote Vereeniging, Prokureur, 1973, Rustenburg
Vorster J A, 45, Hoërskool Lyttelton, Onderhoof, 1967
Vorster J D, 54, N G Pastorie Tafelberg Kaapstad, Predikant, 1964, Jamestown
Vorster J D, 40, Rabestraat 163 Potgietersrus, Geneesheer, 1970, Pretoria
Vorster J E, 38, Hoogestraat 137 Potgietersrus, Boer, 1966
Vorster J E, 27, The Junction Letsitele, Boer, 1967
Vorster J G, 35, Waterval Carnarvon, Boer, 1969
Vorster J H, 32, Glenharte Ingoto/Yskor, Aanlegbestuurder, 1970, Johannesburg
Vorster J M, 48, Vaalreefs Expl Mining Co Orkney, Hysmasjinis, 1969, Springs
Vorster J P, 44, Premium Makelaars Johannesburg, Besturende Direkteur, 1968, Vereeniging
Vorster L F, 28, Landboukollege Glen, Navorser, 1967, Pretoria
Vorster N R, 31, Faurelaan 2 Bloemfontein, Tegniese Asst vir Raadg, Ing, 1975, Zastron
Vorster P A, 38, De Waalstraat 76 La Hoff Klerksdorp, Prokureur, 1977, Pietermaritzburg
Vorster P J, 37, Treurfontein Aliwal-Noord, Boer, 1967
Vorster P J, 45, Vorstershoek Distrik Mafeking, Skoolhoof/Boer, 1976
Vorster P P J, 37, Kirstonia Handelaars PK Bray, Winkelier/Boer, 1967
Vorster S J, 29, Normaalkollege Pretoria, Lektor, 1964, Bloemfontein
Vorster S W, 31, Randsigstraat Richmond Kaap, Hoërskool Onderwyser, 1971, Moorreesburg
Vorster T, 35, Ketelfontein Colesberg, Boer, 1971
Vorster T B, 41, Leeuweg Monumentpark Pretoria, Senior Landdros, 1971, Germiston
Vorster W F, 38, Mopaniestraat Phalaborwa, Geneesheer, 1965, Burgersdorp
Vorster W K, 33, Thorncroftsingel 19 Phalaborwa, Hoërskoolonderwyser, 1971, Pietersburg
Vos J A P, 34, Tweedelaan Edenvale, Senior Onderwyser, 1972, Pretoria
Vos J P, 36, Afrikaanse Springstowwe & Chem Nywerhede Somerset-Wes, Voorman, 1968, Vredenburg
Vos L P G, 42, Munisipaliteit Pretoria, Adj-Stadstesourier, 1965, Rustenburg
Vos S A, 31, Truter Crous Wiggel & Vos Randfontein, Prokureur, 1973, Westonaria
Vosloo C J, 33, Riverside Edenburg, Boer, 1966, Pearston
Vosloo C J, 31, De Put Edenburg, Boer, 1972
Vosloo G J, 33, Mispah Bethlehem, Boer, 1975
Vosloo J, 35, Schoemanstraat 14 Kuruman, Onderhoof (Laerskool), 1970, Stellenbosch
Vosloo J H, 38, Alexandra Marandellas Rhodesië, Boer, 1975, Ottosdal
Vosloo M A, 31, Ventersdorp-Handelshuis, Sakeman, 1968, Salisbury

Vosloo M L, 43, Frederickrylaan 171 Northcliff Johannesburg, Direkteur v Maatskappye, 1971
Vosloo P C, 43, Vosloo & Lindeque Johannesburg, Rekenmeester, 1969
Vosloo W A, 40, Universiteit Stellenbosch, Senior Lektor, 1968, Elsenburg
Vosser P, 33, Hoogestraat Zeerust, Onderwyser, 1969, Marico
Vosser W J, 40, Poskantoor Pietersburg, Superintendent, 1965, Zeerust
Vrey W J H, 34, U O V S Bloemfontein Boersmastraat 45 Universitas, Dosent, 1970, Potchefstroom

W

Wagenaar J P J, 26, Beaconweg 137 Grosvenor Durban, N H Predikant, 1970, Pretoria
Wagenaar H P G, 29 Nas Boekhandel King Williamstown, Bestuurder, 1966, Uitenhage
Wagenaar P M, 36, Kantoor van die Burgemeester Nigel, Sekretaris, 1965, Boksburg
Wagner J F, 47, Volkskas Warden, Bestuurder, 1974, Alberton
Wahl A J, 31, Hoofstraat Merweville, Sakeman, 1967
Walters H A, 43 P/A S A Spoorwegkollege Essenlenpark, Instrukteur, 1969, Malmesbury
Walters J L, 47, Vlakpan Ottosdal, Boer, 1975, Pretoria
Walters P E, 32, Lanzeracweg 13 Karindal/Universiteit Stellenbosch, Snr Lektor, 1972, Piketberg
Walters S S, 33, P/A N G Kerk Salisbury-Suid, Predikant, 1974, Askham
Wandrag J L, 38, Scholtzstraat 43 Universitas Bloemfontein, Ouditeur, 1972, Pretoria
Warmenhoven H W, 38, P/A N C Maritz Tzaneen, Prokureur, 1969, Pietersburg
Warmenhoven W J M, 32, Parkstraat 29, Tzaneen, Apteker, 1967, Lydenburg
Warnich H A, 29, Winkelhaaksvlei Moorreesburg, Boer, 1977
Warnich P G, 39, C M R Port Elizabeth, Predikant, 1965, Hennenman
Wassenaar A D (Dr)
Wassenaar G M C, 32, Universiteit Kollege van Wes-Kaapland, Snr Lektor, 1965, Uitenhage
Wasserfall J H, 44, P/A Human & Pitt Kaapstad, Begrafnisondernemer, 1969
Wasserman I L, 39, Stasieweg Clewer, Skoolhoof, 1973, Witbank
Wasserman J G, 38, Spiesstraat Wepener, Prokureur, 1966, Bloemfontein
Wassermann H S, 44, P/A Dept van Verdediging Pretoria, Kolonel, 1967, Wynberg
Wassermann R, 28, P/A Yskor Pretoria, Beplanner, 1968
Wassermann V D, 34, Dept Landbou Tegniese Dienste Stellenbosch, Snr Lektor, 1967
Watkins F E, 39, Roodeberg Distrik Indwe, Boer, 1973, Lady Grey
Watson A W, 32, Fonteine Paul Roux, Boer, 1971
Weakley Bl, 36, Posbus 34 Harrismith, Ouditeur, 1964, Senekal
Webber H G, 40, P/A S A Polisie Port Elizabeth, Sersant, 1973
Weber H, Bestuurskomitee Middelburg Tvl
Weber H J, 39, Langenhovenstraat 26 Potchefstroom/P U vir CHO, Professor, 1976, Windhoek
Weber P A, Voormalige Besturende Direkteur van Nasionale Pers
Weber P C H, 32, Elliot, Slagter, 1965, Franschhoek
Weeber T M, 30, Kiaatstraat 24 Wilropark/Stadsraad Roodepoort, Eiendomsagent, 1973, Pretoria
Wegner J G, 33, Vennstraat Nelspruit/N J Van Zyl & Vennote, Ouditeur, 1971, Malelane
Wehmeyer R J, 36, P/A Imperiale Koelkamers Pretoria, Rekenmeester, 1975, Nigel
Weich D J V, 32, Jim Fouchélaan 22 Universitas Bloemfontein, Geneesheer, 1974, Malmesbury
Weich H F H, 35, Gainsboroughstraat 4 De La Have Bellville, Geneesheer, 1973, Aliwal-Noord
Weich S J F, 32, 14de Laan 2 Mosselbaai, Geneesheer, 1975, Oos-Londen
Weideman D H J, 30, Normandielaan 77 Bloemfontein, Onderwyser, 1966, Zastron
Weideman I S, 35, Lemoenspruit Luckhoff, Boer, 1973
Weideman J A C, 35, 14deLaan 2 Da Gamapark Simonstad, Vlootoffisier Kmdr, 1972, Saldanha
Weideman J J S, 40, Universiteit Kollege PK Sovenga, Snr Lektor, 1965, Upington
Weideman P J, 42, S A Polisie Pietermaritzburg, Adj-Offisier, 1964, Clocolan
Weideman W J, 45, P/A Magasyndept S A S Johannesburg, Klerk, 1964, Germiston
Weilbach C N, 31, Pilgrimstraat Barberton, Geneesheer, 1967, Lydenburg

Weilbach J, 30, P/A Kantoor v d Eerste Minister, Privaatsekretaris, 1973, Heilbron
Weilbach J F, 39, Pistoria Heilbron, Boer, 1964
Weiss P F D (Prof) (Lid Nr 2902), Direkteur van die Afrika Instituut Pretoria — Voorgestel vir die U R in 1968
Weiss R H O, 30, Utrechtstraat 32 Vryheid, Landmeter, 1969, Pretoria
Welman H, 35, Harmonie Koster, Boer, 1963, Magaliesburg
Welman W P J, 40, Fernhurst Plaas Gatooma Salisbury, Boer, 1968
Welthagen P J, 36, P/A Eiendomsafdeling Volkskashoofkantoor Pta, Bankamptenaar, 1974, Bloemfontein
Wenhold H O, 42, Northlandweg 10 Robertsham Johannesburg, Ingenieur, 1975, Klerksdorp
Wentzel J A T, 42, Onderwyskollege Potchefstroom, Snr Dosent, 1967, Standerton
Wentzel J D, 37, P/A W N N R Pretoria, Navorser, 1965, Pietersburg
Wentzel P C, 42, Driefontein Zoekmekaar, Boer, 1975, Olyfberg
Wentzel W F (Lid Nr 4143) Bloemfontein L U K — Voorgestel vir die U R in 1968
Wentzel W H, 34, Volkskas Dewetsdorp, Rekenmeester, 1966, Ventersdorp
Wepener D A, 43, Duineveld Grootfontein, Boer, 1966, Bethanie
Werner C B H, 37, Kleinfontein Brits, Boer, 1977, Pretoria
Wessels A B H, 30, Winterhoek PK Greytown, Boer, 1967
Wessels B H J, 36, P/A Sanlam Port Elizabeth, Wyksbestuurder, 1965, Kirkwood
Wessels B J, 34, Stalreitherstraat 9 Fichardtpark/O U V S Bloemfontein, Snr Lektor, 1976, Ladybrand
Wessels C C S, 37, Moyesstraat Senekal/P/A Middevrystaatse Suiwel Koöp Bpk, Hoofbestuurder, 1975, Sasolburg
Wessels H D, Lid van die U R se Ekonomiese Komitee in 1973
Wessels H du P, 41, Karsrivier Bredasdorp, Boer/Vert Fedmis, 1976
Wessels H J, 32, Dirkie Uysstraat 17 Malmesbury, Onderwyser, 1970, Warrenton
Wessels H J, 42, S A S & H Plaston, Klerk/Boer, 1963, Excelsior
Wessels H W B, 32, Grasvlei Winburg, Boer, 1965
Wessels I, 34, Brandstraat Thaba 'Nchu/Bartimeaskool vir Bantoe Dowe Kinders, Onderhoof, 1970, Pretoria
Wessels J D J, 51, Hoërskool P J Olivier Grahamstad, Skoolhoof, 1973, Kimberley
Wessels J G H, 38, P/A Fissons Johannesburg, Bedryfshoof, 1969, Vanderbijlpark
Wessels J H, 34, P/A Constantiaskool PK Retreat, Onderhoof, 1970, Parow
Wessels J H W (Dr), 36, Yorkweg Bloemfontein, Oogspesialis, 1963
Wessels J J, 29, Sendingpastorie Amsterdam/N G Sendeling, Predikant, 1971, Ladysmith Natal
Wessels J P, 28, Kerkplein Pastorie Prieska, N G Predikant, 1971, Stellenbosch
Wessels J v d W, 44, Thanda Pers King Williamstown, Bestuurder, 1966, Randburg Tvl
Wessels L, 27, Vegkopstraat 20 Krugersdorp, Advokaat, 1974, Potchefstroom
Wessels L S K, 36, Windhoek Napier, Boer, 1975
Wessels M H, 43, Medfonteinsebou 509 Bloemfontein, Chirurg, 1965, Krugersdorp
Wessels M J, 32, "Roseleigh" Ladysmith, Boer, 1967
Wessels M J L, 39, P/A Vrystaat Koöp/Eikelaan 14 Reitz, Asst Hoofbestuurder, 1976 Bloemfontein
Wessels P, 36, Mopaniestraat 17 Phalaborwa, Prokureur, 1973, Pretoria
Wessels P J, 32, Die Drostdy Lady Grey, Landdros, 1970, Kimberley
Wessels P J, 36, Philamerelaan 31 Durban, Tandarts, 1976, Londen
Wessels P J, 49, Hoërskool Heilbron, Skoolhoof, 1966, Sasolburg
Wessels P W de W, 39, Longleat Vanstadensrust, Boer, 1973
Wessels W H, 30, P/A Landboukollege Potchefstroom, Vakk-Beampte, 1969, Stellenbosch
Wessels W M J, 37, P/A Munisipaliteit Nigel/Nie-Blanke Sake, Bestuurder, 1965, Brakpan
Westerman J F, 43, Witpoort Ottosdal, Onderwyser, 1967
Westraat H J, 26, S A Polisie Port Nolloth, Adj-Offisier, 1968, Beaufort-Wes
Weyers A, 33, P/A O U V S Bloemfontein/Sergeantstraat 19 Universitas Bloemfontein, Lektor, 1975, Graaff-Reinet
Weyers F T, 31, P/A Saaiplaas Volkskool Virginia, Skoolhoof, 1969, Bloemfontein
Whelpton J G, 39, Noristan Laboratorium Pretoria, Streeksbestuurder, 1973
White J H P, 36, Ronkettisirkel 21 Petersfield Springs, Boekhouer, 1966, Sundra
Whiteman M G, 45, P/A Munisipaliteit Vereeniging, Voorman Elektrisieën, 1968

Wiehahn N E, 41, Universiteit Port Elizabeth/Errorylaan 30 Framesby, Professor, 1970, Durban
Wienand V M, 39, Posbus 110 Messina (Skakel vir Broers op Militêre Diens by Greefswald of Modemba 1976)
Wiese P N, 35, Ongwedivaopleidingsentrum Oshakati, Onderwyser, 1977, Thaba 'Nchu
Wiese T J, 51, Hopefield Hertzogville, Boer, 1963, Hartsvallei
Wiese W J (Lid Nr 7685), Bloemfontein, Boer, 1962
Wiid D H, 43, Hickory-Oord Robinacres/R A U Johannesburg, Professor, 1970, Port Elizabeth
Wiid J A, PK Witput — Adverteer vir Dokter en Prokureur vir Hopetown in Omsendbrief
Wiid J J A, 35, P/A Sanlamgroeifonds Bellville, Verteenwoordiger, 1970, Worcester
Wilbers P J E, 32, Fred Nicholsonstraat 319 Les Marais, Onderhoof, 1963, Kempton Park
Wilcocks M S, 29, P/A Opkoms-Meubels Bloemfontein, Onderbestuurder, 1963
Wildenboer L, Mariasburg — Woon 1965 se Bondsraad by
Wildenboer L A, 33, P/A S A Spoorweë Watervalboven, Ingenieur, 1969, Johannesburg
Wildenboer R M, 31, Kensington Woonstel 1405 Morningside Durban/Pauw Botha & Wildenboer, Argitek, 1971, Pretoria
Wilke P G, 39, Morkelstraat 10 Middelburg Tvl, Sakeman, 1973
Wilken A E J, 29, S A S & H Bloemfontein, Klerk, 1965
Wilken L E, 36, Mossiestraat 27 Horison-Uitbr Roodepoort, Onderwyser, 1971, Lichtenburg
Wilken O A, 45, Silvervale Smithfield, Boer, 1969, Wepener
Wilken W J, 35, P/A Theron V D Poel & Kie Kaapstad, Rekenmeester, 1970, Bloemfontein
Wilkens B H, 31, Rietfontein PK Opraap, Boer/Sakeman, 1965
Wille C G, 32, Rietgat Lichtenburg, Boer, 1977
Willemse A J, 35, Sanlam Nelspruit, Versekeringskonsultant, 1973, Pretoria
Willemse B F, 38, P/A Zoeloe Opleidingskool Vryheid, Hoof, 1966, Mapumulo
Willemse C P, 31, N G Pastorie Heilbron, Predikant, 1964, Waverley Pretoria
Willemse J, 29, Enhoek Plaas Chipinga, Boer, 1973
Willemse L W, 37, P/A Volkskas Kaapstad, Rekenmeester, 1966, Malmesbury
Willemse M G, 25, Giddyshome Memel, Boer, 1967
Willemse W H, 37, Bergvlamstraat 8 Skanskop Pretoria/gevangeniswese, Brigadier, 1976
Willer L P, 36, P/A Karbochem Sasolburg, Bedryfsuperintendent, 1974, Bethlehem
Williams J G, 29, 27steLaan 581 Villiera Pretoria, Dosent (Universiteit), 1975
Williams J H H, 48, Gainsboroughstraat 15 Vanderbijlpark/Yskor, Elektrotegnikus, 1976, Johannesburg
Wilms C A, 46, Simonstraat Bethal, Geneesheer, 1964, Pearston
Wilson J G, 34, O T K Bethal, Landboukundige, 1967, Williston
Winterbach D J, 40, P/A Geologiese Opname Pretoria, Hoofgeoloog, 1974, Potchefstroom
Winterbach J P J, 39, Wesstraat 31 Middelburg Tvl, Onderwyser, 1975, Naboomspruit
Winterbach P J, 27, Komatipoort, Onderwyser, 1966, Lydenburg
Wium D J W, 35, Lemoenbult De Doorn, Boer, 1964
Wium D J W, 35, Volmoed De Doorns, Boer, 1975
Wohlitz J F, 47, N G Pastorie Delareyville, Predikant, 1965, Pietersburg
Woite C (Jnr), 39, Aenmaystraat Ventersdorp, Boer, 1971
Wolfaardt F J, 36, Silwerlaan 29 Dersleypark Springs, Onderwyser, 1975, Geysdorp
Wolhuter P, 36, Veenstraat 67 Potgietersrus/Potgietersrus, Tabakkoöp Rekenmeester, 1977, Potchefstroom
Wolmarans C F, 47, Hoërskool Tweeling, Skoolhoof, 1967, Virginia
Wolmarans D J, 45, Bultfontein Hekpoort, Boer, 1976, Pretoria
Wolmarans J B, 33, Sibeliusstraat 21 Vanderbijlpark/Yskor, Hoof Onderwys & Opleiding, 1965, Pretoria
Wolvaardt H A, 28, Bensagebou 102 Trompsburg, Onderwyser, 1967,Smithfield
Wright C P, 28, Impalakoshuis Thabazimbi, Onderwyser, 1966
Wright H R de W, 33, P/A Bank van Johannesburg Kempton Park, Fin Bestuurder, 1975
Wright J N, 35, P/A J N Wright Uitrusters Kempton Park, Sakeman, 1973, Johannesburg

Y

Young C A, 34, Colombowoonstel 72 Scheidingstraat Pretoria, Sakeman/L P R, 1968
Young J A, 35, Roodepoortse Hoërskool, Onderwyser, 1974, Brits
Yssel D, 41, Elandskuil Ventersdorp, Boer, 1967

Yssel G J, 34, P/A S A U K Johannesburg, Personeelhoof, 1964, Pretoria
Yssel J C, 29, Hoërskool Wonderboom Pretoria, Onderwyser, 1966, Lichtenburg
Yssel S G, 42, Elandskuil Ventersdorp, Boer, 1977

Z

Zaaiman S F, 45, P/A Volksblad Bloemfontein, Asst Redakteur, 1964, Zastron
Zaayman W, 39, Volkskas Wolseley, Bestuurder, 1968, Oudtshoorn
Zandberg A J B, 31, S A Polisiekollege Polkol Pretoria, Adj-Offisier, 1971, Britstown
Zeelie J S, 48, Britzstraat 183, Kroonstad/Dept Gevangenis, Majoor, 1977, Pretoria
Zeeman G H, 31, N G Pastorie Villiersdorp, Predikant, 1968, Barberton
Zeeman G H (Lid Nr 10785) N G Pastorie Belgravia Johannesburg, Predikant
Zeeman J P, 35, U O V S Bloemfontein, Lab Tegnikus, 1966, Colenso
Zeeman P S (Prof) Lid van die U R se Wetenskap-Komitee 1973
Zerwick J, 34, P/A Evkom Johannesburg, Snr Adm Beampte, 1974, Middelburg Tvl
Zerwick J W, 32, "Welkom" Christiana, Boer, 1965
Zietsman A J, 27, Pastorie Swellendam, N G Predikant, 1977, Brandwacht
Zietsman A L, 31, PK Pelgrimsrus, Geoloog, 1966, Hennenman
Zietsman E P, 33, Bantjestraat 43 Lichtenburg, Boukontrakteur, 1973
Zietsman M J, 38, Nelspruitse Laerskool Nelspruit, Adj-Hoof, 1970, Marken
Zwiegelaar J S M, 39, Onderwyskollege Durban, Lektor, 1964, Uitenhage
Zwiegers J J, 32, Karnmelkspan Poupanstasie Philipstown, Boer, 1969, Petrusville
Zwiegers P A J, 35, Destragebou Welkom, Tandarts, 1965, Johannesburg
Zwiegers W A, 45, S A S Polisie Johannesburg, Hoofkonstabel, 1965, Durban